The
Empowered
WRITER

Second Edition

The
Empowered
WRITER

K.M. Moran
Eric Henderson

OXFORD
UNIVERSITY PRESS

OXFORD
UNIVERSITY PRESS

Oxford University Press is a department of the University of Oxford.
It furthers the University's objective of excellence in research, scholarship,
and education by publishing worldwide. Oxford is a registered trade mark of
Oxford University Press in the UK and in certain other countries.

Published in Canada by
Oxford University Press
8 Sampson Mews, Suite 204,
Don Mills, Ontario M3C 0H5 Canada

www.oupcanada.com

Library and Archives Canada Cataloguing in Publication

Henderson, Eric, 1951–, author
The empowered writer : an essential guide to writing, reading
& research / K.M. Moran, Eric Henderson. — Second edition.

Includes index.
Eric Henderson is lead author on first edition.
ISBN 978–0–19–900554–3 (pbk.)

1. English language—Rhetoric. 2. Report writing. 3. Academic
writing. I. Moran, Kathleen M., 1955-, author II. Title.

PE1408.H388 2014   808'.042   C2013-907170-9

Cover image: © Purestock / Alamy

Printed and bound in Canada

1 2 3 4 — 17 16 15 14

Brief Contents

Contents

16 Agreement, Pronoun, and Sentence Structure Errors   387

Appendices

Readings

From the Publisher

Oxford University Press is delighted to present the second edition of *The Empowered Writer,* a four-in-one text covering rhetoric, research, and grammar with integrated readings that gives students a detailed yet widely applicable and accessible guide for developing skills in writing and research.

Tailored specifically to college and university students in undergraduate composition courses, *The Empowered Writer,* second edition, offers a detailed and widely applicable method for developing skills in research and writing as well as in personal and business communication. Key principles are illustrated through sample professional and student essays and reinforced through carefully crafted, classroom-tested exercises that encourage students to empower themselves as writers in training: to actively participate in honing their skills, to make informed choices, and to think deeply and critically about how—and why—they write. The new edition boasts a more logical sequence of topics; streamlined coverage in early chapters; practical guidance on giving oral presentations; expanded material on business and workplace writing; and twice as many professional readings to highlight essay techniques and styles.

We hope that as you browse through the pages that follow, you will see why we believe *The Empowered Writer* continues to be the most exciting and innovative new textbook for Canadian students of writing and composition.

❯ Exceptional Features of *The Empowered Writer*

ABUNDANT EXERCISES.   Well over a hundred exercises designed to be completed individually or in groups provide students with ample opportunity to practise and refine their skills. Exercises include

- pre- and post-reading questions and exercises
- end-of-chapter review questions
- documentation exercises
- grammar exercises
- collaborative assignments.

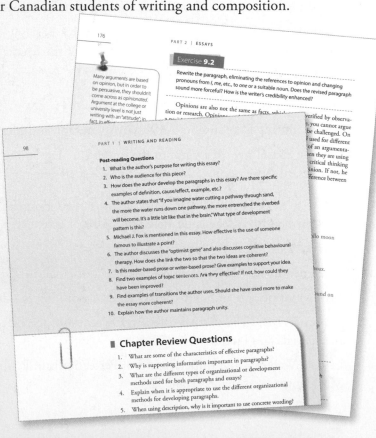

HIGH-INTEREST PROFESSIONAL ESSAYS.

Accessible selections by working writers cover topics of particular interest to students—including local food and hockey violence—encouraging readers to engage with the material. Marginal annotations highlight techniques for students to follow.

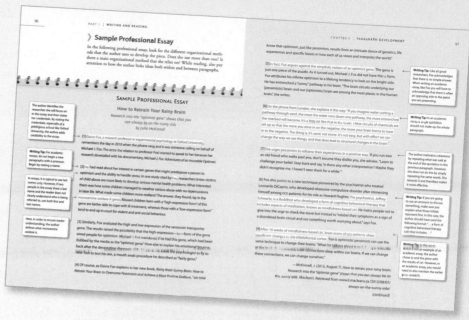

SAMPLE STUDENT ESSAYS.

Numerous examples of student writing, many of which are newly selected for the second edition, illustrate important rhetorical techniques and demonstrate to students that their best work can stand alongside the work of professionals.

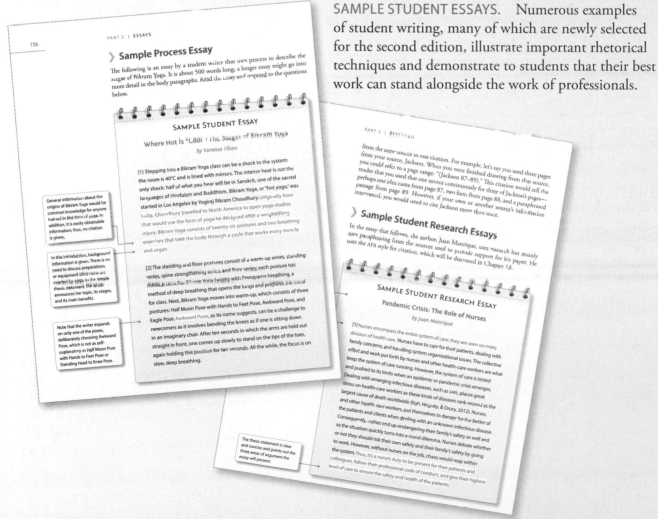

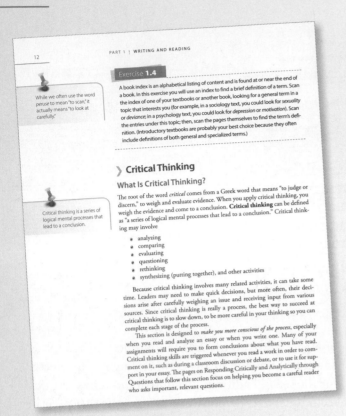

CRITICAL-THINKING FOCUS.   The authors encourage students to think critically about their plans and purposes for writing in order to better structure their work and carry out research more effectively.

THOROUGH COVERAGE OF DOCUMENTATION.   The authors outline both MLA and APA documentation styles, making the book a valuable resource for students in a wide variety of disciplines.

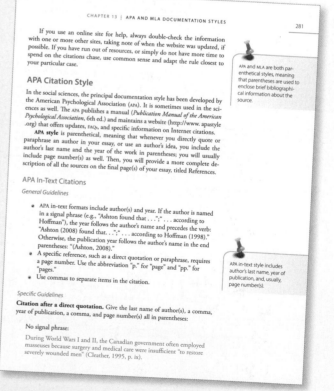

Appendix B
A Checklist for EAL Writers

The following are some English idiomatic expressions and rules for usage organized alphabetically by the major parts of speech. Although articles are not a major part of speech, their usage can be confusing for EAL writers, so they have been allotted a separate section, beginning on page 478.

Adjectives

One-word adjectives usually precede the word(s) they modify, except predicate adjectives that follow linking verbs (see page 335). However, **relative** (adjectival) **clauses** follow the noun they modify and present special challenges for writers.

Adjectives as participles

When a participle ending in *–ed* or *–en* precedes a noun and acts as an adjective, don't drop the ending it requires as a past participle:

Although Parrish lived a *fast-paced* [not fast-pace] life, he had the *old-fashioned* [not old-fashion] habit of stopping and reading a newspaper every day work.

Adjectives and present versus past participles

In verbs related to feeling or emotion, the present participle (ends in *–ing*) is used when the subject *causes* the feeling; the past participle (ends in *–ed* or *–en*) is used when the subject *experiences* the feeling.

The surprise ending of the football game was *exciting*; the few fans left in the stadium were *excited*.

Ago: When you want to refer to a time in the past and relate this time to today, you can use the adjective *ago*; it follows the noun. To refer to a *specific* point in the past, you can give the date (month, day, year) preceded by *on*. See **Times and dates**, under **Prepositions**, below.

CHECKLIST FOR EAL WRITERS. Students of English as an additional language will benefit from an appendix that clarifies common idiomatic words and phrases and matters of usage that native English speakers often take for granted.

HELPFUL MARGINAL NOTES provide useful writing tips, summaries of content, and a running glossary. Marginal definitions, together with definitions that appear in the running text, are compiled in a glossary for handy reference.

EXPLANATORY VISUALS present key concepts in ways designed to assist student comprehension.

The Essay's Introduction

Almost everything you read will begin with an **introduction**. Even if it is not called the "introduction," it will act as one by giving a preview of what follows. It will do that by presenting the main idea and, probably, the organizational pattern of the document—whether it is a book, an article in a scholarly journal, a class essay, a sales proposal, or a résumé. The kinds of introductions students are asked to write are made up of one or more paragraphs that fulfill specific functions, and should, like all paragraphs, be unified, coherent, and well developed.

It is crucial to spend time creating a well-written introduction that will be noticed for its unity and coherence. As it is one of the most important parts of your essay, take the time to write an introduction that will draw the reader into your essay and provide necessary information, satisfying the expectations of your audience.

Functions of the Introduction

Reader Interest: Logical, Dramatic, and Mixed Approaches

The introduction should create reader interest. Although most of your essay's "substance"—your main points and sub-points, the supporting details—will be placed in the middle (body) paragraphs, an ineffective introduction could mean that these details are wasted as the rest of the essay may not be read. Reader interest can be created through two different methods with variations on each.

Logical Introduction

The **logical approach** is the most common and traditional way to create interest. You use the first part of the introduction to build your emphasis. You begin with the general and proceed to the specific; the most specific is your thesis statement, usually the last sentence of the introduction. This is also called the **inverted pyramid** structure. A logical opening helps you establish the topic's relevance and shows where it fits in as your points progressively become more specific.

General or universal statement
More specific statement
Most specific (thesis) statement

FIGURE 6.1 Structure of paragraph introduction

In the following introduction, the writer begins with a general claim and gradually brings the subject into sharp focus—Laos's dependence on hydroelectric power. The pyramidal development is important for general readers who may not know much about Laos and the topic. Pay close attention to how the writer also creates reader interest, as he draws the reader into the topic.

(margin notes:)
An introduction is the opening of a essay that presents the main idea (the thesis statement) and the main organizational pattern.

Reader interest is very important in essay writing. You need to catch the reader's attention and maintain it throughout the essay so that your reader stays interested. If reader interest is not maintained, he or she will finish your essay and all of your hard work will not be viewed. Reader interest is especially important when writing for an instructor. If your essay is entertaining and thought-provoking, your mark will probably be higher than for a more mundane essay.

The logical approach begins with the general aspect of the topic and moves to the more specific as you progress through the introduction. This is repeated as you write your paragraphs.

The logical approach is also called the inverted pyramid approach, as you move from a broad to a narrow focus.

In an expository essay, *fairness* is demonstrated through using evidence objectively. In an argumentative essay fairness is shown by considering opposing views. While presenting a strong case for your views, you can pinpoint the shortcomings and limitations of the opposing views. A fair writer is objective in addressing the other side, avoiding slanted language that reveals bias. While you can demonstrate reliability by avoiding misuse of reason, you can demonstrate fairness by using emotional appeals selectively and without bias (discussed in more detail in Chapter 9).

Connections among the Elements of the Analytical Model

Student writers sometimes have the impression that an effective essay comprises elements that function in isolation. But the opposite is true: it is really one entity with many interdependent elements. As shown in Figure 7.1, each element coexists with the others; you need to think carefully about how each element fits into the whole. A successful essay has many connections among the concepts shown in the diagram. In your own essays, you can ask questions like, "Am I using the kinds of evidence favoured by my discipline? Am I organizing this evidence logically? Have I used enough sources? Is my essay well-structured and is my writing clear and grammatical? Have I used evidence fairly?"

When reading an essay in order to analyze it, you can ask similar questions. When you analyze, you *break something down* into elements so you can look closely at each element. The interdependence of the various elements of the essay is clear. For example, grammatical errors will affect the writer's reliability, which will reduce credibility and weaken support for the claim. If you are aware of how the different elements relate, you should be able to approach your own writing critically have the tools to analyze other writing.

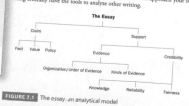

The Essay

Claim — Support
Fact / Value / Policy — Evidence — Credibility
Organization/Order of Evidence / Kinds of Evidence
Knowledge / Reliability / Fairness

FIGURE 7.1 The essay: an analytical model

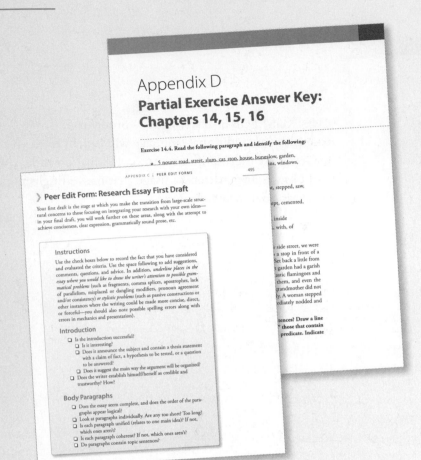

PEER EDITING FORMS are provided to assist students in evaluating the work of their classmates.

A PARTIAL ANSWER KEY enables students to check their progress but leaves some exercises unsolved so that they may be assigned as graded coursework.

❯ For More Information: Online Resources

The Empowered Writer is but the central element in a comprehensive package of learning and teaching tools that includes resources for both students and instructors.

For Instructors

- An **instructor's manual** features chapter overviews, learning objectives, and summaries; examples of key concepts; suggestions for in-class and take-home writing assignments; suggested print and online resources; and much more.

- A comprehensive **test bank** offers instructors access to hundreds of questions in multiple-choice, short-answer, and essay formats.

For Students

- Online **student resources** include chapter overviews; self-grading quizzes, consisting of multiple-choice and short-answer questions with answers; and practice mid-term and final exams.

Preface

There are many books currently available that help students learn how to write at the college or university level. The second edition of *The Empowered Writer* differs by taking a more academic approach to the subject, while addressing the same material. For example, the student samples are genuine, coming from students who have taken courses with us or our colleagues. These samples are either actual essays, summaries, or excerpts, not pieces that follow a journalistic style. The professional essays—which have doubled in number in this edition—also follow the rules set out in this text. While a few of the samples use a journalistic style of writing, students generally are not asked to read about how to write an essay and then asked to analyze a piece that does not follow the same stylistic rules they have been learning.

Critical thinking is an essential skill for any successful writer at this level, and so the term is introduced and explained in detail from the outset, in Chapter 1. The application of critical thinking is then stressed throughout the following chapters. Students are also introduced to the differences between expository writing and argumentative writing, and clear examples, often with annotations, are provided so that the readers can see the differences. In addition, an extensive section about research and how to properly integrate and present sources in an essay outlines the most current practices used in APA and MLA documentation.

Writers at this level are typically required to use a more elaborate writing style than they have been accustomed to using. Unfortunately, many students take this to mean using more words, rather than choosing the most accurate words or phrases. The later chapters help students build on grammar rules they already know, so that their grammatical structures reflect a higher level of writing. A section about style will help students learn to write clearly and concisely, developing a skill that is valued in the workplace.

We have included a chapter to deal exclusively with summary writing, both as a stand-alone task and as a means to incorporate research material in an essay. Again, the student summaries that we have included to illustrate the concepts discussed are genuine, having come from students we have taught. Several of these summaries relate to the full-length essays found in *The Empowered Writer*, so learners can try their hand at summary writing before comparing their product with what other students have produced in the past.

Finally, the book includes chapter objectives, extensive exercises, and chapter summary questions. The new edition also includes post-reading questions at the end of the sample professional and student essays designed to help students to connect content with technique. By involving the student and encouraging the completion of these exercises, we hope that students will apply what they have learned often enough that writing no longer seems an irksome task but a satisfying one.

❯ Acknowledgements

I would like to thank all my students who have helped make this book possible.
You have made this journey so much fun!

K.M. Moran
January 2014

The authors and publisher would like to acknowledge the following reviewers,
along with those reviewers who wish to remain anonymous, whose thoughtful
comments and suggestions have helped to shape *The Empowered Writer*:

Veronica Abbass, Seneca College
Trevor Arkell, Humber College
Jennifer Chambers, Sheridan College
Marie-Joseé Chapleau, College of the North Atlantic
Paula Crooks, Conestoga College
Mark Feltham, Fanshawe College
Lynn Gresham, Conestoga College
Tom Gwin, Red Deer College
Chandra Hodgson, Humber College
Amanda Johnstone, Conestoga College
Louise Lloyd, Conestoga College
Roneen Marcoux, University of the Fraser Valley
Carolyn Speakman, Lethbridge College

The Empowered WRITER

Part 1

Writing and Reading

1 Basic Skills Development for Today's Student: **Writing and Reading**

In this chapter, you will

- learn about how reading, thinking, and writing are involved in the composition process
- learn reading strategies by asking important questions
- learn to understand the value of critical thinking
- learn how to read unfamiliar words in context and improve your vocabulary for writing at the college or university level

The writing process involves more than just putting pen to paper or entering thoughts in a word-processing program. This chapter will explain the importance of thinking, reading, and writing in the composing process. In addition, you will examine how to begin to organize an essay. Finally, the importance of critical thinking in the reading and writing process is discussed, along with guidelines for recognizing word meanings.

〉 Thinking, Writing, and Reading: An Integrated Approach

Student writers and professional writers both know through experience that writing is hard work. This is supported by Thomas Edison's statement that genius is "1 per cent inspiration and 99 per cent perspiration." But the task of writing is easier when you know how to approach it. Composition textbooks, like this one, explain the task of writing by introducing you to practical methods and strategies that make the writing experience more rewarding. The writing skills you acquire now will serve you well in the workplace, such as when you need to compose documents on the job. Good writing, no matter what the situation, involves organizing your thoughts logically, choosing your words carefully, and crafting documents that make sense to the reader.

Good writing, no matter what the situation, involves organizing your thoughts logically, choosing your words carefully, and crafting documents that make sense to the reader.

Writing and Thinking

Writing is inseparable from thinking. Like many writers, you may "think out loud" as you contemplate your topic, or you may read sentences aloud to get a better sense of your thought processes. Such natural responses show this complex relationship between thought and writing, which involves translating abstract ideas into concrete words. Furthermore, once you have set words down on paper or on a computer screen, you have to ask yourself whether these words reflect exactly what you meant to say. Although the words are more concrete than the ideas, getting words onto the page is simply one important step in the process.

Exercise **1.1**

Most people try to master a skill or hobby. Choose a skill or hobby that interests you.

First, write down your spontaneous thoughts and feelings on this skill or hobby without stopping to edit yourself; give yourself 5 or 10 minutes for this. Then, in one or two paragraphs, answer these questions:

What is your goal in pursuing the skill or hobby? Has the goal ever changed? Describe how you attain this goal. Are there different ways the goal could be approached? Which do you enjoy more: working toward a goal or achieving it? Why?

Writing and Reading

Where does reading fit into the writing process? Reading involves more than understanding what each word means. When we read, we interpret the thoughts of the writer according to what we already know. Like writing, it is a complex process.

Some studies have shown that good readers tend to be good writers. Thus, studying the works of other writers can help you improve your own writing. This means you must first clearly understand the writer's language, both the individual words and their combined meaning (the topics Thinking and Writing + Reading, and Word Meanings will be covered later in this chapter). "Active reading" usually involves more than simple comprehension, and most college- and university-level assignments will require you to do more than read for understanding—they will also require critical thinking. Studying the works of other writers can also sharpen your critical thinking skills, as discussed below (Critical Thinking).

Most of what you read is in a finished form (exceptions include your own rough drafts or those of your peers). It's usually possible to see how an essay or article was put together. For example, in every well-constructed piece of writing, you should be able to identify the main ideas. This is especially important if you are summarizing a work, perhaps in order to describe it in your own essay. Also, there may be other features of the work that you can identify—for example, the writer's purpose in writing, the audience for whom it was written, the writer's style, or specific strategies used to communicate meaning or tone. By analyzing any of these features, you can enlarge your own understanding and appreciation of the writing process to become a more effective writer.

By analyzing the features of a written work, you can enlarge your own understanding and appreciation of the writing process to become a more effective writer.

❭ Thinking and Writing + Reading

Most of us read for pleasure, at least sometimes. This reading can include novels, magazines, student newspapers, or Web pages. Even when you read for pleasure, though, you are examining the text more than you may think. On one level, of course, you are reading words for meaning. While you are reading, you are continually interpreting the words—their meanings and associations—which combine to create an overall meaning.

Reading to grasp content is essentially "passive" or "one-way" reading. But this one-way activity becomes two-way when you begin responding to the text. In reading a novel or short story, you may make personal associations—memories, emotions, desires—or experience the simple pleasure of escaping into another world that is, in some way, like your own. These associations are often what help us enjoy reading.

Consider the following text: the beginning of an article about dreams.

Religion was the original field of dream study. The earliest writings we have on dreams are primarily texts on their religious and spiritual significance. Long before psychoanalysts, sleep laboratory researchers, and content analysts arrived on the scene, religious specialists were exploring dreams in a variety of ways: using dreams in initiation rituals, developing techniques to incubate revelatory dreams and ward off evil nightmares, expressing numerous dream images in different artistic forms, and elaborating sophisticated interpretive systems that related dreams to beliefs about the soul, death, morality, and fate.

—Doniger, W., & Bulkley, K. (1993). Why study dreams? A religious studies perspective. *Dreaming: Journal of the Association of Dreams, 3*(1), 69–73.

Look at the literal level of the words. What do the following mean?

- "content analysts"
- "incubate revelatory dreams"

These phrases might have caused you to reach for a dictionary. In reading the paragraph by Doniger and Bulkley, you no doubt went beyond one-way reading. Though you may have formed some personal associations, you probably reacted critically: the writers were making general statements about the use of dreams in religious societies and cultures, and you probably thought about dreams in this or a similar context. If you continued to read the article, you would have made certain **inferences** and drawn conclusions based on the writers' statements and the way they were presented. For example, Doniger and Bulkley provide factual evidence that ancient societies developed highly sophisticated methods for studying dreams. The writers don't directly say that the ancient methods were as complex as those used in today's dream research, but readers could make that inference. As you read on, you would have, perhaps, tested the writers' points for logic and consistency as well as against your own experience by asking questions like:

Inference is a conclusion we make based on the evidence presented; the corresponding verb is *infer*.

1. Is the claim (statement) logical?
2. Is it valid considering the circumstances?
3. Is it truthful?
4. Is it reliable?
5. Is it consistent with previous claims?

When you engage in this process and ask these kinds of questions, you are responding *critically* to a work. (Critical Thinking will be covered later in this chapter.)

Thus we can see that the passage above involves a more critical response than when reading for pleasure. In critical thinking, you use two-way reading to determine the validity of an author's statements, test them by considering the logic and consistency behind them, and decide whether the evidence supports the author's claims.

The main difference between two-way reading and what's called "three-way reading" or **3-D (three-dimensional) reading** is that in the latter you respond *consciously and analytically* to the text. 3-D reading actively makes the connection between the *what* and the *how* of an essay. Being fully engaged in the reading–thinking–writing process develops your writing skills, as well as your reading and thinking skills. A critical analysis requires both a critical *and* an analytical focus.

As a homework assignment, you may be asked to write a response based on a 3-D reading of an essay. As you do the assignment, you complete the cycle of reading–thinking–writing: you read a text; you think about it critically; you write about those thoughts, making them clear and concrete. You can then go back and begin the cycle again by rereading the piece, rethinking it, and, perhaps, further clarifying your thoughts by writing about them again. Responding to essays and thinking about the writers' conscious choices will lead you to reflect on your own writing processes and help you make sound and *conscious* choices in your own writing.

3-D reading at the college and university level means taking a three-step approach to the reading–thinking–writing process where you
1. focus on understanding
2. use critical thinking to test the validity of the statements
3. analyze and evaluate the work, considering the methods and strategies that the writer uses to make it effective (or not)

Active Reading
Reading to Understand Meaning (Content) → *One-Way Reading*
Reading to Respond (Associative/Critical) → **Two-Way Reading**
Reading to Analyze Techniques (Analytical) → ***3-D Reading***

The active reading model above does not mean that 3-D reading is always more difficult than one-way reading. In a scholarly article, for example, it may be quite difficult just to understand the content, and understanding the precise meaning of certain terms might be the key to analyzing the article. But these levels represent a "progressive" approach to reading where it is usually first necessary to understand content before proceeding to respond critically or analytically. Thus, active reading at all three levels is essential to your success in responding to the challenging texts you encounter at the college or university level.

Responding to essays and thinking about the writers' conscious choices will lead you to reflect on your own writing processes and enable you to make sound and *conscious* choices in your own writing.

❭ The Composing Process

Essay writing gives students the opportunity to exercise many kinds of thinking. To come up with a topic and develop it, you will probably begin with a concept. You will try to make connections with other ideas in order to narrow the topic's scope and make it manageable. The thinking–writing process makes you more conscious of how you write in order to make your writing more successful and, hopefully, more enjoyable.

The Traditional Linear Model

The **linear model** is one of the most common models of essay writing. You would use it to create an essay or a report, following these steps:

The linear method breaks down writing into successive stages, each of which involves characteristic activities.

- **pre-writing (inventing):** thinking about and coming up with a topic
- **research:** finding background information and supporting evidence (could involve intensive library resources or simply consist of examining your knowledge about a topic)

- **organization:** determining the order of points; outlining
- **composing (first draft):** writing out your ideas in paragraph form
- **revising (final draft):** revising and editing to achieve the finished version

The essay has an introduction containing a thesis statement, **body paragraphs** with clear topic sentences and examples, and a conclusion that restates the thesis. You will have to choose what information to include and decide how to best organize your thoughts so that your reader clearly understands your ideas.

Body paragraphs are the middle paragraphs of an essay that help prove the thesis by presenting facts, arguments, or other support.

Even if you use the linear model, you might not always follow a predictable order from start to finish. Sometimes no matter how much planning you do, you may find yourself looking for a stronger example, adding a detail, maybe even rethinking your organization. The linear model recognizes that virtually all writing has a goal and distinct stages along the way, though there may be different ways to get to the goal.

Subjects versus Topics

You may be given various subjects and asked to narrow one down to a manageable topic. A subject is a broad category that contains many potential topics. Modern technology, global warming, and energy sources are examples of subjects. A subject could also be more specific than these examples: the Internet, species extinction, and alternative energy sources could also be considered subjects. A topic differs from a subject in being narrower or more focused. Similarly, a thesis is more focused than a topic because it makes a specific comment on the topic or tells the reader how you will approach the topic.

A topic differs from a subject as it is narrower or more focused. Similarly, a thesis is more focused than a topic because it makes a specific comment on the topic or tells the reader how you will approach the topic.

In Chapter 2, you will see how pre-writing strategies can help you to come up with a topic. These strategies sometimes result in a thesis and even in some main points for your essay, but at other times, your thesis will not be clear to you until after you've begun your research. However, your topic *should always* be clear before you begin your research.

Exercise **1.2**

Read through the following list. Decide whether each item in the list is a subject, a topic, or a thesis.

1. The discrepancy between men's and women's basketball coverage is due to sexism.
2. Public transportation is influenced by many factors.
3. Studying abroad can provide valuable life experience.
4. Violence exists in sports.
5. Greed is responsible for the global economic difficulties.

(continued)

6. Jazz is one of America's greatest musical genres.
7. Colleges and universities can change students' lives.
8. If one is illiterate, many career opportunities are lost.
9. Fish are great pets for those who cannot have cats or dogs.
10. Studying the classical languages in school is unnecessary today.

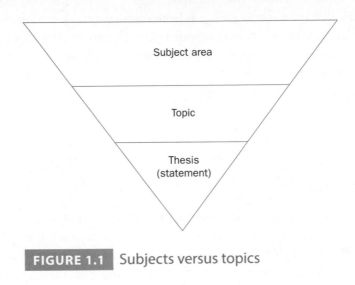

FIGURE 1.1 Subjects versus topics

Topic Hunting

Your instructor may tell you to find your own topic or to narrow a given subject to a manageable topic. In the first case, you will be beginning from scratch. Here are some questions that can help you if you need to come up with a topic from scratch:

- Where do your interests lie? (hobbies, leisure pursuits, reading interests, extracurricular activities?)
- What would you like to find out more about? Curiosity is a good motivator. A topic you are very familiar with doesn't always make a good one for a research essay; your existing knowledge may be incomplete or biased but you may assume that you are fully aware of the topic and that no further research is necessary. This assumption may prevent you from fully exploring the topic.
- Are sufficient sources available? Consider not only research sources but also questionnaires, interviews, experts, statistics, etc.
- What topic might other people like to learn about? What topic could benefit society or a specific group (for example, students at your college or university)?
- Can you think of a new angle on an old topic? A neglected area of an older topic can be a new opportunity for exploration.

By using pre-writing techniques, you can narrow down a subject to a usable topic. However, not every topic can be turned into an effective thesis statement. Some are too broad while others are too narrow. If the topic is too broad, it will be hard to do more than provide a general overview. Your essay may also be difficult to plan and write because there will be so much you could say about the topic. On the other hand, if your topic is too specific, you could be limited by the topic's scope; you may also have problems researching it if there's not much available.

Exercise **1.3**

The following topics are arranged from broadest to narrowest. Place a check mark beside any topics you think could be turned into an effective thesis.

1. species extinction
   threatened species in Canada
   threatened species in Canada's Arctic
   threatened polar bear habitats in Canada's Arctic
   threatened polar bears living near Coats Island in Hudson Bay
2. the Internet
   online gaming
   MMORPGS
   popularity of World of Warcraft
   the contribution of quests to the popularity of World of Warcraft
3. nutrition
   dieting
   fad diets
   the Atkins diet
   loss of muscle mass while on the Atkins diet

The first stage in the linear model of essay writing is pre-writing, an explorative stage in which you may start with nothing more than a subject area, a topic, or perhaps something even less defined. This is where pre-writing strategies can help. These are systematic methods to generate ideas. When you have enough ideas and have made connections among some of them, you may be ready to express your thesis: a statement about your topic that will be the focus of your essay.

Thesis Statement

Nearly all essays need a **thesis statement**, which is the main point of your essay or what you will be attempting to prove. A thesis statement has two parts: the *topic* and *the comment*. It does not just state a topic. For example, "My essay

The thesis statement is the main point of your essay or what you are trying to prove in it.

will be about life in residence at the University of the South Pole" states a topic and does not comment on it. By contrast, the thesis "Life in residence at the University of the South Pole helps prepare one for life after university" makes a comment about the topic. "Life in residence at the University of the South Pole" is the topic; "helps prepare one for life after university" is the comment. It tells the reader how you will be addressing the topic, what your focus will be.

As you continue expanding and exploring your ideas, you will soon be able to construct an outline to show the relationships among the main points. You will then begin your rough draft, trying to create unified, coherent, and developed paragraphs. After you have completed the draft, you will revise it by paying particular attention to grammar, punctuation, sentence structure, and **mechanics**. As you move further along in the process in the linear model, you will be thinking less about the topic itself and more about the methods and forms, each with measurable goals, for crafting an essay. This model can be adapted to a variety of specialized functions, such as business letters.

Scanning versus Focused Reading

College- or university-level reading is not always detailed, microscopic reading. Rather, there are times when scanning is useful just as there are times when you need to read for detail.

First, different subjects may require different kinds of reading: for history, close reading dominates; poetry often requires intensive analysis that even takes words apart; sociology involves seeking particular patterns of information; mathematics and chemistry may have to be read even more closely than poetry; and so on.

But you will not require these levels of precision for everything that you read. Thus, we distinguish between different types of **selective reading**, such as scanning and focused reading, in which you are looking for specific information.

When you **scan**, you read for the gist of an essay or its main points, or to identify another specific feature. To scan effectively, you often need to know where to look. For example, if you want to know the gist of a reading, you might scan the introduction; for main ideas, you might look at the first sentence of each paragraph (this is often a topic sentence that tells you what the paragraph is about). You could also scan a table of contents or list of references for key words. Scanning is not the same thing as idle browsing to spot what interests you. Like focused reading, scanning is reading with a purpose.

In **focused reading**, you concentrate on smaller blocks of text. Sentences are read carefully for detail, and sometimes for tone or style. In this sense, focused reading is specialized reading—you become a specialist (historian, literary critic, sociologist, mathematician) in your reading of the text.

Applied to format, mechanics includes margin size, spacing between sentences, font size and type, and page numbers; applied to writing, it includes abbreviations, capital letters, hyphenation, and numbers.

Selective reading is a reading strategy with a goal, such as scanning for main points or reading for details.

Scanning is a reading strategy in which you look for key words or sections of a text.

Focused reading is a close and detailed (i.e., word-by-word) reading of a specific, relevant passage.

In college- and university-level reading, scanning is often combined with focused reading. Following these stages will help you conduct thorough research:

1. When you begin research, scan catalogue entries, journal indexes, book contents pages and indexes, reference books, and other types of sources in order to find materials to support your essay topic.
2. Once you have located most of your sources, scan them to determine which are the most valuable for your purpose, so that you begin your focused reading with the most useful.
3. Then, scan individual articles, books, and websites to identify the main ideas.
4. After you identify the ideas most relevant to your topic, read closely to understand them and see how they fit with your thesis or with the ideas of other writers.

Scanning and focused reading are most effective when you use them as deliberate strategies. You should ask yourself specific questions as you read in order to get as much from the reading as possible without wasting your valuable time by reading everything closely. Guidelines and strategies for selective reading are discussed in Responding Critically and Analytically through Questions, page 18 in this chapter. Some basic strategies for scanning and focused reading are outlined in Table 1.1.

TABLE 1.1 Basic Strategies for Scanning and Focused Reading	
Scanning	**Focused Reading**
Scanning begins when you know your purpose for reading and what you are looking for.	Focused reading begins when you have identified important or relevant passages.
Knowing *where* to look will help you scan efficiently.	Breaking down the passage will help you find complex material—for example, separating main points from sub-points, and claims from supporting details and examples.
In scanning, you will skip much of the text, isolating only the most relevant areas.	Read the passage first for comprehension; then, apply active reading skills.
With practice, scanning can be done quickly.	Although focused reading is usually slower, frequent practice will enable you to read faster and better understand what the author has written.
Activities associated with scanning include note-taking and cross-referencing.	Activities associated with focused reading include summarizing, paraphrasing, and direct quotation.

While we often use the word *peruse* to mean "to scan," it actually means "to look at carefully."

A book index is an alphabetical listing of content and is found at or near the end of a book. In this exercise you will use an index to find a brief definition of a term. Scan the index of one of your textbooks or another book, looking for a general term in a topic that interests you (for example, in a sociology text, you could look for *sexuality* or *deviance*; in a psychology text, you could look for *depression* or *motivation*). Scan the entries under this topic; then, scan the pages themselves to find the term's definition. (Introductory textbooks are probably your best choice because they often include definitions of both general and specialized terms.)

Critical thinking is a series of logical mental processes that lead to a conclusion.

❯ Critical Thinking

What Is Critical Thinking?

The root of the word *critical* comes from a Greek word that means "to judge or discern," to weigh and evaluate evidence. When you apply critical thinking, you weigh the evidence and come to a conclusion. **Critical thinking** can be defined as "a series of logical mental processes that lead to a conclusion." Critical thinking may involve

- analyzing
- comparing
- evaluating
- questioning
- rethinking
- synthesizing (putting together), and other activities

Because critical thinking involves many related activities, it can take some time. Leaders may need to make quick decisions, but more often, their decisions arise after carefully weighing an issue and receiving input from various sources. Since critical thinking is really a process, the best way to succeed at critical thinking is to slow down, to be more careful in your thinking so you can complete each stage of the process.

This section is designed to *make you more conscious of the process*, especially when you read and analyze an essay or when you write one. Many of your assignments will require you to form conclusions about what you have read. Critical thinking skills are triggered whenever you read a work in order to comment on it, such as during a classroom discussion or debate, or to use it for support in your essay. The pages on Responding Critically and Analytically through Questions that follow this section focus on helping you become a careful reader who asks important, relevant questions.

Applying Critical Thinking

Critical thinking involves making choices, but the most highly developed critical thinking involves making the *best* choice given a range of possibilities.

When you are reading an essay or book, or evaluating a real-life situation, you are usually not directly told what to think. A writer (or situation) might present the evidence and leave you to infer the meaning. When you **infer** (see margin note on page 5 for the definition of this word), you arrive at a probable conclusion based on what you read (or see). The *best* inference is the *most probable* one after all the evidence is weighed.

(see margin note on page 5 for the definition of this word)

Exercise **1.5**

Consider the following situation:

> You invite a new friend for a coffee, but she does not show up. The next day, you meet her unexpectedly and ask her what happened. She pauses for a few seconds and then says matter-of-factly, "Well, actually, I was abducted by aliens, and they just released me."

What do you make of her statement? What inferences are possible? Which are more likely? What could you say or do to ensure that your conclusion is the most probable one? Structure your answer by using the following headings:

Possible inferences:

Probable inferences:

How to ensure that your inference is correct:

You use critical thinking as you read whenever you evaluate and draw conclusions about claims, and about the evidence for or sources of these claims. It is important to remember that critical thinking is a *process of engagement* with a text (or a situation) that may change as you read (or learn more about the situation).

Critical thinking is a *process of engagement* with a text (or situation) that may change as you read (or learn more about the situation).

The critical thinker questions assumptions, including his or her own, tests the evidence, and accepts or rejects conclusions after careful analysis. When questions arise, the critical thinker seeks answers within the text itself, but may also consider relevant personal experience or outside sources. For example, in the situation described above, you might ask the woman's friends about her belief in aliens—or about her sense of humour.

In analyzing an argument, the critical thinker should carefully evaluate all the writer's claims and look for failures in logic or misuse of emotion. (Chapter 9 discusses this subject further.) He or she should also think about points that the writer *doesn't* raise. Is the writer avoiding certain issues by not mentioning them? Expository (fact-based) writing can also produce disagreement and contradictory findings. For example, two different researchers investigating the connection between television viewing and violence may arrive at very different conclusions though the methods of both appear credible. What can account for the differing results? Answering this question involves critical thinking, too.

Reading and Critical Thinking

As we read, we may not be aware that we are thinking critically. But sometimes we clearly use critical thinking, such as when a writer makes a claim that experts have debated for years—for example, that cats are smarter than dogs. Making the best inference requires weighing several factors:

- *The writer's credibility:* Is the writer considered an expert? What is the nature of his or her expertise? Is he or she a researcher into animal behaviour? A veterinarian? An animal trainer? Someone who has owned both dogs and cats? Someone who has owned cats only? Could the writer have a bias? For example, does the author hate dogs?
- *Nature of the thesis or main points:* Specific points are stronger than general ones, and they are often easier to prove. Since there are many different dog breeds, it would be difficult to generalize about the intelligence of *all* dogs.
- *Basis of the statement:* A claim may depend on an underlying assumption, such as a particular definition. There are various ways to define and measure intelligence: physiologically (e.g., the weight of the brain in proportion to the weight of the body) and behaviourally (e.g., trainability, adaptability, independence). Those who think a dog is more intelligent may point to trainability as the intelligence factor, while cat fanciers may point to adaptability or independence. One further thing to determine is whether fact has been separated from fiction.
- *Method:* How does the writer attempt to prove his or her point? Since intelligence can be measured scientifically, a method that measured it would be more credible than one that relied on personal experience—especially since many pet-lovers are opinionated about their pets' intelligence and may not always distinguish between fact and opinion.
- *Support:* A credible writer would need to provide evidence as well as opinion to back up a claim, though research alone does not ensure a writer's credibility. In critical thinking, you must evaluate the nature of the evidence and the way the writer uses it. Typical questions might include: What kind of evidence does the writer use? Does the writer rely too much on one kind of evidence or one source? How many sources are used? Are they current sources (recent studies may be more credible than older ones)? Does the writer ignore some sources (e.g., those that find dogs more intelligent than cats)?

● *Conclusion:* While analysis (taking apart) and questioning are important when you read the work, as you complete your reading, you will be synthesizing (putting together) information in order to say something definitive about it and/or about the writer. *Your goal is to determine whether the weight of evidence supports the writer's claim.* You might consider how weaker points affect the validity of the findings. Are there any gaps or inconsistencies in the chain of reasoning? Is the writer's conclusion logically backed up?

Exercise **1.6**

As discussed above, we use critical thinking and inferences in our everyday lives. The following scenarios call for critical thinking skills by asking us to make inferences.

A. What inferences could be made in each case?

B. Is there a best (i.e., most probable) inference? Justify your choice of the most probable inference. If you believe no inference can be made, explain what kind of information you would need to make an inference.

1. You arrive at your 8:30 class after missing yesterday's class because you overslept. You are surprised to see an empty classroom. As well, there is no one you recognize from class hanging around outside, and there is nothing posted on the wall or door to show that the instructor is ill.

   Inferences:
   a. You have mistaken either the time or the room.
   b. The instructor cancelled class yesterday.
   c. The instructor is ill, but no one put up a notice.
   d. No inference is possible. (What further information is needed?)

2. Matt suggested that he and Dee see a movie tonight. Shrugging, Dee said okay, but when Matt suggested they see a romantic comedy, Dee said she just wasn't in the mood. Matt suggested an action flick, but Dee replied, "You know I don't like them." Finally, Matt suggested a drama starring her favourite actress, but Dee said that she hadn't much enjoyed her last film.

   Inferences:
   a. Matt is pressuring Dee too much.
   b. Dee is finding it hard to decide on a movie.
   c. Dee really doesn't want to go to a movie tonight.
   d. No inference is possible. (What further information is needed?)

3. It was Todd's roommate's turn to cook dinner, but when Todd got home, his roommate was glued to the TV and the kitchen looked untouched. "Wow! Something smells great," enthused Todd.

(*continued*)

Inferences:
a.   Todd has a poor sense of smell.
b.   Todd is sarcastically voicing his displeasure.
c.   Todd is trying to give his roommate a hint that he should start dinner.
d.   No inference is possible. (What further information is needed?)

4.   Brad was helping Kodi train for the 600-metre race by recording his time after every complete circuit of the track. For the first circuit, Kodi was timed at 60 seconds; he did the second circuit in 65 seconds.

Inferences:
a.   He will probably do the third circuit in about 55 seconds.
b.   He will probably do the third circuit in about 65 seconds.
c.   He will probably do the third circuit in about 70 seconds.
d.   No inference is possible. (What further information is needed?)

5.   Lara works at the city's tourist centre, and she is often asked to recommend whale-watching tours. However, her boss has told her she should provide the relevant brochures and not make personal recommendations. She often tells tourists, "I've heard that Whales Galore is awesome, but I've heard a few good things about Spouting Off, too."

Inferences:
a.   Lara favours Whales Galore over Spouting Off.
b.   Lara favours Spouting Off over Whales Galore.
c.   Lara is careful to praise both companies equally in order to satisfy her boss.
d.   No inference is possible. (What further information is needed?)

Exercise **1.7**

The writer of the following informal essay uses critical thinking to analyze the book publishing industry and where it is headed due to the increased use of digital reading devices. Read the essay and answer the questions that follow, using your critical thinking skills and ability to make logical inferences.

Where Are the Books?

[1] Books have lined the shelves of the offices of all my colleagues at every school where I have worked. In my early days of teaching, or when spending a term as a visitor, I'd wander into a learned neighbor's office to get acquainted. The titles and content of those books announced a person's intellectual background and interests. They were instantly and extensively a topic of earnest discussion. If my interlocutor should be interrupted by a call or an assistant popping in, I'd amuse myself by grazing over the titles, scanning the shelves that added up to

an inventory of knowledge. On their shelves and mine, students attending office hours would likewise find easy ice breakers.

[2] When visiting the homes of friends, especially new friends but longer-term friends as well, it has always interested me to see what books are stacked on their shelves, in the living room, the study, along hallways. At parties, these books have been great conversation starters, fountains of discourse and debate. You could even pick them up and hand them over, citing the passage on a given page where you recalled a point being made particularly well.

[3] My wife and I, when house hunting the last time around, inspected two dozen apartments before falling in love with the homey charm of the one where we live now. As an anonymous broker showed us through the absent homeowners' place, we'd scan the stacks of books that gave a sense of the people who lived there–lovers of art history, a denizen of Wall Street, devotees of history, biography, the Civil War. Stephanie and I would joke, when viewing that rare apartment empty of books, that the absence of books was an absence of warmth and that we would not trust the people who lived there. "Where are the books?," we'd ask in bewilderment as we rode down the elevator, never to return.

[4] Today, with reading so often done and "books" acquired digitally, stored in pixels on hand-held devices, we see fewer new titles gracing the offices of colleagues and teachers, the homes of friends. No longer on display, they can no longer be conversation pieces. The average age of books on shelves is rising steadily and even these becoming anachronistic. Shelves are given over to decoration, clocks, cups, bells, photographs. My wife and I wonder, "what will our kids think, 10 or 20 years from now, when they see an apartment without a single book in it?" Maybe nothing. We would be horrified.

[5] But exactly what the future holds is uncertain. One of my recent books, *The Essays of Warren Buffett*, is selling briskly in both print and digital, though with vastly more sales in print than digital, yet it costs $35 in print and half that in digital. Time will tell.

—Cunningham, L. (2013, March 26). Where are the books? *Concurring opinions*. Retrieved from http://www.concurringopinions.com/archives/2013/03/where-are-the-books.html/print/

1. Why do you think the author feels it is important to have icebreakers, such as book titles, when meeting new colleagues?
2. What does the word *interlocutor* mean? Why do you think the author used this rather than a similar word?

(continued)

3. What does the author's opinion of books and the vocabulary he uses tell you about his perception of his audience?

4. In analyzing the essay by using your critical thinking skills, what weight (importance) would you give to (a) Cunningham's credibility, (b) the credibility of the blog where this essay was published, (c) Cunningham's support for his claim, (d) your own experience with books or friends' experiences? List as "most important" to "least important" and support your answer.

5. Cunningham states that when he was house hunting, he felt that he would not trust people who did not have books in their house and that he did not return to look at those places again. Would you feel the same way? How does the author's opinion affect your view of him and how you feel about the blog post?

Responding Critically and Analytically through Questions

Earlier, you learned that active reading can be both a two-way and a three-dimensional process. An active reader interacts with the text. Active reading can be triggered by asking questions about a written work. You can ask them before, during, or after your first reading for content, or during later readings. A question might be about content, such as the date of a historical event mentioned in the reading; others require you to read critically or analytically, perhaps looking at the causes of the event. Active reading typically involves each of these different responses at different times. Of course, your response to any question can change at any point in the reading process as you gather more information.

Before Reading

Pre-reading can give you valuable information to help plan your reading of a text; it can give you an agenda. When you select a source, ask yourself, "How much and what parts of it are useful to me?" Some sources could provide you with methods and points of view for analyzing data.

If you are researching a topic such as the changes in subsidized housing policy during the last 50 years in Toronto, you are going to need documents from the City of Toronto Archives, journal and newspaper articles, and books that cover the general topic of subsidized housing that may discuss Toronto's policy.

If you are researching an aspect of Aboriginal history in Saskatchewan during the 1900s, you may need to consult a range of books, documents, newspaper archives, journal articles, and university archives. Information about the writer could alert you to his or her qualifications, the intended readership, and any biases he or she might have. A science or social science article may contain an *abstract*, a concise summary that precedes the article itself, giving an overview of the writer's hypothesis, method, and results. Reading through abstracts can help you find those articles that are most relevant to your own reading or research interests (see Chapter 11).

What information does the work's title give? As opposed to fiction, the title of a non-fiction work (a book, a journal article, or even a report) needs to tell the reader what the work is about. A work's title can convey a lot of useful information about content, organization, and tone. It may also indicate whether the author plans to tell you about the topic or argue some aspects of it. Of course, you should not decide whether a book will be useful to your research *solely* by its title, but it is often a good starting point. For example, what assumptions can you make about works with the following titles (both deal with globalization)?

Perry-Globa, P., Weeks, P., Zelinski, V., Yoshida, D., & Colver, J. (2007). *Perspectives on Globalization.* Toronto: Oxford University Press.

Clarkson, S., & Wood, S. (2010). *A Perilous Imbalance: The Globalization of Canadian Law and Governance.* Vancouver: University of British Columbia Press.

Both titles contain words that inform their readers about whether the author is discussing a topic or arguing it. The title of the first book suggests that readers will look at different viewpoints about globalization, such as how it affects individuals. The second title indicates that the book will look at globalization from a distinctly Canadian perspective, with a focus on law.

By reading each word of a work's title carefully, you can often determine whether it will be useful to your research.

Exercise **1.8**

Many of your textbooks will include references to journal articles, books, and other media. These may be found under Notes, Bibliography, or Suggestions for Further Reading (perhaps at the end of each chapter). Using a textbook in your favourite subject, choose two journal or book titles listed in it and analyze them word by word. Describe what you think each work will be about.

Other pre-reading questions include the following:

- *How long is the text?* Few people begin an essay without leafing through the pages to find the ending; this impulse reveals how much reading time it will require. You should make sure you have the time to complete your first reading in one sitting to get a sense of the whole. With a longer essay or a book, you can do this with individual sections or chapters.
- *Who is the author?* Do you know anything about him or her? Is he or she featured in your textbooks? Is this a person your instructor has mentioned?
- *What is his or her profession?* Nationality? Are any other important or defining characteristics listed, such as experience in the field?

- *Does he or she belong to or have affiliations with a specific organization, group, or community?* For example, is this person employed by the Government of Canada? Is he or she part of a cultural group being written about or studied?

- *Does he or she seem to be an expert in the field?* What shows you this? Is the author affiliated with an academic institution or organization? Are the author's other works listed?

- *Why was the book/essay written?* Was it written to convince readers of a particular opinion or point of view? If so, how would this affect the way you use it?

- *Is the essay/book divided into parts?* Are there headings throughout the essay? Sub-headings? Do they tell you about content or organization? Extra spacing between paragraphs could indicate divisions. In a book, you would look for chapter titles and, perhaps, sub-headings within individual chapters.

- *When was the essay/book written?* The date might be found in a footnote at the bottom of the first page, or after the essay. In a book, the publication date usually appears on the copyright page (the other side of the title page). A recent date does not necessarily make the work recent; for example, the book may be a reprint of a much earlier edition. On the other hand, if the book has been revised since it was first published, changes or updates may make it especially useful. Essays that appear in an edited collection were probably first published earlier than the collection itself (though essays are sometimes commissioned for a volume and would then bear the same date).

- *To whom is the essay/book addressed?* Who was it written for? If an essay, what publication does it appear in, and what does this information tell you? If the publication is a journal, it could be a refereed scholarly journal: one in which the articles have been evaluated by knowledgeable peers. An article in a refereed journal is usually a reliable source if you are writing a research essay.

- *If a book, who is the publisher?* An academic or a university press? Again, if you are writing a research essay, a scholarly publication might be a more reliable source than a book aimed at a wide, non-specialized audience.

- *What is the level of language used?* Does it seem difficult, specialized? If the answer is "yes," you may have to do a little background reading or exploratory research—at the very least, you will need to read carefully, defining words by their contexts wherever possible and making sure you have your dictionary handy. (Word Meanings will be covered later in this chapter.)

- *Is there an abstract that summarizes the entire essay?* Usually, an abstract precedes an essay. In a book, the Preface, Introduction, or Foreword might give you this information. The editor of an essay collection often summarizes the essays in an introduction or a foreword.

First Reading

It's a good idea to first read the essay or chapter for content and general impressions. Some people like to underline or highlight important passages, but do not mark too much on your first reading. You will be better able to see what is more important and what is less important *after* you've read through the work once. As you read a text the second time, underline or highlight additional passages.

Other people prefer to write comments, thoughts, associations, criticisms, questions, or additions, in the margin of the text (assuming you own the text!). Still others prefer to respond to the text on a separate piece of paper or document, keeping their own notes and the source text apart. If you're not sure which method works best for you, experiment. Responding in some way to the text is the most natural way to make it relevant to you, even if that means you just write abbreviations or symbols such as ?, ??, !, N.B., or *, **, or *** in the margin to indicate levels of importance. Research note-taking will be covered in more depth in Chapter 11.

When reading a text, remember to ask yourself questions, such as the following, that will help you read critically. As you begin reading texts at the college or university level, you are acquiring new critical thinking skills, so it is important to consciously think about these issues. Once you become more familiar with reading and critical thinking, the questions below will become second nature, and you will find that you answer them without even thinking about them.

Your early written responses to a reading can be compared to your first explorative attempts to discover a topic or an approach to a topic during the inventing stage of writing. You may feel tentative about recording your thoughts, but simply writing them down can be helpful; it will give you something to build on as you consider and reconsider the reading.

- *What are your impressions of the first few paragraphs?* Did they draw you into the work?
- *Is there a distinct introductory section?*
- *What is the **tone**?* (i.e., the writer's attitude to the subject matter—for example, familiar, objective, detached, casual, humorous, ironic, formal, informal?). Tone can vary greatly from discipline to discipline or even from journal to journal, with scientific writing typically sounding the most detached.
- *What kinds of words are used?* More specifically, what is the vocabulary level? (Simple, sophisticated, general, specific, specialized?)
- *Is jargon used?* **Jargon** consists of words and expressions used among members of a group or in a particular discipline that its members would understand but that people outside those groups would not necessarily understand. Sometimes jargon becomes part of everyday speech, such as ASAP (from the military) and STAT (from the medical community).

Tone is the writer's attitude to the subject matter—for example, familiar, objective, detached, casual, humorous, ironic, formal, or informal.

Jargon is the language that is specific to a field that those involved clearly know.

- *What kind of essay is it?* (Persuasive, expository, personal, narrative, descriptive, combination of different kinds? Chapter 5 will cover kinds of essays in more detail.)
- *What is the essay/chapter about?* Do you know anything about the subject? Do you know of (or have you read) other works on the subject?
- *Can you identify the thesis?*
- *Can you identify the essay's/chapter's main points?* Are they in paragraph topic sentences, for example?
- *Do the points seem well supported?* Is there always enough detail provided?
- *What kinds of sources does the writer use?* Does the writer use footnotes, endnotes, or parenthetical references?
- *Is the text easy to follow?* Are the points clearly expressed or is the meaning sometimes unclear? Note areas where the meaning is unclear to you. Underline unclear passages with a different-coloured pen or place question marks in the margin. If you are using an electronic copy, highlight the relevant passage. If you are able to convert an online PDF document to a Word document, you may even choose to add comments, using the New Comment function. This will tell you that you need to come back to these passages and give them closer attention. If the passage is not clear, is it due to unfamiliar words? Can you determine word meanings from the context or should you use a dictionary?
- *Does the author always seem confident and certain about what he or she is saying?* Does he or she ever express reservations or doubt? Does he or she ever appear to contradict him- or herself?
- *Does he or she seem to change his or her position at any point?*
- *Does the work shift its focus?* If so, is there an apparent reason for this?
- *Does the work seem to build?* Does it get stronger or weaker? Where?
- *Is there a distinct concluding section?* Is it satisfying? Are the questions that are raised in the introduction addressed in the conclusion?

Exercise 1.9

Using the same material from Exercise 1.8, choose five of the questions on pages 21–22 and further analyze the book or journal. Write a short description (no more than one or two sentences) for each question you have chosen to analyze. Provide examples, if relevant. Would either of the two titles you have analyzed be appropriate for use in an essay? Be prepared to explain why.

❯ Sample Professional Essay

Here is an excerpt from a reader's response to a first reading of an essay on the loss of knowledge in our society. Notice the use of highlighting and annotation.

SAMPLE PROFESSIONAL ESSAY (EXCERPT)

How More Information Leads to Less Knowledge

by C. Thompson

[1] Is global warming caused by humans? Is Barack Obama a Christian? Is evolution a well-supported theory?

> The author uses current issues to attract the attention of an American audience, but these issues also are relevant to a larger audience.

[2] You might think these questions have been incontrovertibly answered in the affirmative, proven by settled facts. But for a lot of Americans, they haven't. Among Republicans, belief in anthropogenic global warming declined from 52 percent to 42 percent between 2003 and 2008. Just days before the election, nearly a quarter of respondents in one Texas poll were convinced that Obama is a Muslim. And the proportion of Americans who believe God did not guide evolution? It's 14 percent today, a two-point decline since the '90s, according to Gallup.

> *Incontrovertibly* means "not open to question or dispute."

> Is this the same in Canada?

> Is the author saying that belief in evolution is decreasing?

[3] What's going on? Normally, we expect society to progress, amassing deeper scientific understanding and basic facts every year. Knowledge only increases, right?

> Notice how the writer asks questions to involve you in the article.

[4] Robert Proctor doesn't think so. A historian of science at Stanford, Proctor points out that when it comes to many contentious subjects, our usual relationship to information is reversed: Ignorance increases.

> *Contentious* means "causing or involving argument"—so do we prefer not to know?

> The thesis is supported by research: more information = more ignorance!

[5] He has developed a word inspired by this trend: *agnotology*. Derived from the Greek root *agnosis*, it is "the study of culturally constructed ignorance."

> Proctor has developed new terminology to explain the growing trend.

(continued)

> Note the bias here. We are only told about anti-Obama groups. Does the pro-Obama side also do this? Do Canadian articles ever show similar political bias?

[6] As Proctor argues, when society doesn't know something, it's often because special interests work hard to create confusion. Anti-Obama groups likely spent millions insisting he's a Muslim; church groups have shelled out even more pushing creationism. The oil and auto industries carefully seed doubt about the causes of global warming. And when the dust settles, society knows less than it did before.

> What are some ways that the truth can be found? What reliable sources would you use?

[7] "People always assume that if someone doesn't know something, it's because they haven't paid attention or haven't yet figured it out," Proctor says. "But ignorance also comes from people literally suppressing truth—or drowning it out—or trying to make it so confusing that people stop caring about what's true and what's not."

> Here is an example the author uses to support the thesis. Are there other examples where the truth has been manipulated to keep readers in the dark?

[8] After years of celebrating the information revolution, we need to focus on the countervailing force: The disinformation revolution. The ur-example of what Proctor calls an agnotological campaign is the funding of bogus studies by cigarette companies trying to link lung cancer to baldness, viruses—anything but their product.

[9] Think of the world of software today: Tech firms regularly sue geeks who reverse-engineer their code to look for flaws. They want their customers to be ignorant of how their apps work.

—Thompson, C. (2009, January 19). How more information leads to less knowledge. *Wired.* Retrieved from http://www.wired.com/techbiz/people/magazine/17-02/st_thompson

Exercise **1.10**

Choose one of the articles that you used in Exercises 1.8 and 1.9. Using the strategies discussed in the section First Reading above, read through the article and make annotations based on the most relevant items in the bulleted list. Once you have completed this, examine the points that you have noted. Identify the strongest points in the essay. Are there particular arguments or statements that you feel are stronger than others? Are there any sections that you feel weaken the essay? Are there any words you do not understand based on the context? If so, do you need to look them up in a dictionary?

Second Reading

In your second reading and successive readings of a work, your ability to apply critical and analytical skills is very important. With practice, these skills will become active in all your reading. Asking yourself the questions listed below as you read will help you develop these skills. As well, these are the kinds of questions we will be asking in Chapter 4, Paragraph Development, and other places in this text that address specific writing skills.

- *Is the introduction effective?* What makes it effective or not?
- *What specific strategies does the writer use to draw you into the work?* (Questions, quotation, anecdote, narration, description, analogy?)
- *Is the author's purpose in writing clear from the start?*
- *What audience is the work written for?* Is the choice of words always appropriate for this audience?
- *Why does the writer use the tone that he or she does?*
- *Is the main thrust of the work argumentative—does it try to persuade you to change your mind about something?* Or, is the intent of the writer to explain or explore something? Or is it something different—to describe something or tell a story, for example?
- *Is the main point of the work (the thesis statement) announced in the introduction?* If so, what is the thesis statement? Can you put it in your own words?
- *How, specifically, are the points backed up?* What kinds of evidence are used? (Examples, illustrations, facts, statistics, authorities, personal experience, analogies?)
- *How does the writer organize the work?* Is one method used more than any other? (Compare/contrast, definition, cause and effect, narration, description, division, other?)
- *Does the author appear reliable?* Trustworthy? Fair?
- *How are the main points arranged?* Is the strongest point placed near the beginning, middle, or end? Is the most effective order of points used?
- *Does the work depend more on logic or on emotion?*
- *Does the writer appeal to a set of values or standards?*
- *Do there appear to be any lapses in logic?*
- *If the points are not always clear, why not?* (Specialized language, insufficient background given, poorly constructed paragraphs, faulty or ineffective writing style, inconsistencies or contradictions in the argument?)
- *Is the conclusion effective?* What makes it effective or not? Does it accurately wrap up the essay? Does it leave you feeling that something is missing?

An anecdote is an incident or event that a writer describes because it is interesting or striking.

Narration relates a scene or an incident and can even include some dialogue.

Description is the use of concrete information, primarily what can be seen, but it can also make use of other senses.

An analogy is a comparison between one object and a second object that is otherwise unlike the first one.

❯ Word Meanings

Dictionaries are an important part of writing, whether you are a professional writer or a student writer, whether you do your writing mostly by hand or use a word-processing program from start to finish. They are also an essential part of the reading life, and every student needs at least one good, recent dictionary, or you may just chose to use reliable online dictionaries. But while a good dictionary is part of the key to understanding challenging texts, it is not the only one.

The texts you read at the college and university level may be more challenging than you are used to. To look up every word you don't understand would require too much time. If you interrupt your reading too often, you may lose your train of thought and/or miss important points. Thankfully, you don't need to know the precise meaning of every word you read; you need to know the exact meanings of the most important words but only approximate meanings for many of the others.

Use a dictionary only when you have no idea what a word means or to confirm a guess; otherwise, try to determine meanings through context clues or similarities with words you already know.

The meanings of important nouns, verbs, adjectives, and adverbs are often revealed through context—the words around them. If an author thinks the typical reader won't know a certain word, he or she may define it or may use a **synonym** or rephrasing to make its meaning clearer. Or the author may let the surrounding words clarify the meaning and **connotation** of the unfamiliar word.

Context clues: Specialized words, such as words borrowed from another language or culture are defined for general audiences:

> The *waribashi* (disposable wooden chopsticks) are provided for free at many Japanese restaurants.

Particularly important concepts may be given an expanded definition:

> *Culture shock*—the cycle of liking, then disliking, then accepting the new culture one is in—is a theory that is widely accepted among linguists and social researchers.

Even in highly specialized writing, the writer may define terms the reader might not know:

> Even though the Danish government eliminated *thimerosal* (the preservative that anti-vaccination people believe causes autism) from its vaccines in 1992, rates of autism have continued to increase. (Thompson, "Science fiction: why are so many radicals rejecting science as a right-wing conspiracy—and embracing irrationality?")

Rather than being stated directly in a clause or phrase that follows, a definition can be implied in a preceding sentence:

Ruttenbur and the soldier have a joint house and property in the game, even though the soldier is married in real life. Such in-game *polygamy* is common. (Thompson, "Game theories")

When a writer doesn't define a word, you may be able to infer its meaning through context—by looking at the words around it and at the idea the writer is trying to express. In the following example, a second statement (following the semicolon) helps to reveal the word's meaning:

Results from the emotions questionnaire indicated that the personality changes were *mediated* by the emotions experienced while reading; a person's emotional state is known to influence his or her scores on personality tests. (Oatley, "The science of fiction")

In the next example, the author's use of *either . . . or* shows us the contrast between two words. Since you probably know that *virtuous* means "morally good," you can infer that *insidious* must mean something bad ("deceptive" or "treacherous"):

We are blinded by cuteness, and the very traits that make a character either virtuous or *insidious* are lost on us. (Poplak, "Fear and loathing in Toontown")

What follows a word may suggest its meaning, not by defining or rephrasing but by expanding or illustrating through examples.

He has a lot of *chutzpah*—his exaggerated swagger, his condescending tone, and his overinflated ego all point to this.

Exercise 1.11

Using context clues, your knowledge of similar words, or a suitable dictionary, determine the meanings of the italicized words in the short passages below. Then, write a one-sentence definition of each word. If you determine the meaning through context or other clues, look up the word in a dictionary and compare your definition with the "official" dictionary definition.

1. In *virtual* spaces, questions of moral behavior seem to have been passed over entirely, perhaps because, until recently, few games have been specifically designed to allow people to virtually participate in morally *reprehensible* behavior. The record-breaking sales of the Grand Theft Auto series guarantee that this will soon change. Such a huge market for the game has shown that there is a collective desire to *immerse* oneself in virtual *misbehavior*. (Andrew Tuplin, "Virtual morality")

2. This is not to *disparage* political activism; the sheer *intractability* of injustice is why we have a moral *imperative* to fight it. But when I started writing about science, I felt, for the first time in a long while, an unusual emotion:

(continued)

optimism. The *dogged* focus on progress, on knowing a bit more about the world than we knew a few years ago, is insanely *infectious.* (Clive Thompson, "Science fiction")

3. Sadly, *segregationist rhetoric* has consistently *hijacked* the debate over black-focused schools, overshadowing what's really at stake. *Proponents* of the concept say it bears no resemblance to segregation, and that they can't afford to worry about the political *optics* when they have the chance to do something—anything—to address the crisis in black education in not only Toronto but the country as a whole. (Andrew Wallace, "The test")

Denotation is the literal meaning of a word.

To sum up, reading carefully to determine both the immediate context and the main idea of the sentence or passage can help you determine a word's meaning. Of course, if you are still in doubt, you should look up the word. By examining a word's **denotations** (dictionary definitions) and at least one of its connotations (the way the author uses it in a particular context) you are well on the way to making it part of your writing vocabulary.

Improving Vocabulary

Just by attending a post-secondary institution, you are broadening your vocabulary. Each profession has its own specialized vocabulary that you will learn as you progress to your final certification. Your instructor may explain these new words, or they may be defined in the glossary of a textbook. Many times you can infer the meaning of a word from the context; however, you usually need to know its specific meaning before you use it yourself. There are a number of ways you can discover the meaning, such as looking it up in the dictionary, or, if you are reading on a digital device, highlighting the word and getting the definition immediately.

Another way to improve your vocabulary is to read. It does not matter what you read! It can be blogs, webpages, graphic novels, or even magazines. Go to your local bookstore, browse through the magazines, and find one that feeds your interest. There are many that represent hobbies, travelling, and even scientific exploration. The more you read, the more you discover new vocabulary. Some magazines, such as *Reader's Digest*, include vocabulary building exercises, and you can find games like these online. You can also look in a thesaurus to discover synonyms for words you already know. Then you can try out the new word when writing an essay. Just make sure the meaning is appropriate by checking it in a dictionary.

Word search puzzles, crossword puzzles, Scrabble, and Boggle are also fun ways to improve your vocabulary. If you are going to do crossword puzzles, start with easier vocabulary levels. (Do not start with the *New York Times* crossword puzzle, as this is one of the most challenging in North America.) You can go online and find many of these for free. You might be surprised at how many words you already know!

Once you have learned new words, it is important to use them so that they become part of your vocabulary. You can maintain a word journal, either on paper or digitally. No matter which form you choose, it is important to add to it and review your new vocabulary regularly. Select new vocabulary that you can work into conversations. Your friends may ask you to explain the meaning, and by doing this, you are helping them increase their knowledge as well. Conversely, you can also learn new words from others in the same way. The important thing is to become comfortable with them. Practise using them as often as possible so that they become part of your everyday vocabulary.

Conversely means "on the other hand." If you don't already know this word, you can add it to your journal.

❯ Sample Professional Essay

The author of the following essay includes many inferences. He expects you to be able to link his ideas to the thesis without him explaining how they relate. While reading, try to identify the main points that appear to be inferences. Once you have completed this, decide whether the inference is clear or if a direct statement would have made the point more clearly.

SAMPLE PROFESSIONAL ESSAY

Almost Famous Canadian Olympians

Anonymity is the rule, not the exception, on the world's
biggest sporting stage
by Jonathon Gatehouse

[1] Don't get her wrong, representing Canada at the Beijing Olympics was one of the great experiences of Sultana Frizell's life. Marching in the Opening Ceremonies, wearing the red maple leaf and, when it came time to chuck her four kilograms of steel, the unimaginable thrill of standing on the field at the Bird's Nest stadium in front of 91,000 people. But the truth was that few were there to watch her, or the other women's hammer throwers. The cheering and the attention was reserved for the men's 400-m heats taking place on the track at the same time. Back home, her event wasn't being carried on TV; it was relegated instead to live streaming on the CBC website. Her parents couldn't even watch. Their house in the countryside near Perth, Ont., only has dial-up.

In informal writing such as this, sentence fragments and comma splices can often be found. If you are not familiar with these, Chapter 14 discusses them in detail.

The author is giving concrete examples to illustrate his thesis.

[2] And Frizell—who shattered her own Canadian record and entered the world's top 10 with a toss of 75.04 m earlier this season—knows that it won't really be any different

(continued)

> The author expects you to infer the thesis, which is that certain sports will not be the noticed at the Olympics.

this time around in London. "When it comes to the Olympics, hammer throwing is definitely the smelly kid on the playground," the 28-year-old says with a laugh. The Games motto—*citius*, *altius*, *fortius*, translates to "faster, higher, stronger." There's nothing in there about "equal."

> The topic sentence clearly supports the thesis.

[3] Anonymity is the rule, not the exception, on the world's biggest sporting stage. There will be 10,500 athletes representing 205 nations competing at the 2012 Summer Games, and the vast majority of them are destined to return home just as overlooked as when they arrived. With 302 medal events in 26 different sports spread out over 17 days, there is simply too much for the average fan to follow. And for every star like Usain Bolt, who became an instant global icon by streaking to victory in the men's 100-m sprint in Beijing, there are hundreds of Olympians who would be overjoyed just to be recognized by anyone other than their friends and family.

> The author gives another example of an overlooked sport in Canada.

[4] Vancouver's Inaki Gomez started out as a swimmer, specializing in the 200-m butterfly, before a car accident early in his teens left him with a damaged disc in his neck and changed his athletic path. Unable to train in the pool, he switched his focus to the track and discovered a talent and passion for race walking. He was the provincial boys champion his last two years of high school. During his time at the University of British Columbia, he placed fifth at the World University Games and was named the school's outstanding male athlete. He is ranked number one in Canada over the 20-km distance, and is aiming to place among the top 15 in the world in London. And in a sport where one foot has to be on the ground at all times, his average pace-per-kilometre is just a tick over four minutes—something few runners can sustain. But all that doesn't buy you much respect. He sees the people gaping as he powers past them on the sea wall in Stanley Park, and hears their sniggering, and sometimes even the taunts and insults. It's part of being a race walker—at least in North America—and you simply have to learn to let it roll off your back. "Anything that anybody would say about our sport we've heard at one point or another," says the 24-year-old. "You become thick-skinned about it."

> Like all good writers, the author acknowledges differences.

[5] There are a few places where the sport is truly cherished. Earlier this spring, Gomez competed at the International Association of Athletics Federations (IAAF) World Cup in Saransk, Russia, a place he refers to as the "Mecca of race walking." The national training centre since Soviet days, and the capital of the Republic of Mordovia, the city is a little off the beaten track—the few images linked to Google maps include a picture of goats standing at the feet of a statue of Lenin—but the locals know their stuff. Gomez was impressed to see banners depicting the sport's greats hanging from the lampposts, and awed by the tens of thousands who lined the streets to watch the race. Their support helped inspire him to a 14th-place finish in the strongest field he has yet encountered in his young career.

[6] Gomez expects the atmosphere in London to be similar—the race walking course runs along the mall in front of Buckingham Palace and it is one of the Games' few unticketed events, open to anyone who cares to come and watch. But he's also realistic about how much attention his own efforts are likely to garner back in Canada. For most fans, race walking is a peripheral sport at best. It would probably take an Olympic medal to even start changing that, but for now Gomez is content with the knowledge that fellow Olympians understand he is every bit as much an athlete as they are. "They know the level of intensity and effort that we put into it," he says.

> The author helps explain why the athletes continue to train despite the lack of recognition.

[7] The enormous scope of the Summer Games—which boasts 11 more sports and almost four times as many athletes as the Winter quadrennial—guarantees not every event will find a place in the sun. But in recent years, the International Olympic Committee has moved to limit the size of the competition, and winnow away some of the less popular pursuits. When BMX bike racing became an official medal event in 2008, it was at the expense of the 1000-m track cycling time trial. Golf and rugby sevens will join the Olympics at Rio 2016, taking the spots of baseball and softball, which were turfed for failing to attract enough nations (and TV viewers), despite their popularity in the Americas and parts of Asia. The churn has been fairly constant over the years. All told, more than 50 sports have now come and gone since the first modern Games in 1896. Rope climbing was a medal event on five different occasions. There was once an Olympic swimming obstacle race where competitors had to clamber over rowboats, and a contest to see who could glide the furthest after diving into the pool. The 1900 Paris Games had a live pigeon-shooting contest—Léon de Lunden of Belgium won gold with 21 confirmed kills. And for three Olympics starting with Los Angeles in 1984, solo synchronized swimming was a sport. Tastes change.

[8] But the temptation to judge sports on the basis of how many spectators or how much media attention they attract does disservice to the athletes. There are no easy paths to the Olympics.

> In an academic essay, paragraphs must be longer than two sentences.

[9] Cory Niefer began shooting competitively 24 years ago, when he was a pre-teen army cadet in Yorkton, Sask. The Canadian air rifle champion for more than a decade, he missed out on a 2008 Olympic berth by a couple of millimetres, placing second at the 2007 Pan Am Games. Sticking with his dream meant enduring another four years of travel and penury, but the 36-year-old will finally be there in London, competing in two disciplines, standing and prone. In preparation, he's taken a year away from his work as a sports psychologist in Saskatoon (the federal government provided him with four months' worth of funding) and thrown himself into training. An average day now begins with an hour of stretching and visualization, followed by two range sessions totalling five hours, and then a couple of more hours in the gym working on his cardio, core

(continued)

strength and flexibility. "As shooters, we have to do our physical training outside of our technical training," he says.

[10] Hitting a one-centimetre-wide bullseye from 10 metres away is no simple matter—just the beating of your heart is enough to throw off your aim. A perfect shot demands that you are both perfectly still and entirely relaxed at the moment you squeeze the trigger. Niefer likens it to holding an incredibly difficult yoga pose. "Most sports are all about movement; ours is about non-movement," he explains. "You can't use your nervous energy or adrenalin." The opening round is more of a marathon, with competitors given one hour and 45 minutes to fire 60 shots. And then when the medals are on the line, it becomes a sprint, 10 shots with no more than 75 seconds between them. "There's a huge mental component," says Niefer. "And that's where my talent really lies."

[11] Donna Vakalis of Toronto will also have to contend with those challenges on the range, but in her case they will come toward the end of a five-event day. The 32-year-old architect is one of two Canadian women competing in the modern pentathlon, which combines fencing, a 200-m swim race, a round of show jumping on an unfamiliar horse, and a three-kilometre run interspaced with stops to shoot at targets with a pistol. "It's probably the Games' most exciting and eccentric event," she says. Introduced by the founder of the modern Olympics, Pierre de Coubertin, in 1912, it is meant to replicate the experiences of a 19th-century soldier carrying a message across enemy lines.

> The author discusses further ways sports are not recognized. How does this situation compare to that in other countries?

[12] Vakalis knows that few Canadians share her enthusiasm for the sport. And the indifference even extends to the federal government and the groups that help Olympians—she receives a total of $6,000 a year in funding from her province and federation and pays for the rest of her training and travel on her credit cards. Attempts to convince her bank to extend her a line a credit have been met with incredulity. And her sponsors are a couple of friends who allow her to live in their home rent-free, and the Toronto company that gives her boxes of power bars. "If you have any riches, you part with them to become a pentathlete," she says. But the scant prospects of fame, fortune or even recognition haven't diminished her satisfaction and excitement over having made it to London. "The reward is the competition itself, and the training," says Vakalis, who started the pentathlon in her teens, long before the women's event became part of the Olympics in 2000. "I'm doing it for me."

[13] Sultana Frizell has a similar explanation for why she continues to sweat and strain in pursuit of excellence, but surely little glory. The hammer throw is the only track and field event that's excluded from the IAAF's "Diamond League," a globe-circling series of stadium competitions featuring large cash prizes. The rationale is that heavy metal balls tear up the infield too badly, and pose a potential threat to other competitors

and officials. Instead, there's the "IAAF Hammer Throw Challenge," nine events in far-flung places like Korea and Senegal, where the winner takes home US$2,000, the silver medallist $1,500, and the third-place finisher $1,000. They're fun, but hardly big time. "For the one in Eugene, Ore., we had about 100 people watching, which was great," says Frizell. "And in the Czech Republic there was a crowd of about 50."

[14] No wonder then that her all-time favourite competition isn't the challenge circuit or even the Olympics, but a festival in Fränkisch-Crumbach, a German town of 3,000 about an hour outside of Frankfurt, that's held each June. The locals set up the throwing cages on a field behind the grocery store and turn out en masse to cheer. There's a beer garden and sausage vendors. "By the end of the competition there are 1,000 drunk-ass Germans who are just so excited you are there," enthuses Frizell. "It's amazing." (Do a little digging on YouTube and you will find a video of the six-foot, 220-lb. former figure skater performing a cartwheel at the medal ceremony to show her appreciation.)

[15] She's looking forward to once again hitting the centre stage in London and competing in front of 80,000 people in the main stadium. And if few people are actually paying attention when her big moment comes, it doesn't really matter. This time her mother will be on hand to watch, just in case there's no TV coverage, or Internet problems back home. And her friends on the field will be cheering. "We know we're not the premier event," she says. "So we try to motivate ourselves. We get excited for each other." After all, even without the hype, it's still the Olympics.

> The author ends with the inference that despite the lack of recognition, the athletes still have attained the dream of competing in the Olympics.

—Gatehouse, J. (2012, July 12). Almost famous
Canadian Olympians: Anonymity is the rule, not the exception,
on the world's biggest sporting stage. *Maclean's*.
Retrieved from http://www2.macleans.ca

Post-reading Questions

1. Now that you have read the article, look at the title, the author, and the name of the publication. Was the title an accurate indicator of what was in the article? What main ideas did you think the author would address? Were these addressed?

2. Go back and read the article carefully, underlining words or phrases you do not clearly understand. Can you infer the meaning from the context? Check your inferences against the dictionary definition. Remember that there is often more than one meaning for a word written in the dictionary, so read through all the definitions to ensure your knowledge is correct.

3. Go through the questions about the second reading on page 25. After reading the article a second time, what differences did you note between the first and second reading?

(continued)

4.   The author begins by discussing Sultana Frizell and then ends with her again. Do you think this was an effective way to end the essay?

5.   What vocabulary did you learn in this article that you could include in your own speaking and writing?

Chapter Review Questions

1.   What approach to essay writing is discussed in this chapter?

2.   Why is reading important in the writing process?

3.   What role does critical thinking play in essay writing? In reading?

4.   What are the different types of reading strategies you may use at college or university? What are the strengths of each?

5.   Why is it important to develop vocabulary? What are some effective ways to build your vocabulary?

The Writing **Situation**

In this chapter, you will

- understand the importance of "purpose" in the writing process
- understand the importance of "audience" in the writing process
- review the steps involved in the writing process
- learn how to write a critical response based on an essay you've read

You need to have a clear understanding of why you are writing and to whom you are writing. This will help you create a strong essay that has your reader in mind. This chapter will help you assess your purpose and audience by introducing you to factors to consider before you begin writing. You will also be introduced to the important steps good writers use when drafting an essay for college or university.

Purpose is your reason for writing, as well as how you will approach the task.

Writing Purpose

Before you begin writing, you need to think about many factors, including your **purpose** for writing and your audience. Purpose is more than your reason for writing. Assessing purpose could involve any number of the questions below and address either broad or specific concerns. If you are uncertain about your writing purpose, try to clarify it—either by asking your instructor or by using techniques such as pre-writing.

- Will you be choosing your own topic or have you been given a specific topic? If the latter, will you have to narrow the topic?
- What kind of writing will you be doing? What form will it take? (Response, essay, research proposal, lab report?)
- What main activities are involved? (Informing, explaining, arguing, narrating, describing, summarizing?)
- Does the assignment stress learning something new, or does it ask you to apply concepts and practices already taught?
- What specific skills will you need to demonstrate? How important is each to the overall assignment? For example, will you have to define, summarize, synthesize, analyze, compare and contrast, or classify? If the assignment includes a specifically worded question or statement, pay particular attention to verbs, such as *evaluate* or *assess*, *summarize*, *explore*, *explain*, *argue for or against*, *discuss*, *describe*. They each indicate a different purpose for the assignment.
- Will you be using your own ideas? Will you be basing these ideas on memory, observation, opinions, readings, class or group discussions?
- Where do your interests lie relative to the topic? How can you find out what they are and develop them further, if necessary?
- What level of knowledge does the assignment require? What level of specialization?
- Will the assignment test originality—new approaches to an old problem? (Inventiveness, imagination, creativity?)
- Should your language be formal, like that of most academic disciplines? Will some informality be acceptable—the use of contractions and/or some informal diction?
- Will you be using other people's ideas? Will you get these from books and articles or other sources? (Interviews, surveys?)
- How much preparatory reading do you expect to do? What kind of reading?
- Will you be submitting work in progress, such as pre-writing assignments, a self-survey, a proposal, an outline, a plan, or a rough draft?

- Is there a specified length? Is it a word or page range? Will marks be deducted if you write outside this range?
- How much time have you been given for the assignment? For example, an in-class exam would require a different assessment of purpose than that of an essay assigned weeks in advance.

Exercise **2.1**

A good way to prepare for an assignment is to think about the questions discussed above so that you understand what is required of you. You can do this as a self-survey, as illustrated in Table 2.1. One way to set up the survey is to divide a page into three columns. In the first column, write abbreviated forms of the most relevant questions (these could vary, depending on the assignment); in the second column, write your responses; and in the third column, briefly state what you know and/or what you need to find out to satisfy the writing purpose.

After receiving guidelines for a research essay project, Simon Walter used some of the questions to clarify his understanding of the assignment, review his knowledge about the topic he wanted to write on—massively multiplayer online role-playing games MMORPGs—and assess his preparedness, as shown in Table 2.1. Walter's research proposal, outline, and final draft will be presented in later chapters.

TABLE 2.1	Self-Survey Table	
Question	Response	Where To Begin/ What Needs To Be Done
Choice of topic?	Was given category (technology); need to narrow topic	I'm interested in writing about MMPORGS, but I need to make the topic more specific; brainstorming works best for me.
Kind of writing?	Formal research essay	I've done some online research in one of my courses but nothing on this scale before.
Main activities?	Informing and explaining, mainly, but I'll be summarizing the results of studies and relating statistics	I need to reread the sections in the text on exposition and summarizing.
Specific skills?	Many skills are relevant: analyzing, synthesizing, & summarizing; evaluating will be important because there are a lot of strong opinions out there about MMPORGS, including their pluses and minuses; I'll likely start by defining MMPORGS and divide RPGS into different categories	We're just starting to cover research, so obviously I need to become familiar with research methods and what's involved in synthesizing information from diverse sources.

(continued)

TABLE 2.1	(Continued)	
Question	Response	Where To Begin/ What Needs To Be Done
Interest and knowledge?	My interest & knowledge levels are high, as I've been a gamer for most of my life, but I'm not very familiar with the academic studies done on RPGS.	It might be hard to be objective all the time since I think that MMPORGS have been given a bad rap by many adults and educators due to recent studies; I need to be careful and not let opinion or bias creep in.
Language?	Formal language, which means no contractions. I need to know if I can use gamer slang, though.	I'm not always sure what is formal versus informal usage; I'll seek clarification from the instructor or the text.
Sources?	5 primary and secondary sources are required; according to the handout, the "4 Re's of research sources" are reputable, reliable, relevant, & recent. We are also supposed to decide ASAP on what citation style we're using.	I'm not sure how many studies have been done on the topic. Because the topic is current, I likely won't be using many books, but I may have to use some online sources, especially publisher's Web pages. Will these be considered reliable sources? I'll have to check. As I'm a humanities student, I'm going to use MLA style.
Preparatory reading?	Not really, other than maybe some background on the gaming phenomenon	Look for encyclopedia entries, books on gaming; talk to friends who are gamers?
Work in progress?	1) proposal; 2) outline; 3) 1st draft; 4) final draft; note dates for peer editing in the syllabus	I know that I will be asked to submit an informal proposal, explaining my interest and knowledge about the topic; by this point, I hope to have narrowed my topic.
Length requirements?	About 1500 words	Can I go over without penalty? How strict is the word count? Right now, it looks hard to do in 1500 words, which is why I need to work on narrowing the topic right away.
Time requirements?	We have 4 weeks before the final version is due with due dates for the stages of the project.	I need to draw up a schedule to visit the library and begin preliminary research. I think I'll need to spend a lot of time on my outline since I find it easier to write a rough draft with a solid outline to work from.

❯ "A" Is for Audience

Audience refers to whom you are writing to and their expectations.

Almost everything is written for an **audience**—readers with common interests, attitudes, reading habits, and expectations. For example, a children's book will look and read much differently than a text you would use for one of your courses. Each is designed for the people using it. The same idea applies to student writers, who must "design" each essay for a particular audience or reader.

Reader-Based versus Writer-Based Prose

Reader-based **prose** is focused on the reader. It makes clear communication a priority and acknowledges the active role of the reader in the communication process. **Reader-based prose** is geared towards the audience the essay was designed for. You need to consider who the audience is and where the reader's interests and values lie.

Prose is ordinary written language. It does not have rhythms or patterns like poetry does.

Reader-based prose is focused on the audience, not the writer.

Exercise **2.2**

Writers want their message—their communication—to be received and accepted. Looking at the writer–reader relationship this way, you could consider it a kind of contract with responsibilities on both sides. What responsibilities would a writer have in this relationship to make it more likely the message will be received and accepted? What responsibilities, ideally, should a reader have in this relationship? Add to the list in Table 2.2, assigning additional responsibilities in this contract. When you've completed the list, share it with classmates.

TABLE 2.2	Responsibilities of Reader/Responsibilities of Writer	
Responsibilities of the Reader	Responsibilities of the Writer
1. to read attentively and closely	1. to use appropriate language and a clear, readable style
2. to test the writer's claims for logic and consistency	2. to reason fairly, logically, and with consistency
3.	3.
4.	4.
5.	5.

If your instructor asks you to write using informal prose, you can address the audience directly by using the pronoun *you*. You may also be able to discuss events by using the pronoun *I*. However, in formal prose, pronouns such as *I* and *you* are usually replaced with *one* or nouns such as *reader*. The reader is often not addressed directly. Read the following sentences and determine whether they are formal or informal and state why. If the prose is informal, rewrite the sentence in formal prose. (Chapter 17 will further elaborate on the distinction between formal and informal prose.)

- Did you enjoy studying Shakespeare in high school?
- All high school students are required to complete at least one art credit in four years.
- When I chose a roommate, I was looking for someone who was responsible. I should have looked for someone who could pay the rent.
- When examining the requirements, one should pay close attention to what needs to be done first.

Writer-based prose, by contrast, is directed less towards its audience and the shared writer–reader role. Private journal writing is one example of a writing activity where there is no need to accommodate a reader.

Writer-based prose is focused on the writer, not the audience.

Exercise **2.3**

Readings and student essays have been included in this textbook. Choose one of these and analyze whether the prose is formal or informal. Are there places where the writer has changed from one type to the other? How does the style of writing affect the way you feel about the piece? Write a paragraph analyzing the reading you have chosen. Focus on whether the prose increases the writer's credibility, as discussed in Chapter 1, page 14. You may also want to use some of the questions posed in Chapter 1 about first and second readings, on pages 21–22 and 25.

Reader-based prose must be error-free and have a clear meaning. Ideas need to be expressed directly and concisely (Chapter 17 will discuss this topic in more detail). In addition, there should be no obvious gaps in logic, nor should you assume a reader knows something just because you know it. In some cases, you may have to define terms or clarify specific points. Even if the intended audience has specialized knowledge about a subject, it is best to assume that *the reader knows a little less about the subject than you do*.

In the following example, the writer should have helped a general reader by giving additional information. A reader could legitimately ask what a "deer tag" is and how it is "filled." Readers should not have to fill in gaps.

In 1998, there were more than 1 million deer tags handed out in Pennsylvania; of these only 430,000 tags were actually filled.

Exercise **2.4**

Read the following sentences and rewrite them, adding detail for the audience, if necessary.

1. Of the 1500 students enrolled, only 750 actually completed the ECE course.
2. In order to improve the world economy, many governments are introducing stimulus packages.

3. More than 75 percent of PET bottles are being thrown into landfill sites.
4. Some people compare Canada's GST to Britain's VAT.
5. 3G networks have become a selling feature for Canada's wireless providers.

Audience Factors

There are basic audience factors to keep in mind as you're writing. Consider the following criteria when you assess your work's purpose or when you think about what level of language and tone to use, how to develop your ideas, how much background to provide, what kind of support to use, and similar matters.

You can characterize an audience according to four criteria:

- *knowledge:* their background, expertise, or familiarity with the topic
- *interest level:* the extent of audience interest or potential interest
- *the reader–writer relationship:* the way an audience would be expected to respond to the writer
- *orientation:* the attitudes and emotional or ethical positions that define a typical reader

By asking these questions and trying to find accurate answers, you will be better able to create reader-based prose.

Meeting audience expectations does not necessarily mean telling its members what they *want to hear*, but, rather, doing everything you can to make it more likely they *will hear* you and understand you. For example, if you don't meet their expectations by using familiar terms or explaining unfamiliar ones, they will be less likely to "hear" you and understand you; hence they may not pay attention to the points you make. It is more effective to write *to* your audience than *for* your audience.

Exercise 2.5

Explore the databases your college or university subscribes to. Many of the articles found on these databases are written for an audience of experts. For example, the *International Journal of Clinical Practice* is written for people in the medical field, and most of the articles use terminology that these professionals are familiar with. Find an article that was written for a specialized audience. Then, using the databases, find an article about the same topic, but which is written for a general audience (you might try searching magazines or newspapers). Compare the prose and writing styles. How are different words used to convey the same information? For example, if the articles were about the use of language, which term would be used for a general audience: *discourse analysis* or *conversation turns*? Which article would you cite more if you were writing to your peers in the classroom?

Your primary audience is the people you are composing the document for, such as your instructor. Although it is tempting to consider your instructor as your sole audience, there may be others, such as other faculty members or

An audience can also vary in its attitudes towards the subject, the writer, or the thesis; these attitudes can range from very positive to very negative.

future employers, who will read your writing as well. Try to write with this larger audience of potential readers in mind. This larger audience is often referred to as the secondary audience.

Of course, it's also important to acknowledge your instructor as a reader by following directions given for the assignment. For example, if you are required to include a title page with the instructor's name and course number on it, omitting this information would be failing to meet his or her expectations. Pay careful attention to the presentation of your essay, since instructors vary in their requirements. For instance, one instructor may require you to use 12-point type while another may accept a size between 10 and 12 points. You will not make a favourable first impression with the first instructor if you use 10-point type.

❯ Sample Professional Essay

The following essay was written for a magazine, so the paragraphs are shorter than those found in an academic essay. However, the author has followed the basics, such as using topic sentences. She has also kept audience and purpose in mind while writing. Once you have read through the essay, try to identify the audience and the author's purpose for writing this essay.

SAMPLE PROFESSIONAL ESSAY

Ring! Your Intuition Is Calling

by Alice Langholt

[1] Everyone has intuition. It's a part of being human. You don't need special psychic abilities, a guru, or hours at a time to learn to hear it. The first step to accessing your intuition is becoming aware of it.

Not all people have the same understanding of the word *intuition*; therefore, the author is providing one so that all readers are starting with the same knowledge.

[2] Intuition is the act of knowing without rational thought processes. This means that knowledge or information has come to you without your deliberately thinking about it or researching the answer. Your intuition is speaking with you every minute of every day. You just need to translate the language it speaks into messages you can understand.

[3] The brain has two sides, and each side does a job. The left brain is in charge of rational thought—logic, thinking things through, making

decisions and calculating. The mind is usually teeming with left-brain chatter throughout the day. When you're thinking of your to-do list, working through problems, doing Internet research, or replaying conversations from earlier, your left brain is taking center stage. For many, this is the inner chatter that goes from waking up until falling asleep at night.

[4] The right brain is the location of your intuition. Emotions, senses, music, art and creative thought are right-brain experiences. Many people get so used to just focusing on left-brain functions that they forget to give the right brain a chance to be heard. Are you too busy to have some creative fun? Do you make time to listen to music, sit quietly and breathe? You can experience right-brain intuition when the left brain takes a break. But quieting your mind is just part of the process. Lots of people tend to dismiss intuitive information when they recognize it because it seems so out of sync with logic. But it is real.

> This statement will be supported by the author later in the article.

[5] Your right brain communicates in a sensory way, different from the language of the left brain's chatter. There are four ways in which your intuition sends messages. The first step is learning which way you are naturally in tune with your intuitive processes.

> This statement is supporting the writer's claim that intuition is real. She is further dividing intuition into four different types to make her statement seem more credible.

[6] Are you a visual person? Do you appreciate and create art? Do you use phrases like, I see, Show me, or We'll see about that? Do you prefer to read rather than listen? These are signs that your intuition may work that way, too. Intuitive information comes through visually via colors, images, vivid dreams, and when your attention is drawn to something you see. Ever been distracted by a word on a page? Has your eye been drawn to something that became significant to you later? These are visual intuitive impressions, known as clairvoyant (clear-seeing) experiences.

> The author is clarifying meaning for the reader and not asking the reader to assume anything. The author is also using questions to develop this paragraph.

[7] Are you a listener? Do you listen deeply to music, play audio books, close your eyes when listening so you can just focus on the sounds? Intuitive audio impressions come through in ringing at important times, a vibration in the ear, or snippets of song lyrics that are significant at just the right time. You might even hear a voice of reason or guidance. This is called clairaudience, or clear-hearing.

(continued)

[8] Are you a feeler? Do you get chills or tingles at important times? Does the hair on the back of your arms or neck stand up when something seems important? Do you sense other people's moods? Do you talk about how a decision feels before you make it? If so, you're naturally tuned in to clairsentience.

[9] Are you a deep thinker? Do ideas just seem to pop into your head? This is the clair that people tend to ignore, but it is a significant part of intuition. Ever think of someone and the person calls? Ever suddenly know something and wonder how you knew? This is your intuition talking.

[10] Figure out which of these intuitive methods of communication is strongest for you. This is the first step.

How can I access my intuition?

[11] Now that you know your natural intuitive strength, the next step is very important. Give it some attention. Just like anything in life, what we pay attention to grows stronger. So just take a few minutes each day to tune into your way of knowing (in a right-brain sort of way). Ask yourself a question. Start out simple. Should we have chicken or fish for dinner tonight? Then quiet down your mental chatter for a moment and tune in to your clair. What do you feel/see/hear/think? Did you feel a tingle when you said chicken? Did you hear any buzz, ring or answering thought? Go with it—don't dismiss it. If not, that's fine. Just go about your day. Before you know it, your attention will be drawn to something that represents either answer—maybe a fish sign on the back of a car, or a commercial for a local chicken takeout. Most important will be that it will grab your attention.

> The writer has been describing how the reader may have experienced intuition; now she is explaining the process.

[12] Another way to access your intuition is to give your left brain a job. That job is to take dictation. Take a piece of paper and write your question at the top. This doesn't have to be a chicken or fish question. It could be something more pressing. What is the best way for me to use my talents in a career?, Should I look for another job? or How can I improve my chances for meeting the man who's my soul mate? are all fair game. Then start writing, without stopping to think. Your right brain will dictate and your left brain will be busy moving the pen into words on the paper.

It sounds simple, but this is a powerful technique for accessing your deepest thoughts and inner guidance. Neale Donald Walsch wrote the entire book, *Conversations With God*, in this way. But anyone can learn to do this by being open to trying. The important thing is not to censor but to let the answer just flow from the pen. If you don't know what to write, just start writing a nursery rhyme until other words come out.

[13] The hardest part of any of this is being open to trying. Don't judge yourself, don't be afraid to be wrong. Just see what happens. Spending a few minutes every day on quieting down the mental chatter and tuning in to your intuitive channels will bring about results that will astound you . Try it and see!

> The author summarizes the essay and reminds the reader both that intuition exists and that it can be accessed. The author is restating the thesis for the audience to remind them of what was stated at the beginning of the essay.

—Langholt, A. (2012, July 17). Ring! Your intuition is calling. *Brain World*. Retrieved from http://www.brainworldmagazine.com

Post-reading Questions

1. How do you think the author would have changed the essay if writing for a specialized audience?
2. What is the author's purpose?
3. How do you think the author viewed the audience? Do you think she believed you would view her topic positively, neutrally, or negatively?
4. Did the author explain points well enough? Could any explanations be improved?
5. How would the inclusion of research have affected the impact of this article?

Writing for the Workplace

While you are in school, it is important to remember that your audience has specific expectations. The same is true once you are working. Your boss has specific expectations, such as the format to follow, and you need to meet them.

Just as in school, communication on the job needs to be clear and concise. You will probably have to revise each message a few times in order to meet these criteria. Remember that people at work are often overwhelmed by the number of messages they see in the day. They need to be able to scan a message to determine its importance. By being clear and concise, you are helping others work more efficiently.

When you are in the workforce, you may be asked to write for a variety of situations. Many companies rely on blogs, social networking sites, and microblog sites, such as Twitter. You may regularly have to compose emails and, occasionally, reports. While all of these seem very different from essay writing, some of the same basic principles apply. Critical thinking skills are extremely valuable, as you have to decide on the purpose of your message, the audience, the tone, and the message itself.

The purpose of your message will dictate whether you want to use an informative approach, much like an expository essay, or whether you want to persuade, much like an argumentative essay. For example, you may want to inform employees of a policy change. If it is a straightforward change, such as switching from paycheques to direct deposit, the informative approach works best. However, if you are changing the start times of shifts, you may have to use the persuasive approach, as many people might be upset about this change.

Always consider your audience when composing a message. You have to think about your primary audience, or the main parties you are composing the message for, such as your boss. But you also have to consider the secondary audience. Many business messages are read by people who are not necessarily the intended audience. For example, you may send your boss an email requesting a change to procedures, such as rearranging desks to facilitate greater communication and collaboration between employees. Your boss may take this to his or her boss, which means you now have a secondary audience. This message may also go to your colleagues, and they are yet another secondary audience. You need to be aware of these different audiences when you are composing your message.

A further consideration for workplace communication is whether the message is going to people in your department or to a more general audience. This understanding will help determine what vocabulary to use. For example, if you are working in the sales department and you are discussing "early adopters" with other people in the same department, you will not need to define this term; however, if you are writing to people who do not know this jargon, you will have to clearly explain that early adopters are customers who are quick to buy new products. It is important to tailor your message to your audience: if your audience already knows words that you define anyway, they will become bored and stop reading; if you do not define words that are new to your audience, they will become overwhelmed, and, again, they will stop reading. No message is effective if no one reads it.

Tone is important when you compose a document. You want to avoid being overbearing or condescending when writing your message. Think of how you would react if you were given your own message. Always be polite. Never compose a message in anger; if you feel you must respond to a message that upset you, leave some time between reading the message and responding to it.

When composing business documents, remember that organization is a key factor, just as when you are writing an essay. Take time to create an outline, even if it is rough. Ensure all the points you want to make are covered. This will help you avoid having to resend messages. It is especially easy to ignore this step with email messages. If you have to send out several messages about the same topic, this wastes everyone's time and signals that you are not an efficient worker or communicator, which can be harmful on the job. No one wants to promote someone who does not communicate well.

Remember that you should consider not only what you know or need to know about your audience, but also your own attitude to them. Is it positive? Neutral? Cautious? Mistrustful? What attitudes will the audience expect you to hold? What attitudes might disturb or offend its members, making them less likely to "hear" you?

Exercise **2.6**

1. What are three characteristics about writing for the workplace?
2. What are the dangers of not understanding your audience?
3. What is the difference between a primary and a secondary audience?
4. In Chapter 1, the importance of titles was discussed. What is the function of the title of a business document?
5. If a message is not clear and concise, what problems can occur?

❭ Stages in Essay Writing

Once you have considered purpose and audience, you are ready to begin narrowing your **topic**. Writing an essay inevitably means working steadily towards a goal. To get there, you will generally complete five stages:

The topic is what the essay is about.

- **pre-writing (inventing):** thinking about and coming up with a topic
- **research:** finding background information and supporting evidence (could involve intensive library resources or simply consist of examining your knowledge about a topic)
- **organization:** determining the order of points; outlining
- **composing (first draft):** getting down your ideas in paragraph form
- **revising (final draft):** revising and editing to achieve the finished version

Although various factors could affect how much time you spend on each stage, you should always plan for enough time on revision to ensure your writing is grammatical, mechanically correct, and clear.

Pre-writing

Pre-writing Strategies

Pre-writing strategies should clarify your thoughts about the subject and enable you to generate useful ideas, some of which you will use in your essay; others you can discard as you further clarify your topic. Pre-writing often brings you to the point where you can write a tentative thesis statement and, in many cases, determine your main points.

Pre-writing helps you clarify your thoughts about a subject, enables you to generate useful ideas, helps you determine your thesis, and may determine your main points.

Pre-writing strategies include questioning about the topic; brainstorming, by yourself or with others; freewriting, in which you write continuously for a specific time without editing yourself; and clustering or mapping, in which you graphically represent your associations with a subject.

Pre-writing can often lead to an outline of your main points. Although pre-writing techniques work similarly, you may find that combining all the strategies together works for you, or you may just use one. Find which works best for you.

- Questioning is often a good strategy for an expository (or explanatory) essay in the sciences or social sciences, in which your thesis can be framed as a specific question or series of questions you will try to answer.
- Brainstorming can be useful for all kinds of essays, but because it can be done in groups, it's particularly useful in collaborative projects where all group members can give input.
- Freewriting can be useful for beginning a personal essay as it enables you to make unconscious or emotional connections.
- Clustering or mapping is often useful for starting an argumentative essay, which relies heavily on logical connections. Unlike brainstorming, questioning, and freewriting, clustering is spatial and enables you to visualize the interrelations among your thoughts.

Questioning and Brainstorming

Brainstorming is writing down words, phrases, or sentences that you associate with a subject.

Asking questions and **brainstorming** are tried-and-true approaches for finding out more about a subject. Although you can pose any questions, asking the traditional journalistic questions *who?, what?, why?, when?, where?,* and *how?* can be helpful for almost any subject, such as "roommates":

Who?: Who make the best roommates? (Worst?)

What?: What are the qualities of an ideal roommate?

Why?: Why are roommates necessary? (Or not?)

When?: When is the best time to start looking for a roommate?

Where?: Where can you find a roommate? Where can you go for privacy when you have a roommate?

How?: How do you go about finding a good roommate? How do you get along with a roommate?

In brainstorming, you write down words, phrases, or sentences that you associate with a subject. You can then begin looking for ways to connect some of the items by asking what they have in common. How can you categorize them? You can often combine brainstorming with other pre-writing methods. For example, if you began by asking the journalistic questions about the subject "roommates," you could brainstorm about the qualities of an ideal roommate, using the question *what?* to generate a list. You could continue to use these two methods by then asking *why* the most important qualities on the brainstorming list contribute to a good roommate.

Although brainstorming can produce a list that looks something like an outline, the object is to come up with as many points as possible and then to connect them in some way. You don't need logical connections to begin with between any one item and the next.

Freewriting

In **freewriting**, you write for a span of time without stopping, usually five to ten minutes. You can freewrite without a topic in mind and see where your thoughts lead you, or you could begin with a specific subject or topic. You may well stray from the topic and write about something else; that is fine. You don't need to censor or edit yourself, or concern yourself with spelling or grammar. You are concerned with flow and process. There is often no need for any punctuation or capital letters: you just write without lifting your pencil from the page, or just continue typing without worrying about tabs. The important principle is that you don't stop. If you cannot think of anything to say, you write something anyway, such as "I can't think of anything to say," or "what's the point in this?" until another idea or association comes to you.

Freewriting means writing without stopping. It is important to let your ideas flow without editing or censoring them.

If you enjoy freewriting and find it beneficial, you can follow it with a looping exercise. In **looping**, you underline potentially useful words, phrases, or sentences; then you choose the best one to focus on as the beginning point for more freewriting. You can also take the most useful phrases, sum them up in a sentence, and begin freewriting using that sentence as a starting point. Although freewriting is a popular pre-writing strategy, you can use it at any point in the composing process—for example, if you get stuck on a particular point or experience writer's block when drafting your essay.

In looping, you underline potentially useful words, phrases, or sentences; then, you choose the best one to focus on as the beginning point for more freewriting.

Freewriting has several functions:

- It can free you from writer's block. A typical problem in beginning to write is feeling you have nothing to say.
- It enables you to express undiscovered feelings and associations; in other words, it gives you access to thoughts or feelings you might not have known about.
- Included with looping, it can help you narrow down a topic and, sometimes, come up with a thesis and main points.

In the freewriting sample below, the writer discovers a potential thesis for an essay. After writing for five minutes, the student was asked to underline anything he thought was usable. In this case, five minutes of writing yielded an interesting topic that was complete enough to serve as a thesis statement (shown by double underlining):

Bureaucracy can be very disturbing you can get parking tickets even when there is no parking left and you are forced to park by the yellow line and you think you'll be gone early enough in the morning where was the bureaucracy when you needed them to make the decision in the first place and it can also lead to you having to take english 100 over again because you didn't get the B- required for the elementary post-degree program even though you feel your writing should be at least a high B or A average and the teacher says just be more clear and some comma errors and gives you a mediocre mark who's to say that the best teachers are the ones who get the A average because I think the best teachers are the ones who know what it's like to struggle because they have learned hard work and they have also learned patience these two things are the most important things being a teacher or they are up there anyway.

—Y.M.

Y.M., who chose to freewrite on "bureaucracy," began with a complaint about parking, which triggered another complaint, concerning his mark in a previous English course. He continued to follow this train of thought as he complained about how the teacher had marked his writing. This led him to consider the qualities of a good teacher, which, he discovered, have nothing to do with marking or education but with the idea of having to struggle and overcome obstacles. Y.M. could then proceed to test this claim by finding evidence to support it.

Clustering

Clustering, or **mapping**, is a technique that represents ideas graphically. On a blank piece of paper, you circle your topic and then think of related words or phrases, which you record and circle, connecting each with the word or phrase that gave rise to it. Using the clustering method can help you develop your main points and provide a structure for your essay. Clustering allows you to form distinct groups of related words and phrases, which you may then develop into main points. You can often see other relationships between circles in one cluster and those in another. In the example in Figure 2.1, dotted lines represent other possible connections.

Figure 2.1 is the result of a group clustering exercise that began with the subject "vitamins" and produced this thesis statement: *Due to media hype and the promise of good health, more people than ever are taking vitamins before they really know the risks involved.* The statement needs further work, but it is a solid start.

Research

If your essay is research-oriented, you will do most of your research in a library or some place where you have access to written and electronic material. However, not all evidence comes from outside sources. Personal interviews and personal observation may also be allowed, and you can do this any place. Also, research

Clustering or mapping involves graphically linking your ideas or thoughts.

All the pre-writing methods could be considered meeting places between you and your topic. Because they are designed to "free up" your thoughts and feelings, don't hesitate to experiment with variants on these methods.

FIGURE 2.1 Clustering diagram about "vitamins"

may involve determining what you already know about a topic and considering how you will use this knowledge in your essay. Research is indispensable to college- and university-level reading, thinking, and writing. Chapter 11 will provide you with a detailed analysis of research methods.

Organization

Organization is mainly about the essay's outline. Knowing how to construct an outline is a valuable skill that can save you time. Referring to an outline in the drafting stage can prevent you from getting off-track. An outline gives you a specific plan and can be reassuring, instilling confidence as you draft your essay. Two kinds of outlines are discussed below: the scratch and the formal **outline**.

Scratch (or Sketch) Outline

A scratch (or sketch) outline represents only your main points, usually indicated just by a word or phrase. It provides a rough guideline and gives you flexibility in developing your points. It may be adequate for a short essay and equally helpful for planning an in-class essay when there is too little time for a formal outline.

Research can come from personal interviews or published sources, such as newspapers or journals.

An outline is a representation of your points and their support. Creating an outline is a crucial stage in essay writing, enabling you to see the arrangement of your ideas before you begin a rough draft.

Formal Outline

The formal outline includes sub-points as well as main points, revealing more of your essay's structure. In a formal outline, you can see at a glance how the parts interrelate—which is especially useful if the essay is long or complex, such as a comparison and contrast or research essay. A formal outline is a good choice if you lack confidence in your organizational skills, since the outline can remind you of the original plan. Chapter 12 will provide an example of an outline.

Exercise 2.7

Read through the student essay "Pandemic crisis" in Chapter 12. While reading the essay, look at the outline for this essay on pages 255–256 also in Chapter 12. Do the paragraphs follow the outline? How do you think the outline helped the writer?

> An outline written before or during the first draft should be considered a working outline in the sense that it may change as your thinking changes or as you come across new evidence. An outline should be considered an organizational help, which can be altered or adapted— not just as an end in itself.

The Value of an Outline

The following section explains how to create an outline. Outlines are a very integral part of writing successful essays. Even seasoned writers use an outline *before* beginning a new piece of work. You do not always need to follow your outline completely, and your outline may change over time, but it is extremely important that, if you want to write a well-organized, articulate paper, you do not skip this step.

Organizing an Outline

An outline is a vertical pattern of ideas and their support. General and introductory points are like headings; under each, you will list ideas connecting to the main points—related, less important points, expansions of the main point, examples, evidence. These can be considered sub-headings. Chapters 9 and 12 will provide detailed discussions of outlines for particular types of essays. Again, Chapter 12 will provide a developed outline.

Although the outline typically proceeds from the general (main) points to the specific (sub)points, another ordering principle is involved: *emphasis*. The order of the points helps determine how much emphasis each receives. For example, the last point to be made in an argument is usually the most emphatic. You can order the points in the body of your essay according to a logical method, such as the strength of the argument presented in each (this is particularly important in an argumentative essay). There are several ways to order your points logically:

- *Climax order:* You begin with your weakest, or least important point and proceed to the strongest, most important point.
- *Inverted climax (dramatic) order:* You begin with your strongest point and end with your weakest.
- *Mixed order:* You begin with a moderately strong point and follow with the weakest argument, before concluding with the strongest.

The number of main points and the strength of the opposing argument are factors that can help you determine which method is best for your topic.

General Guidelines for Creating an Outline

1. Decide on your topic and the main point you want to make about your topic; you can use brainstorming, question–answer, clustering, or freewriting to develop ideas.
2. Divide the outline into introduction, paragraphs for development, and conclusion.
3. Plan for a *minimum* of five paragraphs altogether unless told otherwise or unless your essay is very short.
4. Ensure you have one main idea per paragraph.
5. Divide your main ideas (points) into sub-points (at least two per paragraph) that develop the main idea.
6. Represent the relationship between main ideas and their points of development (or sub-points) graphically by indenting sub-points or, more formally, alternating letters and numbers to show the level of development (e.g., I, A, 1, a).
7. Ensure that the main points themselves are ordered logically and effectively.

Chapter 8 discusses outlining further and provides a template that can be used to help you get started on your outline.

Composing: First Draft

Getting words on paper in sentence and paragraph form is the most challenging stage for most writers. The traditional rough draft is based on the outline.

When you begin your first draft, do not worry if you do not have your introductory paragraph complete. You can just write your thesis statement, and then begin the first paragraph. Start with your topic sentence, and then create sentences for your sub-points. Include the illustrations (such as examples, anecdotes, or statistics) for each sub-point. Then craft a concluding sentence. Repeat this process for each body paragraph. Once you have completed the body paragraphs, try to draft a concluding paragraph. This can be a summary of everything that you have said in the body of the essay. Finally you can turn to writing the introduction.

Remember that these paragraphs are just a rough draft. Sentences can be added or deleted once the draft is complete or even as you continue writing. As you create your first draft, you may find that as you progress through your paper, the organization of the outline is not the most logical. What you thought worked best in the first paragraph may not fit there after all. Feel free to move ideas around. Your outline does not have to dictate exactly how you will write your paper. The outline is there to help ensure your ideas are logical and complete. Additionally, you may discover that a point is not relevant to your essay topic after all. Feel free to eliminate it and add a new idea. Your outline is your guide, but once you actually begin composing your paper, your ideas may branch beyond what you originally considered. This does not mean the outline is useless. In fact, the outline helps you develop your ideas in a more mature fashion.

In the first draft, your focus should be on setting your ideas down.

Composing on the Computer

You can use a computer for creating an outline and for drafting an essay. However, not all people are comfortable with this, so they may outline an essay on paper. There are advantages to both systems. When drafting on paper, even if only an outline, there is more room to add small notes. Some people write a draft on paper so that they can then draw circles and lines between similar ideas. Some feel that seeing an idea on paper helps give rise to creativity, as the blank page becomes a challenge to fill.

Drafting on a computer can save time, as you can often go back and add or revise ideas quickly. You can use different colours and fonts so that you can identify new thoughts or ideas that you want to add to the document. You can also cut whole sections and place them elsewhere to create a better sense of coherence in your paper. However, there are challenges to keep in mind when using computers to write: computers crash, files get lost, and printers run out of ink.

Keeping Copies

When you are composing your document, it is important to keep copies of previous drafts.

When you are composing your document, it is important to keep copies of previous drafts. At various stages of the writing process, save a clean copy and label it clearly so you can find it if you need to go back to it. For example, you will want to save a clean copy of your outline. Save a copy, label it clearly, for example, using the course code, the essay title or topic, and the year, as in *ENG101_HydeOutline1_2014*. Create a system that works best for you.

Once you have created a clean file, copy the whole document and create a new file. Label this and then start to work from this document. Many students, once they have created an in-depth outline, will work from that by adding details and creating a draft of their essay. So, following our example above, you can label the new file *ENG101_HydeDraft1_2014*.

After saving this first draft, again copy the document, and create a new file. You now have a new document to work from as you revise and rework the essay draft. By creating new files as you progress in the drafting of your document, should you decide you don't like the changes you have made, or should you make a mistake and cut information you did not want to delete, you can revert to the older file and start again on a fresh copy.

Alternatively, in most word-processing programs, there are track changes and comment functions you can use to make side notes or write reminders to yourself. These are especially useful in the editing stages of writing. For example, you can add a comment in the margin of your essay, such as "Find a better quote." One thing to keep in mind is that these comments and changes don't always transfer to the subsequent documents when you are saving new drafts.

While you are creating the new files and saving them, also make sure that you pause every 15–20 minutes and save your file to your hard drive on the computer. Also, make sure you save it to another source, such as a USB key. This will ensure that, even if your hard drive crashes, you have saved the document to another safe location. Most colleges and universities allow students access to the school network, so you can save documents there. (Make sure you know exactly where to save your document; saving it to the computer's desktop is generally not a safe location. Get help from the computing staff if you're unsure.) A final alternative is to pay a company to store your data for you. There are many reputable firms that can be found on the Internet. Ask your librarians or IT department staff for suggestions.

Finally, when using the computer, make sure you print out your final paper and read it carefully. Look carefully for typos, spelling errors, and grammar mistakes. You often see errors on paper that are missed when you read on the computer screen.

Revising: Final Draft

The final draft probably is the most undervalued stage of the writing process. Many student writers think the final draft is the place to apply a few necessary touch-ups. They may have assumed they were supposed to "get it right the first time." However, professional writers almost never do, so why should this be expected of student writers?

Remember that usually the first and even the second draft are essentially rough efforts to put your thinking into words.

Remember that usually the first and even the second draft are essentially rough efforts to put your thinking into words. To change the rough into final requires a new focus: the written document. When you revise, you want to build on its strengths as well as repair any weaknesses. This process could involve any or all of the following:

- **F**ine tuning
- **O**verview of purpose and audience
- **C**larifying meaning
- **U**nderscoring ideas
- **S**olidifying structure

The acronym FOCUS can help you recall the parts of the revision process. But keep in mind that while there is no "right" order in revision, "fine tuning" should always be the final stage (even though it appears first in the acronym, to make an easy-to-remember word).

Overview

Conduct an overview of purpose and audience. Ask yourself honestly whether the essay fulfills its purpose and whether it speaks to your intended audience. These questions seldom result in major changes, but you may decide you need to adjust your introduction or make minor changes in the body of the essay. For example, you might find that a point that seemed relatively unimportant in your outline turned out to be very important. You might then need to rewrite a part of the introduction to be consistent with this new emphasis. On the other hand, you might find that you have over-developed a point that is only slightly related to your thesis. You might then decide to delete a part of a body paragraph. You might also now find that some of your words were too informal for your audience and you need to find new words to replace them.

Clarifying Meaning

Try reading complicated or unclear parts of the essay aloud. Will your audience understand your meaning? These unclear passages should receive your close attention. Wherever a sentence seems awkward or too long, consider rephrasing it for directness and clarity.

It is hard to be objective when you look back at what you have written, especially if you have just written it. Leaving some time between completing the first draft and revising will help you see your essay more objectively. Also, getting someone else to read over your paper can give you valuable input, especially if he or she can point to unclear passages. Seeing the places where other people have difficulty will highlight them for close attention. The problem may be as small as a word that is out of place or that means something different from what you thought. Such seemingly small errors can obscure the meaning of an entire sentence and affect the impact of a paragraph. Work on these unclear or awkward passages.

Underscoring/Strengthening Ideas

In your body paragraphs, you introduce and develop your main ideas. These paragraphs should reinforce your thesis and support your points. Reviewing your body paragraphs might mean going back to your notes, outline, or early drafts to see if you can further support an idea that now seems undeveloped. You might decide to include an example, illustration, or analogy to make an abstract or a general point more concrete and understandable. Don't settle for "almost"; ask if *all* your points are as strong as they *could* be.

Getting someone else to read over your paper can give you valuable input, especially if he or she can point to unclear passages. Seeing the places where other people have difficulty will highlight them for close attention.

What if you now see that a point is underdeveloped but you don't know how to go about developing it further at this stage? Remember that you can use pre-writing strategies at any point in the process; their main purpose is to generate ideas. Try a brief pre-writing session to help you expand on the undeveloped point.

Solidifying/Improving Structure

In order to improve your structure, return to your outline. Does your essay's structure reflect your original plans for it? Do you see any weaknesses in the outline you didn't see before? Can you make the structure of the essay more logical or effective? If the essay's structure seems strong, look at each paragraph as a mini-essay with a topic sentence, a well-developed main idea, and a concluding thought. Not all paragraphs need to be constructed this way, but all do need to follow a logical sequence. Is each paragraph unified and coherent as well as adequately developed? Are paragraphs roughly the same length, or are some overly short or long?

The final draft usually focuses on three important stages: (1) reviewing purpose and audience and/or essay re-structuring; (2) checking for correct grammar and clear writing; (3) proofreading.

When you revise, you want to make your essay strong*er*, clear*er*, and *more* readable. When a writer makes a change to a draft it is often because he or she discovered a better way to express an idea. After all, you know much more about your topic now than you did at any other stage in the composing process.

Fine Tuning

Working on the final draft could involve some large-scale adjustments, as described above, and it will almost certainly involve some small-scale ones. In the fine-tuning stage, you shift the focus to the sentence and to individual words. Make sure each sentence is grammatical, your expression is clear and concise, and you have used appropriate transitions between sentences. You can also refine your style by checking for sentence variation. Can you combine short, simple sentences into longer, more complex ones, or can you use different sentence types to make your points more interesting? The final review is proofreading for mechanical errors and typos. Chapter 17 will explain efficient writing and editing strategies, as well as proofreading guidelines.

❯ The Critical Response

Either an in-class or an out-of-class **critical response** assignment may require you to analyze an essay you have never seen before. To do so, you need to exercise your active reading skills, beginning with comprehension of content. A response should demonstrate effective critical thinking and your ability to analyze such elements as the writer's purpose, audience, and strategies. Depending on the nature of the assignment, you may be able to use your own perspective on and/or experience about an issue. You may be asked to focus mainly on the essay itself or on the issue(s) the author raises. Critical responses can vary in length.

A critical response can be considered argumentative: a strong response will convince readers that your thesis is valid and well supported. Although a critical response often clarifies your thoughts about an issue or reveals your feelings about it, you should not force your opinions on the text. The main function of a critical response is to engage with the text and through this engagement to share your views with others.

Below are some of the objectives and conventions of response writing. Remember to pay careful attention to the guidelines you're given, as they can vary greatly from instructor to instructor and from assignment to assignment.

- Your first sentences could include an overview or generalization about the text or the central issue(s) it raises.
- If your reader is unfamiliar with the text, you will need to briefly summarize its main ideas (or its plot, if the text is a literary work or a movie).
- Include a thesis statement in which you briefly state your approach to the essay, topic, or issue.
- Don't forget that you are primarily reacting to *a text* and that the text should remain front and centre in your analysis. If you use personal experience or observation, it should never *replace* analysis but should help support a point.
- You don't need to research the topic, unless your instructor requires this.
- The length of a critical response can vary considerably from a couple of well-developed paragraphs to 500 words or more, depending on the nature of the assignment and length of the work you are responding to.
- You may be required to respond to more than just the text—for example, to another student's response to the text. In that case, you will need to filter your perspective through that of another reader, considering both the validity of his or her views and your agreement or disagreement. Sometimes, the instructor will help get you started by posing specific questions about the text.
- In addition to analyzing what is in the essay, you can consider what is *not* in the essay. What has the writer left unsaid?

The following questions are often relevant to a critical response. (Chapter 1 provides a more complete list of questions applicable to a wide range of readings.)

- Does the author appear reasonable? Does he or she use reason effectively, establishing a chain of logic throughout? Are there failures in logic?
- Does the author succeed in making the issue relevant to the reader? Does he or she appeal to the reader's concerns and values? How does he or she do this? (Or not?)
- Is the tone inviting? (Openly challenging, neutral?)
- Is the order of points appropriate? Are all points well supported?

- What, specifically, would strengthen the writer's argument?
- Does the essay appear free of bias? Is the voice as objective as possible given the argumentative stance? An author may openly declare an opinion. If this is the case, do you think this was a good strategy?
- Does the author acknowledge the other side? How does he or she respond to the opposing viewpoint? (Fairly, effectively?)
- Does the author make emotional appeals? Are any extreme or manipulative?

❯ Sample Professional Essay

The essay below was written in response to an advertisement that the author saw. It is an opinion based on a specific situation he has encountered. Immediately following this essay, there is a student's critical response to it.

SAMPLE PROFESSIONAL ESSAY

An Enviro's Case for Seal Hunt

by Terry Glavin

[1] I saw something the other day that made me sick to my stomach. It was in the February edition of The Grocer, a British retail-food magazine.

> The author is using narration in this piece.

[2] There was an article about a campaign that a group called Respect for Animals is waging to convince consumers to boycott Canadian seafood products. The magazine also carried two huge advertisements from the same outfit.

[3] One of the ads consisted of a photograph of a masked man on an ice floe, and a seal lying prone at his feet. The man was brandishing a club with a spike on the end of it. The words *You Can Stop This* were superimposed upon the picture. The other advertisement proclaimed "Boycott Canadian Seafood & Save the Seals," with a picture of a can of Canadian salmon.

> The author is providing clear details so that the reader can form a mental picture.

(continued)

[4] The Canadian fishing industry exports more than $100 million worth of products into Britain every year. The point of the campaign is to squeeze those sales until the industry begs our government to end the seal hunt.

[5] Here's what makes me sick.

The author's controversial stand is supported here with facts.

[6] The Newfoundland seal hunt is transparently and demonstrably sustainable and humane. There are roughly half a million people in Newfoundland and Labrador, and nearly six million harp seals, which is almost three times as many seals as when I was a kid.

[7] Roughly 6,000 fishermen, mostly Newfoundlanders, but some are from Quebec and the Maritimes, take slightly more than 300,000 harp seals annually. The fishermen share more than $16 million from the hunt at a critical time of year when there's little in the way of fishing income to be had. The seals are harvested for their pelts and their fat, for a range of products, mostly for clothing and for Omega-3 vitamins.

If you are not sure what *abattoir* means, check your dictionary.

[8] The killing is as about as clean as anything you're likely to find in an abattoir. Seals don't spend their lives cooped up in paddocks or feedlots. They live free, and in all but the rarest cases, the ones that die at the hands of a swiler (a sealer) die instantly. The hakapik (a spiked club) is an effective instrument.

The definition of *swiler* is provided here by the author, as it may not be found in many dictionaries.

[9] Even so, most seals are first shot with rifles. The killing of nursing white-coats was banned 20 years ago.

Exploiting empathy

[10] Here's one of those obligatory disclosures: over the years, several environmental organizations—the Sierra Club, the David Suzuki Foundation, Greenpeace, etc.—have subsidized my preoccupation with things that move in the water by having me do research projects for them and so on. With that out of the way, I can now say, if it isn't obvious already, that it's the seal hunt's opponents who turn my stomach.

By disclosing that he has worked with organizations he is now criticizing, he is fending off any possible arguments that he may be biased against the work they do.

[11] It's not just that anti-hunt crusades like this are especially foul in the way they dishonestly misrepresent facts. It's also that they dishonestly

manipulate one of the most redeeming traits the human species has inherited from hundreds of thousands of years of natural selection and cultural evolution—our capacity to expand the embrace of our empathy to include other forms of life.

[12] But far worse than all that, boycott campaigns like this muddy the important distinction between sustainability and sentiment, and between broadly co-ordinated acts of social responsibility and mere lifestyle choices. When we fail to make these distinctions we undermine everything worthwhile that environmentalism has accomplished since it emerged in the early 1970s.

[13] As citizens and consumers in free societies, we are burdened with the duty to make important decisions at the ballot box, in the work we do, and also in the marketplace. Boycotting Canadian seafood to try and stop the seal hunt is the consumer-choice equivalent of deciding to buy a tie-died shirt, move into a Volkswagen van and subsist solely on lentils and tofu.

Serious stakes

[14] Just as the excesses of postmodernist relativism have enfeebled the left over the past quarter-century or so, a corrosive strain of fact distorting, science-hating, Gaia-bothering obscurantism has enfeebled environmentalism.

[15] It was there from the beginning, and it persists most noticeably in animal-rights crusades. It is the environmentalist equivalent of anti-evolution, rapture-seeking Christian zealotry. It has to be attacked wherever it rears its head. There's too much at stake to pretend we can be innocent bystanders here. This is a fight we all have to join.

[16] Here's why.

[17] The last time the planet was in the throes of an extinction spasm this cataclysmic was when the dinosaurs disappeared 65 million years ago. One in every four mammal species, one in eight bird species, one in nine plants, a third of all amphibians and half of all the surveyed fish species on earth are threatened with extinction.

> The author begins discussing extinction in order to support his later points about seal hunting.

(continued)

[18] When Greenpeace was born in Vancouver in 1971, the single greatest cause of species extinction was understood to be habitat loss. Now, the greatest threat to biological diversity is global warming. The last time the atmosphere was accumulating greenhouse gases this fast was 650,000 years ago. The prospects look exceedingly grim—broad-scale ecological disruption, crop failure and famine, desertification and the mass dislocation of some of the most heavily-populated regions of the world.

[19] A key reason environmentalists found themselves so ill-prepared to convince the world to take global warming seriously was that their movement had been corrupted by precisely the same trippy sentiment-mongering that has animated the holy war against the Newfoundland seal hunt, which now turns its sights on Canadian fisheries products.

Where was Greenpeace?

[20] When the founders of Greenpeace were being born, back in the 1950s, the world's fishing fleets were taking roughly 40 million tonnes of marine biomass from the world's oceans every year. By the 1980s, it was 80 million tonnes. Then the seas just stopped giving. Fully 90 per cent of all the big fish in the sea—the tunas, the marlins, the sharks, the swordfish—are now gone.

[21] Of the many fisheries collapses that have occurred around the world in recent years, it is sadly ironic that the greatest single collapse occurred in the seas around Newfoundland, where the bulk of Canada's Atlantic seal hunt takes place. The Grand Banks cod fishery was the largest and oldest pelagic fishery in the history of the human experience.

[22] The cod were mined from the sea by the same big-boat offshore fleets that had caused such devastation everywhere else. A way of life disappeared, and by the early 1990s, tens of thousands of workers were reduced to welfare. While all this was happening, what were environmentalists doing on the Newfoundland coast, in the country where Greenpeace was born, at a time when Greenpeace was at the height of its powers?

[23] They were out cavorting with rich hippies and snuggling up to harp seal pups on the ice floes. They were meditating cross-legged in the snow

and posing for the television cameras and demonizing the good people of Newfoundland, while the seas around them were being emptied of cod. . . .

[24] The whole point of sustainability is to ensure that people can exercise the rights and accept the responsibilities that come with sustainably harvesting the natural resources of the ecosystems within which they live. The harp seal hunt is a living embodiment of that principle. That's why environmentalists should not just give the boycott a pass, or stay neutral, but should actively support and defend the seal hunt.

The author now brings the main point back into focus.

[25] The one consolation we can take from the recent hullabaloo is that it's faltering. Last year, when animal-rightists in the United States boasted that they'd convinced more than 200 restaurants and seafood retailers to boycott Canadian products to protest the hunt, it turned out that only a small minority were doing so. Most of them didn't even know they'd been listed as boycott-compliant.

[26] Also, the European Commission, citing the absence of evidence to support contentions that the hunt is inhumane, has refused, for now, to enforce the European Parliament's proposed ban on seal products.

Contested Council

[27] But the consumer boycott campaign that's just begun in Britain is particularly insidious. Its aim is all Canadian fisheries products, and its targets are Tesco, Sainsbury's, Somerfield and other major retail chains that have already made a commitment to eventually carrying only those seafood products that have been certified by the Marine Stewardship Council (MSC).

[28] The MSC standard remains hotly contested by responsible environmentalists, but its coveted "eco-label" holds out the hope of forcing improvements to fisheries management policies around the world. In Canada, those improvements are increasingly driven by the fishermen themselves, because they want the MSC label on their product.

[29] British Columbia's halibut fishery was turned down once, and has since re-applied, because ground fish management has significantly improved—thanks in no small part to halibut fishermen. Other

(continued)

fishermen are now lobbying federal fisheries officials to improve stock-assessment research to give B.C.'s dogfish fishery a shot at the MSC label. British Columbia's sockeye salmon fisheries have just undergone an arduous certification examination, and a decision is imminent.

[30] If the cuddliness of a particular species harvested in a particular country is allowed to become the factor that determines whether that country's products are considered environmentally acceptable, then everything we won at CITES [Convention on the International Trade in Endangered Species] and in the Brundtland Commission is lost. If those are the kinds of choices we present to everyone from major retailers down to ordinary seafood consumers, then we'll have wasted all our efforts to marshal consumer power to force the sustainable use of the oceans.

[31] It's long past time for conservationists to make a clean, clear, open and unequivocal break with crystal-gazing animal-rights eccentrics and all their camp followers. For them, the conservation of wild resources was always just a flag of convenience. They're dead ballast, so over the side with them.

[32] On the question of the Atlantic harp seal harvest, there's only one defensible and honest position for a conservation-minded citizen to take:

[33] Support the swilers.

—Glavin, T. (2007, March 7). An enviro's case for seal hunt. *TheTyee.ca*.
Retrieved from http://thetyee.ca/Views/2007/03/07/SealHunt/

Post-reading Questions
1. Do you feel the author has clearly supported his argument? Give examples of passages you think prove this.
2. Besides using argument, are there any other organizational patterns you are familiar with that you can find in this essay?
3. Do you feel that the author's disclosure that his research has been funded by environmental organizations helps or hinders his argument? Why?
4. What type of audience do you think Glavin is writing for?
5. What was Glavin's purpose for writing this piece? Did he achieve it?

❯ Sample Student Essay

Below, student Bryan Smith has written a 500-word critical response to Glavin's essay. After you have read the essay and the response, discuss with a partner whether it satisfies the requirements of the critical response essay. Then, write a 350–500 word response of your own to Glavin's essay. If your instructor wishes, you may refer to Smith's response (as he refers to responses of other students in his class).

Remember that the essay you respond to may be written more informally than your critical response to it. For example, the writer may not have cited sources or may have used slang or colloquial language. You should check with your instructor before using an informal style.

SAMPLE STUDENT ESSAY

Response to "An Enviro's Case for Seal Hunt"

by Bryan Smith

[1] Glavin provides a strong argument for the seal hunt in his article, a rare and unexpected standpoint. Though his argument takes on a fire and brimstone tone that gets more offensive as he proceeds, Glavin has me convinced: the seal hunt is wrongly accused. While I feel much of what Glavin says must be taken with a grain of salt, a number of his points make a convincing argument. First, the boycott of Canadian seafood against the seal hunt is doing more damage than good. As proven by the whale and cod crises, boycotts result in over fishing because fishermen have to take more to make profit. Canadian seafood is an entirely different problem; with increasing international fish exploitation off the shores of Canada, the boycott only steps on the toes of activists trying to fight for sustainable local fisheries. Is it any wonder Glavin is calling for responsible activism?

[2] What makes the seal hunt so awful? Indigenous hunters and fishers have been practicing their traditional methods off Canada's coasts for thousands of years with proven moderation and sustainability. Hunting is not everyone's cup of tea, but that doesn't mean it is bad. The seal hunt has gone on for thousands of years as a means of subsistence and economic support in a climate where little else can. It is not only a means

(continued)

of life but also a way of life for many people. If Canada truly is a country that celebrates diversity, condemning hunters and fishers for their traditional means of subsistence and economy is just a little hypocritical.

[3] Simply because Glavin is "ill-tempered" is not a good reason to take the other side of the argument, as some of my classmates have done. Glavin is understandably frustrated—with so much that needs to change in the world, the anti-seal hunt is just another distraction that divides a population that needs to act quickly and in unison. Glavin has clearly put a lifetime into conservationism only to have his work ignored while far-away people denounce what is perhaps the only example of sustainable fishing left. What did you expect Glavin to be? He has every reason to be ill-tempered: change needs to happen now, and it needs to be led by people who are in possession of all the facts, the power to lead, and the experience to do so. Yet distractions bar this from happening.

[4] That said, perhaps Glavin goes too far. The seal hunt has a number of benefits, it seems sustainable, and according to Glavin, it is responsibly carried out. But that doesn't mean some preventative measures should not be taken. Why not put some preventative restrictions on the hunt? With a full and thriving population, we have the time to analyse the effects of maximum kills and season restrictions before such measures have no worth. Thus, perhaps "support the responsible, moderated, and sustainable swilers" might be a better slogan.

Post-reading Questions

1. Has the student written a good response? Give specific examples to support your thoughts.
2. What specific points has he chosen to address from the original essay?
3. Are there any important points that you feel he missed and should have included? Are there any points the student writer should not have included?
4. Do you agree with the student's point of view that Glavin's essay can change people's point of view? Do you feel that Smith could have added more information to strengthen his position?
5. Are there any areas in this critical response essay that are unclear, or did the student judge his audience appropriately?

■ Chapter Review Questions

1. Why is it important to understand your audience?

2. How does formal prose differ from informal prose? Are there times when one is more appropriate than the other?

3. What is the difference between reader-based prose and writer-based prose?

4. Why is it important to have a clear purpose in mind when writing?

5. What are some questions you can ask to determine audience knowledge and interest?

6. What are the different ways you can begin writing your essay? Which one is most effective for you?

7. What are the five stages in essay writing? Why are they all important?

8. What are you asked to do for a critical response assignment?

9. What acronym can you use when revising your final draft?

10. How can revising your draft improve your essay?

Paragraph **Essentials**

In this chapter, you will

- learn how to construct an effective paragraph
- understand why it is important to write coherently
- learn techniques to improve paragraphs
- understand how effective paragraph structure reflects effective essay structure

Like an essay, a paragraph needs to have a beginning, a middle, and an end. If any of these elements is missing, such as the topic sentence, the paragraph could lack unity and coherence, and you could lose the reader's attention. In addition, paragraphs need to be connected to each other to help the reader follow the essay's points. This chapter will help you create unified and coherent paragraphs so you will write an essay that keeps the reader's interest.

Introducing the Paragraph

Like an essay itself, a paragraph must be organized to serve specific functions:

- to introduce an important point
- to develop that point
- to convey both the important point and its development clearly to the reader

A paragraph and an essay each have a beginning, a middle, and an end. The beginning announces what is to follow, usually in the topic sentence of the paragraph or the *thesis statement* of the essay. Without a clear topic sentence, the points will lack force and the paragraph will not be unified.

The middle of the paragraph develops the main point, while the ending provides a satisfying conclusion. The concluding sentence may act as a wrap by summarizing the main idea in the paragraph, much like the conclusion of an essay.

In high school, you may have been taught to end a paragraph by leading into the next one. This, in practice, can be very difficult, and it can become tedious for the reader if you end each paragraph this way. Instead, try to focus on wrapping up the topic in your paragraph effectively before introducing the next topic. Above all, do not try to end a paragraph with one sentence that both concludes your main idea *and* introduces the next one, as this would likely confuse a reader.

Topic Sentence

The **topic sentence** introduces the main idea in the paragraph. Therefore, the topic sentence is usually the most general sentence while the other sentences in the paragraph illustrate or expand on the main idea in some way. The topic sentence is usually the first sentence in the paragraph for the same reason that the thesis statement usually occurs in the introduction (first paragraph) of the essay: it provides a logical starting point and makes the paragraph easy to follow.

> The topic sentence, usually the first sentence in a paragraph, introduces the main idea of the paragraph.

Paragraph Wrap as Conclusion

Using a paragraph **wrap** is a satisfying way to conclude a paragraph as it reminds the reader what the paragraph was about. However, the wrap doesn't just repeat the topic sentence; it reinforces its importance by using different words. In the following paragraph, student writer Jordan Van Horne successfully wraps the main idea, which is introduced in the first (topic) sentence (both sentences are italicized):

> A wrap is the last sentence of a paragraph that sums up the main point, recalling the topic sentence.

> *If speed limits were abolished on highways, the necessity for law enforcement officers to patrol the highway for speeders would be curtailed.* As a result, police chiefs might have more officers to assign to special community projects, such as MADD or drug awareness projects in elementary schools. These officers could spend their time on a variety of social and community projects that would

benefit a large number of youths precisely at the time when they need this guidance. In addition, more officers could be allotted to other important areas that are typically understaffed today, such as surveillance and patrol duty to prevent drug smuggling. *Surely the presence of police in the community or their dedication to large-scale projects such as drug smuggling would be more beneficial to public safety than having them patrol the highways.*

A wrap is especially effective in a longer paragraph where the reader might lose track of the main idea.

Connecting Paragraphs by Using Transitions

A transition connects ideas from one sentence or paragraph to the next.

Always ask yourself if you think the reader can follow your thoughts from one paragraph to the next. Most readers expect a new paragraph to introduce a new topic. However, the relationship between the two topics may not always be clear. When constructing paragraphs, it is important to use **transitions** so that the reader can connect the idea in the current paragraph to what follows. A transition can be a word, phrase, or clause. It can occur at the end of a paragraph as a wrap or at the beginning of the next paragraph as part of the topic sentence. Your instructor may prefer transitions in one position or the other, or leave it up to you. Remember, though, that you must conclude each paragraph so that the reader understands that you are finished discussing that particular topic.

In the following paragraph from a student essay, Marissa Miles begins with a dependent clause (underlined) before introducing the topic for the paragraph (italicized). From the dependent clause, you can see that the previous paragraph focused on the fostering of independence through home schooling.

<u>Although the qualities of independence and self-motivation are important in a home-schooled education</u>, *its flexibility enables the child to learn at his or her own pace, matching progress to the child's natural learning processes.*

The writer of the following sentence combines an indirect reference to the preceding paragraph with the topic sentence of the current one:

Another crucial function of genetic engineering is its application to the pharmaceutical industry.

—Student writer Neil Weatherall

When making connections between paragraphs, avoid brief one-word transitions. They usually are too weak to link two main points, though they can be useful *within paragraphs* to link two sub-points.

All paragraphs should be unified, coherent, and well developed.

In general, when connecting paragraphs, avoid the kinds of transitions used to connect sentences *within* paragraphs, such as *for example, consequently, moreover,* and similar words and phrases (see Transitions between Sentences, below). They are not usually strong enough to connect a paragraph's main idea to the main idea in the next one.

Good paragraphs are unified, coherent, and well developed. Paragraph unity and coherence are discussed below. Because there are many different ways that a main point can be developed in a paragraph or throughout an essay, paragraph development is discussed separately in Chapter 4.

Exercise **3.1**

In each set of sentences, choose which one would make the best topic sentence. Remember that the topic sentence states the main (most general) point to be made in a paragraph.

1. topic: the 100-mile diet

   a. In small communities, stores often use local products to produce their own wares.
   b. Eating locally is one way to sustain the local economy and farming community.
   c. For example, on Vancouver Island, most grocery stores sell dairy products from Island Farms and other regional dairies.

2. topic: cellphones

   a. Recent studies have found that the brain cannot handle all the multi-tasking we try to do.
   b. We interrupt our meals, leave conversations, and forget to concentrate on our driving in order to answer our cellphones.
   c. Cellphones dominate the lives of many people in society today.

3. topic: physical education classes

   a. Physical education classes teach skills and knowledge not usually stressed in other classes.
   b. Skills like physical coordination and teamwork are developed in PE classes.
   c. PE classes allow more opportunities for social interaction, which is an essential skill in building future relationships and careers.

Paragraph Unity

As mentioned in the previous section, each paragraph should focus on *one* central idea announced in the topic sentence. It is usually best to place your topic sentence at the beginning as *the topic sentence anchors thought in the paragraph*. In a **unified** paragraph, all sentences in the paragraph relate to the main idea wherever that idea occurs.

> A unified paragraph focuses on one central idea announced in the topic sentence, and all sentences relate to that one idea.

Paragraphing, however, is not a mechanical process. Although the principle of one idea per paragraph is sound and logical, it may sometimes be difficult to tell where one idea ends and the next one begins. This is especially true in a rough draft where you are trying to get your ideas down and may not always pay attention to paragraph structure. Therefore, when you revise your essay, an important question to ask is whether each paragraph contains one main idea.

Although there is no "perfect" paragraph length, some instructors will give students an ideal range—such as between four and seven sentences—to ensure each paragraph is sufficiently developed but not so long that it becomes complicated and hard to read.

Also, in revising, you may see that one paragraph is much longer than the others. In such cases, you can determine a logical place to divide the paragraph into two smaller paragraphs. In the case of short paragraphs, you should consider combining them as short paragraphs may come across as simplistic and underdeveloped. When combining short paragraphs, be sure to use logical transitions between connecting sentences.

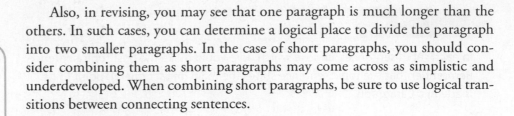

Exercise 3.2

In the following paragraphs, one sentence is off topic, affecting the paragraph's unity. Identify the sentence that doesn't belong, and explain why it is off topic.

1. The requirement to display the N (new driver) sign on your vehicle is a reasonable one. It allows other drivers to recognize that the driver may be inexperienced. These drivers may drive more cautiously around the novice driver. It also alerts law enforcement officials to the fact that the driver is learning how to cope in traffic. However, officers have been known to pull over an N driver even if they have no legitimate reason to do so. Since alcohol consumption is often high in teenagers, the N sign in the rear window enables police to monitor for drunk driving more effectively. The requirement is therefore beneficial for both other drivers and the police.

2. The ability to concentrate during classes can easily be affected by a student's lack of activity. Most students find it difficult to sit around for six hours each day with only a lunch break, during which they might also do nothing but sit and eat. Exercise gives students relief from simply passively taking in information hour after hour. It especially helps children with high energy levels who find it hard to sit still. In addition, exercise is a solution to the ever-growing problem of obesity. By breaking up the day with at least one compulsory period of activity, students will be able to retain more information and perform better academically.

Paragraph Coherence

It is often easy to identify a paragraph that contains more than one idea or an off-topic sentence, but identifying a paragraph that lacks **coherence** may be more difficult. The word *cohere* means "stick together." Someone who is incoherent doesn't make sense; his or her words or ideas don't stick together. By contrast, someone who is coherent is easy to follow. It is the same with a paragraph: one that lacks coherence is hard to follow. The words and the ideas might be jumbled or disconnected. They do not stick together in the reader's mind.

Here is the opening of an essay about the need for a nutritional diet. Although the ideas are quite simple, the paragraph isn't easy to follow. Try to determine why this is the case.

In a coherent paragraph, the writer uses strategies to connect one sentence to the next.

Most children throughout Canada depend on their parents to provide them with the proper nutrients each day. There are many contributing factors that make this ideal unachievable, and this lack can cause children to cultivate a serious disease known as obesity.

Now consider a rewritten version of this paragraph. Do you find it easier to follow? Why?

Most Canadian children depend on their parents for adequate daily nutrition. However, many factors can prevent them from achieving their nutritional ideal, which may result in obesity, a serious medical disorder.

Part of the problem lies in the words themselves: *cultivate* and *disease* are not the best words in this context. However, what also helps the words and ideas stick together is the careful use of repetition and transitions. In the rewritten version, the writer has replaced *this ideal* by *their nutritional ideal*, linking *ideal* back to *nutrition* in the first sentence. By adding the transition *however* and replacing *and* with *which*, the relationship between the ideas becomes clearer.

In this example, student writer Walter Jordan evokes the new awareness of his friend during a camping trip after the death of his friend's grandfather. Coherence here is achieved largely through the use of repetition, rhythm, and balanced structures, all of which are discussed below.

On previous trips, we had noticed the smell of nature when we woke and filled our lungs with fresh air, but this time he noticed the smell of the water and of the rain-sprinkled flowers. We had often looked at the stars on a clear night, but this time he spoke of the deep darkness of the sky, we had always seen the ground we stepped on, but this time he saw the footsteps left behind us.

There are specific strategies you can use to ensure your paragraphs are coherent or easy to follow.

Word Choice

When you consider what words to use, remember that it is not always a case of the right word versus the wrong word. Often, more than one word can convey your intended meaning, so it may be a question of choosing the best word for the given context. Whenever you use a word that is not part of your everyday vocabulary, you should confirm its meaning by looking it up in a dictionary. For written assignments, it's helpful to exchange your writing with someone else and pay attention to any passages that strike your reader as unclear. You will probably know words that he or she will not know and vice versa.

Patterns of Development

Coherent paragraphs often follow a distinct pattern. Paragraphs can follow a spatial, chronological, cause and effect, division, comparison and contrast, or other pattern. Organizational patterns are discussed in detail in Chapter 4.

Understanding the meaning of words is important for both reading and writing. If you do not understand a word when you are reading, this can affect *your* understanding of the essay. If you do not understand the meaning of a word when writing, this can affect *your reader's* understanding of your essay. Strategies for learning word meanings are discussed in Chapter 1, pages 26–27.

Logical Sentence Order

Remember that your writing is closely connected to your thinking and that you need to make your thought process clear to your reader. If one idea does not logically proceed from the previous one, then the paragraph will not be coherent. Similarly, there may be one or more gaps in a paragraph that need to be filled in, perhaps by inserting a sentence.

Repetition and Synonyms

By repeating key words or phrases, you can help the reader follow the main idea in the paragraph. While repetition enables the writer to reinforce the core idea in the paragraph, think of alternative words and expressions, such as synonyms. When looking for a synonym, you can check a thesaurus; however, before you insert the word, make sure it really is appropriate. Check it in a dictionary to ensure it really does mean what you intend. Experienced writers also consider the rhythm of the sentence, often placing the repeated words, or key words, at strategic points in the paragraph.

Using selective repetition is not the same as being repetitious, which can occur when you *needlessly* repeat a word or an idea.

Parallel Structures

Experienced writers also use parallel or balanced structures to achieve coherence. One of the reasons why so many readers can remember the beginnings and endings of Charles Dickens's novels is that Dickens often employed balanced structures: "It was the best of times; it was the worst of times" (*A Tale of Two Cities*). (Chapter 16, page 417, gives more information about parallelism.)

Transitions between Sentences

Transitional words and phrases guide the reader from one sentence to the next, signalling the exact relationship between them. Although adding the right transitional words will give the paragraph coherence, if you fail to use a transition to connect two ideas, the reader may find it hard to follow the paragraph's development. Some of the most useful transitions are listed below:

- *limit or concession:* admittedly, although, it is true that, naturally, of course, though
- *cause and effect:* accordingly, as a result, because, consequently, for this reason, if, otherwise, since, so, then, therefore, thus
- *illustration:* after all, even, for example, for instance, indeed, in fact, in other words, of course, specifically, such as
- *emphasis:* above all, assuredly, certainly, especially, indeed, in effect, in fact, particularly, that is, then, undoubtedly

- *sequence and addition:* after, again, also, and, as well, and then, besides, eventually, finally, first . . . second . . . third, furthermore, in addition, likewise, next, moreover, or, similarly, too, while
- *contrast or qualification:* after all, although, but, by contrast, conversely, despite, even so, however, in spite of, instead, nevertheless, nonetheless, on the contrary, on the one hand . . . on the other hand, otherwise, rather (than), regardless, still, though, whereas, while, yet
- *summary or conclusion:* finally, in conclusion, in effect, in short, in sum (summary), so, subsequently, that is, therefore, thus, to summarize

When you use words or phrases to connect one idea to the next, be careful to punctuate correctly. In some cases, a comma may be correct, but in many other instances, you should begin a new sentence or use a semicolon before the transitional word or phrase. Chapter 15 explains punctuation rules governing transitional phrases.

Do not begin a sentence with the transitions *and, but, or, so,* or *yet.* They should be used to connect two main ideas *within* a sentence.

In spite of their helpfulness, transitional words and phrases can be overused. Too many can clutter the paragraph and the essay. In addition, try to avoid wordy transitions as they, too, produce clutter (examples include *in spite of the fact that, due to the fact that, first and foremost, finally in conclusion, in the final analysis*). Chapter 17, page 442, gives further information about this topic.

Remember, too, that a transitional word or phrase, by itself, is not a substitute for a link in the writer's thought process; it can only assist the reader to move from one idea to the next. As mentioned in the section above about logical sentence order, a writer needs to be careful that there are no gaps in thought and that he or she has written with the reader in mind. The reader needs to be able to follow the writer's logic every step of the way. In the following passage, the writer has left something out, and no transitional word alone could bridge the gap:

> Society relies on an unbiased newscast in order to gain a true perspective on current events. Front-line employees are entering the TV news field underage and under-educated, thus often producing ill-informed reporting.

The writer has quickly moved from a generalization about the need for "unbiased" reporting to an example of one of the causes of "ill-informed reporting" but has not linked the generalization and the example. One logical link would be that newscasts today are sometimes biased or ill-informed. Then the writer can proceed to give examples of or solutions to this problem. As it is, the problem has not been stated clearly.

> Society relies on an unbiased newscast in order to gain a true perspective on current events. However, newscasts today are sometimes biased or ill-informed. This may be because front-line employees are entering the TV news field underage and under-educated, thus often producing ill-informed reporting.

A unified paragraph, then, refers to one central idea; in a coherent paragraph, one sentence leads logically to the next sentence. On the next page are two diagrams that illustrate unity and coherence in which the sentences are represented by arrows:

S1 = sentence 1
S2 = sentence 2
S3 = sentence 3
S4 = sentence 4

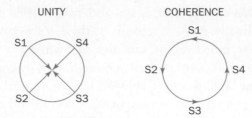

FIGURE 3.1 Unity and coherence

Exercise **3.3**

The following passage contains a gap. Provide a logical link to make it coherent.

> The surprise attack on Pearl Harbor forced the US to be more aggressive in world politics. This interventionist policy has recently evolved into a policy of pre-emptive strikes on those perceived as a threat to US security.

Exercise **3.4**

I. Coherence through sentence order

Combine the sentences below in the most logical order to form a coherent paragraph; one sentence is not relevant to the topic of this paragraph and should be discarded. Supply any necessary links between one sentence and the next. More than one order may be possible. Be prepared to justify the particular order you used to achieve coherence.

1. The roof, to borrow a phrase, is on fire. Next up: a group of mousy tweens who shuffle onstage to present the story of Alan Turing, the computing legend and war hero who was chemically castrated by the British government after being prosecuted for homosexuality.
2. This, and a whole lot more.
3. The 13-year-old is barely audible over the band behind him, but the crowd of some 350 students and parents at Stoke Newington School in London, England, starts to clap along anyway.
4. And it's a mainstay on school curricula across Britain.
5. This is what the UK's LGBT History Month looks like.
6. Max Dineley grips the microphone with a trembling hand and begins to rap.
7. Only eight years after its launch, the initiative numbers more than 1,000 events annually—so many that organizers have given up keeping track.
8. To that end, the group hosted its first town hall at Toronto's 519 Church St Community Centre on March 4.

9. "Who cares if boys are more than just friends, so let this world make amends . . . this is all about love, try to send yourself above!"

10. It was celebrated at 10 Downing St under former Prime Minister Gordon Brown.

11. That's when Max finds his voice.

—Aveling, N. (2012, March 8). Building Canada's queer history month: A look at what activists here might learn from successful UK celebration. *Xtra!* Retrieved from http://www.xtra.ca/public/National/ Building_Canadas_Queer_History_Month-11655.aspx

II. Coherence through transitions

Using transitions can help sentences cohere, or stick together. The following paragraph lacks transitions. Provide logical connections between the sentences by choosing the appropriate transitions from the list below, filling in the blanks. Note: One transition has been given to you, and one transition should not be used in the paragraph.

> Massive energy consumption is having a negative impact on the planet. ___, in the summer of 2006, western Europe experienced some of the hottest weather on record. Moreover, this temperature increase is not an isolated occurrence. ___, almost every credible scientist today believes that the earth is experiencing climate change due to the emissions of greenhouse gases from cars and coal-burning power plants. Ninety percent of the energy used in the US comes from fossil fuels: oil, coal, and natural gas (Borowitz 43), ___ problems arise from other sources, too. ___, nuclear power plants leave radioactive by-products, making storage difficult. ___, dams are not much better as nearby populations must be relocated, and the surrounding habitat is destroyed.

moreover	for example	unfortunately
but	in fact	for example
above all		

Exercise **3.5**

Coherence through use of repetition, parallel structures, and transitions

1. Even though a writer uses a specific organizational method and carefully orders his or her points, a paragraph may not be coherent if there are not enough transitional words and phrases to link these points. In addition, such devices as repetition and even rhythm can help achieve coherence. In the following paragraph, the writer uses transitional words and phrases, repetition, and balanced constructions—all of which make the paragraphs more

(continued)

coherent. If these words and phrases were taken away, much of the paragraph would be unclear. Transitions are in **boldface** type, repetitions are in *italic*, and balanced constructions are <u>underlined</u>.

> **In contrast to** allopathy, in Traditional Chinese Medicine (TCM) organs are viewed as "networks"—**that is**, functional physiological and psychological domains—**rather than** discrete anatomical structures. All our organs are related; **in fact**, *our* body, [our] behavior, and the environment we are in are also interconnected. **In other words**, TCM focuses more <u>on the *context*</u> where the disease exists than on the disease itself. Such emphasis <u>on *context*</u> implies that the way [s] people get sick and can be treated are highly personalized.
>
> People with <u>different *symptoms*</u> may have the same underlying problem, requiring <u>similar treatments</u>; yet people with the <u>same *symptom*</u> may need <u>completely different remedies</u>. While we are equally <u>endowed with our basic parts</u>, our lungs, heart, kidneys, liver, and so on, our way of coordinating these parts is individualized. **For example**, if <u>arthritis</u> is due to an invasion of "heat" (inflammation), it is different from the <u>same condition</u> with a different cause—**for example**, "cold" (reduced circulation) or "dampness" (accumulation of fluids). **In the first case**, practitioners would administer <u>cooling</u> herbs; **in the others**, <u>warming</u> or diuretic herbs would be used.

—Student writer Grace Chau

2. Read the paragraph below to determine how the writer has used transitions and repetition to achieve coherence. Underline transitions and repetitive devices. Identify the topic sentence. One way to achieve coherence is to number your points, although unnecessary numbering can add to clutter. Do you think that the writer of the passage below made a good choice in numbering his points? If so, why?

> Critics of the World Trade Organization (WTO) argue that its approach to globalization causes more harm than good because it undermines democracy. The WTO is undemocratic in several respects. First, ambassadors from member nations are appointed, not elected. Second, the coalition known as the "Quad," comprised of the European Union, the United States, Japan, and Canada, holds almost all the real power. In theory, at least, such decisions as new membership, rule changes, and rule interpretations of WTO rules should be voted for with a three-quarters majority. In practice, however, the Quad determines the WTO agenda. Third, WTO trade talks are held in secret to avoid public criticism and scrutiny. Furthermore, an organization that is not elected controls trade so effectively that it possesses the power to supersede the power of elected communities, states, and even nations on any issue, however ambiguous, related to trade.

—Student writer Tao Eastham

3. Read the paragraph below to determine how the writer has used transitions and repetition to achieve coherence. Underline transitions and repetitive devices. Identify the topic sentence. This paragraph is an introductory paragraph to a chapter of a book. What topic do you think will be developed in the next paragraph? Why?

> The news media's power to trivialize anything that comes to their attention is almost magical. News service advertisements talk about providing a "window on the world" or a report on "history in the making." But the nightly television newscast and the daily newspaper fall far short of these ideals. Instead, we get a fast-paced smorgasbord of unconnected and disembodied news stories where meaning and context are lost in the rapid-fire delivery of colourful prose and dramatic pictures. As a result, much of what passes for news is instead isolated, unconnected, and almost meaningless bits of information—in effect, the news is trivialized. This trivialization operates at both the structural level of news gathering and dissemination, and at the level of individual news stories. We have termed this style "the trivialization effect."
>
> —adapted from R.A. Rutland, *The Newsmongers*

❯ Sample Professional Essay

The following essay was written for a general audience; its purpose is to convince the readers that leisure time is important for everyone. When reading the piece, pay close attention to how the authors meet the criteria for good paragraphs discussed above. For example, look at the transitions they use. As you read, also analyze the coherence of the ideas. Are they linked logically? Is the use of repetition effective? Consider whether transitions could have created the same links. What different words could the authors have used to help the reader better understand their ideas?

SAMPLE PROFESSIONAL ESSAY

7 Ways to Re-Create Your Brain

by Greg D'Eloia and Melissa D'Eloia

[1] In the summer, many of us take vacations and spend more time outside. The benefits of recreation and leisure, however, truly span all seasons. While most people enjoy vacations and such activities as sports, hobbies and exercise, few realize the full spectrum of benefits linked to regular recreation and leisure activities.

(continued)

> As an example, the authors use the transition word *however*. What purpose does it serve here? What other transitions are used?

Writing Tip: The use of repetition helps the reader see the importance of the author's idea.

[2] For decades, scholars and researchers around the globe have documented a compelling body of evidence that suggests regular participation in recreation is essential for our physical, social, cognitive and spiritual development. Recreation improves physical and mental health, builds community and promotes relationships. Recreation encourages us to take risks, to be creative, and to learn and grow from experience. Overall, people who regularly participate in recreational activities report feeling more productive, less stressed and a greater sense of satisfaction.

While the authors do not actually cite this research, they refer to it to reassure the audience that their statements are valid.

[3] Here are a few suggestions to take advantage of the cognitive benefits of recreation and leisure. The following list is based on empirical research that links leisure activities and environments to brain-related benefits:

The authors use headings to help direct the reader's attention to the important aspects of recreation and leisure. However, they still use topic sentences in the paragraphs to organize their ideas.

Go Outside

[4] Outdoor environments help us experience a sense of connection to the natural world. Feeling such a connection is vital to our sense of well-being and peace of mind. The therapeutic value of parks, open space and wilderness in our environments is thoroughly documented by behavioral scientists across a broad range of disciplines. Human beings often miss the solace and wonder of the natural world denied us by modern and urban lifestyles. The simple act of going outside to think for a moment can bring restoration and clarity to cognitive processes cluttered by the hectic pace and confined nature of modern life.

Bring the Outside In

The authors use repetition to reinforce their idea.

[5] Bringing outdoor elements into your office and living spaces can help counteract the deficiency of nature there. Houseplants, herb gardens, aquariums, landscape art and windows with a view can make indoor spaces more comfortable, productive and therapeutic. The use of natural colors, light, textures, images and patterns help create a more pleasant habitat for recently domesticated human beings who still secretly hunger for more natural surroundings.

Let Yourself Play

[6] Research has shown that children need to play in order to foster their imaginations, learn social norms and develop problem-solving and decision-making skills through trial and error. Play is essential to the social, cognitive, emotional and physical development of children and youth. While children's play is characterized by spontaneity, joyfulness and freedom from inhibition, adults play with increasingly specific rules and regulations. Nevertheless, adults also benefit from the opportunities for self-expression, challenge and social connections that come from participating in recreation that is spontaneous, interactive and enjoyable. Some examples of play for adults might include music, painting, theater, games with family and friends—any activity that allows us to change roles and have fun.

Parallelism is used here to define the type of recreation that is beneficial.

Experience Adventure

[7] Do something daring! Seemingly extreme sports like rock climbing, river rafting, snowboarding, surfing, scuba diving and skydiving are all accessible and beginner-friendly for those willing to pay for expert instruction. Perhaps your idea of excitement might be bungee jumping, mountain biking, boating, hot-air ballooning or training for a race. Scientists have established a genetic and neurological basis for thrill-seeking behavior and confirmed that the desire for such experiences is hard-wired into the brain. Chronic thrill-seekers have a greater need for this type of stimulation, in some cases developing compulsions for adventure similar to drug addiction. While some of us are genetically predisposed to crave excitement more than others, everyone's brain responds to the dopamine that gets released when our fight-or-flight instinct gets activated. The thrill of adventure pushes the brain into a state of heightened awareness and a feeling of being truly alive. Warning: These activities may be addictive!

Get Away

[8] Travel can be invigorating and provide insight and perspective. Journeys to unfamiliar places present valuable opportunities to acquire new knowledge and skills. Whether you seek adventure and challenge or rest and relaxation, simply going somewhere different provides an opportunity to inspire, recharge and refresh emotional and mental states. Because the brain reacts to new settings with increased perception and awareness, the newness of each experience makes travel a stimulating and engaging leisure pursuit.

Rest and Relaxation

[9] Be sure to get enough sleep, and remember to relax from time to time. Your brain needs rest and leisure time of its own which only adequate sleep and relaxation can provide. Cultivate the habit of taking a moment to breathe. Explore the brain-body connection through meditation, yoga and visualization techniques.

> The authors use *leisure time* and *relaxation* interchangeably so that there is variation. While repetition can help emphasize ideas, overuse of one word repeatedly in a paragraph becomes tiresome for the reader.

Take Back Your Leisure Time

[10] Free your mind from the digital grid by watching less TV, playing fewer video games, spending less time surfing the web and turning off your smartphone. While there is still relatively little information available about the long-term effects of electronics on the brain, there is no doubt that these devices represent a huge drain on your leisure time and reduce the time you have available for more important things. Cut back on digital recreation to make time for more worthwhile leisure pursuits, such as reading and outdoor recreation.

—D'Eloia, G., and M. D'Eloia. (2012, July 13.) 7 Ways to Re-Create Your Brain. *Brain World*. Retrieved from www.brainworldmagazine.com /7-ways-to-re-create-your-brain/

(continued)

Post-reading Questions

1.   How do the authors maintain paragraph unity throughout this essay?

2.   Have the writers successfully used paragraph wraps? Give some examples to support your point.

3.   Do the authors maintain coherence throughout the essay? What methods do they use to ensure their writing is understandable?

4.   What types of transitions have the authors used?

5.   In the paragraph about play, the authors discuss the importance of play for children. Does this enhance their argument or detract from it? Why?

▌ Chapter Review Questions

1.   Why is it important to create a coherent paragraph?

2.   What are some advantages in using transitions in writing paragraphs?

3.   How are topic sentences and paragraph wraps different?

4.   Why is paragraph unity important?

5.   How can you effectively repeat an idea?

6.   What are some types of transitions that you can use in your writing? How do they differ from each other? How can they help you express your thoughts differently? Create some sentences and try switching transitions.

7.   Create a paragraph about a topic you are interested in by using specific ideas from this chapter. For example, create a clear topic sentence, include at least two sentences regarding sub-topics, and include two transitions between these sub-topics. Then switch with a partner and see if he or she has any suggestions, also based on this chapter.

4 Paragraph **Development**

- learn how to identify different organizational methods for writing both paragraphs and essays
- learn how to develop your essay through substantial paragraphs
- learn how to combine organizational methods within an essay

To write an interesting, informative essay, you need to consider many outside factors, such as audience, and whether the essay is formal or informal. However, you also need to decide how to organize your essay to make it logical and easy to follow. You may decide to use one main pattern for your essay, but different patterns for individual paragraphs. This chapter will introduce you to various organizational writing patterns and help you determine how to organize your essay and its paragraphs into a unified, coherent, and well-developed whole.

Developing Your Essay

As discussed in Chapter 3, an effective paragraph is unified, coherent, and well developed. A unified paragraph focuses on one topic. A coherent paragraph makes sense and provides logical connections so the reader can follow the writer's train of thought. The same applies to an essay as a whole but on a broader scope. An essay focuses on one topic, with each paragraph explaining one particular aspect of the essay topic.

A well-developed paragraph contains supporting information organized in a consistent pattern. Not only does it thoroughly expand on a point, but also the information's organization increases the paragraph's coherence, contributing to the essay as a whole.

The paragraph below, from a student essay about safe injection sites, clearly illustrates these concepts. The author connects drug use and disease, showing unity. Coherence is provided by repeating words, such as *problem*, and by using synonyms, such as *situation*. Finally, the paragraph is well developed, as it illustrates the drug problem in Victoria before the writer discusses the solution to the problem, which is the main focus of the essay.

> Victoria is an urban centre with a heroin and drug-related disease problem. This situation is easy to see when one is walking through the downtown core. The problem may not be as severe as Vancouver's, but it is necessary to take proactive actions to prevent the spread of AIDS and hepatitis. Having been involved with The Youth Empowerment Society downtown and working with street youth in Victoria, I see the need for such a program in Victoria; the personal health of users, old and young, is at stake.
>
> —Student writer Kerry Hinds

Often, a writer chooses to use one main method of development for the essay but uses other methods in supporting roles. He or she may set out to examine a cause–effect relationship, for example, but may use different methods from paragraph to paragraph to introduce, clarify, illustrate, or expand the main points.

Choosing the appropriate **development pattern** is one of the keys to writing a complete and interesting essay. Which pattern should you use for your essay? This will depend on the kind of essay, your purpose in writing, your topic, your audience, your essay's primary organizational method, your main points and their order (climax, reverse climax, or some other), along with many other factors.

Methods for Developing Paragraphs

A topic may guide your choice for organizing an entire essay or individual paragraph. For example, for the topic "Which is more important at college or university: acquiring skills or getting good grades?" you might guess that the essay should be organized using the comparison and contrast method. For the topic

A unified paragraph or essay focuses on one topic.

A coherent paragraph or essay makes sense and provides logical connections so the reader can follow the writer's train of thought.

A well-developed paragraph or essay contains supporting information organized in a consistent pattern.

The development pattern determines how an essay or a paragraph will be organized.

"Solutions to the problem of homeless people," you would know that the essay should be organized using the problem–solution method where you briefly describe the problem and then suggest ways to solve it. On the other hand, if the question was "Do you believe that homeless people today are a problem?" you might develop your essay in a similar way, but the *problem* of homelessness would be much more important than the solutions, which you might mention only briefly or not at all. Even if the topic determines the *main* way that the essay should be developed, there will likely be opportunities to consider different organizational methods or patterns for developing individual paragraphs. These patterns are discussed below with examples.

The topic of the essay may determine the main way you will organize your essay, but each paragraph may be organized using a different pattern.

Analysis and Paragraph Development

When you analyze, you are loosening, then taking something apart in order to look at it closely. Many development methods involve this process. Thus, you analyze when you divide and classify, compare and contrast, and consider problems and solutions, costs and benefits, and the like. Not all methods truly involve analysis—description and narration, for example—but many of them do. Analysis is one of the keys to critical thinking.

You analyze when you divide and classify, compare and contrast, and consider problems and solutions, costs and benefits, and the like.

One way to generate methods of development is to ask questions about the topic, as shown in Table 4.1.

Analysis is one of the keys to critical thinking.

TABLE 4.1	Questions and Methods of Development
Question	Method of Development
What is it?	definition
When did it occur?	chronology
What does it look like?	description
How can it be told?	narration
How do you do it? or How does it work?	process/"how to"
Why should/does it affect me?	personal
What kinds/categories are there?	division/classification
What causes/accounts for it?	cause–effect
What is the result/effect?	cause–effect
What is the answer?	question–answer

(continued)

TABLE 4.1	(Continued)
Question	Method of Development
How can it be shown?	example/illustration
How can it be (re)solved?	problem–solution
What are the advantages/disadvantages?	cost–benefit
How is it like something else?	analogy
How is it like and/or unlike something else?	comparison and contrast

Each of these questions leads to a particular method for developing a paragraph. If, for example, your topic is "fast foods," you could use any of the methods below to develop an essay on this topic.

Definition—What Is It?

Define something in an essay in order to tell the reader precisely what you will be talking about. **Defining** a subject, such as an abstract concept, can also help you understand your topic better and, perhaps, help you organize your main points. By "fast foods," do you mean something like a "Big Mac"? Do you mean store-bought food that is quickly heated and eaten? Both could be considered "fast foods," but they are not the same. Below, the writer concisely defines "cloud computing" for the general audience and then uses the division pattern to expand the definition. (Chapter 8, page 158, provides an example of a definition essay.)

Defining a subject, such as an abstract concept, can help you understand your topic better and, perhaps, help you organize your main points.

Cloud computing is a technology that allows users to access information and documents without being tied to one computer or network. These clouds also allow users to share documents, and anyone can make changes as the need arises. Networks established within companies require users to log in to the company network where data is stored in order to access documents. Storage is often limited on these networks, and documents are difficult to update by many different users. Some people use USB sticks to help them avoid having to constantly access the company network; however, these devices also have limited storage capacity, and the documents are not easy to change when there are multiple users. Cloud computing, on the other hand, means that people can access many different networks and systems, and users can share documents with others easily. Multiple people can access shared documents and make simultaneous changes. Also, storage space can be increased, for a fee, as the user's needs increase. No longer is a person tied to one computer or network.

Chronology—When Did It Occur?

In the **chronological** method, you do more than simply look back to a specific time: you trace the topic's *development over time*. (If you looked back to a specific time and compared an aspect of the subject to that aspect today, you would be *comparing and contrasting*.) When did fast foods first appear, and when did they truly begin to affect people's lives and society? Tracing the evolution of fast foods in the last 15 years might provide evidence that many fast-food restaurants have been forced to expand their choices and reduce their portion sizes to counter the perception that these foods are unhealthy. Applying this method of development, then, could also involve a cause–effect or problem–solution approach; see below.

Chronology means tracing a topic's development over time.

> The earth shook as father and son wrestled high above the clouds; Kronos, the dreaded father who ate his children, battled his powerful son to rule the Earth. However, Zeus, whom the Fates had protected as a child from Kronos' mighty jaws, triumphed once again, becoming, in the words of Homer, "father of gods and men"; his children would honour his victory as a celebration known as Olympia. From 776 BCE the Olympic Games occurred every four years to celebrate Zeus' success. By 260 CE the Games' importance had deteriorated so much that they were held only occasionally, until the Roman Emperor Theodosius outlawed them completely in 394 CE. The Olympic Games were founded on a profound religious significance, specific ideals about athletes, and strict rules that enabled the Games' long existence and prohibited the inclusion of women. As Olympia changed, the founding principles that had originally made Olympia so significant were disregarded, eventually leading to the end of the ancient Games.

—Student writer Courtenay O'Brien

Description—What Does It Look Like?

You can use **description** at any point in your essay to add concrete, physical detail, but description should play a limited role. You could describe something by using the spatial method of organization, a particular kind of descriptive method. In the spatial method, you describe something in a systematic manner—for example, from left to right or as you approach the object. You could describe a fast-food burger from the sesame-seed top bun through its assorted condiments and extras to the plain lower bun. Description can also appeal to the senses. It can create a visual image (such as some of those noted below), an auditory reference (such as the sound of a robin's song), or even a memory of a smell (such as the smell of roses). It is important to be as concrete as possible so that the reader clearly understands what you mean. So instead of using a sentence like *It was a dark and stormy night*, revise so that the reader can "live" the experience, using words such as *The thunder was so loud that the windows rattled, and the rain fell so violently that it bounced off the pavement*. Wording such as this leads to less misunderstanding by the reader.

Description adds concrete, physical detail to an essay.

When Wright came to the site he appreciated the powerful sound of the falls, the vitality of the young forest, the dramatic rock ledges and boulders; these were elements to be interwoven with the serenely soaring spaces of his structure. But Wright's insight penetrated more deeply. He understood that people were creatures of nature, hence an architecture which conformed to nature would conform to what was basic in people. For example, although all of Fallingwater is opened by broad bands of windows, people inside are sheltered as in a deep cave, secure in the sense of hill behind them. Their attention is directed toward the outside by low ceilings; no lordly hall sets the tone but, instead, the luminous textures of the woodland, rhythmically enframed. The materials of the structure blend with the colorings of rocks and trees, while occasional accents are provided by bright furnishings, like wildflowers or birds outside. The paths within the house, stairs and passages, meander without formality or urgency, and the house hardly has a main entrance; there are many ways in and out. Sociability and privacy are both available, as are the comforts of home and the adventures of the seasons. So people are cosseted in to relaxing, into exploring the enjoyment of a life refreshed in nature. Visitors, too, in due measure experience Wright's architecture as an expansion of living.

> The author is presenting a visual image so that readers can imagine the building, even if they have never seen it.

—Hoffman, Donald. *Frank Lloyd Wright's Fallingwater: The House and Its History*, Second, Revised Edition. Mineola, NY: Dover Publications, 1993.

Narration—How Can It Be Told?

A story can lend drama to an argument or be used to illustrate a point. **Narrating** an incident, or even including some dialogue, can be an effective way to introduce or reinforce your topic. Narration is a natural method in personal essays but can also be used in argumentative essays, and even in expository essays, as in the sample below about the legendary origins of coffee. Because description and narration are generally considered more informal, you should ask your instructor before using them extensively in a formal essay.

> Narration can be an effective way to introduce or reinforce your topic.

> Legend has it that one day, Kaldi, an Ethiopian goat-herder, noticed his goats were so frisky when they returned from grazing that they "danced." Curious about the source of their excitement, Kaldi followed them the next day and observed the animals eating the berries of a nearby tree. Kaldi grabbed some berries himself and soon experienced a slow tingle that spread throughout his body. According to the legend, Kaldi was soon "dancing" alongside his goats.

—Pendergrast, Mark, *Uncommon Grounds: The History of Coffee and How It Transformed Our World*. New York: Basic Books, 1999. Print.

> Relating a process focuses specifically on the steps in a sequence.

Process—How Does It Work?

Although a process-analysis essay is usually a fact-based essay that relates the chronological, step-by-step stages of a **process**, this method of development can also be used in an argumentative essay—for example, if you wanted to convince a reader that one games system was easier to operate than another. This method can also be used for less technical subjects—for example, "How to Impress Your Boss, or Professor, in Ten Easy Steps." Remember that relating a process focuses specifically on the successive steps in a *sequence*. Since the production of fast-food burgers is often a regimented process, you could describe this process from the time a customer places an order to the time it is handed to him or her. (Chapter 8, page 156, provides an example of a process essay.)

> The traditional method of painting icons is a long process, requiring a skilled and experienced painter. The artist takes a wooden panel, one with the least amount of resin, knots, and risk of splitting, and covers it with cheesecloth. A gesso is then made from rabbit-skin glue and calcium carbonate (chalk). It is applied to the panel seven to ten times and then polished by hand until it is mirror-like. The original is traced to perfection and then transferred onto the gessoed surface. After this, gold leaf is laid on everywhere it is required (backgrounds and halos, for example). Egg tempera paint is freshly made from powdered pigment and egg yolk and is applied from the darkest dark to the lightest light with an egg-white glaze spread on between each coat.
>
> —Student writer Magda Smith

Personal—Why Should It Affect Me?/How Does It Affect Me?

A **personal essay** is focused on the writer—an aspect of his or her life or a relevant experience. Personal experience in an essay contributes immediacy and, sometimes, drama. But don't use personal experience extensively, unless you are writing a personal essay. In a successful personal paragraph or essay, the writer is able to make personal experience seem relevant to the reader.

To apply your personal experience to fast-food restaurants, you might consider your childhood visits to such restaurants when the busy and exciting atmosphere was more important to you than the food. Below, the writer begins his expository essay on college binge drinking by citing a recent personal experience; such an approach would be particularly appropriate if his audience were mostly college or university students.

A personal essay focuses on an aspect of the writer's life or a relevant experience.

> Exam time is approaching at my college, and stress levels are at an annual high. For this reason, when Friday night arrives, I know I will be drinking—and I definitely will not be alone. Last weekend, my friends and I went to a typical residence party. If I can remember correctly, there were about 15 people noisily crowded into a room the size of a large closet, and many more were herded in the hallways. According to a study in the *American Journal of Public Health*, today's North American college students have the highest binge drinking rate of any group, even when compared to their peers who do not go to school; furthermore, alcohol is associated with many social

problems on college campuses and is the most widespread and preventable health issue for the more than six million students in America (Wechsler et al., 1995, p. 921).

—Student writer Brian Gregg

Classification/Division—What Kinds Are There?

In **classification** or **division**, you begin with many items—for example, commonly known members of the animal kingdom—which you organize into more manageable groups: mammals, birds, fish, reptiles, and amphibians. Each category, such as mammals, could in turn be organized into still smaller units, such as rodents, primates, and carnivores. Fast-food burgers can easily be classified according to their different kinds: hamburgers, chicken burgers, fish burgers, veggie burgers. In the example below, the writer uses classification to break down movies into five designations; the differences could then be analyzed by applying the same criteria to each category.

> Ontario has five categories for rating movies: general, parental guidance, 14A (those under 14 must be accompanied by an adult), 18A (those under 18 must be accompanied by an adult), and restricted. In the "general" category, the language must be inoffensive, though words like "damn" and "hell" can occur occasionally. Violence must be limited and permissible; sexual activity includes only embracing and kissing "in a loving context"; horror is defined by genre—for example, dragons, giants and wicked witches are acceptable.

> —Ontario Film Review Board, http://www.ofrb.gov.on.ca/english/page6.htm

In division, you are more concerned with the whole than with the individual parts. You break a subject down into parts in order to better understand or explain the whole (the subject). For example, to illustrate how essay structure works, you can divide the essay into introduction, body paragraphs, and conclusion. Under Definition—What Is It? above, the writer explains how cloud computing differs from the more traditional ideas of data saving.

Cause–Effect—What Is the Cause? What Is the Result?

You can use the **cause–effect** method to organize an entire essay, or you can use it in one or more paragraphs to analyze a main point. When you deal with causes, you consider the reasons for an occurrence. A cause–effect essay or paragraph might focus on one effect, which would be accounted for by one or more causes. Or you could focus on one cause and consider one or more effects or results arising from this cause. Since fast food has often been blamed for obesity, you could look at studies that link obesity (effect) to unhealthy diets (cause). Cause–effect studies are particularly common in the sciences. The

Classification focuses on a large number of items that can be organized into more manageable groups.

Division breaks the subject down into parts in order to better understand the whole.

A cause–effect essay or paragraph might focus on one effect, which would be accounted for by one or more causes. Or you could focus on one cause and consider one or more effects or results arising from this cause.

antecedent–consequent organizational method uses time–order relationships in a similar way to cause–effect relationships. (Think of "before and after" photographs.) The following essay excerpt discusses one cause for stress in first-year students.

An antecedent is a preceding event, condition, or cause. A consequence is a result.

> A major cause of stress in first-year students is the need to establish a new social base. Students not only find themselves among strangers, but also often have to rely on these strangers for moral support. Consequently, friendships tend to be forged rapidly but superficially. When students inevitably find themselves dealing with mid-terms, assignments, and an increasingly heavy course load, they need close friends and family for support but are forced to turn to these new acquaintances instead. Intense friendships may be formed during such times, but often the stress is insurmountable, leading students to give up and head home.
>
> —Student writer Alexis Parker

Question–Answer—What Is the Answer?

The **question–answer** method is effective when you ask a question in the topic sentence and then answer it in the paragraph. Questions—including the journalistic questions *who?*, *what?*, *when?*, *where?*, *why?*, and *how?*—can be applied to any topic. Posing a relevant question is a good way to engage the reader since it directly invites his or her answer to the question. Below, the writer begins his essay by asking two questions, suggesting that his essay will focus on two related areas of foreign policy:

Consequent means following an event (or antecedent) as a natural effect, result, or conclusion.

> In the post–Cold War era, do military solutions still have a place or is diplomacy able to solve all our foreign policy questions? Does the United Nations still have a useful purpose or will military coalitions like NATO usurp its role entirely? With increasing world tensions and the current American-led wars in Iraq and Afghanistan, many people around the world are asking these questions.
>
> —Student writer Robert Tyre

Questions—including the journalistic questions *who?*, *what?*, *when?*, *where?*, *why?*, and *how?*—can be applied to almost any topic.

Example/Illustration—How Can It Be Shown?

Using concrete **examples** is one of the best ways of supporting a point and clarifying an abstract idea. This method of development can often be combined with other methods, such as cause–effect, cost–benefit, or comparison and contrast. If you were using the cause–effect method and you wanted to develop the point that fast foods save valuable time (an effect), you might talk about the convenience of drive-through lanes at fast-food restaurants as one example; another example might be the use of assembly-line workers. Examples are very important in most writing and may consist of brief expansions of a point or more fully developed explanations.

Using concrete examples is one of the best ways of supporting a point and clarifying an abstract idea.

Brief expansion:

Graffiti art can be seen as a political message on a sidewalk, a limerick on a bathroom wall, a doodle on a desktop, or even a digital image on the Internet.

Fully developed explanation:

In 2012, Lance Armstrong, winner of the Tour de France seven times in a row, admitted to taking performance enhancing drugs. Armstrong admits to using erythropoietin (EPO) and testosterone, as well as utilizing a technique known as blood doping. What many people find hard to believe is how he managed to evade detection during the many years he raced.

Problem–Solution—How Can It Be (Re)Solved?

The **problem–solution** method of development could focus on a problem, a solution to a problem, or both a problem and a solution. A problem with fast foods is its dubious nutritional value. After you state the problem, you could propose ways that fast foods could be made healthier or perhaps give examples of how this is being done today; in this case, you would be combining problem–solution with example/illustration. Studies focusing on problem–solution and cost–benefit (see below) are particularly common in the social sciences where human behaviour is the focus. In the following essay conclusion, the author restates his thesis that Canada's Confederation in 1867 was not so much an effect, or consequence, of various causes, but the best solution to unanticipated problems.

The problem–solution method of development could focus on a problem, a solution to a problem, or both a problem and solutions.

> Politicians were not entertaining the idea of uniting the British North American colonies until numerous problems arose. Political alliances, foreign raids, railway expansion, industrial booms, and the termination of long-standing agreements would have been significant events on their own, but their convergence before 1867 helped push Canada towards Confederation. The most logical solution to these problems was union. Macdonald, Brown, and other nineteenth-century politicians did not strategically plan Confederation, but rather Confederation offered itself as a solution to the problems imposed on them.
>
> —Student writer Chris Hoffart

Cost–Benefit—What Are the Advantages and Disadvantages?

Analyzing something often involves weighing the advantages and disadvantages, the pros and cons. **Cost–benefit** analysis can be applied to almost any topic, since few things in life come without some costs or negative consequences. You could apply cost–benefit analysis to fast foods by focusing on the individual,

Cost–benefit analysis involves studying the pros and cons of the topic.

community, or perhaps even global costs or benefits. In an expository essay, cost–benefit analysis involves the objective weighing of pluses and minuses. However, if you were *arguing* that the benefits were more important than the costs, you might well consider the costs first and *then* the benefits, leaving the strongest argument for the last. If you took the opposing position, you might begin with benefits, as the writer does below in her argumentative essay on genetically modified organisms.

The organizational pattern used for a cost–benefit essay depends on whether the essay is expository or argumentative.

> Some scientists believe that releasing GMOs into the environment could reduce pesticide use since crops could be genetically modified to produce a toxin against the pests. Unfortunately, such a toxin could have adverse effects on other organisms, such as the pollinator species of the plant. Some believe that genetic engineering could reduce hunger in Third-World countries by allowing more food production. However, after growing genetically modified crops, the farmer would be unable to sow the seeds to grow more crops because GMOs seeds are sterile, forcing the farmer to buy new seeds every year—an unrealistic expense. Furthermore, introducing GMOs in Third-World countries would be risky as most countries have limited resources and few safety measures in place for controlling GMOs.
>
> —Student writer Jutta Kolhi

Analogy—How Is It Like Something Else?

An **analogy** is a comparison between one object and a second object that is unlike the first one except for the characteristic being compared. The analogy helps the reader to better understand the original object. You could compare fast foods to the fast pace of modern society itself. Below, the author began his essay on water resource management by using the analogy of a desert to stress the importance of water management in North America.

An analogy is a comparison that helps the reader to better understand the original object.

> Imagine a hot, torturously dry desert. Throughout this arid wasteland, no life exists—not a tree, shrub, or animal alive. Though to many residents of Europe and North America this scenario may seem highly abstract and incomprehensible, it is the reality faced by many equatorial nations, such as China, Africa, Saudi Arabia, and parts of India. Residents of these nations have developed a keen understanding of the importance of water, and how best to manage it to enable a basic level of existence. However, residents of nations more endowed with water, such as Canada, seem largely indifferent to such a reality.
>
> —Student writer François Beaudet

Comparison and Contrast—How Is It Like and/or Unlike Something Else?

Comparison and contrast is a method of systematically drawing similarities and differences between two things. When you compare and contrast, you begin by finding logical bases of comparison and then analyze their similarities and differences. In arguing that one hamburger restaurant is better than

When you compare and contrast, you begin by finding logical bases of comparison and then analyze their similarities and differences.

another, you could compare their prices, their food quality, their cleanliness, and the friendliness of their staff. Early in her comparison and contrast essay, the writer below contrasts two different environmental philosophies by defining each, according to the beliefs of an influential philosopher.

> Conservation is a "shallow ecology" approach to viewing the environment and the role of humans within it. Conceived by Norwegian philosopher and linguist Arne Naess in the early 1970s, "shallow ecology" begins with "an assumption, often unexamined, that human beings are [the] central species in the Earth's ecosystem, and that other beings, as parts of systems, are of less importance or value." Preservation, on the other hand, is based on Arne Naess's "deep ecology" movement, which places humans within ecosystems and holds that humans are different from, but not more valuable than, other species.

—Student writer Bree Stutt

For an example of a comparison and contrast essay, see Chapter 8, page 162.

Exercise **4.1**

Below are 15 general topics. Come up with at least three different topic sentences for each topic; for each topic sentence, use a different organizational method. Here are some examples using the topic "rap music":

Cause–effect: Rap music, with its reliance on ever-changing slang, has expanded people's vocabulary; for instance, one's boyfriend is now called one's "boo."

Definition: Rap music is defined by some as being no more than talking over someone else's music.

Description or narration: The lights were dim, and the crowd, writhing to the rhythm of the bass, was pressing forward to the stage.

Chronology: The style of rap music has evolved considerably since it first gained popularity with North American youth in the early 1990s.

Question–answer: How does rap music manage to offend a broad demographic group while maintaining a strong fan base?

Problem–solution: It may seem somewhat ironic, but it is possible that many of the problems addressed in rap lyrics could be solved through this very same medium.

Comparison and contrast: Rap and hip hop music of the late 1980s and early 1990s, with their offensive lyrics and radical counter-cultural appeal, can be compared in terms of their sociological implications to the rock-and-roll revolution of the late 1960s and early 1970s.

Personal: When I first heard rap music, I found the lyrics offensive and sexist.

Cause–effect: Living in the ghetto, surrounded by "booty" and the "brothers," can sometimes cause young men to chant words to a particular rhythm that has no melody.

Cause–effect: Rap music has been used as a vehicle for an oppressed minority to get its voice heard.

Process: To create rap music you need a DJ to provide the beats by mixing records and an MC who takes the beats and contributes the vocals to make the finished product.

Classification: There are many different forms of rap; these include hip hop, hard core, and R&B.

Definition and division: Rap is a unique form of music that is built around heavy bass beats mixed with sharp, quick lyrics. There is a whole spectrum of rap music, ranging from slow love ballads to fast-paced dance songs.

Cost–benefit: Though rap may lead young people to openly and healthily question authority and the status quo, it can lead some adolescents to commit acts of violence against society.

Analogy: Rap can be compared to the insistent and repetitive chants of an evangelist preacher.

Topics:

alternative schooling	exercise	privacy
animal rights	gas prices	public speaking
eating disorders	global warming	same-sex marriages
email	Internet piracy	sports violence
evolution	organ transplants	stress

Exercise **4.2**

Find an essay in this textbook and choose a body paragraph. (Do not use an introduction or a conclusion.) Read through the paragraph and identify how the author has created a unified, coherent, and well-developed paragraph. Identify where the author connects the paragraph to the next paragraph and to the essay as a whole. Look for transitional words or phrases, and identify the main ideas of the paragraph and the development of these ideas, making sure that you can follow the author's train of thought. Also identify any areas that you feel can be improved. Be prepared to explain your answer with a partner. Your instructor may also ask you to analyze the paragraph and submit it to him or her.

❯ Sample Professional Essay

In the following professional essay, look for the different organizational methods that the author uses to develop the piece. Does she use more than one? Is there a main organizational method that she relies on? While reading, also pay attention to how the author links ideas both within and between paragraphs.

SAMPLE PROFESSIONAL ESSAY

How to Retrain Your Rainy Brain

Research into the "optimist gene" shows that you
can always be on the sunny side
by Julia McKinnell

> The author identifies the researcher she will focus on in this essay and then states her credentials. By stating the credentials, especially of a prestigious school like Oxford University, the author adds credibility to the essay.

[1] Elaine Fox, a research professor in experimental psychology at Oxford University, remembers the day in 2010 when the phone rang and it was someone calling on behalf of Michael J. Fox. The actor (no relation to professor Fox) wanted to speak to her because her research dovetailed with his documentary, *Michael J. Fox: Adventures of an Incurable Optimist*.

> **Writing Tip:** For academic essays, do not begin a new paragraphs with a pronoun. Begin by stating a name.

[2] He had read about her interest in certain genes that might predispose a person to optimism and the ability to handle stress. In one study cited by Fox, researchers knew victims of child abuse are more likely to develop serious mental health problems. What interested them was how some children managed to weather serious abuse with no repercussions in later life. What made some children more resilient? The answer, they found, lay in the monoamine oxidase A gene. Abused children born with a "high-expression form" of this gene are better able to cope with ill-treatment, whereas those with a "low-expression form" tend to end up in court for violent and anti-social behaviour.

> In essays, it is typical to use last names only. However, if two people in the essay share a last name and the reader does not clearly understand who is being referred to, use both first and last names.

> Here, in order to ensure reader understanding, the author defines what *monoamine oxidase* is.

[3] Similarly, Fox analyzed the high and low expression of the serotonin transporter gene. The results raised the possibility that the high-expression—LL—form of the gene wired people for optimism. Michael J. Fox wondered if he had this gene, which had been dubbed by the media as the "optimist gene." How else to explain his emotional bounce-back after the devastating diagnosis of Parkinson's? He asked the psychologist to fly to New York to test his DNA, a mouth swab procedure he described as "fairly gross."

[4] Of course, as Elaine Fox explains in her new book, *Rainy Brain Sunny Brain: How to Retrain Your Brain to Overcome Pessimism and Achieve a More Positive Outlook*, "we now

know that optimism, just like pessimism, results from an intricate dance of genetics, life experiences and specific biases in how each of us views and interprets the world."

[5] In fact, Fox argues against the simplistic notion of an optimist gene. The gene is just one piece of the puzzle. As it turned out, Michael J. Fox did not have the LL form. Fox attributes his infinite optimism to a lifelong tendency to look on the bright side. He has entrenched a "sunny" pathway in his brain. "The brain circuits underlying our [pessimistic] brain and our [optimistic] brain are among the most plastic in the human brain," she writes.

> **Writing Tip:** Like all good researchers, Fox acknowledges that there is no simple answer. When writing an academic essay, like Fox you will have to acknowledge that there is often an opposing side to the point you are presenting.

[6] On the phone from London, she explains it this way: "If you imagine water cutting a pathway through sand, the more the water runs down one pathway, the more entrenched the riverbed will become. It's a little bit like that in the brain. These circuits of chemicals are set up so that the more you zone in on the negative, the more your brain learns to tune in to the negative. The thing is, it's sand, not stone. It's not easy, but with effort we can change the way we see things, and that does lead to structural changes in the brain."

> **Writing Tip:** In an academic essay, a single quotation should not make up the whole paragraph.

[7] She urges pessimists to reframe their experiences in a positive way. If you run into an old friend who walks past you, don't assume they dislike you, she advises. "Learn to challenge your belief. Step back and say, 'Is there any other interpretation? Maybe they didn't recognize me. I haven't seen them for a while.'"

> The author maintains coherence by repeating what was said at the end of the quotation in the previous paragraph. However, she does not do this by simply repeating the same words. She rewords it and therefore makes it more effective.

[8] Fox also points to a new technique pioneered by the psychiatrist who treated Leonardo DiCaprio, who developed obsessive-compulsive disorder after immersing himself among OCD patients for his role as Howard Hughes. The psychiatrist, Jeffrey Schwartz, is a Buddhist who developed a form of cognitive behavioral therapy that includes aspects of meditation, known as mindfulness-based CBT. He trains people not to give into the urge to check the stove but instead to "relabel their symptoms as a sign of a disordered brain circuit and not something worth worrying about," says Fox.

> **Writing Tip:** If you are going to use an acronym to discuss something, make sure you explain what those initials represent first. In this case, the author should have used the following format: "... a form of cognitive behavioral therapy (CBT) that includes ..."

[9] After 10 weeks of mindfulness-based CBT, brain scans of OCD patients show significant changes to the orbitofrontal cortex. Fox is optimistic pessimists can use the same technique to change their brains. "What I'm talking about is real change, reflected at the level of neurons and their connections deep within our brains. If we can change these connections, we can change ourselves."

> **Writing Tip:** In this essay, which is not an example of an academic essay, the author chose to end the piece with the results of CBT. However, in an academic essay, you would need to also mention the earlier gene research.

—McKinnell, J. (2012, August 7). How to retrain your rainy brain: Research into the "optimist gene" shows that you can always be on the sunny side. *Maclean's*. Retrieved from www2.macleans.ca /2012/08/07/ always-on-the-sunny-side/

(*continued*)

Post-reading Questions

1. What is the author's purpose for writing this essay?
2. Who is the audience for this piece?
3. How does the author develop the paragraphs in this essay? Are there specific examples of definition, cause/effect, example, etc.?
4. The author states that "If you imagine water cutting a pathway through sand, the more the water runs down one pathway, the more entrenched the riverbed will become. It's a little bit like that in the brain." What type of development pattern is this?
5. Michael J. Fox is mentioned in this essay. How effective is the use of someone famous to illustrate a point?
6. The author discusses the "optimist gene" and also discusses cognitive behavioural therapy. How does she link the two so that the two ideas are coherent?
7. Is this reader-based prose or writer-based prose? Give examples to support your idea.
8. Find two examples of topic sentences. Are they effective? If not, how could they have been improved?
9. Find examples of transitions the author uses. Should she have used more to make the essay more coherent?
10. Explain how the author maintains paragraph unity.

■ Chapter Review Questions

1. What are some of the characteristics of effective paragraphs?
2. Why is supporting information important in paragraphs?
3. What are the different types of organizational or development methods used for both paragraphs and essays?
4. Explain when it is appropriate to use the different organizational methods for developing paragraphs.
5. When using description, why is it important to use concrete wording?
6. When is using narration acceptable in a formal essay?
7. What is the difference between an essay that discusses causes and one that discusses effects?
8. How are comparison essays and contrast essays different?
9. Examples are important in writing. Why do you think this is?
10. Can more than one development pattern be used in a paragraph? Be prepared to justify your opinion.

Part 2

Essays

5

Kinds of
Essays

In this chapter, you will

- learn about the differences between expository and argumentative essays
- learn how to write an effective in-class essay

Essays are written for a variety of reasons at college and university. You may be given a week or more to prepare an essay; yet on other occasions, you may be required to write an essay within a short period of time, such as during an in-class exam. It is always important to understand what kind of essay you are being asked to write. This chapter will also introduce you to useful terms and guidelines for answering an essay prompt, and it will help you understand how to approach a topic for all essay writing situations.

❯ Expository versus Argumentative Essays

As we saw in Chapter 2, there are many purposes for which you might write an essay. In Chapter 4 you learned about different ways of organizing an essay and its paragraphs. We now look at the two major purposes of essay writing—exposition and argument—and how these purposes influence how an essay will be organized.

Exposition explains or informs; **argument** persuades your audience to change its mind or see your point of view. Although the difference may seem obvious, the dividing line between exposition and argument is not always clear, and many of the same skills and strategies apply to both kinds of essays. Table 5.1 lists some ways that exposition differs from argument.

Here are some elements that exposition and argument share:

- Both can use factual information and reliable sources to support main points.
- Critical thinking is essential to successful expository and argumentative writing.
- In both, your voice should remain objective and your language neutral.

Exposition is informing, explaining, describing, or defining a topic for the audience.

Argument is persuading your audience to change its mind or to see your point of view.

TABLE 5.1	Expository versus Argumentative Writing
In Expository Writing	**In Argumentative Writing**
You use a fact-based thesis (see page 135).	You use a value- or policy-based thesis (see page 135).
You begin with an open mind and see where your exploration takes you.	You begin by considering where you stand on an issue and how you can support your position.
In your body paragraphs, you look at the available evidence and rely on critical thinking for your conclusion.	In your body paragraphs, you draw the reader's attention to supporting evidence but do not ignore or distort contradictory evidence.
Research is usually an integral part of expository writing.	Research is not always necessary in argumentative writing (although your instructor may ask you to include research to strengthen your argument).
If you are writing on a controversial topic, you do not take sides, though you may explain the position of both sides by using objective language.	You try to win your argument fairly, by using logic and making use of emotion only where appropriate.

❯ Types of Essays

When writing an essay, it is important to pay attention to the prompts you are given by your instructor. For example, if you are asked to explain the difference between college and high school, you will write an expository essay. You will probably organize the essay using the comparison–contrast method. You will not, however, attempt to convince the audience that one is better than the other. Your goal is to highlight the differences. If, on the other hand, you are asked to explain whether a business diploma is more valuable than one in journalism, you will use argument and draw a conclusion based on what you have written. Again, you can use a comparison–contrast organizational structure, but with a goal of helping readers understand the validity of your conclusion You don't necessarily have to change the readers' minds; you want them to see that your points have merit. Understanding the prompt given or the nature of the assignment is crucial for your success.

Sample topic for an expository essay:

Explain how the skeletal evolution of the penguin enabled it to adapt to an ocean environment.

In this case, the writer will inform and explain. (Note that the word *explain* is right in the prompt.)

Sample topic for an expository essay that might use some argument:

What we can do to alleviate the impact of global warming on the emperor penguin habitat on Roosevelt Island

How do you think argument might be involved—either directly or indirectly? What assumption is the writer making about the topic that the reader would be expected to agree with?

Sample topic for an argumentative essay:

What must nations do to prevent the destruction of penguin habitat?

Verbs like *must* and *should* usually signal an argumentative thesis.

The In-Class Essay or Examination Essay

You may have to do in-class writing, at least occasionally, during your time in college or university. Typically, you will be given a period of time in which to complete the assignment. You will need to demonstrate both your knowledge of a subject and your writing skills. You may be able to use a text, notes, or a dictionary; or it may just be you, your pen, and some paper (or a computer).

In-class writing serves a practical purpose: demonstrating your ability to think, read, and write under pressure. Although this kind of essay usually tests recall, it also tests other important qualities, such as organization and time management, critical thinking, and adaptability (see Critical Thinking and Adaptability later in this chapter), as well as, possibly, creativity and imagination.

Recall

An in-class or examination essay will require you to remember information from lectures, textbooks, and discussions; however, other factors may also be crucial. Being familiar with the *terminology* of your discipline is vital. This means that you need to be able to communicate effectively in the language of the discipline. You also need to be aware of *basic principles, procedures, and methods stressed throughout the year.* If you are asked to write an essay, you will need to know the basics of essay format and structure. If you are asked to write a summary of a text, you will need to know how to summarize; if you are asked to write a critical response to an essay, you will need to know how to analyze and think critically.

With this type of essay, you should allow enough time for a complete and unhurried review of your notes, highlighted sections of your course texts, and your instructor's comments on previous essays and tests. The goal is to distinguish the essential information from the rest and enable you to focus on what you *need* to know. This type of essay more often tests the *application* of facts than simple recall of basic facts and details. For example, in psychology, you may need to know about B.F. Skinner and his theories of behaviourism, but showing that you understand the implications of his studies and the impact on the field of psychology may be more important than describing how he actually performed his tests.

Organization and Time Management

It is important to spend a few minutes planning your approach to the exam questions so that your essay really answers the questions. Once you have decided how to divide up the exam and how much time to spend on the various parts, stick to your plan. It's common to spend too much time on the first question. If you find yourself doing this, jot one or two points in the margin to follow up on if you have time before the end, and move on to the next question.

Obviously, you should read the general exam instructions carefully before beginning. Resist the urge to dive right in. Read every word and underline key words or phrases to reinforce their importance and to keep them in mind as you write. Of course, the same applies to each question (see Critical Thinking and Adaptability, below). Remember that writing skills are connected to reading and thinking skills. The student who misreads loses credibility as a writer because he or she has not followed directions. This is especially important when

Although in-class writing may test your ability to recall material, it also tests such important qualities as organization, time management, and adaptability.

It is important to prepare for in-class writing with realistic expectations: the goal is to distinguish essential information from the rest and enable you to focus on what you *need to* know.

Write it . . . say it . . . imagine it . . . experience it . . . picture it . . . draw it . . . test it . . . repeat it . . . understand it.

the question makes a distinction of some kind: "Answer *three* of the following five questions"; "Respond to *either* question 1 *or* question 2." Also pay attention to the verb used to introduce or frame the question; *discuss*, *compare and contrast*, and *explain* give you three different instructions.

Finally, plan for at least five minutes per question to look over the exam after you've finished writing to ensure that you haven't left anything out and that the marker will be able to follow your ideas. Final checks and careful proofreading are important—as are small additions, such as transitions to connect ideas. Instructors prefer to read a thoughtfully revised and carefully proofed essay, even one that has some deletions and, perhaps, even a couple of arrows, to one that is tidy-looking but unclear in places. Neatness is important, but completeness and accuracy are more so.

Critical Thinking and Adaptability

Once you have done the necessary planning and are focusing on the individual question(s), you need to

1. distinguish what is important from what is less important
2. focus on strong, well-chosen points and supporting details, adapting the question, if necessary

In the sample essay question below, the writer has underlined the important parts of the question and has already begun to shape her answer by attempting to rephrase or elaborate on the question. At this stage, she is essentially looking for clues, hints, and suggestions for writing.

Before she can proceed from topic to thesis statement, she has to decide on her approach. The subject of Internet piracy is very large, and if she does not put some thought into limiting it, she may find himself becoming too vague. A common weaknesses of in-class essays is the tendency to generalize, or to be too broad. Therefore, first limiting the topic and finding a distinct area to make your own will result in a more manageable essay.

Ask yourself the following questions to help limit and refine a general topic into a topic for your essay:

- What do you personally know about the topic?
- Have you or anyone you know had experience with it?
- How can you explain the topic using your own knowledge or skills?

Finding where you are knowledgeable is the key to refining the topic in order to best use your strengths.

Any essay will benefit from examples and illustrations by giving you solid support for your points. Examples and illustrations will also turn the general and abstract into the concrete and specific. Details are essential. Consider using a pre-writing technique, such as questioning or brainstorming, to generate detail.

The student who wrote the essay below was given 90 minutes, which was enough time to develop an approach to her topic and a thesis statement, and to prepare a scratch outline. Of course, you may not be given this much time to write an in-class essay; as a result, you might not be able to develop each point as thoroughly as this writer has done.

Examples and illustrations will also turn the general and abstract into the concrete and specific.

SAMPLE STUDENT ESSAY

Exam Question

Piracy has been a part of society for centuries. It has been vilified by law makers for as long as it has existed, but it has also been romanticized in literature and in the movies. Pirates have adapted to the changes around them in order to profit from others. They are no longer just "sailing the seven seas," but exist even in cyberspace. Explain what Internet piracy is and describe the ramifications of it to society in general.

Student Answer

[1] The Internet has changed the way people function in daily life. Almost everything can be done online. Shopping, banking, and communicating with others are all tasks that required people to leave their homes, for the most part, up until the mid-90s. Now, these tasks can be done with a computer and an Internet connection. While this is convenient, and arguably, an advancement, unfortunately, this ease of access has also created a new form of pirate in society: the Internet pirate. Unlike the pirates of old, these people profit from someone else's loss without having to leave the comfort of their home, and, for many, the most concerning part about Internet piracy is that virtually anyone can become a "pirate." This form of piracy is just as detrimental to society as traditional forms still practiced.

[2] The most talked about form of Internet piracy involves the theft of music. Until 2011, the music industry was losing money. That did change in 2012, but the profits are not as large as many people seem to think. Making music costs a lot of money. First, there is the musician's share of the profit that must be paid, often in the form of royalties. The cost of the recording sessions must be included in the balance books, as must

(continued)

all the salaries for the people working in the industry. The cost of a CD or music download help cover those costs. However, Internet pirates bypass this by downloading music illegally. Many programs exist that are free and allow music lovers to access digital music without having to pay for their pleasure. While some of these programs or downloads may contain viruses, this does not stop people from accessing them. These pirates often view these activities as victimless crimes, that is not true. Each illegal download costs artists revenue and causes music companies to lose money. Without the money earned from the music being produced, the music industry faces collapse. The more money lost, the fewer large companies are willing to take risks with unknown artists, as their music is not guaranteed to sell. Therefore, society risks missing out on the newest musician who could become the next superstar.

[3] Software piracy grows every year and is of concern to companies that copyright their material. There are many different ways to access pirated software online. Some websites may offer illegal copies of popular software at discounted rates. Keys are provided, which the pirates have created. Sometimes these keys work and sometimes they don't. If one buys a key that doesn't work, it is almost impossible to get the money back. In the long run, pirated software obtained this way can wind up costing as much as the legal versions. Another way that one can obtain software is from peer sharing groups. These people do not see themselves as pirates; however, what they are doing amounts to piracy, as they are stealing the profits from the companies which spend money on research and development.

[4] Another form of piracy that exists on the Internet is that of identity theft. Many people shop and bank online, and while most of the information exchanged is well protected, there are still pirates who hire computer hackers to break through the code that protects an individual's identity. Once one's identity has been discovered, the pirates can then use this information to amass wealth at the expense of the unsuspecting victim. For example, a credit card number can be stolen by a pirate and then used to purchase goods, such as designer clothing, for re-sale. Unless one checks bank or credit card statements

carefully, this piracy can go undetected for months. This is not a victimless crime, as many people wind up paying for this in terms of higher interest rates and service fees. This identity theft can also involve more than just credit cards. Pirates can learn addresses, phone numbers, driver's license numbers, social insurance numbers, and so much more. Once one's identity is compromised in this way, it becomes very difficult to participate in everyday activities until the information is replaced. This type of piracy costs money for both the victim and society, as wages must be paid to those replacing the identification. Once again, society is being made to pay so that a few may profit without ever having to leave home.

[5] Piracy has been a problem plaguing society for centuries and the newest form, Internet piracy, is just as much of an issue as were the pirates on the high seas. Unfortunately though, today's pirates cannot be seen easily, as they often work from the comfort of their homes and steal from unsuspecting victims. These victims can be large corporations, such as those producing music and software, or they can be individual musicians and unsuspecting home computer users. One of the problems is that anyone can become a pirate by simply downloading music illegally. Internet piracy costs everyone money and must be stopped.

—Student writer Lindsay Strummer

Post-reading Questions

1. How did the writer limit the topic? Do you think she has an area of expertise or specialization that she was able to use in order to adapt the topic to capitalize on her knowledge?

2. Identify the thesis statement and the main points (the latter take the form of topic sentences for the body paragraphs). Why do you think she used the order of points she did?

3. Some of the writer's statements could be challenged. Do you think that, within the limits of an in-class essay, the writer has adequately supported her points? How has she done this? Has she failed to do this anywhere?

4. Returning to the exam question, do you think the writer directly addressed what she was asked to address? Suggest other ways that a student writer could respond to the question.

Exercise 5.1

Choose one of the following topics (or one your instructor assigns) and determine which type of audience you are going to address.

- respective audiences for online games (such as The Sims or World of Warcraft)
- the effectiveness of diets
- how tablet computers are changing the way we live
- living in residence versus living in an apartment
- the value of having a Twitter account
- the importance of networking when job hunting
- the value of post-secondary education
- the importance of owning pets

After you have written the essay, determine how you would change it if the audience were different. For example, what would you change if you were to write the essay for your professor or for someone in high school? Give specific examples of what you would change or how you would change it.

❯ Sample Professional Essay

The following expository essay uses process as the organizing principle. The author includes steps so that the reader can see the order the process should follow. He also uses headings to help organize the steps. By looking at the step numbers and the headings, the reader can easily understand what is involved in the process. Notice that the author uses clear examples to help explain his points. There are very clear descriptions included, so that the reader can visualize what is being discussed, which improves the audience understanding. Remember that essays, whether expository or argument, can use a variety of organizational patterns and can even have different organizing patterns in individual paragraphs.

SAMPLE PROFESSIONAL ESSAY

How To Find Sunken Treasure

Modern treasure hunting isn't all about maps and shovels—it takes science, too.
by Erik Sass

[1] **Step 1. Pick a shipwreck.** There are plenty of ships in the sea. According to UNESCP, roughly three million shipwrecks across the globe are just waiting to be found, and at least 100 of them boast potential values that top $50 million. So what's the best case scenario? Finding the *Flor de la Mar*, a Portuguese ship that sank north of Sumatra. The storied treasure includes 60 tons of gold and 200 chests of diamonds, emeralds, rubies and sapphires worth up to $3 billion.

[2] **Step 2. Imagine the riches that could be yours.** Shiny!

[3] **Step 3. Hire professionals.** It may seem like cheating, but most unclaimed treasures are too deep for scuba gear. In fact, salvaging companies invest big bucks in equipment to travel miles below the surface. Odyssey Marine Exploration, one of the world's premier firms, has spent at least $100 million on the essentials, including its 251-foot flagship, the *Odyssey Explorer*. The ship's capable of carrying 60 days' worth of provisions for its 42 crew members; three tow fish for seabed surveys; and two remotely operated vehicles (ROVs) that can dive 4,000 meters and beyond.

[4] All that equipment pays off in sweet government contracts. In 2010, the Brits gave Odyssey salvage work, paired with archeological responsibilities, for the SS *Gairsoppa*—a WWII merchant ship torpedoed about 300 miles southwest of Galway, Ireland, while carrying at least 219 tons of silver. The water's extreme depth has protected the sunken treasure for decades (it's 2.9 miles down, nearly half a mile deeper than the *Titanic*). But the rising price of precious metals has made salvaging the loot an attractive proposition. Today, the *Gairsoppa*'s cargo of bullion, ingots, and coins is worth around $270 million.

[5] **Step 4. Be patient.** Unfortunately, you can't just take barnacle-encrusted money and run. As the folks at Odyssey know, recovery is a lengthy process, made even longer by archeological requirements. Here's how the typical salvage works: First, the team dispatches a remote-controlled submersible to survey the wreck and take photos to create a detailed mosaic of the scene. Marine archeologists then direct a fleet of ROVs to search the ship, recording the distribution of artifacts and cataloging any organisms

(continued)

In this essay, the author includes his thesis statement in the title. Not all process writing follows this format. Most authors have an introductory paragraph that contains the thesis statement.

The author uses both steps and headings to direct the reader's attention to the process and how to complete it.

As well as having a heading, each paragraph has a topic sentence (with the exception of Step 2).

Writing Tip: Always check with your instructor regarding the formality of language needed in your essay. Short forms, such as *the Brits*, and slang may not be acceptable.

Even within the process essay, the author includes yet another process. Here he indicates the steps involved using transitions such as *first* and *then*.

that may call the ship home. When they begin recovering objects, a computer program maps and determines the precise location of each artifact, using a network of acoustic transponders placed on the ocean floor to triangulate locations. Then comes the fun part. Like a high-stakes arcade crane, scientists use ROVs to spray the sediment with gentle water pressure, then suck up the tiny, fragile objects with a low-power vacuum. But that's just the artifacts. Recovering all that precious bullion poses even more technical challenges. Technicians must pluck individual coins and ingots from rotten wooden storage structures and navigate remote vehicles past rusted metal containers. Odyssey began work on the *Gairsoppa* in September 2011, and it's still picking the ship clean. Once it's done the *Gairsoppa* will hold the title of the largest marine salvage of precious metals in history.

[6] **Step 5. Fight for your right to booty.** There's just one hitch in the plunder discovery biz—sometimes the original owners want their loot back. Odyssey recently had to hand over several million dollars' worth of gold and silver it had salvaged in 2007 from the Spanish galleon *Nuestra Senora de las Mercedes*. The Spanish government successfully argued in a U.S. federal court that the treasure still belonged to Spain—although the Spaniards also had to fend off a surprise last-minute claim from Peru, where the metal was mined, refined, and coined. Funny how everyone becomes interested in history when there's a small mountain of gold coins at stake.

> Notice how the author ends with a thought-provoking statement that leaves the reader pondering another aspect of hunting for treasure. However, it is still tied to the original thesis, which is about treasure hunting.

—Sass, E. (2012, September 7). How to find sunken treasure: Modern treasure hunting isn't all about maps and shovels—it takes science, too. *Mental_Floss*. Retrieved from http://mentalfloss.com/article/12482/how-find-sunken-treasure

Post-reading Questions

1. Who do you think the audience is for this essay? Justify your answer with relevant quotations from the article.

2. Do you think the process approach was best for this essay? If so, why? If you think it could have been organized using a different pattern, how would you have written it?

3. The author uses slang in this piece. What do you think his purpose was?

4. Most essays do not include headings. Why do you think the author used these? The author has written a short essay. Do you think it has enough detail? What do you think could have been added to this essay to make it more complete?

■ Chapter Review Questions

1. What is the difference between an expository and an argumentative essay?

2. What is the purpose of writing an argumentative essay?

3. What are benefits of including research in an expository essay?

4. What are some important factors to remember when writing an in-class or exam essay?

5. When you are refining a topic, what are some important factors to consider?

6

Essay
Basics

In this chapter, you will

- learn different ways to introduce an essay
- learn how to create an effective thesis statement
- learn how to write a conclusion that wraps up your essay

You will have probably written many essays by the time you begin

your college or university education; however, the requirements for

essays at this level are more advanced than those at the high school

level. In this chapter, you will examine how to effectively draw your

audience into your essay and keep them engaged through to your

conclusion.

❯ The Essay's Introduction

Almost everything you read will begin with an **introduction**. Even if it is not called the "introduction," it will act as one by giving a preview of what follows. It will do that by presenting the main idea and, probably, the organizational pattern of the document—whether it is a book, an article in a scholarly journal, a class essay, a sales proposal, or a résumé. The kinds of introductions students are asked to write are made up of one or more paragraphs that fulfill specific functions, and should, like all paragraphs, be unified, coherent, and well developed.

It is crucial to spend time creating a well-written introduction that will be noticed for its unity and coherence. As it is one of the most important parts of your essay, take the time to write an introduction that will draw the reader into your essay and provide necessary information, satisfying the expectations of your audience.

An introduction is the opening of a essay that presents the main idea (the thesis statement) and the main organizational pattern.

Functions of the Introduction

Reader Interest: Logical, Dramatic, and Mixed Approaches

The introduction should create reader interest. Although most of your essay's "substance"—your main points and sub-points, the supporting details—will be placed in the middle (body) paragraphs, an ineffective introduction could mean that these details are wasted as the rest of the essay may not be read. Reader interest can be created through two different methods with variations on each.

Reader interest is very important in essay writing. You need to catch the reader's attention and maintain it throughout the essay so that your reader stays interested. If reader interest is not maintained, no one will finish your essay and all of your hard work will not be viewed. Reader interest is especially important when writing for an instructor. If your essay is entertaining and thought-provoking, your mark will probably be higher than for a more mundane essay.

Logical Introduction

The **logical approach** is the most common and traditional way to create interest. You use the first part of the introduction to build your emphasis. You begin with the general and proceed to the specific; the most specific is your thesis statement, usually the last sentence of the introduction. This is also called the **inverted pyramid** structure. A logical opening helps you establish the topic's relevance and shows where it fits in as your points progressively become more specific.

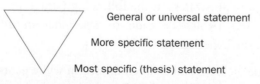

FIGURE 6.1 Structure of paragraph introduction

The logical approach begins with the general aspect of the topic and moves to the more specific as you progress through the introduction. This is repeated as you write your paragraphs.

The logical approach is also called the inverted pyramid approach, as you move from a broad to a narrow focus.

In the following introduction, the writer begins with a general claim and gradually brings the subject into sharp focus—Laos's dependence on hydroelectric power. The pyramidal development is important for general readers who may not know much about Laos and the topic. Pay close attention to how the writer also creates reader interest, as he draws the reader into the topic.

The paragraph begins with a general statement before making specific connections between rivers and their uses by civilizations.

The writer focuses on a specific country and discusses how Laos has used its rivers in the past.

The writer further narrows the topic by mentioning a specific river system and stressing its importance to Laos.

In the thesis statement, the writer announces the essay's main point, the most specific sentence.

Rivers have always been a central part of civilization. From the banks of the Tigris and Euphrates was born the idea of civilization, and almost all subsequent peoples have relied on rivers for trade, transportation, irrigation, fishing, and drinking water. The Lao of Southeast Asia are one such people, living for thousands of years in villages by the many rivers of that country. They have depended on their waterways for clean drinking water, irrigation for their crops, and fishing. The heart of the Lao river system lies in the Mekong River, the longest river in Southeast Asia. Laos is a landlocked country and is therefore doubly reliant on its rivers as a source of trade. Impoverished by war and political turmoil, Laos has turned to its rivers to provide a new, modern resource: electricity.

—Student writer Ian Stock

In another kind of logical approach, you begin by mentioning something familiar to the reader and proceed to the unfamiliar. The following opening illustrates this approach:

> While the intelligence quotient (IQ) has long been a useful tool to determine one's intelligence, a development in the study of human intellectual experience has expanded to include one's emotional state. It is called Emotional Intelligence, or EQ.

—Student writer Chin-Ju Chiang

Dramatic Introduction

In the dramatic approach, the opening of the essay is meant to catch the reader's attention in an interesting or thought-provoking way.

An anecdote is an incident or event that is used because it is interesting or striking.

The writer evokes a scene in order to interest the reader, using both descriptive detail and narration (telling a story).

Putting the reader in the place of "the unknowing spectator," the writer continues to evoke the scene, arousing the reader's curiosity and suspense.

The **dramatic approach** can be used in various ways: you could begin with an interesting quotation (citing from a dictionary is *not* a good example of the dramatic approach), a thought-provoking question, a personal experience, an illuminating statistic, a description of a scene, or a brief narrative, like an **anecdote**.

Unlike the logical approach, here you begin with something quite specific. The object is to surprise or intrigue your reader. The object is to gently surprise, not to shock or startle. Although the dramatic approach is used more often in argument than in exposition, it can be effective in an expository essay as well, as the example below illustrates. In the following paragraph, the student writer creates a scenario that enables the reader to experience an unfamiliar martial art first-hand, just as she experienced it.

> Imagine a circle of adults and children dressed in white pants with different-coloured cords around their waists. Everybody is clapping and singing in an unfamiliar language—entranced by what is unfolding within the circle. Musicians are playing drums, tambourines, and an instrument that looks like a stringed bow with a gourd attached. There is an inescapable feeling of communal energy within the circle. Uncontrollable curiosity lures the unknowing spectator; peering into the circle exposes two people engaged in an intense physical dialogue. Kicks and movements are exchanged with precision and fluidity, which create a dance-like choreography. What is being witnessed is

called a *roda* (pronounced ho-da, it means "circle" in Portuguese). A person's first encounter with this intriguing display of physicality and grace is an experience not easily forgotten. I did not forget my first *roda*, and, consequently, I later began training in this Brazilian form of martial arts—*capoeira* (pronounced cap-where-a).

—Student writer Kerry Hinds

> The writer concisely defines *capoeira* in her thesis statement. Note that her use of personal experience is a strategy designed to create reader interest. Her essay will probably make minimal or no use of personal experience but will explain significant aspects of this martial art form.

Mixed Approach

An introduction could use more than one method to attract interest. This is called the mixed approach.

> You may notice that some academic articles do not use any of the kinds of introductions referred to here. Such an article may begin with a direct and concise statement of the problem or purpose and may even include the study's findings in the introduction. This is often the case with scientific articles designed for those with specialized knowledge of the subject.

Exercise **6.1**

Rewrite the paragraph above using the logical approach. (In order to do so, you might have to do some research into *capoeira*.)

- *Dramatic–logical:* The writer could begin with a question and then proceed to develop the rest of the paragraph through the logical approach.
- *Logical–dramatic:* The writer could use a "reversal" strategy, beginning with a general statement before dramatically turning the tables and arguing the opposite. The writer employs this strategy in an essay that criticizes the use of fur in today's society.

Since the beginning of time, people have depended on fur. Cavemen wore animal skins as clothing; furthermore, after killing an animal, such as a buffalo, the flesh would be eaten and the bones would be used in tool-making. They used as much of the animal as possible due to their spiritual beliefs and because with few other resources, it made sense to waste as little as possible. Wearing fur in that age was a necessity; it was warm, practical, and readily available. Today, it is a far different story. Fur is part of the upscale fashion industry, but killing wild animals for their skin extends beyond fur fanciers; it is a luxury product for more many different consumers today, such as car owners with leather upholstery. There are more than 40 different animal species that are killed for their skin, and not a single one needs to be.

—Student writer Grace Beal

> The writer makes a general statement.

> Using the logical method, the writer adds detail, becoming more specific.

> The writer reiterates her main point before contrasting the caveman's needs with those of society today.

> In her thesis statement, she forcefully announces her argumentative claim: killing animals for their fur today is wrong.

Whatever approach you use, the way that you choose to create interest should be relevant to your topic, your purpose in writing, and your audience. For example, if you were arguing in favour of euthanasia, or another issue with a built-in emotional aspect, and you knew your audience opposed it, a strongly emotional opening might not be a good approach because you could risk alienating your readers.

Other Features of the Introduction

The introduction serves three other important functions:

- *To announce your topic and the main point:* The thesis statement, occurring near or at the end of the introduction, gives the main point of the essay and must have two parts: the topic itself plus a comment on the topic (see The Thesis Statement: Simple versus Expanded, below).

- *To introduce the writer:* The introduction is the place where the reader first comes to know that he or she is in competent hands. The introduction is the writer's first chance to establish credibility, presenting him- or herself as knowledgeable about the topic as well as reliable and trustworthy. One of the ways this comes across is through good writing; another way is by appearing rational, fair, and in control.

- *To indicate how the writer plans to develop the main points:* What organizing method will be used? Organizational patterns include description, narration, definition (saying what something is), chronology (using time order), compare and contrast, and cause–effect, along with the other patterns discussed in Chapter 4, Paragraph Development.

The Opening Sentence

The introduction usually builds up gradually to the last sentence of the introduction, your thesis statement. However, you should not focus all of your energy on the last sentence at the expense of the first sentence. Your opening sentence needs to be carefully crafted too. An ineffective opening may be too general, obvious, too abrupt, overstated (making a false universal claim), or irrelevant. If you start your essay in any of these ways, the reader may be put off and then read your essay much more critically than if you had opened with an effective sentence. Using the analogy of meeting someone for the first time, you could say that an ineffective opening is the equivalent of a weak handshake or an averted glance rather than a firm handshake or direct eye contact.

Too general or broad:

In the twentieth century, many historic events have occurred around the globe, especially in Europe, Asia, and America.

Why is this too broad? Does the phrase beginning with *especially* help to make it more specific? How can the statement be made more effective?

Obvious:

As population continues to rise around the world, the need for transportation will also increase.

What makes this statement too obvious? Is there a way it can be rewritten to make it more appropriate as an opening?

Too abrupt:

Changes need to be made to the current regulations involving the Class 7 driver's licence in British Columbia.

Why is this statement too abrupt? Would it be less abrupt if it were placed somewhere else in the introduction?

First Nations' self-determination and self-government must come from within.

The previous example suggests a strongly partisan point of view that might be quite acceptable if audience members clearly supported this kind of self-government; but it could alienate members of a general or neutral audience. It might be considered overstated. Is there a way it can be adapted to be less abrupt or overstated?

Overstated—false universal claim:

Everyone these days has used a computer at one time or another.

Many people in the world, even in Canada, have not used a computer. There are few situations satisfied by the "everyone" claim. Knowing this, how can the statement be revised?

Be wary of making "everyone" claims unless your statement truly applies to everyone.

Irrelevant, or "So what?":

Few people know that sea otters can live to the age of 15 years.

This could be an effective opening if the statement really fell into the category of "believe it or not"—but it doesn't. How could it be revised so that it is appropriate for a college- or university-level essay?

Writing an introduction requires time and patience. You should not feel discouraged if, after having produced an outline, you cannot quickly come up with a strong introduction. It may be best to return to your introduction after you've written the rest of the essay. In fact, some instructors believe that the introduction should be the last part of the essay you write.

Don't feel discouraged if, after having produced an outline, you cannot quickly come up with a strong introduction. It may be best to return to your introduction *after* you've written the rest of the essay.

Exercise **6.2**

In a group, consider the following opening statements and what makes them ineffective, whether one of the reasons above or something else. How could you revise them to make them more effective and interesting?

1. Franz Anton Mesmer discovered hypnosis in the 1770s.
2. Although email is a modern communications miracle, it is also the biggest nuisance ever invented.

(continued)

3. It is said that ignorance is bliss.
4. I guess we would all like to look like Kate Moss if we could.
5. There are many issues surrounding end-of-life treatment of terminally ill individuals.
6. Leprosy is, without doubt, the most brutal disease known to humanity.
7. Why not buy the best-made sports car the world has to offer?
8. The movement of people away from the Catholic Church today is mostly due to its teachings on issues like abortion, women's equality, and homosexuality.
9. Sports are something we all watch.
10. In all American literature, no character ever gave more thought to moral decisions than Huckleberry Finn does.
11. Most people in our society today dream of growing up, marrying, and getting a good job so they can start a family.
12. Desperate times call for desperate measures.
13. The importance of education has been reiterated many times.
14. Who was Roger Bannister?
15. Fighting is a part of hockey—no ifs, ands, or buts.

The Thesis Statement: Simple versus Expanded

In Chapter 1, you learned that a thesis statement consists of a statement of a topic and a comment on that topic. Now we will look at different kinds of thesis statements and what makes a thesis statement effective. A **simple thesis statement** has the two necessary parts, topic and comment, and no more. This example, which you saw in Chapter 1, is a simple thesis statement:

> Life in residence at the University of the South Pole helps prepare one for life after university.

An **expanded thesis statement** gives more detail, usually by including your main points. Just as a simple thesis statement goes further than a topic, so an expanded thesis statement goes further than a simple thesis statement by answering questions like "how?" or "why?" to account for or justify the main idea—*how* does life in residence prepare one for life after university?—as in the example below:

> Life in residence at the University of the South Pole helps prepare one for life after university by making a student independent, by reinforcing basic life skills, and by teaching one how to get along with other penguins.

A simple thesis statement announces the topic and makes a comment on it.

An expanded thesis statement gives more detail, such as the main points that will be covered in the essay.

Here's an example of a topic, followed by a simple thesis statement and an expanded one that answers the question "why?":

Topic:

School uniforms

Simple thesis statement:

Making school uniforms mandatory has many advantages for students.

Expanded thesis statement:

Making school uniforms mandatory has many advantages for students, as they eliminate distractions, encourage a focus on academics, and reduce competition based on appearances.

A simple thesis statement may be sufficient for a short essay, such as one of fewer than 500 words. A simple thesis statement can be used in a fact-based (expository) essay in which you attempt to answer a question or solve a problem. In an argumentative essay, you try to convince your reader of something. An expanded thesis that announces all your points in the introduction gets you off to a forceful start. Check with your instructor for specific guidelines about simple versus expanded thesis statements.

Effective Thesis Statements

An effective thesis statement should be interesting, specific, and manageable.

- *Interesting:* The thesis is likely to attract the reader, especially the general reader, to the topic and the essay.
- *Specific:* The thesis isn't so general, broad, or obvious that it lacks relevance; it informs the reader about what will follow.
- *Manageable:* The thesis sounds as if it can be reasonably explored in the space of the essay; the writer is going to be able to successfully carry out what is promised in the thesis.

Ineffective Thesis Statements

Although a thesis statement may be ineffective because it is not interesting, specific, or manageable, it may have other problems. An unclear thesis statement may confuse rather than inform. For example, the following thesis statement doesn't clearly express the main points of the essay. In this case, the writer needs to be more detailed and precise.

Pets are important in that they can unify and heal, and are an inevitable part of human nature.

Do we know what the writer means by these assertions? As an expanded thesis statement that includes the main points of the essay, it is inadequate because it will likely baffle readers, not inform them.

Revised:

Pets are important in bringing people together, helping them recover from an illness or depression, and enabling them to express important human values, such as love.

A thesis statement may be unclear because it seems to straddle two topics rather than centre on one. This could be the result of the writer's early uncertainty: he or she may not know the essay's major focus. In revising your essay, you should always ensure that your thesis accurately reflects the essay's main point. In this example, we don't know whether this essay will be about excessive dieting or body image:

Ineffective:

Many youths are obsessed by dieting today due to the prominence our society places on body image.

To successfully revise this thesis, the writer needs to narrow the topic to one specific area, such as the following:

- unhealthy diets and the problems they create
- the effects of body image on youths
- the relationship between body image and dieting

The last topic would likely involve extensive research and might not be manageable within the scope of a medium-length essay.

Avoid a stiff and self-conscious thesis statement that refers directly to the writer or to the essay's purpose:

Ineffective:

I (or, This essay) will examine the phenomenon of online gambling and argue in favour of strict government regulation of this growing industry.

Revised:

Online gambling is of increasing concern to governments today and should be subject to strict regulations.

The thesis you start with shouldn't be considered fixed. As you write your outline or rough draft and uncover areas about your topic you weren't aware of before, you may want to go back and revise your thesis.

A thesis statement can be difficult to write. A clear thesis statement begins with the writer's clear thoughts. As with all writing, clear thinking produces clear expression.

When you use an expanded thesis statement, you need to express your main points in parallel structure; otherwise, it could be hard to follow (see Chapter 16, pages 419–420).

A Thesis Statement Checklist

1. Have you written a complete thesis statement, not just a topic?
2. Does it have two parts? (simple thesis statement)
3. Have you included your main points in the order they will appear in your essay? (expanded thesis statement)
4. Is there enough detail to enable the reader to understand your main points (i.e., is it clearly phrased and not confusing?)
5. Is it clear what *one topic* the thesis will focus on (i.e., it is not vague and doesn't straddle two topics)?
6. Is it worded objectively and not self-consciously (i.e., by mentioning the writer or the essay itself)?
7. Have you arranged your main points in a parallel structure?

Introduction Length

In the introduction you should not *develop* your main points, but that does not mean that skimpy is better. The length of the introduction will depend partly on the length of the essay itself; it may also depend on whether you decide to include the main points of your essay (expanded thesis) or background information. In general, an introduction should not be more than about 15 per cent of the length of the essay, but you should check with your instructor for specific guidelines.

Although the introduction should never overbalance the rest of the essay, there is no reason not to include your main points and express them fully if the introduction seems to call for this. See The Thesis Statement: Simple versus Expanded, page 118.

Exercise **6.3**

A. Look at the following statement of a topic:
   My essay will be about aliens.

   Consider the three following thesis statements and evaluate their effectiveness using the three criteria for effective thesis statements on page 119:

   1. It is probable that aliens exist somewhere in outer space.
   2. It is clear that aliens have infiltrated the highest levels of the Canadian government.
   3. Everyone is curious about the possible existence of aliens.

B. If you were asked to write an essay on the way that the computer influences people, which of the simple thesis statements below would be the best one(s) to use? Rate each according to whether it is interesting, specific, and manageable. Be prepared to explain your decisions.

(*continued*)

1. The computer is one of the most entertaining pastimes we have today.
2. Violence found in computer games is affecting children these days by increasing the number of shootings in schools.
3. The computer has helped change the way we live today compared to the way our grandparents lived 50 years ago.
4. Computers take away our free time by creating a dependency that is very hard to escape from once we are hooked.
5. TV is losing its influence today thanks to the increasing popularity of computers.
6. A computer is a great babysitter for pre-school-age children.

C. Write an effective thesis statement on the topic of the computer's influence, using any pre-writing technique you feel comfortable with and making sure that you follow the three requirements of a good thesis statement.

D. The following thesis statements are either simple or expanded. Identify the type. For the simple thesis statements, add details to turn them into expanded thesis statements.

1. Regular, moderate doses of stress not only are inevitable in today's world but also can be good for you.
2. As consumers, we must keep ourselves informed about the activities of the industries we support.
3. Although poor waste management has already had a significant impact on the planet, through recycling, waste reduction programs, and public education, future damage can be minimized.
4. Education is viewed as a benefit to individuals, but too much education can have negative results.
5. Many people today misunderstand the meaning of success.

Exercise 6.4

In groups, use a pre-writing technique to formulate a simple thesis statement that has all three criteria discussed above. Begin with a choice of broad subjects, such as the ones below. When each group has come up with a thesis statement and written it on a piece of paper, exchange it with another group's and have that group evaluate it according to the three criteria. One mark should be given for each of "interesting," "specific," and "manageable" (half marks are possible). When each group has completed the evaluation process, discuss the ratings and the reasons behind them.

After each group has received feedback on its thesis statement and revised it accordingly, use another pre-writing technique to come up with three main points. Then reword the simple thesis statement so that it is an expanded thesis statement. The thesis statements can again be marked. Expanded thesis statements can be given three marks by awarding a mark for points 4, 5, and 6 in the Thesis Statement Checklist on page 121.

Possible topics: aliens, backpacking, clothes, diet, energy, Facebook, ghosts, humour, indie rock, justice, karma, laughter, malls, nature, organic food, pets, Quebec, relationships, science, taboos, (the) unconscious, virtual reality, waste, xenophobia, youth, Zen Buddhism.

Exercise **6.5**

Evaluate the following introductory paragraphs according to the criteria discussed in the previous pages. Does each function as an effective introduction? Specifically consider the following:

a. Which method(s) did the writer use to create reader interest? (Logical, dramatic, mixed?)

b. Is the opening effective? What makes it effective? (Or not?)

c. Identify the thesis statement. Is it interesting, specific, and manageable? Simple or expanded?

d. Has the writer established credibility? (Shows knowledge, seems reliable or trustworthy?)

e. Is the essay's main organizational pattern apparent (e.g., chronology, comparison and contrast, cause–effect, problem–solution, cost–benefit)? If you wish, you may look back at Chapter 4 to review these patterns.

f. Does the paragraph length seem appropriate?

1. Clothing has always reflected the times, and a prime example is the bathing suit. From their most cumbersome and unattractive beginnings to the array of styles we see today, bathing suits have always reflected the lives of the women who wore them and the society in which they lived. In the last hundred years, roles of the sexes, improvements in women's rights, changes in the economy, and perceptions of body image have all played a part in bathing suit design. —Student writer Stephanie Keenlyside

2. What is it about the Italian Mafia that fascinates millions of people? Could part of the answer lie in Hollywood's depiction of a 5' 9", 275-pound Italian named Bruno Francessi who drives a black Cadillac, wears $3000 silk suits, and claims to have "two" families; or is it the way the media creates celebrity status for Mafiosi people and events? The media and film industry portray a

(continued)

mobster's lucrative lifestyle as the result of thoughtless killings, a regimen of violence and corruption. But to fully understand the mob lifestyle, one must understand how mobsters operate—not what they appear to be on the surface, but the structure, conduct, and economic realities that created their power and enable them to maintain it. As someone who lived close to this power, I know that behind the media perception lies a fundamental belief in and adherence to a system. —Student writer Dino Pascoli

3. The sport of bodybuilding has evolved considerably through the ages. Starting with muscle man competitions, it has now turned into what some would call a "freak show." Bodybuilding is a sport that requires its athletes to display their best aesthetically pleasing physiques on stage; they are judged according to specific criteria. Many factors leading up to the judging itself contribute to the outcome of the competition; for example, nutrition from whole foods and supplements, and low body fat percentage from proper diet and cardiovascular training all contribute to the success of the competitors. Steroids, too, are a major factor in professional events like the International Federation of Bodybuilders (IFBB) competitions, where athletes are not tested for drug use. Anabolic steroid abuse plays a large role in body-building, often resulting in adverse health effects. —Student writer Mike Allison

4. Two 20-year-old Vancouver men were street racing three years ago when one of the cars, a Camaro, struck and killed Irene Thorpe as she crossed the street. The car was going so fast that Thorpe was thrown 30 metres into the air. Both men were convicted of criminal negligence causing death. They were given a two-year conditional sentence to be served at home, put on probation for three years, and had their drivers' licenses revoked for five years. Like most street-racing tragedies, this one was preventable. Though the street-racing phenomenon has been around for decades, it is growing exponentially. Recent movies have glorified this activity, enticing young, inexperienced drivers. The increase in street racing has led to an increase in the injuries to racers, spectators, and innocent bystanders. In addition, racing often results in property damage and is associated with assault, weapons offences, and drug and alcohol abuse. To help combat this growing problem, anti-racing legislation needs to be introduced and strictly en-forced. Furthermore, an education program needs to be implemented and legal racing venues created. —Student writer Maureen Brown

5. Why does my cell phone not work? Why do I get radiation poisoning when I travel by plane? Why is the light switch not working? These are the kinds of questions we ask ourselves when solar flares are striking the earth. Solar flares originate from the sun. Every 11 years, the sun switches its magnetic poles, causing the magnetic fields to twist and turn in the atmosphere above sunspots, which are eruptions on the sun's surface. The magnetic field seems

to snap like a rubber band stretched too tightly. When one of these fields breaks, it can create energy equal to a billion megatons of TNT exploding. The magnetic fields seem to flip and reconnect after they break. Solar flares occasionally head towards the earth, and even though we are 1.5 million kilometres from the sun, these flares can reach us in fewer than two days. While the earth is experiencing a solar flare, multiple problems can occur— from malfunctions of orbiting objects to disruption in power systems and radio signals. While the flares can produce these problems, they can also create the most beautiful and unusual auroras seen around the world. — Student writer Nicholas Fodor

Exercise **6.6**

Evaluate the following introduction according to the criteria discussed in this chapter. For example, you could consider whether the opening is successful, whether the writer creates interest and appears credible, and whether the thesis statement is effective. Then, rewrite it, correcting any weaknesses you find. You can add your own material or ideas, but try not to increase the length of the paragraph (approximately 130 words).

Something drastic needs to be done about obesity among teenagers today! Over the last decade, there has been a disturbing trend toward teenage obesity. Teenagers today would rather lodge themselves in front of the TV or play video games for hours on end than get some form of physical exercise. This problem becomes pronounced in high school because physical education is not compulsory in most schools. However, PE classes have a lot to offer. Participation can reduce the risk of heart failure, improve overall fitness, promote good health habits, improve self-discipline and skill development, boost self-confidence, increase academic performance, and enhance communication and co-operative skills. Obesity is an alarming trend among high school students today and should be a concern to both students and their parents.

❯ The Essay's Conclusion

Functions of the Conclusion

The **conclusion** of an essay should have been prepared for every step of the way—both by the introduction and by the points that have been developed within the essay itself.

The conclusion is the final paragraph of the essay that sums up what was said in the body paragraphs.

A conclusion should be predictable because you have prepared the reader for it, but it should *not* be boring or merely repetitive. A conclusion that simply repeats the thesis statement will be boring. It will leave the reader with the impression of a static, undeveloped argument.

Introduction

Conclusion

FIGURE 6.2 Introduction–conclusion inverted pyramid

In your conclusion, you bring the reader back to reconsider the thesis statement in light of how the thesis has been developed through your main points. The conclusion *recalls* both the thesis statement and what has been discussed in the body paragraphs. It is also a good idea to end with a clincher statement—an idea to remain with the reader. A conclusion often works from the specific to the general, whereas the introduction often starts with the general and works towards the specific (the thesis statement).

Two Kinds of Conclusion

Although they both deal primarily with the thesis, the introduction and conclusion are not like identical bookends with the books (body paragraphs) in between. The conclusion can underscore the importance of the thesis in two ways:

A circular conclusion reminds the reader of the thesis.

A spiral conclusion restates the thesis but also leads beyond it.

- A **circular conclusion** restates the thesis using different words that stress its importance, perhaps by a call to action if you are arguing for a practical change of some kind. It reminds the reader of the thesis and "closes the circle" by bringing the reader back to the starting point. It is particularly important in a circular conclusion not to simply repeat the thesis statement word for word but to show how it has been proven.
- A **spiral conclusion** suggests a specific way that the thesis could be applied, asks further questions, or proposes other ways of looking at the problem; it refers to the thesis but also leads suggestively beyond it. It might point to results of the thesis or suggest follow-up research.

Sometimes, the conclusion can include personal reflection, such as considering the way your thesis has affected you or people you know. This kind of conclusion, however, is more acceptable in personal and some argumentative essays than in expository ones. If you have not used personal experience in the essay, it might be odd to do so in the conclusion.

Specific things to avoid in the conclusion are

- restating the thesis statement word for word
- mentioning a new point; the conclusion should reword the thesis and the main points of the essay in an interesting way, not introduce something new
- giving an example or illustration to support your thesis; examples belong in your body paragraphs
- writing a conclusion that is very much longer than your introduction, but exceptions sometimes occur—especially in the sciences and social sciences where essays may end with a lengthy Discussion section

Set your conclusion beside your introduction to check that it fulfills all the above functions of a conclusion and relates to your introduction in a satisfactory way.

Exercise 6.7

Consider these sets of paragraphs, which form the introduction and the conclusion for three essays. Is it clear from the introduction what the writer will be discussing? What kind of introduction did the writer use? Is it clear from the conclusion what the writer has discussed? What kind of conclusion is each writer using?

Write a brief analysis of how the two parts of the essays intersect yet, at the same time, operate independently. Consider strengths and possible weaknesses. Remember that the paragraphs should not only function as effective specialized paragraphs but also display unity, coherence, and development.

A. An expository essay

Topic: A racial incident in Canada's past

Introduction:

One of Canada's most important features, which figures prominently in its self-presentation to the world, is as a peaceful nation that respects the individual and celebrates multiculturalism. The country is known for its cultural and ethnic diversity. Often, however, Canadians idealize their image and push inequality out of their presentation of their country. However, if we look carefully at the history of Canada, there have been many occasions when the clean image of national tolerance has been seriously undermined, such as in the *Komagata Maru* incident in Vancouver in 1914.

(continued)

Conclusion:

Although much has changed for the better since the beginning of the twentieth century and Canada is justifiably proud of its diversity today, people sometimes ignore past incidents of racial discrimination. Since the *Komagata Maru* incident is not well known, it is important that people hear about it so they can be aware that even in a democratic country like Canada injustice and intolerance have occurred in the past and will continue to occur unless people learn from the past and guard against such incidents. —Student writer Ruth Wax

B. An argumentative essay

Topic: Government-funded screening

Introduction:

Last month, the colour pink sprang up in store windows of retailers nationwide as part of the annual campaign to fund breast cancer research. Breast cancer takes the lives of 44 000 women in the US every year. As a potential carrier of a gene predisposing me to breast cancer, I face the perpetual fear that one day I or my sister could become its victim. It would be almost unthinkable if the mammogram, the screening test for breast cancer, were not covered by our health-care plan. However, for men with a predisposition to prostate cancer, which has been linked to the gene associated with breast cancer, the cost of a blood test to screen for prostate cancer is not covered by the plan. Prevention and early intervention are critical for successful health care, and government-funded coverage for the $35 prostate cancer screening test is essential for men aged 45 and older.

Conclusion:

Today the best hope for a cure to prostate cancer lies in early intervention through the PSA screening test. Although the benefit of screening may be controversial, the evidence is hard to dispute: 80 per cent of patients with elevated PSA levels have prostate cancer. Surgical procedures are rapidly improving, and new options exist to treat complications of surgery or radiation therapy. Until proper medical coverage exists for early detection of prostate cancer, it will continue to cause the second-largest number of cancer-related deaths in men. Gender bias in government-funded cancer screening tests is unacceptable, and public pressure should be exerted for universal access to cancer screening. —Student writer Heather Dyble

C. An argumentative essay

Topic: Smoking and organ transplantation

Introduction:

The atmosphere grew tense in the cramped hospital room as eight-year-old Marla looked up through frightened eyes, trying to be strong for her mother. Everyone was trying to be hopeful, but Marla instinctively knew that she would not be getting a heart transplant in time; the waitlist was long, and an organ match was unlikely. Although Marla was an otherwise healthy girl, there were others on the transplant list who were ahead of her, though not all of them had as good a prognosis. Due to the scarcity of organ donations in comparison to many in need, serious debates have arisen concerning the suitability of some potential heart and lung recipients. Some feel that everyone should have equal right to a transplant and that there should be no pre-conditions relating to what they see as lifestyle choices, such as smoking. Others advocate that smokers should be refused transplants on medical or moral considerations since smokers are more likely to experience complications after surgery. Given the current crisis of long waitlists and variable success rates, lung and heart transplant candidates should be required to quit smoking at least six months prior to surgery in order to reduce smoking-related complications and maximize transplant success.

Conclusion:

The scarcity of organ donations and the length of waitlists have placed an increasing obligation on the part of health-care professionals to ensure the best outcome for their patients. Denying transplants to those who refuse to quit smoking may appear to discriminate against smokers and their lifestyle choice. However, doing so would result in better odds for post-transplant success and would involve the most efficient use of limited health-care services and resources. In short, health authorities should move to institute clear guidelines on pre-surgery smoking restrictions for the benefit of both individuals and the health-care system. —Student writer Annie Gentry

Exercise **6.8**

Choose one of the topics below and create an expanded thesis statement, an introduction, and a conclusion. Begin by brainstorming and creating an outline. Note that the topics are very general to allow you to choose the focus.

1. voting
2. funding for the arts
3. Canada's role on the world stage
4. travel as education
5. volunteerism
6. the effects of events around the world on Canadians
7. funding for intervention programs
8. reality TV shows
9. exercise and health
10. the role of education

❯ Sample Professional Essay

The essay below is a relatively short one. Because of this, you will see that the introduction and conclusion are very short. While reading, ask yourself whether and how the author could have done more to help the reader understand her points.

SAMPLE PROFESSIONAL ESSAY

Alouette Anniversary

by Hillary Windsor

[1] Fifty years ago this autumn, after many small steps, Canada took one giant leap into the future.

[2] The successful launch of the Alouette-I satellite on September 29, 1962, made Canada the third nation (after Russia and the United States) to design and build its own satellite and signalled to the world that our country was going to be a player in the space age.

> The author uses the transition word *but* in order to link paragraphs.

[3] But it wasn't all smooth sailing straight into the stratosphere for the Ottawa-based research and design team, led by the late John Chapman under the auspices of Canada's Defence Research Telecommunications Establishment (later to become Communications Research Centre Canada). Although the team had world-class engineers and scientists working on the project and believed it would succeed, others weren't so sure.

> In an academic essay, a paragraph needs to be longer than just a quotation.

[4] "We were certainly confident," says Colin Franklin, chief electrical engineer of the Alouette-I. "But NASA considered the project too ambitious for the technology at the time. No one believed, outside of ourselves, that it would last."

[5] The public perception of the task facing the team was not much better. Franklin recalls reading an article published shortly before the Alouette's launch that stated all the possible things that could go awry during takeoff and highlighted the amount of money being "wasted" on the project. Still, the team was undeterred. "I remember looking at that article," says Franklin, "and it had absolutely no effect on us."

[6] Despite their assuredness, launch day at the U.S. Pacific Missile Test Range in California was filled with a degree of uncertainty. Franklin, now 84, remembers the moment the team received word of the satellite's successful send-off into orbit aboard a

Thor-Agena rocket. "There was a huge sigh of relief when it was working, " he says. "And then there was jubilation."

[7] From start to finish, the entire Alouette-I project took only 3 ½ years to complete, but it exceeded all expectations. Designed with a nominal lifespan of one year, it spent an impressive 10 active years collecting valuable data about the ionosphere before being decommissioned. Its immediate success kick-started the move to build and launch three more Canadian satellites over the next nine years—Alouette-II, ISIS I and ISIS II—and put Canada in the spotlight.

> While the author has written an expository essay, there is some opinion stated here, which the author indicates using words like *only* and *exceeded all expectations*.

[8] "The creation, launch and incredible success of the Alouette gave Canada an international reputation for excellence in satellite design and engineering," says Franklin, adding that at the time, no one on the team realized the long-term significance. "We were not aware that we were doing anything more than successfully building and launching the program. It was just a huge engineering challenge and an exciting program to be on."

[9] In 1987, Communications Research Centre Canada designated the Alouette-I as one of the 10 most outstanding achievements in the first 100 years of engineering in Canada—a notable tip of the hat that put the satellite in the same company as CPR's transcontinental railway network, the St. Lawrence Seaway and the CANDU nuclear power system.

[10] For many, the satellite's launch remains an iconic moment in Canadian history, shot through with personal meaning. Former astronaut Steve MacLean, the current president of the Canadian Space Agency, recalls hearing about it when he was just seven years old. "My dad worked at the National Research Council, so he made sure we remembered stuff like that," he says. "I collected stamps at the time, and a Canadian stamp with a picture of the Alouette on it came out. It's kind of a symbolic thing for me."

[11] MacLean says that it's hard to predict what the next 50 years have in store for Canada's space industry but hopes that satellites will, in the next five years, provide communications parity for the country, especially in the North.

> The author has skillfully switched from a focus on the past to the future possibilities for Canada.

[12] For his part, Franklin—who's faced down naysayers before—doesn't like to set expectations or limits on what people can accomplish: "People have been spectacularly wrong about forecasting the future before."

[13] In other words, the sky's the limit.

—Windsor, H. (2012, July/August). Alouette anniversary: Celebrating 50 years of Canada's role in space. *Canadian Geographic*. Retrieved from http://www. canadiangeographic.ca/magazine/ja12/canada_50_years_in_space.asp

Post-reading Questions

1. The author starts the essay with a simple thesis statement: "Fifty years ago this autumn, after many small steps, Canada took one giant leap into the future." Is this effective? How could this be improved?

2. Could the author have created a more effective introduction?

3. Does the author use effective topic sentences? Explain.

4. How do the paragraphs differ from what you learned in Chapter 3, Paragraph Essentials?

5. For the conclusion, the author uses the single sentence "In other words, the sky's the limit." How could this be expanded into a full paragraph?

▊ Chapter Review Questions

1. Why is a clear thesis important?

2. What is the difference between a simple thesis statement and an expanded thesis statement?

3. Is a simple thesis statement appropriate for any essay?

4. How do you create a good thesis statement?

5. What is a logical approach to organizing an introduction?

6. When can you use a dramatic approach when writing an introduction?

7. Why should you never start an introduction with an overly broad or obvious statement?

8. Why does an essay need a conclusion?

9. What are two types of conclusions and when would you use each?

10. Why is a well-written conclusion as important as a well-written introduction?

7

The Design of an **Essay**

- be introduced to a generic model of the essay
- discover the differences between three types of claims and where they are used
- learn what kinds of evidence can be used to support your claim
- learn how to increase your credibility with your readers

No matter what type of essay you are writing, your thesis needs to be supported by solid evidence so that the reader can clearly follow your logic. In this chapter, you will learn how to present a claim and then prove it by using appropriate kinds of evidence. By choosing your support carefully, you increase your credibility with the audience, which is another important aspect of essay writing.

❯ The Essay: An Analytical Model

A successful essay can be analyzed, or "broken down," in different ways. For example, as you have seen in earlier chapters, you can divide an essay's structure into introduction, body paragraphs, and conclusion, or you can divide the writing of the essay into five stages. When you write a critical analysis, you may discuss the writer's use of logic and reason, the number and reliability of sources, the tone or style of writing, the writer's background or bias, and the like.

The generic model for the essay presented here will help you know what to look for when you **analyze** other essays. It will also help with your own writing since the elements discussed below are common to most essays—from scholarly studies for specialized readers to the kinds of essays you will write.

There are two main elements to an essay, whether it is argumentative or expository:

When you analyze, you break something down in order to look closely at its elements or to see how the elements connect to make a whole.

- claim: a statement of fact, value, policy (thesis statement)
- support for claim:

  - evidence
  - writer's credibility in presenting that evidence

Whether you are reading an essay or writing one, you will often begin by identifying the claim, a general assertion about the topic on which the essay is based.

Kinds of Claims: Fact, Value, and Policy

Most essays make some kind of **claim**, usually in the thesis statement, and then proceed to prove the claim by various means of support. The writer may present a claim of fact, value, or policy.

A claim is an assertion about your topic that appears in your introduction. It usually takes the form of a thesis statement.

Most topics can be explored through any of these three types of claims, depending on the way the claim is presented. In an expository essay, the claim will be presented as factual. In an argumentative essay, the claim will typically be presented as one of value or policy. If you were writing an essay on the topic of homelessness, for example, your claim could be one of the following:

Factual claim:

Due to the unsettled economic climate, the prevalence of homelessness is increasing in most Canadian provinces.

Value claim:

In a society of excess, our indifference to the problem of the homeless on our doorsteps is an indictment of our way of life.

Policy claim:

To solve the problem of homelessness in our city, council needs to increase the number of permanent shelters, erect temporary shelters in downtown parks, and educate the public about this escalating social problem.

Claim of Fact

A **factual claim** is usually an **empirical** claim that uses the evidence-gathering methods of observation and measurement; it is a claim that can be proven by facts and figures or through the findings of relevant studies. Claims of fact are used in most expository essays.

A factual claim is proven by facts and figures or through the findings of relevant studies.

Empirical means observing and measuring data under controlled conditions in order to reach a conclusion about a phenomenon.

Claim of Value

A **value claim** is an ethical claim and appeals to one's sense of values or a moral system; values might be based on one's religion, philosophical world view, or social and cultural background. A claim of value is supported through a process of reasoning where a certain standard of good or bad, right or wrong, fair or unfair, is accepted as a **premise**.

A value claim is an ethical claim and appeals to the reader's sense of values or moral system.

A premise is a statement assumed to be true.

Claim of Policy

A **policy claim** is usually a call for some kind of action to fix a problem or improve a situation. Although a claim of policy need not be based on a claim of value, it often is. For example, a proposed change to a law or regulation that gives people more control over something in their lives may be rooted in a claim of value. The argument might be that the change will produce a more democratic society in which people have greater freedom to assert their rights.

A policy claim is usually a call for some kind of action to fix a problem or improve a situation.

Support: Evidence and Credibility

A claim will not be accepted without **support**—in other words, without **evidence** to back it up. But evidence alone is not enough. To convince your reader that your claim is justified, you need to demonstrate your credibility. Although many student writers believe that evidence is more important than credibility, the effort of gathering and arranging evidence may be wasted if you do not seem credible.

Evidence, such as that gathered from journals, magazines, and personal experience, gives your claim more support so that the reader believes in what you are stating.

Support in the body paragraphs is provided by the use of ample and credible evidence.

Organization of Evidence

You support your claim through your main points and sub-points. The points will have the best impact when they are organized appropriately and ordered logically (climax, inverted climax, or mixed order, as described in Chapter 2). Organizational methods include definition, division/classification, cause–effect, comparison and contrast, problem–solution, and chronology. (They are discussed in detail in Chapter 4, Paragraph Development.)

Kinds of Evidence

Original sources are known as primary sources.

Depending on your topic, the instructions for the assignment, and the discipline in which you are writing, you may use some kinds of evidence more than others in your essay. Writing in the humanities often relies on **primary**, or original, **sources**. If you write an English essay, for instance, your primary sources are literary works. The primary sources commonly used in historical research are biographies, newspapers, letters, and records from the era being studied.

Social sciences writing tends to focus on facts and figures, statistics and other numerical data, case studies, interviews, questionnaires, and personal observation. Scientific studies may use similar kinds of evidence but frequently rely on experimental methods. Examples are important in just about every discipline.

Using a variety of evidence will likely produce a stronger essay than relying solely on one kind. However, it is important, especially if you are using research, to find hard evidence to support your key points. Hard evidence includes facts, statistics, and statements from authorities (experts). Hard evidence is essential in a factual claim. It is also effective in a policy claim, which will advocate specific actions. It may be less important in a value claim, in which appeals to reason, emotion, and ethics, along with examples, analogies, brief narratives, description, or personal experience could produce an effective argument.

Facts and Statistics

It is hard to argue with facts. For this reason, factual information is the strongest kind of evidence in an essay. If you use facts effectively, you will also enhance your credibility by seeming knowledgeable. Although facts from reliable sources are always relevant to a research essay, they can provide support in an essay not involving research if you are arguing a topic you know a lot about. For example, the student writer of the essay in Chapter 5, pages 105–107, uses several facts, including references to Internet piracy, which she was apparently familiar with. Make sure that you use facts from reliable research sources.

Take extra care when using statistics. Not only should they come from reliable sources, but you should also pay attention to how they are presented in the source in order to assess possible bias or distortion. Use caution with statistics cited by people or organizations promoting a particular cause or viewpoint. For example, surveys conducted by special interest groups can be deceptive.

Consider the case of a union on strike that wants to put pressure on the government by making its case public. It pays for a full-page ad in major newspapers, claiming 93.7 per cent support among the public. The questions to ask are, "Who were the survey's respondents? How many were surveyed? How was the survey conducted?" Perhaps in this situation a small number of people who happened to be walking by the picket lines were stopped and surveyed. Reliable sources reveal their information-gathering methods, which you can evaluate.

You can usually tell whether a source is trustworthy or not. For example, although People for the Ethical Treatment of Animals (PETA) can be considered biased because it strongly opposes practices like animal testing, many statistics it publishes can be considered reliable because they come from reliable sources. In a PETA factsheet criticizing animal research, for instance, the writer cites a 1988 study that appeared in the refereed journal *Nature*, which "reports that 520 of 800 chemicals (65 per cent) tested on rats and mice caused cancer in the animals but not in humans (Lave et al. 631)." In a source like this, however, remember that statistics and factual data are being used for a specific purpose; evaluate them individually with this purpose in mind. Also bear in mind that sources like PETA may report only on those studies that agree with the organization's mission or viewpoint, ignoring contrary findings.

When using facts or statistics that special interest groups and similar organizations have cited in their papers, remember that they use data for a specific purpose. Evaluate the facts and statistics with this purpose in mind.

All the essays in Chapters 9 and 13 use facts and statistics effectively.

Authorities and Experts

An **authority** can be used for support if he or she has direct knowledge of your subject. An authority who is not an **expert** carries less weight. For example, in an essay that argues a scientific or mathematical point, citing Albert Einstein would provide **hard evidence**. In an essay about vegetarianism, citing Einstein would provide soft evidence as he is not considered an expert on the topic. As you research your topic you will discover who the experts are. You may also be able to interview an expert, asking questions related to your claim. See page 259.

An authority can be used for support if he or she has direct knowledge of your subject. An authority who is not an expert carries less weight.

Examples, Illustrations, Case Studies, Precedents

While hard evidence provides direct support, **soft evidence** indirectly supports your points and helps the reader understand them. Kinds of indirect support include examples, illustrations, case studies, and precedents. Analogies, description, and personal experience may also be used if your instructor approves.

We use **examples** in both speech and writing. To support his argument, a teenager arguing for his independence might give several examples of friends who live on their own. Examples should always be relevant and representative. The teenager's parents might refute the examples by pointing out that they are not representative—for example, that one friend, Shawn, has a full-time job and that another one, Giovanna, spent the summer travelling throughout Europe before moving out of her parents' house.

An expert is a specialist in a subject.

While hard evidence provides direct support, soft evidence indirectly supports your points and helps the reader understand them.

In most writing, examples bring a point home to the reader by making it specific and concrete. Examples are especially useful if you are writing for a non-specialist reader, as they make it easier to grasp a difficult or an abstract point. Illustrations, case studies, and precedents are extended examples that can be used to explain or reinforce important points.

Examples are especially useful if you are writing for a non-specialist reader, as they make it easier to grasp a difficult or abstract point.

An illustration is a detailed example that usually takes the form of an anecdote or a brief narrative.

A case study is a carefully selected example that is closely analyzed in order to provide a testing ground for the writer's claim.

A hypothesis is a prediction or expected result of an experiment or other research investigation.

A precedent is an example that refers to the way that a particular situation was dealt with in the past.

An **illustration** is a detailed example that usually takes the form of an anecdote or a brief narrative. In this example, the writer uses an illustration to support his point that, using logic, one can draw different conclusions from the different premises (a statement assumed to be true):

> Consider the example of the hydroelectric dam that the Urra company constructed in Colombia. The dam provides electricity to industry and profit to the companies and people who invest in it. The area flooded by the dam was inhabited by indigenous peoples. The river was a source of fresh water and fish, and on the river's now flooded banks were food plants that sustained them. . . . If an analysis of this situation were based on the premise that all people should be treated equally and with respect, then through reason, the conclusion would be that this was a bad thing for the indigenous peoples living along the river. If, however, the basic premise was that business interests are primary, then the logical conclusion would be that the hydroelectric dam was a good thing.
>
> —Student writer Graeme Verhulst

Case studies are often used as support, particularly in the social sciences, education, and business; they can also be the focus of research studies. A case study is a carefully selected example that is closely analyzed in order to provide a testing ground for the writer's claim. Because case studies are practical, real-life examples, they can be used to support a **hypothesis**. For example, to test the hypothesis that involving youth in decision-making could produce a safer school environment, a Vancouver school planned a series of student-led initiatives and activities. When the results were analyzed, it was found that the students felt safer and had improved their pro-social and conflict resolution skills: the outcome supported the hypothesis.

A **precedent** is an example that refers to the way that a particular situation was dealt with in the past. Judgments in courts of law establish precedents that influence future court decisions. Once you have established an action as a precedent, you then apply it to your argument. The success in using precedents as evidence depends on your ability to convince the reader that both of the following are true:

1. Similar conditions apply to your topic.
2. Following the precedent will produce a desirable result.

For example, if you were arguing that Canada should offer free post-secondary studies to all academically qualified individuals, you could refer to the precedent of Denmark, one of the first countries to provide universal access to post-secondary schooling. Then you must make it clear that

1. The situation in Denmark is comparable to the situation in Canada.
2. Denmark has profited from this system, so Canada will also likely benefit from a similar course of action.

Analogies, Description, Personal Experience

Some kinds of evidence are suggestive and indirect; they cannot in themselves prove a claim. These include analogy, description, and personal experience.

Analogy, a kind of comparison, and description can help the reader understand and relate to a point. Like narration, description may also play a limited role in argument, perhaps to attract interest in the essay's introduction or to set up a main point. (For examples, see Chapter 4, pages 87–88 and 93–94.)

Personal experience could take the form of direct experiences or observation. It can help the reader relate to your topic. You should keep your voice objective when using personal experience; any bias will undermine your credibility. Personal experience can be effective in supporting a value claim. For example, if you had witnessed a dog fight, your observations could strongly support the claim that dog fighting is cruel. Similarly, if you have had personal experience with homeless people by working in a food bank, you could use your experience to help support a related policy claim.

Personal experience can often be effective in supporting a value claim.

Credibility

Demonstrating **credibility** as a writer will strengthen your claim. Three factors contribute to credibility: knowledge of the topic, reliability/trustworthiness, and fairness. Showing your knowledge by itself doesn't make you credible. Consider the analogy of job hunting: when you send out your résumé, you want to impress prospective employers with your experience and knowledge; however, during the interview, the employer will likely ask questions that pertain more to your reliability as an employee than to your knowledge—for example, "Why do you want to work for us? Where do you see yourself in five years? Why did you quit your last job?" Furthermore, when employers check your references, they are sure to ask about your reliability. Similarly with essay writing, once you have shown your knowledge, you must convince the reader that you also are reliable.

Three factors contribute to credibility: knowledge of the topic, reliability/trustworthiness, and fairness

You demonstrate *knowledge* through the points you make in the essay and the kinds of evidence you use to support them. But you can seem knowledgeable without seeming reliable. You show your *reliability* or *trustworthiness* by being able to answer "yes" to questions like the following:

- Is your essay well structured?
- Are your paragraphs unified, coherent, and well developed?
- Is your writing clear? Is your grammar correct? Is your style effective?
- Have you used the rules and procedures of your discipline (if applicable)?
- Have you used critical thinking skills effectively? Are your conclusions logical and well founded?

In an expository essay, *fairness* is demonstrated through using evidence objectively. In an argumentative essay fairness is shown by considering opposing views. While presenting a strong case for your views, you can pinpoint the shortcomings and limitations of the opposing views. A fair writer is objective in addressing the other side, avoiding slanted language that reveals bias. While you can demonstrate reliability by avoiding misuse of reason, you can demonstrate fairness by using emotional appeals selectively and without bias (discussed in more detail in Chapter 9).

Connections among the Elements of the Analytical Model

Student writers sometimes have the impression that an effective essay comprises elements that function in isolation. But the opposite is true: it is really one entity with many interdependent elements. As shown in Figure 7.1, each element coexists with the others; you need to think carefully about how each element fits into the whole. A successful essay has many connections among the concepts shown in the diagram. In your own essays, you can ask questions like, "Am I using the kinds of evidence favoured by my discipline? Am I organizing this evidence logically? Have I used enough sources? Is my essay well-structured and is my writing clear and grammatical? Have I used evidence fairly?"

When reading an essay in order to analyze it, you can ask similar questions. When you analyze, you *break something down* into elements so you can look closely at each element. The interdependence of the various elements of the essay is clear. For example, grammatical errors will affect the writer's reliability, which will reduce credibility and weaken support for the claim. If you are aware of how the different elements relate, you should be able to approach your own writing critically have the tools to analyze other writing.

Breaking down the essay into its essential elements enables you to analyze your own writing processes and those of other writers. It can show you how different elements of an essay contribute to the whole.

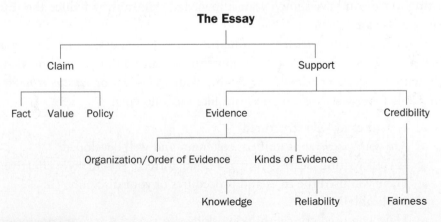

FIGURE 7.1 The essay: an analytical model

Exercise 7.1

It is important to be able to distinguish between a factual claim and a value or policy claim. Although there may not always be a firm line between exposition and argument, you may be asked to write an essay that is either one or the other; and, of course, your reader should recognize what kind of essay he or she is reading. Determine whether the statements below are most suited to argument or exposition by labelling them "A" or "E."

1. British Columbia's environmental policy is better than Alberta's policy.
2. Legislators should impose an outright ban on tablet computers in indoor public establishments and places of business.
3. Diplomacy and militarism are the two main approaches to foreign policy that, though sometimes used independently, are much more effective when used in combination.
4. 3M's tradition, strategy, and corporate image have helped it maintain its top-ten ranking in *Fortune* magazine year after year.
5. Organic farming has many costs, but the benefits seem much greater as this farming method is becoming more popular.
6. Hip hop today acts as a cultural bridge for widely diverse groups of young people to communicate across racial, class, religious, linguistic, and national divisions.
7. In spite of ethical concerns, can the human race really afford to ignore the tremendous potential benefits of embryonic stem-cell research to find cures for many diseases?
8. The government should take steps to regulate the monopolistic practices of airlines today.
9. Probably nobody in the history of psychology has been as controversial—sometimes revered, sometimes despised—as Sigmund Freud.
10. What are the physical effects of artificial and natural tanning? What are the risks involved, and what can be done to educate the public about both?

Exercise 7.2

The 15 simple thesis statements below contain claims of fact, value, or policy. Identify the kind of claim and then write two sentences in which you turn the original claim into the two other kinds of claims. You may make any changes in wording you wish as long as the topic remains the same.

(continued)

Example:

> *Thesis statement:*
> Cellphones are a wonderful modern convenience, but they can be danger-
> ous in cars because they often distract the driver.
> *Kind of claim:*
> Claim of value: the statement asserts that cellphones can be dangerous (a
> bad thing).

A. The recent use of cellphones in cars has increased the number of accidents
    in many urban centres—especially during rush hour.
    Kind of claim:
    Claim of fact: the statement asserts that the number of accidents has
    increased.

B. Cellphones in cars should be prohibited as they are dangerous both for the
    user and for other drivers.
    Kind of claim:
    Claim of policy: the statement advocates an action, though this action is
    based on a value, i.e., that cellphones in cars are dangerous (bad).

    1. It is increasingly necessary to be bilingual in Canada today.
    2. The lyrics of rap music are inherently anti-social and encourage violence.
    3. Women should not be allowed to serve in the military in anything but
        administrative roles.
    4. Whatever one may think of same-sex marriages, it is evident that they
        are here to stay.
    5. After completing high school, one should travel for at least a year before
        proceeding to college or university.
    6. It is necessary to provide more funding for technology in today's class-
        room and to spend less on teachers' salaries.
    7. The current practice of appointing Supreme Court judges in Canada is
        undemocratic.
    8. With the number of sports teams, clubs, and cultural groups on campus,
        students who do not participate in extracurricular activities are not get-
        ting good value for their education.
    9. School uniforms provide many benefits to students and their parents.
    10. The government should subsidize organically grown food.
    11. Recreational use of steroids can cause physical and psychological
        damage to the user.
    12. Before committing more resources to space exploration, we should work
        to solve global problems, such as poverty, that affect people every day.

13. The growing popularity of Eastern medicine today shows that society is tending towards a more natural approach to health care.
14. Parents should have the right, within reason, to discipline their child as they see fit.
15. While advocates of a shorter work week believe that this measure will help our troubled economy, opponents say it will only weaken it and create social problems.

Exercise **7.3**

Taking one of the claims for each statement in Exercise 7.2, determine how you would most effectively support it in the body of an essay. This exercise could take the form of a group discussion, or your group could write out a strategic approach, referring as specifically as possible to those elements under Support in Figure 7.1 on page 140.

Strategies to Consider
Organization of Evidence:
Which patterns of organization/development would you likely use?
What other patterns could be used? (See Chapter 4.)
Kinds of Evidence:
Which kinds of evidence would most effectively back up your claim?
(See pages 136–139.)
Which of the three categories of credibility seem the most important (knowledge, reliability, fairness)? Why? What general or specific strategies could you use to ensure your support was credible?

❯ Sample Professional Essay

The following essay was posted as a blog (the underlined words indicate where hyperlinks were inserted in the online version). As you can see, even writers who use modern technology often follow the basic essay format when writing. This essay begins with comparison and contrast. However, the author uses other methods to expand on the content, such as chronology and description.

SAMPLE PROFESSIONAL ESSAY

Punishing Cheaters Promotes the Evolution of Cooperation
by Eric Michael Johnson

> The author begin with a claim that will be supported later with research.

[1] Humans are one of the most cooperative species on the planet. Our ability to coordinate behavior and work collaboratively with others has allowed us to create the natural world's largest and most densely populated societies, outside of deep sea microbial mats and a few *Hymenoptera* mega-colonies.

> The author uses comparison to discuss cheaters and co-operators.

[2] However, a key problem when trying to understand the evolution of cooperation has been the issue of cheaters. Individuals in a social group, whether that group is composed of bacteria, cichlids, chimpanzees, or people, often benefit when cooperating with others who reciprocate the favor. But what about those individuals who take advantage of the generosity of others and provide nothing in return? These individuals could well thrive thanks to the group as a whole and end up with greater fitness than everyone else because they didn't have to pay the costs associated with cooperating. For decades the idea that cheaters may in fact prosper has been the greatest difficulty in understanding cooperation as an evolved trait.

> **Writing Tip:** When you write an academic essay, make sure you end with a concluding sentence. Do not end your paragraph with a quotation or paraphrase from other research.

[3] However, it turns out that cooperation could be a viable evolutionary strategy when individuals within the group collectively punish cheaters who don't pull their weight. For example, Robert Boyd, Herbert Gintis, and Samuel Bowles published a paper in the journal *Science* in 2010 with a model showing how, so long as enough individuals work together to punish violators, each cooperative individual in the group can experience enhanced fitness as a result.

> The author brings in secondary sources to support his earlier claims.

[4] Before understanding how their model could explain the emergence of cooperative behavior it is first important to look at the two leading explanations for the evolution of cooperation: William Hamilton's (1964) theory of kin selection and Robert Trivers' (1971) theory of reciprocal altruism.

[5] Kin selection proposed that cooperation will emerge in groups that are made up of close relatives. Hamilton's rule, beautiful in its simplicity, proposed that cooperation occurs when the cost to the actor (c) is less than the benefit to the recipient (b) multiplied by the genetic relatedness between the two (r). This equation is written out simply as $rb > c$. Kin selection has been one of the most well tested models that seeks

to explain the evolution of cooperation and has held up among such diverse groups as primates, birds, and social insects (though Edward O. Wilson has recently challenged kin selection as an explanation in the latter).

[6] To put this into context: an alpha male lion and his brother share half of their genes, so have a genetic relatedness of 0.5. Suppose this brother recognizes that the alpha male is getting old and could easily be taken down. If so, the brother could potentially have eight additional cubs (just to pull out an arbitrary number). But, instead, that brother decides to help the alpha male to maintain his position in the pride and, as a result, the alpha ends up having the eight additional cubs himself while the brother only has five. The brother has lost out on 3 potential cubs. But, even so, because he assisted his brother he has still maximized his overall reproductive success from a genetic point of view: $0.5 \times 8 = 4 > 3$. He could have attempted to usurp his brother and, perhaps, had the eight cubs himself but he wouldn't have been in any better of a position as far as his genes were concerned.

> The author decided to give a real-life example to illustrate the formula that he previously cited. This makes the formula easier to understand for non-experts.

[7] Reciprocal altruism follows this same basic idea, but proposes a mechanism that could work for individuals that are unrelated. In this scenario, cooperation occurs when the cost to the actor (c) is less than the benefit to the recipient (b) multiplied by the likelihood that the cooperation will be returned (w) or $wb > c$. This has been demonstrated among vampire bats who regurgitate blood into an unrelated bats mouth if they weren't able to feed that night. Previous experience has shown the actor that they're likely to get repaid if they ever go hungry one night themselves.

[8] Whereas kin selection requires a community of closely related individuals for cooperation to be a successful strategy, reciprocal altruism requires that individuals be part of a single group, with low levels of immigration and emigration, so that group members will be likely to encounter each other on a regular basis. However, neither model can explain the emergence of cooperation in societies composed of unrelated individuals and where there is a constant influx of strangers. In other words, cooperation in human societies.

[9] The more recent model proposed by Boyd et al. seeks to address this very problem. Their paper posits that fitness is enhanced, not by cooperating with close kin or reciprocating a previous act of generosity, but through the coordinated punishment of those who don't cooperate. In a social group individuals are able to choose whether they want to cooperate or defect. Suppose, for example, that a hunter returns from a successful hunt and must decide whether or not to share their gains with other members of the tribe. According to Boyd's model, the cost to the cooperator (c) is less than the overall benefit (b) but is still greater than the benefit to each member of the

> The author introduces recent research to show that earlier theories are supported even today.

group (n): b > c > b/n. If the hunter chose to cooperate, the meat would be divided so that everyone benefits but the hunter still enjoys a slightly larger share. They would also receive a benefit in the future when other hunters had more success than they did (just as they would under reciprocal altruism).

[10] However, if the hunter refuses to share with other members there are two stages to contend with. The first is the signaling stage in which individuals signal their intent to punish those who refuse to cooperate. This is a common occurrence not just in humans but in many animals, especially primates. Baboons, for example, <u>use threat signals</u> such as staring, eyebrow raising, or a canine display to warn others to change their behavior. In humans this can take a variety of forms including angry looks, hand gestures, and/or harsh words. The cost of such signals are fairly low, but still high enough that it doesn't pay to signal and fail to back it up with action if necessary.

[11] If the warning doesn't provide the appropriate result the next stage is coordinated punishment. According to Boyd's model a quorum (τ) of punishers is required to work together to target an individual who refuses to cooperate. In such cases there will be a cost (p) to the target and an expected cost to each punisher of k/npa, where np is the number of punishers. Given that an outnumbered target is unlikely to inflict costs on the punishers, the model assumes that a > 1. What this means is that the higher the number of punishers, the lower the cost to each involved. Furthermore, the punishment doesn't necessarily involve physical attacks. The model allows for punishment to come in the form of gossip, group shunning, or any other nonaggressive action that brings a cost to the uncooperative target.

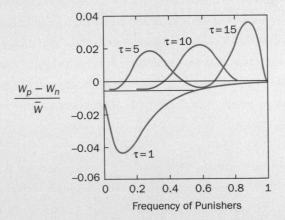

Punishment is an evolutionarily stable strategy when multiple punishers are involved. Source: Reproduced from Boyd et al. (2010). Coordinated punishment of defectors sustains cooperation and can proliferate when rare. *Science.* 328(5978), 617–20.

[12] According to this model a society would be made up of some combination of punishers Wp and nonpunishers Wn. If there were only a single punisher in the group ($\tau = 1$), what

is known as the "Lone Ranger" condition, the fitness cost would outweigh the benefit and punishers would decline in the population. However, for larger values of τ punishment does pay and therefore increasing the number of punishers increases their fitness.

[13] This model has had some empirical support. For example, last year Boyd and Sarah Matthew found that punishing desertion promoted cooperation in raiding parties among the Turkana pastoralists in East Africa. Likewise, Lauri Sääksvuori and colleagues published their results in *Proceedings of the Royal Society* suggesting that this form of enforced cooperation could emerge through competitive group selection. While further empirical tests are needed to confirm Boyd's model, it has the benefit of demonstrating how cooperation could evolve even in large societies where kinship is low and immigration is high: the very factors that were previously thought to confound the evolution of cooperation.

> The author provides support that the hypothetical model works in the real world, but admits that further research is needed. This does not weaken the argument, but in fact shows that the author has done his research and is aware of the limitations of the studies he is citing.

[14] However, given that many indigenous systems are based on restorative justice (in which offenders are brought into a relationship with the victim and must make restitution to regain the society's trust) it's unclear how accurate a model focusing exclusively on punishment would be for understanding the evolution of human cooperation. Nevertheless, Coordinated Punishment now joins other recent approaches, such as Generalized Reciprocity, that seek to reexamine how the common good could emerge out of the selection for individual fitness.

> The author concludes with the shortcomings of the current research, but ends with an idea that the reader can ponder.

Reference: Boyd, R., Gintis, H., & Bowles, S. (2010). Coordinated Punishment of Defectors Sustains Cooperation and Can Proliferate When Rare, *Science*, 328 (5978), 617–620. DOI: 10.1126/science.1183665

> **Writing Tip:** When composing an academic essay, you need to reference all the sources you cited in the paper.

—Johnson, E.M. (2012, August 16). Punishing cheaters promotes the evolution of cooperation. *Scientific American.* Retrieved from http://blogs.scientificamerican.com/primate-diaries/2012/08/16/punishing-cheaters/. Copyright © 2012, Scientific American, a Division of Nature America, Inc. All rights reserved.

Post-reading Questions

1. Is this an expository or argumentative paper? Support your answer with examples from the essay.

2. Do you think this essay would have been different if the author had used a claim of value or policy instead of a factual claim? Why?

3. Why does the author include a graphic in the essay? Does it make it any easier to understand the formulas he discusses?

4. What type of audience is the author writing for? Support your answer with examples from the essay.

5. Does the title of the essay reflect what follows? Can you think of a better title?

■ Chapter Review Questions

1.   What are the two main elements of an essay?

2.   What are the advantages to using certain kinds of claims? When would these advantages occur?

3.   What kinds of evidence can be used in an essay? What is the difference between hard and soft evidence?

4.   Why is a writer's credibility important?

5.   How can you establish your credibility in an essay?

8 The Expository Essay

In this chapter, you will

- learn how to write an expository essay
- be introduced to a template to help you structure an expository essay
- learn how to write process, definition, and comparison and contrast essays

An expository essay seeks to inform readers. It usually requires research, although personal observation or background knowledge can also support a writer's points. Expository essays can follow many different patterns and you, the writer, need to choose the one best suited for your audience and purpose. Among the most common expository essay forms not requiring research are process, definition, and comparison and contrast.

Expository Writing

Expository writing is concerned with *explaining* or *informing*—distinct from arguing or persuading. Much of the reading you do every day is in the form of expository writing. From the time you wake up and turn on your TV or computer to get the latest news, to your review of a textbook chapter at the end of the day, you will have read many examples of exposition.

The main difference between an argumentative essay and an expository essay is that the former tries to convince the reader, to change his or her mind about a subject. The expository essay doesn't try to change the reader's view, but it does try to convince the reader that the thesis is valid by using facts, observation, and clear thinking for support. An expository essay may also use statistics and the findings of research to support the thesis. (Note that the examples of expository essays used in this chapter do not use research; however, your instructor may require it. Always pay attention to instructor requirements, as discussed in Chapter 2.) Expository essays that use research are discussed in depth in Chapters 12 and 13. Effectively integrating research is discussed in Chapter 12.

Types of Expository Essays

There are many types of expository essays. They can

- show the reader the steps in a process
- use definition to help the reader understand the various ways something can be understood
- use comparison and contrast to point out similarities and differences
- use examples to help the reader understand the main points
- classify or divide a subject
- show cause and effect

A template can help you group your ideas so that your final essay is well organized.

An expository essay needs to be well organized; therefore, an essay template, like the one shown in Table 8.1, can be useful. A template can help you organize your thoughts, making the writing process easier. It can also be expanded or contracted to fit your essay's required length. For example, if you need more than five paragraphs (three for the body plus an introduction and conclusion), you simply add more body paragraphs. Also, not all paragraphs will require three sub-points. Some may need only two, while others may include four or more. In addition, each point may have more than one illustration. Chapter 3 explains paragraph composition in more detail, so remember to refer to that when you begin composing after creating your outline.

TABLE 8.1	Expository Essay Template		
Thesis Statement			
	Supporting idea	1.	
		2.	
		3.	
Paragraph 1	Topic sentence		
	Sub-point 1		
	Illustration	(quotation, personal observation, etc.)	
	Sub-point 2		
	Illustration		
	Sub-point 3		
	Illustration		
	Conclusion		
Paragraph 2	Topic sentence		
	Sub-point 1		
	Illustration		
	Sub-point 2		
	Illustration		
	Sub-point 3		
	Illustration		
	Conclusion		
Paragraph 3	Topic sentence		
	Sub-point 1		
	Illustration		
	Sub-point 2		
	Illustration		
	Sub-point 3		
	Illustration		
	Conclusion		
Concluding paragraph	Main ideas to summarize		
	Clincher	Idea to leave reader with	

The sample in Table 8.2 uses the topic "eating disorders" to illustrate this template. The thesis statement is included as well as the first body paragraph. As you can see, the first paragraph uses definition to give the reader the necessary background to understand the rest of the essay. It also has more than three sub-points. The next paragraph, as indicated in the template, will possibly use chronology to establish an increase in eating disorders over a certain time period. The final paragraph may use a cause–effect pattern. Remember that this is just like an outline. Full sentences do not have to be used at this stage, nor do your ideas have to be fully developed. Ideas introduced here can also be modified later. At this point, the main purpose is to write your ideas down and organize them.

An expository essay can use more than one organizing method from one paragraph to the next.

TABLE 8.2	Expository Essay Template: Eating Disorders	
Thesis Statement	Eating disorders are a problem for society	
	Supporting idea	1. explanation of different types 2. why they are on the rise, or at least seem to be 3. medical and psychological impact
Paragraph 1	Topic sentence	When people think of eating disorders, they often think of teenage girls or run-way models who starve themselves, but that is only one of the many disorders.
	Sub-point 1	Anorexia nervosa—most well known
	Illustration	Find medical definition from journals and explain whom it affects and side effects
	Sub-point 2	Bulimia (binge and purge)
	Illustration	Find medical definition from journals and explain whom it affects and side effects
	Sub-point 3	Compulsive overeating
	Illustration	Find medical definition from journals and explain whom it affects and side effects
	Sub-point 4	Selective eating
	Illustration	Find medical definition from journals and explain whom it affects and side effects
	Conclusion	Many different types of eating disorders, but they all have the same outcome.

Exercise 8.1

Look through the following essay topics and create a template for one of them.

1. Narrate the experience of a first-year student during orientation.
2. Describe the causes of tuition increases.
3. Describe the effects of tuition increases.
4. Tell how to alleviate stress during the first year of college or university.
5. Explain how Millennials are different from Boomers.

Three common kinds of expository essays that do not always require research are process analysis, definition, and comparison and contrast. Each is discussed below and is followed by an example of this type by a student writer. Each writer used a variant of the essay template in Table 8.1.

❯ Understanding Your Topic

When you explain or inform, you must be familiar with your topic in order to communicate it to your reader. Like most people, you've probably experienced the awkward situation of trying to explain something you weren't completely sure about—or, perhaps, you've over-explained, and your listener has become impatient or even broken in with "I know that!"

One way to become an expert is to read what other people have written—in other words, to research the topic. (The research process is discussed in Chapters 11 and 12.) You can also become an authority through your personal experience, by practising or doing something for months or even years. Many professional and recreational skills are acquired this way and may be good topics for process essays.

If you wanted to explain these skills to someone, you would first have to consider how much he or she knew about the topic—you would have to consider your audience. You would not write for readers who knew as much as you did, unless you wanted to alert them to a special area they might not know about. For example, you might write an essay about surviving in the extreme cold for either a general audience of winter sports enthusiasts or the more specific audience of out-of-bounds skiers.

Analysis is a common organizational pattern in which you break something down to look at its elements individually or to see how they fit together as a whole. Most methods of essay development involve some kind of analysis. In a process analysis, you break an activity into its *chronological* stages, showing how it is done.

❯ The Process-Analysis Essay

The kind of essay that explains the stages of a process is called **process analysis**. In process analysis, you explain the stages of the process by breaking down the activity and clearly describing the activities involved step by step. You need to consider your topic, audience, and purpose before beginning to write. There are two main reasons to write a process-analysis essay:

- to stimulate reader interest
- to make readers familiar with a process so they can do it themselves

In either case, you need to establish your credibility.

Process analysis can also be used as a method of paragraph development within another type of essay. (See Chapter 4, Paragraph Development, pages 88–89.)

The following is a step-by-step breakdown in the planning and writing of a process-analysis essay. It is followed by a sample student process essay of about 500 words.

A process-analysis essay explains the stages of a process.

Before you write a process-analysis essay, you need to consider the topic itself, your audience, and your purpose in writing. From the beginning, you need to establish your credibility.

You demonstrate your credibility by showing you are knowledgeable, reliable, and fair. See Chapter 7, pages 139–140.

Planning a Process Essay

- After you've decided on a topic, determine your audience's knowledge and interest levels. This will also help you decide on your purpose for writing (i.e., to stimulate your reader's interest or to enable him or her to duplicate the steps in the process).

- Consider the level of detail that is needed. Again, if your main purpose is to stimulate interest, you will need less detail than if you are guiding the reader carefully through each stage. But less detail doesn't necessarily mean your essay will be shorter.
- Consider the way you want to come across to your reader. For example, in an essay about something you're interested in, you can show your enthusiasm. However, you need to do this subtly—not, for example, by using lots of exclamation points! Although a process essay is usually expository, not argumentative, one way to stimulate interest is to mention the practical benefits of the activity/process you're describing (if you stress both benefits and costs, you will be writing a cost–benefit analysis, a different kind of expository essay).
- Before beginning to draft your essay, you need to decide how you're going to address your reader. If your purpose is to teach the reader the steps in a process, it might be natural to use the subject *you*. Remember, though, that your essay should not read like an instruction booklet. Process-analysis essays are designed to be *used*, but their practical function shouldn't override other considerations. Notice in the following set of instructions that each stage is structured as a command; the writer uses a series of **imperative clauses**. The imperative structure may be appropriate for a mechanical set of instructions, but not for your essay.

- Disengage the paper clamp by pushing the wire clamp on the side of the sanding pad towards the sander's body.
- Line up the edge of the sandpaper with the edge of the sanding pad.
- Insert the sandpaper tightly over the foam pad. . . .

Your instructor may want you to avoid the informal *you*, in which case you must use nouns, like *a person*, or *the user*, or third-person pronouns, like *one*. See the sample process essay below.

Writing a Process Essay

- Although an outline is useful in structuring any essay, it is not always essential in a process essay, which is arranged by the order of the stages in the process.
- The introduction may vary depending on audience and purpose. However, it is usually brief and direct. It may provide background information or include preparation instructions, such as listing equipment or tools needed for the activity. As in any essay, you should end the introduction with a clear thesis statement.

An imperative clause or sentence issues a command. Its subject, *you*, is always understood even though it is not expressed. See Chapter 14, page 343.

Using a template like the ones in Tables 8.1 and 8.2, pages 151–152, can help you structure a process-analysis essay.

- Arrange each stage in chronological order (you can number them to make them clear in your own mind, but in your final draft, remove the numbers unless they make the essay easier to follow). Ensure each step is discussed in sequence—don't consider step 2 until you have covered step 1. If any stage is out of order, it will confuse the reader.

- If the process you're describing is broken into many short stages, don't allot one paragraph per stage. Combine two or more closely related stages in the same paragraph, using an appropriate transition to connect one stage to the next. For example, if you were writing on race walking, in a single paragraph you might discuss all the minor changes in the walker's body position from when the heel touches the ground to when the leg is vertical.

- Keep focused on the key details of the process in each paragraph. These may include instructions on what *not* to do or warnings about common mistakes. You also may need to briefly define unfamiliar terms. If the term applies to the entire process, however, the best place to do this would be the introduction.

- Restrict the use of personal experience and description, though these methods of development may sometimes be used in the introduction or conclusion.

- In your conclusion, you could focus on the importance or the benefits of the activity, or you might choose to highlight common mistakes, reinforcing the value of having the proper equipment, of taking safety precautions, and the like.

The following list of 10 topics suggests the range of possible topics for a process essay. If you are assigned to write a process essay, choose a topic according to your expertise and/or interests.

1. choosing an ideal apartment or roommate
2. creating a web page or your Facebook home page
3. buying an iPod or other media player
4. giving a presentation using PowerPoint
5. grooming or bathing a pet
6. organizing a social or educational event for a group you are involved with
7. preparing for a job interview
8. rock climbing, skydiving, or snowboarding successfully
9. travelling abroad on less than $20 a day
10. writing an email to your professor or boss

❯ Sample Process Essay

The following is an essay by a student writer that uses process to describe the stages of Bikram Yoga. It is about 500 words long; a longer essay might go into more detail in the body paragraphs. Read the essay and respond to the questions below.

SAMPLE STUDENT ESSAY

Where Hot Is "Cool": The Stages of Bikram Yoga

by Vanessa Tilson

[1] Stepping into a Bikram Yoga class can be a shock to the system: the room is 40°C and is lined with mirrors. The intense heat is not the only shock: half of what you hear will be in Sanskrit, one of the sacred languages of Hinduism and Buddhism. Bikram Yoga, or "hot yoga," was started in Los Angeles by Yogiraj Bikram Choudhury. Originally from India, Choudhury travelled to North America to open yoga studios that would use the form of yoga he designed after a weightlifting injury. Bikram Yoga consists of twenty-six postures and two breathing exercises that take the body through a cycle that works every muscle and organ.

[2] The standing and floor postures consist of a warm-up series, standing series, spine strengthening series, and floor series; each posture has medical benefits. Bikram Yoga begins with Pranayama breathing, a method of deep breathing that opens the lungs and prepares the mind for class. Next, Bikram Yoga moves into warm-up, which consists of three postures: Half Moon Pose with Hands to Feet Pose, Awkward Pose, and Eagle Pose. Awkward Pose, as its name suggests, can be a challenge to newcomers as it involves bending the knees as if one is sitting down in an imaginary chair. After ten seconds in which the arms are held out straight in front, one comes up slowly to stand on the tips of the toes, again holding this position for ten seconds. All the while, the focus is on slow, deep breathing.

General information about the origins of Bikram Yoga would be common knowledge for anyone trained in this form of yoga. In addition, it is easily obtainable information; thus, no citation is given.

In this introduction, background information is given. There is no need to discuss preparations or equipment since none are needed for yoga. In the simple thesis statement, the writer announces her topic, its stages, and its main benefits.

Note that the writer expands on only one of the poses, deliberately choosing Awkward Pose, which is not as self-explanatory as Half Moon Pose with Hands to Feet Pose or Standing Head to Knee Pose.

[3] Standing series starts with Standing Head to Knee Pose and finishes with Toe Stand Pose. All the poses help increase circulation to the heart and lungs. The floor section follows, starting with Savasana, or Dead Body Pose, in which the mind rests and the body rejuvenates. Every floor posture ends with Savasana to achieve deep relaxation after the Asana (active poses). Those unfamiliar with yoga may find it hard to stay awake during this stage, a real problem because one needs to complete this stage consciously.

[4] In spine strengthening, the two processes of extension and compression are stressed. The entire spine, along with the nervous system and many muscle groups, is worked on with the goal of increased strength and flexibility. This is especially true in the last two poses in this series, the Camel Pose and the Rabbit Pose. The final floor series has only three postures. The last is the Spine Twisting Pose, carefully prepared for by the previous poses to ensure it is performed correctly and without injury. The class ends with Khapalbhati breathing, a method used to expel all the air left in the lungs.

[5] Yoga is said to be a healing process. Although Bikram Yoga may feel like an intense workout, it actually gives one energy while the postures themselves build mental and physical strength, balance, and flexibility. To these benefits, the heated room adds one important one: it allows the muscles to stay warm, helping to prevent injuries. The heat also induces sweating, helping to eliminate toxins through the skin. For the beginner or the seasoned yogi, hot yoga is a "cool" experience.

> The writer begins a new paragraph after completing the stages of the warm-up series.

> The meanings of two Sanskrit words are briefly defined in this paragraph.

> The writer includes a warning about a common problem during one stage of the process.

> In her conclusion, the writer discusses some of the benefits of Bikram Yoga.

Post-reading Questions

1. What kind of reader do you think this essay was written to: very knowledgeable, moderately knowledgeable, or not knowledgeable?
2. Do you think the main purpose of the essay was to stimulate interest or to enable the reader to perform the stages of the activity?
3. Is there anything the writer could have done to further stimulate interest?
4. Is there anything she could have done to ensure that each stage could be duplicated?

❯ The Definition Essay

As you saw in Chapter 4, a definition answers the question, "What is it?" A definition essay helps the reader clearly grasp a concept. It may be about a topic that is often misunderstood or one that is vague or abstract. A definition essay expands and elaborates on a subject, using a variety of organizational methods, such as comparison and contrast.

Definition often provides a necessary starting point in an argumentative essay. Successfully getting your reader to agree with your definition will help establish your credibility as a writer, strengthening your argument. Defining something also enables you to set the terms on which you want your thesis to rest: you take control of a controversial or abstract topic and then go on to develop your thesis through means *other than* definition.

Definition is often an essential part of an expository essay. An essay in the humanities, natural sciences, and social sciences usually begins by defining terms that the writer will employ throughout the essay. The writer must establish the connotation of any terms that can be defined in different ways. Many academic texts—especially introductory textbooks—include a glossary or an index of common terms that is designed to make it easier to apply terms correctly.

It is important to provide an accurate definition in your essay, as definitions sometimes change over time and according to place, as well as according to cultural, national, social, and other factors. For example, the way you would define *privacy* today would likely be different from the way it would have been defined 25 years ago, due partly to technologies that have made it easier for others to access personal information. If you fail to provide the correct definition as it applies to your essay topic, you fail to prove your credibility, which in turn affects the reader's reaction to your essay.

❯ Sample Definition Essay

The following is a student exam essay that uses definition to address the topic of leadership. Read the essay and respond to the exercises below.

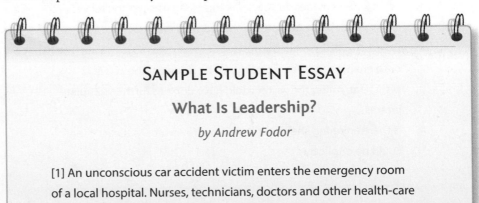

SAMPLE STUDENT ESSAY

What Is Leadership?

by Andrew Fodor

[1] An unconscious car accident victim enters the emergency room of a local hospital. Nurses, technicians, doctors and other health-care

providers swarm around the patient and begin administering tests and procedures. The attending physician stands back to assess, monitor, and give orders to the emergency team. The life of the patient depends on the leadership skills of the attending physician.

[2] Leadership is a skill that actively encourages, directs, co-ordinates, and guides one or more individuals towards the completion of a goal. Leadership is a valuable attribute in nearly all areas of society, such as the military, government, business, education, as well as in families. Although a power structure is often developed to identify or assign an individual, groups of individuals, or organizations to a leadership role, this is not a prerequisite of leadership. For example, the child of a mother undergoing chemotherapy may provide hope, encouragement, and inspiration to his or her family.

[3] A classic example of leadership is a project manager (PM). He or she has a responsibility to complete a project on time, within budget, and to the requirements of the client, usually a third party or company department. The PM must provide direction (a project plan) for his or her team; delegate responsibility to team members (sub-projects); monitor team progress; communicate between management, the project team and the client, as well as manage a number of other tasks (for example, team morale).

[4] There are numerous ways to improve an individual's leadership skills; these can often be accomplished by education (such as workshops) and on the job experience.

As mentioned earlier, an academic essay should not include paragraphs that are only one sentence long. This essay, however, is not academic, so the author does not have to follow the rules so closely.

[5] Leadership is the co-ordination of people, resources, and tasks towards the completion of a goal. Leadership can be demonstrated in many situations, from a doctor trying to save a life in the ER to a university teacher to a military commander. Although leadership is often provided by qualified, educated persons, it may sometimes arise from unlikely sources. Regardless, leadership is a skill that can be developed through experience and education.

(continued)

Post-reading Questions

1. The writer of this piece has tried to use concrete and immediate words to help the reader understand his concept of leadership. Find some examples of this.
2. Do you agree with all the examples given? Are there any that detract from his argument?
3. How does the writer establish his credibility?
4. What type of audience is he writing for? Why do you think that?
5. Explain why this is a good example of a definition essay.

Exercise **8.2**

Write a 500–700 word essay (about the length of the essay on leadership) on one of the following general topics:

1. censorship
2. consumerism
3. freedom
4. human rights
5. justice

6. multiculturalism
7. nationalism
8. self-expression
9. success
10. tradition

The Comparison and Contrast Essay

Comparison and contrast can be used as the primary organizational method in either an argumentative or an expository essay. These kinds of essays can be more challenging than other kinds, so consider using the three-step approach:

1. Ensure that the topics you want to compare are, indeed, comparable. It is not possible to compare the health-care system in the United States to the educational system in Canada. While it is possible to compare the health-care systems of the two countries, such a topic would be too broad and complex for anything much less than a book. However, it might be manageable to compare the health-care systems of two Canadian provinces.

2. After you have determined that the topics are comparable and that the essay is manageable, carefully choose at least three bases of comparison for the main points of your essay, ensuring that each basis of comparison is logical and manageable.

3. Organizing a comparison and contrast essay is especially crucial. To ensure the essay is clearly laid out with the points easy to follow, you can choose between the block and the point-by-point methods.

Point-by-Point and Block Methods

Point-by-Point Method

In the point-by-point method, you consider one basis of comparison as it applies to each subject and continue until you have considered all the bases of comparison. In the following outline, "A" and "B" represent your subjects, or what you are comparing, and the numbers represent your points, or bases of comparison:

1. basis of comparison

   A: subject of comparison

   B: subject of comparison

2. basis of comparison

   A: subject of comparison

   B: subject of comparison

3. basis of comparison

   A: subject of comparison

   B: subject of comparison

Block Method

In the block method, you consider all the points that relate to your first subject of comparison (your first block of material). You then consider all the points as they apply to the second subject of comparison (your second block), in the same order as the first block.

A: subject of comparison

   1. basis of comparison

   2. basis of comparison

   3. basis of comparison

B: subject of comparison

   1. basis of comparison

   2. basis of comparison

   3. basis of comparison

Below, the two methods are applied to the same topic and bases of comparison. Topic: Compare and contrast benefits of walking to benefits of cycling.

Point-by-Point Method

1. transportation
    A: cycling
    B: walking

2. exercise
    A: cycling
    B: walking

3. health
    A: cycling
    B: walking

4. cost
    A: cycling
    B: walking

Block Method

A: cycling
    1. transportation
    2. exercise
    3. health
    4. cost

B: walking
    1. transportation
    2. exercise
    3. health
    4. cost

❯ Sample Comparison and Contrast Essay

After reading this essay, complete the exercises that follow.

SAMPLE STUDENT ESSAY

Tail of Opposites

Meow, meow, or woof, woof?
by Barclay Katt

[1] For most people, it is an easy choice. In fact, it is not really a "choice" at all: it is simply the way it is. There are "cat people" and "dog people" in the world, and neither group speaks the language of the other. They are as separate as curds and whey, and when a cat person meets a dog person on neutral turf, the result is a war of words in which the fur is sure to fly.

It seems that each group disdains the other; in many other ways, each doggedly or cattily proclaims its separate identity.

[2] Just by walking into a house, you can tell whether the owner is a feline fancier or a canine connoisseur. (The fact that you have made it to the front door tells you something; have you ever heard of a watchcat?) The cat owner will show you to the elegant living room. Elegant? Cat owners possess the most costly furniture, but it is invariably armoured by ugly plastic coverings with perhaps a swath of towels wrapped around sofa ends. The dog owner will conduct you swiftly to the humble kitchen table. En route, you will notice the unmistakable "odeur du chien." But in the kitchen, cooking odours will mingle with those of dog, disguising the latter, though not erasing them completely.

[3] Talk to these two different groups of people, and you will again notice a difference. It is not that cat people are snobbish or that they believe themselves superior; the tilt of their noses has nothing to do with it. But there is one thing that they will expect of you: unremitting absorption in the object of their affection—Kitty. You had better be prepared to spend much of your time gazing in adoration at the magnificent specimen. You must also suffer the fastidious attentions of the cat, if it deigns to give them—even if the tribute takes the form of the kneading of its knife-like claws on your thigh.

[4] It is not that dog people are crude or that they have no concern for social graces. But there is one thing that they will expect of you: conviviality, even to the point of garrulousness. Be careful not to turn away from your host too often (resist the temptation to find out where that annoying series of yips is coming from). Dog owners are famous back-slappers, jabbers, and unapologetic probers of your person. But they will never ask you to share the virtues of their pet and will suddenly lose their warmth if you show too much interest. They are possessive of the bond and discourage interlopers.

[5] Most people have been struck, at one time or another, by the way pet owners come to resemble their pets. It is strange why this is so, and never the other way around—that pets come to look more like their owners. For some reason, the face of the cat or dog is more transferable

(continued)

to the human face than the human face is to that of the dog or cat. Here, it must be admitted that the dog owner is at an advantage. As there are far more breeds of dogs than of cats, the observer cannot help but be impressed by the infinite variety of possible faces of dog owners—from pushed-in pug to the full-blown majesty of Irish wolfhound.

[6] Perhaps it is due to these differences that dog owners and cat owners do not seem able to abide one another; they just never can see eye to eye on anything—or whisker to whisker, for that matter—especially where it concerns the superiority of their own pet. Certainly, the day that cat people and dog people do agree on something will be the day that world peace is finally possible.

Post-reading Questions

1. Identify the thesis statement in this essay.
2. Identify the method used for comparing and the basis for comparison.
3. As a member of the intended audience, were you persuaded by the writer of the validity of this point of view?
4. Identify any vocabulary that is unfamiliar and add those to your vocabulary journal (discussed in Chapter 1). Could different words have been used as effectively?
5. Would another organizational pattern be as effective as the one the author used for this essay?

Exercise 8.3

Part of effective essay writing involves being able to identify your audience. Identify the audience characteristics for the above essay. What are some of the clues that help you determine this? How would you change this essay if the requirements were for a more formal essay? (See Chapter 17, Achieving Clarity and Depth in Your Writing.)

❯ Points to Remember

An expository essay may require research, which is discussed in depth in Chapter 11. Even if no research is required, remember that an essay at the post-secondary level is best written in an objective tone. Therefore, a good writer does not use phrases like "I think . . .", or "I believe . . .", or "I feel . . ." Strong writing will convey these ideas to the reader.

Also, remember that in an expository essay you are not trying to convince readers of a particular point of view. You are informing the audience about a subject. Once you have provided readers with information, they may choose to agree or disagree, but your job is to help them understand the topic.

Exercise 8.4

1. In a small group, find an issue that interests all of you. It may be related to your particular area of study, or it may be a current event, such as the changing severity of the weather patterns in Canada. Using your school library's database, look for an article that addresses this. Determine whether it is an expository or argumentative essay. If it is expository, determine what type of essay it is. (Definition, process, compare and contrast?)
2. If you were going to use this article as a source for an essay, would it be better in an expository or argumentative essay? Why?
3. Try to find another article about the same topic that uses a different method for organizing the essay. Is one article more effective than another? Why?

❭ Sample Professional Essay

Pre-reading Questions

While reading the following essay, consider the questions below.

1. What type of organizational pattern did the writer use?
2. How is it similar to, and different from, the essay on leadership on pages 158–159? Does it give the reader a better idea of what leadership is? Does van Vugt use any methods for development that Fodor does not?
3. How could this piece be turned into an argumentative essay?

Before reading this essay, consider the pre-reading questions discussed in Chapter 1, pages 18–21. For example, you could do a brief online search to determine the author's qualifications. You could try to determine the type of magazine in which the work was published and the essay's intended audience. You could also consider essay length and the information contained in the work's title.

SAMPLE PROFESSIONAL ESSAY

The Origins of Leadership

by Mark van Vugt

The title of the essay suggests that the author will be explaining the concept of leadership by looking at its origins—i.e., by tracing its development over time. However, to be certain about his thesis, it is necessary to read the first few paragraphs of the essay.

[1] What makes a good leader? Do different political, economic, and social situations demand leaders with particular styles? How should we judge who is right for the job? Why are we so often disappointed with those in charge?

The writer begins by asking the kinds of questions that might occur to a reader. What does this tell you about the intended audience?

[2] In the run-up to the US elections Americans will doubtless be asking such questions. They are not alone. Leadership is an issue that pervades almost every aspect of our lives, from the family and the office to our local community, national politics, and beyond. No wonder the subject attracts so much attention.

In this paragraph, the writer universalizes his topic, stressing the importance of the issue in our daily lives, not just the lives of Americans.

[3] Despite the seeming glut of information, however, one aspect has been sorely missing—the historical perspective. Until recently, very few people have considered the origins of leadership. Yet to understand how our ancestors acquired the psychological biases upon which leadership is based is to see the concept in a whole new light. In particular, the evolutionary perspective highlights the importance of those who follow and the reasons why leaders and followers may not see eye to eye. It can also indicate what sort of leader is best suited to take charge in a particular situation. It can explain some of our seemingly arbitrary preferences—for tall leaders, for example—and it even suggests why there is a bias towards men as leaders.

In the topic sentence of paragraph 3, van Vugt states how his approach differs from previous approaches to the topic. He mentions three specific areas to be investigated. Can you identify the specific paragraphs in which he follows up on these points?

The author's thesis appears in this paragraph.

van Vugt gives a brief definition of leadership. You could compare this definition with that of Andrew Fodor, the author of the essay "What Is leadership?" (pages 158–159).

[4] In essence, leadership is a response to the need for collective action. How do members of a group decide what to do and how and when to do it? An obvious solution is for one individual to take the initiative and provide guidance while the rest agree to follow. If this strategy promotes survival, then psychological adaptations for both leadership and "followership" are likely to evolve.

Specific examples expand on his point connecting leadership to survival.

[5] In humans these would have included specialised mental mechanisms for planning, communication, group decision-making, competence recognition, social learning, and conflict management. Although such traits are generally associated with higher reasoning, cognitive pre-adaptations for leadership probably evolved long before modern humans ever appeared on the scene.

[6] The foraging patterns of many insects, the schooling of fish and the flying patterns of birds all suggest that species lacking complex cognitive capacities can nevertheless display leadership and followership—perhaps using the simple rule "follow the one who moves first." Our closest animal relatives, chimpanzees, also use leadership to coordinate group movement and to keep the peace or wage war.

[7] The animal evidence supports the idea that adaptations for leadership and followership tend to evolve in social species. In humans, they were probably further shaped by our unique evolutionary history. There were three distinct stages in human development where the nature of leadership altered to reflect cultural and social changes (*American Psychologist*, vol 63, p 182).

[8] The first and by far the longest phase extended from the emergence of the genus *Homo*, around 2.5 million years ago, until the end of the last ice age about 13,000 years ago. Natural selection for certain successful strategies of leadership and followership during this long era is likely to have shaped the distinctly human leadership psychology we still have to this day. Throughout this time, our ancestors probably lived in semi-nomadic, hunter-gatherer bands of between 50 and 150 mostly related individuals. Their lifestyle is widely thought to have resembled that of today's hunter-gatherer societies such as the Kung San of the Kalahari desert and the Amazonian Yanomamo. These groups are fundamentally egalitarian, with no formal leader. Although there are "Big Men"—the best hunters and warriors or wisest elders, for example—the influence of each is limited to their areas of expertise and, crucially, it is only granted with the approval of followers. This suggests that collaboration among subordinates allowed early humans to move beyond the dominance hierarchies found in other primates, towards a much flatter prestige-based hierarchy with a more democratic style of leadership.

[9] With the development of agriculture some 13,000 years ago, groups settled, populations grew rapidly and, for the first time in human history, communities accumulated surplus resources. They needed leaders to redistribute this surplus and to deal with increasing conflict both within and between groups. The power of leaders grew accordingly, and with it the potential to abuse this power. Leaders could now siphon off resources and use them to create cultural elites, while disgruntled followers were less free to move away from exploitative rulers. The result of such changes was a more formalised, authoritarian leadership style and the emergence of the first chiefs and kings, as well as warlords bent on extracting resources through force.

> Notice the way that this paragraph, focusing on the first "stage" of leadership development, is set up by the last sentence of the previous paragraph. van Vugt then allots one paragraph for each stage. Doing so contributes to coherence.

> **Reading/Writing Tip:** The writer doesn't cite all his sources, unlike the writer of an article in a scholarly journal. When you use research sources in your essay, you *must* carefully cite all your sources.

> This paragraph is developed through cause and effect. van Vugt discusses the main effect, or result, of having "surplus resources": the emergence of an "authoritarian leadership style."

[10] The industrial revolution, some 250 years ago, paved the way for the final phase of leadership—the one to which academic discussions of leadership, which tend to focus on business and politics, almost exclusively refer. At the beginning of this era followers were little more than slaves, but as citizens and employees acquired more freedom to defect from overbearing leaders, the balance of power shifted away from authoritarian leaders and back to something more like the egalitarian approach of ancestral times.

> Having traced the origins of leadership, van Vugt asks a question that is relevant to leadership today, answering it by using academic studies and examples throughout the paragraph.

[11] So, what can evolution tell us about modern leadership? The ancestral environment may have equipped us with innate preferences for certain characteristics in our leaders. For a start, we want them to be both competent and benevolent, because these sorts of people will be better at acquiring resources and more willing to share them. We also tend to choose leaders with certain physical characteristics. Other theories of leadership have failed to account for the importance of seemingly arbitrary attributes such as height, age, weight, and health, but these make sense from an evolutionary perspective. For example, ancestral Big Men were probably quite literally that: by dint of their imposing physique, all people would have been more effective peacekeepers and more intimidating foes. Even today we have a bias towards taller leaders (*Journal of Applied Psychology*, vol 89, p 428). In ancestral times elders were likely to have acquired specialist knowledge, and in the modern world older leaders are preferred in situations where knowledge is crucial, such as in running public corporations (*Leadership and Governance from the Inside Out*, edited by Robert Gandossy and Jeffrey Sonnenfeld, Wiley, 2004). Followers may also have evolved a preference for fit and healthy leaders in situations where strength and stamina mattered. That could be why modern voters prefer physically fit and energetic political candidates (*Personality and Social Psychology Review*, vol 10, p 354).

> The author reinforces his thesis that leadership preferences are related to "an evolutionary [i.e., historical] perspective."

[12] More controversially, evolution might explain our bias towards male leaders in most circumstances. When men and women work together, men are quicker to claim leadership roles even when women are better qualified (*Psychological Bulletin*, vol 130, p 711). Moreover, a recent experiment by myself and Brian Spisak, also at the University of Kent (to be published in *Psychological Science* later this year), revealed that groups tend to look to men for leadership when faced with a threat from another group, possibly because inter-group conflict would have been resolved by force throughout most of human history. However, we also found that in situations where there is internal conflict in a group, women are the preferred and most effective leaders. This is confirmed by a recent mock election study which found that people tended to vote for a male president when their country was at war, but a female during peacetime (*Evolution and Human Behavior*, vol 28, p 18). A history of inter-group conflict might have predisposed men to adopt a hierarchical leadership style, while a need for social unity might have equipped women with a more egalitarian, personalised, and communal style. If the predominance of male leaders in many sectors of

> **Reading Tip:** Notice the way van Vugt conveys the speculative nature of his statement. Verbs like *might have predisposed* and *could be* (in the next sentence) suggest uncertainty. Presumably, no studies exist to confirm or refute his statements.

modern life is a vestige of our past, it could be a costly one in an interconnected world in which the emphasis is on interpersonal skills and network-building.

[13] This raises another important aspect of leadership that is often overlooked—that what constitutes good leadership varies according to the situation. The different leadership styles adopted by various organisations, nations, and cultures can be understood in part by considering the specific challenges posed by their particular physical and social environment. In the Netherlands and Australia, for example, where harsh natural conditions force the authorities to collaborate closely with citizens, there is a strong egalitarian ethos. In emergencies such as wars or natural disasters, followers readily defer to the decisions of a single autocratic individual. Indeed, US voters tend to choose hawkish presidents when threatened by war.

> **Reading Tip:** *Egalitarian* and *ethos* may be unfamiliar terms. If they cannot be determined by context, you must use a dictionary. (Hint: If you know what the phrase *collaborate closely* means, you may be able to determine the meaning of *egalitarian*; then you can confirm the meaning by using a dictionary.

[14] All this suggests that leadership and followership are flexible strategies shaped by the interplay between ancient evolutionary pressures and modern environmental and cultural demands. However, there are major differences between modern leadership roles and the kind of leadership for which our psychology is adapted, and this mismatch can be problematic. For a start, our hunter-gatherer ancestors would have deferred to different leaders depending on the nature of the problem at hand. Yet today a single individual is often responsible for managing all aspects of an enterprise. Few leaders have the range of skills required, which may account for the high failure rate of senior managers—in corporate America it runs at 50 per cent (*Review of General Psychology*, vol 9, p 169). Surveys routinely show that between 60 and 70 per cent of employees find the most stressful part of their job is dealing with their immediate boss. This may be partly because ancestral leaders only acquired power with the approval of followers, whereas in modern organisations leaders are usually appointed by and accountable to their superiors, while subordinates are rarely allowed to sanction their bosses. What's more, our psychology equips us to thrive in smallish groups of closely related individuals, which may explain why many people feel indifferent to large organisations and their leaders. Finally, in ancestral societies there would have been minimal differences in status between leaders and followers. In the US, average salaries for CEOs are 179 times those of their workers.

> van Vugt uses the first sentence to summarize previous paragraphs. In the second sentence, he indicates his developmental method for the paragraph: comparison and contrast with the focus on differences (contrast).

> **Writing Tip:** Transitions are used effectively to connect ideas in this lengthy paragraph: *However, for a start, yet*. Can you identify two other transitions in this paragraph?

[15] The upside is that insights from evolution also suggest more effective leadership strategies. In recent years there has been increasing interest in the idea of shared or distributed leadership. Some organisations are finding that executives are more likely to succeed if subordinates are included in the selection process. Meanwhile, effective businesses—including Toyota and Virgin—are designing and structuring their organisations to more closely resemble hunter-gatherer bands. For instance, they delegate decision-making to managers far down the chain of command, creating functional groups of between 50 and 150 members.

> These paragraphs suggest how we can learn from the evolutionary approach to leadership.

[16] By emphasising interdependence and shared interests, values, and goals, a truly transformational leader can change followers from self-interested individuals to committed collectivists. Unfortunately, such people are thin on the ground. Instead, we are often required to defer to leaders whose remit and behaviour is inconsistent with our evolved expectations of leadership. That can be alienating, but at least followers can sometimes do something about it. That is exactly what millions of US citizens will be doing when they exercise their power to vote for a new president.

* * *

[17] Considering leadership from the evolutionary perspective throws a spotlight on followers. The psychology of followership is usually neglected, but it is more interesting than that of leadership. Most of us are destined to be followers, yet we are only starting to understand what makes a good follower and how they influence leaders. A key puzzle is what motivates followers. Why would individuals agree to subordinate themselves when this puts them at a disadvantage compared with leaders in terms of power, status, and resources?

In his conclusion, van Vugt discusses the "psychology of followership," which he explains is a "neglected" area of research. His speculations are probably intended to give his readers, most of whom are followers, something to think about.

[18] The decision to follow may simply be a rational one: if the costs of competing for higher status outweigh the benefits, then following frees up time and energy that can be used more effectively elsewhere. Besides, followers can improve their position relative to leaders by engaging in collective action. Another idea is that complying with and observing leaders may allow followers to prepare themselves for future leadership. Finally, the disadvantages of following are partly offset by the benefits of belonging to a well-led group. So natural selection at the group level might account for leadership.

[19] The relationship between followers and leaders is inherently ambivalent because there is always a risk that leaders will try to coerce or exploit their followers, and that followers will plot to depose their leaders. This tension probably created an evolutionary arms race in terms of the strategies used to gain control. Nevertheless, research shows that people readily adopt leadership/followership behaviour in circumstances that mirror adaptive problems, such as when there are internal group conflicts or external threats (*Journal of Personality and Social Psychology*, vol 76, p 587).

[20] However, there are situations in which leadership is not necessary, and is even resented by followers. Experiments show that unnecessary leadership can actually undermine team performance (*Group Dynamics*, vol 2, p 168). The lesson for businesses and politicians here is that when faced with relatively simple or routine coordination problems, people usually perform better if left alone.

—van Vugt, M. (2008). Follow me: The origins of leadership.
New Scientist, 2660, 20–21.

Post-reading Questions

1. What type of claim does the author start with?

2. What type of essay development pattern does the author rely on for the overall structure of the essay?

3. Has the author followed the essay pattern shown in the expository essay template (Table 8.1, page 151)? If not, how has he deviated from it?

4. Why do you think the author has chosen to support his paper with secondary sources?

5. As with any expository essay, the author is trying to inform the audience. Has he been successful?

▌ Chapter Review Questions

1. What are the different kinds of expository essays?

2. Should an expository essay try to convince the reader of a certain point of view?

3. How can templates help when writing an essay?

4. What are some important points to keep in mind when writing a process-analysis essay?

5. What are some important points to keep in mind when writing a definition essay?

6. What are the two ways to structure a comparison and contrast essay? Why is it important to stick to one method?

The Argumentative **Essay**

In this chapter, you will

- learn the difference between an emotional argument and a logical argument
- learn to identify and avoid common errors of logic
- learn what kinds of evidence can be used in an argumentative essay
- learn why it is important to acknowledge the opposing point of view
- learn how to build a credible argument using specific strategies
- review outlining and learn techniques for creating an outline for an argumentative essay
- learn how to create and deliver oral presentations

Argument requires the use of careful planning and critical thinking skills. Argumentative essays written at college and university rely on logic and reason supported by convincing evidence. Importantly, you need to avoid errors in logic, as these can destroy your credibility with your reader. This chapter will introduce you to some of the most common errors in logic, discuss effective argumentative strategies, and include examples of well-argued essays.

❯ Emotional versus Logical Arguments

People argue every day, and many think they do it well. However, often arguments are emotionally based, such as when parents argue with a teenager about the use of the family car. Arguments can also be based on reason and moral standards. When you read a letter to the editor or a proposal for change, often those with the most impact use a combination of argumentative strategies and make **appeals** to reason, emotion, and ethics.

Even résumé writing involves argument—you are convincing an employer to hire you rather than someone else. An argumentative essay requires the same logical and critical thinking skills that you use every day. Appeals to reason, emotion, and ethics all can be used in **argument**, as the following real-life scenario suggests:

> You are disappointed by an essay grade and arrange to meet your instructor in her office. By your effective use of reason, you try to convince her to change your mark, conceding the validity of some of her criticisms (concessions are used in many arguments). Going through the paper systematically, you focus on points that seem arguable, asking for clarification or elaboration and presenting your counter-claims. As you do, you begin to come across as a responsible, conscientious student: you make an ethical appeal.
>
> You appeal to her as fair-minded, reiterating her helpfulness, your interest in the course, and your desire to do well. In this way, you succeed in establishing common ground, as you would try to do with the reader of your essay. If you argue with integrity, you will leave a good impression. Emotional appeals, such as tearfully bemoaning your stressful life, are apt to be less successful, but subtle appeals may have influence.

In an argumentative essay, the most important appeal is usually to reason and logic. Depending on your topic, ethical appeals play a vital secondary role in establishing your credibility as an arguer. Emotional appeals can also be useful, depending on your topic, your audience, and their placement in the essay.

Although good writers build their credibility by using valid arguments and arguing fairly and ethically, some writers do not argue well because they use faulty logic or rely solely on emotional appeals. At the college and university level, you need to avoid these errors in an argumentative essay, as they affect your credibility and, ultimately, your grades.

> Successful arguments at the college and university level make appeals to reason, ethics, and emotion. Of these, appeals to reason are usually the most important.

Exercise **9.1**

In the scenario below, Ivannia Herrera argues with her roommate over what might seem a trivial issue, a "Tempest in a Teapot"; however, the underlying issues are not trivial. In the course of the argument, some values are seen as more important than others. Although this is an informal argument, it contains many of the features of a formal argument—for example, a claim and supporting evidence. Rebuttals and concessions also are involved (see pages 188–191). Read the argument carefully to find the appeals to reason, emotion, and ethics.

Tempest in a Teapot

Background: My roommate and I share a kitchen and utensils. Each day I make tea in a small stainless steel pot, which has a glass cover and a pouring spout with tiny holes that serve as a strainer. I pour two cups of water into the pot, let it boil, then add the leaves. When the tea is ready, I strain the tea water from the pot, leaving the tea leaves behind. I leave the pot on the counter until the next time I make tea.

The reason for the argument: My roommate has made it plain she does not enjoy seeing the pot with drenched tea leaves in the bottom.

Table 9.1 lists the points that Ivannia and her roommate make during the argument. Which points seem the most convincing to you? Why? Do you think there are any irrelevant points? Are points missing that might have been made?

TABLE 9.1	My Side/Roommate's Side
My Side	Roommate's Side
If I leave the pot with the tea leaves on the counter, I can reuse them three times. Since I make the same type of tea several times a day, it makes sense that I reuse the leaves rather than throw them out, which will cost me more money in the long run.	The pot is left on the counter for many hours. Though it's okay to reuse the leaves, the kitchen looks messy. I don't like the kitchen looking dirty with an unclean pot sitting there every day. Furthermore, I can't use this pot because it is always filled with tea leaves that I can't throw away.
I bought all the pots and pans in this household, and I am happy to share them; however, if you need a pot like this to use regularly, you should consider buying one yourself.	I also bought utensils for the household—and even the computer. I share these things and understand the concept of sharing. I think that having roommates means having to compromise.
I think of myself as a clean person, and I contribute greatly to the cleanliness of the household. I think that your having to look at a small pot is a small "defect," considering. . . . Drinking tea is part of my daily life, and I enjoy it. As well, it costs me $6 per month; if I were to discard the tea each time, I would be spending $18 per month, and I can think of better ways to spend those extra $12!	I am not saying that you should throw away the tea leaves, but just find a better way to use them so they are not in sight and taking over the pot. I think that the cleanliness of my living space is a reflection on me, which is why I want a clean environment. I do not like seeing a messy pot, and that is my "defect." I also think I should be able to use the pot if I like, and I can't with the leaves in it.
We both agree on the need to compromise. I'm willing to compromise and buy a ball strainer that can hold the tea leaves inside for as long as need be. It is a small ball attached to a chain; the ball divides in half, the tea leaves are put in one half, the ball is closed, and it is placed inside a cup filled with boiling water. I suggest we compromise and each pay half for the ball strainer.	I'm happy to pay for half of it, as long as you keep the ball with the tea leaves in a cup in your own room. That way, you can bring it out anytime you want tea, but it will be out of my sight.

Argument, Opinion, and Facts

Although the discussion above illustrates an ordinary occurrence, it contains the necessary elements of argument. However, the sample paragraph below is based solely on opinion and cannot be considered an argument. Although her topic can be argued, the writer oversimplifies and uses **generalizations** that are not backed up by evidence.

Be careful in making generalizations. When you make a generalization, something that is applicable to all people in a large category, make sure it does truly apply to *all people* in the category.

Sports Utility Vehicles, commonly called suvs, can also be called Stupid Useless Vehicles.

They were designed for people who wanted to travel over different types of terrain in all kinds of weather. A Jeep is a perfect example of this type of vehicle.

If suvs were used for their intended purpose, then they would be beneficial.

However, most people who purchase them seem to live in towns and cities, and the suvs never seem to be dirty, which shows they are not used off-road.

Many of these vehicles are driven on highways with rarely more than one passenger, and these overly large vehicles use precious resources and pollute the environment.

Unless people can prove that the suv is going to be used for the purpose for which it was designed, they should not be allowed to purchase one.

> The writer starts by abruptly stating an opinion that not all readers will share.

> The writer uses a fact and an example, but also introduces opinion with the adjective *perfect*, weakening the statement.

> The writer fails to support this point, which is based simply on moral high ground—she also uses flawed reasoning in assuming there is one "intended purpose" for these vehicles.

> The writer makes a broad generalization that cannot be argued against. Facts or statistics are more effective in convincing the reader that a claim is valid.

> Again, the writer uses a generalization and provides no support.

> The writer ends using opinion only, which is ineffective.

As the example above demonstrates, opinion is not the same as argument. Many arguments are based on opinion, but in order to be persuasive, they shouldn't come across as *opinionated*. Everyone has opinions, but not everyone argues well. Consider the following passage in which the writer makes it clear to the reader that he is opinionated; in doing so, however, he shows poor argumentative skills. In being overwhelmed by opinion, the reader may well miss his points.

> Institutions of higher learning are meant for people hoping to broaden their interests and knowledge in order to contribute to society. I, myself, agree with this principle, and I also agree that a degree can help me acquire a job and be good at it. Along with this, I do not doubt that these institutions facilitate higher cognitive functioning. What I do not agree with is the approach that these institutions have towards the sciences. In fact, I categorically oppose the favouritism that is always shown to the sciences whenever financial matters are considered.

Many arguments are based on opinion, but in order to be persuasive, they shouldn't come across as *opinionated*. Argument at the college or university level is not just writing with an "attitude"; in fact, in effective arguments, writers express themselves objectively, using neutral language.

In your own argumentative essays, always clearly separate fact from opinion. When you use opinion, it should be supported— by logic and/or reliable evidence, such as facts.

Exercise 9.2

Rewrite the paragraph, eliminating the references to opinion and changing pronouns from *I*, *me*, etc., to *one* or a suitable noun. Does the revised paragraph sound more forceful? How is the writer's credibility enhanced?

Opinions are also not the same as facts, which can be verified by observation or research. Opinions can be challenged. As you will see, you cannot argue a position on a topic that has no opposing view—it cannot be challenged. On the other hand, facts can be interpreted in different ways and used for different purposes. Facts, therefore, can be used to support the thesis of an argumentative essay. However, effective arguers are always clear about when they are using facts and when they are using opinion. In reading, use your critical thinking skills to ask if the writer always clearly separates facts from opinion. If not, he or she might be guilty of faulty reasoning. To help clarify the difference between opinions and facts, examples are given below.

Fact (not challengeable):

The moon is 378,000 kilometres from earth's equator.

Fact:

According to moon landing conspiracy theories, the 1969 Apollo moon landing was faked.

Opinion (challengeable):

The Apollo moon landing didn't actually take place; it was all a hoax.

Fact:

On November 13, 2009, NASA announced that water had been found on the moon.

Opinion:

Now that water has been found on the moon, humans should set up colonies at the moon's poles by 2050.

Exercise 9.3

Consider the two pairs of statements above on the topic of humans on the moon. In small groups, discuss the ways that fact differs from opinion in each case. Come up with other topics and write two statements for each, one of which represents a fact and the other of which represents an opinion.

Exercise **9.4**

Recall a recent argument. Begin by briefly describing the circumstances that led to it. Then, divide a page in half vertically and summarize each point raised by "your side" and "the other side" (see Table 9.1). Simply report what was said (do not embellish with interpretations of what was said)—each side's point of view and the counter-argument, if any. When a new point begins, draw a horizontal line to separate it from the next point. Then analyze the strengths and weaknesses of each point. Did the point make an appeal to reason? Did it make an emotional appeal? An ethical one? Was an opinion supported? Were facts used to support an opinion? Were the points logically related to one another? Was the argument resolved? If so, how? Write a paragraph response to the argument, analyzing flaws, such as simplifications and generalizations. In your analysis, try to be as objective as possible to *both* sides.

Faulty Reasoning

It is easy to make mistakes when first trying to write an argumentative essay, so it is important to first understand **faulty reasoning** and how to avoid it. Also, if you know what mistakes to avoid when you argue and how arguments can go wrong, you will be in a better position to point out flaws in your opponent's argument. Once you have become familiar with some of the common problems that affect argumentative essays, you will learn how to create arguable claims and support these claims by well-reasoned points and specific argumentative strategies.

Faulty reasoning can result from an argument that is not valid, a lack of proof for a claim, or opinion not clearly separated from fact.

A fallacy is a misleading or unsound argument.

Logical, Emotional, and Ethical Fallacies

Ineffective arguments that use logical, emotional, or ethical **fallacies** detract from the writer's credibility: we do not trust someone who misuses logic or reason. For example, we might well mistrust a person who argued that because some students are underage, all college and university campus pubs should be closed.

Misuse of emotional or ethical appeals are unfair to the other side: emotional fallacies *exploit* emotions and so are very different from valid appeals to emotion. People frequently misuse emotion. We have all been told that the emissions from vehicles affect the environment and that larger vehicles are more harmful than smaller ones. But that fact alone does not mean that all drivers of pick-up trucks or SUVs in the city should be condemned, as the writer of the paragraph on page 175 stated. The vehicles have several uses within a city: for example, a landscaper might need an SUV for work. By stating that *all* people driving large vehicles in the city do not care about the environment, one is guilty of misusing emotional or ethical appeals.

Misuse of emotional or ethical appeals are unfair to the other side: emotional fallacies *exploit* emotions and so are very different from valid appeals to emotion.

Some fallacies are based on faulty inductive reasoning, for example, cause–effect fallacies, such as "If I wash my car, it will rain." Others are based on the faulty use of deductive reasoning where general or universal statements are made that may not be true, such as "All people who ride bicycles are environmental-ists." (Inductive and deductive reasoning are discussed on pages 186–188.)

Table 9.2 lists common argumentative fallacies that misuse reason, emo-tion, or ethics. You should avoid these in your own writing and look for exam-ples of them in the argument of your opponent. In some arguments, more than one type of fallacy may be involved.

TABLE 9.2	Argumentative Fallacies		
Types	Term	Definition	Example
Irrelevant	Red herring	It attempts to distract or sidetrack the reader, often on an ethical matter. In the example, there may be some valid-ity to the point, but it should not form the basis of an argument.	He cheated on his exam. How can we trust him to participate in our group project?
	Straw man	It misrepresents an opponent's main argument by substituting a false or minor argument in its place. The point is to get the audience to agree.	Thaddeus Tuttle points out that while women have not achieved wage parity with men, they often take maternity leave, which means they don't work as much as men. (Among its flaws, this argument ignores the basic principle of equal pay for equal work.)
Emotional	Band wagon	It argues in favour of something be-cause it has become popular.	Everyone is using a smartphone now. I have to get one too even though my old phone works just fine.
	Dogmatism	This common type of argument asserts a point without supporting evidence on the basis of a firm, perhaps passion-ate, belief.	I believe that everyone should oppose whale hunting. (In argumentative essays, it's best to avoid the self-conscious refer-ence to your opinion; instead, you should let your points talk for you.)
	Either/or	It suggests that there are only two available options.	You are either with me or against me. (These arguments often also lack logic.)
Logical	Circular	An argument that does not move forward or that continues in a circle. The main point is just repeated, but not expanded.	Applied degrees are now available at some community colleges in Canada. They are only offered there because community col-leges teach applied skills.
Evidence	False analogy	It compares two things that are, in fact, not alike. While a true analogy can pro-vide support for a point, to draw a true analogy, you need to have a real basis for comparison, which does not exist in the example.	How can people complain about circuses that use wild animals in their acts? We keep animals, such as cats, which were once wild, in small spaces in our homes.

TABLE 9.2	(Continued)		
	False cause	It asserts that simply because one event preceded another one, there must be a cause–effect relationship between them.	Tamara forgot to wear her lucky watch for the exam; consequently, she failed. (Superstitions can arise when people assume a causal relationship between two events. Of course, there are causal relationships between many events; for example, if Tamara walked in front of a car and was hit, then obviously her action resulted in her injury. A false cause assumes a connection without valid evidence.)
	Hasty generalization	It forms a conclusion based on little or no evidence.	I talked to two people, both of whom said the text was useless, so I will not buy it. (Perhaps many people bought the text, so two people may not be a good sample.)
	Predicting	It denies that an effect arises from a cause because it hasn't happened yet—therefore, it's not going to. The arguer projects into the future without considering probability or other evidence.	I did well on the last test and I didn't study much; therefore, I don't need to study much for the final exam.
	Tradition ("that is the way we have always done it")	It argues for a course of action because it has been followed before, even if the same conditions no longer apply.	You should not compose your essay on a computer. Hand writing it is much better.

There are certainly many occasions when, for example, you will be able to successfully argue that the ends do justify the means, where there may be only two alternatives to consider (either/or), or where a point can be explained using an analogy. For example, as discussed below (page 182), analogies and other comparisons are often used in argument, but if the basis for comparing two things is faulty, the writer's credibility will be affected.

When writing an argument essay, using the fallacies listed above can weaken your position greatly. A reader could easily think, "Wait a minute; that doesn't make sense." When you use argument, you want your statements to be forceful and effective—not to arouse suspicion.

Writers need to look closely and objectively at the *way* they argue and ensure that their arguments are always based on logic and that their appeals to emotion are always moderate, not extreme or exaggerated. The writer who watches out for the first will appear reliable and trustworthy; the one who watches out for the last will appear fair.

Writers need to look closely and objectively at the *way* they argue and ensure that their arguments are based on logic and that their appeals to emotion are moderate.

Exercise 9.5

Silencing

A writer sometimes resorts to logical or emotional fallacies because these can "silence" the reader—no logical response is possible since the reasoning is flawed.

Each of the following statements is based on faulty reasoning. Try to determine why it fails the test of reason and why it would not be effective in an argumentative essay. If it seems to be an example of one of the fallacies listed in Table 9.2, decide which one; in some cases, more than one fallacy might be involved.

1. In our family, males have always been named "Harold" and females "Gertrude"; therefore, you should name your twins "Harry" and "Gerty."
2. If you don't get a degree in law, medicine, or business these days, you're never going to make any money.
3. When I serve you dinner, it's terrible not to eat all of it when you consider that one-third of the world's population goes to bed hungry.
4. The teacher hasn't called on me to answer a question for three consecutive days; it looks like I don't need to do the reading for tomorrow.
5. I know I went through the red light, officer, but the car in front of me did, too.

Using Slanted Language

Slanted language reveals the writer's bias, affecting his or her credibility. It can take direct forms, such as accusatory language, or be more indirect.

In addition to misusing logic and emotion, a writer can show a lack of objectivity by using slanted or loaded language. Such language shows that the writer is not objective, and it detracts from his or her credibility. **Slanted language** can take many forms from extreme direct statements to qualifiers (adjectives or adverbs) that subtly convey a bias. When slanted language is direct and offensive, it is easy to spot. For example, if you dismissed the other side as "evil" or their argument as "horrible" or "disgusting," you would reveal your bias. If you use slanted language, readers could easily take offence and question your fairness.

However, slanted language can be less obvious, for example, when words play unfairly on the connotations, rather than the denotations, of language—in other words, on the negative implications of particular words, rather than on their literal meanings. A writer's careful and conscious use of a word's connotations can be effective in an argument, but if the purpose is to distort the truth, then the writer's credibility will be at stake. For example, in the passage below, "removed from office" has a more negative connotation than "voted out of office" (a phrase the writer could have used instead). The italicized words in the following reveal slanted language:

In the recent election, the *reigning* political *regime was removed from office* as a result of the *atrocities they had committed* against the people of the province. The voters believed the new government would improve things, but when you achieve such easy victory there is a tendency to overlook the reason for your victory: the people who elected you. Today, the government is ignoring the middle class, *betraying* the very people who *naively* voted them into office.

Exercise 9.6

The following paragraphs suffer from faulty logic and/or emotional appeals, as well as slanted language. In groups, analyze the arguments, determine what fallacies and inconsistencies make them ineffective, and suggest improvements to make the argument stronger. More important than identifying the precise fallacy is identifying which statements are illogical or make unfair appeals to emotion.

1. Genetically engineered foods are being sold in most supermarkets without anyone knowing that we are being used as guinea pigs for the corporations developing this technology. The general public is being kept in the dark entirely, and the way that this food is being sold is through one-sided advertising. The public is being told that genetically engineered foods are a safe and effective way to grow a lot of food faster by inserting genetic material of one species into another. Though the proponents of genetically engineered foods attempt to convince the public that this technology will save lives, the reality is that major biotechnology companies are developing genetically engineered food crops to maximize their profits. Corporations would have us believe that the reason why 19,000 children starve to death daily is because of inefficient agricultural practices, but the world currently produces enough food today to provide a decent diet for every person on this planet. In spite of this fact, genetically engineered foods are being sold as the cure for Third-World starvation. This, however, is simply not true. The motives of the companies selling genetically engineered foods are not to save the lives of starving people, but to line their own pockets by profiting from the biotechnological industry. As a society, we should move to force governments to ban the development of genetically engineered foods before it is too late.

2. The legalization of marijuana would destroy society as we know it today. The typical Canadian would be exposed to many harsh drugs, such as coke, crack, and heroin, due to the increased acceptance of drugs within the community. Rehabilitation clinics for chronic drug users would be a huge drain on the economy. There would have to be new laws and screenings implemented to prevent people from working with heavy machinery or operating a motor vehicle while impaired by marijuana. Canadian business owners would be dissatisfied with many of their employees, and then discrimination would rear its ugly head. Firing someone for smoking marijuana and not being productive at work is not discrimination; however, the point would be made that it is. Clearly, our society would sink to a despicable level if this drug were legalized.

Creating Your Argument by Claims and Support

To create an effective argument, you can use a variety of general strategies, including

- making a claim of value (something is right or wrong)
- making a claim of policy (a policy or practice needs to be changed)
- interpreting facts, such as statistics, to support your claim
- providing evidence from the experts
- supporting your points with credible examples, such as case studies
- supporting your points using soft evidence, such as analogies, description, or personal experience
- defining a term or concept, especially if the term could be misunderstood
- comparing your ideas to other ideas that the audience understands

Using these strategies while avoiding fallacies will help you create an essay that builds your credibility as an arguer.

One way to help make a point easier for a reader to understand or relate to is to use an analogy (comparison) or description. For example, author Elizabeth Bowen used the following analogy in her book *The House in Paris:*

> Memory is to love what the saucer is to the cup.

Analogy can often help the reader visualize your argument, making a point easier to understand. However, you need to make sure you use an analogy that the audience can relate to.

Description may also play a limited role in argument, perhaps to attract interest in the essay's introduction or to set up a main point. Student writer Leslie Nelson began her essay on adolescent depression this way:

> Imagine a deep, dark hole that stretches forever without end. There is no light at either end of this hole; there is nobody else in this hole except you. Imagine living in this hole for hours, days, weeks, years. Imagine believing that you will never escape. Most teenagers find themselves in this hole—depression—at least once in their adolescent life, a time when nothing seems to go right.

If you use personal experience, it is important to keep your tone objective. See Chapter 7, page 139. Check with your instructor before you use personal experience.

Definition can also help your readers understand how you are using a concept or term. For example, in writing a paper about the value of post-secondary education, you might want to define what this concept means to you. Does it include university, community college, and private degree-granting institutions (such as the ones you see commercials for on television), or does it include only university and community college?

Comparison and contrast can help a reader visualize something by setting it alongside what he or she knows. The example below comes from an essay in which a student writer explains how houses in Japan are cleaner than in North America because people do not wear shoes in the house. She compared and contrasted tatami flooring with something she thought her readers would be already familiar with. (This example also uses description.)

> Tatami, or rice mat, flooring is common in Japan. Tatami is similar to the rice mats that one can buy for use on the beach; however, tatami does not fold up. The rice matting is placed on large wooden frames and fastened securely to these frames. One mat is difficult for most adults to pick up alone. An average room can have six or eight mats on the floor.

Any of these strategies can be used to support your argumentative thesis. However, the beginning point for argument, as in most college and university writing, is in the introduction where you state your major claim, your thesis.

Arguable Claims

What is needed for a valid argument? First, you need an *arguable topic*. If you and a friend start debating whether a homemade hamburger tastes better than one from the frozen food aisle, who is right? How can you determine this? If you are using only subjective standards (such as what you *think* tastes better), obviously neither you nor your friend is "right" because the topic is not arguable—you both are just stating an opinion, which cannot alone form a reason-based argument. On the other hand, you could base your argument on the respective nutritional values, fat content, or additives and preservatives.

Second, the topic needs an *opposing viewpoint*. You could not easily write an argumentative essay on the benefits of good health, as there is no opposing view. In the same way obvious claims, such as "computers have changed a great deal in the last decade," are unarguable. Also, just because a subject is controversial does not always mean that it is arguable. For example, an argument that justifies computer hacking or the writing of viruses likely is not valid.

Specific, Interesting, and Manageable Claims

You also need to ensure that the claim, like all thesis statements, is specific, interesting, and manageable. Below, we focus on a sample argumentative claim, showing the kinds of questions you can ask to help you develop a strong and effective thesis for an argumentative essay. To review claims and thesis statements, see Chapters 6 and 7.

Specific Claims

A specific claim states clearly and precisely what you will be arguing. The reader should know whether the claim is one of fact, value, or policy. The claim must not be vague.

The limited use of personal experience is often effective in argument. However, simply using the pronoun *I* or *my*, as in "I believe . . ." or "my opinion is . . ." is not the same thing as using personal experience as evidence.

A topic that can be argued (1) is based on objective, not just subjective, standards, and (2) has an opposing viewpoint.

A specific claim states clearly and precisely what you will be arguing. The claim must not be vague.

Vague claim:

Parents of children who play hockey would like to see fighting eliminated from the game at all levels.

Is this claim specific? Although it is arguable and has an opposing viewpoint, it is not specific enough to suggest the kind of argument to follow or even if the essay will be focused on argument rather than exposition: *parents*, *would like to see*, and *at all levels* are vague. Also, the phrase *eliminated from the game at all levels* does not seem connected to the rest of the claim. What has this got to do with the parents who presumably don't like seeing their children fight? An expanded thesis statement can help make the claim more specific (see Chapter 6). In the following revised thesis statement, the claim is expressed more clearly through specific words as well as the inclusion of main points. As well, *should* clearly reveals a policy claim.

More specific argumentative claim:

Fighting should be prohibited in hockey, since violence gives young hockey players a negative role model and reinforces a "win at all costs" mentality.

Although precise wording helps make a claim more specific, it is often a good idea, as mentioned above, to follow the claim by defining concepts central to your argument. In the claim above, the writer might define what is meant by *fighting*. Does a fight start when the hockey gloves are dropped, or when there is excessive physical contact, or when a third player joins in? Definition enables the writer to narrow the topic, to make it more specific.

An "all or none" kind of claim is also non-specific. Where your claim is too broad, you should either use qualifiers to restrict its scope or reword it to make it more realistic. Qualifiers include words such as *usually*, *often*, *sometimes*, *in part*, *many*, *some*, *several*, *a few*, and many others. In addition, you can use verbs and verb phrases that qualify and limit, such as *contribute to*, *may*, *play a role in*, and *seems*.

Interesting Claims

To be interesting (as well as specific), a claim should be drafted with a specific audience in mind. Who in your opinion might be interested in the topic but not share your viewpoint?

Is this claim interesting? To be interesting, a claim should be drafted with a specific audience in mind. In the claim about fighting in hockey, the intended audience is hockey parents as well as minor hockey coaches, managers, and other leaders, people who can make changes. Many die-hard fans of professional hockey would not be interested in the main point of the argument, as it applies mostly to children. Those who never watch hockey or don't have children playing hockey probably would be even less interested. Similarly, an argument how best to prevent eutrophication and growth of single-celled algae in China's lakes and reservoirs might be interesting to biologists, but probably not to the average reader.

Along with audience interest, also consider the viewpoint of your audience. Are most people to whom the argument is addressed likely to agree with you? Disagree? Be neutral? Will they possess general knowledge of the topic? Is the topic a current one that most will have heard of? These kinds of questions will be even more relevant when you come to structure your essay and support your claim. For example, if your audience will include many opponents of your claim, it may be important to establish **common ground** and to convince them that you have similar values and goals. See Rebutting the Opposing View, on page 188, for specific audience strategies.

Establishing common ground is a strategy in argument to show an opponent that you share common concerns or basic values.

Manageable Claims

Although the manageability of a claim will be determined partly by whether it is specific and interesting, it will also depend on the essay's length, what support is available, and the complexity of the issues raised by the claim.

Factors in manageable claims include essay length, support available, complexity of the topic, and practicality of the claim.

Policy claims, which try to persuade people to take action, go beyond simply proving something is bad or unfair. Often needed are realistic solutions or at least suggestions that these kinds of solutions exist. Is the proposal realistic? To say that a government should increase funding to post-secondary education by 25 per cent is probably not realistic. If the change you propose isn't realistic, it may be best to change your claim to one of value or else reword it. Your supporting points may be complex, but the thesis statement itself must be workable and clear to the reader.

The claim about hockey violence was found to be arguable, specific, and interesting (to its intended audience), but is it *manageable*?

> Fighting should be prohibited in hockey, since violence gives young hockey players a negative role model and reinforces a "win at all costs" mentality.

It would be too complex and unmanageable to address banning fighting in hockey at both the professional and minor levels. Realistically, would the role model argument motivate the executives of professional hockey to ban fighting? To make the statement manageable, the writer could focus *either* on the way that fights in professional hockey undermine its players as role models *or* on the consequences of fighting in minor hockey.

Remember that all claims need to focus on one main topic, not to straddle two related topics. In addition to being specific, interesting, and manageable, all claims must be focused and clear.

Value claim:

> Fighting in professional hockey gives young hockey players a negative role model since violence reinforces a "win at all costs" mentality.

Reworded policy claim:

> Fighting should be prohibited in minor hockey below the midget level since violence reinforces a "win at all costs" mentality.

A Closer Look at Reason

Two main kinds of reasoning are used in arguments: inductive and deductive reasoning. Using inductive reasoning, you reach a general conclusion based on observable evidence. Using deductive reasoning you reach a conclusion by stating a general principle, the major premise, and applying it to a specific case, the minor premise.

Inductive Reasoning in Practice

Inductive reasoning is sometimes called *scientific reasoning* because scientists and other researchers use it to answer questions about the natural world and make predictions about natural phenomena.

Inductive reasoning is also called scientific reasoning. Scientists often rely on collecting and analyzing specific data to reach a conclusion. We also use inductive reasoning daily to draw conclusions. Consider the following example:

> Recorded observations:
> on June 5 the sun set at 9:16
> on June 6 it set at 9:16
> on June 7 it set at 9:17
> on June 8 it set at 9:17
> on June 9 it set at 9:18
>
> Prediction/Claim:
> on June 10, the sun will set at 9:18

It is possible to make this prediction because we have observed specific data about the setting sun.

If we had simply recorded the times that the sun set on June 5 and 6, we might conclude that the sun would also set at 9:16 on June 7, which would be incorrect: we would be drawing a conclusion without enough evidence. On the other hand, if we made our first set of observations in Edmonton, Alberta, on June 5 and 6 and the second set in Regina, Saskatchewan, on June 7 and 8, the conclusions would also be incorrect because the method for evidence gathering would be flawed.

Two questions to ask yourself when using inductive reasoning are (1) Have I provided enough support for each statement I make? and (2) Have I been logical and consistent in the way I have used reason (my reasoning method)? Several examples of flawed inductive reasoning are illustrated in Table 9.2, pages 178–179—for example, "hasty generalization" and "false cause."

Most research studies focusing on causes and effects, such as clinical trials to confirm the causes of a disease or to test a new drug, work by induction to discover a probable cause or effect.

Logical fallacies in inductive reasoning can develop where

- there is not enough evidence to make a generalization
- the means for gathering the evidence are flawed or biased

Again, a fallacy of this type in an essay can affect your credibility, so it is important to always use sound reasoning and to consider the validity of every statement.

Deductive Reasoning in Practice

The **deductive reasoning** process can be broken down into three parts:

- *major premise:* a general statement of a principle
- *minor premise:* a specific statement about the topic
- *conclusion:* a statement that combines the major premise and the minor premise

Below is an example of a logical argument based on the deductive method.

Major premise: It is wrong not to treat all people with respect.
Minor premise: In building the dam, the Urra company did not treat the indigenous peoples with respect.
Conclusion: The Urra company was wrong to build the dam.

We can see examples of faulty reasoning every day, and, unfortunately, they can have negative consequences. Many forms of stereotyping are based on faulty deductive reasoning.

Major premise: People who spend more than two hours a day at their computers are geeks.
Minor premise: Brandon spends more than two hours a day at his computer.
Conclusion: Brandon is a geek.

Most logical arguments combine inductive and deductive reasoning. Arguing well is a challenge; to succeed, you need to test the logic of your own reasoning as you proceed from one point to the next.

In deductive reasoning, you use a general statement and a specific statement to arrive at a conclusion.

Ask yourself two questions when using deductive reasoning: (1) Does the major premise (general statement) apply to the people or situation described? (2) Is it a valid generalization? Faulty logic, like that used in the example about the sun, weakens your credibility. Several examples of faulty deductive reasoning are illustrated in Table 9.2, pages 178–179—for example, "either/or" and the "tradition" fallacy.

Exercise **9.7**

Detective Work: Read the following short scenarios and analyze how the police reached their decision (i.e., analyze their reasoning methods) or why the investigation failed. How might *inductive* methods have been involved? If inductive methods were flawed, was the problem related to a lack of evidence or faulty methods of evidence gathering? How might *deductive* methods have been involved? If deductive methods were involved, what generalization was used as a major premise?

1. *Scenario:* After a robbery at an expensive and seemingly burglar-proof home, the police investigation settled on two possible suspects. One suspect had been seen near the house near the time of the robbery but had never previously been arrested. The second suspect had not been seen near the house but was unable to account for his movements that night; furthermore, he had two prior robbery convictions. *Result:* Police brought the second man in for questioning.

(continued)

2. *Scenario:* Police believed they would easily be able to determine the suspect of an assault when they discovered blood samples on the floor and wall of the crime scene. But the crime scene officer, who was working on his first case, neglected to prepare the samples correctly, and they deteriorated. *Result*: Police were unable to come up with a suspect.

Rebutting the Opposing View

When you write an argumentative essay, you should present the opposing viewpoint. In the past, you may have been told not to introduce the opposing side, as this could weaken your argument. However, by addressing the other side, you are showing the reader that you are aware of it and that your own points are strong enough to counter your opponent's. In a **rebuttal**, you raise and argue against the points on the other side in order to strengthen your own argument. Your rebuttal may be determined by

The rebuttal is that part of your argument in which you raise the points on the other side, usually in order to strengthen your argument and to appear fair.

- the topic itself
- your audience
- your purpose in arguing

Topic-Based Rebuttal

If the reader is likely familiar with the topic and the major points of debate, it is a good strategy to raise each point and rebut it; see Strategy B: Point-by-Point Rebuttal, below. On the other hand, if your reader knows little about the topic, it may be best to acknowledge only the major counter-argument(s), while ensuring that your points are stronger and more numerous. If the main arguments on the other side are obvious to anyone, however, there may be little point in giving space to them in your essay.

Audience-Based Rebuttal

If your audience is made up of mild opponents and the undecided, it may be wise simply to acknowledge the other side and counter it by a strong argument, employing Strategy A: Acknowledgement. If, however, you are addressing strong opponents, you should acknowledge their side and perhaps even make concessions (see below). An important aspect of rebuttal is to anticipate your opponents' objections. Analyzing the views of your opponent should show that you find them inadequate. Consider using Strategy B: Point-by-Point Rebuttal, then, if your audience strongly opposes your thesis.

Showing how opponents can benefit by agreeing with your thesis is a common argumentative strategy.

Being sensitive to your audience might mean stressing the ways readers can benefit from considering your view. If your topic is a highly charged one, such as providing safe injection sites for drug users, you may begin by arguing your weakest points and work up to your strongest points. This way, you address all types of opponents, from the weaker to the stronger.

Whether the reader is undecided, mildly opposed, or strongly opposed, you should work to establish **common ground**. This can be done by showing that you share basic values with your readers, though you may disagree with the action to be taken. Making **concessions**—partly agreeing with their argument— shows your reasonableness and willingness to compromise.

Purpose-Based Rebuttal

The primary goal of an argumentative essay is not always to win the argument, and an argument should not be judged successful only when it silences the opposition. An argument may be an opportunity to engage in dialogue with others who share your concern about the topic, to enable your reader to see another side or dimension of an issue in order to view it with greater tolerance. Long-lasting change can often result when the arguer is open and flexible, while a "pin the opponent" approach may result in nothing more than a fleeting victory. The open approach to arguing can be particularly effective with value-based claims.

Two Strategies for Rebuttal

Strategy A: Acknowledgement

Acknowledging the other side is important in most arguments. In cases where you need only acknowledge the opposition, you will have to decide how much space to devote to this. In the following example, student writer Laura Benard briefly characterizes the opposing viewpoint by using only a prepositional phrase ("Despite their aesthetic value") ahead of her thesis statement. She presents no real rebuttal but treats the opposing argument, that people use pesticides to make their lawn look attractive, as obvious:

> Despite their aesthetic value, the negative impacts of maintaining lawns by means of pesticide, lawn mower, and water use are so great that lawn owners should adopt less intensive maintenance practices or consider lawn alternatives.

A writer will often put the acknowledgement in the form of a dependent clause that contains the less important (opposing) information, followed by his or her own claim expressed in an independent clause. "Although some may argue . . . [major point of opposition argument], the fact is/I believe that . . . [your thesis]."

It is often necessary to provide background for the reader or a brief summary of the opposing view. In such cases, the writer can begin with this view, then follow with his or her own argument. To decide how much space to spend on the opposing view, consider how objective you want to appear versus the importance of presenting a strong argument of your own.

When you establish common ground, you show that you and your opponent share basic values; using this strategy may make opponents believe your side and theirs are not far apart.

When you make a concession or concede a point, you acknowledge its validity. Doing so enables you to come across as fair and reasonable. Arguers often concede a minor point in order to follow with a strong point of their own.

A concise method of acknowledging your opponent is to summarize the argument in a phrase or dependent clause and follow with your own summarized thesis in an independent clause.

When you give background information or summarize the opposing view, make sure you use an objective tone and neutral language. It is a good idea to summarize as concisely as possible while stating that side's points clearly and fairly.

Strategy B: Point-by-Point Rebuttal

You should address several of the strongest points on the other side if they have strong support or if your purpose is to arrive at a compromise or find common ground. In both cases, you would raise individual points, usually beginning with the opponent's point, and then responding to the weaknesses in the opponent's position. If your purpose is to win the argument, you will stress the opposing arguments' inadequacies and inconsistencies, and draw attention to any fallacies. If your purpose is to find common ground, you will still point out the weaknesses in the opposing viewpoint, but in the form of helpful, constructive criticism. In both cases, though, your voice should be unbiased and objective.

In the excerpt below, student writer Spencer Cleave addresses a common argument supporting the US embargo against Cuba. After a concession (italicized below), he introduces two counter-claims, developed in the succeeding paragraph, that attempt to undercut the original claim:

> Many supporters of the maintenance of the trade embargo against Cuba contend that the Cuban government fails to uphold the human rights of its population. *It is true that Cuba has had a number of human rights violations in its past. Thus, it is conceded that Cuba is also morally at fault on certain issues.* However, many reforms have recently been made by the government in an attempt to remedy its human rights problems. These efforts show that the government has a desire to improve the conditions within its own nation. Furthermore, it would be in the best interest of the US to applaud the Cuban government in any human rights improvements, thus giving the image of a co-operative partner.

Because the opponents of your topic may have a strong and often-debated case, you may choose to address the main points of their argument systematically, summarizing these points and refuting them with facts and statistics. Such would be the case with some environmentalists who have been vocal in their public opposition to wind farms. David Suzuki responds to their claims systematically throughout his essay. Suzuki also uses emotional appeals, concessions, and appeals to common ground (see page 194).

As mentioned earlier, argument is important in all aspects of our lives. The case study that follows is adapted from an information campaign of a medical service company in response to a government decision to restructure the company's services. Although the form of the argument is very different from that of an essay, notice that the necessary parts of an argument are included and that also in other ways it conforms to the basic argumentative model discussed above. Numbers and letters have been added to show its outline structure.

If you use a point-by-point rebuttal, you do not have to respond to *all* your opponent's points. In shorter essays, you may not have the space to rebut any more than one point. As well, the opposing side might have only one strong argument, in which case it would be counterproductive to mention other points.

CASE STUDY

"Please Sign Our Petition": A Case Study

We Need Your Support! Please Sign Our Petition

The government plans to fundamentally change how laboratory services are delivered. These plans jeopardize the lab services you depend on.

These plans could also compromise one of the best lab systems there is—one that has been serving patients in communities across our province for more than 45 years.

I. What the Government Is Planning:

A.	B.	C.
It has already announced a 20 per cent cut in the fees it pays to community labs for the testing services we provide.	It is planning to dismantle the existing province-wide system and create six independent lab delivery systems—one within each of the health authorities.	It is planning to establish a bidding process that would see each health authority going to tender for all outpatient lab services.

II. What This Means to Patient Care:

A.	B.	C.
1. Alone, the magnitude of the fee cuts will affect patients and patient care. 2. The government's other plans will bring a period of complete instability, turning today's system upside down.	The government's plans will result in six fragmented systems—potentially providing six levels of service and access—and six new bureaucracies to manage them.	Applying a competitive bidding process to laboratory medicine comes at a very high risk. Price is always a major factor in any competitive bidding process, and lowest bids come with reduced access service levels.

As with most arguments, the claim is announced early. It is a policy claim, as the reader is asked to take an action—sign a petition. However, it is based on a value claim, that government plans could "compromise one of the best lab systems." To support this, the company cites facts and statistics in the bulleted list, showing that the labs provide essential services.

The argument begins by summarizing three points of the opposing position. Systematically, the points are refuted in the next two sections. For example, point A is countered by two points under What This Means to Patient Care (point A). The argument is developed through cause and effect: a 20 per cent cut (cause) will affect patients and patient care.

(continued)

In addition to countering the major points of the government's argument, the company is concerned with establishing its credibility. Topic II addresses patient care, focusing concern directly on the reader. Topic III Point C attempts to find common ground in an effort to show fairness to the government side: *We fully support the government's goals.*

Section IV serves as a conclusion to the argument. The information in points A, B, and C, in effect, summarize the claim by rewording it: in the claim/thesis, the phrase *jeopardize the lab services you depend on* is used; compare—*affect lab services and service levels, value the services we provide,* and *protecting the lab services you rely on.* Point C makes an emotional appeal with its deliberate choice of the words *care* and *protect.*

III. Our Concerns:

A.
The government based its plans on flawed, faulty, and unsubstantiated data.

B.
We don't understand why the government chose to dismantle a system that works well, instead of building on its strengths.

C.
We fully support the government's goals. However, we don't agree with the way it is trying to achieve these goals.

IV. What We've Done

A.

1. We've told the government repeatedly that we support its goals and can help them achieve them. We've told the government to put its plans on hold so that we can talk to them about less disruptive alternatives.

2. We've told patients and physicians about the government's plans and how they could affect lab services and service levels.

What We're Doing Now

B.

1. We're asking people who value the services we provide to show their support by signing our petition.

2. If you want to know more about the government's plans and our concerns, please visit our website.

C. If you care about protecting the lab services you rely on—please sign our petition.

Community lab facts [statistical evidence to back the claim]:
- For more than 45 years, physicians and their patients have relied on the quality cost-effective diagnostic testing and information services community labs provide.
- The testing and information services we provide help doctors diagnose, treat, and monitor their patients.
- Every day, the 1,600 people working in community labs
  - provide a selection of several hundred different tests, from routine to specialty diagnostics.
  - support early discharge hospital programs by providing access to lab testing at home and in the community.

- perform more than 55,000 tests on the 16,000 patients who visit one of our labs.

- visit more than 700 patients in their homes and in long-term care facilities, at no charge to the patient or health-care system.

- deliver more than 5,000 specimens to public testing agencies at no cost to the patient, agency, or health-care system.

- transmit lab results electronically via Path NET to more than 3,000 physicians.

- support our services through an extensive collection and transportation network, information technology, and analytical expertise that's taken years to develop.

Exercise **9.8**

In collaborative groups or individually, analyze the case study above and evaluate its effectiveness, using the questions below as guidelines.

1. Consider your own position towards the issues. Do you have any knowledge about this or similar issues relating to government decisions about health care (or education)? How do government decisions affect you and/or other consumers of these kinds of services? What are the sides of the debate? Which side do you support? How might your prior knowledge and opinions affect your response to this argument or others like it?

2. Is there anything that would have made the argument more effective? Be as specific as possible.

3. Are there any questionable appeals to emotion or ethics? Are there any logical fallacies? Why do you think the company does not give specific information in main point III sub-point A: "The government based its plans on flawed, faulty, and unsubstantiated data"?

4. Analyze the refutation, bearing in mind topic, audience, and purpose. Why do the authors employ strategy B to refute the three points mentioned in the first main point (I), which gives background about the government's position?

5. What specific changes would you make if you were writing this argument as a formal essay? In what ways does it differ from a formal essay? (See Chapter 17 for some of the characteristics of informal writing.)

(continued)

6. Imagine that one year has passed. The government is proceeding with its plans; some lab employees have lost their jobs, and there are dire predictions in newspaper editorials that our health care will be directly affected. How do you think the company's argument will change in response? Write a revised claim that reflects the new current conditions. Choose one specific form: informal brochure for distribution, letter to the editor/editorial, or argumentative essay.

❭ Sample Professional Argumentative Essay

In the following essay, noted scientist and environmentalist David Suzuki argues for wind turbines. Note his use of point-by-point rebuttal and many other rebuttal strategies discussed in this chapter.

SAMPLE PROFESSIONAL ARGUMENTATIVE ESSAY

The Beauty of Wind Farms

by David Suzuki

> Suzuki makes an emotional appeal in his introduction, describing an idyllic scene; however, in the last sentence, he uses an unexpected statement to get the reader's attention.

[1] Off the coast of British Columbia in Canada is an island called Quadra, where I have a cabin that is as close to my heart as you can imagine. From my porch on a good day you can see clear across the waters of Georgia Strait to the snowy peaks of the rugged Coast Mountains. It is one of the most beautiful views I have seen. And I would gladly share it with a wind farm.

> Here Suzuki discusses the opposition to wind farms, and in the next paragraph he offers his rebuttal.

[2] But sometimes it seems like I'm in the minority. All across Europe and North America, environmentalists are locking horns with the wind industry over the location of wind farms. In Alberta, one group is opposing a planned wind farm near Cypress Hills Provincial Park, claiming it would destroy views of the park and disturb some of the last remaining native prairie in the province. In the UK, more than 100 national and local groups, led by some of the country's most prominent environmentalists, have argued that wind power is inefficient, destroys the ambience of the countryside and makes little difference to carbon emissions. And in the US, the Cape Wind Project, which would site 130 wind turbines off the coast of affluent Cape Cod, Massachusetts, has come under fire from famous liberals, including Senator Edward Kennedy and Walter Cronkite.

[3] It is time for some perspective. With the growing urgency of climate change, we cannot have it both ways. We cannot shout from the rooftops about the dangers of global warming and then turn around and shout even louder about the "dangers" of windmills. Climate change is one of the greatest challenges humanity will face this century. It cannot be solved through good intentions. It will take a radical change in the way we produce and consume energy—another industrial revolution, this time for clean energy, conservation and efficiency.

> In this paragraph, the writer introduces the logic behind his argument.

[4] We have undergone such transformations before, and we can do it again. But first we must accept that all forms of energy have associated costs. Fossil fuels are limited in quantity and create vast amounts of pollution. Large-scale hydroelectric power floods valleys and destroys animal habitat. Nuclear power is terribly expensive and creates radioactive waste.

> Here Suzuki uses an appeal to common ground.

> In this paragraph, Suzuki offers factual summaries to bolster his argument.

[5] Wind power also has its downsides. It is highly visible and can kill birds. The fact is, though, that any man-made structure can kill birds—houses, radio towers, skyscrapers. In Toronto alone, it is estimated that 10,000 birds collide with the city's tallest buildings every year. Compared with this, the risk to birds from well-sited wind farms is very low.

> Suzuki begins the paragraph by offering a concession (wind farms kill birds), following it with a rebuttal (other structures kill *more* birds). In the next paragraph, he acknowledges that the opposition does have valid points by making another concession. He shows his understanding that not all his audience agrees with him.

[6] Even at Altamont Pass in California, where 7000 turbines were erected on a migratory route, only 0.2 birds per turbine per year have been killed. Indeed, the real risk to birds comes not from windmills but from a changing climate, which threatens the very existence of bird species and their habitats. This is not to say that wind farms should be allowed to spring up anywhere. They should always be subject to environmental impact assessments. But a blanket "not in my backyard" approach is hypocritical and counterproductive.

> Here Suzuki uses statistics to show that his opponents' argument is not as strong as his.

[7] Pursuing wind power as part of our move towards clean energy makes sense. It is the fastest-growing source of energy in the world—a $6 billion industry last year. Its cost has dropped dramatically over the past two decades because of larger turbines and greater knowledge of how to build, install and operate turbines more effectively. Prices will likely decrease further as the technology improves.

> Now that the writer has acknowledged the opposition, he moves on to support his argument by facts and statistics.

[8] Are windmills ugly? I remember when Mostafa Tolba, executive director of the United Nations Environment Programme from 1976 to 1992, told me how when he was growing up in Egypt, smokestacks belching out smoke were considered signs of progress. Even as an adult concerned about pollution, it took him a long time to get over the instinctive pride he felt when he saw a tower pouring out clouds of smoke.

> In these two paragraphs, Suzuki uses comparison to convince the reader of the validity of his viewpoint.

(continued)

[9] We see beauty through filters shaped by our values and beliefs. Some people think wind turbines are ugly. I think smokestacks, smog, acid rain, coal-fired power plants and climate change are ugly. I think windmills are beautiful. They harness the power of the wind to supply us with heat and light. They provide local jobs. They help clean our air and reduce climate change.

> Suzuki's conclusion returns us to his first paragraph, playing on the hypocritical saying "not in my backyard."

[10] And if one day I look out from my cabin's porch and see a row of windmills spinning in the distance, I won't curse them. I will praise them. It will mean we are finally getting somewhere.

David Suzuki is a scientist, environmentalist, broadcaster, author and chair of the David Suzuki Foundation (www.davidsuzuki.org).

—Suzuki, D. (2005). The beauty of wind farms. *New Scientist, 186* (2495), 20–21.
© 2005 Reed Business Information—UK.
All rights reserved. Distributed by Tribune Media Services.

Post-reading Questions

1. Does the author use inductive or deductive reasoning? Support your answer.
2. Is Suzuki's rebuttal about other structures killing more birds effective? Why or why not?
3. Who do you think makes up most of Suzuki's audience? Why do you believe this?
4. The author states, "I believe windmills are beautiful." Do you think this statement of opinion bolsters or detracts from his argument? Why?
5. Even if you disagree with the author, do you believe he has made this essay interesting?

〉 Organizing an Outline for Argument

When outlining and drafting an argumentative essay, you should pay attention to the order of your main points. Ensure that they are ordered logically in a way that suits your argument. Recall from Chapter 2 the different ways to order your points:

- *climax order:* least important to most important
- *inverted climax:* most important to least important
- *mixed order:* strong point, then weaker point, then strongest point

Table 9.3 provides a template that you can follow to organize an argumentative essay, based on the classical five-part argumentative model. You do not have to include all the elements listed there; for example, it may not be necessary to include background if the issue is well known to most readers. Also, you can put the elements in a different order. Of course, in your own essay, you may allot more than one paragraph for any of these areas, especially for "lines of argument."

If you include a rebuttal, it may not need much space. Depending on the topic and other factors, you might choose to place it before your main points. If you use strategy A to acknowledge the other side, you could do that in either the Introduction or the Background section. With strategy B, you could begin a point-by-point rebuttal in the first or second body paragraph.

The order of your points is often vital to argument. In the climax order, you begin with your weakest point, saving the strongest point for your final body paragraph. In the often-used mixed order, you begin with a moderately strong point, follow with a weaker one, and conclude with the strongest.

TABLE 9.3	Argumentative Essay Template
Introduction	• gain reader's attention and interest
	• include your claim
	• suggest the primary developmental method (if there is one)
	• establish your credibility (knowledge, reliability, and fairness)
Body paragraph 1: Background	• present background information, if relevant
Body paragraph 2: Lines of argument	• present good reasons (logical, emotional, and ethical appeals) in support of thesis
	• use all relevant evidence—facts, statistics, examples, views of experts/authorities
	• present reasons in specific order related to argument
Body paragraph 3: Rebuttal	• consider opposing points of view
	• note both advantages and disadvantages of opposing views; may use concessions or common ground
	• argue that your thesis is stronger than opposing view and more beneficial to the reader
Conclusion	• summarize argument
	• expand or elaborate on the implication of your thesis
	• make clear what you want the reader to think or do
	• possibly make final strong ethical or emotional appeal

Exercise **9.9**

From the following topics, choose one for which you can prepare an outline using the template above, narrowing the topic down if necessary. Make sure you choose a position that you can argue with a value or policy claim; do not create an expository essay with a factual claim. If possible, conduct some research before creating the outline and include relevant quotations or paraphrases in your outline.

1. bullying
2. communication
3. physical activity among teens
4. recycling programs
5. social networking sites
6. technology in schools
7. civics courses
8. space exploration
9. salaries of sports celebrities or CEOs
10. nuclear weapons

❯ Sample Student Argumentative Essay

This argumentative student essay uses minimal research. For examples of argumentative essays that use little or no cited research, see pages 59, 105, and 194.

To conserve space, the essay is not double spaced and the References section is not on separate pages. The essay does not follow correct essay format requirements for title pages or identification information. For the correct ways of dealing with these issues, see Chapter 17, Essay Presentation, page 469.

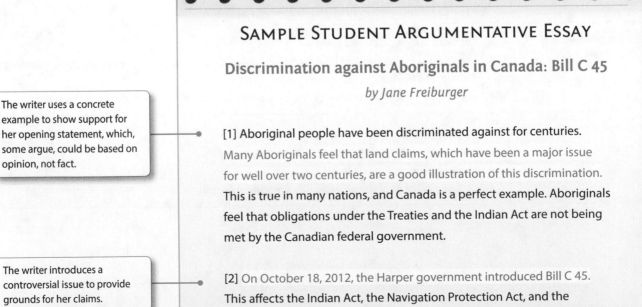

SAMPLE STUDENT ARGUMENTATIVE ESSAY

Discrimination against Aboriginals in Canada: Bill C 45

by Jane Freiburger

The writer uses a concrete example to show support for her opening statement, which, some argue, could be based on opinion, not fact.

[1] Aboriginal people have been discriminated against for centuries. Many Aboriginals feel that land claims, which have been a major issue for well over two centuries, are a good illustration of this discrimination. This is true in many nations, and Canada is a perfect example. Aboriginals feel that obligations under the Treaties and the Indian Act are not being met by the Canadian federal government.

The writer introduces a controversial issue to provide grounds for her claims.

[2] On October 18, 2012, the Harper government introduced Bill C 45. This affects the Indian Act, the Navigation Protection Act, and the

Environmental Assessment Act. These changes have angered many Aboriginal people as they believe that more laws and legislation that will further erode treaty and indigenous rights and the rights of all Canadians (News C., 9 questions about Idle No More, 2013). Many Aboriginals feel that this bill discriminates against them by taking the decision-making powers away from them, showing that non-aboriginals know what was best for them, which is discrimination.

[3] Bill C 45 alters the Indian Act which includes changes to land management on reserves, making it easier for the federal government to control reserve land (Gotz, 2012). Bill C 45 also alters the Navigable Waters Protection Act. This Act was used to protect 2.5 million rivers and lakes and now only covers 97 lakes and 62 rivers. This leaves rivers, lakes and oceans vulnerable to exploitation and it leads the way to mining and the controversial Enbridge Northern Gateways pipeline to move forward (Fotheringham, 2013). Again, this alteration is felt to be discrimination, as the people who live on these lands will not be consulted before their lives are disrupted.

> The author uses a fact to support her argument.

[4] In order to protest this loss of rights, many Aboriginals and non-aboriginals participated in the "Idle No More" campaign in order to bring awareness of the latest issue of discrimination to the Canadian public. Unfortunately, both Prime Minister Stephen Harper and the media added to the discrimination issue. During this protest, Prime Minister Stephen Harper typified Aboriginals as arrogant imperialists and denied that colonization exists. Minorities have always been a focus of the media, particularly framing them as the problem. It is part of the way the news is created rather than it being the people who carry personal prejudices. This type of structural discrimination is not intentional, but it is harmful (Kunz, 2013). In the Idle No More protest, this message was very apparent, supporting the Aboriginal claim of discrimination.

> Again, the writer uses facts to support her argument.

[5] Among the non-aboriginal population, there is a clear misunderstanding of what the Aboriginals are trying to attain. A recent poll from Ipsos Reid found that about two-thirds of Canadians believe Canada's Aboriginal people's received too much support from federal taxpayers, they believe that Aboriginal peoples are treated well by the government and most of the problems native people face are brought on by themselves. On the other hand the poll also found that two-thirds of

> The writer begins with a controversial statement, but then quickly supports it with research.

(continued)

Canadians believe the federal government must act now to improve life of Canada's Aboriginal peoples (Akin, 2013). This poll shows the ignorance on the part of most Canadians, and adds to the discrimination that exists.

[6] Discrimination is an ugly aspect of any society, but it is even more disturbing when it is perpetuated by world leaders and the media. Aboriginal people in Canada have suffered through discrimination for far too long, and they have had far too many rights taken away. The Idle No More protest was their way of standing up and fighting back against the "others" in society who believe that they know better than the troublemakers in society. In order to stop this problem in society, people need to stop listening to those in authority and start studying the issues on their own.

References

Akin, D. (2013, January 15). Idle No More: Canadian public opinion set against First Nations protesters. Retrieved from *Toronto Sun*: http://www.torontosun.com/2013/01/15/idle-no-more-canadian-public-opinion-set-against-first-nations-protesters

Fotheringham, N. (2013, January 5). Canada's Bill C-45 reduces protected waterways from 2.5 million to 62 rivers and 97 lakes. Retrieved from GreenMoxie: http://www.greenmoxie.com/canadas-bill-c-45-reduces-protected-waterways-from-2-5-million-to-62-rivers-and-97-lakes/

Kunz, F. a. (2013). Newscasting: "Problematizing" Minorities. In U. o. Waterloo, Centre For Extended Learning SOCWK 301 R (p. 38). Waterloo: The University of Waterloo Book Store and Media.doc.

News, C. (2013, January 5). 9 questions about Idle No More. Retrieved from CBC News Canada: http://www.cbc.ca/news/canada/story/2013/01/04/f-idlenomore-faq.html

Post-reading Questions

1. How does the author of this piece establish her credibility?
2. Can you find any examples of the fallacies listed in Table 9.2 in this essay?
3. How does the author gain your attention in this essay?
4. Does the author argue a value, a policy, or a claim in this essay?
5. Which type of order does the author use for organizing this essay?

❯ Oral Presentations

An oral presentation is often based on argument. You are trying to convince your audience that your point of view is a valid one, so you will need to use the same organizational patterns as if you were creating an argument essay.

While in school, you may be asked to present information to your class, which can be based on an essay you have written, or which may be about another topic entirely. Oral presentations, while challenging, are good practice for the workplace, as many proposals or reports result in oral presentations. For example, you may have found a new way to increase productivity and you want the company to allow you time to research it. Your boss may ask you to present your proposed study to a group of directors. Often the most efficient way to do this is orally, so you will have to present your rationale, proposed timeline, and hypothesis. Most often, this information will be accompanied by visuals, such as a PowerPoint presentation. There are guidelines for creating effective presentations, and these same guidelines apply to classroom presentations as well.

Oral presentations are often used in the workplace to present new ideas to a large audience.

Creating a Presentation

The most important consideration for any oral presentation is the amount of time you have to speak. Often, for meetings, you will be given a brief time slot, but other times, such as when presenting a report, you will be given more time, such as 30 minutes. Make sure you use this time wisely. If your presentation is too short, your audience will wonder, at best, what you have left out, and, at worst, what you have missed and how much you really know about the topic. If the presentation is too long, you risk your audience becoming bored and tuning you out before you make all your key points. In addition, a too-long presentation at work will probably make the meeting run longer, which no one wants. As well, many workplace presentations need to allow time at the end for questions, so plan accordingly. Classroom presentations, on the other hand, often do not have this requirement.

Good presenters are well organized, and they make sure the audience can clearly follow their ideas.

Oral presentations are unlike a written document, where the reader can go back over a point that may have been misread or misinterpreted. Listeners do not have that luxury, so make sure your points are clear and precise. Also, make sure they are ordered in a logical way, such as from the least important to the most important. To help your audience clearly understand your presentation, be sure to include transitions or markers to draw their attention to a point. When using an illustration, use a marker such as *for example*. When moving to new points, use words such as *additionally* or *on the other hand*. For the most important point, make sure you clearly indicate this to the audience with a marker such as *the most important aspect*. Successful use of these transitions or markers will help the audience clearly understand your movement from point to point.

When making an oral presentation based on research, remember that less is more. Present only your most important information with illustrations. For example, if you are presenting a report, spend time explaining the background information, but do not delve into details, such listing other studies on the same topic. For example, if you are presenting a report about the rise of the concept of multi-tasking, you might discuss how this has evolved since the 1980s and the advent of the personal computer. However, in an oral presentation, you may not go much further nor list all the articles you reviewed to reach your analysis of the evolution. Move on to discussing some of your methods of study, such as how you chose a specific group to study, but again omit detail. Again, if you are studying students' ability to multi-task, you would tell the audience your basic criteria for choosing students, such as age, years of study at the school, and perhaps their majors, but you can leave out other criteria such as cultural background or hobbies. You will want to focus most of your time on the findings of the study, and this is where visuals are extremely helpful. You can use charts and graphs to make your findings stand out for the audience. You may want to present a pie graph showing the success rates of those who do and do not multi-task. Leave some time at the end to discuss possible ramifications of this study and where research can continue to build on your findings.

When presenting research, only discuss the most relevant parts of the research.

On the other hand, if you are presenting an essay as an oral presentation, begin with your thesis. This will help the audience orient themselves to the topic. Do not spend time leading up to your thesis, as the audience may not understand when you actually reach your thesis. After this, present the main points from your essay with brief illustrations. If you have a relevant quotation, pause briefly to allow the audience time to absorb it. Remember that they are probably seeing it for the first time and will need to reflect on it to understand its importance. Do not forget to state your conclusion clearly. Unlike in an essay, in a presentation, you can use a marker such as *in conclusion*. This helps your audience understand that you are wrapping up. If you don't use a marker, the audience may not realize the importance of your closing remarks.

Finally, visuals can add a great deal of impact, but only if they are appropriate and not overwhelming. As a general guideline, do not use more than one visual per minute, as the audience needs time to see a visual and to absorb it along with what you are saying.

Keep your visuals simple. When creating visuals, each slide or screen shot should contain a minimal amount of information. For example, you can use the "five by five" rule. There should be no more than five lines of text and each line should have no more than five words. Of course, if you use a quotation, it should be on a slide by itself. If you are using graphs or pie charts, include only the most relevant data. Do not create a pie chart that has more than five segments, as the audience will not be able to differentiate the segments on a more complicated chart. Put only one chart or graph on each slide (with relevant documentation if the data is not from your own research).

When creating visuals, less is better.

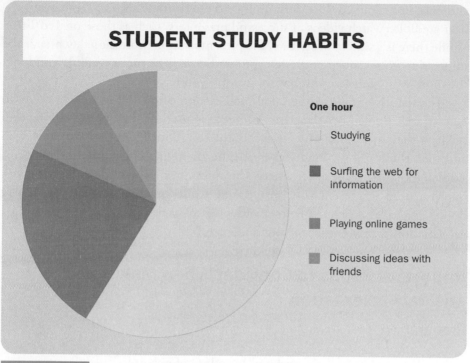

STUDENT STUDY HABITS

One hour

- Studying
- Surfing the web for information
- Playing online games
- Discussing ideas with friends

FIGURE 9.1 Sample slide of a pie chart graphic

While oral presentations can be stressful, if you remember the guidelines you should be able to create a successful one.

Delivering a Presentation

Many studies have shown that, in business, the people who communicate effectively are the ones who receive promotions. Use oral presentations as a stage for your abilities.

It is important to practise before you get up in front of the audience. Nerves play an important role in the success or failure of a presentation. For example, when you practise the presentation on your own, you are probably more relaxed than when standing in front of an audience. Therefore, you are probably speaking more slowly. Many a student has timed a presentation at home only to find it is much shorter when presented to the class. If you find you are speaking too quickly while presenting, pause, take a deep breath, and slow down.

Of course, the other problem many presenters face is forgetting their material. This is another reason why practice is important. The more familiar you are with your material, the less likely you are to forget it. It is a good idea to memorize the first few lines of your presentation; you can make a positive first impression by establishing eye contact with your audience, which is vital if you want to keep your audience engaged.

When planning for your oral presentation, how you look is also important. Dress for success. You may not need to wear a suit, but if you appear before your

Knowing your material and being able to engage the audience are essential for success.

audience in a rumpled shirt, torn jeans, and old running shoes, you may not appear credible. Watch videos of successful presenters, such as those on Ted Talks. While there is a variety of style, all the presenters look professional, which is the impression you want to create for your audience. The more credible you look, the more your audience will believe in what you have to say.

The success or failure of an oral presentation often lies in the work you do beforehand. Remember that your audience is used to slick presentations everywhere they turn. Think of the successful YouTube videos that you have seen and then think of how long you watch the amateurish or poorly done videos. Audiences expect to be entertained. This does not mean you have to tell jokes, but you need to present your material in a relevant, meaningful way. If you do this, and if you practise beforehand, you are well on your way to creating a presentation that will interest your audience.

Important Points to Consider When Making an Oral Presentation

Preparation

- Know your material and practise a lot beforehand.
- Make notes to help you remember the key points and organizational structure of your topic.
- Create clear, easy to see visuals with necessary citations.
- Check your visuals for errors.
- Practise your presentation out loud and time it.
- Decide when you will address any questions that are asked. Will you encourage the audience to ask questions as they think of them, or would you prefer them to ask at the end of the presentation?
- Choose clothes that are appropriate for your audience.

Delivery

- Speak slowly and clearly. Make sure you are loud enough for everyone in the room to hear what you are saying.
- Let the audience know when you will address questions.
- Allow your audience time to read your visuals, but do not read them word for word yourself.
- Discuss only relevant details.
- Watch your audience for signs of engagement and adjust to them. For example, if they did not seem to really understand a point, expand on it. If they look bored, move on to a new point.
- Address all questions from the audience.
- Thank your audience for their time at the end of your presentation.
- Keep within your time limit.

■ Chapter Review Questions

1. Why is it important to understand your audience?

2. How does formal prose differ from informal prose? Are there times when one is more appropriate than the other?

3. What is the difference between reader-based prose and writer-based prose?

4. Why is it important to have a clear purpose in mind when writing?

5. What are some questions you can ask to determine audience knowledge and interest?

6. What are the different ways you can begin writing your essay? Which one is most effective for you?

7. What are the five stages in essay writing? Why are they all important?

8. What are you asked to do for a critical response assignment?

9. What acronym can you use when revising your final draft?

10. How can revising your draft improve your essay?

11. How do essays and oral presentations differ?

12. Why is it important to use simple visuals?

13. When delivering oral presentations, what are some key points to remember?

14. How can you prove to your oral presentation audience that you know your information?

15. Why is timing important when giving oral presentations?

10 Summarizing Other Writers' Work

In this chapter, you will

- learn the difference between a summary, a paraphrase, an abstract, and an annotated bibliography
- discover the steps used in writing a summary
- learn how to paraphrase
- learn how to create an annotated bibliography

In college and university classes, students are often asked to summarize or to paraphrase another author's work. This material can then be integrated into your essay, which can add variety and credibility to your writing. This chapter will help you learn how to write effective summaries and paraphrases. In addition, you will learn how to use and write abstracts and annotated bibliographies.

> What Is a Summary?

A summary is a short overview or outline of a longer piece of writing. You can write a summary of a sentence, a paragraph, an entire essay, or a long report. Throughout your time at college or university, instructors will often ask you to write an extended summary of an article or a passage from a textbook to ensure you understand the writer's ideas. This type of exercise can also help you develop both reading and writing skills.

The summary

- accurately reflects the original
- includes the main idea(s) of the original
- does not add anything that wasn't in the original
- is in your own words

When you write an essay, you might include a short summary of another writer's work for several reasons:

- to use a source's main idea(s) as background information
- to set up a point of your own (to show how it is similar to or different from the other writer's position, for example)
- to explain the other writer's position as it relates to your thesis

When summarizing, you are acting partly on behalf of the original writer. Careful representation of these ideas is a sign of a good summary.

You may already have experience writing summaries. When writing essays in the past, you may have concluded by summarizing your thesis and main points.

In the student essay "What is leadership?" in Chapter 8, the author summarizes his definition of leadership in the concluding paragraph. (The paragraph is broken down into separate sentences here.)

Leadership is the co-ordination of people, resources, and tasks towards the completion of a goal.

> The author restates his definition using wording that is different from that used earlier in the essay.

Leadership can be demonstrated in many situations, from a doctor trying to save a life in the ER to a university teacher to a military commander.

> The author gives relevant examples referred to in the essay to illustrate his thesis.

Although leadership is often provided by qualified, educated persons, it may sometimes arise from unlikely sources.

> The author reinforces yet another aspect of his thesis, again using different words.

Regardless, leadership is a skill that can be developed through experience and education.

> After an appropriate transition, the author concludes with his belief, which has been stated earlier.

Summary writing skills are used both in essays and for stand-alone exercises. Your instructor may ask you to summarize an essay you have read. You may

> Although you may have experience summarizing your thesis and main points in your own essays, an important college or university writing skill is learning the steps in summarizing the ideas of other writers.

also be asked to complete various summaries and construct an annotated bibliography in writing a research paper. In addition, a well-written essay often includes paragraph summaries rather than direct quotations (which are discussed in Chapter 12). All of these activities have one thing in common: you are presenting your audience with someone else's ideas. However, you are doing this in your own words, so you must first clearly understand the material you are summarizing.

It is important that you understand terminology used at the college and university level. While some of the terms presented below may seem to overlap, you need to recognize the differences between summary and paraphrase so that you provide your instructor with what he or she wants.

Terms Related to Summarizing

In general, a **summary** is the rephrasing of somebody else's ideas. A summary is always shorter than the original and must be mostly or completely in your own words.

A paraphrase is the rephrasing of someone else's ideas completely in your own words; however, unlike a summary, it is close to the length of the original.

An abstract is an overview of your purpose, methods, and results. It is often found at the beginning of a journal article, such as those found on the databases in your school library.

An annotated bibliography is an *expanded* bibliography (*annotate* means "to note"). It concisely summarizes similar works in the field of study.

Paraphrases, abstracts, and annotated bibliographies are discussed in more detail beginning on page 219.

How to Write a Summary

Summaries may seem intimidating if you haven't written one before. However, the book reports you wrote when you were younger are very similar to what you will be doing when writing a summary. The main difference though is that you will not be adding an analysis of what you have read, so you will not be recommending anything at the end of a summary.

A well-written summary

- accurately reflects the original
- retains the meaning of the original piece
- includes the main idea(s); includes sub-points if it is a longer summary
- omits examples and illustrations, unless very important
- uses the same order as in the original
- does not add anything that was not in the original

A summary is a shorter rephrasing of an original work.

- keeps the relative importance of ideas the same as in the original
- uses concise prose
- is mostly your own words, but you may use some words from the original (though no more than you strictly have to). You *must place quotation marks* around any phrases that you cite directly. If you cite more than *three* consecutive words, you should place them in quotation marks.
- is approximately 10–30 per cent of the length of the original. However, if the work you are summarizing requires more expertise than your audience has, you may occasionally need to write a summary that is longer than 30 per cent. In addition, you may have to add a few transitions to make the summary easy to follow. Add no more than necessary for clarity, however.

Writing a summary need not be a difficult task, as long as you follow the steps below. These apply for a summary of any length.

1. Read the entire work for the first time to learn its purpose, thesis statement, intended audience, purpose, etc. Make sure you pay attention to the title, as this often signals the content of the piece. Headings also indicate main points.
2. Reread the piece, noting its major points. While reading, write these points in your own words to create a summary. The length will depend on how you are using the summary. For example, a quotation may be only a sentence or two long, or you may be required to write an extended summary (discussed on page 213). If you are writing a short summary, make sure you have captured only the most important points.
3. Reread the article and your summary to make sure you have accurately stated the points as the original author intended.
4. Make sure you have used your own words. Do not use the original sentence structures and insert synonyms. This is considered plagiarism, which will be discussed in Chapter 12. Create your own sentence structures.
5. Edit and proofread before you use your summary.

Summary Length

A summary is shorter than the original work. Summary length can range from one sentence to several paragraphs or even several pages; depending on how you use the summary. For example, you may want to summarize an entire paragraph in one sentence, rather than quoting the whole paragraph in your

Summary length is dictated by the intended use. A summary can be as brief as a sentence or two, or can be a longer extended summary.

essay, because the paragraph may include irrelevant material that could distort your purpose and distract your reader. At other times, you may be asked by your instructor (or your boss) to summarize an entire report or lengthy essay in a one-page document to be shared with others. In the examples found in this chapter, you will see summaries of various lengths, accompanied by related exercises.

Summarizing Your Sources

When you summarize from a secondary source, you take the important parts of somebody else's work to use in your own essay. Always ensure that you give credit to your source. During the research stage, it is a good idea to summarize all the main sources you plan to use, as well as to carefully record significant direct quotations. This can save you from having to find the sources again when you begin writing. Summarizing from a book, an article, or an Internet source puts the main points before you when you come to write your essay, enabling you to *demonstrate your understanding of the source and its applicability to your thesis statement.* Summarizing the content of a source also avoids the practice of *too much* direct quotation.

Summaries and Argument

If the purpose of your essay is to persuade its reader, rather than present factual information, you may need to carefully distinguish between fact and opinion. For example, one professional writer began an essay in this way:

> In the course of two years' research for a book on how we think about pain, I've spoken to neurologists, doctors, artists, therapists of every stripe, as well as psychologists—the front-line workers. And frankly, I preferred the people selling healing magnets to most of the psychologists. They were bad communicators. They couldn't make eye contact. They seemed more interested in certain folds in the brain than in helping human beings cope with pain.

> —Jackson, Marni, "Every breath you take: A former hospital pain
> specialist puts his faith in the powers of meditation."
> *Maclean's* 16 August 1999 Print.

If, in such a case, you did not acknowledge the writer's words as opinion, you would seriously misrepresent her:

A distorted summary:

Psychologists generally communicate badly and are shifty-eyed.

However, you could acknowledge the author's argument this way:

Correct:

Marni Jackson preferred "the people selling healing magnets" to the majority of psychologists she spoke to.

Using Signal Phrases

A **signal phrase** can be used to clearly attribute a statement to one or more people. Carefully choose a signal verb that reveals whether the writer is explaining or arguing—verbs like *prefer*, *believe*, *claimed*, and *argued* all suggest opinion, whereas *says*, *states*, *described*, and *found* do not. (Signal phrases are discussed in more detail in Chapter 12.) In using appropriate verbs or phrases like *according to*, you are showing the writer's attitude towards the subject. But do not characterize the writer's stance as negative or assume that the writer has a bias. A summary should *represent*, not judge. The writer may be opinionated; when representing those opinions, you should not express your *own* opinions.

Sample Sentence Summaries

The following summaries show how to condense a paragraph into a sentence or two. This type of summary is useful when you want to include key ideas in your essay but do not want to quote extensively. Bear in mind that your instructor may require more detail.

Sample 1:

Helen Thompson was one of the first women to obtain a Ph.D. from the University of Chicago. Her thesis, *The Mental Traits of Sex* (1903), illustrates the main arguments in the similarities tradition. These include the importance of overlap between genders, the requirement of highest methodological standards to demonstrate difference, the search for social explanations of difference, and the demonstration of the specificity of difference.

—Kimball, M.M. (1994). The worlds we live in: Gender similarities and differences. *Canadian Psychology/Psychologie canadienne, 35*(4), 388–404.

Summary:

Helen Thompson's 1903 thesis, *The Mental Traits of Sex*, shows the importance of scientific and social study of the similarities and differences between men and women.

A signal phrase indicates that what follows is taken from another source.

When you summarize, be especially careful *not* to

- be too general or vague; be *specific* but *not detailed*

- distort the writer's meaning in any way; use *your words* but *the writer's ideas*.

The summary begins by noting the author, the date of publication, and the title of it to show where the information came from.

The summary points out the two types of studies that were performed in order for the author to arrive at her conclusions.

Notice how the author of the summary uses different words and a different sentence structure to state the main points of the above paragraph.

Sample 2:

It is time for some perspective. With the growing urgency of climate change, we cannot have it both ways. We cannot shout from the rooftops about the dangers of global warming and then turn around and shout even louder about the "dangers" of windmills. Climate change is one of the greatest challenges humanity will face this century. It cannot be solved through good intentions. It will take a radical change in the way we produce and consume energy—another industrial revolution, this time for clean energy, conservation and efficiency.

—Suzuki, D. (2005). The beauty of wind farms. *New Scientist*, *186*(2495), 20.

Summary:

In order to fight global warming, people have to choose to become actively involved and not complain about the changes that will be necessary.

Exercise **10.1**

Examine the following summary sample below, taken from "The worlds we live in: Gender similarities and differences," by Meredith M. Kimball. It is not a strong summary. First, consider how it fails to meet the criteria discussed above. Then, write a summary that does meet these criteria.

Original passage:

Throughout the history of feminism, from Wollstonecraft to the present, two views of gender differences have been advocated (Cott, 1986). In one, similarities between the sexes have been emphasized, whereas in the other, women's special characteristics that differ from men's have been emphasized.

Summary:

The history of feminism, from Wollstonecraft to the present, shows two different views of gender differences (Cott, 1986). Similarities between the sexes are highlighted in one, but women's special characteristics have been spotlighted in the other.

Exercise **10.2**

Choose a paragraph from one of the readings in this textbook. Summarize it in one or two sentences.

The Extended Summary

The extended summary uses many of the same principals mentioned above

- accurately reflects the original
- retains the meaning of the original piece
- includes the main idea(s); includes sub-points if it is a longer summary
- omits examples and illustrations, unless very important
- uses the same order as in the original
- does not add anything that was not in the original
- keeps the relative importance of ideas the same as in the original
- uses concise prose
- is mostly your own words, but you may use some words from the original (though no more than you strictly have to). You *must place quotation marks* around any phrases that you cite directly. If you cite more than *three* consecutive words, you should place them in quotation marks.
- is approximately 10–30 per cent of the length of the original. However, if the work you are summarizing requires more expertise than your audience has, you may occasionally need to write a summary that is longer than 30 per cent. In addition, you may have to add a few transitions to make the summary easy to follow. Add no more than necessary for clarity, however.

For an extended summary, you apply the rules for summarizing to an entire work or a main part of it. Although an extended summary is too long to use in an essay, it shows your ability to identify key ideas and put them in your own words.

When writing an extended summary, you'll have to decide whether to include all the main ideas or just the most important ones. However, if you are using the summary in an essay, only use the parts relevant to your thesis.

How to Write an Extended Summary

A summary contains the main ideas of the source, so can be thought of as a miniature version of its longer, more detailed original. Writing such summaries sharpens your reading and analytical skills. As you read a work for summarization, you will first be concerned with understanding its meaning. You must not only understand and synthesize the information—as you need to do any time you read for content—but also separate the most important ideas from the less important ones.

You can write an extended summary using seven steps.

1. Read the work for the first time to learn its purpose, thesis statement, intended audience, purpose, etc. Take note of the author, his or her professional credentials, and any other sources used. This can help you determine purpose, etc.
2. Reread it, noting its major points, along with the most important sub-points and/or key examples. From these points write an outline. Use your own words for this.

3. Reread the article and your outline to make sure you have not missed any of the main points.

4. Following your outline closely, write a summary that includes the thesis statement and all the main points (if you're summarizing the entire piece). If you are writing a summary of a specific length and have room for more than the main points, pick the most important sub-points or developments of ideas to reach the required length.

5. Check your wording against the original. Have you unconsciously used any of the original writer's wording? Have you accurately reworded the points? Have you put quotation marks around phrases and sentences taken directly from the original?

6. Create the title for your extended summary (if required). The title of the summary should include the title of the document you are summarizing, as well as the original author's name. The preferred method is "Summary of 'Title of Essay,' by [Name of Author]." After giving these elements in the title, you may not need to mention them again in the summary itself.

7. Edit and proofread your summary.

When you have written the summary, check it over to ensure that it is essentially in your own words and that you have put quotation marks around words and phrases taken directly from the source.

It is best to leave time between each step. Sit down and do step 1 all at once. Minimize the distractions around you, as you want to make sure you understand the writer's meaning. Then take a break. If you have enough time, leave a few hours, or even a day, between step 1 and step 2. But if the work is short, and you feel you can concentrate well, you can move on to step 2 at the same time.

A summary, at its minimum, should contain the work's thesis statement and, depending on the length, the main ideas. The thesis statement should appear at the end of the introduction of the original, and the main ideas are often the topic sentences of major paragraphs. Remember, though, that the topic sentence might not be the first sentence of a paragraph—indeed, some paragraphs might not even have a topic sentence. Furthermore, not every paragraph will contain a main idea, so the number of paragraphs in the original might not match the number of points in your outline.

〉 Extended Summary Samples

In the first summary, based on the essay "Fighting hockey violence will give you a concussion," the main ideas are listed in an outline, and then a summary was written from these ideas. In the second summary, based on the student essay about romantic relationships (page 313), the outline stage is omitted.

SAMPLE PROFESSIONAL ESSAY

Fighting Hockey Violence Will Give You a Concussion

by Jeffrey Simpson

[1] Specialists in diagnosing and treating concussions should know about the perils of bashing heads against a brick wall. But, nonetheless, bravo to those who know about concussions for having recently recommended an end to fighting in hockey.

[2] Medical experts, minor hockey executives and former National Hockey League players who suffered from concussions recently gathered in London, Ont., to try to improve safety in the game. They made many suggestions about better head protection, but they also said: Stop the fighting.

[3] Concussions can be caused by many aspects of hockey, and by numerous rules that leave heads inadequately protected. Shots to the head are endemic in hockey, and the NHL has always been fitfully attentive, at best, in trying to protect against them. But some damage to the head, even the occasional death, occurs from fighting as a player's head is struck, either by a fist or when he falls against the ice.

[4] The medical experts were right: An end to fighting would reduce head injuries. But just as threatened legal cases against on-ice thuggery have come to naught, so medical advice won't change the cultivated culture of violence in professional hockey.

[5] Fighting, however, is to professional hockey as hearts are to Valentine's Day. People just love it. Those noble souls who wish to ban it will give themselves concussions trying to end it, although the case against fighting, rationally speaking, is overwhelming.

[6] Those who gathered at the concussion conference were bashing their heads against not just one wall but many. There's the wall of tradition; fighting has always been there. There's the wall of the NHL Players' Association, some of whose members are fighters, lacking any other skill that would give them

(continued)

a job in professional hockey. There's the wall of the owners, who know—and rightly so—that fighting means excitement, and excitement means money. There's the wall of commissioner Gary Bettman, who knows that fighting puts bums in seats. And, sad to say, there's the wall of the fans.

[7] Attend an NHL game in any arena. When a fight starts, fans throughout the building rise, shout and gesticulate as vigorously as when a goal is scored. A few Canadians like to insist that fighting really only appeals to Americans. Fighting exists in hockey to sell the game in U.S. markets where people carry guns, watch football players smash each other and where television is overrun with violence.

[8] Alas, such an argument merely reflects Canadian conceit about Americans in general, and American hockey fans in particular. Watch a fight in any Canadian city with a professional team, or attend a junior hockey game where fights break out even more frequently than in the NHL. Canadian fans eat up fighting.

[9] It's in Canada, don't forget, where the highest media priests who defend fighting reside. And not only in Canada, but on the CBC. As if Don Cherry were not already the country's leading cheerleader for fisticuffs, the CBC went out and hired the worst general manager of the past 20 years, Mike Milbury, as an "analyst." He quickly joined Mr. Cherry in trotting out the old cliches about the indispensability of fighting as an outlet for aggression. He then added his own denunciation of "pansification" in hockey, for which he had his knuckles rapped.

[10] Fortunately for literate hockey fans, there is TSN, where the quality of hockey commentary vastly outstrips anything on the CBC. On that hockey-savvy network, there are some defenders of fighting in hockey, but the brilliant Pierre McGuire opposes it and, of course, he is right. Even on TSN, however, the highlight package each night usually features a brawl or two, rather than some extraordinary defensive play or slick passing move.

[11] Fighting is not endemic to hockey, except for the evident fact that the sport allows it. Fighting could be eliminated with the snap of a finger if owners and players didn't believe that the fans want fighting. It is, after all, the only professional sport that allows fighting. Hockey is no rougher than football or Australian-rules football or rugby, where to fight is to be expelled from play. The argument that fighting is a necessary outlet for aggression is wholly bogus.

[12] Go to the Hockey Hall of Fame, or watch films of classic encounters of yesteryear. You won't remember the fighters, but rather the skilled players. Today, the NHL markets the Sydney Crosbies and Alexander Ovechkins for national and international purposes. But the owners also watch us, the fans, and our reaction to fighting. We, or at least most fans, like it.

[13] It used to be that North American players fought and Europeans did not. True, most of the fighters remain North American, but we have passed on bad habits to a handful of Europeans, too. The Cherryfication of hockey that glorifies fighting has spread, and will not be stopped, notwithstanding the excellent advice of the concussion experts.

—Simpson, Jeffrey. (2009, February 14). Fighting hockey violence will give you a concussion. *The Globe and Mail* A19.

When you decide on the main points of the source you are summarizing, paraphrase them as you construct an outline. Remember that the final summarized version must be in your own words and that words and phrases quoted directly must be placed in quotation marks.

Outline:

[1] A conference was held in London, Ontario, about player concussions in hockey.
[2] Concussions occur because of fights or falls, and the NHL is not consistent in protecting players.
[3] Medical professionals think ending fighting in hockey would help prevent head injuries.
[4] However, many do not want to see an end to fighting—the players, especially those whose only skill seems to be fighting, the owners, who know fighting draws the fans, and many of the fans themselves.
[5] While Canadians like to think that fighting in hockey is something Americans like, this is untrue because you see fighting at all levels of hockey in Canada, from the junior leagues to the professionals.
[6] Broadcasters, like CBC, hire people like Don Cherry, who are advocates for fighting in hockey.
[7] Other networks try to focus more on the game itself, but in the end, even they provide the fight highlights of games.

[8] Hockey is the only sport that allows fighting. In other sports, players are kicked out of the game if they fight.

[9] Unfortunately, fighting in hockey has spread from North America to Europe and this fighting trend does not seem about to stop.

Note that in the original piece, there are many illustrations, such as the passage that discusses Don Cherry and Mike Milbury. Much of the information in this passage is used to support the writer's thesis and does not need to be included in the summary. Also, some of the passages in the article just elaborate on the main points, so the writer summarizing the piece chose to leave those out.

Summary of "Fighting hockey violence will give you a concussion," by Jeffrey Simpson

The medical dangers of hockey fights are well-documented, yet these fights continue to occur. The danger of concussions from fights and falls in hockey has become severe enough that medical professionals, hockey executives, and former players attended a conference to discuss this issue in London, Ontario. These people all feel that fighting should be eliminated from the game because it is so dangerous. However, there are many others, such as owners, players themselves, and fans, who want to see fighting remain in hockey. Some Canadians argue that Americans are the ones who like the fighting, but this is not true, as fighting is seen in all levels of hockey in Canada, and Canadian broadcasters often show game highlights that focus on the fighting. While fighting is not necessary in sports (in many sports, players are penalized for fighting), hockey seems to encourage violence. This violence is spreading from North America to Europe, and no one seems able to stop it.

—Student writer Krystal Noonan

The following sample is an abstract/summary of the essay about media use in romantic relationships, which is found in Chapter 13, page 313.

Summary of "'I luv u :)!': A Descriptive Study of the Media Use of Individuals in Romantic Relationships," by Sarah M. Coyne, Laura Stockdale, Dean Busby, Bethany Iverson, and David M. Grant

In this study, we address the communication technologies individuals within romantic relationships are using to communicate with one another, the frequency of use, and the association between the use of these technologies and couple's positive and negative communication. Participants consisted of individuals involved in a serious, committed, heterosexual relationship. The Relationship Evaluation Questionnaire instrument was used to assess a variety of relationship variables. The majority of individuals within the study frequently used cellphones and text messaging to communicate with their partner, with "expressing affection" being the most common reason for contact. Younger individuals reported using all forms of media (except for e-mail) more frequently than older participants. Relationship satisfaction did not predict specific use of media but predicted several reasons for media use. Additional analyses revealed that text messaging had the strongest association with individuals' positive and negative communication within their relationships. Specifically, text messaging to express affection, broach potentially confrontational subjects, and to hurt partners were associated with individuals' view of positive and negative communication within their relationship. Implications of the results are discussed.

❯ Other Types of Summaries

Paraphrase

A **paraphrase** is usually about the same length as the original. You would normally paraphrase an important part of a text, perhaps a whole paragraph or even, occasionally, more. A strict paraphrase is entirely in your own words and the ideas appear in a different order from the original. Because a paraphrase doesn't omit anything of substance from the source, it is unlike a summary, whose main purpose is to condense the original while keeping its basic meaning.

Below is an example illustrating the differences between summarizing and paraphrasing an original paragraph taken from an essay written by student Barclay Katt, titled "Tail of opposites."

> Most people have been struck, at one time or another, by the way pet owners come to resemble their pets. It is strange why this is so, and never the other way around—that pets come to look more like their owners. For some reason, the face of the cat or dog is more transferable to the human face than the human face is to that of the dog or cat. Here, it must be admitted that the dog owner is at an advantage. As there are far more breeds of dogs than of cats, the observer cannot help but be impressed by the infinite variety of possible faces of dog owners—from pushed-in pug to the full-blown majesty of Irish wolfhound.

Summary:

Many have noticed that people who own pets often look like their animals, but this comparison is found more often with dog owners than cat owners.

Paraphrase:

It has often been observed that those who own pets look like their animals. However, pets seldom resemble the people who own them. Perhaps this is because people see animals in human faces, but not humans in animal faces. People who own dogs are compared most often to their pets because there are more kinds of dogs than cats. Therefore, people can see many types of breeds in human faces, such as a pug or an Irish wolfhound.

A summary is shorter than the original, but when you are paraphrasing, the length remains the same.

A paraphrase restates the source's meaning using only your own words. Paraphrase when you want to cite a small amount of material that is directly relevant to your point. When you paraphrase, you include *all* of the original thought, but you rephrase it.

Just as you do when summarizing, in paraphrasing, you must use your own words. Unlike a summary, though, a paraphrase is the same length as the original work.

Exercise **10.3**

Take the paragraph from one of the readings that you summarized above in Exercise 10.2 and paraphrase it.

Abstract

An abstract is an overview of your purpose, methods, and results. It can include key phrases or even whole sentences from the full work. Not all the material needs to be reworded.

An **abstract** is an overview of your purpose, methods, and results. You write it *after* you have finished your essay or, at least, after you have arrived at your conclusions. However, an abstract appears before the beginning of the essay; it is placed after the title and author notation and before the introduction, enabling readers to decide whether they wish to read the whole essay.

An essay abstract is generally 75–100 words. An abstract for a scientific paper is typically at least twice as long (150–250 words); some are even longer. A writer will often incorporate key phrases or even complete sentences from the full work into the abstract. You will often find abstracts at the beginning of papers in peer-reviewed journals. When you search databases, you can look at the abstracts to determine whether an article may be of some use to you for your own essay; however, do not use the abstracts alone for your research. Scan the whole article to ensure that it does, in fact, relate to your topic.

Articles in peer-reviewed journals have been evaluated by experts before publication.

Exercise **10.4**

1. Using your school's databases, find articles that have abstracts. Choose two articles that you find easy to understand by scanning the contents.
2. Read the abstract for one article and then read the complete article.
3. Read the second article without looking at the abstract first.
4. Compare your understanding of the two articles. Was it easier to understand the first or the second article?
5. Finally, without looking at the abstract for the second article, try writing a one-paragraph summary (i.e., an abstract) of the article and then compare it to the actual abstract. How different are the two?

Annotated Bibliography

An annotated bibliography summarizes similar works in a field of study. It includes a concise summary of the content, focusing on the thesis statement and major points or findings. It can also include an appraisal of the study's usefulness.

An **annotated bibliography** is an *expanded* bibliography. An annotated bibliography often accompanies a large research project, such as a book, dissertation, or other major study. It can take the form of a critical survey, demonstrating the variety of approaches that other writers or researchers have taken to the subject. While an abstract concisely summarizes your own work for potential readers, an annotated bibliography concisely summarizes similar works in the field of study—they tell readers where the writer's particular piece of the puzzle fits into the whole.

Because an annotated bibliography may contain hundreds of entries, each entry must be brief. Generally, the entry provides a concise summary of content, focusing on the thesis statement and major points and findings. If the entry refers to a book-length study, the main points may take the form of major section or chapter headings. Sometimes, an annotated bibliography appraises each work's usefulness or contribution to the field of study.

Following is a sample annotated bibliography entry of the essay "The imperfection of perfectionism: Perfectionism as a maladaptive personality trait," by Erin A. Walker (from Chapter 13).

> The author discusses perfectionism and its negative implications from a social psychological viewpoint. She separates perfectionism into "normal" and "neurotic" types, and then discusses the characteristics and suspected causes of perfectionism. Walker cites studies that demonstrate its negative effects, such as its connections to depression and difficulties in intimate relations. Information from psychological studies is effectively integrated into the paper to support the author's points. She uses logically ordered sub-topics to present a successful overview of current social psychological findings concerning perfectionism. [82 words]

Exercise **10.5**

Create an annotated bibliography using the articles from Exercise 10.4 above.

❯ Summarizing at the Workplace

Preparing a summary is not only a classroom activity. While working at a job, you may also be asked to summarize information for colleagues or your boss. You may be asked to attend a seminar or conference and come back and report what you learned. You obviously will not give people a very detailed account of the event. Nor will you give your opinion about how beneficial it was. Instead, you will need to apply the same rules you learned here and provide a summary of the important information you learned.

Exercise **10.6**

Look at the following memo and write a summary to present to your instructor. Try to keep the summary length at 10 per cent of the original.

MEMO

TO: Juan Alexandros, District Supervisor
FROM: Gail Fromme, Human Resources Manager
DATE: November 12, 2010
SUBJECT: CHANGES TO WORKPLACE ASSESSMENTS

As of January 1, we will be implementing a new system to evaluate the managers in each district. This new evaluation includes the latest in psychological testing, which we feel will better predict who will succeed as a manager and whom we need to eliminate.

I will be sending out the new forms within the next few days, once our legal team has vetted them. Please do not share these forms with the staff, as District Supervisors will be the only ones using them.

The company would like you to inform the managers that changes will be made to the yearly evaluations. Please notify them that the new evaluations will

1. include feedback from the staff they manage
2. include a minimum of 15 hours on-site supervision by the District Supervisor
3. require a self-evaluation, which will be compared to the staff feedback
4. include a visit to the head office to meet with an evaluation team

Once you receive the new evaluation package, which will include all the necessary new forms, as well as detailed instructions, please take the time to read everything carefully. Any questions you have will be answered at the training session we will be having in mid-December. In the meantime, feel free to call me at ext. 267 between 8:30 and 4:00, Monday to Thursday.

❭ Sample Professional Essay

The following article contains elements of a summary. Tamsin McMahon, the article author, summarizes the main ideas from the book *The Locavore's Dilemma*. However, McMahon goes on to present various aspects of the local food movement and includes quotations from interviews with other parties interested in the subject. While reading the article, note whether the author used adequate transitions between ideas and also between what was summarized from the book and what is new material.

SAMPLE PROFESSIONAL ESSAY

Is Local Food Bad for the Economy?

The Locavore's Dilemma, *a controversial new book by two Canadian academics, is attracting its fair share of criticism*
by Tamsin McMahon

[1] The North American farm is experiencing a cultural renaissance, or so say the stories of urban twentysomethings swapping the comforts of the city for overalls and buckets of manure, of municipal bylaw officials debating the merits of backyard chicken coops, to say nothing of the explosion of farmers' markets, community gardens, high-end restaurants specializing in local food, and the home-delivery services of fresh produce from nearby farms.

[2] The push for sustainable agriculture and local food trumpeted by everyone from Michelle Obama to the Canadian authors of *The 100-Mile Diet* seems innocuous enough as a way for us to end our dependence on a corn-based diet of junk food and soft drinks, as well as curb rising rates of childhood obesity by teaching us to appreciate how our food gets from the farm to the table.

[3] Know your farmer, proponents of local food say, and you'll make better choices about what you put in your mouth, support the local economy and save the environment in the process. As Michael Pollan, the *New York Times* writer and champion of the local food movement, is fond of saying, "Pay more, eat less."

[4] Enter two previously little-known Canadian academics with a controversial new book that argues that, far from making our communities healthier and more self-sufficient, the local food movement will destroy our economies, ruin our environment and probably lead to more wars, famine and incidences of food poisoning.

> This is the point at which the author begins the summary.

[5] *The Locavore's Dilemma*—the title is a play on Pollan's bestselling *The Omnivore's Dilemma*—by University of Toronto geography professor Pierre Desrochers and his wife, Hiroko Shimizu, who has a master's in International public policy, argues that much of the gains the world has made in food security and standards of living have come from the evolution of our food system from small-scale subsistence agriculture to international trade among large and specialized producers, the corporate-driven agribusiness that so many food activists despise.

> Here the author of the summary is explaining who the book authors are and giving credentials to show that the book is written by people who know about the subject.

This is the main idea of the book.

[6] To Desrochers and Shimizu, corporations that control huge swaths of the North American food supply—the McDonald's and Wal-Marts of the world—have made food safer and cheaper by creating economies of scale that can help support technological advancements such as more sophisticated automated farm equipment, safer pesticides and fertilizers, genetically modified seeds that produce higher yields, and more advanced food-safety practices that have cut the rate of outbreaks of food-borne illness by a hundredfold in the past century.

[7] Food activists, they contend, would rather turn back the clock on those modern developments, close the doors to trade and return to a world where families toiled the land, pesticide- and fertilizer-free, and then squeaked by on what they could earn from selling their goods at the local farmers' market. It's a recipe, the authors say, for economic and social disaster.

The summaries you write for school will not include quotations from interviews.

[8] Today's locavores—the term for those who support local food—"don't ask the most obvious question, which is, if things were so great in our great-grandmothers' time, why did things change so much since then?" Desrochers says in an interview. "If it was only an educational movement, I wouldn't have any problem with it. But increasingly, it's becoming a way to stick it to the man. What are activists going to do when Wal-Mart offers fair trade coffee and organic food? They will have to find another way to get back at corporations."

[9] Local food movements have a long history, as successive generations rediscover the romantic idealism of living off the land as their ancestors did, from Henry David Thoreau heading to the woods in *Walden*, to Depression-era policies to turn vacant city lots into urban potato patches, to wartime "Victory Gardens." These movements were all popular for a few years and usually floundered when government funding ran out or farmers found living off the land too difficult. Today's movement, which Desrochers traces back to the economic boom times of the 1990s, is all well and good, he says, until the tumultuous global economy eventually forces us to spend less on groceries. "The main message we want to send to idealistic young farmers is don't count on charity to build your business. The movement might be popular right now, but I'm not sure it will last down the road."

Again, the author turns back to the original ideas in the book.

[10] Desrochers's and Shimizu's argument is largely a treatise on the benefits of the free market and globalization, the belief that the only way to feed an ever-growing global population is to produce more food on less land with fewer resources, which means the family farm will continue to die a gradual death in favour of corporate agribusiness.

[11] To understand just how far we've come, they argue, consider that in a "short" several thousand years we've gone from needing 1,000 hectares (nearly 2,500 acres) of land to feed a single person to just one-tenth of an acre in today's globalized food chain. In the past 60 years, the world's population has exploded from 2.5 billion to seven billion,

and the percentage of the population going hungry on a daily basis has dropped from 40 per cent to less than 15 per cent. Desrochers and Shimizu argue that if we were still using 1950s technology to produce our food, we would need to plow an extra land mass the size of South America just to feed the world's population.

[12] Take local food to its most extreme conclusion, Desrochers says—grow only food that's truly native to North America—and we'd all be eating a lot of blueberries, seeds, squash, and not much else. The most dramatic examples of economic and social destruction from policies to promote local food over international trade, he says, include the nationalist policies of Mussolini's Italy, Hitler's Germany, and Japan of the 1930s, when rice prices rose 60 per cent above the international rate as the country pursued agricultural self-sufficiency.

[13] Not surprisingly, an argument that compares locavores to Hitler has attracted its fair share of critics, who mostly accuse Desrochers and Shimizu of either being in the pockets of corporate agribusiness—Desrochers says the couple's only remuneration came from their publisher—or of harbouring a personal vendetta. Shimizu was born and raised near Tokyo and the couple wrote *The Locavore's Dilemma* after they took issue with a Toronto speech by a visiting professor from the University of British Columbia, in which he said Japan was one of the world's most "parasitic" countries because it imported so much of its food. Desrochers grew up in a farming community in Quebec's St. Lawrence Valley and worked for a time at the Quebec Farmers' Union ferrying new immigrants from Montreal out to the countryside to pick berries. Among his biggest supporters, he says, have been people who grew up on a farm and later left it. Two of his biggest detractors have been his brother, François Desrochers, a former Quebec MLA for the Action démocratique du Québec, who represented the rural riding of Mirabel, and his father, whom he describes as a "typical Quebec nationalist who wants Quebec to be self-sufficient."

> Again, the author deviates from a typical summary that has been discussed in this chapter by including the opposite side of the argument and criticism for the book's authors.

[14] Local food supporters say the authors have painted an unfair picture of the locavore movement by focusing on its most extreme elements. "The book is very, very manipulative," says Debbie Field, executive director of FoodShare, a Toronto community food program that sells about 4,000 local food boxes and feeds about 141,000 children in a school nutrition program. "It does not bring us light, it is throwing oil on the fire. It's just making things more complicated." Field says critics of the local movement too often assume that local food always has to cost more and that all locavores are against using modern technology on the farm. "I know a lot of young farmers in Ontario and they're some of the most technically sophisticated people in the world," she says. "They're not about going back to some mythical slavery past. It's about creating new, environmentally sustainable food."

> **Writing Tip:** Even in a non-academic essay, a writer needs to start with a topic sentence so that the readers know what the paragraph will be about.

[15] Most local food supporters take a more balanced approach between promoting local and imported fair trade food, she says. For instance, FoodShare, which is

supported by private donations and government funding, bought $1.5 million worth of produce last year, with $500,000 of it from local producers. Only about half of the food in FoodShare boxes and 30 per cent of the food sent to schools is local. This year, FoodShare included imported strawberries and apples because unseasonably warm and wet weather wreaked havoc with local crops. "I don't want a child eating potato chips from southern California instead of strawberries and apples from southern California if our strawberry and apple crops are destroyed," Field says. "We're not saying, 'Don't eat the mango,' but they're saying, 'I'm not going to eat that local strawberry, even if it's the same price.'"

The author has again returned to summarizing an idea from the book.

[16] Among the most popular and controversial aspects of today's local food movement is the concept of "food miles," the distance food travels from the farm to the table, which serves as a rallying cry for environmentalists concerned over greenhouse gas emissions and climate change. Desrochers calls the food-miles argument a "misleading distraction" in the debate over food policy. Research from the U.K. comparing local tomatoes with those imported from Spain showed the U.K. tomatoes, which had to be grown in heated greenhouses, emitted nearly 2,400 kg of carbon dioxide per ton, compared to 640 kg for the Spanish tomatoes, which could grow in unheated greenhouses.

[17] Other studies have found that food miles represent just four per cent of total emissions related to food, with most of the emissions coming from producing food and from consumers driving to the grocery store to buy it. Air transportation accounts for just one per cent of food miles, with much food transported in the cargo holds of passenger jets, while marine container ships are one of the most fuel efficient ways to transport large shipments of food, Desrochers says.

[18] Studies on food miles need to be taken with a grain of salt since many are industry-funded, says Don Mills, president of Local Food Plus, which certifies local organic and sustainable farms in Ontario. Those studies also assume that produce shipped to Canada in the winter hasn't been kept in cold storage elsewhere, he says. Critics willing to dismiss the food-miles argument also ignore the tax dollars spent building the infrastructure to ship food long distances. "An awful lot of public infrastructure and public policy goes into food no matter how you shake it out, and that's why you see huge money being spent lobbying by large agricultural producers to get some policy outcome," he says.

[19] A better measure than food miles or even food prices, he says, is the amount of energy, in fuel, put into growing food compared to the energy, in calories, that people get from eating it. By that standard, Mills says, research shows large, highly automated farms use more fossil fuel energy than small farms that use manual labour. "Small subsistence fallow farming is incredibly productive from a [fuel] calorie perspective,"

he says. "There's lots of ways to measure the world, and we may have to balance the predominance of economic measurement with a notion of energy balance."

[20] Like it or not, Mills says, the debate around food policy is here to stay, mostly because food represents a core part of society's value system that eclipses the traditional economic arguments of industries such as manufacturing. "I would argue that food is different. It has a more important place in humanity and in culture than widgets," he says. "If we can figure out issues around food transportation, around energy, around how we treat our produce with pesticides, around how we treat our [farm] labour, we'll be well on our way to sorting through a number of other spheres as well. If we get food right, we'll get a lot of other things right."

> **Writing Tip:** In an academic essay, do not end a paragraph with a quotation. You need to provide a concluding thought.

[21] Such arguments are one of the biggest dangers of the local food movement, counters University of Manitoba agricultural professor Ryan Cardwell. It's one thing for food activists to want to spend more on groceries at their local farmers' markets. It's another when they push governments to use tax dollars to support local agricultural production, either through direct subsidies or through programs that require public institutions such as schools, prisons and military bases to buy and serve only local food. "My concern is when advocates of local food try and influence policy and government money and regulations to address a policy objective," he says. "If you want to address an issue like urban poverty or greenhouse gas emissions, then you should pick the policy that best addresses them, and local food really doesn't answer any of them."

> **Writing Tip:** In an academic essay, do not end a paragraph with a quotation. You need to provide a concluding thought.

[22] Another argument of the local food movement that Desrochers disputes is that local farming is inherently healthier and safer than the mass-produced counterpart, since farmers tend to use fewer pesticides and they have a duty to their local community. In contrast, he says, large corporations have brands to protect and budgets to devote to scrupulous food-safety practices, compared to small farms, which usually aren't worth suing if they cause outbreaks of food-borne illnesses like *E. coli* or salmonella. He cites Jensen Farms, the family farm in Colorado whose pesticide-free cantaloupes were linked to an outbreak of listeria last year that killed at least 30 people.

> Again, the author returns to summarizing an idea from the book.

[23] Large farms and food processing plants are also susceptible to outbreaks of food-borne illness—Maple Leaf Farms paid $25 million to settle claims from a 2008 listeria outbreak—but Desrochers argues they're easier to trace and correct than illnesses caused by small farms since they generate more media coverage and government oversight.

> **Writing Tip:** When you write for academic purposes, your paragraphs need to be longer than one sentence.

[24] "You see young organic farms grow their stuff in manure and bring it to the barn where all the doors are open and wash everything with a hose, all the various

vegetables together," he says. "As [Loblaw executive chairman] Galen Weston said, farmers' markets are beautiful places, but eventually they will kill people."

[25] Getting to know your farmer is a noble aim, but most visitors to farmers' markets have very little understanding that the food they buy from local growers is often not produced under the same conditions as those they can find at the grocery store, says Mary Shelman, director of Harvard University's agribusiness program. "Most people assume you can take it home and eat it out of the bag before they wash it," she says. "That's actually frightening to me because people don't respect that it actually came out of a field full of rabbits and deer and birds who aren't too discriminating about where they take a bathroom break." Larger commercial farms tend to have fewer problems of animal contamination because they're required to fence off animal pathways.

> The author of this article has gone to other sources to provide support for the argument put forth in the book.

[26] One of the advantages of the decline of the family farm has been to move agriculture away from the large population centres, where diseases can easily spread back and forth between humans and animals, Shelman says. "If everyone had chickens in their backyard and there was an outbreak of bird flu, that would take care of every chicken."

[27] Neither, says Desrochers, is local food inherently more secure than that from commercial farms or foreign exports, as many food activists argue. Historically, societies that relied solely on their own agriculture were more susceptible to famine than those who opened their doors to international trade, mainly because if one country had a poor harvest it could always import food from a country that had a good season. Advancements in transportation—first the railway and later the airplane—have only helped eradicate food shortages and famines in developed countries by ensuring that fresh food can always be readily shipped anywhere.

> Another idea from the book is being summarized.

[28] Rather than closing borders or encouraging more local agriculture, Desrochers and others argue, food security requires encouraging economic development, so consumers can spend less of their incomes on food. Already the amount of disposable income spent on food has dropped from 23 per cent in 1930s America to 9.4 per cent today. By promoting less productive, small-scale agriculture, Desrochers says, locavores are encouraging a type of farming that will require huge tracts of wilderness to be destroyed to create farms in order to accommodate an anticipated doubling in the global food supply needed to feed the world's population by 2050. As it stands, he says, each year more agricultural land is reverting to wilderness than is consumed by urban sprawl.

> Here the author is combining ideas from the book with other outside sources to increase the credibility of the argument.

[29] True North American food security, says Shelman, would mean converting large parcels of urban land to agriculture use. "If you look at all the land that is devoted to

huge houses and driveways and pools in the backyard and beautiful landscaping, you can make the argument that ultimately for food security we have to be willing to give up other parts of the way we live," she says.

[30] Ultimately, though, Shelman says the local food movement is driven less by nationalism and more by consumers' need to connect with their food and have confidence in how it's produced, whether locally or abroad. That will keep the movement a potent force for years to come. "Local could mean it has to be in my backyard, or it could be local in the same sense that I have confidence in my food even if I'm eating artisan cheese that's been produced in Ireland and Italy," she says. "As long as I know the story, that is local. That's really what people are looking for, somebody to put a face on agriculture and farming. We're more confident in people than we are in faceless institutions."

> —McMahon, T. (2012, July 9). Is local food bad for the economy? *Maclean's*. Retrieved from http://www2.macleans.ca/2012/07/09/is-local-food-bad-for-the-economy/

Post-reading Questions

1. Was it easy to understand when the author switched between new ideas and the summary of the book?
2. How did the summary aspects of this article add to your understanding of the basic argument of the book?
3. Do you think a summary of the book alone would have been as effective as this article in presenting the author's point of view?
4. Is the author's point of view clear? How do think McMahon feels about the local food movement? Use examples from the article to support your idea.
5. Why do you think the author chose to write an article like this rather than a typical summary as outlined in this chapter?

∎ Chapter Review Questions

1. What are the key characteristics of a summary?
2. Can you use the original author's words when writing a summary?
3. What is an extended summary?
4. What steps can you follow in writing an extended summary?
5. What is the difference between summarizing and paraphrasing?
6. What is an abstract?
7. What is an annotated bibliography and when is it used?
8. How can summarizing be useful in the workplace?

Part 3

Research

11 Research

In this chapter, you will

- learn how to conduct research for your essay topic
- learn how to determine whether your sources are reliable
- learn how to use the Internet for research
- discover what other types of resources are available for researching your topic

At college and university, each essay you write will need a strong thesis that is supported by research. By adding relevant, reliable outside information, you demonstrate to the reader that you are familiar with the topic, and if you research well, you show that you are becoming an expert in that field. This chapter explains how to begin a research essay by exploring what you know about a topic. It then addresses how to conduct research and where to find reliable and credible sources.

❯ Developing Research Skills

This chapter is designed to help you develop your research skills so that you can support your thesis using what other people, such as scientists and other researchers, have discovered about your topic. You may decide to summarize or paraphrase parts of published works, as discussed in Chapter 10, or to use direct quotations (discussed in Chapter 12). Much of this chapter addresses expository essay writing, but can be applied to argumentative essays as well (Chapter 9).

Research, which comes from the French *rechercher*, meaning "to seek again," is an important part of most expository essays and some argumentative essays. In order to use research effectively in essays you need to *look again*—explore, check, and recheck. Once you have all your information, you need to **synthesize** it. You put together the evidence provided by your **primary** and **secondary sources** to create your essay.

While a successful argumentative essay relies on the *effectiveness* of your *argument*, the *presentation* of your *information* is vital in an expository essay. You should find ways to make the essay interesting and appealing to the reader. Don't just assemble the facts and add transitions between ideas. You need to find out what someone else has discovered or thinks about the topic, and then rewrite their points in your own words. This means that, at the college or university level, exposition usually involves research.

In an expository research essay, you will generally use claims of fact, so you need to find reliable information, analyze what various researchers have discovered about the topic and, on the basis of their conclusions, come to a reasoned conclusion of your own.

It is often said that great thinkers stand on the shoulders of giants. This means that they build on the knowledge of the researchers and thinkers of previous generations. The Wright brothers did not just wake up one day and decide to build an airplane. They studied previous designs and ideas, such as Samuel Langley's aerodrome. Langley himself had no doubt studied gliders and other designs for flying machines. This is an example of what we call "progress" in the sciences, the social sciences, and the humanities. The most knowledgeable experts depend on the findings of others to help in their own explorations; the research they do, in turn, adds to the store of knowledge, enabling them to contribute to their chosen field.

Writing a research essay involves drafting an outline, adding and checking citations, and assembling and presenting the information you have found in the most effective way. When you are drafting the essay, you may begin linearly with an outline, but you will probably then go back and add research and check citations. You will also need to go back and make sure that you have accurately represented your research and that you have focused on the most relevant and important aspects. The following section will help you proceed with greater confidence.

When you research, you explore a topic to find out what others, especially experts, have written or said about it.

Synthesis is putting together ideas from different sources.

Primary sources are original sources; secondary sources comment on those sources. Primary sources include literary texts, historical documents, surveys, questionnaires, and interviews. Secondary sources include authoritative written sources such as books and journal articles, but can also include oral presentations and conference papers.

When you write an essay for college or university, your instructor judges it not only on grammar and mechanics but also on your critical thinking. Therefore, your essay is not just a rewrite of what others have said, but a combination of your thoughts and theirs.

While exposition implies research, research implies synthesis—putting together what you have learned.

Research—Finding and Exploring

Your first step in writing a research paper often involves choosing a topic (unless your instructor has provided one for you) and finding possible sources. At this early stage, it is helpful to write a summary of your purpose as well as a tentative list of source material. Your instructor may even ask for a brief proposal. A research **proposal** is a document that tells the instructor what topic you want to study. You write the proposal after you have done sufficient background research to ensure there is enough information for you to proceed. You may even be asked to provide relevant citations to show that you have done the required preparation. You should explain what the focus of your paper will be, perhaps even providing a working thesis. This may change as you begin to write the essay, but it shows that you have a specific direction in mind. Providing the reason why you chose the topic is important. If the topic is not assigned, make sure, as Simon Walter does below, to include why the topic is relevant to you. If the topic is assigned, do not simply state this as the reason. Explain why your particular focus is of interest to you. Your proposal should be a few paragraphs in length so that you are able to fully expand on your topic.

The paragraphs below were submitted by student writer Simon Walter to explain why he chose to write about massively multiplayer online role-playing games (MMORPGs) for a research paper, "The virtual life: An overview of the effects of MMORPGs on individuals and countries," in Chapter 12. Also, see Walter's self-survey in Table 2.1, pages 37–38.

A research proposal announces a topic, a purpose, and research sources.

[1]   When choosing my topic, I immediately drew upon video games as a topic I was both interested in and motivated to write about, most likely because I have been involved in gaming for most of my life.

[2]   My interest in MMORPGs specifically is not from personal experience, however. In fact, it is mostly because of my graduating year in high school; I found a large portion of my friends' circle sucked into the vortex which is the world of MMORPGs such as Everquest and World of Warcraft. I was a fairly active kid both academically and athletically in high school, and though I considered myself a gamer, I could never understand how so many people could almost completely disappear from their real lives to make synthetic ones online. Mostly, it was frustration with losing a lot of friends to a video game and the fact that I had too many commitments going on to join them, even if I wanted to.

[3]   Of course, that period of my life is past, but curiosity about the nature of those games remained; I wanted to know how a video game could have such an allure. I knew why I was attracted to certain video games, but I wanted to know why others could spend so much time with these MMORPGs. Then I starting noticing new "research" coming out concerning them and an overall dislike for them in the circles of other gaming genres.

[4] All this contributed to my choosing MMORPGs as a topic: I wanted to learn what traits exactly defined an MMORPGs, why it consumes so much time, and, finally, the reasons for an increasingly negative media bias on the subject.

[5] I don't consider myself an authority on video game culture, but I believe I'm a well-informed participant. I like the idea of gaming as both a technological and social movement. As my thinking on the topic progresses, I am starting to study the politics behind MMORPGs more than simply the positive and negative effects. My essay will be less comparative and more analytical in its approach. I have come across many articles studying the effects of long-term gaming in a country and am fascinated by many journalists' attempts to incorporate not just the game, but the gamers themselves, into the economics of a country. My essay began as an interest derived from a basement hobby, but I ended up choosing a particular facet of the issue which I find fascinating and current: the economic component.

Proposals like the one above help you in the "finding and exploring" stage of essay writing. Even if you are not asked to submit a proposal, you will have to think about the topic and use the pre-writing strategies you find the most effective. Some key questions can help you get started.

By asking yourself key questions about the topic, you will discover what you already know and what you need to find out.

Questions to ask:

- What am I interested in?
- Do I know enough to explore a topic thoroughly?
- If I don't know very much, how can I obtain background information?
- What am I hoping to contribute to this subject area?
- Who is my audience?
- What kind of sources would be appropriate given my topic and my audience?
- Where will I find my source material?
- Do I know of the major authors in the field, or how can I find these authors?
- Have I given myself sufficient time to research, synthesize, organize, compose, document, and revise?

Synthesis I—Integration

After you have found your sources, you begin to *assimilate* the information. By taking notes and summarizing where appropriate, you show that you can accurately represent another person's ideas and integrate them with your own ideas. This vital stage of the research essay is discussed in this chapter and in Chapters 10 and 12. When you have finished taking notes and understand the information, you are ready to begin organizing your essay.

To assimilate means to take other people's ideas and incorporate them into your essay.

Questions to ask:

- Is my research geared towards supporting my points?
- Have I understood the results of the studies I've looked at and/or the positions of the experts whose works I have read?
- Are all my sources credible? Are there many recent ones?
- Have I summarized adequately and/or quoted accurately all sources I might use?
- Which sources are the most important?
- How do the different experts' views or conclusions fit together?
- Are there opposing positions? Do some findings challenge others, for example?
- How do they help me explore the topic?
- Has my research changed my view of my topic? If so, how? Do I need to change my thesis?

Successful writers create outlines to help them organize their thoughts early in the writing process.

Organization—Arranging

Every essay needs a structure; usually this will take the form of an outline, a kind of blueprint for the writing stage. Outlines for expository essays are discussed in Chapter 2. It could also take the form of a template like the kind discussed in Chapter 8. See Chapter 12 for an example of a student outline.

Questions to ask:

- Do I have enough support to begin an outline? If so, what kind of outline template should I use?
- Is there a natural organizational method I should use? (Chronology, cause–effect, problem–solution?)
- Do my points thoroughly explore the topic?
- Are some points inadequately developed to produce substantial paragraphs?
- Are all areas of my research relevant to the points I want to make?
- What points are most essential and what sources are most relevant?
- Am I off topic anywhere?
- Does the structure I chose reflect my purpose? Does it reflect my audience? Is it logical?

Synthesis II—Composing

During the first-draft stage you integrate your sources into your essay. Here, synthesis takes place at the level of language. Thus, how you use summary and paraphrase (Chapter 10) and direct quotations (Chapter 12) will be important.

Questions to ask:

- Am I overusing my sources? Underusing them?
- Which sources should be summarized, which paraphrased, and which quoted directly? (This will depend on various factors including length, importance, and phrasing of the source.)
- Am I using my sources effectively? Have I used the best information from them? Have I represented this information correctly?
- Can I use ellipses (see Chapter 12) to omit less important parts of the source?
- Am I providing smooth transitions between my sources and my own writing?
- Is the language level roughly the same throughout? Is it appropriate for my audience?
- Are direct quotations grammatically integrated and easy to read?
- Have I double-checked quotations for accuracy?
- Is my own writing clear, grammatical, and effective? (See Chapters 14–17.)

Documenting—Following Rules

In this stage of the research essay, you must document sources using an appropriate format. The two main scholarly formats for referencing are those of the Modern Language Association (MLA) and the American Psychological Association (APA) style. These resources should be available in your college or university library or bookstore, or online. See Chapter 13 for specific documentation formats for both APA and MLA styles.

With APA and MLA, you can include a source on the References page or Works Cited page only if you have used it in your essay.

Questions to ask:

- What documentation style is expected for this essay?
- Where is information on documenting to be found?
- If I am using electronic sources, am I clear on acceptable methods for documenting them? (Has my instructor given me guidance or directed me to specific sites or sources?)
- Do I know what needs to be documented and what does not?
- Is it possible that the reader could confuse my own ideas or observations with information taken from another source?
- Have I carefully documented other people's words and ideas but without cluttering the essay with unnecessary citations?

Formal research requires you to analyze, compare, assess, and/or synthesize the work of experts in your subject area, generally by discussing multiple approaches to a problem.

What Is Research?

You have been conducting research informally for some time now. Chances are you did not just randomly choose the school you are now attending or the program you are enrolled in. You probably read brochures, talked to people—perhaps to current students, graduates, or school counsellors. This information was no doubt helpful, but you probably also relied on *factual evidence*: programs, prerequisites, tuition fees, housing, and campus size. You may have consulted objective experts, such as people who have researched the different schools, ranking them according to various criteria.

This process of decision-making based on research is a life skill, and the critical skills of analysis, judgment, and evaluation are involved in the decision-making process. Research assignments in college or university require similar skills but involve formal research that requires you to analyze, compare, assess, and/or synthesize the work of experts in your subject area, generally by discussing multiple approaches to a problem. Simply rephrasing these sources or summarizing your own opinions or experiences is not necessarily research.

As discussed in previous chapters, one common approach to organizing a research paper is to compare and contrast the similarities and differences between two or more ideas. Another method is to evaluate the strengths and/or weaknesses of a point of view based on criteria that you create or borrow from experts. The following example involves both comparison and contrast, and evaluation.

1. Identifying a problem:

   Many people are now using e-devices to read. Researchers claim that students do not understand material as well when using these devices.

2. Stating a claim or the thesis about this problem (what the writer will explore or prove):

   E-readers are affecting the way students understand material.

3. Describing the points made by one or more "experts" concerning the claim:

   Researcher A claims that his study demonstrates that students are not understanding material being read when using an e-device. He presents information gathered from a study comparing the reading comprehension levels between students who used an e-device and students using paper.

   Researcher B asserts that students comprehend material well regardless of whether they use e-devices or paper. She presents her study showing no significant difference in the reading comprehension levels between students who used e-devices and those using paper. She goes on to claim that those using e-devices actually gained more knowledge through the use of hyperlinks embedded in the text and the ability to access online dictionaries.

4.   Reaching a decision on the merits of these experts' approaches to the thesis:

Researcher B's arguments are more convincing than those of researcher A. Researcher B is able to show that students gained a better understanding of the topic because of the additional features available when using e-devices.

5.   Concluding with your judgment on the thesis, either by rating the experts' approaches or by suggesting a new way of thinking about the problem:

Researcher B has provided a strong argument that the use of e-devices for reading actually benefits students. While this is a relatively new field, this researcher created an additional parameter to study, which sheds light on the way students are using e-devices, rather than just testing reading comprehension, as researcher A did.

Who Are These Experts—and Where Can You Find Them?

Experts are people who are experienced or well educated, who have published or produced significant work about a subject. A documentary filmmaker may be an expert; his or her film may provide information for your essay. A writer for a magazine or newspaper may also be an expert; so, too, a person interviewed on radio or television could be very familiar with a topic, through his or her research, knowledge, or personal experience. Library shelves are filled with the publications of experts, and the Internet may be another source of expertise. Since the number of these experts may be enormous, you need standards for screening the quality of their information. In the case of the filmmaker, for example, you could consider the following criteria for credibility:

Experts are people who are experienced or well educated, who have published or produced significant work about a subject.

- An important part of research is to select sources whose work has been analyzed by their colleagues. Anyone who can run a camera can make a documentary film. Are there any reviews in journals or other commentaries about the film? These can show you what the filmmaker's colleagues think about this film.
- Is the film part of your institution's collection or available through a reputable organization like the National Film Board?
- Since you are writing a research paper in an educational context, you may wish to consider the filmmaker's academic credentials.

Another criterion used to measure the usefulness of research material is *publication date*. Since attitudes and analyses change over time, more recent information gives you the latest developments in your field. A further advantage in beginning with recent material is that the source often will refer to previous studies that might be useful. Sometimes just scanning the Works Cited or References section at the end of a recent work will suggest other potential sources.

❭ A Note about the Internet

When conducting research, ask your instructor about publication dates. Is there a limit to how far you can go back? Does an article have to be published after a certain year? Depending on the field, research conducted 10 years ago might be extremely dated or relatively new.

When assessing the credibility of a secondary source, especially an Internet source, consider the following quotation from George Orwell's *Animal Farm*: ". . . some animals are more equal than others." Anyone with basic computer skills can publish online, which creates both new opportunities and new challenges for researchers. For instance, if you enter the phrase "essay writing blogs" in a search engine, you will no doubt discover numerous blogs related to this topic; however, is the author an expert? Is he or she credible?

Searching the Internet for android device prices and using it for academic research require different criteria; for research you need to find trustworthy authors. The Internet has countless sites created by individuals, companies, and institutions with very few controls to guarantee the accuracy or fairness of the information. To retrieve quality information, you must assess the reputation of a site's creator and double-check the information in other sources.

Not all Internet sources are of equal value. If you are using the Internet for research, make sure you use a credible source.

Many thoughtful and well-respected authors use the Internet to reach others who share their interests; however, it is important to judge a website author's motivation carefully. Some of the information available on the Internet simply promotes the author's unsupported point of view or contains inaccurate information. Therefore, its usefulness is limited. Ask yourself, "Is the author providing a reasoned argument or just an opinion?" Be aware that personal blogs and Listservs are largely designed for conversation and opinion rather than the promotion of academic research.

Some Internet resources that you might want explore include

- college or university websites
- blogs and discussion boards
- personal email with respected professionals

A uniform resource locator (URL) is the address of specific Internet content.

URLs containing ".edu" or a Canadian university or college name followed by ".ca" are often useful, scholarly sites.

College or university library websites provide a wealth of accurate scholarly information, so an excellent strategy for beginning researchers is to use them to find appropriate online material. The final part of a website's **uniform resource locator** (URL) directs you to these websites. The addresses of degree-granting American educational institutions always end with the domain ".edu."

Canadian schools' websites generally contain a shortened version of their name, followed by ".ca."

Your professor may require that all sources you use need to be peer reviewed, like those found in professional journals. But if peer-review is not a requirement, you may be able to use blogs, discussion boards, or even personal email correspondence. Blogs can provide you with interesting information. Many professionals publish regular blogs covering a variety of topics from vacation tips to psychological issues to "How to" guides. It is important to remember, though, that anyone can publish a blog, and its information could be biased or false. Only use blogs that generally support what your other research has indicated, whether it supports your thesis or not. Avoid blogs that are inflammatory. For example, if you were writing about gaming, as Simon Walter did, you would avoid blogs that state that gamers are introverts who are not able to function properly in social environments. This type of blog is designed to incite discussion based on the writer's opinion but will probably not be focused on research.

Much like blogs, discussion boards can be a useful research source. Again, you can find discussions on the Internet about virtually any topic. Professionals and laypeople alike can belong to any discussion group, and the opinions they post can help you understand what others feel is important in the area you want to study. Discussion boards can also guide you to relevant current research for your topic, or they can introduce new areas that you hadn't considered. Again, be aware that anyone can post to discussion boards as long as he or she belongs to that particular group. Not all posts will be appropriate to use as a research source.

Finally, personal email can also be used as a source for many essays. If you know of a person who is well respected in a particular field that you are studying, you may decide to contact him or her and ask questions about your topic. It is generally a good idea to do this only after you have thoroughly researched the topic. By doing the background work ahead of time, you can ask pointed questions that can then be integrated into your essay. For example, if you are writing about child development and you are interested in Jean Piaget's theories, you can ask your source why he or she thinks Piaget's theories have fallen out of favour. The answer can then be used in your essay as support for your argument. It is important to remember with personal email, though, that you may not get the answer instantly, so leave enough time for your contact to respond. Do not leave this until the last minute. You may want to provide a window of time you would like the response in, but be reasonable, as your contact may be extremely busy.

Another very popular source is Google Scholar. This site is geared more toward research than other search engines, including Google and Yahoo, which are often more commercially focused. Some of the sources on Google Scholar are peer reviewed, which adds credibility. Once you have determined your topic,

Discussion boards and blogs can be useful, as the authors can give you an idea about what is considered important in that particular field.

Personal email to a respected member of a particular field can also be used for research essays.

you can type in key words and relevant articles will appear. Google Scholar also lets you search related articles, which may give you a broader view of your topic or provide a new direction for your research. Once again, remember that not all sources are equal. Some are better than others. Once you have done some research in the field, you will be able to start discerning which are acceptable and which are not.

One source to avoid citing is Wikipedia. This is a good source to start with if you are unsure about your topic and want some basic information. However, like all wikis, it is created by volunteers who add content. While most of the information is accurate, not all is reliable. Sometimes Wikipedia provides links to scholarly papers that can then be used in your research essay. However, make sure that the link does indeed lead to a scholarly article and not just further Wikipedia pages.

While Wikipedia is a place to start, do not cite it in an essay.

〉 Researching Your Topic

Exploring

The first stage in researching a topic is to determine the major authors in your subject area and what they say about your topic. As well, you need to know where they provide this information, so that you can quote or paraphrase what these experts have to say and document them in your essay.

A useful first step when conducting research is to use a general work, such as a textbook.

Finding important authors and works in your area may be easier if your instructor can recommend them. However, in most cases, especially if you are free to choose your own topic, beginning and narrowing the search will be something you do yourself. Looking for a general work, such as a textbook, in your subject area is a useful first step. General works frequently include extensive bibliographies (alphabetical listings of works used or consulted), which you can scan for relevant titles and authors. Consult works in the library's reference section, such as indexes, encyclopedias, dictionaries, and comprehensive guides in your area. Most books in a library's reference section can't be taken out of the library, but they can direct you to more specific sources that can be taken out. However, some of these reference sources may also be available electronically through the library, so check with the librarians.

Internet search engines and subject directories can also provide excellent starting points, providing you with general topics that you can narrow down. If you are having trouble finding information about your topic, use the glossary section of your textbook, which contains key words relevant to your chosen topic.

A working bibliography is a useful tool. It will help you keep track of the sources you have already looked at.

When you find potentially useful sources, you can add them to your **working bibliography**, a list of books and articles you plan to look at. When you find a book on the list, scan the index and the table of contents to determine how helpful it will be. If it looks promising, read the Introduction, Preface, or Foreword. The author often summarizes his or her approach and, sometimes, provides chapter-by-chapter summaries in the introductory section. In Chapter 1, you learned about useful reading strategies, such as scanning, that you can use when conducting research. With articles, read the abstract (Chapter 10).

Your working bibliography may not look much like the final list of works you actually use, but it often leads you to the most relevant sources. Remember to note the date of the work's publication (in books, found on the copyright page—the other side of the title page). If possible, use more recent works, not only because they will be up to date but also because they may draw on relevant previously published works and provide you with other useful sources.

Research Note-Taking

Keeping clear records during the research phase of the essay-writing process will allow you to read material efficiently as well as save time (and your sanity) when you write your paper. You should make notes as you research your sources, ensuring that you record the following information:

1. a direct quotation, a summary, or a paraphrase of the writer's idea; if it is a direct quotation, make sure you put quotation marks around it
2. the complete name(s) of the author(s)
3. the name(s) of editor(s) or translator(s), if applicable
4. the name of the book, journal, magazine, newspaper, or website affiliation or sponsor
5. the name of the specific article, chapter, section, or website
6. full publication details, including date, edition, or translation; for a journal article, this could be the volume and issue number; for Internet sites, this could be the date the site was started or updated
7. the name of the publisher and the company's location (including province, state, or country) for books
8. for Internet sites, the day you viewed the page and either the URL or the **digital object identifier** (DOI)
9. the call number of a library book or bound journal for later reference, if needed
10. the page numbers you consulted, both those where you found specific ideas and the full page range you read (or some other marker for unnumbered online documents, such as paragraph numbers or section heading)

An abstract is a short summary that precedes most academic journal articles.

When you are taking down information, don't forget to record your observations, comments, and queries. You will need bibliographic details, of course, but you will also need to synthesize the ideas of the source with your own ideas as your essay develops; you will have to relate the information to other sources and to your own thesis statement.

It's important to keep source material separate from your own comments—by writing your responses on another piece of paper or by writing your comments in pencil or a different-coloured pen. *Always give clear directions to yourself when you take down this information.*

Digital object identifier (DOI) is a number-letter sequence that begins with the number "10" and is often found on documents obtained electronically through databases. It is the last element in a citation, just like a uniform resource locator (URL).

Organizing Research Notes

There are many ways to organize your notes, but this is an extremely important aspect of research. It is very frustrating to be trying to complete a research paper and not being able to find one key piece of information. One method is to write these notes on index cards (remember to number them). You can also record notes in a journal and use tabs to section the book into particular headings. On a computer, you can create a record-keeping system, either by using a database program like Access or by simply creating multiple document files in a folder. In addition, there are a number of software programs available that can assist you in organizing your research. Programs such as Scribe (http://www.scribes .com) imitate the card file system. Others, like EndNote (http://www.endnote .com), Bibliographix (http://www.bibliographix.com), and Nota Bene (http:// www.notabene.com), are databases.

Another program you can use to keep track of material is called RefWorks (http://www.refworks.com). You can enter the bibliographic information into the systems and it will create a References or Works Cited page (depending on whether you specify APA or MLA style, which are discussed in Chapter 13). Creating such a document can help you retrieve information if you misplace your notes. Before submitting a final essay, review all the entries to ensure you have eliminated any sources you decided not to use.

Learning programs such as these take time, but they generally offer helpful extra features like the automatic formatting of citations and references or bibliographies. If you choose to record your notes electronically, you should back up your work regularly in case of technical failure.

Cross-Referencing

It is important to keep your research notes organized so that you can retrieve information quickly at a later date without having to go back and reread material.

Cross-referencing your notes can make it easier to retrieve your information when you are writing your essay. You can create a list of central or key words, names, or themes, and record where in your notes these occur. You can cross-reference by writing notes in a margin or by using index cards or computer files. Some students draw themselves a visual aid like a mind map (graphic organizer) on a large sheet of paper to connect their key words. Some word-processing programs include a cross-referencing feature for single documents (in Word 2010, for example, this is found under Insert). The computer programs mentioned previously often have built-in, key word–based cross-referencing systems.

Some Useful Research Strategies

Assimilating

- Begin the research by gathering definitions of the key words in your thesis statement.

- Read or view everything with the thesis statement always in mind. Resist getting sidetracked by reading unconnected material, however interesting it might seem.
- Judge whether or not a book will be worth your time by looking up your cross-referencing key words in the index at the back of the book. Read the abstracts of journal articles to similarly determine their usefulness.
- Consider how you can connect the information from different sources by using transitional words and phrases like *because, as a result of, on the other hand,* or *in contrast.* This will help you select points that flow logically.
- Try to find an example to support every major statement you wish to make. An example can be a quotation, a paraphrase, or a larger concept that forms a comment on or solution to your thesis statement.

Arranging

- When you've finished your first round of research, write an outline that lays out the structure of your paper by creating primary and secondary headings corresponding to the major elements of your thesis statement. Under the headings, list the lines of reasoning that support these points and the examples that support each of them. You can also use the template provided in Chapter 8
- Decide how many pages you will allot for each section of the paper, taking the instructor's requirements for paper length into serious account.
- Look over your outline. Do you have sufficient examples to support all your major statements? Review the assigned word count. Do you have enough material in your study notes to fill the pages? If neither of these things appears to be true, perhaps you need to do more research. On the other hand, if you have too many key points and several examples for each one, now is the time to choose the strongest ones in order to meet length requirements.
- Consider laying out your paper in a word-processing program according to the suggested page number count. If you use the manual "page break" option (under "Insert" in most programs) to create document sections that follow your outline, you'll easily be able to judge whether you're writing too much or too little for any portion of the paper.
- Design a timeline for each of the steps in your paper if you haven't done so in a research proposal. This will help ensure that you don't spend too much time on any segment of the paper.

Table 8.1, page 151, provides a template that you can use for arranging the information from research sources. You can either use this one or create your own electronically. Having a few copies on hand will make it easier if you rearrange material. Use a clean copy and record changes there, rather than erasing or crossing out information. This way you can make sure nothing gets left out by mistake.

Using Contradictory Evidence

In the initial research stage, you will need to find sources relevant to your topic; however, not all studies on a given topic come to the same conclusion. If your primary purpose is to explain or investigate a problem, you will have to assess the different findings, trying to discover why the findings are different, perhaps by analyzing their respective strengths and weaknesses. This process of assessing, a critical thinking skill, is a fundamental part of the research process.

In the humanities, your thesis is often based on your interpretation of the findings, so you must carefully show how the interpretations of other academics differ from your own. An excellent strategy when discussing conflicting results is to acknowledge another interpretation and use it as a springboard into your own interpretation. Contradictory interpretations should not simply be dismissed without explanation; it is better to acknowledge them and qualify them, possibly by briefly discussing their limitations. If you do not address contradictory studies, the reader may assume that you do not know enough about the topic, reducing your credibility. For example, there have been many recent studies that attempt to show the health benefits of vitamins. If you are investigating the benefits of vitamin E in preventing heart disease and have found that credible evidence exists, you still need to acknowledge contradictory studies and explain how these findings fit into your claim about the value of vitamin E.

Researching a topic can be a challenging process—possibly a trial run for the kind of work you will do later in your academic or professional career. If you experience doubts or uncertainties at any stage of the process, talk to your instructor as soon as possible. Don't wait until the day before your paper is due!

〉 Sources of Research Material

There are many different kinds of source materials available; most of the important ones are discussed below.

Primary and Secondary Sources

The distinction between primary and secondary sources is crucial as essay assignments frequently include a requirement that both primary and secondary sources be identified and referenced. Primary sources are the original compositions of authors. Personal documents, such as letters and diaries, and initial scientific articles reporting on a work are also considered primary sources. A secondary source is another writer's analysis of and commentary on a primary source. An article that cites someone else's research, or a textbook that explains others' theories, are both secondary sources. An encyclopedia entry is also a secondary source.

At the college and university level, in order to write a well-researched paper, you need to acknowledge a different point of view if there is one. If you ignore contradictory findings, your instructor may tell you that you have not researched the topic adequately.

Primary sources are the original compositions of authors, but secondary sources cite someone else's research or theories.

When using texts accessed online, it is important to remember that multiple translations/editions often are available, and the online version may not be the most accurate or accepted one. Check with your instructor before you go ahead and use Internet material as a primary source.

Start Your Research by Looking at Secondary Sources

An efficient way to construct a general framework of research from your thesis statement is to access reference sources such as indexes, almanacs, encyclopedias, dictionaries, and yearbooks. These can provide you with concise summaries of statistics, definitions, and biographies, and they also generally provide a reading list of the principal primary and secondary sources. As mentioned, the paper copies of these books are found in the reference section of a library and usually can't be taken home. However, this type of information is widely available on the Internet. For instance, a Google search of *black hole* and *encyclopedia* returns results that include the *Encyclopaedia Britannica*, the *Columbia Encyclopedia*, *Encarta Encyclopedia*, and numerous online library-based sites offering further links to information on the subject. The *Britannica* entry includes a listing of relevant books, articles, websites, magazine articles, and videos on black holes.

Books

Once you've developed a basic understanding of your topic, you can look for books that refer specifically to your thesis statement. Continue your research by locating books mentioned in your preliminary search of reference materials. A book can be written on a single topic; can be a compilation of articles, essays, or chapters by a number of authors around a topic; or can be a collection of pieces by a particular author that have already been published individually. Books can be located by searching a library's catalogue, or sometimes can be found online by doing an author or title search, or by using a database. For instance, Project Gutenberg (http://gutenberg.org) has digitally republished more than 30,000 ebooks, ranging from the contemporary *Human Genome Project, Y Chromosome*, by the Human Genome Project, to the nineteenth-century novel *The Hunchback of Notre Dame*, by Victor Hugo.

Periodicals

Periodicals are published regularly—for instance, monthly, yearly, or daily. Examples include newspapers, magazines, journals, and yearbooks. Unless you are writing about an extremely current aspect of contemporary culture, you will probably be concentrating on periodicals called **journals**, which publish articles written by academics, scientists, and researchers. The most respected journals are **peer reviewed**, which means that other experts in that field have assessed the work prior to its being published.

Locating Journal Articles

Scholarly journals are the places where researchers publish their findings in order to share their ideas—and advance their careers. As a result, there are thousands of scholarly journals publishing a wealth of research on just about any

Periodicals are newspapers, magazines, journals, and yearbooks; a yearbook is a book of facts or statistics published every year.

A journal is a periodical that publishes the results of experts' research.

topic you can imagine. However, finding these articles online can be a challenge, because the journals generally are distributed only through expensive subscriptions. College and university libraries subscribe to some of the journals that they consider most valuable and then allow students, faculty, and staff access to them either in paper editions or online.

Locating a paper copy of a journal article generally begins with a library's catalogue search. Let's say you have selected an article from the bibliography of a well-known textbook on your topic. In order to find the article, you'll need some detailed information that makes up what is called a **citation**, which includes much more than the author's name and the name of the journal. The following components of a citation illustrate what you will need:

Author(s) Name(s): Zigler, E.F. & Gilman, E.
Publication Year: 1993
Article Title: Day care in America: What is needed?
Journal Name: *Pediatrics*
Volume and Issue Number: 91, 1 [an issue number is not always required in your citation, but you should record it in case it is needed]
Page Numbers: 175–178
The complete citation written in APA style (see Chapter 12) looks like this: Zigler, E.F., & Gilman, E. (1993). Day care in America: What is needed? *Pediatrics*, *91*(1), 175–178.

Most library catalogues are designed so you can select "journals only" in the search options and then search for the journal name (as opposed to the article title or author name). You will be given a call number that will direct you to a location in the library where you will find either unbound or bound (into a book) journals. Look up the volume month or issue, and then follow the page numbers to the article. If you are unsure how to do this, ask for help. The librarians or library technicians are trained and experienced in finding sources, so they can show you how to search quickly and efficiently.

Internet Searches

College and university libraries also subscribe to **databases** and indexes that contain the full texts of journal articles, which you can save directly onto your computer's hard drive. These databases collect many different journals together and let you access and search many journals.

Databases also may house a blend of scholarly and non-scholarly information, including popular magazines, newspapers, and non-peer-reviewed journals, along with government-produced documents. In addition,

If an article appears in a peer-reviewed journal, it has been assessed by experts in the field before it is published.

A citation is needed after a quotation, a paraphrase, or a summary. This is done so that the reader knows this information is not yours, but from another source. A citation includes the author name, publication date, title, and where the information came from.

A database is a collection of related data organized for quick access.

databases supply links to the growing number of journals that don't publish a paper version at all and are available only online: electronic journals, or e-journals.

When you are using journal articles, never cite from an abstract, and only use full-text articles. When using a database for research, if possible, indicate that you want full-text articles, as searches can produce articles for which only the abstract is available.

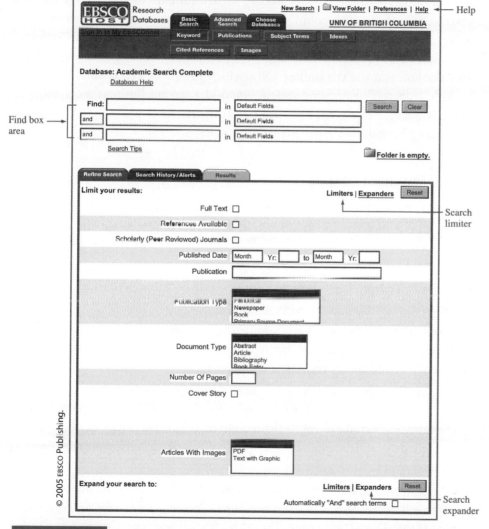

This database screen shows how databases typically organize research information. By entering a word or phrase in the Find box, you can retrieve any article that contains your keywords in either the title or the body of all of the thousands of periodicals available through EBSCOhost.

Needless to say, the list of articles found through a search can be enormous and overwhelming. For this reason, EBSCOhost allows you to select limiters on your search, including a time period of publication and the option to search only peer-reviewed journals. There is also an advanced search window, which permits you to define various combinations of keywords and search limiters or expanders.

Each academic discipline has specialized databases and indexes that concentrate on publications that are particularly relevant to that field. You can ask your instructor to direct you to the most appropriate databases or search your library's website for discipline-related listings. When you need help in your search, use the database's help button.

FIGURE 11.1 Screenshot capture of EBSCOhost research database page

Most databases let you search using **keywords** (including authors' names) and search options.

Boolean operators are used to customize your search. Search limiters include the words AND and NOT. If you type the word AND between two or more search terms, your results will include both search terms; if you type the word NOT between search terms, your results will omit what follows NOT. If you use OR as a search expander, each result will include *at least one* of the terms.

Let's say you were undecided about the topic you wanted to explore but were seriously considering researching either caffeine or alcohol. A database search on "caffeine OR alcohol" using EBSCOhost turns up 27,388 entries. This is far too many to be useful, so you then enter only one search term, "caffeine"; this yields 1,658 entries. Thinking that you might want to compare caffeine and alcohol, you use the limiter AND, which produces 116 results. In order to exclude "tobacco" from your search, you add a second limiter, "NOT tobacco" and hit Search. Using the two limiters (caffeine AND alcohol NOT tobacco) produces 93 results—a more manageable start.

Some Popular Databases

BioMed Central indexes hundreds of journals offering peer-reviewed research about biology and medicine. It is an open-access site that is free for everyone.

Business Source Elite is a database assembled for business schools and libraries, which incorporates scholarly journals and business periodicals relating to marketing, economics, and accounting.

CANSIM (Canadian Socio-economic Information Management) Database (Statistics Canada) is a comprehensive database from Statistics Canada containing nearly 18 million government documents.

EBSCOhost is a database service for more than 9,500 journals on a vast range of discipline areas that allows Internet-style (Boolean logic) searching. EBSCOhost is the academic database you want to start with, and it might be the only one you need. It is widely available through college or university library sites; see your institution's library site for login directions.

ERIC (Educational Resources Information Center) is a large database that pertains to education and is best known for its expert summaries on educational topics (ERIC Digest Records). The ERIC Social Sciences Citation Index lists more than 1,725 social and behavioural sciences journals published after 1995.

Health Source Nursing/Academic Edition offers full-text articles from more than 500 health and medical journals and indexes the abstracts of more than 850 publications.

IEEE/IEE Electronic Library makes available full-text technical journals, conference proceedings, and active standards in engineering, physics, computer science, and materials sciences. Over 3 million full-text documents are available.

InfoTrac provides indexing and abstracts for 1550 academic journals as well as news and general interest publications, along with full-text articles from more than 500 social sciences, technology, and humanities journals.

Ingenta is an excellent source for journals in the humanities, sciences, social sciences, and education. It features full-text articles from almost 12,000 publications.

Lexis-Nexis Academic Universe contains full-text articles from nearly 2,000 sources such as company reports, newspapers, transcripts of broadcasts, wire services, newsletters, journals, legal case law, government documents, as well as some valuable reference texts.

Newspaper Source allows access to a range of full-text articles from 40 international newspapers, including *The Christian Science Monitor*, transcripts from many news broadcasters, and 330 regional American newspapers.

Project Muse offers full-text articles from more than 100 scholarly journals in the humanities, the social sciences, and mathematics. It also contains ebooks. Articles are available from 1995.

ProQuest provides access to thousands of current periodicals and newspapers that are updated daily; it contains full-text articles from as early as 1986.

Psyc INFO, operated by the American Psychological Association, offers citations (not full-text articles) for reports, articles, dissertations, and book chapters relating to psychology in fields such as education, business, medicine/nursing, and sociology.

WorldCat, operated by a consortium of more than 9,000 universities, libraries, and colleges, allows users to view or borrow audiovisual materials, books, films, government documents, computer files, and research reports in 400 languages. This "database of databases" has thousands of full-text articles and an interlibrary loan service for non-digitized items.

Notes on Library Research

With the wealth of research information available electronically, it may seem unnecessary to go to a college or university library in person. In reality, libraries continue to be valuable resources for researchers at all levels of expertise, partly because they have books not available online. As well, they are staffed by professionals who understand how information is organized and interrelated. Most libraries have reference librarians who can save you time and direct you to sources you might never come across on your own. Reference librarians and library technicians have been specially trained and often know of different ways to retrieve information. Help desks are staffed with these people specifically to help students find information.

Libraries often run courses to familiarize students with the specific systems the college or university uses, so it is a good idea to find out when these are being held and sign up for a session or two. Participating in the same session more than once is often helpful, as the information can be overwhelming, and you can learn things you missed the first time.

Reference librarians and library technicians have been specially trained and often know of different ways to retrieve information. Help desks are staffed with these people specifically to help students find information.

Furthermore, libraries hold many important records, including the following:

- indexes for many periodicals, images, films, microfiche files, and videos
- theses and dissertations (book-length documents written by university students as part of their advanced degree requirements)
- historical documents, including maps and public records
- collections of textual and graphic material on special subjects, sometimes including original documents
- clipping files from newspapers and magazines
- bound volumes of journals
- collections of audio and film or video recordings

In addition, libraries store print information that has been gathered, sometimes over centuries, that is too expensive or fragile to digitize. Even for documents that are considered essential, the gradual transition to electronic record-keeping means that much important information created before 1985 is available only in paper form at a library. If your college or university library is small, or if you are attending a newer school, ask about borrowing privileges at other schools close by. You may be able to access those libraries using only your student card, or you may be able to get special permission to use another school's library if they have information your own does not. Another option that may be available is the interlibrary loan. If your college or university has this service, you may be able to borrow documents from other libraries without having to go there yourself. The documents will be delivered to your school library where you can then pick them up. However, you do need to plan ahead, as it can take several days to a week or more to get the document.

Using electronic sources to access journals that publish paper versions has another wrinkle that can frustrate inexperienced researchers: these publications often hold back their latest year's editions from databases in order to maintain their paid subscriptions. This means that it is still necessary to view the most current issues on paper; and remember, accessing recent studies is vital, especially if your subject is a topical one.

Although the nature of research has changed dramatically with the increasing availability of online resources, it is best to think of the cyber–paper relationship as complementary. Relying *only* on the Internet is inadvisable, and some instructors may specify how much electronic research is allowable.

Alternative Information Sources

Although this section has emphasized research information that is written, many disciplines accept support for your thesis from visual or audio media, such as television, film, video, works of art, performances, surveys or questionnaires,

When searching for information, do not leave it to the last minute or you will be competing for help with other students who have the same deadline.

interviews, and observations. Using these alternative sources of information requires the same attention to detail in note-taking as when using traditional materials, and most citation styles provide instructions for citing and referencing non-textual research information. As these approaches to research are more acceptable by some disciplines than by others, if your essay outline emphasizes alternative information sources, review it with your instructor early in the writing process.

Interviewing

If you have direct access to a noted authority in your field, interviewing can be an effective form of research. The main advantage of an interview, whether face-to-face, by telephone, or by email, is that you can ask questions specific to your research rather than having to search many potential sources for this particular information. Interview subjects can be treated the same way as other expert sources of knowledge; that is, their words can be summarized, paraphrased, or quoted directly. There are also specific methods for documenting interviewees. The college or university community—including, perhaps, one of your professors—is an ideal place to look for experts.

■ Chapter Review Questions

1. What is the difference between primary and secondary sources?
2. Why is it important to know the experts in the field you are researching?
3. What is the difference between a database and the Internet?
4. What sources, other than books, can you find at a college or university library?
5. What is a Boolean operator?
6. What is the difference between a popular magazine and a journal?
7. What does it mean if an article is peer reviewed?

12 Using Your **Research**

When you are writing a research paper, you need to use outside sources (primary, secondary, or both), as discussed in Chapter 11. However, good writers do not mechanically insert the material: they integrate it seamlessly into their work, making the essay more readable. Several ways to integrate sources are discussed in this chapter. When using primary or secondary sources to support your thesis, you must make sure that you use these sources correctly so that you do not plagiarize, which is a serious academic offence. This chapter explains plagiarism and outlines the steps to take to ensure you acknowledge the work of others properly.

❭ Outlines for Research Essays

How do you know when you have enough support for your points and can begin an outline? The answer may depend on the assignment itself, as your instructor may be expecting a specific or minimum number of sources. Otherwise, you should probably have at least one source (direct quotation, paraphrase, or idea) to support each main point. Whereas an argumentative essay depends on effective reasoning and various kinds of evidence—including examples, illustrations, analogies, anecdotes, and *perhaps* the findings of secondary sources—an expository essay usually relies heavily on outside support. Therefore, it may be a good idea to include such sources in your outline, as the student writer does in the outline below. Being specific in your outline will make it easier to write your first draft, when you will focus on integrating the sources with your own words.

Below is the outline for the student essay on page 266. Note that the student provided his main points and then added the relevant research that he was going to use. This is a very brief outline but included enough detail for the student to elaborate on points once he began writing the essay. Note that this outline closely follows the template, which can also function as an essay outline, found in Chapter 8. Following this template will help you produce a paper that is argued logically.

> An outline for an essay requiring research may include the sources you will use to support your main points.

Sample Student Outline

Outline for Pandemic Crisis

by Juan Manrique

Thesis and comment: nurses' duty—be present for patients and colleagues, follow professional code of conduct, ensure health and safety of patients

Topic sentence: obligations to patients and colleagues
   A.   Patients' advocates—Hyland, Willard
   B.   Collaboration with others in health care field—Baggs & Schmitt
   C.   SARS and work overload—Registered Nurses' Association of Ontario

Concluding sentence: nurses need to be ready to help out to meet obligations

Topic sentence: nurses' rights for personal obligations without interfering with professional obligations

(continued)

> A. Protecting family
> B. SARS and what nurses did—Registered Nurses' Association of Ontario
> C. Rented apartments for example
>
> Concluding sentence: meeting both obligations is possible
>
> Topic sentence: nurses' professional standard of care
>
> A. Ontario College of Nurses guidelines and standards
> B. Refusal to perform duty is abandonment and misconduct—College of Nurses of Ontario
> C. Definition of misconduct—College of Nurses of Ontario
> D. Professional misconduct may mean losing privileges
> E. Ontario's Occupational Health and Safety Act/SARS and refusal to work
>
> Concluding sentence: nurses are always required to care for patients
>
> Topic sentence: maintenance of quality care during infectious disease outbreak
>
> A. Sufficient staffing levels required—Irurita
> B. Productivity and teamwork—Rafferty, Ball, & Aiken
> C. Teamwork and increased motivation—Rafferty, Ball, & Aiken
> D. Collaboration and teamwork increase quality of care
>
> Concluding sentence: more nurses means better quality of care
>
> Topic sentence: shortage of nurses affects quality of care
>
> A. Shortage affects productivity as nurses are overloaded
> B. Collaboration between nurses decreases
> C. SARS example: Singer, Benatar, Bernstein, Daar, Dickens, MacRae, Upshur, Wright, & Shaul
>
> Concluding sentence: those left working during shortage are not able to perform well
>
> Conclusion: Nurses' duties include providing quality patient care, following a professional code of conduct, and providing the highest level of care

Plagiarism

What Is Plagiarism?

Plagiarism is an issue that you will hear about over and over again. You will probably hear it so often that you will become tired of it, perhaps even before the first week of classes is over. Your college or university library may have handouts or online resources about plagiarism. If your school has a writing centre, tutors there can explain it or provide a handout. Finally, your composition instructor (and this text) will address it. Why is it so important to understand plagiarism?

Much has been written recently about society's disregard for copyright laws. Millions of people download music or movies. Studies have shown a rise in student cheating, and some say more than half of high school students have cheated on tests. File sharing is common, with sites such as YouTube making it possible to post videos directly from its site to your Facebook or Google+ account. Lines have blurred between personally owned material and that which is protected by copyright. However, in academia, this sort of "sharing" is not acceptable. Borrowing someone else's words or ideas without acknowledging the source is plagiarism.

Intentional plagiarizing is a serious academic crime with equally serious consequences. Intentional plagiarizing includes using, without acknowledging, sections, sentences, or even just phrases from a website, a book, a newspaper article, a magazine, etc. It also includes using a friend's essay and turning it in as your own or buying one from the Internet. Another example is reusing a paper you have written for another class. Unintentional or inadvertent plagiarizing usually leads to the same consequences, even if the reason for the plagiarism was careless note-taking, improper documentation, or a lack of knowledge about plagiarism itself. Therefore, it is important to cite information that is taken from other sources, either primary or secondary.

The consequences for plagiarizing can range from a zero for that particular paper to failing the course to being expelled from your school. It is often easy for an instructor to detect plagiarism because there may be a shift in tone or word use. When an obvious clue like this shows up, many instructors will then type the questionable phrase into a search engine and see if the exact wording matches anything on the Internet. Many colleges and universities now subscribe to services such as "Turnitin." You may be required to provide an electronic copy to such a service before submitting your essay. Such sites maintain an electronic copy of your essay and compare it to thousands of documents. If any matches are found, the results will be posted electronically for you and your instructor to see, along with the sources that match.

Plagiarism occurs when you

- fail to cite an idea, a paraphrase, or a summary
- use the exact language of the source without putting it in quotation marks
- use the identical structure of the original

In the section below, examples of plagiarism are shown. In Chapter 13, you will find complete information for citing the most common sources used in research essays.

Plagiarism is the intentional or unintentional use of someone else's work as if it were your own.

All secondary sources require parenthetical citations and an alphabetical listing in the Works Cited section at the end of your essay (MLA) or the References section (APA). You must cite secondary sources—whether you quote from them directly, summarize them, paraphrase them, or just refer to them in passing—by using the appropriate style of your discipline.

Remember that plagiarism does not apply just to the words of the source, but also to any idea you obtain from a source. You are plagiarizing if you use the language of the source without enclosing it in quotation marks or if you closely imitate the structure of the material cited—even if you changed the words.

Plagiarism, whether intentional or unintentional, usually leads to the same harsh consequences, which may even be a zero in the course or expulsion from your school.

To Cite or Not to Cite?

Fortunately, you may not need to cite *everything* you include in your essay. Anything that falls under the category of "general knowledge," even if you obtained the information from a specific source, does not need to be cited. If you were writing an essay about Amelia Earhart, you would not have to cite a source when stating that she disappeared while attempting to fly around the world: it is a well-known fact. You would, however, have to cite a source that gives a theory about where she vanished, as this has not yet been determined, and many theories exist about where her remains might be.

If there is a reasonable presumption that a typical reader would not know a fact, then cite the source. If, however, a fact would be *easily obtainable* by a reader from a number of different sources (even if a typical reader would not know it), it may not be necessary to cite it. Your instructor may be able to tell you how many sources constitute "easily obtainable" information; a minimum number often given is three.

General knowledge can vary according to audience. If you are writing for an audience with a medical background, for example, you may not need to cite the fact that the active ingredient in marijuana is tetrahydrocannabinol; if you are writing a paper for historians or political scientists, you may not need to cite the fact that British Columbia became a Canadian province in 1871 because your readers could easily obtain this information. If the general knowledge or the easily obtainable standards do not apply, make the citation.

Plagiarism Sample 1

Original:

Anybody who will look at the thing candidly will see that the evolutionary explanation of morals is meaningless, and presupposes the existence of the very thing it ought to prove. It starts from a misconception of the biological doctrine. Biology has nothing to say as to what ought to survive and what ought not to survive; it merely speaks of what does survive. —Stephen Leacock, "The Devil and the Deep Sea: A Discussion of Modern Morality"

Language of the source unchanged:

A person willing to see *the thing candidly* would realize that morals cannot be accounted for through evolution.

Sentence structure unchanged:

Biology does not distinguish between what should and should not survive; it simply tells us "what does survive."

When trying to determine whether to cite information in your essay, remember these two principles: if the fact is *easily obtainable* by the reader or if it is *general knowledge* for your audience, you do not need to provide a citation.

Acceptable paraphrase:

An honest appraisal can tell a person that morals cannot be accounted for through evolution . . . . Biology tells us only "what does survive," not what should and should not survive (Leacock 57).

Plagiarism Sample 2

Original:

Previous studies by the American Psychological Association show cheating is relatively infrequent in elementary school, but increases as children become adolescents and progress through grade levels. The increasing incidence of cheating correlates almost perfectly with increasing pressure from teachers to get good grades. —Minsky, A. (2009, 9 August). Cheating stats getting out of control: Researcher. *CanWest News*. Retrieved from CBCA Current Events.

Language of the source unchanged:

As students progress to higher grades, cheating correlates almost perfectly with increasing pressure.

Language changed, but sentence structure unchanged:

Students cheat more because of mounting pressure to achieve high marks.

Acceptable paraphrase:

As students advance from one grade to the next at school, they often feel that they need to perform well, and this pressure seems tied to the frequency of cheating.

A good strategy for avoiding plagiarism (and for learning the information) is to carefully study the passage you want to use; then, close the text and write out its points from memory completely in your own words. Finally, look at the passage again, ensuring that it is different from what you have written in its structure as well as in its language—and that you have accurately restated the thought behind it.

❯ Integrating Secondary Sources

Using secondary sources enables you to support your argument and demonstrate your familiarity with source material. Your essay, interwoven with citations in the correct format, reveals your skills as a reader, researcher, and writer.

You can treat secondary sources in three major ways:

1. You can summarize the source, or the section of it that is most directly relevant to your point.
2. You can paraphrase the source.
3. You can cite from the source directly.

Summary, Paraphrase, Direct Quotation, Mixed Format

You can choose how to integrate secondary sources with your own ideas. Using a variety of methods is usually best; however, there are general guidelines to help you make choices. In all cases, remember that the source must be identified either in a signal phrase (see below) or in a parenthetical citation.

Summarize

Summarize if you want to use a source's main idea(s) to provide background information, to set up a point of your own (to show similarity or difference, for example), or to explain a point relevant to your discussion. You can summarize passages of just about any length—from one sentence to several pages. For more about summaries, see Chapter 10, page 207.

Paraphrase

A paraphrase restates the source's meaning using only your own words. Paraphrase when you want to cite a relatively small amount of material that is directly relevant to the point you wish to make. When you paraphrase, you include *all* of the original thought, but rephrase it. For more about paraphrases, see Chapter 10, page 219.

Direct Quotation

Direct quotation is used when the source itself and the exact wording are important. This could be due to specialized vocabulary in the cited passage or the unique way that the source uses language or expresses the idea.

Block quotation is a method of setting off a large quotation (four or more lines, or 40 or more words) in your essay. The quotation is set in a paragraph by itself indented one half-inch from the left margin.

Direct quotation is used when the source itself *and* the exact wording are important. This could be due to specialized vocabulary in the cited passage or the unique way that the source uses language or expresses the idea. You can use direct quotations for small amounts of text or for larger ones. If you choose to quote four or more consecutive lines, use the **block quotation** format in which you indent one half-inch from the left margin. You double-space the text, *but do not use quotation marks*. The usual procedure is to introduce the block quotation by a complete sentence followed by a colon. For examples of block format, see the student essay on page 272. See also Mixed Quotation Format below.

Use single quotation marks to indicate a word or passage in your source that is in quotation marks:

Use single quotation marks to indicate a word or passage in your source that is in quotation marks.

> Sarah said "John told me to just 'walk away,' rather than argue with Peter."

The single quotation marks around *walk away* inform the reader that quotation marks were used in the original.

Direct quotations are most effective when used for one of the reasons stated above. Avoid direct quotations if there is no compelling reason to use them; summarize or paraphrase instead. You demonstrate your ability to understand and synthesize sources when you summarize and paraphrase.

Avoid using direct quotes if

- the idea in the passage is obvious, well known, or could be easily accessed
- the material is essentially factual and does not involve a particular *interpretation* of the facts
- it can be easily paraphrased

Avoid large blocks of quoted material. Some instructors discourage this practice by not including direct quotations in your total word count. Direct quotations used *selectively*, however, are an essential part of most essays.

The following are examples of direct quotations that are unnecessary or ineffective. The preferable alternatives are given after them.

"About one-third of infants are breast-fed for three months or longer."

Paraphrase:

Approximately 33 per cent of infants receive breast-feeding for at least three months (Statistics Canada).

"The greenhouse effect is the result of gases like carbon dioxide, nitrous oxide, and methane being trapped in earth's atmosphere."

Paraphrase:

The accumulation of such gases as carbon dioxide, nitrous oxide, and methane in the atmosphere has led to the greenhouse effect.

The following are examples of direct quotations that are effective.

Albert Einstein once said, "It always seems to me that man was not born to be a carnivore."

The fact that you are quoting as well-known a personality as Einstein, even though he is speaking from personal opinion, would make direct quotation a good choice—but not an essential one. However, in the following instance, precise wording matters and gives authority to the passage:

"Neither capital punishment nor life imprisonment without possibility of release shall be imposed for offenses committed by persons below 18 years of age" (UN Convention on the Rights of the Child).

Many facts can be paraphrased rather than quoted directly. Avoid quoting long passages of statistical information; this can easily distract the reader. Paraphrasing the material is usually better.

Mixed Quotation Format

In a **mixed quotation format**, you use a mixture of paraphrase and direct quotation to effectively show your familiarity with a source and your confidence in integrating words and ideas smoothly into your essay.

> Although in his tribute to Pierre Elliott Trudeau in *The Globe and Mail*, Mark Kingwell recalls the former prime minister as "the fusion of reason and passion, the virility and playfulness, the daunting arrogance and wit, the politician as rock star," behind this he finds "the good citizen."

Compare with the original text below. The text crossed out shows what was not used.

> ~~It's hard to say anything about Trudeau now that has not been said a thousand times before~~: the fusion of reason and passion, the virility and playfulness, the daunting arrogance and wit, the politician as rock star. ~~All true; all banal.~~ But underneath all that I find ~~a more resonant identity, one which is at once simpler and more profound:~~ the good citizen.

When you use direct quotations, you must ensure that the quoted material is integrated grammatically, clearly, and gracefully. See below for examples. For information on how to use ellipses or brackets to integrate quotations, see Signal Phrases, Ellipses, and Brackets below.

Examples:

Ungrammatical:

Charles E. Taylor discusses the efforts of scientists "are defining a new area of research termed artificial life" (172).

Grammatical:

Charles E. Taylor discusses the efforts of scientists to "[define] a new area of research termed artificial life" (172).

Unclear:

Art critic John Ruskin believes that the highest art arises from "sensations occurring to them only at particular times" (112).

Clear:

Art critic John Ruskin believes that artists produce the highest art from "sensations occurring to them only at particular times" (112).

Punctuate a direct quotation exactly as it is punctuated in the original, but do not include any punctuation in the original that comes *after* the quoted material. Note the omission of the original comma after *recklessness*.

Original:

"Any accounting of male-female differences must include the male's superior recklessness, a drive, not, I think, towards death . . . ."

Directly quoted:

In his essay "The Disposable Rocket," John Updike states that "[a]ny accounting of male-female differences must include the male's superior recklessness."

To test whether you've integrated a quotation properly, remove the quotation marks and make sure that the sentence is grammatical. Don't forget to put the quotation marks back in when you've finished, and also ensure that any changes you made to the original are indicated through brackets or ellipses.

Signal Phrases, Ellipses, and Brackets

Signal Phrases

The examples above under Mixed Quotation Format use signal phrases to introduce direct quotations. Signal phrases contain the source's name (*Taylor, Ruskin*) and a signal verb, such as *recalls, discusses,* or *believes.* Signal phrases alert the reader to exactly where the reference begins. They can also guide the reader through a complex issue that involves different findings or interpretations. The following paragraph contains two citation formats: the first reference contains a signal phrase; the second one does not.

Signal phrases include the source's name and a signal verb; they "signal" an upcoming reference.

MLA style:

Richard Goldbloom states that a surveillance video taken in Toronto showed that in more than 20 per cent of incidents where bullying was involved, peers actively became part of the bullying (2). Furthermore, recent statistics show not only the pervasiveness of the problem but that outsiders perceive bullying as a problem in schools today (Clifford 4).

This is an example of a signal phrase.

The reader would easily be able to separate the two sources at the transition word *furthermore*, so a second signal phrase is unnecessary.

If you are using APA style, the signal phrase will include the year of the work's publication after the author's name.

APA style:

Asch and Wishart (2004) state that the Slavey communities had grade schools by the 1960s, and people left their homes to live in communities so as to retain social benefits (p. 186). As children and parents were reminded, a half-dozen absences from school could result in fines and jail for the parents and the loss of family allowance payments (*The Catholic Voice*, 2000, p. 5).

Ellipses

If only part of a quotation is relevant to your essay, you can omit unnecessary words. For example, if you find a quotation that discusses two points and you want to discuss only one, you can leave out the part that is not relevant. In fact, keeping it in might confuse the reader. However, if the information is important, make sure that leaving it out would not be misleading. You may hear people say that they have been quoted "out of context." This could mean that when they were quoted, relevant information was left out, perhaps to deliberately create a bias that did not exist in the original.

You can use **points of ellipsis** (. . .) to indicate that you have omitted one or more words from a direct quotation. Three spaced dots (periods) show an ellipsis (omission). Four dots with a space at the beginning of the sequence (*childhood requires* . . . .) indicate that the omitted text includes all the remaining words up to the period at the end of the sentence. The fourth dot is also used if you omit one or more complete sentences.

If a parenthetical citation follows an ellipsis, the fourth dot (i.e., the period) will follow the citation:

> "Going green might cost a lot, but refusing to act now will cost us the Earth . . ." (BBC News par. 5).

You can use points of ellipsis before or after the original punctuation to show exactly where you have dropped material:

> But some damage to the head occurs from fighting as a player's head is struck, . . . either by a fist or when he falls against the ice.

Brackets

Square brackets (or just **brackets**), as opposed to **parentheses** (round brackets) indicate a change or an addition to a direct quotation. Brackets can indicate a stylistic change (e.g., upper case to lower case), a grammatical change (e.g., the tense of a verb), or a change for clarity's sake (e.g., adding a word to make the context clearer). The following illustrates these kinds of changes (although you would probably paraphrase a passage that contained as many brackets and ellipses as this):

> The text states that "[a]ll secondary sources require parenthetical citations and an alphabetical listing . . . at the end of [the] essay . . . . [Students] must cite secondary sources, whether [they] quote from them directly,

You can use points of ellipsis (. . .) to indicate the omission of one or more words within a direct quotation. You add a fourth dot if you omit all the words up to and including the final period.

As a general rule, do not use an ellipsis (. . .) *before* the beginning of a direct quotation.

summarize them, paraphrase them, or just refer to them in passing by using the [MLA or APA] style . . . ."

The original text:

All secondary sources require parenthetical citations and an alphabetical listing in the Works Cited section at the end of your essay (MLA) or the References section (APA). You must cite secondary sources, whether you quote from them directly, summarize them, paraphrase them, or just refer to them in passing by using the style preferred by your discipline.

You may occasionally use brackets to explain an unfamiliar term within a direct quotation:

Emergency room nurse Judith McAllen said, "we triage [prioritize by severity of injury] patients if it's a non-emergency, and don't treat them on the basis of their arrival time."

Avoid using brackets any more than is strictly necessary.

Inserting "sic" (which means "thus") between square brackets tells the reader that what immediately precedes [sic] occurs in the original exactly the way it appears in your quotation. One use of [sic] is to call attention to an error in the original:

As people often say, "Vive le [sic] différence!".

[Sic] here calls attention to the article error: *le* should be *la*. In APA documentation style, italicize "sic" within brackets: [*sic*].

Parentheses, like dashes, are a form of punctuation (they may enclose text that explains or expands on something, as these parentheses do); square brackets (usually just called *brackets*) tell the reader that a change has been made to the original passage or that something has been inserted.

Parentheses would be incorrect in the passage shown here.

〉 Documentation: Citations

Necessary versus Unnecessary Citations

You now know *what* needs to be documented; basic APA and MLA guidelines for *how* to document follow in Chapter 13. However, understanding *where* and *when* to document can also be confusing. If you document too much, your paper will not flow well. However, if you do not properly document your in-text sources, you will be plagiarizing.

Parenthetical citations (the parentheses you see after a quotation, paraphrase, or summary that contain bibliographic information) are intended to convey as *much* information as possible about the source while interfering as *little* as possible with the essay's content and readability. The general rule is that you cite enough to give the reader the information needed, while avoiding unneeded citations. If it is clear what specific source is being referred to without a citation, do not give one.

Do not cite every statement or fact from a source if you use that one source for consecutive references. In fact, you can sometimes combine a few references

Parenthetical citations are intended to convey as *much* information as possible about the source while interfering as *little* as possible with the essay's content and readability.

from the same source in one citation. For example, let's say you used three pages from your source, Jackson. When you were finished drawing from that source, you could refer to a page range: "(Jackson 87–89)." This citation would tell the reader that you used that one source continuously for three of Jackson's pages—perhaps one idea came from page 87, two facts from page 88, and a paraphrased passage from page 89. However, if your own or another source's information intervened, you would need to cite Jackson more than once.

Sample Student Research Essays

In the essay that follows, the author, Juan Manrique, uses research but mainly uses paraphrasing from the sources used to provide support for his paper. He uses the APA style for citation, which will be discussed in Chapter 13.

> This essay uses APA format.

> The student begins with a broad statement intended to capture the reader's interest. He then goes on to expand this and explain the nurses' roles further.

> The thesis statement is clear and concise and points out the three areas of argument the essay will present.

SAMPLE STUDENT RESEARCH ESSAY

Pandemic Crisis: The Role of Nurses

by Juan Manrique

[1] Nurses encompass the entire system of care; they are seen on every division of health care. Nurses have to care for their patients, dealing with family concerns, and handling system organizational issues. The collective effort and work put forth by nurses and other health-care workers are what keep the system of care running. However, the system of care is tested and pushed to its limits when an epidemic or pandemic crisis emerges. Dealing with emerging infectious diseases, such as SARS, places great stress on health-care workers as these kinds of diseases rank second as the largest cause of death worldwide (Koh, Hegney, & Drury, 2012). Nurses, and other health-care workers, put themselves in danger for the better of the patients and clients when dealing with an unknown infectious disease. Consequently, nurses end up endangering their family's safety as well and so the situation quickly turns into a moral dilemma. Nurses debate whether or not they should risk their own safety and their family's safety by going to work. However, without nurses on the job, chaos would reap within the system. Thus, it's a nurse's duty to be present for their patients and colleagues, follow their professional code of conduct, and give their highest level of care to ensure the safety and health of the patients.

[2] Nurses have an obligation to their patients as well as to their colleagues. Aside from caring for and curing patients, nurses are the patients' advocates. Nurses ensure patients are receiving the highest quality care, while ensuring patients' take part in the decision-making for their care (Hyland, 2002; Willard, 2008). Nurses also have a duty to assist and collaborate with other nurses and health-care workers. For example, the collaborations between nurses and physicians in intensive care units are essential in lowering mortality rates among patients (Baggs & Schmitt, 2007). However, shortages of nurses and doctors limit the level of collaboration if the number of patients exceeds management capabilities a hospital. The SARS crisis in Canada in 2003 exposed just how short the country is on nurses and doctors. Many people were admitted to hospitals, but the hospitals weren't able to keep up with the quality care demands of the patients. Nurses were basically overloaded with work, which led to miscommunications, poor synergism, medical errors, and nurses quitting from burnouts (Registered Nurses' Association of Ontario, 2003, p. 4). Therefore, nurses capable of working should be present to help their fellow nurses and doctors by easing the amount of workload on each health care worker, and to meet the quality care demands of the patients.

[3] Nurses also have the right to care for their own personal obligations. However, nurses should do it in a way that won't affect patient care. There are many ways to protect family without interfering with their professional duties. For example, during the SARS outbreak, health care workers distanced themselves from family (Registered Nurses' Association of Ontario, 2003, p. 5). Many health care workers rented apartments and kept in touch with family through phone calls, emails, web chats, etc. (Registered Nurses' Association of Ontario, 2003, p. 5). By looking at what health care workers have done in the past, it is clear that managing both professional and personal obligation is possible.

[4] Nurses must always abide by their professional standard of care at all times. In Ontario, the College of Nurses sets the rules and regulations, and practice guidelines for nurses. One rule in particular is regarding refusal of assignments and discontinuing nursing services, which basically states that refusing to care for patients is considered abandonment and an act of professional misconduct (College of Nurses of Ontario, 2009,

---

The topic sentence is broad enough to allow elaboration, but the student also creates parameters for the discussion.

The student's statements are supported by outside evidence, which makes the argument stronger.

The author uses a specific example from researchers to support his earlier statement.

The student uses a concrete example that most Canadian readers are familiar with and then supports his statements with evidence obtained by researchers.

The conclusion wraps up what has been stated in the paragraph. The student chooses to end with a paragraph wrap, rather than trying to end the paragraph and introduce the next one.

Notice the use of the transitional word also. This indicates that the student is moving to a new topic.

The student elaborates on what he means by "personal obligations."

Again, concrete examples obtained from research are given to support the point being made.

Note that the student is using information from a professional body that directs nurses' behaviour.

(continued)

p. 4). Professional misconduct for nurses is the failure to give care for their patients (College of Nurses of Ontario, 2009, p. 4). Any nurse deemed of professional misconduct may lose their privilege of practice as a nurse. However, according to Ontario's Occupational Health and Safety Act (OHSA), nurses may argue that they have the right to refuse to care for patients, if he or she feels it's unsafe for their own well-being (p. 4). For example, there were nurses that refused to care for patients during the SARS outbreak (Shiao, Koh, Lo, Lim, & Guo, 2007, p. 6). However, according to section 43 (b) of OHSA, the right to refuse is not valid if there is potential in harming the health and safety of another human being (Ontario, 1990). Therefore, nurses that discriminate and distance themselves from patients are breaking professional standards. No matter what condition a patient has, nurses should always see patients equally and give equal care to all.

[5] Maintaining high quality care during an outbreak of infectious disease is extremely important. For nurses to effectively give patients quality care in times of great stress, sufficient numbers of staff nurses must be available. An ample amount of nurses allow for better communication and coordination, which will lead to higher productivity among health care workers and care for patients (Irurita, 1999, p 7). Productivity is measured by the level of teamwork that goes on in patient care and within the entire hospital (Rafferty, Ball, & Aiken, 2001, p. 34). Another benefit of teamwork is an increase in the nurses' motivation and so forth with their quality care for patients increases as well (Rafferty, Ball, & Aiken, 2001, p. 35). Therefore quality care increases with more collaboration, teamwork, and consistency of caregivers. With more nurses at work, the level of quality care given to patients will remain at a steady rate as a result of high productivity within the hospital.

[6] However, shortage of staff nurses will have an inverse effect on the quality of care given to patients. The shortage of nurses will limit the level of productivity within the hospital. The level of consistency of caregivers will be low as a result of nurses being overloaded with assigned patients. Collaborating with other staff nurses will also be very difficult since every nurse will have their hands full. The SARS outbreak in Canada caused the number of working nurses to decrease. Many nurses became sick and some stopped working because of their fear for their own health and safety (Singer, Benatar, Bernstein, Daar, Dickens, MacRae,

---

Marginal notes:

After presenting the relevant information, the student then summarizes what the research says.

Here the student is providing an answer as to how to maintain quality care and therefore is discussing one aspect of his topic sentence.

One way that the student can improve his writing is to provide his own commentary between materials cited from outside sources.

Again, note the use of the transition *however*. This clearly tells the reader that another aspect of the topic will be examined.

The student is discussing one area that will be affected by the shortage of nurses.

Note the use of paraphrasing to explain what the researchers have said.

Upshur, Wright, & Shaul, 2003, p. 1343). Unfortunately, the nurses at work were forced beyond their professional limits, which started to have an inverse effect on their ability to perform quality care.

[7] In outbreaks of diseases such as SARS, nurses and doctors are at the front line defending people. Nurses shouldn't abandon patients because of fear for their own safety. To be a qualified nurse is to be able to tackle any risky situation for the better of the patients' health and safety. A nurse should know well in mind that working in a hospital brings new challenges to overcome every day. Outbreaks of diseases should not be seen as any different from all the other challenges faced on a regular basis. In fact, in a crisis situation, nurses shine in preventing chaos while maintaining quality care for patients. Without their helping hands, kind hearts, and brilliant minds, quality care and order in the hospital would likely be impossible to accomplish. Thus, it's a nurse's duty to be present for their patients and colleagues, follow their professional code of conduct, and give their highest level of care. After all, nurses form the pillars of society's health care.

> The author does not begin his concluding paragraph with *in conclusion* but instead chooses to repeat information used throughout the essay. This is the type of sentence that instructors are looking for at the beginning of the conclusion.

> The student repeats his thesis in new words and then ends with a thought-provoking statement that leaves the reader thinking further about the issue.

References

Baggs, J.G., & Schmitt, M.H. (2007). Collaboration between nurses and physicians. *Journal of Nursing Scholarship, 20*(3), 145–149. Retrieved from http://onlinelibrary.wiley.com

College of Nurses of Ontario. (2009a). *Professional misconduct.* Retrieved from http://www.cno.org/Global/docs/ih/42007_misconduct.pdf

College of Nurses of Ontario. (2009b). *Refusing assignments and discontinuing nursing services.* Retrieved from http://www.cno .org/Global/docs/prac/41070_refusing.pdf

Hyland, D. (2002). An exploration of the relationship between patient autonomy and patient advocacy: implication for nursing practice. *Nurse Ethics, 9*(5), 472–482. Retrieved from http:// onlinelibrary.wiley.com.libaccess

Koh, Y., Hegney, D., & Drury, V. (2012). Nurses' perceptions of risk from emerging respiratory infectious diseases: A Singapore study. *International Journal of Nursing Practice, 18*(2), 195–204. doi: 10.1111/j.1440-172X.2012.02018.x

Ontario. (1990). *Occupational Health and Safety Act.* Retrieved from http://www.e-laws.gov.on.ca/html/statutes/english/elaws_ statutes_90o01_e.htm

(continued)

Rafferty, A.M., Ball, J., & Aiken, L.H. (2001). Are teamwork and professional autonomy compatible, and do they result in improved care? *Quality in Health Care, (10)*2, 32–37. Retrieved from http://qualitysafety.bmj.com

Registered Nurses' Association of Ontario. (2003). SARS *Unmasked: Final report on the nursing experience with* SARS *in Ontario.* Retrieved from http://www.rnao.org/Storage/24/1891_SARS_Report_June_04.pdf

Shiao, J. S., Koh, D., Lo, L., Lim, M. K., & Guo, Y. L. (2007). Factor predicting nurses' consideration of leaving their job during the SARS outbreak. *Nurse Ethics, 14*(1), 5–17. Retrieved from http://nej.sagepub.com

Singer, P. A., Benatar, S. R., Bernstein, M., Daar, A. S., Dickens, B. M., MacRae, S. K., Upshur, R. E. G., Wright, L., & Shaul, R. Z. (2003). Ethics and SARS: Lesson from Toronto. *BMJ, 327*(7427), 1342–1344. Retrieved from http://www.bmj.com

Willard, C. (2008). The nurse's role as patient advocate: Obligation or imposition? *Journal of Advanced Nursing, 24*(1), 60–66. Retrieved from http://onlinelibrary.wiley.com

In the following essay, the writer, Simon Walter, uses some of the different methods discussed above to integrate sources. He has used the MLA style for citation, which will be explained in further detail in Chapter 13. Post-reading questions follow the essay.

SAMPLE STUDENT RESEARCH ESSAY

The Virtual Life: An Overview of the Effects of MMORPGs on Individuals and Countries

by Simon Walter

[1] In the *South Park* episode "Make Love, Not Warcraft," Stan's father says, "you've been on your computer all weekend. Shouldn't you go out and socialize with your friends?" Stan, from his computer, angrily replies "I *am* socializing! I'm logged on to an MMORPG with people from all over the

world getting EXP with my party using Teamspeak." Though sometimes crude in its contemporary satire, *South Park* tackles serious issues, and their ridicule of *World of Warcraft*, the most popular online game to date, is one such issue. The increasing popularity of online gaming today begs the question: when worlds are created online, what befalls the offline one?

[2] MMORPGs (Massively Multiplayer Online Role-Playing Games) are recent developments; the first modern MMORPG was released by a South Korean Company in 1996 (Jin and Chee 38). Thus, the current generation of gamers has received the first exposure to these massive online worlds and, consequently, will be the first to feel their effects. Consumer reception has been astounding; the popular MMORPG *Everquest* makes more than $5 million per month in subscription fees—revenue unheard of in any other gaming genre (Day 111). With the realization that incredible profits can be made, researchers are finally receiving enough company funding to regain ground against the anti-video-game movements of China, the United States, and other developed countries (Golub and Lingley 66; Anderson and Dill 774). In the modern world, the effects of online gaming are a relatively new area of study; some countries are beginning to criticize the MMORPG genre as an unhealthy pastime for socioeconomic reasons, but this criticism is often the product of rumour rather than research. As of now, countries are ambivalent about the MMORPG issue, and this indicates the need for objective research to find reliable results in lieu of international speculation.

[3] Unlike first-person shooters or real-time strategy games, MMORPGs are "persistent state worlds." The game does not stop when the player does; the world continues whether one is logged in or not (Day 111). Success becomes time-dependent. Players, in order to be better than others, must log more game-time than other players. As Yee notes, the game is functioning twenty-four hours a day; server operating costs are exorbitant, and "pay to play" monthly subscriptions are typical of the genre ("The Labor of Fun" 70). Gamers are in control of a character with various skillsets. The tasks associated with improving a character in an MMORPG are often repetitive and simple, demanding large quantities of time for improvement. Attributes, equipment, and wealth are gained through trading, hunting creatures, and producing goods. This often demands hours of a player's time before his or her character is

(continued)

competitive with others on the server. The most powerful items in the game are often rare and exclusively available as treasure from the most powerful creatures. This makes "raids" and "quests"—parties of players hunting together—an intrinsic part of the MMORPG genre. According to Putnam (qtd. in Williams), "time spent in front of [the computer] is time spent away from human contact" (14). However, the social aspect of the game is a defining characteristic of the genre: massive intersections of humanity trade, fight, and socialize in MMORPGS. Most feature complex, player-driven economies as important to the game as the stock exchange to the real world, including the sale of rare weapons, staple items, and unique skills; this can lead one to question the asocial stigmata associated with gaming. *Star Wars Galaxies*, an older MMORPG, permits users to produce pharmaceuticals:

> [4] Everything that is bought or sold has to be bought or sold by another player . . . . Manufacturers must decide how broad or narrow their product line should be, how to price and brand their products . . . whether to start a price war with competitors or form a cartel with them . . . . It takes about 3 to 6 weeks of normal game play to acquire the abilities and schematics to be competitive in the market, and the business operation thereafter requires daily time commitment. (Yee, "The Labour of Fun" 69)

[5] This large amount of time dedicated to life-like endeavours (amassing wealth, developing skills, conversing and journeying with friends) sets MMORPGS apart from any other game genre. The virtual world of an MMORPG never ends, and one's success is measured against other players' wealth, skill, and experience—all attributes that are achieved through time and dedicated play.

[6] This staggering time demand has prompted the United States to oppose MMORPGS. Gaming as a whole is interpreted as an impediment to normal youth development both socially and physically. The anti–video games movement links gaming to poverty, increased aggression, obesity, and even physical addiction (Anderson and Dill 788). However, Nicholas Yee argues that, according to his findings, "there is no one discrete point where a player becomes suddenly addicted . . . . The claims that MMORPGS are completely healthy or completely addictive are both extreme to the point of absurdity, and are not supported by the empirical data provided"

("Ariadne—Understanding MMORPG Addiction" 7). Yee has headed the
Daedalus Project, a continuing study of the psychological effects of
MMORPGS on gamers, which has spanned six years and involved 40,000
MMORPG players (*The Daedalus Project*). Though gaming is undoubtedly
a sedentary practice, MMORPG players are no more at risk of physical
problems than gamers of another genre. Earlier research indicated
gaming takes an individual's time away from family and friends; from this,
researchers extrapolated the theory that simply *because* they consume
more time, MMORPGS are more threatening to the American family. New
findings, however, suggest that the decline of arcades, bowling, and
other offline activities has encouraged online gaming's rise to popularity
in America (Williams 15). It is evident that the United States is only just
beginning to see the benefit of legitimate research into online gaming.

[7] Unlike the US, which believes MMORPGS hazardous to the individual,
China sees MMORPGS as a threat to national stability. Social venues—
bars, coffeehouses, community halls, cybercafés, and even churches—
constitute "third places" (Williams 14), social areas that are not home or
work. The People's Republic of China fears that MMORPGS will become the
next "third place" (Golub and Lingley 66). In a government like China's,
the existence of a "social sphere" outside of government censorship
that ignores international borders could constitute a threat to national
sovereignty and state control (66). China is, therefore, in the process of
actively demonizing the practice of online gaming and stigmatizing its
players: "Gaming addiction is likened to addictive drugs, not only at the
level of the individual; it is also regarded as a social problem . . . .
[T]he Internet is therefore linked not simply to addictive drugs in general
but to opium and opium's long association with a wide range of social
problems in China" (63). In short, China views online gaming as a new
breed of opium: a substance that made the Chinese and their culture
subservient to both Europeans and the Japanese in the 19th century
during the Qing Dynasty (64). With the number of individuals online
increasing exponentially, the Chinese fear that the next generation
of youth will define themselves through online means that require
independence from parents, the traditional wellspring of Chinese values
(69). With the One Child Policy already creating a contracting population,
it is easy to see why the last thing China needs is the MMORPG. Their
youth may develop under reduced national influence in the face of a

(continued)

transnational world inside MMORPGS and the Internet; their diminished working class may end up spending valuable time and money on a foreign game company—money and time consequently exported out of the Chinese economy. The MMORPG and the virtual medium it provides are thought to undermine Chinese sovereignty.

[8] Though China and the US both oppose MMORPGS, one country has embraced online gaming fully: South Korea. First, gamers have not been marginalized; they are adored like North American sports stars, and it is possible to live opulently as a professional cyber-athlete there.[1] As of March 2007, 89.4 percent of South Korean households were connected to broadband Internet. Of those, 74.6 percent confirmed the connection had been used for online games (Jin and Chee 46). Second, South Korea was the home of the first modern MMORPG, *Kingdom of the Winds*, in 1996 (38). Therefore, one would assume South Korea would be the first to suffer its effects, yet the negative response of China and the US has not occurred in South Korea. This could be because South Korea's online game industry has allowed foreign investment through the "transnationalization" of its domestic online game industry (45). It was one of the first industries to be recognized as a means of stimulating the economy during the Asian economic crisis of 1997, continues to be subsidized by the South Korean government, and is hailed by popular culture as an economic saviour (47). Whether the same physical and psychological negatives that have been widely publicized in other countries are present in Korean youth is hard to determine because research has been superficial with a more "celebratory emphasis [on] positive business . . . due primarily to the accelerated pace of development" (39). In short, South Korea partly owes its developed status, stable economy, and next-generation identity to the development of its online gaming industry; why bite the hand that feeds you? South Korea provides compelling evidence that MMORPGS are not all negative. In fact, for a country that needed to break out of an economic crisis and join the technology movement of the 21st century, they were a godsend.

[9] To find controversy concerning MMORPGS, one merely has to compare countries. Reception of the new genre is not evenly spread worldwide. Panic in North America over obesity, sedentary lifestyles, and socially

---

[1] South Korea is particularly fond of the real-time strategy game *Starcraft* and televises matches between the most skilled players.

isolated youth has increased with the introduction of a more time-consuming video game. On the other side of the world, China views the international nature of MMORPGS and the Internet as a political and socioeconomic threat. Meanwhile, South Korea continues to enjoy a cultural revolution and an economic boom in the 21st century. While research has shown that perceived health hazards during gaming are a diagnosable phenomenon, more recent research suggests MMORPGS are no more dangerous than any other genre. While their characteristics make them a more time-dependent hobby, no substantial evidence suggests that MMORPGS are more or less harmful than another type of game. Furthermore, negative traits expressed by individual players associated with the genre are minimal and open to interpretation. Thankfully, the presence of more in-depth research on the horizon may clarify the costs and benefits of MMORPG use, perhaps even putting current controversy to rest.

Works Cited

Anderson, Craig A., and Karen E. Dill. "Videogames and Aggressive Thoughts, Feelings, and Behaviour in the Laboratory and in Life." *Journal of Personality and Social Psychology* 78.4 (2000): 772–90. Print.

Day, Grantley. "Online Games. Crafting Persistent State Worlds." *Entertainment Computing* 34.10 (2001): 111–12. Web. 1 Mar. 2009.

Golub, Alex, and Kate Lingley. "'Just Like the Qing Empire': Internet Addiction, MMORPGS, and Moral Crisis in Contemporary China." *Games and Culture* 3.1 (2008): 59–75. Web. 4 March 2009.

Jin, Dal Y., and Florence Chee. "Age of New Media Empires: A Critical Interpretation of the Korean Online Game Industry." *Games and Culture* 3.1 (2008): 38–58. Web. 4 Mar. 2009.

"Make Love, Not Warcraft." Writ. Trey Parker and Matt Stone. *South Park*. Comedy Central. 4 Oct. 2006. Television.

Williams, Dmitri. "Why Game Studies Now? Gamers Don't Bowl Alone." *Games and Culture* 1.1 (2006): 13–16. Web. 1 Mar. 2009.

Yee, Nick. "Ariadne—Understanding MMORPG Addiction." 2002. Web. 1 Mar. 2009. <http://www.nickyee.com/hub/addiction/home.html>.

———. *The Daedalus Project*. Palo Alto Research Center. 2007. Web. 4 Mar. 2009. <http://www.nickyee.com/index-daedalus.html>.

———. "The Labor of Fun: How Videogames Blur the Boundaries of Work and Play." *Games and Culture* 1.1 (2006): 68–71. Web. 1 Mar. 2009.

(continued)

Post-reading Questions

1. Go through the essay and identify the different ways the writer incorporated his sources. Find two examples each of direct quotation, paraphrase, summary, and mixed quotation format.

2. Did the writer rely too much on one particular method for integrating his sources? Explain why you think he did or did not, pointing to specific instances.

3. Find at least two examples each of ellipses, indicating material omitted from a direct quotation, and brackets, indicating changes to a direct quotation.

4. How effective was the essay's introductory paragraph? Why do you think the writer chose to quote from a popular television program?

5. How much background information does Walter give about his topic? What does this tell you about his intended audience?

6. Do you think the writer presented both sides of the debate fairly and reliably?

7. Look at the Works Cited list. Do you feel that Walter has included enough sources? Do they seem reliable? Be specific.

Exercise 12.1

Look through a textbook from one of the courses you enjoy. Find a section that you think you could write an essay about. Choose five or six passages that you could use for this essay. Then, using the techniques for integrating sources discussed in this chapter, create direct quotations, summaries, paraphrases, and examples of mixed quotation format for these passages.

Exercise 12.2

In a small group, select a topic that you are interested in. Go online or to the library and find some sources that would be relevant to that topic. After skimming through your sources, create an outline for a research essay.

■ Chapter Review Questions

1. Why is outlining an important part of essay writing?

2. Why is it crucial to cite your sources?

3. What kind of information does not require a citation?

4. Summarize in two or three sentences the paragraphs under the heading What Is Plagiarism? on page 256.

5. What are the three main ways of integrating information from a source? What are their differences?

6. When should you avoid direct quotations in essays? When should you use them?

7. What are signal phrases and why are they important?

8. What is the "mixed quotation format" method of source integration?

9. How could you indicate a grammatical change to a direct quotation in order to integrate it smoothly with your own writing?

10. What are ellipses and when should you use them?

13

APA and MLA
Documentation Styles

In this
chapter,
you will

- learn how to cite sources according to APA and MLA styles
- learn how to create a References page and a Works Cited page
- see examples of writing that uses APA and MLA styles

As you saw in Chapters 11 and 12, when you write a research essay,

you need to add information from outside sources to help support

your points. While the previous chapter dealt with how to integrate

these sources into your essay, this chapter will introduce you to the

two major citation methods, the APA and MLA styles, enabling you

to give proper credit to your sources. Common formats, including

electronic ones, are shown with examples of each. APA and MLA

sample essays are included to illustrate how to correctly use these

styles in your own essays.

〉 Choosing Your Citation Style

The purposes of **citations** and **references** are

- to give appropriate credit to the work of others
- to establish your own credibility as a researcher
- to show where your own work fits into other work in the field
- to avoid plagiarism, a form of theft, and certainly one of the most serious academic crimes, with severe penalties for anyone who knowingly or unknowingly plagiarizes
- to enable readers (such as markers) to trace or verify your sources
- to find the reference again if you need it for further research
- to enlarge on a matter (in a footnote or an endnote) that would be disruptive if placed in the text

A citation includes the author name, publication date, title, and where the information came from.

A reference gives complete retrieval information for a source used in an essay.

Handbooks are published for both APA and MLA citation styles (as well as many other styles) and contain extensive guidelines for use. However, usage rules are updated every five years or so. This is done for a variety of reasons. For example, in the 1980s, the Internet did not exist as the research tool we have today. Therefore, rules had to be adapted to fit the changing technology and the ways people retrieved information. Even the arrival of Web 2.0 has created new procedures, as many websites are no longer static and contain a broader range of materials that can be used as sources for essays.

College and university libraries provide a range of current style manuals. Ensure that you use the most up-to-date edition. If you want to purchase your own book, be aware that older editions and second-hand copies may not provide accurate rules.

Different areas of academia favour distinct styles. Below is a list of some of the more common areas. However, your department or your instructor should be the final guide in your choice of citation style.

APA (American Psychological Association)

- business
- education
- psychology
- social sciences and some sciences

MLA (Modern Language Association)

- English literature
- philosophy
- religion

CSE (Council of Science Editors)

- science

In addition to the major styles, some subject areas have their own style specifications:

- chemistry
- engineering
- history
- mathematics
- medicine
- music
- sociology

Although there are many subtle differences among the various styles, the main elements of a citation usually include

1. the name(s) of the author(s)
2. the page number or a similar locator of the information cited
3. the year of publication
4. other publication details

Most styles require an abbreviated citation in the sentence where the reference appears. In parenthetical styles, the information is enclosed in parentheses. Further details are given in an alphabetized list at the end of the essay under a heading such as References, Works Cited, or Bibliography. The following references have been styled according to the rules of each handbook or manual.

Social Sciences:

American Psychological Association. (2010). *Publication manual of the American Psychological Association* (6th ed.). Washington, DC: Author.

Humanities:

The Modern Language Association. MLA *Handbook for Writers of Research Papers*. 7th ed. New York: The Modern Language Association, 2009. Print.

❯ The Major Documentation Styles

In the following APA and MLA sections, the basic standards for documenting sources are shown with examples to illustrate format. For examples not given below, you can check updates on the APA and MLA websites. As well, you can consult a college or university reference librarian or your instructor for hard-to-find formats. Make sure you follow the most up-to-date guide.

If you use an online site for help, always double-check the information with one or more other sites, taking note of when the website was updated, if possible. If you have run out of resources, or simply do not have more time to spend on the citations chase, use common sense and adapt the rule closest to your particular case.

APA Citation Style

In the social sciences, the principal documentation style has been developed by the American Psychological Association (APA). It is sometimes used in the sciences as well. The APA publishes a manual (*Publication Manual of the American Psychological Association*, 6th ed.) and maintains a website (http://www. apastyle .org) that offers updates, FAQs, and specific information on Internet citations.

APA style is parenthetical, meaning that whenever you directly quote or paraphrase an author in your essay, or use an author's idea, you include the author's last name and the year of the work in parentheses; you will usually include page number(s) as well. Then, you will provide a more complete description of all the sources on the final page(s) of your essay, titled References.

APA In-Text Citations

General Guidelines

- APA in-text formats include author(s) and year. If the author is named in a signal phrase (e.g., "Ashton found that . . ."; " . . . according to Hoffman"), the year follows the author's name and precedes the verb: "Ashton (2008) found that. . ."; " . . . according to Hoffman (1998)." Otherwise, the publication year follows the author's name in the end parentheses: "(Ashton, 2008)."
- A specific reference, such as a direct quotation or paraphrase, requires a page number. Use the abbreviation "p." for "page" and "pp." for "pages."
- Use commas to separate items in the citation.

Specific Guidelines

Citation after a direct quotation. Give the last name of author(s), a comma, year of publication, a comma, and page number(s) all in parentheses:

No signal phrase:

During World Wars I and II, the Canadian government often employed masseuses because surgery and medical care were insufficient "to restore severely wounded men" (Cleather, 1995, p. ix).

The author, Cleather, is not named in a signal phrase, so the parenthetical citation includes the author's name.

You can use a signal phrase to set up your reference (see page 263). After the author is named in the signal phrase, follow with the year. The page number is placed at the end of the reference.

Signal phrase:

According to Stambouli and Traversa (2002), "each gallon of gasoline produced and used in an internal combustion engine releases roughly 12 kg of CO_2," (p. 299).

The authors are named in the signal phrase "According to Stambouli and Traversa (2002)," so the parenthetical citation consists only of the page number. Note that the year follows the authors' names in parentheses.

Block quotation. A quotation that is at least 40 words begins on a new line and is indented one half-inch from the left margin. Quotation marks are not used, and the quotation is double spaced. The author's name, the year of publication, and the page number appear in parentheses at the end of the quotation *after* the final period.

. (Ellis & Bochner, 2000, pp. 81–82)

A paraphrase includes all the content of the source put entirely in your own words. When you paraphrase material, your citation must include the page number.

Citation for a specific reference (such as a paraphrase). State the last name of author(s), year of publication, and the page number(s) in parentheses:

Most of the profits from BC's aquaculture industry go to Norwegians, who control 92 percent of the industry (Macdonald, 2009, pp. 148–149).

You do not include a page number in a citation that refers to the work as a whole rather than to specific page(s).

Citation for a non-specific reference. An example of a non-specific reference might be an author's thesis statement or the main findings of a study. It will apply to the essay as a whole rather than to a specific page in the work. Give the last name of author(s) and the year of publication in parentheses.

Conservation biologists agree that protecting habitats is the most effective way to conserve biological diversity (Primack, 2000).

The information does not come from a specific page.

An indirect source is one that is cited in another source. Always prefer original sources, but if you have to cite information from an indirect source, make sure you use the phrase *as cited in* followed by the place where you got the information.

Citation referring to an indirect source. If it is necessary to refer to a source found in another work, include the original author in the sentence, along with the name(s) in parentheses of the source of the information. This is followed by the phrase *as cited in* and year of publication. In the References section, list the details for the indirect source.

Francis Bacon (as cited in Lindemann, 2001) observed that language affects our thinking when he said that "words react on the understanding" (p. 93).

Personal communication, including interviews. Give the author's name, including first initial(s), the phrase *personal communication*, and a date all in parentheses:

(J. Derrida, personal communication, September 20, 2000).

Note that personal communications are cited only in the text of your essay; they are not listed in the References section.

Multiple sources in one citation. You may cite more than one relevant source in a single citation if the point you are making applies to both. Order the sources alphabetically by last name and separate them by a semicolon.

The practices of teaching composition in college have not radically changed in the last few decades (Bishop, 2005; Williams, 2007).

You may include more than one source in a single citation. Separate sources by semicolons.

APA In-Text Citations by Format

Kinds of Authors

Work by one author (book or article). In parentheses, give the author's last name, a comma, year of publication, a comma, and page number(s) (if required). Note that a book with both an author and an editor will usually be cited by author.

(Bloom, 2002, p. xviii).

Work by two authors. State the last names of both authors with an ampersand (&) between them, a comma, a date, a comma, and a page number in parentheses:

(Higgins & Wilson-Baptist, 1999, p. 44).

When naming the authors in the text of your essay, as in a signal phrase, use the word *and* instead of an ampersand:

Higgins and Wilson-Baptist (1999) argue that "a tourist exists outside of experience. A traveller, though, submerges herself in the new" (p. 44).

Works by three, four, or five authors. List the last names of all authors in parentheses for the first citation. Later citations need the last name of the first author followed by the abbreviation *et al.* with the publication year in parentheses. If the authors are mentioned more than once in a paragraph, the year of publication is not included after the first reference.

(Higgins, Wilson-Baptist, & Krasny, 2001)

second citation in the paragraph: (Higgins et al.)

When you refer to a work with more than one author in a citation, use an ampersand (&) to separate the last author's name from the preceding name.

Work by six or more authors. State the last name of the first author followed by the abbreviation *et al.*, a comma, and the publication year in parentheses:

(Terracciano et al., 2005)

To cite six or more authors, give the name of the first author followed by *et al.*

Two or more works by the same author in the same year. Add letters alphabetically in lower case (*a*, *b*, *c*, etc.) to distinguish works published in the same year:

. . . self-enforced discipline (Foucault, 1980a, p. 37)

The *a* after the year, above, indicates that you have used at least two works by the same author in 1980 and would correspond with the entry for 1980a in your references page.

Two authors with the same last name. Include the authors' first initial(s) separated from the last names by commas:

(Sinkinson, S., & Sinkinson, B., 2001, pp. 225–237)

Group or organization as author (corporate author). Documents published by companies and government departments may not list an author. If the group title is long or is well known by an acronym or abbreviation of the name (for example, the United Nations Children's Fund is commonly known as UNICEF), for the first citation include, in parentheses, the entire title where the author's name would appear; follow with the acronym in square brackets, a comma, and the year of publication. Use the abbreviation with the year of publication throughout the rest of the paper. If the group name is not well known, use the full name with publication year each time.

(American Educational Research Association [AERA], 2001)

later citations: (AERA, 2001)

If no author is given, use the name of the group or organization in place of the author's name.

Work with an unknown author (including many dictionary and encyclopedia articles). Put the first few words of the title of an article or chapter in quotation marks and follow with a comma, and the year of publication.

("Plea to City Hall," 2003)

Author is anonymous or not named. Cite in the same way as a named author:

(Anonymous, 1887, p. 12)

APA In-Text Citations: Electronic Sources

The most challenging aspect of citing online documents is that they often lack page numbers. If paragraph numbers are given, cite by paragraph number preceded by the abbreviation *para.* If neither page nor paragraph numbers are available but the document includes section headings, cite the heading title in quotation marks and include the paragraph number(s) in which the material occurs.

Many articles retrieved from a database are viewed as Portable Document Format (PDF) files. In such cases, use the page numbers in the document. They are usually the same as the page numbers of the print version (if one exists).

Sample in-text Internet citation. Include the author's last name, a comma, the year the site was mounted or updated, a comma, a heading title (if applicable), a comma, and page or paragraph number in parentheses:

(Gregoire, 2000, "Bones and Teeth," para. 5)

Internet site without an author or without a date. Use the title or an abbreviated form of the title in quotation marks, a comma, the year the site was mounted or updated, a comma, and a page or paragraph reference. Use the abbreviation *n.d.* if the date that the site was created is absent.

("Muchinfo's Poll," 2002, para. 16)

(Hannak, n.d., para. 2)

APA In-Text Citations: Non-textual Sources

Film, video, audio, TV broadcasts, and musical recordings. Use the most senior production person's name, a comma, and the year of public release or broadcast in parentheses:

(Coppola, 1979)

Installation, event, performance, or work of art. Use the format followed by other non-textual resources, such as name of artist(s), a comma, and a date of presentation or creation:

(Byrdmore, 2006)

APA Citations in the References Section

In APA style, the References section, containing complete retrieval information, appears at the end of your essay. It begins on a new page that continues the page numbers of your essay. The References list is double spaced, with a one-inch margin.

Omit redundant words like *Publishers*, *Inc.*, and *Co.* after the publisher name, but write out complete names of associations, corporations, and university presses. Some of the most common abbreviations include

- ed. (edition)
- Ed. (Editor), Eds. (Editors)
- No. (Number)
- p. (page), pp. (pages)
- para. (paragraph)
- Pt. (Part)
- Rev. ed. (Revised edition)
- Trans. (Translator[s])
- Vol. (Volume), Vols. (Volumes)

Guidelines

- The title is centred an inch from the top of the page.
- The list is alphabetized by author's last name; each entry begins flush left with the margin; subsequent lines are indented half an inch from the margin. Items are not numbered.

If you cannot locate page or paragraph numbers in an electronic document, give the section heading in quotation marks and count by paragraphs from the heading to the paragraph(s) that the information is from.

- The standard APA citation begins with the author's last name followed by initial(s), not given name(s). Titles of full-length works are italicized.
- Capitalize the following elements of work titles: the first word, the first word after a colon, all proper nouns, and acronyms like NFB or CBC, regardless of how the original is capitalized.
- Capitalize each word in titles of journals except for prepositions (*in*, *of*, *to*, etc.), articles (*a*, *an*, *the*), and conjunctions (*and*, *or*).

Sample book entry. List book and report data in the following sequence: author, date of publication, title of book, place of publication, publisher:

> Fries, C. C. (1962). *Linguistics and reading*. New York, NY: Holt, Rinehart & Winston.

Sample journal entry. List journal article data in the following sequence: author, date of publication, title of article, title of journal (italicized), volume number (italicized), issue number (if required), page range, and DOI or URL:

> Valkenburg, P. M., & Jochen, P. (2007). Who visits online dating sites? Exploring some characteristics of online daters. *CyberPsychology and Behavior, 10*, 849–852. doi:10.1089/cpb.2007.9941

A DOI (digital object identifier) is included in many journal articles whether in print or electronic format. It enables readers to quickly locate documents on the Internet. See page 290.

Kinds of Authors

Work by one author. See above, "Sample book entry."

Work by two authors. Use an ampersand (&) to separate the authors, and invert the names of both authors. Place commas between the last name and the initial, and before the ampersand. Conclude with a period:

> Luckner, J., & Nadler, R. (1992). *Processing the experience*. Dubuque, IA: Kendall/Hunt Publishing.

Work by three to seven authors. List all the authors:

> Festial, L., Ian, H., & Gomez, S. (1956). *When economics fails*. Minneapolis, MN: University of Minnesota Press.

Work by eight or more authors. List the first six authors and the last author with three points of ellipses (. . .) between the sixth and the final author:

> Terracciano, A., Abdel-Khalek, A. M., Ádám, N., Adamovová, L., Ahn, C. K., Ahn, H. N., . . . McCrae, R. R. (2005). National character does not reflect mean personality trait levels in 49 cultures. *Science, 310*, 96–100. doi:10.1126/science.1117199

Two or more works by the same author. Works by the same author are arranged chronologically, earliest to latest. Works with the same publication year

The order for most final-page citations is author's last name and initial(s); publication date; title of work; and publication details, which vary depending on whether the work is a book, a journal article, or an electronic document.

With two to seven authors, invert all authors' names and use an ampersand (&) between the second-last and the last name.

Unless there are more than seven authors of the article, include all authors' names in the citation.

are arranged alphabetically by first major word of the title. Below, the earliest article is listed first; the *h* in *history* precedes the *P* in *Power*, justifying the order of the second and third items.

> Foucault, M. (1977). *Discipline and punish: The birth of the prison.* A. Sheridan (Trans.). New York, NY: Random House.

> Foucault, M. (1980a). *The history of sexuality* (Vol. 1). R. Hurley (Trans.). New York, NY: Random House.

> Foucault, M. (1980b). *Power/Knowledge: Selected interviews and other writings 1972–1977.* C. Gordon (Ed.). Brighton, England: Harvester Press.

Work by two authors with the same last name. Alphabetical order of initials determines sequence. If two works have the same first authors, the order is determined by the last name of the second author.

> Jason, L. A., & Klich, M. M. (1982). Use of feedback in reducing television watching. *Psychological Reports, 51,* 812–814.

> Jason, L. A., & Rooney-Rebeck, P. (1984). Reducing excessive television viewing. *Child & Family Behavior Therapy, 6,* 61–69.

Group or organization as author (corporate author). Use the full group name in place of the author's name. If the organization name begins with an article (e.g., *The*), omit it.

> Education International. (2008). *Guide to universities & colleges in Canada.* Victoria, BC: EI Education International.

Work with an unknown author (non-electronic source), such as an entry in a reference book. List alphabetically by the first major word in the title. When an author is listed as "Anonymous," alphabetize by the letter *A.*

> Interveners. (1993). In *Canadian Encyclopedia* (Vol. 11, pp. 344–348). Ottawa, ON: Smith Press.

No date. Replace date in parentheses by *n.d.*

Source Type

Work with an editor. Begin with the editor(s) name followed by *Ed.* (one editor) or *Eds.* (more than one editor) in parentheses:

> Corcoran, B., Hayhoe, M., & Pradl, G. M. (Eds.). (1994). *Knowledge in the making: Challenging the text in the classroom.* Portsmouth, NH: Boynton/Cook.

When a work has a group author, rather than an individual author, the group name takes the place of the author's name.

When there is no author in a non-electronic source, the entry is listed alphabetically by the first major word in the title. (This does not include words such as *The*.)

Chapter or other type of selection, such as an essay, in edited volume. Begin with the author name, year, and chapter (or essay) title. Follow with the name(s) of book editor(s), not inverted and preceded by *In*. The abbreviation *Ed.* or *Eds.* follows, and the citation concludes with the book title, page range (in parentheses), and publication information.

> The usual order for an essay or other selection in an edited book is author name, year, essay title, book editor's name preceded by *In*, the abbreviation *Ed.*, book title and page range, and other publication details.

> Sanders, D. E. (1984). Some current issues affecting Indian government. In L. Little Bear, M. Boldt, & J. A. Long (Eds.), *Pathways to self-determination: Canadian Indians and the Indian state* (pp. 113–21). Toronto, ON: University of Toronto Press.

Translated work. The translator's name is placed in parentheses after the work's title and is followed by *Trans.*

> Lacan, J. (1977). *Écrits: A selection.* (A. Sheridan, Trans.). New York, NY: W. W. Norton. (Original work published 1966)

To cite a republished book in the text of your essay, use both the original and the current publication dates:

> (Lacan, 1966/1977)

> If there is a new edition of the work, include the edition number in parentheses after the title.

Volume in multivolume work. Include the volume number after the title:

> Bosworth, A. B. (Ed.). (1995). *A historical commentary on Arrian's history of Alexander* (Vol. 1). London, England: Oxford University Press.

If referring to more than one volume, give the specific volumes or range (e.g., *Vols. 1–3*).

Second or subsequent edition of a work. Include the edition number after the title:

> Suzuki, D. T., Griffiths, A. J., & Lewontin, R. C. (1989). *An introduction to genetic analysis* (4th ed.). New York, NY: W. H. Freeman.

> Whether you include the issue number in a citation depends on whether each issue is numbered separately (include issue number) or the numbering continues from the previous issue (do not include issue number).

Article in a journal with continuous pagination. If the numbering continues from the previous issue, include the volume but not the issue number. Page numbers in journals are not preceded by *p.* or *pp.*

> Garner, R. (2003). Political ideologies and the moral status of animals. *Journal of Political Ideologies, 8,* 233–246.

Article in a journal that is paginated by issue. If every issue begins with the page number *1*, include both volume (italicized) and issue number (in parentheses and not italicized).

> Unlike journal and magazine articles, newspaper articles require the abbreviation *p.* (page) or *pp.* (pages) with all page numbers included. The exact publication date is given (i.e., year, month day).

> Trew, J. D. (2002). Conflicting visions: Don Messier, Liberal nationalism, and the Canadian unity debate. *International Journal of Canadian Studies, 26*(2), 41–57.

Article in a magazine. Cite the complete date beginning with the year; follow with a comma and the month or month and day. Include the volume and issue number if available.

> Knapp, L. (2007, September/October). Licensing music to the film and television industries. *Canadian Musician, 29*(5), 49–56.

Article in a newspaper. List the author if given; if no author is given, begin with the title. The abbreviation *p.* or *pp.* is used for newspapers. If the article breaks off and continues later in the work, give all page numbers, separated by commas, or the page range. A letter to the editor or an editorial follows the same format and includes specific information in square brackets after the title (e.g., *[Letter to the editor]*).

> Lawyer seeks mistrial for client accused of illegal midwifery. (2003, April 20). *National Post*, p. A8.

Book/movie review. Follow article format but include in brackets the title of the book and the reviewer's name preceded by "Review of" and the medium (e.g., *[Review of the DVD . . .]*).

> Mihm, S. (2009). Swindled: The dark history of food fraud, from poisoned candy to counterfeit coffee [Review of the book *Swindled: The dark history of food fraud, from poisoned candy to counterfeit coffee*, by B. Wilson]. *Business History Review, 83*(2), 379–381.

Government document. If the author is unknown, begin with the name of the government followed by the agency (e.g., ministry, department, Crown corporation) and the document name:

> British Columbia. Office of the Auditor General. 2005. *Salmon forever: An assessment of the provincial role in sustaining wild salmon*. Victoria, BC: Author.

Because the publisher is the same as the author (i.e., Office of the Auditor General of British Columbia), *Author* replaces the publisher's name in the example above.

In cases or reports, such as government documents, the report number can be placed after the work's title (e.g., *Research Report No. 09.171*).

Indirect source. List the work the citation comes from, not the original text. See page 282.

Personal communication. Because they cannot be reproduced or verified, personal communications (including emails, phone calls, interviews, and conversations) are not included in the list of references.

APA Internet Citations in the References Section

The 6th edition of the APA manual recommends that online sources include the elements of print sources in the same order with exact location information

Because they cannot be reproduced or verified, personal communications (including emails, phone calls, interviews, and conversations) are not included in the list of references.

added as needed. If available, include the DOI, which is found with other publication information, such as journal title and volume number, and/or on the first page of the article. The DOI is a number-letter sequence that begins with *10*. It forms the last element in your citation sequence and, like a uniform resource locator (URL), is *not* followed by a period.

Since not all publishers use this system, cite the URL using the home page of the journal or book publisher if the DOI is unavailable or if your instructor tells you to do so. If the document would be hard to locate from the home page, provide the exact URL or as much as is needed for retrieval. APA does not usually require your date of access for Internet sources, but you should confirm electronic links before including them in your paper. More information on electronic reference formats recommended by the APA is available at http://www .apastyle.org/manual/related/electronic-sources.pdf.

Sample electronic reference. Citation formats follow those of print sources with the title of the website replacing the journal title.

> Czekaj, L. (2009, February 7). Promises fulfilled: Looking at the legacy of thousands of black slaves who fled to Canada in the 1800s. *InnovationCanada.ca*. Retrieved from http://www.innovationcanada.ca/en/

Note the absence of a period after the URL. If it is necessary to break the URL from one line to the next, break *before punctuation*, such as the period before "innovation canada" above; never use a hyphen to break a URL unless it is part of the URL.

Group or organization (e.g., corporate or government) **website.** If there is no author, list by the organization's name:

> Environment Canada. (August 12, 2009). 10 things you should know about climate change. Retrieved from http://www.ec.gc.ca/cc/default .asp?lang=En&n=2F049262–1

The complete URL is given because it would be hard to locate the document from the organization's home page.

> Article in online-only journal:

> Rye, B. J., Elmslie, P., & Chalmers, A. (2007). Meeting a transsexual person: Experience within a classroom setting. *Canadian On-Line Journal of Queer Studies in Education*, *3*(1). Retrieved from http://jps.library. utoronto.ca/index.php/jqstudies/index

The home page of the journal has been used for retrieval information.

Article from a database (with a DOI). The name of the database is not usually required:

> Martel, M. (2009). "They smell bad, have diseases, and are lazy": RCMP officers reporting on hippies in the late sixties. *Canadian Historical Review*, *90*, 215–245. doi:10.3138/chr.90.2.215

Article from a database (no DOI). The home page of the journal is used; the name of the database is not usually required:

> Barton, S. S. (2008). Discovering the literature on aboriginal diabetes in Canada: A focus on holistic methodologies. *Canadian Journal of Nursing Research*, *40*(4), 26–54. Retrieved from http://cjnr.mcgill.ca/

No author or date. Place *n.d.* in parentheses:

> Hegemony. (n.d.). In *Merriam-Webster online dictionary*. Retrieved from http://www.merriam-webster.com/dictionary/hegemony

> Electronic-only book:

> Radford, B. (n.d.). *Soil to social*. Retrieved from http://on-line-books.ora .com/mod-bin/books.mod/javaref/javanut/index.htm

In the example, above, the first part of the article is in quotation marks, indicating that a direct quotation is part of the title. If there is a DOI, or if there is no DOI and you include the name of the journal, the name of the database can be omitted.

Electronic version of print book. Do not include publication details of the print version but include the reader version, if applicable, and either the DOI or the URL:

> Douglass, F. (1881). My escape from slavery [MS Reader version]. Retrieved from http://etext.lib.virginia.edu/ebooks/

Message posted to online forum, discussion group, or blog post:

> Koolvedge. (2009, August 8). Reply to massacre in Peru [Web log message]. Retrieved from https://www.adbusters.org/blogs/dispatches/ massacre-peru.html#comments

> If you use a video blog post, indicate this in square brackets: [Video file].

APA *Citations for Non-textual Sources*

Lecture or other oral presentation. Include the name of the lecturer, the date (in the order year, month day), the title (or topic) of the lecture, followed by *Lecture presented at* and location details, such as the sponsoring agency (or department if at a college or university) and/or building name, name of the school, and location of the school:

> Armstrong, M. (2009, April 2). *Darwin's paradox*. Lecture presented at David Strong Building, University of Victoria, Victoria, BC.

Film, video. Use the following order: producer, director, year, and title of film followed by *Motion picture* in square brackets. Conclude by giving the country of origin and studio.

> Coppola, F. F. (Producer & Director). (1979). *Apocalypse now* [Motion picture]. USA: Zoetrope Studios.

Episode from a television series. Use the following order: writer, director, year, and title of episode followed by *Television series episode* in brackets. Conclude by giving the city and broadcasting company.

Lindelof, D. (Writer), & Bender, J. (Director). (2005). Man of science, man of faith [Television series episode]. In J. J. Abrams (Executive producer), *Lost*. New York, NY: American Broadcasting.

Music. Use the following order: writer, copyright year, and title of song followed by the recording artist in brackets (if different from the writer). Conclude by giving the album title preceded by *On*, the medium of recording in brackets, the country of origin, and the label. If the recording date is different from the copyright year, provide this information in parentheses.

Morrison, V. (1993). Gloria. On *Too long in exile* [CD]. UK. Polydor.

❯ Sample Student Research Essay (APA)

In the following student essay, Erin Walker uses extensive research to investigate a problem in her field of study, social psychology. She cites her sources by using APA style.

To conserve space, the essays in this chapter are not double spaced and the References, Works Cited, and Notes are not on separate pages; in addition, the essay does not follow standard essay format requirements for title pages or identification information (see Chapter 17, Essay Presentation on page 469).

SAMPLE STUDENT RESEARCH ESSAY

The Imperfection of Perfectionism: Perfectionism as a Maladaptive Personality Trait

by Erin A. Walker

[1] What does it mean to say that one is a perfectionist? Does it mean that one does everything perfectly? As it is commonly understood, the term "perfectionist" carries the connotation that the perfectionist does everything perfectly, but this is not the case. According to perfectionism experts in social psychology, the term refers to a mentality, or set of cognitions, that are characteristic of certain people. According to Hollender (as cited in Slade & Owens, 1998), perfectionism refers to  "the practice of demanding of oneself or others a higher quality of performance than is required by the situation" (p. 384). Although the

---

APA Note: Walker refers to an indirect source here. The page reference follows the direct quotation.

After addressing the common perception of perfectionism, the writer gives one definition of the term, explaining, however, that its connotation is misleading. Her thesis, like her title, makes it plain she will use research to investigate the problems of one type of perfectionism, "maladaptive perfectionism."

term might suggest that perfectionism would be a desirable trait, this quality is, in fact, underappreciated and often unrecognized for its harmful effects on the lives of people who are maladaptive perfectionists. Perfectionism not only is associated with mental illness but also can contribute to problems in areas of life such as academic success and intimate relationships.

[2] When research on perfectionism first began, perfectionism as a social psychological construct was conceptualized as two dimensional: there was "normal" perfectionism and "neurotic" perfectionism. Normal perfectionism was characterized by setting realistic standards for oneself, taking pleasure in hard work, and having the capacity to be less selective when necessary. Neurotic perfectionists, on the other hand, set unrealistically high demands for personal achievement, feel chronically dissatisfied with their efforts, and have inflexible personal standards (Hamachek, 1978, p. 28). Clearly, normal perfectionism can, at times, be highly adaptive, whereas neurotic perfectionism is typically maladaptive. Normal perfectionism can be an adaptive quality insofar as it propels a person toward excellence and meeting important goals, whereas neurotic perfectionism is maladaptive in that it can foster self-defeating behaviours, concerns over how others view the self, and excessive worry over mistakes (Slade & Owens, 1998, p. 373). Slade and Owens summarized the similarity and differences between adaptive and maladaptive perfectionism when they wrote,

> [3] [f]or both types of perfectionists, the setting of high standards is a common feature. The crucial difference is that the normal perfectionist, when achieving these standards, feels pleased and satisfied, whereas the neurotic perfectionist can never do enough to feel satisfied with his or her performance. (p. 374)

[4] Finally, research by Hewitt and Flett (1991) suggests that there are three dimensions to perfectionism, termed self-oriented perfectionism, other-oriented perfectionism, and socially-prescribed perfectionism. Self-oriented perfectionism, "is not simply the tendency to have high standards for oneself; it also includes the intrinsic need to be perfect and compulsive striving for perfection and self-improvement"

In this paragraph, the author uses comparison and contrast, outlining the kinds of behaviours that separate the two types of perfectionists.

Writing Tip: Walker uses strategies for coherence in this paragraph, including transitions (*on the other hand, clearly*) and parallel structures

APA Note: When two or more authors are named in the text of your essay, you don't use the ampersand (&) symbol. Notice that the previous citation is only a general one, so no page number is needed. Below, Walker uses a specific reference, so the page number is included.

Long direct quotations are set up in block format. They are indented and do not include quotation marks. Because a signal phrase was used (*Slade and Owens summarized*), the parenthetical citation includes only the page number.

Writing Tip: In order to deal with complex material, Walker uses the classification pattern, discussing three "dimensions," or categories, of perfectionism. She then discusses them in the order they are listed in the topic sentence.

(continued)

APA Note: APA style, often used in the social sciences, particularly psychology, includes the publication year in most references; however, when you use a source more than once in the same paragraph, you do not need to repeat the year. Because the same source is used consecutively in this paragraph, only the page numbers are required after the first reference.

Walker uses two sources in this paragraph, integrating them effectively through summary and mixed quotation format. She uses brackets to make necessary grammatical changes. Note that she provides a page reference here as she has paraphrased specific content.

In contrast to the previous paragraph where the specific wording seems important, Walker uses only summary here, putting the main ideas in her own words.

Reading Tip: Try to determine the meanings of specialized words like *etiology* and *longitudinal* (in the last sentence of this paragraph) by context. The meanings of other challenging words, like *avert* and *propensity*, can be determined the same way.

APA Note: Multiple sources can be combined in a single citation; semicolons separate the sources.

Reading Tip: Essays using APA style can be hard to read because of the number of multi-authored studies in the social sciences and sciences. A good strategy is to ignore parenthetical citations when you read an article for the first time, returning to them later if you need more information.

(p. 468). Not surprisingly, other-oriented perfectionism is the opposite, with outward-directed perfectionistic expectations. Other-oriented perfectionism, then, is characterized by one "hav[ing] unrealistic standards for significant others, plac[ing] importance on other people being perfect, and stringently evaluat[ing] others' performance" (p. 457). Finally, socially-prescribed perfectionism involves "the perception of other people's imposed expectations . . . [and] a perceived incontingency between one's own behaviour and the unrealistic standards prescribed by others" (p. 468). Considering the two-dimensional concept of perfectionism described above, other-oriented perfectionism is a new concept, while self-prescribed perfectionism would map on to normal or adaptive perfectionism, and socially-prescribed perfectionism would coincide with neurotic or maladaptive perfectionism (Slade & Owens, 1998, p. 377).

[5] Research on theories of perfectionism has not been as prolific as investigations into the types of perfectionism. However, one conceptualization by Slade and Owens (1998) suggests that perfectionism may have three roots: social contingency, avoidance, and rule-governing. With social contingency, perfectionism may develop upon repeated reinforcement of skilled (or unskilled) behaviour. Otherwise, perfectionism may be an avoidance behaviour, whereby children will over-perform in response to inconsistent parenting, so that they will not have to learn what punishment would result from imperfect achievement. Finally, perfectionism may be a form of rule-governed behaviour, in that a child may infer correctly or incorrectly, through implicit or explicit cues, that only perfectionistic behaviour will be rewarded; as a result, the child will become perfectionistic.

[6] While Slade and Owens (1998) have taken a behaviourist perspective as to the etiology of perfectionism, other researchers have proposed the common psychoanalytic theory of perfectionism arising from faulty parenting. That is, perfectionism results from overly critical (Flett, Hewitt, & Singer, 1995; Frost, Lahart, & Rosenblate, 1991; Rice, Ashby, & Preusser, 1996, as cited in Kawamura, Frost, & Harmatz, 2002), demanding (Rice, Ashby, & Preusser, 1996), and authoritarian (Flett, Hewitt, & Singer, 1995) parenting. Recently, Kawamura, Frost, and Harmatz (2002) found that

maladaptive perfectionism is associated with authoritarian parenting, and suggested four reasons for this. First, parental approval often determines a child's sense of self-worth, and the child may develop an obsession with perfection as one way to avert parental criticism (Burns, 1980; Driscoll, 1982; as cited in Kawamura, et al., p. 325). Second, it was proposed that after a while, authoritarian parenting may instil in a child a similar propensity for self-criticism. Third, it is possible that authoritarian parenting is merely a mistaken perception on behalf of independently perfectionistic children. Finally, Kawamura et al. proposed that perfectionism may develop as "perfectionists are constantly focused on their own mistakes, [and] can more easily recall instances in which their parents were also harsh and critical in their evaluation of them" (p. 325). Since research on perfectionism only began in earnest approximately 25–30 years ago (Slade & Owens, 1998), there has not yet been longitudinal research that can provide solid evidence for particular types of parenting leading to perfectionism, although logically, a psychoanalytic theory seems most plausible.

[7] Given the nature of perfectionism and its pervasiveness, it is not surprising that recent research has shown associations between perfectionism and mental illness. Research by Rice, Vergara, and Aldea (2006) has found that "[s]elf-critically perfectionistic evaluations were associated with poorer self-regulation capacities and worse adjustment" (p. 469). Furthermore, maladaptive perfectionists were found to hold more inflexibly dichotomous perceptions of people and issues, as well as themselves, and to report greater amounts of stress in their lives (Rice et al.). It was proposed that these problems result due to perfectionists' problematic coping styles and stress-management efforts (Dunkley, Zuroff, & Blankstein, as cited in Rice et al.), attributional style (Chang & Sanna, 2001, as cited in Rice et al.), and social problem-solving (Chang, 2003, as cited in Rice et al.). In addition, a study by Kawamura, Hunt, Frost, and DiBartolo (2001) found that anxiety—in the form of social anxiety, trait anxiety, and worry—was associated with maladaptive perfectionism. This study also revealed an association between adaptive as well as maladaptive perfectionism, and Post-Traumatic Stress Disorder (PTSD) (Kawamura et al., 2001). Surprisingly, the authors found that depression is related to adaptive perfectionism, although this correlation

Writing Tip: Walker numbers some of her points in this paragraph to make the ideas easier to follow.

After summarizing the research, Walker concludes that one theory is more "plausible" than another.

Notice that all the sources in this paragraph are current ones (in contrast to the previous paragraph, which discussed theories of perfectionism). By looking at the topics of both paragraphs, can you infer the reason for this?

APA Note: Walker uses one source—Rice, Vergara, and Aldea—often in this paragraph. In her first reference, she names all authors; for later references she uses the abbreviation *Rice et al.* Can you identify one other source in this paragraph where she uses the same formats?

(continued)

is not as strong as the association between depression and maladaptive perfectionism (Kawamura et al.). Therefore, it is clear that perfectionism, regardless of type, is associated with facets of mental illness, although maladaptive perfectionists appear to be more seriously afflicted than are adaptive perfectionists.

[8] A logically related correlate of the association between perfectionism—as a personality problem—and mental illness is academic success. Rice and Dellwo (2002) found that maladaptive perfectionists reported less emotional, academic, and social well-being compared to adaptive perfectionists and non-perfectionists. Adaptive perfectionists, on the other hand, reported greater self-esteem, academic integration, and social integration—although, consistent with Kawamura, Hunt, Frost, and DiBartolo's (2001) finding, this group did evidence higher levels of depression than did non-perfectionists. There was no difference found in GPA, however, in the three groups. The authors concluded that

> [9] [t]he emotional and interpersonal correlates of maladaptive per-
> fectionism suggest that this comparable level of academic achieve-
> ment comes with decided costs to well being . . . . [Maladaptive
> perfectionists] feel considerably worse and do not consider them-
> selves to be as academically well-integrated as the other students.
> (Rice & Dellwo, 2002, p. 194)

[10] Finally, it is likely that, due to its permeating nature, perfectionism would affect one's intimate relationships. Considering more specifically what effect perfectionism might have on intimate relationships, Martin and Ashby (2004) proposed that, due to their fear of revealing personal inadequacies and tendency to perceive their efforts as unsuccessful, or not achieving their personal standards, maladaptive perfectionists would have a fear of intimacy in close relationships. This research was deemed necessary due to the overwhelming evidence that intimacy, an element of social support, has been shown to buffer effects associated with maladaptive perfectionism, such as anxiety and depression (Martin & Ashby). As suspected, the authors found that compared to non-perfectionists, maladaptive perfectionists show an increased

Writing Tip: Walker has used two appositives in this sentence, surrounding them with commas. An example of non-essential information, an appositive can be taken out of the sentence without changing its meaning.

Writing Tip: This paragraph is unified by its focus on one significant study, Martin and Ashby (2004), which was conducted to test the findings of previous studies. Walker then explains the result of the Martin and Ashby study: their prediction was confirmed. She summarizes the authors' explanation for their findings and concludes with a paragraph wrap.

fear of intimacy. Martin and Ashby proposed that the reason for this is that maladaptive perfectionists, feeling personally inadequate, feel exposed and vulnerable in close relationships, therefore leading to a fear of intimacy. They will "fear the honest self-disclosure necessary for the development of intimacy in family relationships and romantic partnerships" (Martin & Ashby, p. 372) due to their need to disguise personal flaws that they perceive as unacceptable and a tendency to overcompensate in response to their perception of inferiority to intimate others. Clearly, maladaptive perfectionism has important, negative repercussions on an individual's intimate relationships.

[11] As a personality characteristic, perfectionism is often a psychologically harmful quality. Although adaptive perfectionism has been associated with positive elements such as the pursuit of excellence, it has also been associated with increased levels of depression as compared to non-perfectionists. Maladaptive perfectionism is that much more detrimental to an individual's life in that it is associated with more elements of mental illness and with difficulty in academics and intimate relationships. Since, as Costa and McCrae (1986) point out, personality is relatively stable, research on perfectionism is needed to better understand and help people suffering from this trait.

> Walker briefly summarizes her thesis and main points in her circular conclusion, focusing on both types of perfectionism, but mostly the maladaptive type. In her last sentence, she makes a brief appeal for further research.

References

> **APA Note:** Under the heading "References," the writer alphabetically lists all her sources. APA replaces author's first names by initials, and the first letters of most words in article titles are not capitalized. Walker has used journal articles in her research, ensuring that her information is current.

Bieling, P. J., Israeli, A. L., & Antony, M. M. (2004). Is perfectionism good, bad, or both? Examining models of the perfectionism construct. *Personality and Individual Differences, 36*, 1373–1385. doi:10.1016/S0191-8869(03)00235-6

Costa, P. T., & McCrae, R. R. (1986). Personal stability and its implications for clinical psychology. *Clinical Psychology Review, 6*, 401–423. doi:10.1016/0272-7358(86)90029-2

Hamachek, D. E. (1978). Psychodynamics of normal and neurotic perfectionism. *Psychology: A Journal of Human Behaviour, 15*(1), 27–33.

Hewitt, P. L., & Flett, G. L (1991). Perfectionism in the self and social contexts: Conceptualization, assessment, and association with psychopathology. *Journal of Personality and Social Psychology, 60*, 456–470. doi:10.1037/0022–3514.60.3.456

> **APA Note:** APA encourages the use of a DOI (digital object identifier) for both print and online journal sources where it is available.

(continued)

Kawamura, K. Y., Frost, R. O., & Harmatz, M. G. (2002). The relationship of perceived parenting styles to perfectionism. *Personality and Individual Differences, 32*, 317–327. doi:10.1016/S0191-8869(01)00026-5

Kawamura, K. Y., Hunt, S. L., Frost, R. O., & DiBartolo, P. M. (2001). Perfectionism, anxiety, and depression: Are the relationships independent? *Cognitive Therapy and Research, 25*(3), 291–301.

Martin, J. L., & Ashby, J. S. (2004). Perfectionism and fear of intimacy: Implications for relationships. *The Family Journal: Counseling and Therapy for Couples and Families, 12*(4), 368–374.

Rice, K. G., Ashby, J. S., & Preusser, K. J. (1996). Perfectionism, relationships with parents, and self-esteem. *Individual Psychology: Journal of Adlerian Theory, 52*(3), 246–260.

Rice, K. G., & Dellwo, J. P. (2002). Perfectionism and self-development: Implications for college adjustment. *Journal of Counseling and Development, 80,* 188–196.

Rice, K. G., Vergara, D. T., & Aldea, M. A. (2006). Cognitive-affective mediators of perfectionism and college student adjustment. *Personality and Individual Differences, 40*, 463–473. doi:10.1016/j.paid.2005.05.011

Slade, P. D., & Owens, R. G. (1998). A dual process model of perfectionism based on reinforcement theory. *Behaviour Modification, 22*(3), 372–390.

APA Note: If each journal issue is numbered separately (i.e., begins with page 1), you must include the issue number after the volume number; the issue number is put in parentheses with no spacing after volume number; it is not italicized. Contrast this example with the one above it that does not include issue number.

APA Note: Where consecutive entries begin with the same last name and author initials, order is determined by the last name of the second author.

MLA Citation Style

In the humanities, the principal documentation style has been developed by the Modern Language Association of America (MLA). The MLA publishes two manuals that define its style. The MLA *Style Manual and Guide to Scholarly Publishing* is designed for publishing academics. The MLA *Handbook for Writers of Research Papers*, 7th edition (2009), is compiled specifically for student researchers in such disciplines as cultural studies, English, and modern languages. The Association also maintains a website (http://www.mla.org) that offers guidelines on Internet citations and updates. If you use an online source for documentation, ensure it is reliable and follows the guidelines of the *Handbook*'s 7th edition.

MLA style is parenthetical, meaning that whenever you directly quote or paraphrase an author in your essay, or use an author's idea, you include the author's last name and the location of the reference (usually a page or paragraph number) in parentheses. Then, you provide a more complete description of all the sources on the final page(s) of your paper, titled Works Cited.

MLA In-Text Citations

Guidelines

MLA in-text formats include author(s) and page number(s) (e.g., "Ashton 17"). If the author is named in a signal phrase (e.g., "Ashton found that . . . ."; "according to Hoffman"), only the page number will be in parentheses: (17).

MLA in-text formats include author's last name(s) and page or paragraph number(s).

- Do not use page abbreviations (*p, pp*); in page ranges, drop the redundant hundreds digit in the second page number (e.g., 212–47, *not* 212–247), but use both tens digits (e.g., 34–37).
- Leave one space between the author's last name and the page number. Do not use commas to separate items unless you need to include both an author and title in the citation or if you need to separate author from paragraph number in an electronic source.
- Readability and efficiency are key principles in the MLA system: parenthetical references should not intrude in the text, but clearly indicate the cited source(s).

Specifics

Citation for a direct quotation, paraphrase, or summary. Give the last name of the author and the page number in parentheses:

A paraphrase includes all the content of the source put entirely in your own words.

No signal phrase:

During World Wars I and II, the Canadian government often employed masseuses because surgery and medical care were insufficient "to restore severely wounded men" (Cleather ix).

You can use a signal phrase to set up your reference (see page 263). Since a signal phrase names the author, the citation requires only the page number.

Signal phrase:

According to Stambouli and Traversa, "each gallon of gasoline produced and used in an internal combustion engine releases roughly 12 kg of CO_2" (299).

Block quotation. In MLA style, a quotation that is longer than four typed lines is indented one inch from the left margin. Quotation marks are not used, and the quotation should be double spaced. The author's name and page number appear in parentheses at the end of the quotation and *after* the final period.

An indirect source is one that is cited in another source— not the original one. Always prefer direct sources, but if you have to cite information from an indirect source, make sure you use the phrase *as qtd. in* (*qtd.* is an abbreviation for *quoted*) followed by the place where you got the information.

. (Ellis and Bochner 81–82)

Citation referring to an indirect source. If it is necessary to refer to a source found in another work, include the original author in the sentence, along with the name(s) in parentheses of the source of the information. This is preceded by the abbreviation "qtd. in" and followed by page number(s):

> Francis Bacon observed that language affects our thinking when he said "words react on the understanding" (qtd. in Lindemann 93).

In Works Cited, list details for the indirect source (in this example, for Lindemann).

Personal communication, including interviews. These kinds of communication need the interviewee's last name only, in parentheses:

> (McWhirter)

Multiple sources in one citation. You may cite more than one relevant source in a single citation if the point you are making applies to both. Order the sources alphabetically by last name and separate them by a semicolon.

> The practices of teaching composition in college have not radically changed in the last few decades (Bishop 65; Williams 6).

However, if the citation is lengthy, consider moving the entire citation to a note (see MLA Notes, page 311).

MLA In-Text Citations by Format

Kinds of Authors

Work by one author (book or article). Give the author's last name and page number in parentheses. Note that a book with an author and an editor will typically be cited by author.

> (Bloom 112)

Work by two authors. Give the last names of both authors with the word *and* between them, in addition to a page number all in parentheses:

> (Higgins and Wilson-Baptist 44)

Work by three and by more than three authors. Include the last names of all authors with commas between them. When following this format for citing three authors, the word *and* is placed between the second and third names in the list in addition to page number(s) in parentheses. For more than three authors, include all names as above or give only the last name of the first author with the abbreviation *et al.*, and page number(s) in parentheses.

> (Higgins, Wilson-Baptist, and Krasny 102); (Terracciano et al. 96)

If you cite two sources in the same sentence, placing the citation after each source may help with clarity: e.g., "One study looked for correlations between GPA and listening to music (Cox and Stevens 757) while another study related academic performance to three types of music (Roy 6)."

Two or more works by the same author. Give the author's last name, along with a shortened version of the work's title separated by a comma, and a page number:

> "self-enforced discipline" (Foucault, *Power/Knowledge* 37)

Two authors with the same last name. Include the authors' first initials along with page number(s):

> (S. Sinkinson and B. Sinkinson 225–37)

Group or organization as author (corporate author). Documents published by companies and other groups may not list an author. MLA style recommends including the entire name of the organization in the sentence itself, if possible, in order to avoid overly long citations. For example, the organization commonly known as UNICEF would appear as the United Nations Children's Fund (along with a page number in parentheses). However, it is also acceptable to shorten the organization's name and place it in parentheses, accompanied by the page number in the same manner as a standard author citation.

If no author is given, use the name of the group or organization in place of the author's name—in the sentence itself, if possible.

> The United Nations Children's Fund reports that indigenous children are at exceptional risk of becoming refugees (204).

> Some child protection advocates suggest that indigenous children are at exceptional risk of becoming refugees (UNICEF 204).

For specific references from electronic documents without page numbers, use paragraph number(s) if visible, separated by a comma from the author's name; the abbreviation for *paragraph(s)* is *par(s)*. If sections are numbered, use these, preceded by a comma and the abbreviation *sec.*

Work by an unknown author (including many dictionary and encyclopedia entries). Begin with the title, if it is short, followed by the page number, in parentheses. When the title is lengthy, a condensed version can be used. Distinguish articles from complete works by placing article titles in quotation marks.

> ("Plea to City Hall" 22).

MLA In-Text Citations: Electronic Sources

The most challenging aspect of citing online documents is that they often lack page numbers. If your source is the entire website, place the author's name within the sentence without a citation. If you are citing a specific quotation or paraphrasing and the document uses paragraph numbers, use these (preceded by the abbreviation *par.* [one paragraph] or *pars.* [more than one] with a comma and space between author's name and *par.*). If sections are numbered, you may use these numbers (preceded by the abbreviation *sec.*). If the reference is specific but the document has neither numbered pages nor paragraphs or section headings, the work must be cited without a page, paragraph, or section reference.

Citation of entire website. Give the author's last name within the sentence:

> In his article, Dillon compares reading practices for print media to those for electronic media.

Many articles retrieved from a database are viewed as Portable Document Format (PDF) files. In such cases, use the page numbers in the document. They are usually the same as the page numbers of the print version (if one exists).

If you are referring to a website itself, rather than a specific part, include the author's name within the sentence and do not use any numbering.

Citation from specific passage. The specific location is given in the parenthetical citation:

> One firmly entrenched belief is that reading screens will never replace reading books and other print media (Dillon, sec. 1).

Internet site without an author. A site without an author's name follows the guidelines for a print document without an author and uses the site title to direct readers to the source of any information.

> ("LHC Machine Outreach")

MLA In-Text Citations: Non-textual Sources

Film, video, audio, TV broadcasts, musical recordings, and other non-textual media. Place the name of the individual(s) most relevant to your discussion in the text. In the case of a film, this could be the director, performer, screenwriter, or other contributor. If your focus is on the whole work, use the title.

> Francis Ford Coppola's film *The Conversation* explores the psychology of surveillance.

In the Works Cited section, the entry would be alphabetized under *C* for *Coppola*, the film's producer.

MLA Citations in the Works Cited Section

In MLA style, the Works Cited section containing complete retrieval information appears at the end of your essay and begins on a new page that continues the numbers of your essay. The Works Cited list is double spaced, with a one-inch margin. Omit words like *Press*, *Inc.*, and *Co.* after publisher name (but university presses should be abbreviated *UP* for *University Press*). Some of the most common abbreviations used in MLA style include

- assn. (association)
- ch. (chapter)
- ed. (editor[s], edition)
- fwd. (foreword)
- introd. (introduction)
- P (Press)
- par. (paragraph), pars. (paragraphs)
- pt. (part)
- rev. (revised)
- rpt. (reprint)
- sec. (section)
- trans. (translator)
- U (University)
- vol. (volume)

Guidelines

- The title is centred an inch from the top of the page without underlining or bolding.
- The list is alphabetized by author's last name; each entry begins flush with the margin with subsequent lines indented half an inch.
- The standard MLA citation begins with the author's last name, followed by a complete first name (unless the author has published only initial[s]). Italicize book titles and titles of other complete works, such as plays, films, and artistic performances—along with journal titles and websites; place quotation marks around titles of articles, essays, book chapters, short stories, poems, web pages, and TV episodes.
- All first letters of major words in the title are capitalized, even if the source did not do so.
- The medium of publication or a similar descriptor is included, usually as the last element.

Sample book entry. List book (pamphlet or brochure) data in the following sequence: author; title (italicized); place of publication; shortened version of the publisher's name created by removing articles like *A* or *The* and abbreviations; year of publication; publication medium:

> Fries, Charles, C. *Linguistics and Reading*. New York: Holt, Rinehart and Winston, 1962. Print.

Sample journal entry. List journal article data in this sequence: author; title of article (in quotation marks); title of journal (italicized); volume number; issue number; year of publication; inclusive pages; publication medium:

> Valkenburg, Patti M., and Peter Jochen. "Who Visits Online Dating Sites? Exploring Some Characteristics of Online Daters." *CyberPsychology and Behavior* 10.6 (2007): 849–52. Print.

The order for most Works Cited entries is author's last name and first name; title of work; publication details, which vary depending on whether the work is a book, a journal article, or an electronic document; and medium of publication.

Kinds of Authors

Work by one author (book). See above, "Sample book entry."
Work by two or three authors. Only the first author's complete name is inverted, with a comma before *and*:

> Luckner, John, and Reldan Nadler. *Processing the Experience*. Dubuque: Kendall/Hunt, 1992. Print.

Work by more than three authors. MLA style provides two possibilities: (1) the complete names of all authors, reversing the name of the first author only and including a comma between the authors' names, or (2) the complete name of just the first author plus the abbreviation *et al.* ("and others"):

Festial, Lawrence, Harold Inch, Susan Gomez, and Komiko Smith. *When Economics Fails*. Minneapolis: U of Minnesota P, 1956. Print.

Or:

Festial, Lawrence, et al. *When Economics Fails*. Minneapolis: U of Minnesota P, 1956. Print.

Two or more works by the same author. Works by the same author are arranged chronologically from earliest to most recent publication. The author's name appears in the first listing only, with three dashes substituted for it in the additional citation(s).

Foucault, Michel. *Discipline and Punish: The Birth of the Prison*. Trans. Alan Sheridan. New York: Random, 1977. Print.

———. *The History of Sexuality*. Trans. Robert Hurley. 3 vols. New York: Random, 1978. Print.

Work by two authors with the same last name. Alphabetical order of first names determines sequence. If two works have the same first authors, the order is determined by the last name of the second author:

Srivastava, Sarita, and Margot Francis. "The Problem of 'Authentic Experience.'" *Critical Sociology* 32.2–3 (2006): 275–307. Print

Srivastava, Sarita, and Mary-Jo Nadeau. "From the Inside: Anti-Racism in Social Movements." *New Socialist* 42 (2003). 18 May 2006. Web. 8 Dec. 2009.

The order in the example, above, is determined by the last name of the second author, *Nadeau*.

Group or organization as author (corporate author). Use the full group name in place of the author's name. If the organization name begins with an article (e.g., *The*), omit it.

Education International. *Guide to Universities & Colleges in Canada*. 2000 ed. Victoria: EI Education International, 2000. Print.

Work without an author, a publisher, or a publication location (non-electronic). If the work being cited does not provide an author's name, it is preferable to list it alphabetically by the title. For missing publication details, use the following abbreviations: *N.p.* means "no place" if inserted before colon and "no publisher" if inserted after; *N.d.* means "no date." Use square brackets to identify any information that isn't from the source; if the information may be unreliable, add a question mark.

No author name (unsigned encyclopedia entry):

"Interveners." *Canadian Encyclopedia*. 1985 ed. Print.

No publisher:

Webb, Noah. *The Great Haileybury Forest Fire*. [Ontario?]: n.p. 1971. Print.

The entry above has no known publisher; the place of publication is tentatively identified as Ontario.

No publishing place or date:

Case, Michael. *Opus Dei*. N.p.: Slipshod P, n.d. Print.

Source Type

Work by author with an editor or a translator. Begin with the author's name unless you refer primarily to the work of the editor (for example, his or her introduction or notes); original publication date can be included after the title. Follow the same format for a translated work. *Ed.* is used for one or more editors.

Referring primarily to the text:

Hawthorne, Nathaniel. *The Scarlet Letter*. 1850. Ed. John Stephen Martin. Peterborough: Broadview, 1995. Print.

The first date indicates the year the book was originally published.

Referring primarily to editor's work:

Martin, John Stephen, ed. *The Scarlet Letter*. By Nathaniel Hawthorne. 1850. Peterborough: Broadview, 1995. Print.

Translated work. The abbreviation *Trans.* precedes the translator's name after the work's title:

Calvino, Italo. *Why Read the Classics?* Trans. Martin McLaughlin. New York: Pantheon, 1999. Print.

Chapter or other type of selection, such as an essay, in an edited volume. Begin with the author's name and chapter (or essay) title. Follow with the book title and book editor(s) names, not inverted and preceded by *Ed.* The citation concludes with publication information, the complete page range, and publication medium:

Sanders, Douglas E. "Some Current Issues Affecting Indian Government." *Pathways to Self-Determination: Canadian Indians and the Indian State*. Ed. Leroy Little Bear, Menno Boldt, and J. Anthony Long. Toronto: U of Toronto P, 1984. 113–21. Print.

If you use more than one work from the same collection, you can economize by creating one entry for the work as a whole and abbreviated entries for specific works.

Main entry:

Little Bear, Leroy, Menno Boldt, and J. Anthony Long, eds. *Pathways to Self-Determination: Canadian Indians and the Indian State.* Toronto: U of Toronto P, 1984. Print.

Specific entry for Sanders, above (other works would be set up the same):

Sanders, Douglas E. "Some Current Issues Affecting Indian Government." Little Bear, Boldt, and Long. 113–21.

Introduction, preface, foreword, or afterword. Begin with the author of the introduction, etc. followed by the section name (not in quotation marks). The title of the complete work comes next, then the work's author preceded by *By*.

Scholes, Robert. Foreword. *The Fantastic: A Structural Approach to a Literary Genre.* By Tzvetan Todorov. Trans. Richard Howard. Ithaca: Cornell UP, 1975. v–xi. Print.

Volume in multivolume work. State the volume number if you use one work; if you use more than one, give the number of volumes used in place of the specific volume number:

Bosworth, A. B., ed. *A Historical Commentary on Arrian's History of Alexander.* Vol. 1. London: Oxford UP, 1980. Print.

If you used two volumes, *2 vols.* would replace *Vol. 1*, above. In your essay, the parenthetical reference would include author's name, volume number followed by a colon; after a space, include the page number(s).

Second or subsequent edition of a work. Include the edition number after the title (or editor, translator, etc.):

Suzuki, David, Aaron Griffiths, and Rebecca Lewontin. *An Introduction to Genetic Analysis.* 4th ed. New York: Freeman, 1989. Print.

Book published before 1900. The publisher's name can be omitted; between the place of publication and year, insert only a comma.

Baring Gould, S. *Old Country Life.* 5th ed. London, 1895. Print.

Article in a journal. Whether the numbering of the journal continues with each succeeding issue (continuous pagination) or begins with the number *1* for every issue, you should include both the volume and issue numbers. Of course, if the journal does not number both volumes and issues, one of these will be missing.

Trew, Johanne Devlin. "Conflicting Visions: Don Messier, Liberal Nationalism, and the Canadian Unity Debate." *International Journal of Canadian Studies* 26.2 (2002): 41–57. Print.

Article in a magazine. Cite the complete date (day, month, year) if the magazine is issued every week or every two weeks; if issued monthly or every two months, include month and year. If the article breaks off and continues later in the work, cite the first page number followed by a plus sign—not the whole page range (e.g., *12+* indicates the article begins on page 12 and continues somewhere after page 12).

Knapp, Lonny. "Licensing Music to the Film and Television Industries." *Canadian Musician* Sept./Oct. 2007: 49–56. Print.

Article in a newspaper. Cite the author if given; if no author is given, begin with the title. Give the day, month, and year; give the page number preceded by a section number or letter if more than one section. If the article breaks off and continues later in the work, cite first page number followed by a plus sign as for a magazine article (above). A letter to the editor follows the same format and includes *Letter* after the title.

"Lawyer seeks mistrial for client accused of illegal midwifery." *National Post* 20 April 2003: A8. Print.

Book/movie review. Follow the reviewer's name by title of review; if there is no title, continue with *Rev. of* and book/movie title followed by *by* and the author's (director's) name. Conclude with publication information.

Mihm, Stephen. Rev. of *Swindled: The Dark History of Food Fraud, from Poisoned Candy to Counterfeit Coffee*, by Bee Wilson. Business History Review 83.2 (2006): 379–81. Print.

Government document. If the author is unknown, begin with the name of the government followed by the agency (e.g., ministry, department, Crown corporation) and document name:

British Columbia. Office of the Auditor General. *Salmon Forever: An Assessment of the Provincial Role in Sustaining Wild Salmon*. Victoria: Office of the Auditor General of British Columbia, 2005. Print.

Indirect source. Cite the work where you found the citation rather than the original text. This example refers to the indirect source citation "(qtd. in Lindemann 93)" that appeared under MLA In-Text Citations, "Citation referring to an indirect source."

Lindemann, Erika. *A Rhetoric for Writing Teachers*. 4th ed. New York: Oxford UP, 2001. Print.

Personal communication, including interview. Include a description of the communication. TS below stands for "typescript":

Carr, Emily. Letter to Lawren Harris. 12 December 1940. TS.

MLA Web Publication Citations

When you type in a URL, most word-processing programs automatically flag it as a hyperlink. This means that the URLs are underlined and usually show up in blue. If you are reading the document electronically and click on the hyperlink (and if you are connected to the Internet), you will automatically be taken to that URL. However, in print documents, you must delete the hyperlink. Therefore, before printing your essay, make sure all URLs show up as plain text and not as hyperlinks.

As online sources often change or even disappear, the MLA recommends that you download or print research material that may become inaccessible later. In cases where some relevant information is unavailable (such as page or paragraph numbers), cite what you can to enable the reader to access the source. Note that a URL surrounded by angled brackets is used only if the source would be otherwise hard to locate. (If you need to divide the URL between two lines, break it after single or double slashes.) The date of access, however, is a basic part of web citations.

Sample electronic citation. Title of the website follows the work's title, which is then followed by the site's publisher or sponsor; if that name is unavailable, use *N.p.* The first date is that of the website or the latest update. The date that follows publication medium (Web) is the date of your latest access:

> Czekaj, Laura. "Promises Fulfilled: Looking at the Legacy of Thousands of Black Slaves Who Fled to Canada in the 1800s." *InnovationCanada.ca.* Canada Foundation for Innovation, 7 Feb. 2009. Web. 19 Apr. 2009.

Group, organization (e.g., corporate or government) **website.** If there is no author, list by the organization's name:

> Environment Canada. "10 Things You Should Know About Climate Change." 12 Aug. 2009. Web. 15 Aug. 2009. <http://www.ec.gc.ca/cc/default.asp?lang=En&n=2F049262–1>.

The first date in a web entry is the date of the site itself or most recent update; the second is the date you last accessed the site.

The URL is included because the page would be hard to locate otherwise.

Article in online-only journal. Online-only journals may not include page numbers, in which case use the abbreviation *n. pag.* ("no pagination") after the website date:

> Rye, B. J., Pamela Elmslie, and Amanda Chalmers. "Meeting a Transsexual Person: Experience within a Classroom Setting." *Canadian On-Line Journal of Queer Studies in Education* 3.1 (2007): n. pag. Web. 21 Oct. 2008.

In addition to the information included in the print version, journal articles retrieved from a database require database name and date of access, which follows medium of publication.

Internet article based on a print source and retrieved from a database. In addition to the information required for the print version of a journal article, the name of the database and date of access are included:

> Barton, Sylvia S. "Discovering the Literature on Aboriginal Diabetes in Canada: A Focus on Holistic Methodologies." *Canadian Journal of Nursing Research* 40.4 (2008): 26–54. *Ingenta.* Web. 11 May 2009.

Work online that first appeared in print. Include details of the print source and follow with the title of the website, publication medium, and date of access:

Douglass, Frederick. "My Escape from Slavery." *The Century Illustrated Magazine* Nov. 1881: 125–31. Electronic Text Center, University of Virginia Library. Web. 14 Jan. 2010.

Letter or email. If the letter is published, cite it as you would a work in an edited volume, adding the date of the letter. If it is a personal letter or email, include a description, such as "Message to the author" (if you received it) and date. If the message is a typed letter, use *TS* (typescript) as publication medium.

Barrett, Anthony. "Re: *Lives of the Caesars*." Message to the author. 15 Aug. 2008. Email.

Message posted to online forum, discussion group, or blog post. Follow the guidelines for "Sample electronic citation" above. If no title is given, the entry should include a generic label after the author's name.

Koolvedge. Online posting. *Adbusters.org*. Adbusters Media Foundation, 8 Aug. 2009. Web. 30 Aug. 2009. <https://www.adbusters.org/blogs/dispatches/massacre-peru.html#comments>.

The author in the example above did not include a first name, so this information cannot be given.

MLA Citations for Non-textual Sources

MLA style has been updated to include specific citation formats for a variety of non-textual information sources. As a general rule of thumb, the person(s) most relevant to your discussion should be featured in your citation, along with an abbreviated description of their role. For example, if your paper is about actors, you can cite their contribution in a film either alongside or instead of naming the director.

Lecture or other oral presentation. Begin with the name of the speaker, the title of the presentation, the meeting and/or sponsor (if applicable), location detail, and date. Conclude with the equivalent of publication medium (e.g., *Lecture, Reading*).

Armstrong, Nancy. "Darwin's Paradox." Department of English. David Strong Building, University of Victoria, Victoria. 2 April 2009. Lecture.

Film or video. Begin with the work's title unless you are referring mainly to one person's contribution (for example, a performer or writer). Follow with the name(s) of the most relevant individuals and conclude with the distributor's name and year of release.

Citing the film:

Apocalypse Now. Dir. Francis Ford Coppola. United Artists, 1979. Film.

Citing a specific individual:

Brando, Marlon, perf. *Apocalypse Now*. Dir. Francis Ford Coppola. United Artists, 1979. Film.

The abbreviation *perf.* stands for "performer."

Performance (e.g., play, concert). Begin with the title of the performance and follow with relevant information, usually the writer, director, and main performers. Conclude with the company name, theatre, city, date of performance, and the word *Performance*.

Macbeth. By William Shakespeare. Dir. Des McAnuff. Perf. Colm Feore and Yanna McIntosh. Stratford Shakespeare Festival Company. Festival Theatre, Stratford, ON. 1 June 2009. Performance.

If you are citing one individual's contribution, begin with that person's name (see "Film or video," above).

Episode from a television or radio series. Use the following order: title of episode (in quotation marks), title of program (italicized), network, call letters of local station, and city, if relevant. Conclude by giving the broadcast date and medium of reception.

"Man of Science, Man of Faith." *Lost*. Dir. Jack Bender. CTV. CFTO, Toronto, 21 Sept. 2005. Television.

Information relevant to the episode (e.g., the writer or director) follows episode title; information relevant to the series follows series title.

If you are citing one individual's contribution, begin with that person's name (see "Film or video," above).

Music. Use the following order: performer (or other most relevant individual), recording title, label, year of issue, and medium (e.g., CD, LP):

Morrison, Van. *Too Long in Exile*. Polydor, 1993. CD.

If you are citing a specific song, place its name in quotation marks after the performer's name; use a period before and after song's name.

Work of visual art. Use the following order: artist, title (italicized), date of composition (or *n.d.* if this is unavailable), medium of composition, name of institution that contains the work, and city:

Escher, M. C. *Drawing Hands*. 1948. Lithograph. Cornelius Collection, National Gallery of Art, Washington.

Interview. Begin with the name of the interviewee and follow with the interviewer's name preceded by *Interview by*. Conclude with publication details.

Murakami, Haruki. Interview by Maik Grossekathöfer. *Spiegel Online International* 20 Feb. 2008. Web. 8 Dec. 2009.

If you are the interviewer, begin with the interviewee, followed by the type of interview (e.g., *Telephone Interview*) and date of interview.

MLA Notes

MLA permits either footnotes (at the bottom of the page) or endnotes (at the end of the document) as a way of including information you feel is valuable but does not fit well within the text. You may footnote in order to further explain a point, to cite multiple sources, to suggest additional reading, or to cite related points of interest. These notes are indicated by a superscript (raised) number directly to the right and above the word most related to the note, or at the end of a phrase; they are numbered consecutively through your paper. Format the notes to match the rest of the document by double-spacing and indenting each note. For an example of a student essay that includes notes, see page 274.

Exercise **13.1**

The following exercises ask you to apply information from Chapters 10, 12, and 13. They test your ability to use summary, paraphrase, direct quotation, mixed quotation format, block format, signal phrases, ellipses, brackets, and APA and MLA in-text citations.

Part I

Following the instructions given in this text, complete A, B, and C, creating sentences that show your understanding of how to use sources.

The excerpts for Part I are from the website article "Comets May Have Led to Birth and Death of Dinosaur Era," by Hillary Mayell. It was published in *National Geographic News* on 16 May 2002. The information for part A is taken from paragraphs 1 and 2 of the source; part B is taken from paragraph 4; part C is taken from paragraph 3.

A. Paraphrase the following in one or two sentences. Do not use a signal phrase or any direct quotations. Use MLA style for the parenthetical citation.

Comets slamming into the Earth may be responsible for both the birth and the death of the dinosaur era, an international group of researchers report. There is a considerable amount of evidence that a bolide [a comet or asteroid] collision with Earth triggered the end of the dinosaur era 65 million years ago.

B. Paraphrase the following sentence, but include one direct quotation that is no more than eight words (choose the most appropriate words for the quotation). Use a signal phrase to set up the paraphrase (i.e., source's name and signal verb).

(continued)

"We have been able to show for the first time that the transition be-tween Triassic life-forms to Jurassic life-forms occurred in a geological blink of an eye," said Paul Olsen, a geologist at the Lamont-Doherty Earth Observatory of Columbia University.

C.   Using brackets, grammatically integrate the direct quotation into the com-plete sentence. Do not use a signal phrase.

The cause of the end of the dinosaur age might have been "a giant ball of ice, rock, and gases smashed into the supercontinent Pangaea."

Part II

Integrate the passage below as if you planned to use it in your essay, following the instructions. Use a signal phrase and APA style, which includes the source's name, year, and signal verb, followed by a direct quotation of the passage. In sentence three, omit (1) "oral contraceptives, transoceanic phone calls" and (2) "just to mention a few," indicating to the reader that material is omitted. Format the quotation in the most appropriate way—i.e., either as part of the text or in block format.

(The author is David Suzuki; the name of article is "Saving the Earth"; the date of publication is June 14, 1999; the quotation is from page 43 of *Maclean's*.)

In this century, our species has undergone explosive change. Not only are we adding a quarter of a million people to our numbers every day, we have vastly amplified our technological muscle power. When I was born, there were no computers, televisions, jet planes, oral contracep-tives, transoceanic phone calls, satellites, transistors or xerography, just to mention a few. Children today look at typewriters, vinyl records and black-and-white televisions as ancient curiosities.

Part III

A.   Paraphrase the passage below, which is from page 43 of the same Suzuki essay as in Part II, and cite using APA style. Include one direct quotation no longer than three words as part of your paraphrase. Do not use a signal phrase.

B.   Summarize the passage in one sentence of no more than 20 words (there are 54 words in the original); begin with a signal phrase and use APA style. Do not use any direct quotations.

In biological terms, the globe is experiencing an eco-holocaust, as more than 50,000 species vanish annually, and air, water and soil are poisoned with civilization's effluents. The great challenge to the millen-nium is recognizing the reality of impending ecological collapse, and the urgent need to get on with taking the steps to avoid it.

❭ Sample Academic Essay

The following excerpt from an academic article is annotated to show some of the similarities and differences between academic essays and the kind of essays you will write. Academic essays, which usually appear in academic journals and can be accessed electronically through your school's databases, are longer and more complex than most student essays. Many of the challenges they present, however, can be overcome by knowing where to look for information. Following the steps below will make the reading process easier:

1. Read the title and abstract to get an idea of the essay's purpose, topic, and results or findings. If the essay includes specific headings, they may also give useful information.

2. Read the introduction, especially the last paragraphs, where important information is placed.

3. Read the Conclusion or Discussion section (or, if it is not labelled as such, the last few paragraphs) in which the findings are summarized and made relevant, applying the strategies discussed in Chapter 1, Scanning versus Focused Reading, page 10.

4. If you know the essay will be crucial to your own research, you can now go back and read the other sections closely.

5. Before reading this essay, you can review the questions discussed in Chapter 1, Responding Critically and Analytically through Questions, page 18.

SAMPLE ACADEMIC ESSAY

"I luv u :)!": A Descriptive Study of the Media Use of Individuals in Romantic Relationships

by Sarah M. Coyne, Laura Stockdale, Dean Busby, Bethany Iverson, and David M. Grant

Abstract (summary)

In this study, we address the communication technologies individuals within romantic relationships are using to communicate with one another, the frequency of use, and the association between the use of these technologies and couple's positive and negative communication. Participants consisted of individuals involved

> **Reading Tip:** Closely reading the title of an academic essay can be a useful pre-reading activity. Before the colon, the authors use text-speak to show the area of research and to grab the reader's attention. After the colon, they elaborate on the study being done.

> **Reading Tip:** Like many academic articles in the social sciences, this one includes an abstract or summary written by the authors. (See page 220.) It gives background information, briefly explains how the research was carried out, and gives the results.

in a serious, committed, heterosexual relationship. The Relationship Evaluation Questionnaire instrument was used to assess a variety of relationship variables. The majority of individuals within the study frequently used cell phones and text messaging to communicate with their partner, with "expressing affection" being the most common reason for contact. Younger individuals reported using all forms of media (except for e-mail) more frequently than older participants. Relationship satisfaction did not predict specific use of media but predicted several reasons for media use. Additional analyses revealed that text messaging had the strongest association with individuals' positive and negative communication within their relationships. Specifically, text messaging to express affection, broach potentially confrontational subjects, and to hurt partners were associated with individuals' view of positive and negative communication within their relationship. Implications of the results are discussed.

> **Reading Tip:** Academic writers often begin by summarizing work done by other scholars in the field.

[1] Every day, over a billion text messages are sent through mobile phones around the world (Bargh & McKenna, 2004). In the past, the "digital divide," or the gap between higher socioeconomic groups and lower economic groups' access to new technology and media, was a reality in the United States, but the last decade has provided an ever-shrinking gap between these groups (Strasburger, Wilson, & Jordan, 2009). The majority of American households have access to the Internet creating the possibility of communication through e-mails, instant messaging, chat rooms, and other sites (Bachen, 2007). Social networking sites such as "MySpace" and "Facebook" are growing in popularity and reach (Sheldon, 2008). More public libraries, schools, and businesses are providing access to the Internet, shrinking the digital divide even further. It seems that the majority of Americans have an endless array of communication possibilities and outlets within their grasp.

[2] According to the sociotechnological model, to understand the impact of new communication technologies on the family, researchers must address the characteristics of the new technology, individual traits of the users, family factors, and extrafamilial influences (Lanigan, 2009). The combination of these factors provides a more complete understanding of the effects of both verbal and nonverbal communication technologies on the family. Although several studies have examined the use of newer forms of technology in parent/child relationships, little research has focused on couple relationships, arguably one of the core components of most families. Accordingly, in this study, we examined how individuals in romantic relationships use different types of newer forms of technology (both computer-mediated and noncomputer-mediated) to connect with their romantic partner.

Computer-Mediated Communication

[3] Recently, researchers have focused on the effects of computer-mediated communication (e.g., email, social networking sites) on friendships and relationships. For example, Walker, Krehbiel, and Knoyer (2009) found that the majority of communications done through MySpace were friendly inquiries or greetings and expressions of affection and encouragement. Frequent Internet use has been associated with increased sociability across multiple cultures and contexts (Räsänen & Kouvo, 2007) and closeness in friendships, particularly among shy individuals (Valkenburg & Peter, 2007).

[4] Although little research has placed computer-mediated forms of communication in a family context, a few studies show that such communication can have mixed results. For example, Mesch (2003) found that adolescent Internet use was not related to overall time spent with parents; however, their Internet use was negatively correlated to family closeness even when controlling for the amount of time spent together.

> **Reading Tip:** This paragraph, as in many academic essays, includes some challenging words. If words like *computer-mediated* cannot be determined by context, you will need to look them up in a dictionary.

[5] Other research has focused on romantic relationships, particularly on the formation of such relationships via technology (e.g., Scott, Mottarella, & Lavooy, 2006; Sprecher, 2009). Other researchers (Manago, Graham, Greenfield, & Sallmkhan, 2008) have examined how computer-mediated communication might enhance relationship displays online. Furthermore, a few studies have shown how Internet use might influence feelings in relationships. For example, Baym, Zhang, Kunkel, Ledbetter, and Lin (2007) found that type of communication (whether via Internet or phone conversation) had no effect on relationship satisfaction. Other researchers have found that the use of Facebook is associated with increased jealousy in relationships (Muise, Christofides, & Desmarais, 2009).

[6] Although this literature gives us a small glimpse into the ways technology has influenced relationships, researchers have not examined the association between individuals' normative media use and their perceptions of romantic relationship outcomes. Whether such computer-mediated communication is common among individuals in romantic relationships is unknown. Likewise, the effects of using such communication on individuals' feelings of connectivity and satisfaction within their relationship are also unknown. One of the primary aims of the current research was to assess both the frequency of computer-mediated communication in romantic relationships and the potential benefits or consequences of using such communication to connect with a romantic partner.

Noncomputer-Mediated Forms of Communication

[7] The use of cell phones to communicate is quickly becoming one of the most common and easiest ways to connect with others (see Green, 2003; Ling, 2004).

Both actual cell phone conversations and the use of texting are extremely popular, especially among the adolescent and emerging adult populations (e.g., Kamibeppu & Sugiura, 2005). When emerging adults were asked why they preferred mobile phone conversations and text messaging over other forms of communication they explained that non-face-to-face communication gave them the option of talking to multiple people at once, to leave large gaps in the conversation, to conceal truth, and the ability to immediately clarify misunderstandings (Madell & Muncer, 2007). These individuals also claimed that there were often misunderstandings when they used this form of communication, but they felt it gave them more time to ponder and articulate what they were trying to express.

[8] The potential "misunderstanding" on the part of the receiver may be particularly likely for a text message, as compared to face to face and actual phone conversation. Tone of voice and facial cues have been found to be important aspects of interpersonal communication that help enhance the clarity of messages (Zuckerman, Amidon, Bishop, & Pomerantz, 1982). When verbal and textual communication and nonverbal communication did not correspond, misunderstandings were likely to occur (Lanigan, 2009). "Mismatch," or when senders' facial cues do not match the message of the sender, was related to negative couple outcomes (Van Buren, 2002). Couples who experienced low levels of mismatch within their face-to-face communication had more stable and satisfying relationships than couples with greater mismatch (Koerner & Fitzpatrick, 2002). It is possible that new communication technologies are inherently prone to misunderstandings because they do not contain these vital nonverbal aspects.

[9] Most research has focused on general cell phone and texting trends, as opposed to placing this form of communication in a relational context. In one qualitative study, Pettigrew (2009) found that the majority of couples claimed that text messaging had benefited their relationship and allowed them to remain in constant contact with one another. This study, however, was entirely descriptive and did not address the issue of whether such communication was actually related to core relationship communication or satisfaction. Some scholars studying traditional communication methods have found that the sheer amount of overall couple communication alone was significantly correlated to relationship satisfaction, especially for women (e.g., Rehman & Holtzworth-Munroe, 2007). Therefore, it is possible that the use of mobile phones represents a convenient way for couples to connect throughout the day and to increase their levels of communication when apart. This added opportunity for communication might suggest a positive consequence on couple relationships. As stated before, however, cell phone use, and especially texting, might be associated with more frequent misunderstandings in communication that may have a negative effect

Like most essays this one includes important information near the end of the introduction. The authors discuss the shortcomings of other comparable research and then end with their purpose or thesis. Although this thesis may look different from the ones that you write, it fulfills the same purpose of informing the audience about what will follow.

on the relationship. Accordingly, one of the primary aims of this study was to examine the frequency and potential consequences of cell phone use (both conversations and texting) in romantic relationships.

Theoretical Approach and Research Questions

[10] In accordance with the sociotechnological model (Lanigan, 2009), communication technologies and the family can only be understood when the characteristics of the technology, the individual traits of the user, family factors, and extrafamilial influences are taken into account. Technological characteristics include the accessibility, scope or malleability, obtrusiveness, resource demands or costs, and gratification potential of any communication technology. Individual traits include the personality, personal goals, attitudes toward technology, processing styles, and general demographics such as age, gender, and income of the individual using the technology. Family factors are demographics such as how many people are in the family, stage of development, how many people within the family use the technology, and family processes. Finally, extrafamilial influences include community and workplace acceptance of communication technologies. All these factors work together to influence how strongly these communication technologies impact the family (Lanigan).

[11] The sociotechnological model is particularly pertinent when addressing new communication technologies such as social networking sites, blogs, text messaging, and e-mails (as in this study) for several reasons. First, the characteristics of all these technologies make them highly accessible and rewarding for families to use. The majority of families own cell phones and have access to the Internet either within their homes or in the community, making texting, social networking sites, and other forms of Internet communication highly accessible and cost-effective. Furthermore, these communication technologies are very adaptive and can be used in multiple situations and circumstances. Families are also very likely to see these communication technologies as rewarding and gratifying because they are new, trendy, and make it possible for families to constantly be in contact with one another. Finally, extrafamilial influences such as work and the community tend to be very supportive of these communication technologies, making them much more likely to have an impact on the family.

[12] We focused on only one aspect of the family, namely romantic relationships, in this study. In accordance with the sociotechnological model, however, we examined technological characteristics (e.g., type of media, context of use),

The authors clearly state their area of research so that the reader understands exactly what was being studied.

individual characteristics (e.g., demographic variables), and family factors (e.g., relationship satisfaction) to assess the frequency of use and impact of computer-mediated (e.g., social network sites, e-mail, blogging) and noncomputer-mediated (cell phone/texting) forms of communication on relationship communication and satisfaction. As stated earlier, little is known regarding how individuals in romantic relationships use newer forms of technology to communicate with each other. This study has the potential to shed some light on not only the ways media is used within relationships but also the potential consequences of such use. Within the context of the sociotechnological model, we will focus on two research questions outlined below.

[13] RQ1: How often are cell phones, text messaging, e-mail, instant messaging, social networking sites, blogs, and webcams used within romantic relationships to communicate? Are there any demographic (i.e., gender, age, ethnicity, educational attainment) or relationship (e.g., length, status, satisfaction) differences in use?

[14] RQ2: What is the relationship between the use of communication via technology and relationship satisfaction and communication?

Method
Participants
[15] Participants were drawn from the entire population of respondents (approximately 5,124 people) who completed the Relationship Evaluation Questionnaire (RELATE; Busby, Holman, & Taniguchi, 2001) in 2009. Individuals completed the RELATE online after being introduced to the instrument through a variety of settings. Some participants were requested to take the RELATE as part of a class, others completed it as part of a workshop for couples, some individuals completed it after finding it on the Web, and some completed it as part of an assessment package given by a professional therapist or clergy member.

[16] Because of the relationship variables that were analyzed in this study, the only individuals retained in the sample were participants in a heterosexual relationship who were in a serious/steady dating relationship or who were engaged or married. This also included individuals who were separated or remarried but were currently in a serious relationship. We also eliminated any participants with missing values on any of the variables used in this study to more appropriately evaluate the models without resorting to any type of substitution processes for missing values. This resulted in a final sample size of 1,039 participants.

Method

Results

Discussion

[17] To our knowledge, this is the first study to describe different forms of media use within romantic relationships. On the whole, individuals are using the media to frequently connect with their romantic partner, primarily through the use of cell phone conversations or texting. The sociotechnological model states that characteristics of the technology determine the impact these technologies have on the family (Lanigan, 2009). Cell phones, as compared to other types of media, are probably the most accessible form of media, making contact both quick and easy throughout the day. Likewise, workplace and communities tend to be highly supportive of cell phone use, with some companies even giving cell phones to their employees as a way to maintain contact. Contact through e-mail, social networking sites, or instant messaging all occur in romantic relationships, but not as frequently. We also found that individuals rarely use blogs or webcams to contact their partner. Thus, on the whole, this study shows evidence of a high amount of media use specifically to contact romantic others, although some forms (cell phones) are used more frequently than others.

[18] We also assessed the reasons why individuals use the media to connect with their partner. The most common reason by far was to express affection. Our analysis with texting for using the media in this context was specifically related to positive forms of communication, showing that the media can act as a positive force in many relationships. It is likely that technology has increased the ease with which affection can be expressed, with individuals being able to covertly text a quick "I luv U :)!" during an office meeting or call while doing the weekly shopping. Although face-to-face expressions of affection are undoubtedly necessary, it would appear that individuals can add to these positive communications by using the media to continue to express affection.

[19] Conversely, about a quarter of our sample reported using the media to discuss serious issues, with around 10% using it either to apologize or to broach a potentially confrontational subject. Still fewer (only 3%) reported using the media to hurt their partner, by sending mean text messages for example. In our texting analysis, using the media to both hurt one's partner and broach confrontational subjects was related to more negative forms of communication. Any type of antagonistic or cruel behavior may have a negative effect on relationships, and it appears that such behavior in the context of texting is no different. The lack of nonverbal cues and face-to-face interactions are not enough to overcome the damaging effects of cutting words. Whether texting mean things to a partner is "better" than saying them face to face is unknown and

For the sake of brevity, most of the Method and Results sections of this research paper have been deleted.

Researchers and other academic writers do more than report their findings: they often interpret them for their reader should be a focus for future research. Our results, however, revealed that texting hurtful messages could have a negative effect on communication and indirectly on relationship satisfaction. Thus, it seems unlikely that the use of this particular technology would completely buffer the effect of saying (or in this case texting) hurtful messages to one's partner. Although such behavior did occur in the context of relationships, it should be noted that, on the whole, these results show that media use is very common among individuals involved in romantic relationships and that most contact via the media is very positive.

[20] When examining demographic differences, we found a few significant findings for gender, ethnicity, and religion. The largest findings, however, were for age, length of relationship, and educational status. Given that younger individuals are also likely to have shorter relationships and less education, these latter findings are likely a reflection of the age of the individual. Specifically, younger individuals (17–25) reported using all forms of media to communicate with their partner more than older couples. This is especially likely in the case of texting, with older adults (61+) rarely, if ever, texting their partner while young adults (17–25) reported texting their partner more than once a day on average. This is not surprising given the popularity of newer forms of technology among emerging adults (e.g., Kamibeppu & Sugiura, 2005). Older individuals may be contacting their partner through more traditional forms of communication (i.e., landlines, notes); thus, these routes should also be examined in the future.

[21] Interestingly, married individuals reported using almost all types of media (texting, IM, social networking, blogs, and webcams) more frequently than couples who were dating. Married individuals likely have a host of responsibilities regarding both the relationship and family that need to be discussed during the day. Technology provides a very quick and accessible way to deal with concerns at any time. Dating couples likely have less of a need to deal with as many issues throughout the day; accordingly, their contact through technology is less frequent. Furthermore, a high amount of contact via the media early on in the relationship may seem like overkill to some couples who are still just getting to know each other.

[22] Although relationship satisfaction did not predict media use per se, it did appear to have an influence on several reasons for using the media. Individuals who were more satisfied in their relationship reported using the media more frequently to express affection toward their partner. It is likely that highly satisfied individuals are more likely to express affection toward their partner in multiple contexts; the media simply provides yet more ways. Less satisfied individuals, however, were more likely to report using the media to attempt to broach a confrontational subject with their partner. Again, these individuals

may simply have more confrontational subjects to talk about in their relationship. For example, after an argument, individuals might send a text message to their partners to gauge their feelings on the topic of discussion. Contact via the media has the potential to be less intense and less emotionally charged than face-to-face contact. Given the negative relationship with satisfaction, positive communication (as found in our texting analysis), and the potential "mismatch" that often occurs with media and real intent, however, it is likely that using the media in this context is not as successful as other forms of communication. Research should certainly address this issue in the future.

[23] Although it is somewhat unusual to use the same variable, relationship satisfaction, as a predictor and an outcome in the same study, as our data are correlational it is clearly possible that media usage is a result of the overall quality of a relationship and/ or media usage could contribute to overall relationship quality. In our study, we tested both options and also found that the purposes for using media did influence overall relationship satisfaction through positive and negative communication.

Limitations and Implications for Applied Professionals

[24] This study has several limitations. All the data collected were self-report in nature; thus, future research should obtain partner reports or observational data regarding media use. Also, the sample was not random, and therefore, some of the results might be unique to the sample characteristics of this study. Even with the shortcomings of the sample and data gathering techniques, we were able to provide important findings about different types of technology use in relationships. Very little is known about the types of technologies individuals use to communicate, the types of individuals who use the different technologies, and the influence these usage patterns have on relationship variables and outcomes. This article is only a beginning down the pathway of discovery regarding technology, communication, and relationships. The rapid changes occurring with our communication technology are challenging to keep up with as individuals, let alone as scholars who must design and conduct research that explores these changes, hopefully before some other type of technology has emerged and become dominant. Already some forms of technology, such as instant messaging, seem to be falling out of favor before we even knew much about how it was being used and what impact it had on relationships.

[25] We expect with the ubiquitous nature of cell phones and texting that this type of communication will remain common and might become the primary way many couples stay in touch with each other for the near future. It seems an ideal time to explore the impact of this type of technology use on relationships, as there are still many couples who use it little and many couples who use it almost hourly. So far, our findings demonstrate that it can have both a positive and negative effect on relationships

depending on the intent. In this regard, it does not appear to be different from other forms of communication, but long-term effects need to be studied, especially as texting may be prone to miscommunication because of the missing nonverbal channels. How do couples address miscommunication when it comes from texting as compared to face-to-face communication? Do they initiate communication through a phone call or wait until they are face to face to iron out the problems? How does this influence their overall relationship? As media technologies continue to grow in scope and reach, it is important to understand how media may influence the creation, shape, trajectory, or overall strength or weakness of a relationship.

> One of the functions of the conclusion in an academic essay is to analyze and interpret the results, applying them to real-world situations. This is a major difference between an academic essay and a student essay, in which the conclusion is usually concerned with recalling and reinforcing the thesis.

[26] Our study also demonstrates the potential for including media more in the educational and therapeutic endeavors of practitioners. The problem with many interventions is that they occur too infrequently and require individuals to go to an inconvenient location, the practitioner's office, instead of being provided in their homes. Already the RELATE and Couple CARE (Halford, Moore, Wilson, Dyer, & Farrugia, 2004) programs are being provided over the Internet and by using phones, and couples are responding to this type of intervention (Halford et al., 2010). The room for innovation with these technologies for adapting educational and therapeutic interventions is almost limitless. Practitioners could easily use automated prompts to individuals or couples to gather information through a quick assessment over cell phones or to remind family members to interact around certain topics or in certain ways. In addition, the development of apps for smart phones could provide much more advanced forms of communication that are triggered at certain times of the day, such as when certain responses are given to a question or when certain things are observed in their relationships. Although using media to adapt interventions is sure to provide challenges with compensation, boundaries, confidentiality, and other issues, there are unique opportunities with these technologies to meet couples where they are at, when they need it, and in ways they are already communicating that may very well redefine intervention as much as phones, the Internet, and texting have redefined how family members stay in touch with each other.

References

Arbuckle, J. L. (2008). *Amos 17.0 user's guide*. Chicago, IL: SPSS.

Bachen, C. M. (2007). Just part of the family? Exploring the connections between family life and media use. In S. R. Mazzarella (Ed.), *20 questions about youth and the media* (pp. 239–252). New York: Peter Lang.

Bargh, J. A., & McKenna, K. Y. A. (2004). The Internet and social life. *Annual Review of Psychology*, *55*, 573–590.

Baym, N. K., Zhang, Y. B., Kunkel, A., Ledbetter, A., & Lin, M. (2007). Relational quality and media use in interpersonal relationships. *New Media & Society*, *9*, 735–752.

Busby, D. M., & Gardner, B. C. (2008). How do I analyze thee? Let me count the ways: Considering empathy in couple relationships using self and partner ratings. *Family Process, 47,* 229–242.

Busby, D. M., Holman, T. B., & Niehuis, S. (2009). The association between partner- and self enhancement and relationship quality outcomes. *Journal of Marriage and Family, 71,* 449–464.

Busby, D. M., Holman, T. B., & Taniguchi, N. (2001). RELATE: Relationship evaluation for the individual, cultural, and couple contexts. *Family Relations, 50,* 308–316.

Byrne, B. (2001). *Structural equation modeling with AMOS.* Mahwah, NJ: Erlbaum.

Gottman, J. M. (1999). *The marriage clinic: A scientifically based marital therapy.* New York, NY: W.W. Norton.

Green, N. (2003). Outwardly mobile: Young people and mobile technologies. In J. Katz (Ed.), *Machines that become us: The social context of personal communication technology* (pp. 201–218). New Brunswick, NJ: Transaction.

Halford, W. K., Moore, E. M., Wilson, K. L., Dyer, C., & Farrugia, C. (2004). Benefits of a flexible delivery relationship education: An evaluation of the Couple CARE program. *Family Relations, 53,* 469–476.

Halford, W. K., Wilson, K. L., Watson, B., Verner, T., Larson, J., Busby, D., & Holman, T. (2010). Couple relationship education at home: Does skill training enhance relationship assessment and feedback? *Journal of Family Psychology, 24,* 188–196.

Hoyle, R. H., & Panter, A. T. (1995). Writing about structural equation models. In R. H. Hoyle (Ed.), *Structural equation modeling: Concepts, issues, and applications* (pp. 158–176). Thousand Oaks, CA: Sage.

Kamibeppu, K., & Sugiura, H. (2005). Impact of the mobile phone on junior high-school student's friendships in the Tokyo metropolitan area. *CyberPsychology and Behavior, 2,* 121–130.

Koerner, A. F., & Fitzpatrick, M. A. (2002). Nonverbal communication and marital adjustment and satisfaction: The role of decoding relationship relevant and relationship irrelevant affect. *Communication Monographs, 69,* 33–51.

Lanigan, J. D. (2009). A sociotechnological model for family research and intervention: How information and communication technologies affect family life. *Marriage and Family Review, 45,* 587–609.

Ling, R. (2004). *The mobile connection: The cell phone's impact on society.* San Francisco, CA: Morgan Kauffman.

Madell, D. E., & Muncer, J. J. (2007). Control over social interactions: An important reason for young people's use of the Internet and mobile phones for communication? *CyberPsychology & Behavior, 10,* 137–140.

Manago, A. M., Graham, M. B., Greenfield, P. M., & Salimkhan, G. (2008). Self presentation and gender on MySpace. *Journal of Applied Developmental Psychology, 29,* 446–458.

Mesch, G. A. (2003). The family and the Internet: The Israeli case. *Social Science Quarterly*, *84*, 1038–1050.

Muise, A., Christofides, E., & Desmarais, S. (2009). More information that you ever wanted: Does Facebook bring out the green-eyed monster of jealousy? *CyberPsychology & Behavior*, *12*, 441–444.

Pettigrew, J. (2009). Text messaging and connectedness within close interpersonal relationships. *Marriage and Family Review*, *45*, 697–716.

Räsänen, P., & Kouvo, A. (2007). Linked or divided by the web?: Internet use and sociability in four European countries. *Information, Communication, and Society*, *10*, 219–214.

Rehman, U. S., & Holtzworth-Munroe, A. (2007). A cross cultural examination of the relation of marital communication behavior and marital satisfaction. *Journal of Family Psychology*, *21*, 795–763.

Scott, V. M., Mottarella, K. E., & Lavooy, M. J. (2006). Does virtual intimacy exist?: A brief exploration into reported levels of intimacy in online relationships. *CyberPsychology & Behavior*, *9*, 759–763.

Sheldon, P. (2008). The relationship between unwillingness-to-communicate and students' Facebook use. *Journal of Media Psychology: Theories, Methods, and Application*, *20*, 67–75.

Sprecher, S. (2009). Relationship initiation and formation on the Internet. *Marriage & Family Review*, 45, 761–782.

Strasburger, V. C, Wilson, B. J., & Jordan, A. B. (2009). *Children, adolescents, and the media*. Thousand Oaks, CA: Sage.

Valkenburg, P., & Peter, J. (2007). Online communication and adolescents well being: Testing the stimulation verse displacement hypothesis. *Journal of Computer-Mediated Communication*, *12*, 1169–1182.

Van Buren, A. (2002). The relationship of verbal-nonverbal incongruence to communication mismatches in married couples. *North American Journal of Psychology*, *4*, 21–36.

Walker, K., Krehbiel, M., & Knoyer, L. (2009). "Hey you! Just stopping by to say hi!" Communicating with friends and family on Myspace. *Marriage and Family Review*, *45*, 677–695.

Zuckerman, M., Amidon, M. D., Bishop, S. E., & Pomerantz, S. D. (1982). Face and tone of voice in the communication of deception. *Journal of Personality and Social Psychology*, *43*, 347–357.

▮ Chapter Review Questions

1. Why are citations needed in an essay?

2. What are some of the different citation styles?

3. Can you combine different citation styles?

4. Why is it important to use the most current style guide when documenting your sources?

5. What is the difference between an in-text citation and a References/Works Cited entry?

6. What order is used in the References/Works Cited to list the sources used in your essay?

7. What are the basic elements of APA in-text citations? How does the use of a signal phrase affect this?

8. What are the basic elements of MLA in-text citations? How does the use of a signal phrase affect this?

Part 4

Grammar

14 Sentence Essentials

In this chapter, you will

- review the importance of using correct grammar
- be introduced to the parts of speech: what they are and why they are important
- be introduced to sentence structure
- learn the four errors of sentence incompletion and how to avoid them
- be introduced to phrases and clauses and their roles in the sentence
- learn the errors of sentence combining and how to join sentences correctly

In this chapter and the two that follow, you will be introduced to the basic concepts for understanding and using English grammar and punctuation. First, you will study the parts of speech, phrases and clauses, and then the sentence itself. In Chapter 15, you will find guidelines for using commas, semicolons, colons, and apostrophes. In Chapter 16, you will refine your skills by learning how to craft grammatically correct sentences.

❯ Grammatical Groundwork

Correct grammar will *always* help create a channel of clear communication between writer and reader. Grammar errors may cause misunderstandings, and they can make your work look sloppy.

In general, the rules of grammar apply to all writing across all courses. That means you will need to follow proper grammar rules for all your academic writing, not just for English. Academic writing is **formal writing**, so the rules of formal usage and correct grammar need to be applied. In this chapter and the next two, we approach grammar formally but without excess terminology.

Although formal grammatical rules are stressed throughout, not all your writing at college or university will be formal. For example, when you take notes on a lecture, you may be concerned solely with content, using point form or even just key phrases. You might correspond with classmates by email, in which case you will probably write more informally, using "casual," everyday language.

Informal writing may also apply to certain kinds of business, technical, or journalistic writing. Some of the readings in this book are designed for a wider reading public than are academic papers and may employ more informal language and looser sentence structure. In all your writing assignments, your instructor is the final judge on the level of formality required. For more information on the differences between formal and informal writing, see Chapter 17, page 448.

Academic writing is formal writing, and that means that the rules of formal usage and correct grammar need to be applied.

Exercise **14.1**

Find three examples of formal prose and three examples of informal prose. Try to find an example of both from each of the following: a magazine, a newspaper, and a book. Share your excerpts in groups, considering how each could be changed into informal prose or how it could be rewritten as acceptable formal prose. Consider such factors as vocabulary, sentence length and variety, tone of voice, and audience. Then, consider which ones might be rewritten as conversation.

To help you identify these three writing styles, think in terms of different kinds of audiences—you can think of a specific person or persons whom you are writing for: e.g., a friend, for informal prose or conversation; a workplace acquaintance, such as your boss, for semi-formal prose; and the chairperson of the English or Communications Department for formal prose.

Guidelines for usage determine what words are suitable for a typical reader or listener. The typical reader of academic prose is different from the typical reader of a popular book, an office memo, a blog, or an email. Therefore, the level of usage is usually different.

Exercise **14.2**

Listen to the speakers around you. Find three samples that illustrate how the rules governing speech can be different from those governing semi-formal and formal writing. Again, consider factors such as vocabulary, sentence completion, tone of voice, and audience.

〉 The Grammar of Reading and Writing

As a reader, your comprehension depends on your ability to recognize grammatical and other linguistic "signposts" that are part of the English language. The processing of grammar is, therefore, part of the act of reading. To illustrate this point, read this stanza from Lewis Carroll's nonsense poem "Jabberwocky":

> "Beware the Jabberwock, my son!
> The jaws that bite, the claws that catch!
> Beware the Jubjub bird, and shu
> The frumious Bandersnatch!"

Do you understand what a "Jabberwock" is? The grammar clues tell us it is a concrete noun and probably alive. The meaning of *frumious* is not found in a dictionary, but again, the reader sees that it is modifying the proper noun *Bandersnatch*, which again is a concrete noun and probably a person or thing.

As a writer, you are responsible for ensuring that readers can understand your message, so you need to become familiar with grammatical rules if you are to write effectively. Knowing and applying these rules will help open up the channel of communication from you, the writer, to your reader.

In addition to ensuring the reader's clear understanding of your message, the proper use of grammar makes a good impression. Just as dressing for the occasion increases your prestige, the proper use of language creates a positive image. If your document contains errors, the reader assumes that you, as the writer, are either careless or uneducated, and therefore your opinion and research are not worthy of attention.

The fastest, least complicated way to learn English grammar is to start with the basic *concepts* that underlie the rules of grammar. The pages that follow teach a concept-based grammar, beginning with the smallest word-units in the sentence: the parts of speech. From there, we look at what a simple sentence is, how to recognize phrases and clauses, and how to join clauses to form more complex sentence types.

❯ Introducing . . . the Parts of Speech

Before considering the sentence, the basic unit of written communication in English, you need to be able to identify what makes up a **sentence**. The sentence can be divided into individual words, which, in turn, can be categorized as different parts of speech. Being able to identify the parts of speech will also help you understand larger units within sentences, such as phrases and **clauses**. The seven major **parts of speech** are

- nouns
- pronouns
- adjectives
- verbs
- adverbs
- prepositions
- conjunctions

Many words can be used as more than one part of speech. For example, the word *fish* is a noun (a thing), but *fish* also is a verb (to perform the act of fishing). When *fish* as a noun is placed in front of another noun, as in *fish market*, it functions as an adjective (modifying the concept "market").

Articles, such as *a, an,* and *the,* and determiners, such as *this* and *her,* precede nouns and function as adjectives. Interjections, such as *oh!* and *hey,* are not grammatically related to the rest of the sentence. They express surprise or emotion and should not be used in formal writing unless they form part of a quotation.

A sentence is a group of words containing a subject and a predicate that expresses a complete thought.

A clause is a group of words containing both a subject and a predicate.

The parts of speech are the names given to each word and its function in a sentence.

Articles modify nouns.

Interjections express surprise or emotion.

The Parts of Speech at Work

When you are hired by an organization and given a job title along with a detailed job description, the job title is what you will be called; but the full job description explains your responsibilities, duties, or functions within the organization. The parts of speech, too, have specific, assigned roles within their organizational structure, the sentence.

The tables that follow identify the parts of speech, along with their major functions. Learning to identify the categories of the parts of speech and being aware of their functions within the sentence (their job descriptions) will enable you to apply the rules of grammar.

Nouns and Pronouns

Nouns and pronouns are the *significant* words in a sentence because they name people, places, things, and ideas.

TABLE 14.1 Nouns and Pronouns	
Identification	Functions
Noun: name of a person, a place, a thing, or an idea. • A *proper* noun is a name and begins with a capital letter. • A *common* noun refers to a class or a general group and is not capitalized. • A *concrete* noun refers to a physical object or something experienced through the senses. • An *abstract* noun refers to a concept, an idea, or an abstraction. • A *count* noun refers to something that can be counted. • A *non-count* noun refers to something that can't be counted. • A *collective* noun refers to a group comprising individual members.	1. **Subject:** performs the action of the verb (the *doer* of the action); sometimes called the simple subject to distinguish it from the complete subject that includes the simple subject plus its **modifiers** 2. **Object** (also called the **direct object**): receives the action of the verb 3. **Object of a preposition** (also called the **indirect object**): is usually preceded by a preposition (such as *in, between, with*) 4. **Subject complement:** follows a linking verb (often a form of *to be* such as *is, are, was, were*) and can be linked to the subject 5. **Appositive:** is grammatically parallel to the previous noun or noun phrase
Pronoun: usually takes the place of a noun in a sentence. For a list of kinds of pronouns, see below.	Since pronouns generally replace nouns, they share the functions of nouns.

Functions of Nouns

1. Subject. The subject noun usually performs the action (except in the passive construction; see Chapter 17, page 426).

The subject of a clause or sentence usually performs the action of the verb.

A modifier is a word or phrase that describes or limits another word.

In the following examples, the subject is in **bold**; the action word, the verb, is *italicized*.

> **Dan** *stood* at the front of the line-up.
> **She** *awoke* before dawn.
> The **rain** in Spain *falls* mainly on the plain.

The subject usually comes before the verb but sometimes follows it, as, for example, in some questions:

> *Was* the final **exam** difficult?

The object of the verb is the receiver of the action of the verb.

2. Object of the verb is also called the **direct object**. It is the receiver of the action of the verb.

In the following examples, the object is in **bold**; the verb is *italicized*.

> James *beat* **Dan** into the movie theatre.
> Erin *let* **him** into the house.
> They *chopped* the **logs** for firewood.

3. Object of the preposition (also called **indirect object**). The noun/pronoun is usually preceded by a preposition.

In the following examples, the object is in **bold**; its preposition is *italicized*.

She gave a present *to* **her nephew.**
The rain *in* **Spain** falls mainly *on* the **plain.**
I never heard *of* **it** before.

When a noun or pronoun acts as the object of a preposition, it is usually preceded by a preposition.

The object of a preposition or indirect object most frequently tells for whom an action is done.

4. Subject complement (completion). This is the noun or pronoun that "completes" the subject after a linking verb.

In the following example, the subject complement is in **bold**; the linking verb is italicized; the subject is underlined.

<u>Rayna</u> *was* the first **person** to get a job after graduation.

5. Appositive. This is a noun, noun phrase, or pronoun that is grammatically parallel to a preceding noun/pronoun and that rephrases or (re)names the preceding noun.

In the following example, the appositive is in **bold**; the preceding noun is *italicized*.

Madeline's *cats*, **Evie and Nanny**, have very different personalities.

A subject complement gives more information about the subject.

The subject of the sentence is *cats*; the names of the cats are in apposition to the subject (the names are not part of the simple subject).

Kinds and Functions of Pronouns

A **personal pronoun** refers to a person or a thing; in the possessive case, it can function as an adjective.

He ran all the way to the sea.
She sat down because her feet were blistered.

A noun appositive names the previous noun.

A **relative pronoun** introduces a dependent clause that *relates* the clause to the rest of the sentence; the clause usually functions adjectivally: *that, which, who.*

The book, *which* I lost on the bus, was about Greek history. The student *who* found it returned it to me.

An **interrogative pronoun** introduces a question: *how, what, which, when, why, who, where.*

Where is the book I lost on the bus? *How* can I thank you enough for returning it?

A personal pronoun refers to a person or a thing and replaces a noun in a sentence.

A relative pronoun introduces a dependent clause that *relates* the clause to the rest of the sentence.

An interrogative pronoun introduces a question.

A demonstrative pronoun points to a noun and makes the reference clearer: for example, *this book* versus *that book*.

An indefinite pronoun can be used in place of a noun for an unspecified individual or group.

A reflexive pronoun is one that uses *–self* at the end, such as *himself*. It can be used only if the person has already been referred to earlier in the sentence.

A **demonstrative pronoun** points to a noun; it can function as an adjective: *this, that, these, those.*

> **This** is the *day* of reckoning.
> **This** *day* will be long remembered.

An **indefinite pronoun** refers to an unspecified individual or group, and its possessive is formed in the same way as for nouns: *any, some, whoever.*

> It is *anyone's* guess when the boat will arrive.

A **reflexive pronoun** has the form of a personal pronoun with the *–self* suffix; it refers to the subject as the receiver of an action. In the following example, the subject is *italicized* and the reflexive pronoun is in **bold**.

> *Ben* congratulated **himself** on his successful election.

You cannot use a reflexive pronoun unless you have already mentioned the noun or pronoun that is it refers to.

> Incorrect: The gift was given to John and *myself*.
> Correct: The gift was given to John and *me*. [A personal pronoun is needed, not a reflexive one.]

A reciprocal pronoun refers to the separate parts of a plural antecedent.

The antecedent of a pronoun is the noun it replaces.

A **reciprocal pronoun** refers to the separate parts of a plural antecedent. In the following example, the reciprocal pronoun is in **bold** and the **antecedent** is *italicized*.

> *People* need to accept and tolerate **one another**.

Verbs

A verb conveys an action, a state of being, or a condition. There are three different kinds of verbs, each having different functions.

The various tenses of English verbs are illustrated in Appendix A.

Functions of Verbs

The main verb in a sentence expresses an action, a condition, or a state of being.

Helping verbs combine with main verbs to form different tenses.

1. The **main verb** in a sentence expresses action, condition, or a state of being. Some kinds of action are not necessarily visible—*think, imagine,* and *suggest* are examples of action verbs in which the "action" is interior or mental. Verbs may be modified by adverbs or adverbial phrases.

2. A **helping verb** (also called **auxiliary verb**) combines with a main verb. The two most common helping verbs are *to be* (*am, are, is, was, were, will be,* etc.)

TABLE 14.2 Verbs	
Identification	Functions
Verb: conveys an action, a state, or a condition, or precedes another (main) verb. The different kinds of verbs have different functions.	1. The **main verb** may be transitive (take a direct object) or intransitive (do not take a direct object) and usually conveys an *action*, not necessarily physical, in the **predicate**. 2. A **helping or auxiliary verb** precedes a *main verb* to form more complex *tenses* (indications of the time, continuance, or completeness of the action); to express a *mood* such as obligation, necessity, probability, or possibility; or to show *voice*, i.e., whether the relation of verb to subject is active or passive. 3. A **linking verb** is followed by a predicate noun or adjective that refers back to the subject.

The predicate contains the verb and object (and indirect object), or subject complement.

and *to have* (*have, has, had*, etc.) Forms of *to be* are used in the *progressive* tenses; forms of *to have* are used in the *perfect* tenses (see Appendix A).

A **modal** is a verb form placed before the main verb to express necessity, obligation, possibility, probability, or a similar condition: *can, could, may, might, must, ought to, shall, should, will,* and *would* are modals.

You *should* finish your homework.

A modal verb expresses necessity, obligation, possibility, or probability.

3. A **linking verb**, such as *to be*, is used to connect subject and predicate in one of six ways:

- expressing identity: Today *is* Saturday.
- expressing condition: I *am* upset.
- expressing state: These *are* my colleagues.
- expressing opinion: We *are* for freedom of speech.
- expressing total: One and one *are* two.
- expressing cost: The fundraiser *is* $200 a plate.

A linking verb joins (links) a subject to a noun or adjective that follows the verb.

Verbs that imply "to be" also may function as linking verbs:

Mildred becomes [begins to be] faint as the night grows [continues to become] cold.

Compare: "He *acted* the part of Hamlet *splendidly*."
With: "He **acted** *sick* by staying home from school."

In the first sentence, *acted* is a main verb used transitively (takes the object *part*); it is modified by the adverb *splendidly*. In the second sentence, *acted* is a linking verb—he acted [behaved as one who *is*] sick—the verb implies "to be"—and thus is followed by a subject complement, the predicate adjective *sick* (see "Subject complement" in Table 14.3).

Modifiers: Adjectives and Adverbs

Adjectives and adverbs modify, or give more information about, nouns and verbs.

TABLE 14.3	Modifiers: Adjectives and Adverbs
Identification	Functions
Adjective: a word that modifies a noun. It precedes a noun or follows a linking verb; it answers the question *which?*, *what kind?*, or *how many?*	1. An **adjectival modifier** describes or particularizes a noun and precedes it. 2. A **subject complement** (also called the *predicate adjective*) follows a linking verb (see "Noun" in Table 14.1) and modifies the subject.
Adverb: a word that modifies a verb, adjective, adverb, or even an entire sentence; it often ends in *-ly* and answers the question *when?, where?, why?, how?, to what degree?,* or *how much?*	1. An **adverbial modifier** describes or particularizes a verb and may precede or follow it; an adverb may also modify an adjective or another adverb; a *sentence* adverb may be the first word of the sentence and modify the entire sentence. 2. A **conjunctive adverb** may be used to connect two independent clauses.

An adjectival modifier describes a noun and usually precedes the noun it modifies. An adjective can also follow a linking verb, where it modifies the subject.

Functions of Adjectives

1. An **adjectival modifier** usually precedes the noun it modifies. An adjective can also follow a linking verb, where it *modifies the subject*. In the following examples, the adjective is in **bold** and the modified noun is *italicized*.

They attended the **delightful** *party*.

2. A subject complement modifies the subject and follows a linking verb. In the following example, the adjective is in **bold**, the linking verb is *italicized*, and the subject is underlined.

> The <u>party</u> *was* **delightful**.

Functions of Adverbs

1. An **adverbial modifier** describes a verb, an adjective, or an adverb. Many end in *-ly*.

> In this example, the adverb, in **bold**, modifies the verb, *italicized*.
> Jake *turned* **suddenly**.
> In this example, the adverb, in **bold**, modifies the adjective, *italicized*.
> That looks like a **very** *contented* cow.
> In this example, the adverb, in **bold**, modifies another adverb, *italicized*.
> They lived **quite** *happily* together.

An adverbial modifier describes a verb, an adjective, or an adverb.

2. Some adverbs can also act as conjunctions to connect two independent clauses. These are most commonly called **conjunctive adverbs**. Do not confuse them with regular conjunctions (such as *and*, *or*, and *but*), which can join words, phrases, and clauses.

A conjunctive adverb joins two independent clauses.

> Richard was hired by the publicity firm on Monday; *however*, he was fired on Tuesday.
> Note the semicolon separating the clauses and the comma after *however*.

Joiners: Prepositions and Conjunctions

Prepositions and conjunctions connect different parts of a sentence.

TABLE 14.4	Joiners: Prepositions and Conjunctions
Identification	Functions
Preposition: a small word/short phrase that often refers to place or time.	A **preposition** joins the noun or pronoun that follows to the rest of the sentence.
Conjunction: a word/phrase that connects words, phrases, and clauses of equal or unequal weight or importance. For a list of common subordinating conjunctions, see page 346.	1. A **coordinating conjunction** joins *equal* units, including independent clauses; there are seven coordinating conjunctions. 2. A **subordinating conjunction** joins *unequal* units, including independent and dependent clauses. 3. A **correlative conjunction** joins two *parallel* units.

Function of Prepositions

A **preposition** joins a noun or pronoun to the rest of the sentence and helps add information to the subject or predicate. Where there is a preposition, you will usually find an object of the preposition (noun or pronoun) following. Prepositions introduce prepositional phrases, which function as *adjectives* or *adverbs* depending on what part of speech they are modifying. A prepositional phrase never contains the subject of the sentence. In the following examples, the preposition is in **bold**, the object of the preposition is *italicized*, and the prepositional phrase is underlined.

> You will find the letters **in** the attic.
> She worked **during** the summer *vacation*.
> They laughed **at** *him*.

The noun or pronoun that follows a preposition will usually function as the object of the preposition. Many prepositional phrases, such as *as well as, in spite of, on account of,* are not listed as prepositions (see list in margin). The complete phrase acts as one preposition and they can often be recognized by the fact that a noun or pronoun follows.

Functions of Conjunctions

Conjunctions have two main joining functions: they can join equal or unequal units.

1. A **coordinating conjunction** joins *equal* units—word to word, phrase to phrase, clause to clause. An important use of coordinating conjunctions is to join *independent clauses* in compound sentences. In the following example, the coordinating conjunction is in **bold**:

> Tanya objected to their new roommate, **but** Bronwyn liked her.
> Note the comma before the conjunction.

Coordinating conjunctions are often referred to as the FANBOYS (**F**or, **A**nd, **N**or, **B**ut, **O**r, **Y**et, **S**o).

2. A subordinating conjunction joins *unequal* units. It usually begins a *dependent* clause and joins it to an *independent* clause. In the following examples, the subordinating conjunction is in **bold**. Note the comma in the second sentence.

> He plans to exercise his option **once** the season is over.
> **Once** the season is over, he plans to exercise his option.

3. Correlative conjunctions occur in pairs and require parallel structure. In the following examples, the correlative conjunctions are in **bold**:

> **Either** you will support me, **or** you will not be able to borrow my car.
> **Both** Ali **and** his father work at the community centre on Saturdays.

Exercise **14.3**

In this exercise, the goal is to create grammatically correct sentences; how-ever, they may not make a great deal of sense, much like the nonsense poem "Jabberwocky" given above. Try to make the sentence as funny as possible. Divide yourselves into four or eight groups. Each group is to come up with a list of ten examples of *one* of the following parts of speech (nouns, verbs, adjectives, or adverbs). When deciding on the list, try to avoid common words in favour of unusual or funny ones (e.g., nouns: *gelatin*, *dumpster*; verbs: *ooze*, *pout*; adjectives: *crinkly*, *repulsive*; adverbs: *tritely*, *gluttonously*). Keeping your textbook closed, create your list and decide the order you will use them in. After each group has completed the list, choose one member of the class to read the sentences below. As the blanks come up, one member of the part of speech group will read their group's chosen word. For example, in sentence 1, the "verb group" will provide their chosen word when the blank comes up, and then the "adjective group" will provide their chosen word, and so on until the sentence is complete. Remember: the idea isn't to try to "make sense" but to create strange sentences that are grammatical!

A subordinating conjunc-tion joins a dependent clause, which contains less important information, to an independent clause, which contains more important information.

A correlative conjunction always consists of two parts. Both must be used in order to complete the sentence. Common examples include *either/or, neither/nor, not only/but also, both/and.*

1. If you do not ____ your ____ _____, someone might ____ ____ your ____.
        verb   adj noun   adv verb   noun

2. We all occasionally ____ ____, but some _____ ____ ____their _____ every day.
                verb adv   noun (pl) adv verb   noun

3. The ____ ____ looked ready to ____ ____ into the ____ ____.
        adj noun   verb adv   adj noun

4. Before you ____ your ____ ____, it's best to ____ your ____ ____.
            verb   adj noun   verb   noun adv

5. The ____ ____ that ____ on the _____ _____ ____.
        adj noun   verb   noun verb adv

Exercise **14.4**

Read the paragraph below and underline the following:

5 nouns   2 adverbs
2 pronouns   4 prepositions
6 verbs   2 conjunctions
3 adjectives

(*continued*)

Once we left the main road and turned down a narrow side street, we were in nothing more than an extended slum. The car came to a stop in front of a house that was far better than any of the others around it. Set back a little from the street, it was a well-kept bungalow. The cemented front garden had a garish marble fountain in the middle, with an arrangement of plastic flamingoes and penguins around it. The windows had heavy bars across them, and even the front door had an extra door of iron bars in front of it. My grandmother did not get out; instead she had the driver toot his horn imperiously. A woman stepped out of the front door, and when she saw the car, she immediately nodded and smiled and went back inside.

Selvadurai, Shyam. "The Demoness Kali." *Short Fiction & Critical Contexts*. Ed. Eric Henderson and Geoff Hancock. Don Mills: Oxford UP, 2010. 384. Print.

〉 Introducing . . . the Sentence

Because the sentence is the basic unit of written (though not of spoken) communication, you need to know how to identify incomplete sentences in your writing so you can make them complete in formal writing. In order to know what an incomplete sentence is, you need to first consider the concept of the sentence.

What Is a Sentence?

It's not always easy to identify a complete sentence. Which of the following is a sentence?

> Write!
> Right!

Now, consider this pair:

> Seeing as believing.
> Seeing is believing.

Although you may have been able to correctly identify *Write!* and "*Seeing is believing*" as complete sentences, the examples show that just the appearance of a word or group of words isn't a reliable guide to identifying a sentence. In commands, the subject *you* is implied (see below, page 343); therefore, *Write!* means *You write!* and is a complete sentence. A **sentence fragment** is the term for a less-than-complete sentence. *Right!* and *Seeing as believing* are examples of fragments. *Right!* is missing both subject and predicate: *You are right!* is complete. *Seeing as believing* is a noun phrase; there is no predicate.

A sentence fragment is an incomplete clause. There are four main types.

Some textbooks define a sentence as a complete thought. Most complete sentences express a completed thought or idea, but if we define a sentence simply as a complete *thought*, we need to know what a thought is. As well, sentences certainly can contain more than one "thought."

Which of these word groups is a sentence?

Rules of grammar.
Grammar rules!

If we accept *rules* in the second example as a colloquialism (an informal expression) that produces the meaning "grammar helps students get high grades," then the second word group would form a sentence. The first, however, is not a sentence because nothing is happening and no comment *about* the rules of grammar is being made. Some groups of words can be recognized as sentences because a word or words suggest something is happening or a relationship is being observed.

The word *rules* in the second sentence tells us something the writer is observing about grammar. The first word also is necessary to make the sentence complete; it indicates *what* rules. So, you can say that complete sentences need two things:

1. A *subject* that answers the reader's question "What or who is this about?"
2. A *predicate* that tells us something the subject is doing or what is being observed about it.

A sentence, then, is a word or group of words that expresses a complete thought.

More important, it can be defined grammatically: a sentence is a group of words that contains at least one subject and one predicate and needs nothing else to complete its thought.

One question to ask to determine the subject of a sentence is "Who or what is doing the action in the sentence?" When you ask this question, you are attempting to connect a verb, the main part of the predicate, to a noun or pronoun, the main part of a subject. Consider a very simple sentence:

Dogs bark.

The answer to the question "Who or what is doing the action in the sentence?" is "Dogs." So, *dogs*, a noun, is the subject.

To determine the predicate of a sentence, you can ask the question, "What does the subject do?" The answer is "bark." A predicate will always include a *verb*. The line in the sentence below divides the subject from the predicate.

Dogs | bark.

This sentence, *Dogs bark*, is very brief. How can we make it longer and more interesting? Adding words or phrases to the subject make it more informative

Although verbs often convey an action, some verbs do not express what a subject is doing but express a condition or state of being. The most common of these verbs are forms of *to be*: *is, are, was, were, has been, have been, will be*, etc. Because you will use these verbs often, you need to become familiar with them and recognize them as examples of a particular category of verb (see Functions of Verbs, 3, page 335).

A sentence is a group of words that contains at least one subject and one predicate and needs nothing else to complete it.

but doesn't usually change its basic structure. The line between subject and predicate will remain; the difference will be that a reader will know more about the dogs. Similarly, we could add words or phrases to the predicate so we would know more about their barking.

Dirty, dangerous dogs | bark balefully behind the barn.

The reader has been told that the dogs are dirty and dangerous. The predicate also has more information: the reader has been told *how* the dogs bark (*balefully*) and *where* they bark (*behind the barn*). The longer sentence illustrates that more interesting statements can be made by adding words or phrases, modifiers, to the subject and to the predicate. The subject together with its adjectival modifiers is called the **complete subject**; the main noun or pronoun alone is sometimes called the **simple subject** to distinguish it from the complete subject.

Another way you can give more information in a sentence is to add more subjects and predicates. When you add one or more subject-predicate units, the sentence is no longer simple. While simple sentences convey one complete thought, more complex sentences can convey more than one complete thought.

The first thing to check in your writing is that you are writing in complete sentences, which means you must make sure that the sentence you write has two parts, a subject and a predicate.

When you look to see whether the word group has a subject, make sure you don't mistake a noun or pronoun in a prepositional phrase for a subject. (See "Fragment 2—add-on fragment," page 344.) In the sentence below, there are two nouns in the complete subject, *end* and *troubles*. The first noun is the true subject; *troubles* is preceded by the preposition *of* and cannot be linked with the verb *is*.

The *end* of our troubles | *is* in sight.

The subject together with its modifiers is called the complete subject; the main noun or pronoun alone is sometimes called the simple subject to distinguish it from the complete subject.

A prepositional phrase consists of a preposition and a noun or pronoun; it modifies a noun or a verb. The noun or pronoun that immediately follows the preposition will not be the subject.

Exercise **14.5**

Which of the following are complete sentences? Draw a line between the subject and the predicate. Mark with an "S" those that contain only a subject and a "P" those that contain only a predicate. Indicate an "N" if there is neither subject nor predicate.

1. The empty cup on the bench.
2. Signed his name to the bottom of the petition.
3. A spider in the web.
4. Dropped the egg while running the egg and spoon race.
5. A ripe-smelling orange.
6. Faith heals.
7. Is unable to drive to school today.
8. The high levels of the lake.
9. Can grammar rules be bent?

10. Thousands of tourists around the world.
11. Close the window!
12. A parasite.
13. Don't eat pizza every day.
14. All dressed up with no place to go.
15. This grammar should be easy to master!

The Invisible-Subject Sentence

The need for a subject and a predicate in every complete sentence suggests that the minimum English sentence must contain at least two words. The imperative sentence, which is a command, is one exception. It may consist only of a predicate (verb). The subject, which is always implied, is the pronoun *you*, although it is invisible. For example, in the imperative sentence, *Listen! you* is understood to be the subject: *[You] listen!* In the command, *Go to the store! you* is understood to be the subject: *[You] go to the store!* Notice that *you* could be plural, that is, the command could be to more than one individual; indeed, all readers of the sentence could be implied.

Four Errors of Incompletion

The way to make sure your sentences are complete is to check that there is a noun or pronoun subject to connect with a verb in the predicate. However, checking for fragments can be a little more complicated than this. To help you recognize *all* kinds of fragments in your writing, they are divided into four types below.

Fragment 1—lacks subject or predicate. In this type of fragment, discussed above, either a subject or a predicate is missing.

In sentence 10 in Exercise 14.5, *Thousands of tourists around the world*, something essential is missing. What about the tourists? Do they exist? Are the tourists doing something? What did they look like? Who saw them?

To answer any of these questions is to complete a thought—and the sentence. For example,

One kind of fragment is missing a subject *or* a predicate.

> Thousands of tourists around the world experience jet lag.
> The Taj Mahal is seen by thousands of tourists from around the world.

In the first example, a predicate has been supplied. In the second example, a subject, *The Taj Mahal* and a verb, *is seen*, have been introduced, and the *thousands of tourists from around the world* have become part of the predicate, with the preposition *from* added for clarity. The following sentence, like the one above, is incomplete because it consists only of a subject. In this case, the noun *driver* is followed by a word group that expands on the subject. The subject is not doing anything.

A driver who never stops at a red light.

Who never stops at a red light tells us what kind of driver he or she is but goes no further. To turn this into a complete sentence, you would need to complete the thought by adding a predicate.

A driver who never stops at red lights *is dangerous.*

Exercise 14.6

Come up with two other ways to complete the fragment above; then, complete the following fragments, all of which lack a predicate.

1. The store that I missed
2. The brilliant idea that came to me in the middle of the night
3. A marching band that is able to rouse everyone
4. The kind of doughnut that doesn't have a hole in the middle
5. The rugby towel that was on the ground

Add-on fragments may begin with a word like *especially*, a phrase like *such as*, or a prepositional phrase. They lack a subject and predicate. Add-on fragments may begin with transitional words and phrases: *also, as well as, besides, especially, except (for), for example, including, like, such as,* and similar words. They may also begin with prepositions like *on, in,* and *to.*

Fragment 2—add-on fragment. Add-on fragments contain neither a complete subject *nor* a complete predicate. Writers can mistake them for complete sentences because in speech a pause is usual between them and the preceding sentence; you may mistakenly associate a pause or drawn breath with a new sentence. The easiest way to fix these kinds of fragments is to make them part of the previous sentence or to supply missing essentials, such as a subject and predicate. Punctuation may not be needed; at other times, you can use a comma or a dash.

Fragment: Exaggerated images of fitness are everywhere. Especially in teen-oriented magazines.

Corrections: Exaggerated images of fitness are everywhere, especially in teen-oriented magazines.
Exaggerated images of fitness are everywhere—especially in teen-oriented magazines.

Fragment: Sewage contains more than 200 toxic chemicals that are flushed down sinks or toilets. Not to mention the runoff from roads.

Correction: Sewage contains more than 200 toxic chemicals that are flushed down sinks or toilets, not to mention the runoff from roads.

When you begin a sentence with a word like *in*, *to*, or *at* (i.e., a preposition), check to see that the sentence expresses a complete thought and includes both a subject and a predicate.

Fragment: On top of the biggest sundae.

Who or what is there and what is taking place?

Corrections: The cherry was on top of the biggest sundae.
On top of the biggest sundae, the waiter placed a cherry.

Fragment 3—*-ing* fragment. A third kind of fragment occurs when an **incomplete verb form** ending in *–ing* or *–ed/en*, or a base verb form, is mistaken for a complete verb. To avoid sentence fragments, always ensure you write a *complete* verb form.

Here are some examples of incomplete verb forms:

- *listening, studying, thinking, being* (present participle form of verb)
- *given, thought, written, taken* (past participle form of verb)
- *to begin, to tell, to be, to look* (infinitive form of verb)

A third kind of fragment occurs when an incomplete verb form ending in *–ing* or *–ed/en*, or a base verb form, is mistaken for a complete verb.

While *complete* verb forms can be joined to a subject by adding a helping verb, incomplete verb forms can't:

Incomplete: She listening, they given . . .

Complete: She *was listening*, they *are given* . . .

Helping verbs such as *are*, *was*, *has*, or *had* combine with main verbs to create different verb tenses.

A common sentence error is mistaking the *–ing* part of a verb form for a complete verb form. The following are examples of fragments with incomplete verb forms:

Dogs running around the fenced-in play area.

What are the dogs doing? If you said "they are running," you have changed the fragment into a complete sentence by adding the helping verb *are*:

Dogs | *are running* around the fenced-in play area.

Fragment: As a new doctor fascinated by innovative surgery procedures.

Correction: As a new doctor, he | *was fascinated* by innovative surgery procedures.

The three incomplete forms mentioned above can act as nouns, adjectives, and adverbs in a sentence—but not as verbs.

Incomplete verb form as noun: Eating sensibly | is the best way to lose weight.

Learn how to recognize incomplete verb forms in your writing. Doing so will help you avoid this kind of sentence fragment. See also Appendix A (verb tenses).

Eating is the noun subject of this sentence.

Incomplete verb form as adjective:

My growling stomach | told me it was time to eat.

Growling is an adjective modifying *stomach*, the noun subject. Note that there is another incomplete verb form in this sentence, *to eat*, which is acting as an adjective, modifying *time*.

An independent clause is equivalent to a simple sentence: it has a subject and a predicate and needs nothing else to complete it.

A dependent clause contains a subject and a predicate, but it expresses an incomplete thought because the information it contains is dependent on information in the independent clause. By itself, it cannot form a complete sentence.

Common subordinating conjunctions and relative pronouns:

after	though
although	unless
as	until
as if	what
as long as	whatever
as soon as	when
as though	whenever
because	where
before	whereas
even though	wherever
ever since	whether
if	which
if only	whichever
in case	while
in order that	who
once	whoever
since	whom
so that	whose
that	why

Exercise **14.7**

To the remaining fragments in Exercise 14.5, add a subject and/or predicate to create grammatically complete sentences.

Fragment 4—dependent clause fragment. A dependent clause fragment is the most common type of fragment. That is because, at first glance, a dependent clause looks a lot like a grammatical sentence.

An **independent clause** is equivalent to a simple sentence: it has a subject and a predicate and needs nothing else to complete it. A **dependent clause** also contains a subject and a predicate, but it expresses an incomplete thought because the information it contains is *dependent on* information in the independent clause. That is one way you can tell a dependent from an independent clause. (Recall that one definition for a complete sentence is that it expresses a complete thought.)

Another way to identify a dependent clause is by the word it begins with— a subordinating conjunction or a relative pronoun. Common subordinating conjunctions and relative pronouns are listed in the margin.

A dependent clause fragment sounds incomplete and leaves us wondering about the missing part.

Consider this fragment:

Because he was late.

You can think of a dependent clause as searching for an answer to a question—in this case, *What happened because he was late?* When you provide that information in an independent clause, you will have a complete sentence. You can also test a sentence for completeness by asking whether the word group is true or false. *Because he was late* can be neither true nor false due to missing information.

Because he was late for work, he lost some pay.

The subordinating conjunction that introduces the dependent clause indicates the relationship of that clause to the independent clause, such as one of cause–effect (*as, because*), time (*before, since, when, while*), or contrast (*although,*

though, whereas). (For more information about subordinating conjunctions as joiners, see page 338.) If you take away the subordinating conjunction, you are left with a subject and a predicate and a sentence that expresses a complete thought. Another way to fix a dependent clause fragment, then, is to take away the subordinating conjunction; you will have a simple sentence expressing one idea. However, it may not be the idea you intended to convey:

> He was late for work.

This is a complete sentence, but it does not explain the consequences of his being late.

Note that a dependent clause could precede or follow the independent clause. The placement of the dependent clause often determines whether you use a comma to separate it from the main idea (see page 364).

To test whether you have written a dependent clause fragment, answer these questions. (1) Does the idea sound complete? (2) Can you answer "true" or "false" to it? If the answer to 1 or 2 is no, it is probably a fragment. (3) Does it begin with one of the words in the margin box above?

Exercise **14.8**

The following may or may not be sentences. If they are not, identify what kind of fragment each illustrates (lacks subject or predicate, add-on fragment, *-ing* fragment, dependent clause fragment). If they are fragments, make them into complete sentences with a subject and a predicate and needing nothing else to complete them.

1. Completing the test on time.
2. Huge tears rolled down his cheeks.
3. Being that she worked late.
4. Whenever they called her into work.
5. He promised to call on her tomorrow. To see if she was still all right.
6. He must be guilty. Since he's already confessed.
7. I won't watch TV tonight. Unless I find something interesting.
8. Introducing our next prime minister.
9. A murder of crows, along with a flock of sheep.
10. Swimming on her back.

After you've checked your answers (see Appendix D), complete the exercise by doing questions 11–25.

11. Walking beside the tracks, he eventually reached the town.
12. Because trips create memories.
13. Stress can make us victims of illnesses. Including mild to life-threatening ones.
14. The student sauntered into class. After he opened the door and cautiously peeked inside.
15. Which is an example of a dependent clause.
16. For example, the famous TV show *The Walking Dead*.

(continued)

17. This is the information age. When ideas are literally at your fingertips.
18. The objection was overruled. As the judge felt that the jury need to hear the statement.
19. Learning about people from different ethnic groups.
20. Painting is a good hobby and helps people see the world more clearly. Such as the increased perception of shadows.
21. Golf courses always include obstacles. These being water hazards and sand traps.
22. Almost all Canadians agree that snow is great. But not when shovelling.
23. Although there are options in today's schools for Aboriginal students to learn about their culture.
24. Sounds and textures are common features of dreams. While smell and taste are usually absent.
25. 2016 is the year of the Ram. Which is a Chinese Zodiac symbol.

Exercise **14.9**

The following passage contains four sentence fragments. Underline them. Then, correct them by joining them to complete sentences or by adding information.

> When considering college or university. Many students must decide where to live. If they are going to school close to home, they may decide to continue living with their families. Listening to their parent's advice. However, if the school is far away and commuting is not possible, students must decide whether to live in the school residence or in an apartment. Residences are convenient. Especially if there is a meal plan available. Meal plans that are nutritious. Apartments might be a better idea though, especially if students need to work. Not all residences are close to where jobs are. Privacy might be an issue in residence. Not all students can get their own rooms. Apartments may provide privacy, but only if there is no need for roommates. Many factors need to be considered when choosing where to live.

❭ Introducing . . . Phrases and Clauses

Phrases and clauses are grammatical units within the sentence. They are larger than the individual parts of speech but usually smaller than a complete grammatical sentence. (The exception is an independent clause, which is equivalent to a simple sentence.)

Prepositions join nouns and pronouns to the rest of the sentence, while conjunctions handle the other joining functions. Coordinating conjunctions join two or more independent clauses while subordinating conjunctions and relative pronouns join dependent and independent clauses. By joining clauses, you can form different sentence types.

Phrases

Phrases function as nouns, verbs, adjectives, and adverbs. When a **phrase** acts as one of these parts of speech, it is important to remember that it does so as a unit, though each word *within* the unit may be a different part of speech and have a function distinct from that of the phrase as a whole.

Phrases | function (as a unit) (within the sentence).

As a unit and *within the sentence* are functioning as adverbs, modifying the verb *function*. (Recall that adverbs modify verbs.) The first phrase answers the question *how?* while the second answers the question *where?* of the verb. But though each phrase is acting as an adverb, the individual words within the unit have distinct functions, none of which is adverbial.

as = preposition
within = preposition
a = indefinite article
the = definite article
unit = noun (object of preposition *as*)
sentence = noun (object of preposition *within*)

Prepositional Phrases

A **prepositional phrase** will act as either an adverb or an adjective. As you've seen above, a group of words that includes more than one part of speech can, as a unit, modify a verb. If it does, it is said to be functioning *adverbially* (as an adverb) within the sentence.

She drove me (into town) so I could do my laundry.

The prepositional phrase *into town* begins with the preposition *into* and is followed by the noun *town*, the object of the preposition. But if you look at the phrase as a unit, you can see that *into town* is functioning as an adverb modifying the verb *drove* by explaining where the action took place: Drove where? Into town.

Similarly, a group of words can modify a noun or pronoun, in which case it is functioning *adjectivally* (as an adjective).

Consider the prepositional phrases (indicated by parentheses) in this sentence:

An obsession (with *Star Wars*) | led to her career (as an astronomer).

A phrase is a group of grammatically linked words that lacks a subject or a predicate or both. It functions as a single part of speech.

A prepositional phrase consists of a preposition and a noun or pronoun (the object of the preposition). The phrase can act as an adverb to modify a verb or as an adjective to modify a noun or pronoun.

When a word is functioning adverbially, it is acting as an adverb, which modifies verbs, adjectives, and other adverbs.

An adjectival phrase usually *follows* the noun or pronoun it modifies. This order is different from that of a one-word adjective, which usually *precedes* the noun it modifies.

"With *Star Wars*" is a prepositional phrase that gives us more information about (i.e., modifies) the noun *obsession*. It is functioning as an adjective.

with = preposition
Star Wars = proper noun (object of preposition *with*)
The second phrase, *as an astronomer*, modifies the noun *career*, functioning as an adjective.
as = preposition
astronomer = noun (object of preposition *as*)

Prepositional phrases do not contain the actual subject of a sentence. In the following sentence, *at the beginning of class* does not contain the actual subject even though it begins the sentence.

> *At the beginning of class*, students in Japan bow to their teacher.

The subject here is *students*, and *at the beginning of class* is a prepositional phrase answering *when* they bow. Since it answers *when?* of the verb *bow*, you know it is acting adverbially in the sentence.

Noun and Verb Phrases

A noun phrase is a group of words that acts as a noun in a sentence. It can be either the subject or an object in the sentence.

In this example, the indefinite pronoun *some* combined with its modifier, *of the injured*, makes up a **noun phrase**. The entire phrase, *some of the injured passengers*, functions as the subject in this sentence because it tells us *who had to be hospitalized*.

> Some of the injured passengers | had to be hospitalized.

A phrase, then, can function as a noun subject or object.

Finally, consider the following sentence, in which a **verb phrase** acts as a unit in the sentence, conveying the action of the subject *we*:

A verb phrase is a group of words that acts as the verb in a sentence.

> We *will be looking* carefully for the person with a red flag on her backpack.

Verb phrases are very common, since you will often need to use helping verbs with main verbs to create different tenses beyond the one-word simple tenses (verb phrases are *italicized*):

Simple present: I *think*, you *say*, she takes . . . .
Simple past: I *thought*, you *said*, she *took* . . . .
Present progressive: I *am thinking*, you *are saying*, she *is taking* . . . .
Past perfect: I *had thought*, you *had said*, she had taken . . . .

For more information about the tenses, see Appendix A.

Exercise **14.10**

First, identify the word groups in parentheses as adverbial, adjectival, noun, or verb phrases. Then, identify the subject of the sentence.

1. Tomorrow, (the class time) will be changed (for the rest)(of the semester).
2. (Some of the food) (in the fridge) (has spoiled.)
3. The store (in the mall) (with the latest fashions) (has closed).
4. A search (of the abandoned house) (turned up) several cartons (of stolen goods).
5. (The 2018 hockey season) (will belong) (to the Leafs).

In addition to forms of *to be* and *to have*, verb phrases occur when modals, a special kind of helping verb, combine with main verbs to convey ability (*can, could*), possibility (*may, might*), necessity (*must, have*), and other meanings.

Clauses

A word group larger than a phrase that can be broken down into two grammatical units, a subject and a predicate, is called a **clause**. In the following sentence, the subjects are in bold, the verbs are italicized, and the conjunction is underlined. Clauses can be combined to create sentences that are generally longer than simple sentences.

A clause is a group of words containing both a subject and a predicate.

> **Frances** never *answers* questions in class <u>unless</u> the **teacher** *calls* on her.
> First clause: Frances never answers questions in class
> Second clause: unless the teacher calls on her

The first part of this sentence could stand alone as a sentence, as it has a subject, *Frances*, has a predicate verb, *answers*, and needs nothing else to complete its thought. The second part could not stand alone as a sentence—the word *unless* makes it a dependent clause fragment.

Thus, this sentence illustrates two different kinds of clauses: (1) an **independent clause**, which can stand alone as a sentence, and (2) a **dependent clause**, which cannot stand alone as a sentence. It is especially important to be able to distinguish an independent clause from a dependent clause in order to avoid writing a sentence fragment. As discussed under "Fragment 4—dependent clause fragment" (page 346), a dependent clause contains an idea subordinate to (dependent on) the idea of the main clause.

An independent clause can stand alone as a complete sentence; a dependent clause cannot stand alone as a complete sentence.

Using Conjunctions to Join Clauses

An independent clause by itself is equivalent to a **simple sentence**. *Frances never answers questions in class* is a simple sentence consisting of an independent clause. Clauses are used as building blocks to construct more complex sentences. The function of a coordinating conjunction is to connect *equal* units, such as

A simple sentence consists of one subject and one predicate.

two independent clauses. The function of a subordinating conjunction is to connect *unequal* units, such as an independent clause and a dependent clause. Different rules for punctuation apply to independent and dependent clauses connected this way.

Exercise **14.11**

Identify all independent and dependent clauses in the following sentences by underlining independent clauses and placing parentheses around any dependent clauses. For help, you can refer to the list of subordinating conjunctions, page 346; these kinds of conjunctions introduce dependent clauses. Remember that pronouns, such as *I* or *it*, can act as subjects.

1. Despite the professors giving harder tests, students are still passing.
2. Even though I was born in Canada, I don't like winter.
3. I ran through the rain after I realized I'd left my umbrella at home.
4. In most parts of North America, Daylight Saving Time begins in March.
5. The struggle for democracy will continue until all the rebels are captured.
6. While it is important that students volunteer, mandatory volunteerism does not instil a sense of civic duty.
7. Driving is a privilege; however, most people see it as a right.
8. Studying grammar does not guarantee good grades, but it certainly helps.
9. Until the semester is over, Candice cannot begin work.
10. Ecstasy was in the news a lot a few years ago, though harder drugs posed more risk to users.

Sentence Patterns

The basic sentence pattern is the simple sentence. As you have seen, a simple sentence consists of a subject and a predicate, and is equivalent to an independent clause. Other sentence patterns are formed by joining clauses together.

Compound Sentence

A compound sentence has two or more independent clauses joined by a coordinating conjunction (one of the FANBOYS).

A sentence formed by two or more independent clauses joined by a coordinating conjunction is called a **compound sentence**. We can see these kinds of conjunctions (*italicized*) operating as joiners in the following examples:

The books were sorted into piles, *and* the piles were placed in the corner.
My grades were good in the first semester, *but* in the second semester, they dropped.
I have no clean clothes left, *so* I need to go home to do my laundry.

A sentence can have two subjects or two verbs and still be a simple sentence (but not two subjects *and* two verbs). A coordinating conjunction joins equal units, so as well as joining two independent clauses, it can join two nouns that are the subject of one verb or two verbs governed by one subject. Such **compound-subject** and **compound-predicate** constructions can occur in simple sentences. However, a compound *sentence* contains two independent clauses, *each* with its own subject and verb.

Here is an example of a simple sentence with a compound predicate:

John finished his test and walked quickly out of the room.

Note that there is no comma before the conjunction *and* because the two verbs it connects are parts of the same clause. The compound sentence below contains two subjects and two predicates:

John finished his test, and *he* walked quickly out of the room.

Don't use a coordinating conjunction to begin a sentence. Words like *and*, *but*, and *or* should occur only *within* a sentence where they join two equal units, such as two independent clauses.

Incorrect: The popularity of Facebook is undeniable. And it shows no sign of abating.
Correct: The popularity of Facebook is undeniable, and it shows no sign of abating.

A sentence with one noun and two verbs is still a simple sentence.

A compound subject consists of two nouns, two pronouns, or a noun and a pronoun.

A compound predicate is two verbs governed by one subject.

Complex Sentence

A sentence formed from an independent clause joined by a subordinating conjunction to a dependent clause is called a **complex sentence**. In a complex sentence, two or more subordinating conjunctions may connect two or more dependent clauses to an independent clause. We can see these kinds of conjunctions operating as joiners in the following examples:

Plagiarism is a problem at many universities *where* much research these days is conducted through the Internet.
Although much work has gone into developing artificial organs, the results, to date, have been disappointing.

A complex sentence is created by joining an independent clause to a dependent clause by using a subordinating conjunction.

In the first sentence, *where* is the subordinating conjunction that begins a dependent clause and joins it to the preceding independent clause. In the second sentence, the dependent clause comes first, but the subordinating conjunction *although* nevertheless joins the dependent to the independent clause. (You can just as easily start a sentence with a dependent clause as with an independent one.)

In the next example, an independent clause is followed by two dependent clauses; *after* and *that* are the subordinating conjunctions that join them:

Common subordinating conjunctions and relative pronouns:

after	though
although	unless
as	until
as if	what
as long as	whatever
as soon as	when
as though	whenever
because	where
before	whereas
even though	wherever
ever since	whether
if	which
if only	whichever
in case	while
in order that	who
once	whoever
since	whom
so that	whose
that	why

A compound-complex sentence is created by combining a compound sentence with a complex sentence.

Ena began taking night classes *after* her company announced *that* there would be layoffs in the near future.

You need to carefully distinguish clauses in order to punctuate them correctly. For example, in this sentence, a dependent clause intervenes between the subordinating conjunction *that* and the rest of the dependent clause. The dependent clause that interrupts is italicized:

The car, *because it was new*, was her pride and joy.

Compound-Complex Sentence

The last sentence type, a **compound-complex sentence**, combines a compound sentence (independent clause + coordinating conjunction + independent clause) with a complex sentence. It will contain two independent clauses along with one or more dependent clauses. For example,

The woodwinds warbled, the brass bellowed, *and* the strings sang sweetly, *though* the timpani thundered, almost drowning out the other instruments.

Exercise 14.12

Examples of the simple, compound, and complex sentence types appear below. For compound and complex sentences, underline independent clauses, circle conjunctions, and put parentheses around dependent clauses. Identify each sentence type.

1. The class average was low in the first semester, but it has gone up this semester.
2. Until a few months ago, she had never eaten Thai food.
3. Summer is the time for outdoor sports, and winter is the time to hibernate.
4. Tom wanted to give Jane a gift but had no money.
5. Salmon oil is a supplement that lowers cholesterol.
6. An essay should convince someone about a point of view or teach him or her a new idea.
7. Mandarin is spoken in mainland China, and has become popular in North American schools.
8. His library privileges have been suspended until he pays his fines.
9. She looked her subject up on Wikipedia and has not gone further.
10. She is convinced that she will get an "A" in the course.

Exercise **14.13**

To demonstrate your familiarity with the different kinds of clauses and joiners, construct compound, complex, and compound-complex sentences from the independent clauses (simple sentences) below. After you have joined the clauses in the most logical way, identify the sentence type: compound, complex, or compound-complex. Ensure that you have at least one example of each type of sentence. Small changes can be made so that it is easier to make up complex sentences, and sentence order may be changed.

1. They intended to eat at Benny's Bistro.
   They saw a long line-up outside Benny's.
   They went to Kenny's Kitchen instead.
2. There may be nearly two million kinds of plants in the world.
   There are likely at least as many different kinds of animals.
   No one can know how many species have evolved, flourished, and become extinct.
3. Timothy Findley's story "Stones" takes place in Toronto.
   Norman Levine's "Something Happened Here" takes place in northern France.
   Both stories describe the tragic assault by Canadian troops on Dieppe during the Second World War.
4. We may suspect that earth is not unique as a life-bearing planet.
   We do not as yet have any compelling evidence that life exists anywhere else.
   We must restrict our discussion of the presence of life to our own planet.
5. Cooking has become a popular hobby.
   Many celebrities have cooking shows.
   These celebrities have written cookbooks that promote their shows.

Errors of Combining

A fragment in formal writing suggests the writer does not fully understand what a sentence is, but sometimes writers run one sentence into another, suggesting they don't know where to end the sentence. The two major errors in ending a sentence are the **run-on sentence** (sometimes called "the fused sentence") and the **comma splice**, or the comma fault.

A run-on sentence is one that has no punctuation between independent clauses.

A comma splice occurs when a comma is used to join two independent clauses.

The Run-On Sentence

The writer of a run-on sentence joins two sentences without stopping. Doing this is like running a stop sign without changing speed. The writer charges through the end of the first complete thought and into the second one without separating them. This writer doesn't place a period at the end of the first sentence and so doesn't capitalize the first letter of the word that should begin the second sentence.

A sentence may contain one, two, or more subject–predicate units, but these units (independent clauses) must be joined correctly with commas and conjunctions so the reader can distinguish one main idea from another. Otherwise, they must be separated by a period to form separate sentences.

Incorrect:

The cruise to Alaska was full Tom and Yumi decided to fly to Jamaica instead.
The Dene peoples live in Northern Canada they speak different languages.

Once you determine where the first clause ends and the second one begins, make them into two simple sentences or use a comma and the appropriate coordinating conjunction to join them.

Correct:

The cruise to Alaska was full. Tom and Yumi decided to fly to Jamaica instead.
The cruise to Alaska was full, *so* Tom and Yumi decided to fly to Jamaica instead.
The Dene peoples live in Northern Canada. They speak different languages.
The Dene peoples live in Northern Canada, *and* they speak different languages.

The run-on sentences below contain two complete thoughts or two main ideas. Lines indicate the division between subject and predicate; diagonal lines show where the first sentence ends and the second begins, and where a period or a comma and coordinating conjunction should be placed.

Incorrect:

Many people | have smartphones // smartphones | are very practical devices.
The poverty line | is very low in Canada // many people | live below the poverty line.

Correct:

Many people have smartphones. Smartphones are practical devices.
Many people have smartphones, as they are practical devices.
The poverty line is very low in Canada. Many people live below the poverty line.
The poverty line is very low in Canada, but many people live below it.

The Comma Splice

An error more common than the run-on sentence is the comma splice—the joining of two complete sentences by only a comma. This error is like slowing down at a stop sign without coming to a full stop, then charging through. The comma has many uses *within* the sentence, but, by itself, a comma cannot be used to connect two sentences.

The simplest way to avoid comma splices is to find where one complete thought (independent clause) ends and the next begins and either place a period there or use a comma and a coordinating conjunction. Comma splices sometimes occur when two clauses are very closely related or the second clause seems a continuation of the first one. In formal writing, it's important to be able to separate two independent clauses.

Incorrect:

Models today are very thin, they look ill.
The population is rising, some think the earth cannot sustain itself.

Although the second clauses in these sentences are closely related in meaning to the preceding clauses, they are not part of those clauses and must be separated from them by something stronger than just a comma. As you will see in Chapter 15, a "stop" form of punctuation, such as a semicolon or colon, may be a good choice in these cases:

Correct:

Models today are very thin. They look ill.
Models today are very thin; they look ill.
The population is rising. Some think the earth cannot sustain itself.
The population is rising; therefore, some think the earth cannot sustain itself.

Remember that a pronoun generally replaces a noun that precedes it in a sentence. Like a noun, a pronoun can act as the subject of a clause. In the following sentences, a pronoun is the subject of the second clause. Lines indicate the division between subject and predicate; diagonal lines show where the first sentence ends and the second begins, and where a period or the comma and coordinating conjunction should be placed.

A run-on sentence isn't just a long sentence: it's a major grammatical error in which two subject–predicate units (two "sentences") are not properly separated.

A comma splice isn't just a problem in comma usage; it's a major grammatical error in which a comma alone is used to separate two complete thoughts.

Incorrect:

Working in a busy office environment | was completely new to her, // she | had always worked at home.
Censorship | does not just mean getting rid of swearing and nudity, // it | can also mean blocking an idea or a viewpoint.

Correct:

Working in a busy office environment was completely new to her. She had always worked at home.
Working in a busy office environment was completely new to her, *for* she had always worked at home.
Censorship does not just mean getting rid of swearing and nudity. It can also mean blocking an idea or a viewpoint.
Censorship does not just mean getting rid of swearing and nudity, *but* it can also mean blocking an idea or a viewpoint.

Remember that if you wish to use a comma to connect two independent clauses, you must also use one of the seven coordinating conjunctions (FANBOYS). You cannot use a comma before words such as *however, therefore,* or *thus* to join two independent clauses. That would also produce a comma splice. For the correct form of punctuation with these and similar words and phrases, see page 373.

Exercise **14.14**

Fix the sentences by using a period to make two separate sentences (if you already know the rules for using other forms of punctuation to join independent clauses, you can use them). Also, identify whether the sentence is run-on or contains a comma splice.

1. I read two books in two days I did nothing else but read.
2. I couldn't use my laptop today, I forgot to plug it in before the battery was dead.
3. I was frightened during my first driving lesson the instructor yelled at me.
4. It's easy to punctuate sentences, just put a comma whenever you pause.
5. She finished watching the movie then took the bus home.
6. Magazine are available for digital download, this is better for the environment.
7. Technology continues to evolve but we can't always predict whether this is good or bad.
8. Humans are imitators, conforming is something they are good at.
9. Many immigrants want to learn about Canadian culture they take courses about it.
10. Binge drinking is a serious problem, many students engage in this behaviour.

Exercise **14.15**

Determine what is wrong in the following sentences. It could be a fragment or a run-on sentence, or it could contain a comma splice; then, make the correction.

1. He managed to pass the year though he seldom did his homework, what will happen to him next year is anyone's guess.
2. The opening ceremonies were delayed. On account of rain.
3. She has decided to work at a fast-food restaurant. Not a great place for tips.
4. Movies provide entertainment for people, different people prefer different genres such as horror.
5. Since she bought the new tablet.
6. The only way a person can learn. To pay attention to what is going on in class.
7. He was too tall and thin to excel at sports. Except basketball, of course.
8. The concept that "bigger is better" is part of our culture, it is promoted by both advertisers and the media these days.
9. Understanding the theory of relativity and its impact on our daily lives.
10. Justin Trudeau may eventually be as well known as his father, Pierre had charisma and charm.

After you've checked your answers, complete the exercise by doing questions 11–25.

11. The Romans were willing to change their religious beliefs quite easily, the Greeks, however, were less willing to do this.
12. Although video games can eat up your time if you are not careful.
13. The computer is not the only way to access email today, telephones and tablets may come equipped with email capability.
14. It seems that the North American mass media prescribes two roles for women, they can be sex objects or passive housewives.
15. Martial arts are attracting more people than ever before. Especially those who want to gain self-control and self-awareness.
16. We can no longer turn our backs to what is happening in the north It is time to take action.
17. BlackBerry is located in Waterloo, Ontario, it employs people from around the world.
18. Her message about crime was lost on the audience, they wanted to hear about terrorism.
19. Part of a long line of police officers.
20. Speaking in public is distressing for some, the most common fear is that people will laugh even if the presentation is serious.
21. Speakers in the House of Commons need to speak loudly, their message will not be heard otherwise.
22. One of the most tragic events of the twentieth century. The detonation of the atomic bomb over Hiroshima.

(continued)

23. Podcasts are current, up to date and appear automatically, thus they can be enjoyed anywhere at any time.
24. I have been to London and Paris neither city is in Europe though.
25. Many factors contribute to poverty. Including geographic factors, disease, and lack of education or health care.

Exercise **14.16**

Identify the sentence errors in the following paragraph; they may include fragments, run-on sentences, and comma splices. Then, correct them.

The "Freshmen 15" is not a recent phenomenon this refers to the weight students typically gain during their first year at college or university. What concerns doctors now is the amount of weight gained during this time. In the 70s and 80s, students typically gained 5 pounds, now it is up to 15. This is a very unhealthy weight gain. Once the weight is gained. It is very hard to lose. Because of this. Cafeterias are starting to offer more nutritional meals with fewer calories. Student councils are beginning to be proactive, and inform students of the dangers of excess weight gain. School gyms are offering more classes to help students battle this weight gain. In the future, many hope that the "Freshman 15" becomes non-existent.

■ Chapter Review Questions

1. What is a noun? A noun phrase?
2. What is a verb? A verb phrase?
3. What is an adjective?
4. What is an adverb?
5. What is a preposition? Prepositional phrase?
6. What is the difference between a coordinating and subordinating conjunction?
7. What are the different types of sentence patterns?
8. What are the two essential parts of a sentence?
9. What are the different types of sentence fragments?
10. What is the difference between a run-on sentence and a comma splice?

15

Commas and Other
Forms of Punctuation

While some punctuation rules change slowly over time, not all the uses you see every day are correct. Therefore, this chapter will introduce you to the current standards for properly using punctuation. Once you have studied the rules, you may even begin to notice other people's mistakes in using commas, semicolons, colons, dashes, parentheses, and apostrophes. Later in the chapter, you will be shown how to avoid some of the common punctuation errors that writers make. Various exercises will help reinforce the punctuation rules you need to know in order to write error-free documents.

❯ Do Commas Matter?

Does the precise placement of those visually challenged marks on paper *really* matter? The short answer is "yes" because readers look for commas in specific places to help them read. When a comma is missing or is placed where it shouldn't be, the reader might have to reread the sentence, looking for another cue to its meaning. Furthermore, if you make comma errors, your writing will appear unreliable. For example, missing commas in the short sentences below could confuse a reader. Read each incorrect sentence and then look at the correct version that follows. See how much easier it is to understand the correct versions.

> Incorrect: The year before a deadly virus ravaged much of the countryside.
> Correct: The year before, a deadly virus ravaged much of the countryside.
> Incorrect: Although dating services may ask you for a photo appearance is less important than personality.
> Correct: Although dating services may ask you for a photo, appearance is less important than personality.

As a student, you will be writing essays or reports for many of your classes. As a future working professional, you may write letters, email, reports, summaries, memoranda, or other documents that need to be punctuated. Correct comma use guides the reader through the sentence, clarifying the relationships among its parts.

Myths about comma use abound, such as the "one breath rule," which states that wherever you naturally stop to pause, you should insert a comma. However, commas assist the typical silent reader more than the one who reads aloud. If you are coaching yourself to read a speech, you may want to place commas where you plan to pause for breath, but in formal writing, the "one breath rule" is simply too vague to be of use; it can even lead you astray.

The word *comma* comes from the Greek word *komma*, meaning "cut" or "segment." In general, commas separate (segment) the smaller or less important units in a sentence. Working with coordinating conjunctions, however, they are also used to separate large units, independent clauses. In a sentence, commas separate

- items in a series
- independent clauses
- parenthetical (types of non-essential) information
- adjectives, dates, addresses, titles, and the like

Commas separate the smaller or less important units in a sentence. Working with coordinating conjunctions, they are also used to separate large units, independent clauses.

Rule Category 1: Use Commas to Separate Items in a Series

This rule category applies to three or more grammatically parallel items whether single words—such as nouns, verbs, or adjectives—phrases, or clauses. For example:

Commas separate three or more items in a series: words, phrases, and clauses.

A series of three nouns:

It doesn't matter whether the items in the series are words, phrases, or clauses.

A series of three predicates:

Every Saturday, Davina gets up, drowns herself with coffee, and stumbles to the door before she realizes what day it is.

A series of three clauses:

Flowering plants produce seeds, ferns produce spores, and coniferous trees produce cones.

A series or list is *three* or more of something. When you refer to *two* of something with a joiner in between like *and*, you do *not* usually use a comma unless *and* is joining two independent clauses. The grammatical name for a group of words consisting of two of something (such as two nouns or two verbs) is a **compound**.

A list or series contains *three* items; commas separate the items. A compound contains *two* items; a comma is not used unless the items are two independent clauses with a word like *and*, *or*, or *but* in between.

The comma before the last item in a series of three or more items, referred to as the *serial comma*, is often omitted in informal writing.

My three favourite months are May, June and September. [informal]

However, the serial comma often makes a sentence much easier to follow. It should *not* be omitted if the last element or the one that precedes it is a compound (contains two items). In this example, the last item in the list is a compound, a single thing, *toast and jam*, consisting of two elements: *toast* and *jam*:

Always include the serial comma, the comma preceding the conjunction joining the last and second-last items in a list, unless your instructor tells you otherwise.

She ordered orange juice, an omelette with cheese, and toast and jam.

The serial comma is especially helpful to the reader where the second-last or the last item is significantly longer than the other items.

The two-year specialization includes 10 half-courses, two full courses that involve internships in health care facilities, and a research paper.

Rule Category 2: Use Commas to Separate Independent Clauses

Rule category 2 applies to three related situations: (2a) two independent clauses joined by a coordinating conjunction, (2b) introductory words, phrases, or clauses when an independent clause follows, and (2c) some conclusions when an independent clause precedes the conclusion.

2a. Use a comma after an independent clause when that clause is followed by another independent clause with a coordinating conjunction in between. In other words, use a comma before the coordinating conjunction in a compound sentence.

Use a comma before the coordinating conjunction in a compound sentence.

> The course was supposed to be offered in the fall, *but* it was cancelled.
> The grocery store is two kilometres away, *so* he never walks.
> Dyana was the best dancer on the cruise ship, *and* she won an award to prove it.

Remember that the comma goes *before*, not after, the coordinating conjunction.

Short independent clauses. Exceptions to this rule may be made if the second clause is very short or if the clauses are so closely related that they could be considered compounds (i.e., the ideas are hard to separate).

For example, the comma may be omitted between *dress* and *and* because the clauses are short:

> "She wore the dress and I stayed home," sang Danny Kaye in the movie *White Christmas*.

2b. Use a comma after an introductory word, phrase, or clause when an independent clause follows it.

A sentence adverb is an adverb that modifies the complete independent clause that follows it.

> After six years as committee chair, it was time for her to retire.
> In order to get the maximum enjoyment from his stereo equipment, Curtis put it in a room where the acoustics were excellent.

In the following example, the introduction is one word, a **sentence adverb**, an adverb that modifies the independent clause that follows it:

> Unfortunately, we have run out of mineral water.

Introductory dependent clause. When you begin the sentence with a dependent clause that is followed by an independent clause, a comma follows the dependent clause introduction (italicized below).

Use a comma after an introductory word, phrase, or clause when an independent clause follows it.

> *While the drinking age is 19 in most provinces,* it is only 18 in Alberta.

When she first encountered the Canadian educational system, she was surprised by the many differences between the North American and Japanese systems.

Compare with rule 2c, below.

2c. In general, use a comma before a concluding word or phrase when an independent clause precedes it.

W.J. Prince wrote to his client Larry Drucker, asking direction in the case.

Rule 2c will apply when a statement is followed by a reference to the person or group that made the statement:

"We still think of a powerful man as a born leader and a powerful woman as an anomaly," Margaret Atwood once said.
Students who participate in sports or social activities at school are more likely to consider themselves satisfied with their lives compared to those who do not, according to a recent study.

Concluding dependent clause. Rule 2c does not usually apply when an independent clause is followed by a dependent clause. So, if you begin with a dependent clause and follow with an independent clause, you use a comma to separate the clauses, as rule 2b above states. However, if you *begin with an independent clause and conclude with a dependent clause*, you do *not* generally use a comma. However, a dependent clause that begins with *although, though, even though*, or *whereas* suggests a contrast with the independent clause and *should* usually be preceded by a comma.

The sleek Siamese cat lay on the sofa *where it was sunny*. [no comma; general rule]
The sleek Siamese cat lay on the sofa, *whereas the old Labrador retriever curled up by the fire*. [clause begins with *whereas*, suggests contrast]

Rule Category 3: Use Two Commas to Separate Parenthetical Information

When you place something in parentheses, you signal to the reader that this information is less important than the other parts of the sentence. Commas operate similarly to separate less important from more important information. The three rules below will help you decide whether the information is non-essential (additional) or essential; then, you can punctuate accordingly.

3a. Use commas before and after non-restrictive (non-essential) phrases or clauses. Restrictive and non-restrictive clauses often begin with the relative pronouns *who, whom, which*, or *that*. They follow nouns, which they modify.

Combining rules: In the following sentence, independent clause rules 2a and 2b are illustrated:

In America, [2b] 20 per cent of homeless children repeat a grade in school, [2a] *and* another 16 per cent of these children are enrolled in special education classes.

In general, use a comma before a concluding word or phrase when an independent clause precedes it.

Combining rules: In the following sentence, independent clause rules 2b and 2c are illustrated:

By banning the use of cellphones, [2b] Newfoundland and Labrador encouraged its drivers to focus on the road, [2c] reducing the number of collisions.

In general, use a comma when you begin a sentence with a dependent clause and follow with an independent clause, but do not use a comma if you begin with an independent clause and follow with a dependent clause.

Relative pronouns introduce dependent (adjectival) clauses.

A non-restrictive clause contains information that can be left out of the sentence without affecting the meaning of the sentence.

A restrictive clause contains information that is necessary for the reader to understand the sentence.

In clauses beginning with *who*, *which*, or *that*, use two commas around the clause if it can be omitted without changing the meaning of the sentence.

Although the information in a **non-restrictive clause** may be important, it *can* be left out without changing the main point of the sentence. By contrast, a **restrictive clause** is *essential* to the meaning of the sentence. If you left it out, the sentence would mean something different or would be ungrammatical.

Look closely at clauses that begin with *who*, *which*, and *that* in order to punctuate them correctly. When the clause gives additional (non-essential) information, separate the clause from the rest of the sentence by commas. If it gives essential information, do not use commas. Consider these sentences:

1. Tony, who often wears a leather jacket, was identified as one of the rescue team.
2. A man who wore a leather jacket was identified as one of the rescue team.

The main idea in sentence 1 is that Tony was identified as part of the rescue team. Tony's leather jacket may be important elsewhere in a larger narrative, but in this sentence it is not part of the main idea; therefore, the information about his jacket is enclosed by commas. Note that *two* commas are required, just as two parentheses would be required.

In sentence 2, the information about the jacket is essential to the identification of this person on the team. If you were to leave out the clause *who wore a leather jacket*, the sentence would mean simply that a man, not a woman, was on the rescue team. That's the way you can test whether information in clauses beginning with *who*, *which*, or *that* is essential: if you omit the clause and the sentence says something different, you've proven that the information is essential. Try omitting the *who* clause in the following:

Incorrectly punctuated:

Many students, *who take out loans*, have a heavy debt burden on graduation.

If you take out what is between the commas (in italics), you are left with a sentence that says simply, *Many students have a heavy debt burden on graduation.* That's different from the more specific statement about those students *who take out loans*. No commas should be used because *who take out loans* is essential information in this sentence.

Note: Use *who* to refer to people in restrictive and non-restrictive clauses. Use *which* to refer to non-humans in non-restrictive clauses and *that* to refer to non-humans in restrictive clauses.

The actor *who* [not *that*] appeared in the movie *Outbreak* also appeared in *Sweet Home Alabama.*

3b. Use commas to set off appositives. These are nouns—words or phrases—that are grammatically parallel to a preceding noun or phrase. They name, rephrase, specify, or explain the noun or noun phrase that comes just before. Appositives are underlined below.

> Her first work, <u>a short story collection called *Drying the Bones*</u>, was given outstanding reviews.

> Seal hunting, <u>a traditional means of livelihood among Inuit</u>, has been criticized by some environmentalists.

Use commas around true appositives. Sometimes, however, the second noun completes the first noun, giving essential information. In this case, you do not set off the second noun by a comma. If in doubt, take the second noun or noun phrase out of the sentence and see if the sentence is complete without it and makes grammatical sense.

Can you explain why commas are placed around *king of the beasts* in the following sentence but not before *Aesop*, the name of the Greek writer? Which is the true appositive? Hint: try taking *king of the beasts* and *Aesop* out of the sentence to test for essential versus non-essential (additional) information.

> Correct: The lion, king of the beasts, is the subject of many fables by the ancient Greek writer Aesop.

Although they are not strictly appositives, you can use the appositive rule for words and phrases that can be considered "subsets" of a larger set—this would include examples in phrases beginning with *such as* and *including*.

> The celebration of certain holidays, such as Christmas and Halloween, has been banned by several local school boards.

3c. Use commas to set off adverbs and adverbial phrases that interrupt the flow of the sentence from subject to predicate and from verb to object or subject complement. Such words or phrases often emphasize or qualify a thought. See page 374 for a list that includes *after all, for example, however, in fact, indeed, needless to say, therefore*, and many more.

> "I must say that your performance on the aptitude test demonstrates, beyond a doubt, that you would make an excellent engineer."

Sometimes, especially in informal or semi-formal writing, using two commas around a small word or phrase that interrupts the sentence may produce clutter. Except in the most formal writing, commas around adverbial interruptions can be omitted if they directly follow a coordinating conjunction, such as *but*, to avoid three commas in close proximity.

> Commas can be omitted: Leslie worried about her driver's test, but in fact she aced it.
> Not incorrect, but cluttered: Leslie worried about her driver's test, but, in fact, she aced it.

Use *who* to refer to people in restrictive and non-restrictive clauses. Use *which* to refer to non-humans in non-restrictive (inessential) clauses and *that* to refer to non-humans in restrictive (essential) clauses.

Use commas around nouns that (re)name the previous noun and with which they are grammatically parallel.

Combining rules: In the following sentence, the appositive rule 3b and independent clause rule 2a are illustrated:

His first purchase, [3b] the painting of the Northern Ontario landscape by Tom Thomson, [3b] is now worth thousands of dollars, [2a] but he says he will never sell it.

Use commas around words and phrases that interrupt the flow of the sentence.

Coordinate adjectives are those in a series that can be moved around in the list, and the meaning of the sentence does not change.

Non-coordinate adjectives are those in a series that cannot be moved around because the meaning will be changed.

Use a comma between two coordinate (equal and interchangeable) adjectives.

Rule Category 4: Conventional and "Comma Sense" Uses

There are a number of other comma rules that must be followed that don't often fit into a neat category like those above. These consist of the following:

4a. Use commas to set off the name of the person you are addressing directly:

I can tell, Naomi, that you really do understand the math concepts taught last week.

Stylistic convention more than grammar dictates that you use commas between coordinate adjectives before a noun, with dates, addresses, titles, and before and after direct quotations.

4b. Adjectives modify a noun and usually precede it. When a series of adjectives is **coordinate**, or equal and interchangeable, you separate them by a comma. When the series is **non-coordinate**, or unequal and not interchangeable, you do not use a comma.

Coordinate adjectives: big, friendly dog; tall, white tower; proud, condescending man
Non-coordinate adjectives: white bull terrier; welcome second opinion; incredible lucky break

One way to confirm that adjectives are coordinate is to mentally place the word *and* between the adjectives, such as *big (and) friendly dog*. If this makes sense, then the adjectives are coordinate and commas are required. Applying this test to *white (and) bull terrier* does not work, as the phrase contains non-coordinate adjectives; therefore, commas are not used.

4c. Use a comma to separate a quotation from the rest of the sentence, as in attributions (i.e., where a source is named):

The sign says, "trespassers will be prosecuted."
"I am not a crook," said Richard Nixon.

4d. Use a comma to distinguish names and locations in addresses:

The Prime Minister of Canada, 24 Sussex Drive, Ottawa, Ontario, Canada

Convention also dictates that you place a comma *after* the name of a province, territory, or state if the sentence continues:

I lived in Calgary, Alberta, until I moved back to Ontario.

4e. Use a comma in a date to separate the day and year:

October 7, 1951 but 7 October 1951; October 1951

A comma is not used if you begin with the day and follow with the month and year, nor is it used with the month and year alone.

4f. Use commas to separate degrees, titles, and similar designations:

Sabrina Yao, M.D., Ph.D., F.R.C.P.S.

4g. Use commas to separate groups of three digits in numbers in a non-metric format:

The output of chemical wastes was 13,890,457 tons per day for that factory.
In 2006, the population of Nunavut was 29,474, according to Statistics Canada.
The US Defense Department listed 2,356 casualties earlier in the year.

In the metric system, there is a space rather than a comma between every three digits in a number of more than four digits (the space is optional with four-digit numbers):

13 890 457; 29 474; 2356

Your instructor can tell you whether to use metric or not when writing. Otherwise, use the industry standard for your profession.

Commas are used between some elements in addresses, dates, degrees, and numbers, and between quotations and their source.

4h. Place commas and periods *inside* quotation marks. Other punctuation marks are placed *outside* quotation marks. (In the UK, the convention is to place commas and periods outside quotation marks).

The new topic, "Where Ecological Ends Meet," has been posted.
We have been told that our meals "are not gratis"; however, the company has paid for our transportation.

Place commas and periods *inside* quotation marks. Other punctuation marks are placed *outside* quotation marks.

4i. In some cases, you will have to apply "comma sense." If a sentence seems confusing when you read it over, it may be necessary to insert a comma. Commas in the following sentences ensure the sense intended.

In 1971, 773 people were killed in an earthquake in Peru.
He told the student to come now, and again the following week.

Exercise **15.1**

Add commas to the following sentences, if and where required. Also, name the rule category discussed above. There is one comma rule to apply in each sentence.

1. After her inaugural speech several members of the House rose to congratulate her.
2. The optional package includes bucket seats dual speakers and air-conditioning.
3. We have collected more than $20 000 and there is a week remaining in our campaign.
4. Metaphors similes and personification all are examples of figurative language.

Combining rules: In the following sentence, the rule for comma use with quotations (above) and the independent clause rule 2c are illustrated:

"You should always put periods and commas inside quotation marks, " [4b] said Professor LeGuin, [2c] "though this system is predominant in North America and may not apply in other countries."

(continued)

5. As one can see the tower is leaning four-and-one-half metres to the south.

6. Hardly daring to breathe Nelson took a quick look at the valley far below him.

7. Although many are called few are chosen.

8. The magnificent country estate is hidden behind a long elegant row of silver birches.

9. "We can't achieve peace in our time if we assume war is inevitable" he said.

10. Her house was a newer one with dark wood trim and large open rooms.

11. As well as the Irish many Africans were forced to leave their families behind during times of famine.

12. Because of the humidity levels it feels hotter than the actual temperature.

13. Joe Clark the former prime minister has a famous wife.

14. Even though many people are aware of global warming and climate change fewer are aware of the term "carbon footprint."

15. James Earl Jones who is the voice of Darth Vader in *Star Wars* is a well-known actor.

16. *The Globe and Mail* is a popular paper across Canada whereas the *Toronto Star* was created for the Toronto and area market.

17. Trust is important in any relationship and it always takes time to develop.

18. The types of RNA required for protein synthesis are messenger RNA transfer RNA and ribosomal RNA.

19. People have immigrated to Canada from countries in Asia Europe the Middle East and Central and South America.

20. The committee studying the proposal is a mixture of health officials journalists and politicians.

21. Caffeine a stimulant is unregulated and completely legal.

22. Since climate change is a global problem it requires global solutions.

23. Diesel-powered cars have long been on the North American market yet they have never been widely accepted by the typical motorist.

24. The aggression effect of a video game depends on the type of game the way it is played and the person playing it.

25. Now a widely accepted theory evolution was discounted when Charles Darwin published *On the Origin of Species* in 1859.

Exercise **15.2**

Add commas to the following sentences, if and where required. There is more than one comma rule to apply in most sentences.

1. I had planned to go to Calgary,but my bus was delayed for more than four hours,so I decided to go back home.

2. Juliet studied medicine at the University of Western Ontario in London, Ontario, before becoming a doctor near Prince Albert, Saskatchewan.

3. Like Jane Austen's character Emma, the heroine of *Clueless*, Cher, is less superficial than she first appears.

4. Nick and Nicole were married on April 20, 1995, but they separated two years later.

5. Jessica Julep, the mayor of Nowhere, Nova Scotia, provided inspirational leadership.

6. The simple sentence, as we've seen, is easily mastered by students, but compound sentences necessitate an understanding of various forms of punctuation.

7. The waste of our resources, including the most precious resource, water, is the major environmental problem that Canada is facing today.

8. British general, Sir Frederick Morgan, established an American-British headquarters which was known as COSSAC.

9. The book with the fine red binding (on the highest shelf) is the particular one I want.

10. Agnes Campbell Macphail, the first woman elected to Canadian Parliament, served for 19 years, beginning her career in 1921.

11. The first steam-powered motorcycle, known as the "bone-shaker", led to the bikes we use today.

12. Following successful completion of the English test, another skills test is taken, which is in a written format.

13. He combed through directories of professional associations, business and trade associations, and unions, looking for possible contributors to his campaign.

14. Oliver Wendell Holmes, an American, was known as a master essayist, but Canadian Barry Callaghan, is also internationally respected as an essayist.

15. After visiting her ancestral homeland, China, and meeting her sisters from her mother's first marriage, Amy Tan wrote the novel: *The Joy Luck Club*.

16. The soldier with the red coat in the picture, fought on the side of our enemies, the Americans.

17. In 1885, the Canadian government introduced a racist bill, the Chinese "head tax", which forced every Chinese person entering the country to pay a $50 fee.

18. Currently ranked fourth behind heart disease, stroke, and respiratory infections, AIDS is set to become No. 3, say researchers in a new report.

19. Leslie Hornby, known as "Twiggy", became a supermodel overnight and was identified by her skinny 90-pound body.

20. Jeff Deffenbacher, PhD, a specialist in anger management, thinks that some people have a low tolerance for everyday annoyances.

Add commas in the paragraphs below, following the rule categories as discussed above and avoiding comma splices. A few commas have been included to help with comprehension, but they may be incorrect.

1. If you asked people to name the most gruelling and challenging race in the world most of them would probably say that it was an auto race such as the Indianapolis 500, few people would name the Tour de France which is a bicycle race. Thousands of cyclists however vie for an elite position in this annual event. Even with the modern advances in bicycle technology cyclists still find the course very challenging, it offers a variety of climbs including slight inclines hills and steep grades. The Tour de France has a history that dates back about one hundred years, in the years to come the race will continue to challenge inspire and glorify new riders.

2. Autism is a much misunderstood problem, often children with autism are viewed as a "handful" and "hyperactive." Very little is known of its causes and characteristics can vary making a diagnosis difficult. In children it is even harder because normal children can exhibit some of the characteristics associated with autism. Although autism can cause many behavioural difficulties autistic children can still live near-normal lives if they are surrounded by understanding caregivers. Working with autistic children can change a person and make one realize the need for better understanding and education. Treating autism can be difficult because often there is no feedback from the patient. Over the years there have been many ideas of how to treat autism but not all were correct and have at times made treatment problematic.

❭ Other Forms of Punctuation

The careful use of semicolons, colons, dashes, and parentheses gives your writing polish and precision. The colon and semicolon are stronger, more emphatic marks of punctuation than the comparatively mild-mannered comma. For stronger breaks, for longer pauses, and to show emphasis, learn where to use these marks in your writing.

Semicolons

As discussed, one of the major functions of commas is to separate independent clauses in a compound sentence. Two rules for semicolons also involve independent clauses; the third rule is to separate items in a series that contains commas.

1. To join independent clauses. You may use a semicolon rather than a comma and a coordinating conjunction to join independent clauses if there *is a* *close relationship between the clauses.* Using a semicolon to join two independent clauses, rather than a comma + a coordinating conjunction, signals to the reader the close connection between the ideas in the two clauses. Consider the following examples:

1. Strong economies usually have strong school systems, and investment in education is inevitably an investment in a country's economic future.
2. Strong economies usually have strong school systems; weak economies generally have weak school systems.

In sentence 1, the second clause is logically related to the preceding one; however, they have different subjects and are not so closely related that a semicolon would be called for. In sentence 2, however, both clauses are concerned primarily with the relationship between economic strength and school systems. That focus in each clause justifies the use of a semicolon.

A semicolon is often used if you want to stress a contrast between two independent clauses as in the examples below:

1. Scott was impatient to get married; Salome wanted to wait until they were financially secure.
2. Japanese food is generally good for you; fast food is not healthy.

Note that the semicolons in both sentences could be replaced by a comma and the coordinating conjunction *but*—they could *not* be replaced by a comma alone.

Here are other examples where a semicolon would be a good choice to stress the close relationship between independent clauses:

Gymnastics is not just any sport; it's one of the most challenging and physically taxing of all sports.
Some children may have lost a parent due to illness or divorce; others may have been cared for by grandparents or other relatives.

2. To join independent clauses by using a conjunctive adverb. To review, the rules for independent clauses we have looked at so far demonstrate many options for connecting important ideas.

- You can begin a new sentence after you have expressed your first idea. This is particularly useful if you are conveying a lot of information that makes it hard for a reader to follow or if the sentence is just too long.
- You can join the two clauses by using a comma + a coordinating conjunction.
- You can use a semicolon in place of a period and a new sentence or in place of a comma + a coordinating conjunction if you want to stress the closeness of the ideas in the independent clauses.

A fourth option is **using a semicolon with a conjunctive adverb/ transitional phrase followed by an independent clause**. There are many

Use a semicolon to replace a comma + a coordinating conjunction in closely related independent clauses.

Do *not* use a semicolon to separate an independent clause from a *dependent* clause. The rules for punctuating independent and dependent clauses are given on pages 364-5

Use a semicolon before words like *however* and *therefore* if they are joining independent clauses. Follow the joining word/phrase by a comma.

Here are some of the most common conjunctive adverbs and transitional phrases:

accordingly	likewise
afterward	meanwhile
also	moreover
as a result	namely
besides	nevertheless
certainly	next
consequently	nonetheless
finally	otherwise
for example	on the
if not	contrary
in addition	on the other
in fact	hand
in the	similarly
meantime	still
further(more)	subsequently
hence	that is
however	then
indeed	therefore
instead	thus
later	undoubtedly

Don't put a semicolon before words like *although* or *whereas*; don't put a comma after these words. They do not join independent clauses but introduce *dependent* clauses.

conjunctive adverbs and transitional phrases that are frequently used, and the most common ones are listed in the margin. While the list is not complete, all existing conjunctive adverbs/transitional phrases can be used to connect two independent clauses.

1. My roommate lacks charm, friendliness, and humour; *still*, he is an excellent cook.
2. A recent study has found a surprising correlation between a rare form of sleeping disorder and those with telephone numbers that include the number six; *however*, the conclusion is being challenged by several researchers.

Adverbs like *however* and *therefore* can act as ordinary adverbs (interrupters) or as conjunctive adverbs (joiners), as described above. A common error is to confuse these uses. The following sentence pair illustrates this distinction. In sentence 1, commas are required because the adverb occurs in the clause as an interruption between the subject *he* and most of its predicate. In sentence 2, a semicolon is required before the conjunctive adverb because *however* is joining two independent clauses:

1. Dr. Suzuki will not be in his office this week; he will, *however*, be making his rounds at the hospital.
2. Dr. Suzuki will not be in his office this week; *however*, he will be making his rounds at the hospital.

In the following sentences, the word that changes its function from interrupter to joiner is *therefore*:

1. The CEO has been called away for an emergency briefing; her secretary, *therefore*, will have to cancel her appointments.
2. The CEO has been called away for an emergency briefing; *therefore*, her secretary will have to cancel her appointments.

At first, it seems that the only difference between these sentences is word order: in sentence 1, *therefore* is the third word of the clause, whereas in sentence 2, it begins the second clause. If you look closely, though, you can see that changing its position can change its function. In sentence 2, an independent clause precedes and follows *therefore*, requiring the semicolon before and the comma after. (The comma is required since *therefore* introduces an independent clause.)

Be careful not to confuse the words and phrases discussed above with another large group of joiners, subordinating conjunctions, which join dependent to independent clauses (see pages 353-4). *Although* and *whereas* are sometimes mistaken for conjunctive adverbs, but they are subordinating conjunctions and cannot be used to join two independent clauses.

3. To separate items in a series: the serial semicolon. A semicolon can be used *between items in a series if one or more of the elements contain commas*. Without semicolons, these sentences would be confusing:

Her company included Alex Duffy, president; Marie Tremble, vice-president; John van der Wart, secretary; and Chris Denfield, treasurer. Bus number 1614 makes scheduled stops in Kamloops, BC; Valemont, BC; Jasper, Alta.; and Drayton Valley, Alta., before arriving in Edmonton.

You may also use semicolons to separate *items in a list* where each item is a long phrase or clause, especially if there is internal punctuation. Using semicolons to separate the items makes this sentence easier to read:

> The role of the vice-president will be to enhance the school's external relations; strengthen its relationship with alumni, donors, and business and community leaders; implement a fundraising program; and increase the school's involvement in the community.

A semicolon can be used between items in a series if one or more of the elements contain commas, or if one of the elements is much longer than the others.

Exercise 15.4

The following sentences are punctuated correctly. The italicized word or phrase is either an ordinary adverb acting as an interrupter or a conjunctive adverb (joiner). Rewrite the sentence by moving this word/phrase to another place in the second clause in which its function will be different. Punctuate accordingly.

Example:

Original: The weather this summer was very wet; *however*, it did not make up for the drought we have experienced.

Rewritten: The weather this summer was very wet. It did not, *however*, make up for the drought we have experienced.

Or: The weather this summer was very wet; it did not, *however*, make up for the drought we have experienced.

1. One of my roommates rode her bicycle to school most of the time; she was more physically fit, *as a result*, than my other roommate, who didn't even own a bicycle.
2. SPCA officers work for but are not paid by the government. It is donations, *in fact*, that provide their salary.
3. If homelessness continues to increase, it will be costly for taxpayers; *moreover*, homelessness affects downtown businesses.
4. Many professional golfers have used the same caddy for years; *for example*, Steve Williams has caddied for Tiger Woods since 1999.
5. Scientists tend to strongly support stem-cell research. Most evangelical Christians, *however*, just as strongly oppose it.

Note that this is the only rule for using semicolons that does not involve independent clauses. You can use semicolons to join independent clauses in one of the two ways discussed above or to separate items in a series where, otherwise, confusion might result.

Colons

It is often said that while a semicolon brings the reader to a brief stop, the colon leads the reader on. The colon has three main uses: (1) to set up a quotation, (2) to set up or introduce a list or series, and (3) to separate an independent clause from a word, phrase, or clause that answers, completes, or expands on what precedes it.

1. To set up a quotation. When you use direct quotations in your essays, you can set them up formally with a colon:

You may use a colon to set up a direct quotation if the thought is complete and fully expressed before the colon.

> The *Oxford English Dictionary* defines the word "rhetoric" this way: "The art of using language so as to persuade or influence others."
> Health Canada has made the following recommendation for dentists: "Non-mercury filling materials should be considered for restoring the primary teeth of children where the mechanical properties of the material are safe."

Direct quotations can also be set up less formally. In such cases, a comma may be required or no punctuation at all. To determine which, treat the complete sentence as if it contained no quotation and see if one of the rules for using commas applies:

> According to the American Academy of Dermatology, "a tan is the skin's response to an injury, and every time you tan, you accumulate damage to the skin."
> The most general definition of evolution is "any non-miraculous process by which new forms of life are produced" (Bowler 2).

In the first sentence, a comma rule dictates the use of a comma before the quotation; in the second sentence, there is no rule that would necessitate a comma before the quotation. A comma after *is* would be incorrect.

2. To set up or introduce a list or series. The most formal way to set up a list or series is to make a complete statement and follow with a colon and the list of items:

> In 1998, the CBC outlined three challenges for the future: to attract more viewers to Canadian programming, to increase the availability of "under-represented" categories, and to direct its resources towards this kind of programming.

Avoid the temptation to insert a colon just before you start the list unless what precedes it is completely expressed. Normally, you would *not* use a colon after *including* or *such as*, or right after a linking verb like *is* or *are*, though these words are often used to set up a list or series.

> Incorrect uses of the colon:
> Caffeine withdrawal can have many negative effects, such as: severe headaches, drowsiness, irritability, and poor concentration.

One of the questions the committee will attempt to answer is: Does our current public health system work?

A comma is also incorrect after *such as* or *including*.

3. To separate an independent clause from a word, phrase, or clause that answers, completes, or expands on what precedes it. What follows a colon may answer, complete, or expand on what is asked or implied in the preceding independent clause. This could be as little as a word or as much as an independent clause. Like the comma and semicolon, then, the colon can be used to separate independent clauses; however, what follows the colon must answer a question asked in the previous clause:

> There is only one quality you omitted from the list of my most endearing characteristics: my modesty. [answers *what quality?*]

> David's driving test was a memorable experience: he backed over a curb, sailed through two stop signs, and forgot to signal a left turn. [answers *why was the test memorable?*]

> The New Testament of the Holy Bible gives the ultimate rule for Christians: to treat others the way you want them to treat you. [answers *what rule?*]

If what follows the colon is at least the equivalent of an independent clause, it may begin with a capital letter. It is perfectly acceptable to begin with a lower case letter, however, as in the examples above.

You may use a colon to separate an independent clause from a word, phrase, or clause that answers or completes what precedes it.

Remember that unless you are using semicolons to separate items in a series, what *precedes and follows a semicolon* should be an independent clause.

What *precedes a colon* should be an independent clause that makes a complete statement.

Dashes and Parentheses

Although some people use dashes and parentheses interchangeably, their functions are different. Imagining this scenario might help: you are in a crowded room where everyone is talking. Somebody takes you aside and begins speaking in an unnaturally loud voice about the latest rumour. You look around. People are listening, which is the design of the person talking. A couple of minutes later, somebody else approaches and very discreetly begins whispering the same information in your ear.

Using dashes is like giving information that is meant to be overheard, to be stressed. But parentheses are more like asides. They convey additional information which is not important enough to be included in the main part of the sentence.

Dashes, then, set something off and can convey a break in thought. You can use dashes sparingly to emphasize a word or phrase; two dashes (one dash if the material comes at the end of a sentence) will draw the reader's attention to what is between the dashes.

You can type two hyphens to indicate a dash—if you don't leave a space after the second hyphen, your computer may automatically convert the hyphens to an em-dash like this: —.

Don't use one hyphen if you want to set off a word or phrase. Hyphens are a mark of spelling—not punctuation.

Use parentheses sparingly to include a word or phrase, even occasionally a sentence, that isn't important enough to be included as part of the main text; where dashes emphasize, parentheses de-emphasize.

You may also use parentheses to refer to a source in a research essay:

> "Crayolas plus imagination (the ability to create images) make for happiness if you are a child" (Robert Fulghum).

For information about parenthetical documentation methods, see Chapter 13.

Punctuating parenthetical insertions depends on whether the statement in parentheses is (1) complete in itself, or (2) part of the larger sentence. If the parentheses enclose *a complete sentence*, the period should be placed *inside* the second parenthesis, as the information pertains only to what is between parentheses. The following sentence illustrates this rule. (The period in this sentence goes inside the second parenthesis.)

In the second case, punctuate the sentence just as you would if there were no parentheses. The sentence below illustrates punctuation that has nothing to do with the parenthetical insertion but is required to separate independent clauses. Notice the absence of the capital letter beginning "both":

> Cassandra wanted to be an actor (both her parents were actors), but she always trembled violently as soon as she stepped on a stage.

Use dashes and parentheses sparingly in your writing.

You may use dashes occasionally to set off words from the rest of the sentence.

You may use parentheses to include less important information of the sentence.

Exercise **15.5**

Using the rule categories discussed above, replace commas in the sentences below with the most appropriate form of punctuation (semicolon, colon, dash, parentheses). In some cases, the commas are correct and should not be replaced.

1. April showers bring May flowers, May flowers bring on my asthma.
2. A developing salmon goes through four stages, the alevin, the fry, the smolt, and the adult.
3. Every essay needs three parts, an introduction, a body, and a conclusion.
4. He paused to admire the splendid sight before his eyes, the ruins of Montgomery Castle.
5. Mayumi tended to look on the good side of things, Glenn usually saw the bad side.
6. The following is not a rule for comma use, put a comma wherever you pause.
7. It is probable, though not certain, that she will be promoted to the rank of corporal next year.

8. It was the best of times, it was the worst of times.

9. Marselina has a fine ear for music, unfortunately she can't sing a note.

10. In my health sciences class, we studied the four main food groups, dairy products, meats, carbohydrates, and fruits and vegetables.

11. Whenever I order designer clothing for my boutique, I shop in Toronto, Canada, Buffalo, New York, and London, England.

12. The Online Dictionary defines animal cruelty this way, "treatment or standards of care that cause unwarranted or unnecessary suffering or harm to animals."

13. The tuition increase has affected many lower income families, therefore, there is an even greater demand for student loans.

14. Brian never tired of misquoting Shakespeare, "the quality of mercy is not stained."

15. Virginia Woolf had this to say about the essay, "Of all forms of literature it is the one which least calls for the use of long words."

After you've checked your answers, complete the exercise by doing questions 16–30.

16. First advice to those about to write a novel is the same as Punch's to those about to wed, don't (Victor Jones).

17. The Romans were willing to change their religious beliefs quite easily, however, the Greeks were less willing to do this.

18. In compound sentences, use a comma to join independent clauses where there is a coordinating conjunction, use a semicolon where two such clauses are not joined by a coordinating conjunction.

19. His plans for the new development included the following, an apartment complex, single-family residences, a 60-store mall, and a multi-use recreation centre.

20. Oil, electricity, and solar power are popular sources for heating homes in Ontario, however, the most popular is natural gas.

21. The tour includes visits to the following museums, the Prado in Madrid, Spain, the Louvre in Paris, France, and the Rijksmuseum in Amsterdam, the Netherlands.

22. It was the ideal summer job, you were outdoors in lovely weather, you were active, and the pay was more than reasonable.

23. School cafeterias often offer unhealthy options, such as hot dogs, which have virtually no nutritional value, hamburgers, which have a high fat content, and poutine, known as "heart attack in a bowl."

24. The zero emissions of a battery-electric vehicle come with a drawback, the emissions are only as clean as the means used to generate the power.

25. This year's conference on the environment is intended to focus concern on three main areas, global warming, pollution, and the destruction of natural habitat.

26. The art of writing the news lead is to answer as many of the following five questions as possible, Who?, What?, Where?, When?, and How?

27. The current figures of mercury absorption have been announced by the ADA, however, the group's review has been criticized as misleading.

(continued)

28. A lack of essential nutrients can result in deficiencies, for example, a vegetarian may have iron deficiency.

29. As rainwater travels downwards through the soil, it may collect a number of pollutants, furthermore, an extended period of time may elapse before this pollution is discovered.

30. Freewriting can be a useful means of overcoming blocks, it can help you write when you're not in the mood, it can generate ideas, even if you are the kind of writer who has a hard time coming up with main points, and it can energize your writing.

Exercise **15.6**

Correct or add commas in the following passages. Among your changes and additions, include *at least* one semicolon and one colon in each passage. Some commas have been included to help with reading; however, they may not be correct.

1. Cocaine an alkaloid obtained from coca leaves is a stimulant to the nervous system, unfortunately it is one of the most addictive drugs and it is possible to overdose and die on first use. Among the 3 million users today 500 000 are highly addicted. Cocaine users describe the high as a euphoric feeling, they feel energetic and mentally alert, however this feeling wears off in as little as 20 minutes. User responses to the drug vary but may include the following, hyperactivity elevated blood pressure and heart rate and increased sexual interest. Large amounts of cocaine such as more than 100 milligrams can cause bizarre erratic and violent behaviours.

2. Labour shortages during the late nineteenth century in Canada became an impediment to progress and something had to be done to fix this problem. For white politicians and business owners the solution seemed obvious, exploit cheap labour. Chinese immigrants provided exactly what was needed to boost the labour scene, they were male unskilled and cheap. Between 1881 and 1885 approximately 17 000 Chinese immigrants arrived in Canada, Chinese men were employed in masses, their jobs included those in mining forestry canning and above all railroad construction. Sir Matthew Begbie the Chief Justice of BC said "Chinese labourers do well what white women cannot do and what white men will not do."

❯ Punctuation Prohibitions

Several common errors in punctuation are summarized below. Learning the rules for punctuation and being aware of these common errors will greatly enhance your writing skills.

No-Comma Rules

Do *not* use a comma to separate simple compounds (two words, phrases, or clauses joined by a conjunction like *and*). Writers sometimes make this mistake because they are thinking of the rule for items in a series: recall that a series consists of *three or more* items. A separate rule applies to compound sentences where a comma is required before the coordinating conjunction.

> Incorrect:
> Some of the heaviest damage from steroid use occurs to the heart, and the liver. [two nouns]
> Logging reduces the number of old-growth forests, and destroys these habitats. [two predicates: "reduces . . ." and "destroys . . ."]

Do *not* use a comma to separate the subject and the predicate. This error is probably the result of writers mistakenly applying the "pause" non-rule.

> Incorrect:
> The only way our society is going to be fixed, is if we change our laws.
> One advantage in using helicopters to fight fires, is the accuracy of their drops over the scene of the fire.

It is easy to be distracted by parentheses and mistakenly insert a comma between a subject and a predicate. In the example below, another option would be to add a comma after "Medicine" and remove the parentheses:

> Incorrect:
> The American College of Sports Medicine (a body that advances research into exercise and sports), considers all physically active females at risk for developing eating disorders.

Do *not* use a comma alone to join independent clauses or with a word other than a coordinating conjunction. This produces a comma splice, a serious grammatical error.

> Incorrect:
> Football is one of the most popular sports in North America, it is also one of the most brutal of all sports.
> You must use the buttons provided at the bottom of the pages to navigate through the application, otherwise, you could lose your connection. [from an online application form]

No-Semicolon Rules

Do *not* use a semicolon if what follows the semicolon is a fragment. In the first two examples below, what follows the semicolon is an incomplete verb form (an *–ing*). In the third sentence, what follows is a prepositional phrase: *such as* and two nouns. An independent clause should follow a semicolon unless semicolons

A semicolon should be both preceded and followed by an independent clause unless semicolons are being used to separate items in a series.

are being used to separate items in a series. In all the sentences, a comma should replace the incorrect semicolon to separate the independent clause from the concluding phrase.

> Incorrect:
> When the media portrays minorities, it often stereotypes them; leading audiences to reinforce the stereotype through their behaviour.
> Valuable land is destroyed when it is cleared for grazing; reducing habitats for other animals.
> For many years, Canada has been a leader in multiculturalism, along with a few other countries; such as the United States and England.

Do *not* use a semicolon to introduce a list or series; a *colon* is correct.

> Incorrect:
> Shakespeare's last plays are sometimes called romances and include the following; *Cymbeline*, *A Winter's Tale*, and *The Tempest*.

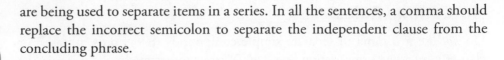

Apostrophes

The apostrophe is a mark of spelling that indicates the possessive and shows where letters have been omitted in a contraction.

Technically, the **apostrophe** isn't a mark of punctuation; it is a mark of spelling that indicates the possessive case of nouns and some indefinite pronouns. It is also used to show the omission of one or more letters. The apostrophe, then, has two main uses: (1) to indicate the possessive and (2) to show where letters have been omitted, as in a contraction.

1. Apostrophes for Possession in Nouns

The **possessive** case in nouns and pronouns indicates ownership and similar relationships between nouns, such as association, authorship, duration, description, and source of origin. The possessive indicates that the second noun belongs to or is associated with the first noun. When an apostrophe and *s* are added to a noun to show the possessive, the noun is functioning adjectivally and can be replaced by the corresponding possessive adjective. Most pronouns, however, do not show the possessive through an apostrophe.

The possessive case indicates relationships such as ownership.

> the hard drive of the computer = the computer's hard drive (*its* hard drive)
> the landlady's apartment (ownership) (*her* apartment)
> the tenants' rights (association) (*their* rights)
> Dvorak's *New World Symphony* (authorship) (*his* symphony)

Singular Nouns

Singular nouns take an apostrophe + *s* to indicate the possessive; plural nouns that end in *s* take an apostrophe without *s*.

The usual rule with a *singular* noun, including proper nouns (nouns that begin with a capital letter) ending in *s*, *ss*, or the *s* sound, is to add *'s* to make it possessive.

> the attorney's portfolio; Mr. Price's car; the week's lesson

Plural Nouns

With a plural noun, an apostrophe is added after the *s* to make it possessive.

the islands' inhabitants; the Hansons' children; the Gibbses' marriage certificate; two weeks' lessons; the readers' perceptions

Make sure you carefully distinguish between singular and plural nouns when applying the rules for possessives:

"company" is singular + *'s* → the company's profits (one company)
"companies" is plural + *'* → the companies' profits (more than one
company)

"society" is singular + *'s* → our society's attitude towards war (one society)
"societies" is plural + *'* → past societies' attitudes towards war (many
societies)

A few plural nouns do not end in *s*. They are treated as singular nouns for the possessive: *children, women, men, people*:

the popular children's book; the women's group

Proper Nouns Ending in *s*

Because it may look and sound awkward to add an apostrophe + *s* to a proper noun ending in *s*, some authorities would write *Tracy Jarvis' book*, meaning *the book of Tracy Jarvis*. Others would follow the rule for singular nouns by adding an apostrophe + *s*: *Tracy Jarvis's book*. Whichever rule you follow, it's important to be consistent in applying it.

Joint Ownership

In the case of *joint ownership*, where both nouns share or are equal parties in something, only the last noun should show the possessive. Ensure from the context that both nouns reflect a truly equal, shared relationship. In the following sentences, the assumption is that Salem and Sheena shared duties as hosts at one party but that the general manager and the district manager were paid separate wages.

I attended Salem and Sheena's party.
Morana raised the general manager's and the district manager's wages.

These educators do *not* share the same belief or theory:

Incorrect: Piaget and Montessori's beliefs about how children learn were similar in many ways.
Correct: Piaget's and Montessori's beliefs . . . .

Apostrophes are sometimes misused with plural nouns. Avoid the following incorrect uses:

Incorrect: I have 6 CD's.
The 1990's were a decade of extravagant spending.
The lemon's are on sale this week.

Exception: Apostrophes can be used for clarity with numbers, letters, or symbols to indicate the plural:

Adrian got two A's and three B's on his transcript.

Apostrophes with Indefinite Pronouns

Like nouns, but unlike other kinds of pronouns, many indefinite pronouns take an apostrophe + *s* to show the possessive:

In times of stress, it is not in *one's* best interest to act quickly or reflexively. [i.e., the best interest of one]

2. Contractions

The second main use of the apostrophe is to show missing letters. People often confuse the contraction *it's* (*it is*) with the possessive form *its* (as in *I gave the dog its bone*). The contraction *who's* (*who is*) is sometimes confused with the possessive form *whose* (*the man whose house I'm renting*). Contractions are not generally used in formal writing. You should check with your instructor to see if they are acceptable in your assignment.

The apostrophe is *not* used to indicate the possessive of *pronouns* (except for indefinite pronouns, as discussed above).

Indefinite pronouns, unlike personal pronouns, take an apostrophe + *s* to indicate the possessive: e.g., *one's beliefs*.

Don't confuse *its*, the possessive pronoun, with *it's*, the contraction for *it is*.

Exercise **15.7**

Decide which nouns in the following sentences require the possessive; then add apostrophes and make any other necessary changes.

1. In South Africa, the current crime rate is using up much of the countrys GDP.
2. Parents and teachers often complain about televisions influence in todays society.
3. The Crosses house is up for sale, and its list price is $179 000. (The last name is Cross.)
4. Ones education should not depend on the financial resources of ones parents.
5. The schools biggest draw for new students was the brand new recreation complex.
6. The course I took required two hours homework a day.
7. The mayors biggest asset is her commitment to the citys future growth.
8. In anorexia nervosa, a patients fingernails and teeth may be damaged due to a lack of calcium.
9. Ryans and Jessicas birthday is on the same day.
10. Apples, oranges, mangoes, and tomatoes are the stores specials today.

After you've checked your answers, complete the exercise by doing questions 11–25.

11. Its a shame that Lennys parents werent able to attend their sons graduation ceremonies. (Lenny is an only child.)

12. I dont know whether this etching is his or hers, but theres no doubt its worth a lot in todays market.

13. Its true there are four *ss* and four *is* in the word "Mississippi," but there are only two *ps*.

14. This weeks classifieds had several jobs for legal secretaries, all requiring three years experience in solicitors work.

15. Zebra stripes always make me homesick for my Uncle Filbert, whos in jail for stealing his brothers life savings. (one brother)

16. The instructor found Bens copy of Shakespeares play *The Winters Tale* in the recycle bin after the last class.

17. As a child whose parents were relatively well off, I thought all my relatives lives were as easy as mine.

18. Our societys fascination with celebrities lives is a product of the medias daily obsession.

19. Books, music, and DVDs can be found on Amazon.com, one of the Internets most popular sites.

20. The young man stated his churchs mission is to spread Jesus message to people throughout the world.

21. Drugs called immunosuppressants can interfere with the bodys ability to fight infection.

22. Nowadays, rap is used to express a persons experiences, feelings, and opinions.

23. Climate change is caused by harmful chemicals that trap the suns energy in the earths atmosphere.

24. The Smiths and the O'Neils won the trip to see the Seattle Mariners play the Blue Jays in the Mariners home town.

25. The introductory paragraph should capture the readers interest while developing the writers credibility.

Exercise **15.8**

Punctuate for correctness and effectiveness, using commas and other forms of punctuation as appropriate. Minimal punctuation has been provided in places to aid in understanding; however, some punctuation may be incorrect. Correct all errors in apostrophe use. The passage concerns the response to an investigative article entitled "Spin Doctors," posted on the Canadian news and information website *Canoe*.

Reader reaction was swift and impassioned. The sites traffic which averages 65 to 70 million views each month experienced an additional 50,000 page views within the first 10 days of the posting. The investigation drew

(*continued*)

more than 400 letters to the editor hundred's of emails to the message boards and more than 16,000 responses to an online poll.

The intensity of the response surprised veteran investigative journalist Wayne MacPhail the articles author. Although the sheer volume of letters was unexpected it proved to him that there was an audience for online journalism in Canada. MacPhail has experimented with hypertext reporting since the late 1980s but outside of "Spin Doctors" he believes that by and large newspapers have done a "woeful job" of building an audience for Web-based investigative reporting . . . .

Unlike it's media rivals Canoe has never made journalism it's only or even its most important focus. A headline announcing the top story of the day appears underneath the Canoe banner but there are so many other things to do, shopping email contests Web utilities and lifestyle tips all compete with the news.

The CNEWS section isnt necessarily the first place people are expected to go on the network though it is usually at the top of the highlighted sections. It is also part of the site that changes the most during daylight hours. In other words when CNEWS changes the entire home page changes. A "This Just In" feature was recently added but theres no set schedule for posting stories. Despite this expansion of the news section Canoes promotional material drives home the message that the site is about much more than current events. One recent ad reads, "shop chat email read, in that order."

▮ Chapter Review Questions

1. What are the comma rules?
2. When should you not use a comma?
3. Identify at least one comma use that you did not know or that you had previously learned incorrectly.
4. When do you use semicolons?
5. When should you not use a semicolon?
6. When do you use colons?
7. When should you not use a colon?
8. Why do you use dashes or parentheses?
9. What are the rules for apostrophe use?
10. Provide examples of incorrect apostrophe use that you have seen outside the classroom.

16 Agreement, Pronoun, and Sentence Structure Errors

In this chapter, you will

- learn about subject–verb agreement
- learn how to fix different kinds of pronoun errors
- understand how the incorrect use of pronouns can show gender bias
- understand how modifiers can affect clarity
- learn how to use parallelism to create clear sentences

The grammar rules discussed in this chapter are ones that are easily missed when you write your rough draft. Mastering these rules will increase your credibility as a writer and help you create documents that are easy to understand.

A verb must agree with its subject, and a pronoun must agree with its antecedent.

A verb must agree with (i.e., match) its subject in number—that is, a singular subject requires a singular verb, and a plural subject requires a plural verb.

Look ahead in the sentence to find the subject if the sentence begins with *Here/There is . . .*, is set up as a question, or uses a delayed subject construction.

A delayed subject appears after a prepositional phrase and the verb.

❯ Agreement

A verb must agree in number with its subject: they must be both singular or both plural. Similarly, a pronoun must agree in number, person, and gender with its antecedent. These forms of **agreement** reinforce the close connection between a subject and the verb it governs, along with the close connection between a noun and the pronoun that replaces it.

Subject–Verb Agreement

You will not usually have to stop and think about whether a verb agrees in number with its subject, especially if English is your first language. However, determining whether a subject is singular or plural is not always straightforward. In the specific instances explained below, the rules help the writer apply the important principle of **subject–verb agreement**.

Finding the Subject

Usually, the subject of a sentence or clause is the noun or pronoun that performs the action of the verb (or that exists in the state or condition expressed by the subject complement). In most cases, the subject precedes the verb and is easy to find.

> *Kevin and Nigel* are happy that they passed the exam.

Sometimes the subject is harder to spot for one of the following reasons.

1. The sentence begins with *Here is/are, There is/are, There has/have been*, etc. The subject follows the verb, not precedes it, and you will have to look ahead in the sentence to the first noun/pronoun to determine whether the subject is singular or plural.

> There *are* many *reasons* for supporting the legalizing of marijuana.
> Here *is* one *person* who supports raising the drinking age.

2. The sentence is phrased as a question. You may need to look ahead to determine the number of the subject.

> What *is* the main *reason* for legalizing marijuana?
> Where *are* all of the *people* who are in favour of raising the drinking age?

3. The subject is delayed. Because the sentence begins with a prepositional phrase, the noun(s) in the phrase may seem to form the subject, but the subject will be found later in the sentence. You can always rearrange these kinds of sentences to confirm that you have, in fact, used a **delayed subject** construction.

> With the dependence on caffeine *come withdrawal symptoms*.

Sentence rearranged with subject first:
Withdrawal symptoms come with the dependence on caffeine.
Among Graham's favourites *was the recent album* by Green Day.

Sentence rearranged:
The recent album by Green Day *was* among Graham's favourites.

4. The subject governs a linking verb that has a plural complement. Don't be distracted by what follows the verb; the subject alone determines whether the verb is singular or plural.

Tanning *salons are* not the safest way to get a tan these days.
The *topic* for discussion tomorrow *is* the pros and cons of indoor tanning.

5. The subject is followed by one or more prepositional phrases containing nouns and/or pronouns. People sometimes forget that the common word *of* is a preposition and that the following noun or pronoun will be the object of the preposition, not the subject. If there are several nouns before the verb, backtrack carefully to find the noun or pronoun that governs the verb. You can put parentheses around the distracting words.

A long *list* (of items, including vegetables, fruits, meats, and several kinds of bread,) *was* handed to Tao.
The *roots* (of his dissatisfaction with the course) *go* very deep.

If several nouns precede the verb, make sure you identify the true noun/pronoun subject before deciding whether the verb should be singular or plural.

Mistaking the Subject

In the examples under 3, above, the nouns *dependence* or *caffeine* in the first sentence and *favourites* in the second sentence could be mistaken for the subjects of *come* and *was*, respectively; however, they are preceded by prepositions. A noun or pronoun that directly follows a preposition cannot act as a subject; it will be the object of the preposition.

A related problem occurs when a writer mistakes a prepositional phrase or even a dependent clause for a subject. The sentences below can be fixed by omitting the preposition and beginning the sentence with the noun subject:

Incorrect: By choosing to take a few correspondence courses may afford a student athlete greater flexibility in meeting academic requirements.

By choosing has been mistaken for the subject.

Correct: Choosing to take a few correspondence courses may afford a student athlete greater flexibility.
Incorrect: With the development of the computer led to automated robots on the production line.

With the development of the computer has been mistaken for the subject.

> Correct: The development of the computer led to automated robots on the production line.
> Incorrect: Although Edna thinks of her children at the last moment before her death does not change the fact she is still willing to leave them.

Although Edna thinks of her children at the last moment before her death, a dependent clause, has been mistaken for the subject. A dependent clause contain its own subject.

> Correct: Although Edna thinks of her children at the last moment before her death, she is still willing to leave them.

Edna thinks of her children at the last moment before her death, though this does not change the fact she is willing to leave them.

See also Precision and Logic (page 451).

Rules for Subject–Verb Agreement

1. A compound subject joined by the conjunction *and* usually requires a plural verb form.

> Thanh *and* his friend *are* visiting Ottawa.

Occasionally, a compound subject expresses a single idea.

> *Rhythm and blues was* always popular with younger audiences.
> *To compare and contrast* the roles of setting in the novels *is* sure to be a question on the exam.

In both examples, the compound subject can be treated as a singular subject since both elements are so closely connected that they can't be separated or their meaning would change.

2. When the nouns or pronouns in a compound subject are linked by the conjunction *or* or *nor*, along with the correlative (or paired) conjunction *either . . . or* or *neither . . . nor*, the verb form is determined by the noun or pronoun nearest the verb. These conjunctions suggest a choice between one thing or the other much more than *and*, which clearly suggests two or more of something, requiring the plural verb.

> The chairs *or the table is* going to auction.
> Neither famine nor *floods are* going to force the people to leave their homes.

If you changed the order of the nouns making up the compound subject in the above sentences, you would need also to change the number of the verb.

3. A prepositional phrase can also be used to join two nouns in a compound subject. *As well as, along with, in addition to, together with,* and *combined with* are examples of such phrases. These phrases do not have the strength of the conjunction *and.* When you use one of these joiners, you stress the first element more than the second one. Logically, then, the verb is *singular* if the first element of the compound is *singular.* If the writer of the following sentence wanted to stress equality, the sentence should read "The instructor *and* her students *are . . . .*"

> The *instructor, as well as* her students, *is* going to be attending the symposium on the environment.
> The Australian *prime minister, along with* his ministers for education and foreign affairs, *is* set to arrive tomorrow.

When using a compound subject, look at the word(s) doing the joining to determine whether the subject is singular or plural.

4. A **collective noun** refers to a group. It is singular in form but may be either singular or plural in meaning, depending on context. If the context suggests singular, then the verb form is singular; the same applies, of course, for plural. Examples of collective nouns include *audience, band, class, committee, congregation, family, gang, group, jury, staff,* and *team.*

Whenever the context suggests the members of the group are to be thought of as *one unit,* all doing the same thing or acting together, the verb form is *singular;* when the members are considered as *individuals,* the corresponding verb form is *plural.*

A collective noun may be singular or plural depending on context. If in doubt, consider it singular.

> The jury *is* out to consider the evidence before it.
> After the lecture, the class *are* going to be able to ask questions of the guest speaker.

Most often, a collective noun is considered singular, so, if in doubt, choose the singular form. If a plural verb with a collective noun sounds odd, you can rephrase the subject so that the collective noun functions adjectivally before an appropriate plural noun.

> After the lecture, *class members are* going to be able to ask questions of the guest speaker.

5. In the following phrases, the verb form will be singular, even though the noun or pronoun that follows will be plural: *each of, either/neither of, every one of, one of,* and *which one of.* The verb form following *the only one who* also will be singular.

> *One of* our 115 students *has* written an A+ essay.
> Alec is *the only one of* those attending who *has* difficulty speaking before a large group.

6. An **indefinite pronoun** refers to non-specific individuals or objects. Most indefinite pronouns are considered singular and take a singular form in agreement. *Anybody, anyone, anything, each, either, everybody, everyone, everything,* *neither, nobody, no one, nothing, one, somebody,* and *someone* are singular indefinite pronouns. Unlike other pronouns, many indefinite pronouns use the apostrophe to express the possessive:

> *Everybody's* opinion is welcome.

Compare with:

> *His or her* opinion is welcome; *their* opinions are welcome.

Some experts believe that when context clearly warrants the use of plural agreement with the antecedents *everyone* and *everybody*, as in the second sentence below, you may use the plural pronoun.

> When the pepper was spilled, *everyone* rubbed *their* noses.

Most indefinite pronouns are considered singular even though they may refer broadly to many people, objects, etc.

7. There is a separate rule for phrases involving portions and fractions + *of,* such as *all, any, a lot, a variety, a number, (one-)half, more, most, much, none, part, plenty, some,* and *the majority/minority.* The form of the verb depends on whether the noun or pronoun following *of* is singular or plural.

> *None of the missing* **pieces** *have* been found yet.
> *Some of the* **losses** incurred with the companies' merger *are* being absorbed by the shareholders.
> *Half of the* **pie** *is* gone.
> *One-third of the* **employees** *are* out on strike.

8. Subjects referring to distance, time, money, weight, or mass will usually be *singular;* also, when the subject is *the number of,* the verb is *singular* (in contrast with rule 7).

> *Twelve miles is* not a great distance to an experienced hiker.
> *The number of* people attending the courses *has dropped* in the last two years.

When the subject is *a number of,* the verb will be singular or plural depending on whether the noun/pronoun following *of* is singular or plural; when the subject is *the number of,* the verb will be singular.

9. Some nouns end in *s,* but because they usually refer to a singular concept or subject, they require the singular form of the verb. Examples include *athletics, billiards, darts, economics, gymnastics, mathematics, measles, mumps, news, physics, politics,* and *statistics.*

> *Statistics is* an inexact science.
> No *news is* good news.

Depending on their context, many of these nouns can be considered plural and should then take a plural verb form. For example, *statistics* could refer to a set of facts, rather than to one subject:

> The *statistics* on global warming *are* alerting politicians to the need for worldwide action.

Whether the titles of artistic works or the names of companies are singular or plural in form will not affect the verb. A singular verb will be needed to agree with the subject.

Most errors in subject–verb agreement occur in one of these three situations:
- use of a compound subject
- use of an indefinite pronoun as the subject
- words between the subject and the verb

Montreal Stories is a collection of Mavis Gallant's fiction; McClelland & Stewart *is* the publisher.

10. The following will be plural and will require the plural form of the verb: *both*, *few*, *many*, *parts of*, *several*.

A well-educated *few seem* to care about correct grammar and punctuation these days, but *both are* essential parts of the writing process.

Most errors in subject–verb agreement occur in one of these three situations:

- use of a compound subject
- use of an indefinite pronoun as the subject
- intervening words between the subject and the verb

❯ Pronouns at Work

Pronoun–Antecedent Agreement

Most problems in **pronoun–antecedent agreement** apply to personal pronouns, such as *she*, *he*, *they*, and *them*, as well as to the possessive form of pronouns, *its* and *their*. The antecedent of a pronoun is the noun it replaces, and a pronoun must agree with its antecedent noun in number. If you have difficulty finding the antecedent, see if it, or an equivalent form, can be substituted for the pronoun in the sentence:

Testing for the antecedent:

The first thing that usually strikes us about *a person* is his or her [a person's] physical appearance.
The dieter should realize that diets will only work when he or she [the dieter] restricts his or her [the dieter's] caloric intake.

Most of the rules for subject–verb agreement also apply to pronoun–antecedent agreement. For example, a compound antecedent requires the plural form of the pronoun or possessive pronoun.

Connie *and* Steve *have* invited me to *their* cottage.

If the compound subject includes the word *each* or *every*, the singular form should be used.

Each book and magazine in the library *has its* own entry.

When two antecedents are joined by *or* or *nor*, the pronoun agrees with the closest antecedent (see Rules for Subject–Verb Agreement, rule 2, page 390).

Neither the prime minister *nor his advisors were* certain how to implement *their* proposal.

As with subject–verb agreement, a collective noun antecedent requires the singular pronoun form if it is thought of in the collective sense, as a unit; if the

Personal pronouns refer to persons. The *first person* refers to the one *doing* the speaking or writing; *second person* refers to the one *spoken to*; *third person* refers to the one *spoken about*.

The antecedent of a pronoun is the noun it replaces, and a pronoun must agree with its antecedent noun in number.

Their is an adjectival form of the pronoun *they*. The rule for pronoun–antecedent agreement also applies to possessive adjectives, such as *their*, which are formed from pronouns.

context suggests that individuals are being referred to, the pronoun will take a plural form (see Rules for Subject–Verb Agreement, rule 4, page 391).

> Our hockey team will play *its* final game against *its* archrivals. [The team will be playing as a unit.]
> The team will be receiving *their* new jerseys Friday. [Individual team members each will be given a jersey.]

With a pronoun referring to a portion or fraction, agreement depends on whether the noun following *of* is singular or plural (see Rules for Subject–Verb Agreement, rule 7, page 392).

> Studies show that a large *number of college and university students are* cheating on *their* exams and essays; however, a much larger number are not.

If the pronoun has an indefinite pronoun antecedent such as *anybody, one,* or *someone,* the singular form will apply, as it does with subject–verb agreement (see Rules for Subject–Verb Agreement, rule 6, page 391).

> *One* should be careful about pronoun agreement, or *one's* teacher will certainly point out the error to *one.*

Although grammatically correct, the sentence above could be improved by using a personal pronoun to replace the indefinite pronoun *one.* However, you must be careful to use a *singular* pronoun to replace an indefinite pronoun like *one* as the writer of this sentence has failed to do:

> Incorrect: *One* should be careful about pronoun agreement, or *their* teacher will certainly point out the error to *them.*

In the sentence below, a singular pronoun replaces the singular antecedent *one*—but the sentence is incorrect because the possessive adjective *his* and the personal pronoun *him* refer to only one gender. In the next section, we discuss problems that can arise when you want to replace an indefinite pronoun or a generic singular noun by a singular pronoun.

> Incorrect: *One* should be careful about pronoun agreement, or *his* teacher will certainly point out the error to *him.*

Problematic Pronouns: Inclusive Language

In recent years, the efforts of many to avoid gender bias have driven them to a neutral or **gender-inclusive**, but grammatically incorrect, use of the plural personal pronouns *they, them,* and *their* instead of singular pronouns. Using both correct pronouns in the form *him or her* or *his or her* is awkward compared to the inclusive *him,* but is preferable to an incorrect *their* and better than a form that may appear sexist. In the sentence below, the writer has used both singular forms to replace the antecedent *student.*

Gender-inclusive language is the careful use of terms and grammatical forms that include both genders. When an antecedent is either a generic singular noun or an indefinite pronoun, the personal pronoun that follows must be both singular *and* gender-inclusive. This often means using two personal pronouns, such as *he or she,* etc.

A student must footnote *his or her* references, or the teacher will expect *him or her* to correct the oversight.

The problem of pronoun–antecedent agreement is especially common among student writers when the antecedent noun is either an indefinite pronoun or a singular noun referring to a person where gender is unspecified—a generic noun such as *reader, writer, student, teacher, individual, character,* or *person*. Here are three options to consider when you have used an indefinite pronoun or a generic singular noun and want to follow with a pronoun.

Option 1. Replace the plural pronoun with *both* singular personal pronouns (or possessive adjectives). This option is nearly always acceptable in academic writing, but can be seen as awkward and repetitive in journalistic and workplace writing.

> Incorrect: Anybody not willing to put in long hours for little pay should give up *their* idea of becoming a writer.
> Correct: Anybody not willing to put in long hours for little pay should give up *his or her* idea of becoming a writer.

Option 2. Change the singular antecedent into the equivalent plural form and use the plural pronoun.

> *Those* not willing to put in long hours should give up *their* ideas of becoming writers. [Note the plural *ideas* to agree with *those* and *their*.]

Option 3. Revise the sentence to use the gender-neutral pronoun *you*. This option is not always possible and may occasionally sound too informal for academic writing.

> If you are not willing to put in long hours for little pay, you should give up *the idea* of becoming a writer.

Exercise 16.1

In the short paragraph below, fix pronoun–antecedent agreement errors, using at least one of each of the three options discussed above.

> If a child begins to perform poorly at school nowadays, they will likely be sent to a school counsellor to deal with the situation. Everyone assumes that attention deficit disorder is the culprit, and they just as automatically assume that drugs are the answer. On the other hand, perhaps the child is just not interested in a particular subject, or they do not understand the material. Parents, in turn, treat the child as if he is the problem instead of listening to him to find out how he can be helped.

Exercise **16.2**

Chose the correct form of the verb and/or pronoun in the sentences and make any other necessary changes in agreement. Rewrite the sentence if that will produce a better result.

1. Everybody who supported the motion raised (his/her/their) hand.
2. Neither the film's director nor its producers (was/were) on hand to receive (his/her/their) prestigious award.
3. The instructor as well as the students (thinks/think) the room is too small.
4. It is unfortunate when a person no longer cares what others think about (him/her/them).
5. One should never expect to succeed unless (one/they) (is/are) willing to persist—even against the odds.
6. It is the tried and true that (provides/provide) the ultimate refuge in mediocrity.
7. Everyone who works during the year (is/are) obliged to file (his/her/their) income tax return.
8. Her set of baby teeth (was/were) complete when she was only 18 months old.
9. He was one of those few candidates who (was/were) able to win re-election.
10. None of the company's products (requires/require) testing on animals.
11. Lining the side of the highway (is/are) a lot of billboards advertising fast-food restaurants.
12. Every specimen of the horned grebe (has/have) a distinctive tuft on each side of (its/their) head.
13. Media and information technology training (provides/provide) students today with important communication skills.
14. Neither team members nor their coach (expects/expect) the season to last another game.
15. The maximum number of people allowed on this elevator (is/are) 30.

Exercise **16.3**

Most of the following sentences contain one or more subject–verb agreement and/or pronoun–antecedent agreement errors. Correct the sentences as needed.

1. Every person in the community should have the right to attend a university and create new opportunities for themselves.
2. Especially unique to adolescent depression are physical symptoms, such as headaches.
3. The tonal quality of Amati's violins are excellent, but not perfect.
4. Over the past week, there has been some unexplained occurrences on the girls' floor of the residence.

5. Small class sizes and a low student population means few opportunities to meet new people.

6. A typical poem by Emily Dickinson leaves the reader searching for another line or even another stanza to satisfy their craving for closure.

7. Use of the leaves of the coca plant for its stimulant effects dates back thousands of years.

8. A coalition of neighbourhood organizations, students, and unions are currently forming to oppose the university's proposed plan.

9. Everyone who has purchased tickets is eligible for the grand prize, but they must be residents of Canada to claim their prize.

10. If a child is denied the opportunity to play, how can they develop emotionally and physically?

11. Participation and public education is necessary in a true democracy.

12. When a person contracts jaundice, their skin as well as the white part of their eyes turn yellow.

13. Another round of intense labour negotiations have not produced a settlement, so each union member has been told to do his duty on the strike line.

14. Before rendering its unanimous verdict, the jury was polled individually.

15. Almost nothing shapes a person's true character as much as their home.

16. The nature and role of human resources in organizations have undergone tremendous change in the last two decades.

17. In P.K. Page's poem, it is apparent that the landlady's prying nature and lonely life has made her forget her place.

18. Stereotyping and the use of degrading language in the book serves to reinforce its theme.

19. His overriding concern with rules and regulations, together with his excessive neatness and demand for order, suggests a mild obsessive-compulsive complex.

20. A person who continually disregards others' feelings will pay for their neglect sooner or later.

21. The encouragement of curiosity, questioning, and discussion is vital to the success of today's school environment.

22. In Japanese culture, a person's reputation along with their social standing depend on the concept of "saving face."

23. Medieval universities established a system of education and academic credentials that continue to function in today's universities.

24. The give and take in any relationship is the most important factor in sustaining it.

25. Although the Canadian Forces is still one of the best-trained military in the world, the training standards and morale of the forces is declining, according to some people.

❭ Other Problems with Pronouns

In addition to agreement problems, there are other potential pronoun pitfalls: errors in *pronoun reference*, *pronoun case*, and *pronoun consistency*.

Pronoun Reference

For a moment, consider life without pronouns.

A Lost Loonie Leads to a Lesson Learned

Alex and Alex's lawyer, Alan, left in Alex's limousine for Loonies Unlimited to buy Alex's landlady, Alice, a litre of light lemonade. Alice told Alex and Alan to also buy a litre of light lemonade for Alice's long-time lodger, Alison. When Alex and Alan alighted at Loonies Unlimited, Alex and Alan were alarmed that Alex had left Alex's loonie in Alex's loft. So Alphonse, of Loonies Unlimited, allowed Alex and Alan only one litre of lemonade, along with a length of limp licorice, and Alphonse loudly lamented Alex's and Alan's laxness.

The principle for pronoun reference is simple: each pronoun should refer clearly to a specific antecedent.

Exercise 16.4

Newsflash: the pronoun has just been invented! Rewrite the above paragraph, replacing as many nouns as possible with pronouns, ensuring that it is clear what noun (antecedent) the pronoun is referring to. If in doubt about the clarity of antecedents, refer to the section that follows.

As discussed, a pronoun usually takes the place of a noun. Therefore, when replacing nouns, *each pronoun you use in your writing should refer clearly to its antecedent*—this is called **pronoun reference**. In formal writing, you must pay attention to this principle. A pronoun replaces a specific noun; *the relationship between pronoun and antecedent must always be clear*.

You can test for pronoun reference errors in your writing by seeing whether you can replace a pronoun by a specific noun that precedes the pronoun in the sentence (i.e., its antecedent):

Pronoun replaced by specific noun:

As reality shows have become more popular, they [reality shows] have become more and more bizarre.

Unclear which noun acts as antecedent:

Reality shows have become more popular while their participants have become more and more bizarre; consequently, they [reality shows? participants?] can no longer be believed.

There are four kinds of pronoun reference errors, which can be repaired in different ways.

1. No reference (missing antecedent). This error occurs where the pronoun has no apparent noun antecedent. Consider this sentence:

Following the prime minister's speech, *he* took several questions from reporters.

The personal pronoun *he* apparently replaces *prime minister's*, which is a possessive adjective. Pronouns replace nouns, not adjectives. In the following sentence, the noun antecedent is implied but not actually stated; grammatically, the reference is missing:

One thing that Canadians are especially proud of is *its* national health-care system.

If the antecedent is missing, the sentence can be revised so the pronoun has an antecedent.

Where there is no antecedent, one must be provided or the pronoun changed into an appropriate noun.

After the *prime minister* spoke, *he* took several questions from reporters.

Or:

After speaking, *the prime minister* took several questions from reporters.
One thing that *Canadians* are especially proud of is *their* national health-care system.

A tendency in speaking, and sometimes in informal writing, is to use the impersonal third-person pronoun *it* or *they* to refer vaguely to some unmentioned authority. In formal writing, you should avoid this habit:

They say there's nothing like a nice car to make you popular.

If a sentence begins with a prepositional phrase, the noun that is the object of a preposition cannot be the antecedent of a pronoun later in the sentence. The grammatical antecedent will be missing, and the sentence will have to be revised to include an antecedent/subject of the clause. The examples below illustrate this problem (and its solutions), which sometimes occurs in a rough draft when you try to get ideas down quickly.

Incorrect: With the new Formula One scoring system, it keeps fans excited throughout the season.

Correct: The new Formula One scoring system keeps fans excited throughout the season.

Or:

With the new Formula One scoring system, fans remain excited throughout the season.

2. Remote reference. A reader should not be expected to connect a pronoun to a noun when they are separated by more than one sentence.

> In George Orwell's prophetic book *1984*, people's lives were watched over by television screens. These screens, along with brainwashing techniques, enabled people to be kept under firm control. *It* is an example of dystopian fiction.

The pronoun *it*, in sentence three, takes up the thread too late. Many nouns have intervened, causing the reader to have to hunt for the antecedent. Repetition of the noun is often the best solution where the antecedent is far away from the pronoun.

3. Ambiguous (squinting) reference. This error occurs when the pronoun seems to refer to two or more nouns, either of which could be the antecedent.

> When *Peter* gave *Paul his* driver's licence, *he* was very surprised to see that it had expired.

Who was surprised in this sentence? The pronoun *he* could refer to either *Peter* or *Paul*.

Other examples:

> The problem for readers aspiring to look like the models in women's magazines is that their photos have been airbrushed. [*Their* has two grammatical antecedents: *readers and models*.]
> In 1916, a member of the Russian parliament denounced Rasputin before his colleagues. [Does *his* refer to the member's colleagues or to Rasputin's?]

While it is sometimes possible to correct ambiguous reference by repeating the noun intended to act as the antecedent, the result is not always pleasing:

> When *Peter* gave *Paul* his driver's license, *Peter* was surprised to see that it had expired.

Rewriting may be the better solution:

> On giving his driver's license to Paul, Peter was surprised to see that it had expired.
> The problem for readers aspiring to look like the models in women's magazines is that the models' photographs have been airbrushed.

If the antecedent could grammatically be one of two possible nouns, you may need to rewrite the sentence so the antecedent is clear.

In 1916, a member of the Russian parliament denounced Rasputin before the House.

4. Broad reference (vague reference). This error occurs when the pronoun (often *this*, *that*, or *which*) refers to a group of words, an idea, or a concept, rather than *one specific noun*.

> Incorrect: Children these days are too prone to lazy habits, such as watching television. *This* shows we have become too permissive.

This replaces too much—in effect, the whole preceding clause. The following, though, would be quite acceptable in anything but the most formal writing, even though the pronoun *which* doesn't replace a specific noun here, but rather the fact that she *received top marks*. The meaning of the sentence, however, is clear.

> She received top marks for her final dive, *which* gave her the gold medal in that competition.

In the following sentence the pronoun *this* refers to an idea, rather than a noun antecedent, making the meaning of the second independent clause unclear.

> Incorrect: Many older drivers are re-tested if they have had medical problems, but *this* needs to go further.

Broad reference often requires a sentence rewrite. Sometimes, the easiest way is to provide a noun and change the demonstrative pronoun into a demonstrative adjective. (A demonstrative adjective has the same form as a demonstrative pronoun—*this*, *that*, *these*, *those*—but, as an adjective, it precedes a noun as a modifier, rather than take its place.)

> Correct: Children these days are too prone to lazy habits, such as watching television. *This tendency* shows that we have become too permissive.
> Correct: Many older drivers are re-tested if they have had medical problems, but *this re-testing* needs to go further.

While there is perhaps a "broad" allowance for broad reference error, depending on the level of formality required, *it* is a personal pronoun, and, like all personal pronouns, should always have a clear noun referent.

> Poor: We try not to mention specific businesses by name in our article; however, it can't be avoided in some situations.
> Better: We try not to mention specific businesses by name in our article; however, we can't avoid names in all situations.

If the antecedent appears to be an idea rather than a specific noun, you need to add a noun that sums up the idea to the part of the sentence where the error occurs.

Exercise **16.5**

Broad pronoun reference errors are particularly distracting when they occur repeatedly as a writer tries to develop a point. Read the following paragraph, and then revise it to fix the errors in broad pronoun reference:

> Genetically modified foods have been engineered to flourish in harsh environments. *This* will help alleviate the need for usable farmland as *this* will enable farming to occur on lands once considered unsuitable for growing crops. *This* will be a major benefit to many nations in Africa, Asia, and South America where there is a shortage of food and available land.

Exercise **16.6**

Working backward: To reinforce the principle that pronouns require clear antecedents, make up antecedent nouns for the pronouns to replace and construct sentences/clauses containing the nouns to precede these sentences/clauses.

Example:

He just shrugged off all she had to say in her defence.

Preceding sentence:

Lucinda explained her behaviour to Ted, but he just . . . .

1. She had long, brown hair down to her waist. (antecedent for *she*)
2. He found him sleeping soundly on the kitchen floor the next morning. (*he*, *him*)
3. They lived as if nobody else mattered but themselves. (*they*)
4. This will be her chance to prove whether she is good enough to make the team. (*she*)
5. They have a responsibility to educate the public. (*they*)
6. His attorney decided on a "not guilty" plea. (antecedent for possessive adjective *his*)
7. She awoke suddenly to the sound of gunfire. (*she*)
8. They make a delightfully odd couple. (*they*)
9. She will eat only the most expensive kind of deluxe cat food. (*she*)
10. After hearing their protests for a long time, he finally agreed to take them along. (*their*, *he*, *them*)

Exercise **16.7**

Identify the kind of pronoun reference errors in the following sentences; then, correct the errors by making necessary revisions. In the first five sentences, the pronoun that needs to be changed is italicized.

1. *It* says in my textbook that pronouns should always have a clear referent.
2. Whenever a staff meeting is called, *they* are required to attend.
3. Racism is a disease that will continue to plague society until *it* is non-existent.
4. Sixty per cent of our pesticides are used on cotton, and *this* is our major ground water pollutant.
5. During Roosevelt's Pearl Harbor speech, *he* identified the US as a peaceful and tolerant nation.
6. I know it said *No Parking*, but I went ahead and parked there anyway. They gave me a $20 fine.
7. Her second novel was far different from her first. It was set in the remote Hebrides.
8. Previous Afghan successes were significant victories; for example, they last waged war against the powerful Soviet Union.
9. Some psychologists and researchers believe in the "innate" theory of prejudice. According to this theory, ingrained prejudice is cross cultural and awareness of race is one of the earliest social characteristics to develop in children. These findings may help account for its popularity.
10. During the dinosaur age, they lived in a rapidly changing environment.

After you've checked your answers, complete the exercise by doing questions 11–20.

11. It is the right of everybody to have access to knowledge, and this means access to the education of choice.
12. In Chapter 21 of my textbook, it analyzes the success of the Liberal Party in Canada.
13. Supervisors may discourage workers from reporting injuries since they receive annual bonuses for low injury rates.
14. Children often hide their compulsive behaviours from friends and family due to feelings of shame, causing them to remain undiagnosed.
15. To experienced "gamers," the quality of the video card is crucial; this is because the latest games require a high standard of video card.
16. The Catholic kings of Spain rallied the country to fight their enemies, the Moors. This became known as the "Reconquista."
17. Huck Finn was the physically abused son of Pap, who harasses Judge Thatcher when he is drunk. This creates sympathy in the reader, which makes him more likeable.
18. By teaching today's youth safe and healthy approaches to sexuality, it will elevate their self-esteem.
19. Part of the appeal of driving an SUV is that they are big and look impressive beside the "merely mortal" car.
20. Japanese smokers consume more than twice the number of cigarettes as American smokers do, and it continues to increase steadily.

Pronoun Case

Some personal, relative, and interrogative pronouns change their form to reflect their function in the sentence. The grammatical term for this form is **pronoun case**. You need to be aware of those situations in which you look at the pronoun's function in order to use the correct form.

Personal Pronouns

Personal pronouns refer to persons. The first person refers to the one doing the speaking or writing; second person refers to the one spoken to; third person refers to the one spoken about. Most nouns can be considered third person and can be replaced by third-person pronouns.

Table 16.1 can be used to distinguish between one group of pronouns and another group. It's important to be able to distinguish between them because the role that a personal pronoun plays in a sentence will determine whether you use the pronoun form from the first group (subjective) or from the second one (objective). Notice that the second-person pronoun *you* doesn't change its form, so it's the first- and third-person pronouns you will be concerned about.

Consider the pronoun forms under Subjective–Singular and Subjective–Plural in Table 16.1:

He was swimming in the pool.

He is the subject of the sentence, the third-person singular masculine form of the pronoun. *He* is correct because it is the subject of the clause/sentence, so it is said to be in the subjective case. The following sentence illustrates what happens when the pronoun plays a grammatical role other than subject:

I was swimming in the pool with *her*.

The subject *I* is first-person singular. But the other pronoun in the sentence is acting as the object of the preposition *with*. When it acts as the object of a verb or of a preposition, it is in the objective case.

Personal pronouns refer to persons. The *first person* refers to the one *doing* the speaking or writing; *second person* refers to the one *spoken to; third person* refers to the one *spoken about.*

The first and third forms of the personal pronoun and two other pronouns (*who* and *whom*) change their form, or *case*, to express their grammatical function in the sentence.

TABLE 16.1	**Personal Pronouns**			
Pronoun Person	Subjective–Singular	Subjective–Plural	Objective–Singular	Objective–Plural
First person	I	we	me	us
Second person	you	you	you	you
Third person	he, she, it	they	him, her, it	them

If you are in doubt about the correct form of a personal pronoun, determine the grammatical role it is playing in the sentence and then use the corresponding case form.

> *She* spoke so softly to the teacher that it was difficult for *him* to understand *her*.

She is the subject of the verb *spoke*; *him* is the object of the preposition *for*; *her* is the object of the infinitive *to understand*.

Notice the different pronouns in these two sentences:

> Anna, the King, and *I* are going out for Chinese food tonight. [*I* is part of the subject.]
> Anna arrived late for her dinner with the King and *me*. [*Me* is part of a prepositional phrase; it is the object of the preposition *with*.]

There are two steps to deciding which form to use:

1. Determine the grammatical relationship involved: Is the pronoun the subject of a clause/sentence, or the object of a verb, preposition, or infinitive?
2. Then, choose the appropriate form (subjective or objective). Until the forms become familiar, you can refer to Table 16.1.

Although the principle of pronoun case with personal pronouns is quite straightforward, it can be tricky to apply in compounds.

> Tina and [I? me?] plan to attend Mavis's wedding on May 15.

Strategy: Isolate the pronoun from the noun to determine the correct form:

> ~~Tina and~~ I plan to attend Mavis's wedding on May 15.
> Mavis's wedding will be a joyous occasion for ~~Tina and~~ me.
> We ~~students~~ believe firmly that our rights should be given back to us.
> Our rights should be given back to us ~~students~~.

Possessive Pronoun

Another example in which pronouns change their form is the possessive (adjectival) form of nouns and pronouns (e.g., my *uncle's* pet alligator; *his* pet alligator).

> The book doesn't belong to Anthony but to Kristy; it is *hers*.

Hers is the noun form of the possessive pronoun replacing the antecedent *Kristy*. The adjectival form is seen in the following sentence:

> The book doesn't belong to Anthony but to Kristy; it is *her* book.

Never use an apostrophe when you use a form like *hers* ("belonging to her") or *theirs* ("belonging to them").

Table 16.2 completes Table 16.1 by listing the possessive forms of pronouns and the noun (complement) forms.

TABLE 16.2	Possessive Pronouns with Adjectival and Noun Forms			
Pronoun Person	Adjectival- Singular	Adjectival- Plural	Subject Complements, Singular	Subject Complements, Plural
First person	my	our	mine	ours
Second person	your	your	yours	yours
Third person	his, her, its	their	his, hers, its	theirs

Relative Pronouns

A relative pronoun introduces a dependent clause and usually functions adjectivally, modifying the preceding noun. This clause is called a relative clause.

A **relative pronoun** *relates* the dependent clause it introduces to the noun that it follows. A **relative clause**, then, usually functions as an adjective, modifying the preceding noun. Of the major relative pronouns (*who, whoever, which, whichever, that*), only *who* and *whoever* change their form depending on whether they are being used as the subject of the clause or as the object of either the verb or a preposition in the clause.

To determine the case of a relative pronoun, look at *the role the relative pronoun plays within the clause*; in other words, the answer to whether you use *who* or *whom* will be found *in the clause that the relative pronoun introduces.*

If the pronoun is the subject of the clause, use *who*; if it is the object of the verb or of the preposition in the clause, use *whom*.

If either the pronoun *who* or *whoever* is the subject of the clause or is the subjective completion, use the subjective form. If the pronoun is acting as an object of the verb or of a preposition in the clause, use the objective form: *whom* (*whomever*). Consider these two sentences; italics indicate the dependent (relative) clause:

1. The old man shouted at *whoever happened to be within listening distance.*
2. The old man should be free to shout at *whomever he chooses.*

In sentence 1, *whoever* is the subject of the clause it introduces (*whoever happened to be within listening distance*). In sentence 2, *he* is the subject of the clause, and the relative pronoun is in the objective case. If you see that the relative clause has a subject, you can be certain that the relative pronoun will *not* be the subject of the clause. In sentence 2, *he* does the choosing and is the subject of the verb; *whomever* is the object of the verb.

One test for case is to substitute the third-person form of the personal pronoun for the relative pronoun in the relative clause. *Whoever* (relative pronoun) *happened to be within listening distance* would become *he/she* (personal pronoun) *happened to be within listening distance.* In sentence 2, the relative clause would read, *he chooses he*, which is incorrect.

Determining pronoun case with relative pronouns always involves determining the function of the relative pronoun that begins the clause. Which is correct?

1. Jeong-Gyu is someone who, we firmly believe, will go far.
2. Jeong-Gyu is someone whom, we firmly believe, will go far.

Answer: Sentence 1 is correct. *Who* is the subject of the relative clause *who will go far*. *We firmly believe* is not part of the relative clause but part of another clause (with another subject) that interrupts the relative clause.

Jeong-Gyu is someone who ~~, we firmly believe,~~ will go far.

Interrogative Pronouns

The **interrogative pronouns** (*who, whoever, which, whichever, what*) are always asking questions. Once you know how to determine the case of the relative pronouns *who and whom*, the interrogatives shouldn't give you too much trouble. Again, you need to determine their function to determine pronoun case. Of the three interrogatives, it is *who* and *whoever* that change, depending on their function in the sentence.

The interrogative pronouns, *who, which,* and *what,* introduce questions.

With whom did you go out on Saturday night? [object of the preposition]
Who says you should never reveal your feelings? [subject of the verb]
Whom would you recommend for the new opening? [object of the verb]

If a pronoun is part of a prepositional phrase, it will normally follow the preposition. However, it's possible to structure the sentence so the pronoun precedes the preposition (e.g., *Whom is the note for?*) If you end a sentence with a preposition, you can rearrange the sentence so the preposition comes *before* the pronoun. It is then clear that the *objective case* should be used for the pronoun.

The function of the interrogative pronoun in the sentence determines whether *who* (subjective form) or *whom* (objective form) is used.

Whom did Professor LeGuin direct the question to?

The more formal usage makes it easier to determine case:

Rearranged sentence:

To whom did Professor LeGuin direct the question?

It is now clear that *whom* is the object of the preposition *to*.

Exercise **16.8**

Choose the correct form of the pronoun.

1. Management often forgets about the needs of (we/us) wage-earners.
2. (Who/whom) should run for office this election?

(continued)

3. I have no intention of speaking to (they/them).
4. The person (who/whom) finishes first will be rewarded.
5. You recommend (who/whom) for the position?
6. As she entered the room, a mysterious feeling came over (she/her).
7. Margaret Laurence was a novelist (who/whom) entertained her readers with well-developed plots and realistic characters.
8. People (who/whom) use memory aids tend to be better spellers.
9. The instructor explained the different cases of pronouns to Gail and (I/me).
10. "Hey, buddy, (who/whom) did you mean to refer to when you used that insulting term?"

After you've checked your answers, complete the exercise by doing questions 11–25.

11. (Whoever/whomever) fails to address the most important issue— unemployment—will find themselves among the unemployed.
12. The last person (who/whom) she wanted to see at the track meet was her former coach.
13. My fifth grade teacher always let her favourite students—Mallory, Cindy, and (I/me)—help her with clean-up.
14. I wanted to ask her (who/whom) the note should be addressed to.
15. The young narrator's goal is to bring back a present for his friend's sister (who/whom) he admires from afar.
16. Chris's rival, Mike, lasted longer in the ring than (he/him).
17. We were allowed to invite (whoever/whomever) we wanted to the party.
18. I proposed that Geordie and (I/me) would stack chairs after the meeting.
19. The only "mother" (who/whom) the kitten has known is Madeline, (who/whom) rescued it from traffic.
20. The newly renovated house is a very pleasant place for my brother and (I/me) to live.
21. During his career, Jackie Robinson was subjected to racial hatred from many people (who/whom) he came in contact with.
22. Prejudices decrease when children observe non-prejudiced behaviour by peers (who/whom) children associate with during their pre-teen years.
23. Christy so drastically changes his personality that his own father can barely believe it is (he/him).
24. "[I]n these fits I leave them, while I visit / young Ferdinand, (who/whom) they suppose is drowned." —Shakespeare
25. Choose the grammatical poem:

a. Roses are red,	b. Roses are red,
Butterflies are free;	Birds can fly;
You must choose	You must choose
Between him and me.	Between he and I.

Pronoun Consistency

A pronoun must agree in number, gender, and person with its antecedent—this is called **pronoun consistency**. In many instances, you will refer to different persons in the same sentence, and it's acceptable to do so, as long as the change isn't arbitrary. On the other hand, if you want simply to replace a preceding noun with a pronoun, the pronoun should be the same *person* as its antecedent. Nouns are usually treated as third person and are replaced by third-person pronouns.

> Pronoun consistency is the principle that a pronoun must agree in number, gender, and person with its antecedent.
>
> Do not needlessly switch from one person of pronoun to another. If an antecedent is a noun, use the third-person form to replace it.

Incorrect: During final exams, if *students* must go to the washroom, raise *your* hand so *you* can be escorted there. [*Students* is third person; *your* and *you* are second person.]
Correct: During final exams, if *students* need to go to the washroom, *they* should raise their hands . . . .

Or, more informally:

During final exams, if *you* need to go to the washroom, raise *your* hand . . . .

A further example:

Incorrect: It is possible that *our* desire to make life easier for *ourselves* will, in fact, make *humans* redundant.
Our and *ourselves* are first person; *humans* is third person.
Correct: It is possible that our desire to make life easier for ourselves will, in fact, make us redundant.
It is possible that the desire to make life easier for *humans* will, in fact, make *them* redundant.

Incorrect: Educators today should teach students learning skills, such as how to manage your money.
Correct: Educators today should teach *students* learning skills, such as how to manage *their* money.

Exercise **16.9**

The following paragraph contains errors in pronoun consistency, along with some awkward use of third-person pronouns. When you rewrite the paragraph, strive for correctness and effectiveness. First decide which person you want to refer to consistently. This decision might be based on the level of formality you want to use (first- and second-person pronouns, such as *I/me* and *you*, are considered more informal than third-person pronouns, such as *he/she* and *him/her*).

(continued)

You can definitely learn a lot from educational TV; we can learn things that we cannot learn from written texts. If one is a major in commerce, for example, and if he or she watches the business news, he or she can understand the commerce textbook better by applying what he or she learns from the news. Similarly, I think that watching sports programs can provide people with excitement. Watching sports can also give us a better understanding of the game. On the other hand, if one chooses to watch comedy all the time, people are not going to gain any real benefits. I feel comedies are generally meaningless.

❯ Sentence Construction Errors

Writing in complete sentences and using the appropriate conjunctions to join clauses will help you form grammatical sentences. However, there are other potential problems in constructing sentences. Major sentence construction errors are discussed below under four categories: (1) misplaced modifiers, (2) dangling modifiers, (3) faulty parallelism, and (4) faulty comparisons.

Misplaced modifiers and dangling modifiers are examples of errors that can result when the first principle is not adhered to. Faulty parallelism and faulty comparisons result when the second principle is not followed (see note in margin).

Misplaced Modifiers

The main function of adjectives is to modify nouns, while the main function of adverbs is to modify verbs. Prepositional phrases can also function as adjectives or adverbs. A **misplaced modifier**, then, can be an adjective, an adjectival phrase, an adverb, or an adverbial phrase. It is misplaced when it is mistakenly placed next to a part of speech it is not intended to modify.

The meaning of a sentence in English heavily depends on word order, or **syntax**; it is partly through syntax that writers communicate their meaning and that the reader understands the message.

Adjectival Modifiers

The usual position for a one-word adjective is immediately before the noun it is intended to modify, but an adjectival phrase or clause usually follows the noun it modifies. Most misplaced adjectival modifiers are phrases or clauses. Consider the following examples of misplaced modifiers:

Incorrect: They headed for a child in the front row *with a long overcoat.*

It is the child, not the front row, wearing the long overcoat. The adjectival phrase should follow the noun *child.*

Sentence construction errors result from forgetting two basic principles in English grammar:
1. A modifier should be placed as close as possible to the word it is intended to modify.
2. Coordinate (equal) elements in a sentence must be grammatically parallel and complete.

A misplaced modifier is an adjective, an adjectival phrase, an adverb, or an adverbial phrase that is too far away in the sentence from the word it should modify, possibly giving the sentence an unintended meaning.

Syntax means the way words are put together into sentences in a language.

Correct: They headed for a child with a long overcoat in the front row.

Incorrect: The furnace thermostat is located upstairs, *which displays the temperature settings.*

In this sentence, the adjectival (relative) clause, *which displays the temperature settings*, is placed next to the adverb *upstairs* instead of the noun *thermostat.*

Correct: The furnace thermostat, which displays the temperature settings, is located upstairs.

Adverbial Modifiers

Misplaced adverbs and adverbial phrases are more common than misplaced adjectives and adjectival phrases because adverbs can often be moved in a sentence without affecting meaning. However, moving them does sometimes affect meaning, and it is safest to place them right before or after the word or phrase they are supposed to modify.

The meaning of the following sentence could be misconstrued:

Incorrect: Students should buy this book because it will give them all the information they need to know about writing *in a convenient form.*

Presumably, the writer did not mean "convenience in writing," but that the book "will give them . . . information . . . in a convenient form."

Correct: Students should buy this book because it will give them, *in a convenient form*, all the information they will need to know about writing.

Consider the following example:

Incorrect: The conviction carries a penalty of 8 to 10 years in *two provinces.*

Because of the misplaced prepositional phrase, the writer seems to be saying that on being convicted, the criminal will have to "do time" in two provinces. Either of the following rephrased sentences is correct:

Correct: In two provinces the conviction carries a penalty of 8 to 10 years.
Correct: The conviction carries a penalty in two provinces of 8 to 10 years.

Fixing Misplaced Modifiers

When the misplaced modifier *in two provinces* in the last example is placed before or after the verb it should modify, *carries*, the problem is fixed. The solution to misplaced modifiers, whether an entire clause, a phrase, or a single word, is simple: move them.

The following misplaced modifier makes the sentence awkward or misleading:

Incorrect: The instructor marked the essay I wrote unfairly.
Correct: The instructor unfairly marked the essay I wrote.

Or:

I thought the instructor marked my essay unfairly.

When you are writing quickly, trying to get your ideas down, a misplaced modifier can occur anywhere in a sentence; however, they often occur at the end, almost as an afterthought. That is the place to begin checking:

Incorrect: Cars today produce large amounts of toxic chemicals that can damage human cells *if inhaled*.
Correct: Cars today produce large amounts of toxic chemicals that, if inhaled, can damage human cells.

A misplaced modifier should be placed as close as possible to the word(s) it is intended to modify.

One-Word Modifiers

You need to be especially careful in placing one-word modifiers in the sentence, especially with limiting adverbs such as *only*, *almost*, *just*, *even*, *nearly*, *barely*, *merely*, and the like.

Does one little word out of place *really* affect the meaning of the sentence? Consider how the meaning of the following statement changes, depending on where the "little" word *only* is put:

Jared didn't do *his homework* yesterday.

Six Answers to the Question: Is Jared a Lazy Student or a Conscientious One?

1. Only Jared didn't do *his homework* yesterday.

Everyone but Jared did his or her homework; *only* is an adjective modifying *Jared*.

2. Jared only didn't do his homework.

The meaning of this sentence is unclear. It could mean the same as sentence 1 or that Jared did other things—but not his homework. It could also mean that the fact Jared didn't do his homework wasn't important.

3. Jared didn't *only do his homework* yesterday.

Now *only* is an adverb modifying the verb *do* and suggests that Jared did do his homework and other things as well.

4. Jared didn't do *only his homework* yesterday.

Placing *only* before *his homework* means that Jared definitely did his homework and other things as well. It might also mean that Jared was involved in doing someone else's homework in addition to his own.

5. Jared didn't do his *only homework* yesterday.

Placing *only* between *his* and *homework* implies that Jared didn't have much homework, but he didn't do it.

6. Jared didn't do his homework *yesterday only.*

Perhaps Jared is not such a lazy student after all: the only day he didn't do his homework was yesterday!

Dangling Modifiers

Misplaced and **dangling modifiers** can be the grammatical equivalent of life's most embarrassing moments: a modifier that is misplaced or dangling can give the communication a quite different, sometimes humorous, meaning from the intended one. The sentence below seems to refer to precocious parents:

Incorrect: When only seven years old, my parents decided to enroll me in a Highland dancing course.

Now, consider the following sentence from a résumé, which never mentions the applicant at all:

Incorrect: When not working or attending classes, my hobbies are gardening, doing macramé, and bungee jumping.

As dangling modifiers are often *–ing* participle (adjectival) phrases, they are sometimes called **dangling participles**. Grammatically, they modify the closest noun. These adjectival phrases, then, are dangling because the intended noun or noun phrase is not in the sentence. That's why it doesn't help to move the modifier.

The way to correct dangling modifiers is either (1) to provide the noun or noun phrase in the independent clause to give the modifier something to modify, or (2) to turn the dangling phrase into a dependent clause with a subject.

Correct: When only seven years old, I was enrolled by my parents in a Highland dancing course. [method 1]
Correct: When I was only seven years old, my parents decided to enroll me in a Highland dancing course. [method 2]
Correct: When not working or attending classes, I enjoy several hobbies, including gardening, doing macramé, and bungee jumping. [1]
Correct: When I am not working or attending classes, my hobbies include gardening, doing macramé, and bungee jumping. [2]

Grammatically, a dangling modifier modifies the closest noun, often giving the sentence an unintended meaning.

A dangling participle is a modifier in a sentence that is not modifying anything, as the noun or noun phrase it should modify is not in the sentence.

While a misplaced modifier frequently appears at the end of a sentence, a dangling modifier usually is found at the beginning—somewhat less often at the end—of a sentence, and even occasionally in the middle. With a misplaced modifier, the needed information is in the sentence, and the modifier needs to be moved as close as possible to the word or phrase it is intended to modify. With a dangling modifier, the essential information *is not in the sentence*. The examples below will show you how to identify dangling modifiers by asking the appropriate questions.

In this example, poetic description is undercut by the statement that the clouds are arriving in Calgary, when more likely the writer is describing his or her arrival.

> Incorrect: When arriving in Calgary, the clouds had scattered, and the sky was aglow with bands of pink and red.

In the next example, the book seems to have written itself.

> Incorrect: Though a well-known writer, his latest book failed to make the best-seller's list.

The question to ask in the first example is, Who is arriving in Calgary? In the second, we can ask, Who is the well-known writer? Since the answers are not in the sentences, the modifiers must be dangling. In each case, the missing information needs to be provided in the independent clause, or the dangling phrase needs to be turned into a dependent clause that can modify the independent clause that follows.

> Correct: When arriving in Calgary, I saw that the clouds had scattered, and the sky was aglow with bands of pink and red. [1—information has been provided in the independent clause]
> When I arrived in Calgary, the clouds had scattered, and the sky was aglow with bands of pink and red. [2—dangling phrase has been changed to a dependent clause]

> Correct: Though a well-known writer, he failed to make the best-seller's list with his latest book. [1]
> Though he was a well-known writer, his latest book failed to make the best-seller's list. [2]

In the following example, the dangling modifier is at the end of the sentence:

> Incorrect: Verbal and non-verbal skills are greatly enhanced when living in a foreign country.

Who is living in a foreign country? This information is missing, so the participial phrase *when living* is dangling. To correct it, add information:

Correct: When living in a foreign country, you are able to enhance your verbal and non-verbal skills. [1]
Verbal and non-verbal skills are greatly enhanced when you live in a foreign country. [2]

Exercise 16.10

The intended meanings of the following sentences are obscured or distorted due to modifier problems. Working in groups, identify the particular problem (misplaced or dangling modifier) and determine the grammatical (incorrect or ambiguous) meaning(s) of the sentences. Then, fix the sentences using one of the methods above.

1. A striped hat was on his head that came to a point.
2. As we were leaving, he promised to visit us with tears in his eyes.
3. Although unambitious and downright lazy, I have never known Sam to break his word.
4. His ego was further inflated by being awarded first prize in the Ben Affleck look-alike contest.
5. Every character has a purpose in Shakespeare's play, big or small.
6. When asked what my favourite sport is, I usually say that it is running without any hesitation.
7. Stepping out of the airplane, the fresh air was most invigorating.
8. Gabriel Kolko describes peace in Vietnam after the war in his book.
9. Opening the door unexpectedly, his eyes fell upon two of his employees sleeping in front of their computers.
10. Teacher Laurie McNamara posed for the photographer with Principal Dan Saunders, who gave her a kidney last month, in the Cloverdale Elementary School hallway.

Exercise 16.11

Correct the following sentences, each of which contains a modifier error. In some instances, it will be necessary to reword the sentence for clarity and correctness.

1. In our city, shady characters lurk on quiet corners that offer a variety of drugs.
2. Over the years, several world-class cyclists have had spectacular careers, such as Eddie Merckx and Greg LeMond.

(continued)

3. Running down the street without a care in the world, two pedestrians had to quickly move out of his way.

4. Being a member of the Sikh community, my paper will be given a strong personal focus.

5. Built in mere minutes, you will have a fully interactive website for your business or for your personal use.

6. Benefits will only result from a smoke-free environment.

7. Germany has built an extensive network of highways through its countryside, known as the Autobahn.

8. Trying to find a job today, employers are stressing verbal and written communication skills more than ever before.

9. People's rights to privacy should be forfeited when caught in criminal behaviour.

10. This species of snake will eat frogs, mice, and small pieces of meat in captivity.

After you've checked your answers, complete the exercise by doing questions 11–25.

11. Walking through the streets of Srinigar, devastation and fear are immediately evident.

12. As a beginner, my instructor taught me about the respect one karate student must show to another.

13. Tylenol and Aspirin effectively reduce pain when experiencing a fever.

14. Speaking from experience, tans that dye the top layer of the skin last for about one week.

15. Moving to Nebraska at the age of 10, Jim Burden's narrative reveals the reflections of a child.

16. Being an Elizabethan playwright, I am certain that Shakespeare would have been a major influence on Marlowe.

17. Adolescents essentially experience the same depressive symptoms as adults do.

18. As a serious snowboarder, it is exciting to observe the growth of this sport.

19. In John Donne's "Death, Be Not Proud," Death has a personality that is usually only given to a human being.

20. The boy in *Araby* returns home empty-handed without the highly valued object, in this case, a gift for Mangan's sister that most quests require.

21. Darwin's theory of evolution may be contested on the grounds that species may cease to appear abruptly.

22. Another example of imagery of light and dark in *Heart of Darkness* occurs when Marlow encounters an African dying in a clearing with a white scarf.

23. Based primarily on the work of Karl Marx, socialists see the creation of profit as a complex process.

24. Having an emotional personality, Beethoven's music identified him as a nineteenth-century Romantic.

25. A mother and her daughter were recently reunited after 18 years in a checkout line.

The Parallelism Principle

Balanced constructions give a sentence grace and strength, while unbalanced constructions make a sentence weak and unstable, as a misaligned wall in a building undermines a building's stability. A sentence must be constructed so that words and phrases parallel in the logic of the sentence are parallel in the grammatical structure of the sentence.

Coordinate elements are *equal* elements. **Parallelism** ensures that the elements in a sentence that have the *same grammatical function* are expressed in parallel structures.

When studying paragraph coherence (Chapter 3), you looked at using repetition and balanced structures. Learning the fundamentals of parallelism in this section will help ensure that your writing is both grammatically correct and easy to read.

Experienced writers have mastered the principles of parallel structures and use them routinely in their writing; balanced structures are rhetorically effective structures. Consider, for example, the following excerpt from Francis Bacon's essay "Of Youth and Age" (1601), which is made up almost entirely of parallel words, phrases, and clauses. Without parallel elements, shown by italics, this paragraph would be very hard to follow:

Parallelism is the principle that the elements in a sentence that have the *same grammatical function* are expressed in parallel structures.

> A man that is *young in years*, may be *old in hours*, if he have lost no time. But that happeneth rarely. Generally, youth is like the *first cogitations*, not so wise as *the second*. For there is a youth *in thoughts*, as well as *in ages* . . . . Young men, in the conduct and manage of actions, *embrace* more than they can hold; stir more than they can quiet; *fly* to the end, without consideration of the means and degrees; *pursue* some few principles, which they have chanced upon absurdly; *care not* to innovate, which draws unknown inconveniences; *use* extreme remedies at first; and, that which doubleth all errors, *will not acknowledge or retract* them; like an unready horse, that will neither *stop* nor *turn*. Men of age *object too much, consult too long, adventure too little, repent too soon*, and seldom *drive* business home to the full period, but *content* themselves with a mediocrity of success.

Student writer Allison McClymont was able to use parallel structures to create a dramatic opening for her essay on school uniforms.

> In the hallways of today's high school, students congregate in various cliques, using their dress as an indicator of their conformity: there are the "jocks" in their letterman jackets, the "nerds" in their high pants and suspenders, the "cheerleaders" in their short skirts and sweaters, and the "arties" in their paint-covered hippie clothes. Other easily identifiable cliques include the "gangsters," the "preppies," the "mods," the "punks," the "weirdos," and "the band geeks."

Read the following sentences. Although their meanings are clear, they don't *sound* balanced. In fact, they're not balanced because the important words in the compound or list aren't all the same part of speech: each sentence contains an error in parallel structure. The words you need to pay attention to are italicized:

Incorrect:

1. Ian would prefer *to snack* on some chips than *eating* a regular dinner.
2. The basic human needs are *food, clothes, shelter*, and *having a good job*.
3. After her 10-kilometre run, she felt *weak, tired*, and *she badly needed water*.
4. Our cat enjoys *watching* TV, *looking* out the window, and *to sleep* at the foot of our bed.
5. Neither a *borrower* be, nor *lend* to others.

Identifying and Fixing Parallelism Problems

Use a two-stage approach to identify and fix non-parallel structures in your writing:

In the first stage, identify structures where there should be parallelism: *lists, compounds, correlative conjunctions*, and *comparisons*. For example, in the following sentence, there is a compound object of the verb *prefer*:

1. Ian would prefer *to snack* on some chips rather than *eating* a regular dinner.

You should check to see whether all the elements are parallel whenever you use a list (3 or more items), a compound (2 items), correlative (paired) conjunctions, or a comparison (which has two parts).

In the second stage, when you have identified the part(s) of the list, etc. that are not grammatically parallel, make them so. The two objects of the verb *prefer* in the sentence 1 above are not expressed in parallel form: *to snack* and *eating*. Either the verbal noun (infinitive form of the verb acting as a noun) or the gerund can function as an object, so either of these changes is correct:

Correct: Ian would prefer *to snack* on some chips than *to eat* a regular dinner.

Or:

Ian would prefer *snacking* on chips to *eating* a regular dinner.

Identify in the following sentences the parts of speech that have the same functions:

2. The basic human needs are *food, clothes, shelter*, and *having* a good job.

Now, use four nouns in the list to make it grammatically parallel:

Correct: The basic human needs are *food, clothes, shelter*, and *a good job*.

3. After her 10-kilometre run, she felt *weak, tired*, and *she badly needed water*.

Using three predicate adjectives, make this list parallel:

After her 10-kilometre run, she felt *weak, tired*, and *very thirsty*.

You could also fix the sentence by using three independent clauses:

After her 10-kilometre run, *she felt weak*, *she was tired*, and *she badly needed water*.

4. Our cat enjoys *watching* TV, *looking* out the window, and *to sleep* at the foot of our bed.

Use three gerunds (*–ing* verb forms acting as nouns) to make the list parallel:

Our cat enjoys *watching* TV, *looking* out the window, and *sleeping* at the foot of our bed.

Next, correct the sentence by using three infinitives:

Our cat likes *to watch* TV, *to look* out the window, and *to sleep* at the foot of our bed.

5. Neither a *borrower* be, nor *lend* to others.

Using two verbs after the correlative (paired) conjunctions *neither* and *nor* makes the sentence parallel:

Neither *borrow* from nor *lend* to others.

You could also follow Shakespeare's example in his play *Hamlet* and use two nouns after the conjunctions:

Neither a *borrower* nor a *lender* be.

When checking for parallel structure, consider first the structurally essential words like nouns and verbs (not their modifiers). But if adjectives or adverbs appear in a list *by themselves* without words to modify, ensure they are in parallel form. Look at any larger grammatical units, such as prepositional phrases, which also should appear in parallel relationships with other prepositional phrases. Similarly, dependent clauses should be parallel with other dependent clauses and independent clauses with other independent clauses.

The examples below apply the two-step method to lists, compounds, correlative conjunctions, and comparisons.

Parallelism in a List or Series

A list or series comprises three or more items. So, whenever you list something, you need to check for parallel structure. For example, if you use an expanded thesis statement that lists your essay's main points, you need to ensure that all the items in the list are grammatically parallel.

Incorrect: Research into cloning should be encouraged as it could lead to cures for diseases, successful organ transplants, and put an end to infertility problems.

Correct: Research into cloning should be legalized as it could lead to | cures for diseases, | successful organ transplants, | and solutions to infertility problems.

The elements are now parallel. Notice that to avoid repeating the word *cures*, a word with a similar meaning has replaced it.

Note: Length is not necessarily a factor in parallelism: for example, a simple noun would normally be considered parallel with a noun phrase (but not with a prepositional phrase) because they have the same grammatical function.

The following sentence contains two nouns preceded by adjectives and a noun followed by an adjectival (prepositional) phrase. The important words here are the nouns:

Discipline in single-sex schools has been shown to directly affect | regular *attendance*, good *grades*, and *standards for dress and behaviour*.

The following thesis statements include lists where the items are not parallel:

Incorrect: The major forms of eating disorders involve the compulsion to count calories, to constantly exercise, and the need to alter one's appearance.
Correct: The major forms of eating disorders involve the compulsion | to count calories, to constantly exercise, and to alter one's appearance.
Incorrect: Buddhism teaches that one's karma can be affected by many things: your generosity to those less fortunate, your behaviour to strangers, and if you treat even your enemies with respect.

The list of "noun, noun, clause" needs to be changed to "noun, noun, noun."

Correct: Buddhism teaches that one's karma can be affect by many things: your *generosity* to those less fortunate, your *behaviour* to strangers, and *respect* even for your enemies.

You also need to be careful that items in a list are *logically*, as well as grammatically, parallel. The following list contains five nouns/noun phrases, but not all of the items are logically parallel. Which item does not belong in the list? Why?

Incorrect: Common injuries in the meat-packing industry include chemical burns, broken bones, lacerations, amputations, and even death.
Correct: Common injuries in the meat-packing industry include chemical burns, broken bones, lacerations, and amputations. Some accidents even result in death.

More informal lists that use bullets, numbers, or point form also require parallel structure. Choose a set up or starting point; then, ensure that each bulleted item has the same grammatical function and, if necessary, form.

Incorrect:

Before choosing a graduate program, a student should investigate

- the number of graduate students who receive financial support
- the expertise of faculty in the student's desired specialty
- course work required
- do research opportunities exist for graduate students?

Starting all items in the list with a noun or noun phrase would make the list grammatically parallel:

Correct:

- financial support . . .
- expertise of . . .
- course work . . .
- research opportunities . . .

Compounds

You need to apply the principle of parallel structure to **compounds**. A coordinating conjunction, such as *or*, *and*, or *but*, can signal a compound, as can a prepositional phrase joiner such as *as well as*; in a comparison, *than* or *as* may join the two elements of a comparison.

A compound consists of two of the same parts of speech acting as a grammatical unit.

Once you've identified a compound, look at the important word or phrase in the first element of the compound and ensure that the second element that follows the joiner uses the parallel grammatical structure. Several examples of compounds follow.

> Incorrect: It is actually cheaper | to convert a used vehicle into an electric vehicle than | buying a new gas-powered model.
> Correct: It is actually cheaper | to convert a used vehicle into an electric vehicle than | to buy a new gas-powered model.

Some compounds that cause trouble are those with helping verbs. In these cases, it may be helpful to draw a line where the first element begins and another where the second begins (after the conjunction). Then, see if both parts line up with the main verb that follows; you can draw a line there too. The main verb in the sentence below is *worked*:

> Incorrect: The prohibition of marijuana and the laws in place for it | *do not* and | *have never* | worked.
> Test: The prohibition of marijuana and the laws in place for it | *do not* . . . worked and *have never* worked.
> Correct: The prohibition of marijuana and the laws in place for it *do not* **work** and *have never* **worked**.

Sometimes a compound phrase ending in a preposition doesn't line up with what follows. Here is an example of a compound in which the words that follow the verbs don't line up with the object. Again, the presence of a coordinating conjunction can alert you to these tricky kinds of compounds:

Incorrect: Most people under 30 *are familiar or have heard of* the rapper Eminem.
Correct: Most people under 30 | *are familiar with or* | *have heard of* | the rapper Eminem.
Incorrect: "We have to change our production methods to make sure the products we sell are *as good* or *better as* any in the world," said the Minister of Agriculture.
Correct: "We have to change our production methods to make sure the products we sell are | *as good as* | or *better than* | any in the world," said the Minister of Agriculture.

Correlative Conjunctions

A specific kind of compound involves correlative conjunctions. These are joiners that work in pairs (*either . . . or, neither . . . nor, both . . . and, not . . . but, not only . . . but also*). Logically, the part of speech that follows the first half of the compound should also follow the second half. It might be helpful to draw a line after each conjunction:

Incorrect: A college diploma today is an investment *not only* in students' financial resources *but also* | their time.

What follows *not only* is a prepositional phrase that begins with *in*; therefore, a prepositional phrase, not just a noun (*time*), must follow the second member of the pair:

Correct: A college diploma today is an investment *not only in* students' financial resources *but also in* their time.
Incorrect: The lack of classroom availability means *either* constructing new buildings *or* lower the number of students accepted into programs.
Correct: The lack of classroom availability means *either constructing* new buildings *or lowering* the number of students accepted into programs.

Comparisons

Under Compounds we looked at comparisons as compound structures requiring parallelism. However, sometimes faulty comparisons have less to do with grammar than with logic.

Because comparisons are always made between one thing and another thing, both these elements must be fully expressed for the comparison to be complete. Often either the comparison is left incomplete or the terms being compared are incompatible; that is, they cannot be compared because there is no basis for comparison.

Note: *Than* is the word for comparisons, not the adverb related to time, *then*. Other words and phrases can also signal comparisons: *compared to, similar (to), different (from), as, like,* etc.

You need to ask if the two parts of a comparison are grammatically parallel, if both parts of the comparison are fully expressed, and if the two objects of the comparison can logically be compared. In this sentence, the reader is left to assume whom males are being compared to.

> Incomplete: An unfortunate stereotype is that males are more scientific and less intuitive.
> Complete: An unfortunate stereotype is that males are more scientific and less intuitive than females.
> Incompatible: I have found that students are less judgmental at university compared to high school.

You can ask what precisely is being compared to what and if the comparison is logical; in this case, grammatically the writer is comparing a perceived trait of *students* at university to high school itself. People must be compared to people.

> Compatible: I have found that people are less judgmental at university than they are at high school.

The two sides of the comparison are now complete and compatible.

> Incompatible: In the study, men's running times were recorded for 30 more years than women.

What is being compared here? Are the terms comparable? The writer is comparing running times (for men) to women.

> Compatible: In the study, men's running times were recorded for 30 more years than women's times.

Exercise **16.12**

In the word groups that follow, there are three or four main points related to a topic. Build parallel structures in thesis statements for each topic. Make whatever changes are necessary to achieve parallelism and use whatever order of points seems natural.

Topic 1: Why I like toe socks:

- warm and comfortable
- they are the latest fashion in socks
- come in many colours and designs

(continued)

Topic 2: The advantages of yoga:

- to relax and reduce stress
- to exercise
- also can meet people in yoga classes

Topic 3: The importance of computers to students:

- they provide entertainment
- cutting down on homework time is important
- you can obtain a wealth of information quickly

Topic 4: Living with roommates:

- they can create a lot of mess
- invade your personal space
- you can talk to them about your problems

Topic 5: The benefits of coffee:

- coffee helps you wake up
- it improves your mood
- it improves your concentration

Topic 6: The comparison of two recreational drugs:

- their possible dangerous side effects
- who uses them
- the effects they produce in the user

Topic 7: The facts about organically grown food:

- the way organically grown food is farmed
- the cost of these kinds of foods
- their nutritional value

Topic 8: The advantages of home birthing:

- allows the parents to maintain control over their surroundings
- a positive and friendly place for the child to be born
- is as safe as a hospital birth if common sense is used

Topic 9: School uniforms are beneficial:

- promote school identity and school pride
- they save parents money and hassle
- reduce the pressure of students to conform to the latest fashions
- to make it easier for school authorities to enforce discipline

Topic 10: The legalization of marijuana:

- it is less addictive than some other illegal drugs
- the Canadian government has already made it legal under certain circumstances

- governments could increase their revenue by selling it
- making it legal would reduce crime since people wouldn't have to obtain it illegally

---

Exercise 16.13

The sentences below contain parallelism errors. Identify the kind of error (series, compounds, correlative conjunctions, or comparisons) and fix the errors.

1. A good journalist is inquisitive, persistent, and must be a good listener.
2. Music can directly affect your thoughts, emotions, and how you feel.
3. In this essay, I will be looking and writing about the role of women in the military.
4. Tiddlywinks is not only a game of considerable skill but also strategy.
5. Television can affect children in a variety of negative ways since children often lack judgment, are naturally curious, and easily influenced.
6. There are three main qualities that a leader must possess: a leader must be enthusiastic, organized, and have creativity.
7. Aman never has and never will be good at golf.
8. She was not only the best teacher I have ever had, but also I was impressed by her modesty.
9. Tremors may occur on either or both sides of the body.
10. There are many reasons why people choose to or enjoy watching television.

After you've checked your answers, complete the exercise by doing questions 11–25.

11. A recent study has found that Caucasian children acquire self-awareness at an earlier age than other ethnic groups.
12. Alyssa's trip to London involved such pleasures as Buckingham Palace, feeding the pigeons, visiting her relatives, and those quaint London accents.
13. I enjoyed watching *The Last Samurai*, *The Last of the Mohicans*, and *Braveheart* was also enjoyable.
14. I want to emphasize that my work as MP in this riding has not, and will not, be affected by political developments.
15. When Jim has the choice of either jumping or to stay on the doomed ship, he chooses to jump.
16. Physical education teaches children not only to work well together but also patience and discipline.
17. Smoking should be banned because it raises health-care costs, physically harms both smokers and non-smokers, and because cigarette production damages the environment.

(continued)

18. Users of ecstasy report feeling euphoric, energized, intensified pleasure, and increased sensory awareness.
19. What made Beethoven's music different from other composers was his expressive style.
20. Recent studies suggest that wellness depends on three main factors: feeling good about yourself, your everyday eating habits, and being comfortably active.
21. Although two very different American writers, Nathaniel Hawthorne's and Mark Twain's works are nevertheless similar in many ways.
22. Differing viewpoints in a work of fiction not only add conflict, but they can also reveal differences in characters' ages, genders, and upbringings.
23. Those who exercise regularly show a decrease in anxiety, depression, fatigue, and elevated vigour.
24. In Sonnet 130, Shakespeare stresses the reality of his mistress rather than portraying her as something she is not.
25. According to a recent poll, the premier has more support among college students than the general public.

Passive Constructions

A passive construction is indirect. It displaces the subject and therefore can add unnecessary words to a sentence, In general, the passive voice should be avoided, though it may be acceptable or even preferable when you do not want to stress the subject or if the exact subject is unknown.

Passive Constructions: The Lazy Subject

In a passive construction, the subject of the sentence is not doing the action. Instead, the noun that receives the action is the subject and this is placed at the beginning of the sentence.

In a **passive construction**, the subject of the sentence is *not* doing the action. Ordinarily, the subject *is* acting, as in the following:

Ezra placed the book on the table.

To change the sentence so that the object becomes the (non-active) subject requires changing the word order and adding words:

The book was placed on the table by Ezra.

Note the differences between these two sentences. The direct object, *book*, has become the subject, and the original subject, *Ezra*, is now at the end of the sentence, the object of the preposition *by*. The verb form has changed too. The sentence now has a subject that is acted on rather than itself acting. The passive subject sentence requires more words to provide the same information. Effective, direct English is geared towards the *active*, not the passive, voice.

Exercise **16.14**

Go to your school's database and find some annual reports distributed by companies. See if you can find any examples of passive voice constructions.

The passive voice uses a form of the verb *to be* followed by a past participle. If the actor is named, it will be the object of a prepositional phrase that begins with *by*. Although you can identify the passive by the verb forms that compose it—the past, present, or future form of *to be* plus a past participle—don't confuse the identifying verb forms of the passive with a construction in which a form of the verb *to be* is used along with the past participle as a predicate adjective. For example, in the following sentence, the subjects are clearly the actors; you can't add the preposition *by* after *determined* or after *pleased*. This sentence uses an active construction:

Dana was determined to succeed at any cost; I am pleased to see him succeed.

In the following sentence, there are three indicators of a passive construction:

The door was opened by a tall, sinister man.

1. The subject (*door*) is not doing the action expressed by the verb *open*.
2. The preposition *by* precedes the actor (*man*).
3. The simple past of *to be* combines with the past participle of the main verb to form the passive voice of the verb.

To change a passive to an active construction

1. Move the subject so that it follows the verb as the direct object.
2. Move the object of the preposition *by*, the actor, to the beginning of the sentence/clause to replace the passive subject.
3. Remove the identifying passive forms of the verb and the preposition *by*.

A fast way to change a passive into an active construction is to move the noun or pronoun that follows *by* to the beginning of the sentence. The other changes will be easier to see once you've done this.

A tall, sinister man ~~was~~ opened the door ~~by~~.

Here's a slightly more complicated example:

Passive: The special commission was informed of its mandate by a superior court judge last Monday.
Active: A superior court judge informed the special commission of its mandate last Monday.

In its active form, the sentence contains fewer words, and the thought is expressed more directly. As a general rule, *don't use the passive voice if the active will serve.* However, these are times when the passive is acceptable or is even the better choice:

1. When the subject isn't known or is so well known it doesn't matter.

> Pierre Trudeau was first elected prime minister in 1968.

> It is unnecessary to mention that the voters or the electorate elected him.

2. When passivity is implied, or if the context makes it seem natural to stress the receiver of the action.

> When a cyclist completes a hard workout, massages are usually performed on the affected muscles.

> In this sentence, the massages are more important than the person giving them.

> Acceptable passive: The woman was kidnapped and held hostage by a band of thugs.
> Questionable passive: Several of the thugs were picked out of a line-up by the woman.

In the first sentence, the woman obviously is the passive recipient of the action of the thugs; in the second sentence, she is doing the action. Therefore, in the second sentence, the active is preferred:

> Active: The woman picked several of the thugs out of a line-up.

Occasionally, you may choose the passive voice because the rhythm of the sentence requires it, or because it is rhetorically effective.

> The books obviously had been arranged by a near-sighted librarian.

In this sentence, the librarian's near-sightedness is important; the placement of the adjective near the end of the sentence gives it emphasis.

There are cases in academic writing, especially in the sciences, in which it is unnecessary to mention the author of a study or the researcher; the passive may be used to stress the object of the study or the method of research.

> Through case studies, a comparison of two common methods for treating depression will be made.

In the following examples from academic writing, the passive is preferred either because the actor doesn't matter or because the writer wants to stress the receiver of the action:

> In 1891 the science of embryology was shaken by the work of the cosmopolitan German biologist and vitalist philosopher Hans Driesch (Bowring, 2004, p. 401).

Don't use the passive unless you want to deemphasize the actor (active subject). A passive construction stresses the noun that is acted upon.

The emergence of second-hand smoke (SHS) [as a cancer hazard] has been offered as a viable explanation for the increased enactment of local smoking restrictions (Asbridge, 2003, p. 13).

Exercise **16.15**

The following sentences use passive constructions. Determine which are appropriate and which are inappropriate in the passive voice. Change unnecessary uses of the passive voice to form active constructions. (In some sentences, the actor or "active" subject is not part of the sentence, so you may have to add it to the sentence (see example sentence below). Be prepared to justify your decisions to leave some sentences as passive constructions.

Example:

Passive:

The suspect's behaviour had been watched for more than one month.

The suspect's behaviour had been watched [by the police] for more than one month.

Active:

The police had watched the suspect's behaviour for more than one month.

Decision:

Leave as passive because *suspect's behaviour* is more important to the meaning than *the police*.

1. I was given two choices by my landlord: pay up or get out.
2. It was reported that more than 1,000 people were left homeless by recent flooding.
3. The manager's protest was heard by the fairness committee.
4. The tree was buffeted by the wind, which tore off one of its lower branches.
5. Beethoven's Third Symphony, *The Eroica*, originally was dedicated to Napoleon, but the dedication was erased after Napoleon proclaimed himself emperor.
6. Education needs to be seen by the government as the number one priority.
7. Many acts of self-deception were committed by Bertha, the protagonist of "Bliss."
8. The belief in a powerful and infallible Creator is commonly held today.
9. Poverty in First Nations communities must be addressed by the federal, provincial, and First Nations' governments.
10. There are two ways of looking at rights-based ethics that were put forward by Emanuel Kant.

Exercise **16.16**

The following five paragraphs contain various errors that have been discussed in Chapters 14–16. Identify the errors indicated and then make corrections.

1. Identify and correct the following:

    a. comma splice
    b. one comma use error
    c. error in pronoun case
    d. broad pronoun reference
    e. missing pronoun antecedent
    f. two pronoun–antecedent agreement errors
    g. apostrophe omitted
    h. ambiguous pronoun reference
    i. failure to use gender-neutral language

    In my family, my father and sister play video games as much as me. They have become very complex, and can even improve problem-solving in children. By progressing through increasing difficulty levels, it can help childrens thought processes. On the one hand, if the child goes straight to the hardest setting, they may feel discouraged, on the other, if the child tries to systematically progress through increasing levels, they can learn the mechanics of the game step by step. This can help in the study of math, as the child may learn to persevere until he finds the solution.

2. Identify and correct the following:

    a. comma error
    b. subject–verb agreement error
    c. fragment
    d. two parallelism errors
    e. misplaced modifier
    f. dangling modifier
    g. pronoun inconsistency
    h. comma splice

    Having a job and earning one's livelihood is a necessary goal in life, it is one of the reasons you acquire an education. At the place where I work however, many people come in expecting to find a job lacking presentation skills. Many are poorly dressed, do not know how to behave, and they may not speak grammatically. Untidy, disorganized, and unprepared, I still have to match them with a prospective employer. They lack the skills to present themselves to others and knowing what to do in public. Although they may be highly intelligent people.

3. Identify and correct the following:

   a. comma splice
   b. misplaced comma
   c. parallelism error
   d. two apostrophes omitted
   e. fragment
   f. two pronoun–antecedent agreement errors

   Logic can be defined as "the science of the formation and application of a general notion." Meaning that logic is apt to vary according to ones way of seeing certain things as important. A vegetarians logic, asserts that it is completely unnecessary—not to mention cruel—to eat animals in our day and age. Today's meat eater also has their logic. For them, meat is to be enjoyed, the taste of the food and the social interaction involved is to be cherished. We need to allow time in our busy lives to eat more and feeling guilty about it less.

4. Identify and correct the following:

   a. four comma errors
   b. one error in use of a semicolon
   c. comma splice
   d. pronoun case error
   e. error in apostrophe use
   f. dangling modifier

   The Myers-Briggs personality test is based on the work of Swiss psychologist, Carl Jung, and two Americans; Isabel Briggs Myers, and her mother Katharine C. Briggs. Myers developed the tests, and tried them out on thousands of schoolchildren; she wanted to see how the test results would correlate with vocation. Consisting of a series of questions requiring a yes or no response, she tested a group of medical students, who she followed up on 12 years later and who confirmed the test's validity. Variations of Myer's test are sometimes given by employers today, however, the results should not be the sole means for a hiring decision.

5. Identify and correct the following:

   a. comma splice
   b. one other comma error (missing or misplaced)
   c. one punctuation error other than comma
   d. parallelism error
   e. two apostrophe errors
   f. subject–verb agreement error
   g. pronoun–antecedent agreement error
   h. broad pronoun reference error

(continued)

According to the principle's of Buddhism, neither sensual pleasures nor self-mortification bring about enlightenment, instead, the "Middle Way" is the path between these extremes; this can be understood through the "Four Noble Truths." These truths are: the truths of suffering, of the origins of suffering, of the cessation of suffering, and finding the path to end suffering. The Buddhas teaching asks each individual to examine their own conscience, and to come to a conclusion about the nature of truth.

Exercise **16.17**

Identify then correct the error(s) in each sentence. If there is more than one error, choose the "more than one error" option.

1. Written through the eyes of a young boy, one can see the perspective of the indigenous peoples.

    a. dangling modifier
    b. misplaced modifier
    c. pronoun–antecedent agreement
    d. comma error

2. The daily stresses of students, such as project or assignment due dates, teaches you to manage your time wisely.

    a. subject–verb agreement
    b. pronoun inconsistency
    c. more than one error
    d. parallelism

3. Parents sometimes push their children so hard to excel that they lose interest altogether.

    a. error in use of colon
    b. pronoun reference error
    c. more than one error
    d. subject–verb agreement

4. My roommate thinks it would be better for society, if all drugs were decriminalized.

    a. dangling modifier
    b. comma error
    c. subject–verb agreement error
    d. none of the above

5. Contributors to homelessness include the lack of good-paying jobs, increasingly large families and, probably the most important factor, which is the cost of living in a large city.

   a. dangling modifier
   b. more than one error
   c. comma error
   d. parallelism error

6. One of the most tragic events of the twentieth century. The detonation of the atomic bomb over Hiroshima.

   a. sentence fragment
   b. comma splice
   c. pronoun reference
   d. none of the above

7. With the increasing media focus in the 1980s on the plight of homeless women, came the need for more research, unfortunately, this research was not comprehensive.

   a. comma splice
   b. more than one error
   c. pronoun–antecedent agreement
   d. parallelism error

8. Optometrists have been reshaping the cornea in order to correct vision for 50 years.

   a. parallelism error
   b. error in comma use
   c. misplaced modifier
   d. subject–verb agreement error

9. Information on airlines, currency exchange, and other passenger services are available on this website.

   a. subject–verb agreement
   b. comma error
   c. more than one error
   d. run-on sentence

10. Many people are intrigued by the lives movie and TV heroes seem to live; these viewers tending to be teenagers.

    a. more than one error
    b. error in semicolon use
    c. parallelism error
    d. sentence fragment

Exercise **16.18**

Identify the error (a, b, c, or d) and correct it in the sentence (there is one error in each sentence).

1. Anorexia <u>starts</u> when <u>a person</u> decides to take control over <u>their</u> <u>body</u> weight.
           a   b   c   d

2. There <u>are</u> three types of turbine engines used in aircraft<u>;</u> the <u>turbojet</u>, the
          a   b   c

    turbofan<u>,</u> and the turboprop.
         d

3. Work <u>songs</u> and street <u>vendors</u> <u>cries</u> <u>are</u> examples of traditional
           a   b   c   d
    African-American music styles.

4. <u>Reforms</u> of the UN Security Council <u>include</u> abolishing the veto or <u>to extend</u>
       a   b   c
    the Council beyond the <u>current five</u> members.
                                d

5. Results from a recent study <u>showed that</u> patients <u>suffering from</u>
                                a   b

    osteoarthritis, <u>who listened to music for 20 minutes each day,</u> reported
                                    c

    <u>a 66 per cent</u> reduction in their perception of pain.
         d

6. As a <u>known</u> anarchist<u>,</u> <u>Chomsky's views</u> <u>have been</u> much debated.
           a   b   c   d

7. The brain of <u>a drug addict</u> <u>is</u> physically <u>different from</u> <u>a non-addict</u>.
                 a   b   c   d

8. The tobacco in cigarettes is not <u>the only</u> problem<u>,</u> <u>cigarettes</u> contain many
                                       a   b   c

    dangerous chemicals <u>as well</u>.
                   d

9. By teaching <u>today's</u> youth safe and healthy approaches to sexuality<u>,</u> <u>it</u> will
                a   b c

    elevate <u>their</u> self-esteem.
            d

10. Holly Hunter, the actress <u>who</u> <u>I</u> most admire<u>,</u> appeared in several
                                a b   c

    <u>award-winning</u> movies.
         d

■ Chapter Review Questions

1. How do you find the subject of the sentence?

2. Does a prepositional phrase that follows a subject affect the verb form?

3. What is a compound subject? How is a verb form affected by a compound subject?

4. When is a collective noun followed by a plural verb form?

5. Are most indefinite pronouns considered singular or plural? Why?

6. What are the three situations that cause most subject–verb agreement errors?

7. Why is the sentence *One should always finish their homework* incorrect?

8. How can you check for pronoun–antecedent errors?

9. What are the four kinds of pronoun reference errors?

10. When is it correct to use *who* in a sentence or clause? When would the use of *whom* be correct?

11. What are misplaced modifiers? Give an example.

12. What are dangling modifiers? Give an example.

13. What is parallelism and why is it important?

14. What is a compound?

15. When should you use passive sentence constructions?

17
Achieving Clarity and
Depth in Your Writing

In this chapter, you will

- learn the importance of clarity in all your writing
- learn strategies for cutting unneeded words and phrases
- learn ways to avoid constructions that weaken sentences
- learn the value of using direct and forceful language
- learn the difference between formal and informal diction
- learn strategies to introduce variety and emphasis
- learn successful proofreading techniques
- learn a format for presenting your essay
- learn the correct usage of confusing words

Many beginning writers believe that once they have completed their draft, their essay is ready to be turned in. Unfortunately, these students forget about a crucial stage of essay writing—revision. Papers can always be revised for clarity, precision, and conciseness. This chapter will help you create stronger essays that are clear, direct, and reader-focused.

❯ Effective Style: Clarity

What is **style**? If you have written a research essay, you will know that the word *style* is applied to documentation formats, such as the rules for citing sources using MLA or APA guidelines. Style is also a term applied to individual writers—say, a dense, sophisticated style versus a spare, terse style. Although every writer has a unique writing style, when you are writing factually with a specific purpose for a specific audience, you need to put **clarity**, or clear writing, above your personal writing style.

Clarity depends on various factors. If you were writing for a general audience on a specialized topic and used words that were unfamiliar to most readers, you would not be writing clearly, though a specialist might understand you. Word choice and level of language, then, are important factors in clear and effective writing. But they are not the only factors discussed in this chapter.

The "art" of writing clearly is really not an art or talent at all; it is the result of hard work and attention to detail. Few writers—experienced or inexperienced—write clearly without making several revisions. Much of the **revising** process, in fact, consists of making the language reflect the thought behind it.

One of the differences between experienced and inexperienced writers is that the former expect to spend much of their time revising their prose; they ask, Can this be put more clearly? Student writers should ask themselves that question, too. If the answer is "yes" or "maybe," try paraphrasing it (putting it in other words). Can you do this easily? Does your paraphrase express the point more clearly? When you paraphrase something you've written, you often find that the second version is closer to what you intended to say.

When you are writing for an audience, it is not enough that *you* understand your ideas. *Your readers* need to understand what is being written. Therefore, revise your work with this thought in mind.

What, then, is clear writing? Writing that is clear is grammatical, concise, direct, precise, and specific. When you revise, you not only can ask yourself, *Is the writing clear?*, but also the following questions:

- *Is it grammatical?* Chapters 14–16 have provided most of the information you need to write understandable, grammatically correct sentences.
- *Is it concise?* Do you use as many words as you need and no more? Have you used basic words and simple constructions that reflect what you want to say?
- *Is it direct?* Have you used straightforward language? Is the structure of your sentences as simple as possible given the complexity of the point you are trying to express?

Style is the way that one writes.

Writing that is clear is grammatical, concise, direct, precise, and specific.

The "art" of writing clearly is really not an art or a talent at all; it is the result of hard work and attention to detail. Few writers—experienced or inexperienced—write clearly without making several revisions. Much of the revising process, in fact, consists of making the language reflect the thought behind it.

When you are writing for an audience, it is not enough that *you* understand your ideas. *Your readers* need to understand what is being written. Therefore, revise your work with this thought in mind.

- *Is it precise?* Does it say exactly what you want it to say? When you are writing for a reader, *almost* or *close enough* is *not* enough. Would another word or phrase more accurately reflect your thought?
- *Is it specific?* Is it as detailed as it needs to be? Is it definitive and concrete—not vague or abstract?

Writers who carefully work to make their writing more grammatical, concise, direct, precise, and specific will likely produce an essay that is clear. However, experienced writers aim also for forceful writing; therefore, they may introduce variety and emphasis in their writing.

Do not use more words than necessary to express an idea.

Exercise **17.1**

The following is a paragraph from an argument essay. Try to find examples that illustrate stylistic problems summarized above. How could the writer be more concise, direct, precise, and specific?

> Foie Gras is considered a delicious delicacy by some, yet it is viewed with disdain by others. Foie Gras is duck or goose liver pate, which is very fatty. It is created by force feeding the ducks or geese with a corn-based food. Tubes are forced down the animal's throat and then it is forced to consume more food than it would normally, either in the wild or in captivity. Many organizations in both Europe and North America are calling for a ban on the sale of foie gras in order to encourage the immediate cessation of this form of animal cruelty. In some states, such as the glorious state of California, this force feeding has been outlawed by the courts. Some chefs, including celebrity chefs, refuse to use foie gras, as they firmly believe that the force feeding practice is unnecessarily cruel and a terrible thing. If more people were aware of the cruel and inhumane treatment of the poor ducks and geese, then maybe they would stop supporting this cruel and inhumane industry. It is our necessary duty to inform the uninformed population.

Exercise **17.2**

Go to the student essay in Chapter 12, "The Virtual Life: An Overview of the Effects of MMORPGS on Individuals and Countries." Read through the essay and find examples showing how the writer addressed his audience. Also, note any places where the writer used variety in his sentences or paragraphs to make his essay more interesting and his points more forceful.

Why should so much effort be devoted to concise and direct writing? For one thing, such writing will be easy to follow and will keep the reader's interest. Unnecessary repetition and other kinds of clutter may cause a point to lose its sharpness. Have you ever read a novel that was filled with what you considered unnecessary details? How interested were you in the book? If you were like most readers, you probably stopped reading and moved on to another, more interesting book. Redundancy and unnecessary detail cause the same reaction in your readers.

Just as concise and direct writing makes you seem reliable, indirect writing may give the impression that you lack confidence in what you're saying, that you are just trying to impress the reader, or that you are trying to use more words to reach a word limit. Finally, when you use more words than you have to or express yourself in a roundabout way, you increase the odds of making grammatical and mechanical errors.

When you use more words than you have to or express yourself in a roundabout way, you increase the odds of making grammatical and mechanical errors.

Cutting for Conciseness

To achieve conciseness, cut what is inessential. How do you determine what is unnecessary? The simple test is to check whether you can leave something out without changing the meaning and the effectiveness of your statement.

Many common stylistic patterns that student writers adopt, especially in their early drafts, are described below under specific categories. Your instructor may indicate problems with conciseness by putting parentheses around what is unneeded or by writing *wordy* or *verbose* in the margin. You should not think of this as criticism so much as advice directing you to more readable writing.

Student writers may also unconsciously shift the stress away from the main nouns and verbs—where it should lie. Certainly it is not always wrong to use two of the same parts of speech consecutively, and to banish all passive constructions would unreasonably limit writers. The pages that follow are intended as guidelines, strategies to consider as you revise your essay.

Doubling Up: The Noah's Ark Syndrome

Writers sometimes suffer from "double vision." When they write, two words automatically pop up: two verbs, two nouns, two adjectives, or two adverbs. Experienced editors offer this formula: one + one = one-half. In other words, when you use two words when one is enough, you are halving the impact of that one word. When you do choose to use two of the same parts of speech, ensure that the two words don't convey the same thing.

> The administrative officer came up with an ~~original,~~ innovative suggestion for cost-cutting. [Anything innovative is bound to be original.]

> The event will be held at ~~various~~ different venues.

Ensure that one of the words doesn't include the meaning of the other, as in the second example above. This applies to phrases with words that are unnecessary

If a second noun, verb, adjective, or adverb doesn't make your meaning clearer, delete it.

because the meaning of the phrase can be understood without them. Be especially wary of verb–adverb combinations; ensure that the adverb is necessary.

The airport was ~~intentionally~~ designed for larger aircraft. [Can a design be unintentional?]

She ~~successfully~~ accomplished what she had set out to do. [The word *accomplished* implies success.]

Here are some common verb–adverb pairings and other combinations that usually are redundant. The unneeded words are in parentheses:

(anxiously) fear	gaze (steadily)
(better/further) enhance	(harshly) condemn
(carefully) consider	hurry (quickly)
(clearly) articulate	plan (ahead)
(completely) surround	ponder (thoughtfully)
climb (up)	praise (in favour of)
combine/join (together)	progress (forward/onwards)
descend (down)	protest (against)
dominate (over)	refer/return/revert (back) to
drawl (lazily)	rely/depend (heavily) on
dwindle (down)	sob (uncontrollably)
emphasize/stress (strongly)	(strictly) forbid
(eventually) evolve (over time)	(successfully) prove
estimate/approximate (roughly)	(suddenly) interrupt
examine (closely)	(symbolically) represent
fill (completely)	(totally) eradicate/devastate
finish (entirely)	unite (as one)
gather/assemble (together)	vanish (without a trace)

Be wary, too, of such repetitive adjective–noun pairings as the following:

(advance) warning	(past) memory
(brief) encapsulation	(positive) benefits
(dead) carcass	(powerful) blast
(fiery) blaze	(sharp) needle
(future) plan	(terrible) tragedy
(knowledgeable) specialist	(timeless) classic
(mutual) agreement	(total) abstinence
(new) beginning	

Redundancies are evident in such familiar phrases as *consensus of opinion, end result, end product, in actual fact, this point in time, time frame, time period, time span, years of age*, etc.

Unnecessary nouns are redundant. These nouns steal the thunder from other parts of speech, including other nouns and verbs.

Exercise **17.3**

Listen to your favourite radio station or watch one of your favourite TV shows. Pay attention to the language used by the advertisers and the announcers or actors. How often did you hear examples of "doubling up?" Write down some of the most frequent examples and be prepared to share these with the class.

1. The world of politics demands that you kowtow to the ineptitude of others.
2. The efforts of conservationists in the fields of ecology and biodiversity are leading to renewed efforts to save old-growth forests.

In each sentence above, the most important noun has been displaced by a weaker noun. In sentence 1, we are not really talking about a *world*, but about *politics*. In sentence 2, the noun *fields* is redundant because *ecology* and *biodiversity* are fields of study.

Phony Phrases

Phony phrases are redundant prepositional phrases. Look for them after verbs and nouns.

Unnecessary: For now, the patient's kidneys are functioning *at a normal level*.
Better: For now, the patient's kidneys are functioning *normally*.

The prepositional phrase *at a normal level* can be replaced by the adverb *normally*. Here the phony phrase is introduced by the preposition *for*:

Unnecessary: The bill was legislated in 1995 *for a brief period of time*.
Better: The bill was *briefly* legislated in 1995.

A cluster of non-specific nouns, such as *level, scale, basis, degree*, and *extent*, are connected to phony phrases beginning with *on*, *to*, or other prepositions. Watch for prepositional phrases that include these words, for example, *on/at the international level, on a regular basis, on the larger scale, to a great/considerable degree/extent*. The phrase likely can be replaced by an appropriate adverb.

If you can sum up a prepositional phrase by a one-word adverb or adjective, use the one-word modifier.

Unnecessary: Jindra checks voice mail *on a regular basis*.
Better: Jindra checks her voice mail *regularly*.

A relative clause is adjectival and may sometimes be replaced by a corresponding adjective preceding the noun.

Unnecessary: Most bodybuilders follow a strict diet that is high in protein.

That is high in protein is a relative (adjectival) clause modifying *diet*.

Better: Most bodybuilders follow a strict, high-protein diet.

The Small but Not-So-Beautiful

Even small words, such as prepositions and articles, may be omitted. Writers may think they make an ordinary phrase sound just a little bit more impressive. In the examples below, parentheses indicate words that can be omitted:

He was (the) last out (of) the door.
(The) taking (of) life can never be condoned.

Look at the following passage and consider what can be deleted—big words and small—without changing the meaning of the sentence:

The city of Toronto has one of the most ethnically diverse of cultures in all of North America. The entire city, including the surrounding areas, has a population of 5,500,000 people, and is also the home of a variety of sports teams that play in professional leagues and non-professional leagues.

The word *that* can be used as a pronoun (demonstrative and relative), an adjective, and a subordinating conjunction. It can often be omitted if the subject of the second clause introduced by *that* is different from the subject of the preceding clause. By methodically checking your first draft for unnecessary *that*s, you can often improve sentence flow.

I thought (that) Silas was going to go to the same school (that) his brother went to.

Unravel the meaning of the following statement:

It's certain that that *that* that that person used was wrong.

Those Un-intensives

An *intensive* is a word or phrase that adds emphasis to the word or expression it modifies but has little meaning on its own. In all levels of formal writing, intensives should be avoided if they do not truly add emphasis. The intensives in the following sentence are unneeded:

She is ~~certainly~~ a(n) ~~very~~ impressive speaker.

Words like *certainly* and *very* are overused and may add nothing to the sentence. Many intensives are adverbs modifying verbs or adjectives. In some instances, you can simply use a stronger verb in place of a weak verb and an

If you can delete "clutter words" like *of* or *that*, do so.

Overused intensives include the following:

absolutely	incredibly
actually	inevitably
assuredly	indeed
certainly	interestingly
clearly	markedly
completely	naturally
considerably	of course
definitely	particularly
effectively	significantly
extremely	surely
fundamentally	totally
highly	utterly
in fact	very

Other overused qualifiers include the following:

apparently	overall
arguably	perhaps
basically	quite
essentially	rather
generally	relatively
hopefully	seemingly
in effect	somewhat
in general	sort of
kind of	virtually

intensive, or a stronger adjective in place of the intensive plus a weak adjective; or a better option may be to get rid of the intensive, as in *it was a very strange idea.*

Unnecessary: He was very grateful for his warm reception.
Better: He was gratified by his warm reception.
He appreciated his warm reception.

Words and prepositional phrases that may clutter:

aforementioned	in regard(s) to
amidst	in terms of
amongst	in the final analysis
analogous to	in view of the fact that
as a result of	irregardless
as to	notwithstanding the fact that
at this point in time	oftentimes
cognizant of	pertaining to
consequent to	so as to
despite the fact that	subsequent to
due to the fact that	that
each and every	the majority of
in accordance with	thusly
in as much as	whether or not
in connection with	whilst
in comparison to	with regard(s) to
in conjunction with	with respect to
in reference to	

> Instead of using adverbs like *very*, *highly*, *really*, or *extremely* before adjectives, see if you can find a stronger adjective or simply delete the adverb.

Writing Directly

Writing should get straight to the point. Indirect writing stresses the less important parts of the sentence.

Black Hole Constructions

Inappropriately passive constructions not only use too many words but also place the stress where it doesn't belong, weakening the entire sentence. Other indirect constructions can also weaken a sentence. You can consider them the black holes of writing: they swallow up the substance of the sentence.

1. ***It was . . .***

It was Mary Shelley who wrote *Frankenstein* in 1816.

As simple as this sentence is, it begins weakly by displacing the logical subject, *Mary Shelley*, and substituting *it was*. The sentence is stronger and more direct when the most important noun is made the subject:

> Avoid starting sentences with *it is* or *there are* constructions. Using these weak beginnings may make your reader lose interest.

Mary Shelley wrote *Frankenstein* in 1816.

If a relative pronoun (*who*, *which*, or *that*) follows the displaced subject, consider getting rid of the "empty" subject (*it was*, *there is*, *here is*) and the relative pronoun to make the statement more direct and concise. Occasionally, you may want to use this and similar constructions for rhetorical effect. In such cases, emphasis, rather than directness, may determine your choice.

> Unnecessary: There are a variety of different strategies that you can use to reduce excess verbiage in your writing.
> Better: You can use various strategies to reduce verbiage in your writing.

2. *One of* —a redundancy to be avoided:

> Poor: The path you have chosen is one of danger and uncertainty.
> Better: The path you have chosen is dangerous and uncertain.
> You have chosen a dangerous, uncertain path.

3. *The reason . . . is because*, which is both illogical and redundant:

> Incorrect: The reason Jessica is lucky is because she has a horseshoe on her door.
> Correct: Jessica is lucky because she has a horseshoe on her door.

Numbing Nouns

Writers sometimes fall into the habit of using a weak verb and a corresponding noun rather than a verb that directly expresses the meaning. In each of these cases, a direct verb replaces a weak verb phrase:

Weaker Constructions	Stronger Constructions
I *had a meeting* with my staff, and I am now asking you to *provide a list* of all your clients.	I met with my staff, and now ask you *to list* all your clients.
Inexperienced writers *have a tendency* to be wordy.	Inexperienced writers *tend* to be wordy.
She *made changes* to the document, *making clear* what was ambiguous.	She *changed* the document, *clarifying* ambiguities.
Sam *offered comfort* to Amanda, who *received a failing grade* on her essay.	Sam *comforted* Amanda, who *had failed* her essay.
Canada *made a significant contribution* to the war effort in France and Belgium.	Canada *contributed significantly* to the war effort in France and Belgium.

Notice how many sentences in the sample paragraph in Exercise 17.1 contain weak openings. They affect the entire paragraph, making it hard to read.

Weak verb + noun constructions begin with common verbs like *have*, *make*, or *take* and follow with a noun object, which can usually be made into a strong verb.

Note: in the weak phrase *has an effect on*, where *has* is the verb and *effect* is the noun, remember that the corresponding verb form is *affect*.

> Global warming *affects* shifting major weather patterns. Its *effects* are being widely felt throughout the globe.

Nouns that pile up in a sentence can create a numbing effect. This is especially true with nominals, nouns formed from verbs. There is nothing wrong with using a polysyllabic noun formed from a verb—unless a more concise and direct alternative exists.

Clear expression in literary essays is sometimes a challenge to students who are unfamiliar with terms or tempted to make a point sound complex and, thereby, significant.

> The conflict between Billy and Claggart ultimately serves as a device in the interruption of the reader's attempts at a coherent interpretation of the novel as an ideological message. In addition to problematizing definitive interpretations, this technique effectively secures a lasting relevance for the novel.

The thought in these sentences can be expressed more directly and clearly by omitting words and reducing the number of nominals.

> The conflict between Billy and Claggart challenges a coherent ideological reading of the novel, making definitive readings difficult and ensuring the novel's relevance.

Avoid a succession of long words if shorter, basic words can do the job equally well.

TABLE 17.1	Verb, Nominal, Example	
Verb	Nominal	Example
accumulate	accumulation	Nominal: The (accumulation of) evidence is overwhelming. [The nominal can simply be deleted.]
classify	classification	Nominal: We will now proceed with the classification of Vertebrata. Verb: We will now classify Vertebrata.
intend; install	intention; installation	Nominal: Our intention is to complete the installation of the new system this month. Verb: We intend to finish installing the new system this month.

Euphemisms

Many ancient cultures used **euphemisms** to avoid naming their enemies directly. They believed that naming gave power to those they feared, so they invented

A euphemism is a word or phrase substituted for the actual name of something—usually in order to make it more acceptable or to give it dignity. It is an example of indirect writing.

ways around saying their names; the word *euphemism* comes from the Greek word that means "to use words for good omen." We sometimes do the same today out of consideration and kindness to those who may be suffering, as a way of speaking about taboo subjects and objects, or as a form of satire or irony. For example, the euphemisms for *die* are numerous, *to pass away* or *pass on* being the most common.

Although euphemisms can be used to protect us from the unpleasant, they can be used also to falsely reassure. For example, *urban renewal* avoids the implications of *slum clearance, revenue enhancement* has a more positive ring than *tax increase*, and *collateral losses* attempts to sidestep the fact that civilians have been killed during military action.

We also sometimes use euphemisms to try to give more dignity and a sense of importance to special objects, actions, or vocations: *pre-owned automobile* for *used car* and *job action* for *strike*. The Plain English Campaign once awarded a Golden Bull Award to the writers of a document that described the act of laying a brick in a wall as "install[ing] a component into the structural fabric."

The following classified ad uses some wordy and euphemistic language:

> We are seeking an individual who possesses demonstrated skills and abilities, a sound knowledge base coupled with the experience to provide service to mentally challenged teenagers with "unique" and significant challenging behaviours.

The requirements of the position could have been written in half the words:

> Applicants need proven skills, knowledge, and experience to serve mentally challenged teenagers with challenging behaviours.

A special category of "acceptable euphemisms" are those that we, as a society, agree should be substituted for expressions that have acquired inappropriate connotations. For example, to refer to someone in a wheelchair as a *cripple* inappropriately stresses the disability and its limitations. More sensitively and more accurately, this person *has a physical disability* or *physical challenge* (the person is not the disability).

Exercise **17.4**

In groups, think of 10 euphemisms (they can be ones you've heard of or made-up ones). Then, read them to the rest of the class and have them guess what they are meant to describe.

Exercise **17.5**

The following sentences can be revised for conciseness and directness. Make whatever changes you think are necessary and be prepared to justify them.

1. Tanya has been invited to provide us with a summary of the significant main points of her findings.
2. The totally unexpected tsunami turned the fields into either a large waste land or a large junk yard.
3. Gretta was decidedly overjoyed after being the unexpected recipient of an income tax refund in excess of $1,000.
4. The protagonist of *Life of Pi* was confronted with the necessity of making the decision about whether he wanted to continue on living or not.
5. It was because of her clear, beautiful voice that she was made the winner of the singing contest.
6. The disappearance of even one single species at the lower end of the food chain can have dire adverse effects in many instances on the survival of various other species.
7. Although Copernicus's radical idea that the earth made revolutions around the sun was once considered an extreme heresy and was ridiculed mercilessly by his peers, the idea eventually gained gradual acceptance.
8. The fact is that for many students of above-average intelligence, school can seem tedious and dull so they begin to act up in class and cause other students who are not as smart to miss the important and salient points of the lesson in question.
9. Perhaps in the heat of emotion the act of capital punishment would seem to be a feasible idea, but when you come to think of it rationally, this act would accomplish virtually next to nothing at all.
10. In protest of their salary freeze, all of the teachers who teach at the high school in Oak Bay have made the unanimous decision not to undertake any tasks of a supervisory nature until the school board has conducted a fair and impartial salary review.
11. Vehicles that have the four-way drive feature option are an extremely practical and pragmatic form of transportation for the majority of the Canadian population in this day and age.
12. There are many people in our society today who have serious drug addictions that take complete and utter control over their lives.
13. From the beginning of its conception, Canada has been a country concerned with promoting an active multicultural society, although the reality of unity within the country is still a large, unanswered question in the minds of most of the people of Canada.

(continued)

14. A French scientist by the name of Louis Pasteur was the first individual to make the discovery that microbes were harmful menaces to the well-being and healthy functioning of the human body.

15. The reason yoga allows us to live a healthy lifestyle is due to the fact that it provides a strong basis for the efficient functioning of the body's endocrine system.

Exercise **17.6**

Rewrite the following passage, aiming for concise, direct writing.

Dear Employers,

The Youth Resource Centre, in conjunction with the Federal Human Resource Department of Canada, has opened the Hire-A-Student office once again this summer, staffing Summer Employment Officers working towards finding the best possible student employees for any jobs that you may have available to post with us at the Centre.

Our service, conveniently situated at 147 High Street, is a totally free service to both employers posting jobs in the Centre and to students and youths trying to secure employment opportunities throughout the community. The service is a means for you the employer to help advertise any positions you may have available, and is additionally a way to assist students who are showing initiative in finding possible long-term or limited-term seasonal employment.

We are not a solicitation firm, and this is the point that we need to emphasize to the greatest extent. Our service is absolutely free of charge, and our intention is first and foremost to try and find employment for students who seem serious about working, as well as to offer a free alternative to posting jobs in newspapers and ad agencies that could end up costing you an excessive amount of money through advertising ventures.

Working Toward Precision: Wise Word Choices

For most writing assignments in college and university, you will be required to use **formal writing**, also known as formal **diction**. Because you may be used to writing informally when using the Internet or when text messaging—even, perhaps, from your high school English courses—you may puzzle over the ways that informal writing differs from formal writing. In informal writing

- language may be close to speech or chatty with **colloquialisms**, **idiom**, or even slang

- contractions are acceptable (e.g., *don't, can't, shouldn't, it's*)
- the first-person (*I, me*) and second-person (*you*) voice may be used
- sentence fragments may be used occasionally for dramatic effect
- short paragraphs are the rule rather than the exception
- citations for research sources are not given

In your essays, you should avoid contractions, unless your instructor tells you otherwise. Certainly, unless you are quoting someone, you should always avoid slang, colloquialisms, and jargon. For example, you would not use any of the following in a formal essay:

do drugs	pan out
down side	price tag
fall for	put a positive spin (on something)
give the green light	put (someone) down
go to great lengths	put on hold
go overboard	quick fix
grab the reader's attention	stressed (out)
mindset	upfront
no way	the way to go
obsess (about something)	tune out
okay	way more (of something—*a lot* is also
opt for	colloquial)

Diction is related to word choices and level of language; formal and informal writing are examples of different kinds of diction.

Colloquialisms are words and expressions acceptable in conversation but not in formal writing.

An idiom is a phrase whose meaning is understood only within the context of the phrase itself. For example, *his bark is worse than his bite* can be understood only by looking at the overall meaning and not by the meanings of the individual words.

Avoid merely qualitative words and phrases, such as *great, incredible, beautiful, terrible*, and the like; they are non-specific. You also should refrain from using words and expressions that might suggest a gender, sexual, racial, cultural, or other kind of bias.

Of course, your word choices involve much more than thinking about the level of formality. Effective writers choose their words and phrases carefully. In the following three examples from student essays, the writers did not choose carefully:

The mass production of plastics and ready-to-use products is growing at a *stagnating* [sic *staggering*] rate.

Avoid using informal verbs such as *saw, has seen*, etc., when you mean *resulted in or occurred* (e.g., *The policy that was implemented two years ago has seen a 40 per cent drop in violent crime.* Revised: *The policy that was implemented two years ago has resulted in a 40 per cent drop in violent crime.*).

Note: *staggering* is informal; the writer could have used *rapid, rapidly increasing*, or *exponential*, or a specific rate, such as *doubling every five years*.

The Shakespearean sonnet is an *oppressed* [sic *compressed*] form of poetry.
After successfully completing police officer training camp, the applicant can finally *swear* [sic *be sworn in*] and become a police officer.

Exercise **17.7**

Read the following paragraphs taken from the essay "An enviro's case for seal hunt," found in Chapter 2. Highlight or underline examples of informal language use and then try to provide more concise wording for these examples.

> There was an article about a campaign that a group called Respect for Animals is waging to convince consumers to boycott Canadian seafood products. The magazine also carried two huge advertisements from the same organization.
>
> The Newfoundland seal hunt is transparently and demonstrably sustainable and humane. There are roughly half a million people in Newfoundland and Labrador, and nearly six million harp seals, which is almost three times as many seals as when I was a kid.
>
> Here's one of those obligatory disclosures: over the years, several environmental organizations—the Sierra Club, the David Suzuki Foundation, Greenpeace, etc.—have subsidized my preoccupation with things that move in the water by having me do research projects for them and so on. With that out of the way, I can now say, if it isn't obvious already, that it's the seal hunt's opponents who turn my stomach.

Rather than make extreme blunders, more often you choose a word that is not quite precise for your purpose. These kinds of "near misses" can distract or confuse the reader. You should not let the search for the exact word prevent you from fully expressing your ideas in a first draft. But when revising, you should look up the meanings of all words you're in doubt about—even if you're only a little unsure.

You can use a thesaurus to look for words similar in meaning to avoid repeating a word too often. But a thesaurus should always be used along with a reliable dictionary. Most thesauruses, such as the ones that come with word-processing programs, simply list words similar in meaning; they do not provide connotations for the words.

Some dictionaries help you to be precise not only by defining the main entry but also by providing distinctions among similar words. In addition to illustrating the way a word is used by making examples, many mid-sized dictionaries distinguish the main entry from other words with similar meanings. For example, the *Gage Canadian Dictionary*, which lists more than six meanings for the adjective *effective*, also defines two words similar to *effective* in meaning but different in connotation:

Syn. adj. 1. **Effective, effectual, efficient** = producing an effect. **Effective**, usually describing things, emphasizes producing a wanted or expected effect: *several new drugs are effective in treating serious diseases*. **Effectual**, describing people or things, emphasizes having produced or having the

Writers often use words that have specific associations or implications. A word's *connotation* includes its possible meanings in its given context.

power to produce the exact effect or result intended: *his efforts are more energetic than effectual*. **Efficient**, often describing people, emphasizes being able to produce the effect wanted or intended without wasting energy, time, etc.: *A skilled surgeon is highly efficient*.

Similarly, the *Student's Oxford Canadian Dictionary*, which lists seven meanings for the adjective *nice*, offers the following examples of words that may be more appropriate or more forceful than *nice* in certain contexts:

we had a delightful/splendid/enjoyable time
a satisfying/delicious/exquisite meal
a fashionable/stylish/elegant/chic outfit
this is a cozy/comfortable/attractive room
she is kind/friendly/likeable/amiable
our advisor is compassionate/understanding/sympathetic
a thoughtful/considerate/caring gesture

When you read an unfamiliar work, it is a good idea to try to guess a word's meaning by its context and then check it in a dictionary if you need to. As a writer, you should *always* check a word's meaning if you're even a little unsure whether it's the right word.

Precision and Logic

Choosing your words carefully will help make your writing precise. But sometimes, imprecision may result from illogical thinking or from writing down an idea quickly. To be sure whether something you've written really makes sense, you need to look carefully at the relationship among the parts of the sentence, especially at the relationship between the subject and predicate. **Faulty predication** exists if a verb cannot be logically connected to its subject. In general, avoid the phrases *is when* and *is where* after a subject in sentences that *define* something. For example, in the following sentence *faulty predication*, which is a thing, is illogically referred to as a time or a place:

Faulty predication occurs where a verb cannot be logically linked to its subject.

Incorrect: Faulty predication is when/where a verb cannot be logically connected to its subject.
Correct: Faulty predication occurs where [i.e., in a sentence] a verb is not logically connected to its subject.
Faulty predication is an illogical juxtaposing of a subject and a verb.

Consider this comment on the setting of Joseph Conrad's *Heart of Darkness*:

The Congo represents an inward journey for the character Marlow.

The Congo is a country as well as a river. How can a country or a river represent a journey? Of course, a *trip* through a country or on a river could represent an inner journey.

In one kind of faulty predication, an inanimate object is falsely linked to a human action.

Some opponents claim that PE programs are unwilling to accommodate the needs of all students.

The programs aren't "unwilling," since this implies a will, though teachers or administrators may be unwilling.

Some opponents claim that the administrators of PE programs are unwilling to accommodate the needs of all students.

Sound should also play a role in word choice. You should avoid placing words with similar sounds in close proximity (the "echo effect").

Endorphins enable the body to heal itself and *gain pain* relief.

You should also be wary of unintentional puns in a work of scholarship:

The first experiments in music therapy were *noted* during World War I.

Also, keep the **tone** objective; do not write ironically or sarcastically, though you may be tempted to do so in an argumentative essay. Your reader may not share your attitude. Besides, the hallmark of both expository and argumentative writing is an objective voice, one that is unbiased.

Inappropriate tone: It is well known that college students under stress need to exercise their livers on the occasional Friday night.

Tone shows the writer's attitude toward the subject.

Exercise **17.8**

Circle every example of informal diction in the following paragraph; then, rewrite the paragraph using formal diction. There may be one or two places where the word or phrase is colloquial but necessary due to context or the fact it can't be rephrased easily.

> Hosting the Olympic Games is a once-in-a-lifetime opportunity, and it seems like a great idea. It would create world recognition for a world-class city, helping to really put it on the map. On top of that, it would be a fun and exciting time for the citizens of the surrounding area. However, after sober second thought, it is clear that while the Games might pay for themselves, who will pay for the upgrades necessary to get the city in good shape for the Games? Even with the government chipping in for a fair amount of the costs, because that city would be dealing in billions of dollars, even a small chunk of that cost is a lot of money. These small chunks would come from the pockets of the taxpayer, some of whom are not big fans of the Games at all. But although these direct costs are bound to be steep, it is the hidden costs of the Games that will be the real killer.

Verbs with Vitality

Verbs are the action words in a sentence. Look at the verbs in your sentences. Could you replace them with stronger, more descriptive verbs? Could you re-place verbs like *be* and *have*, which convey a state or condition, with verbs of action? Common verbs, such as *do*, *make*, *go*, and *get*, are not specific. Could you replace them with more precise or emphatic verbs?

The most common verb in English, *to be*, takes many different forms as an irregular verb—*am, is, are, was, were, will be*, etc.—and appears frequently as a helping verb. Your writing will be more concise if you omit the forms *being* or *to be* whenever they are unnecessary.

> The results of the study can be interpreted as ~~being~~ credible.
> She dreamed of a carriage ~~being~~ pulled by two fine horses.
> Hypnosis has been proven ~~to be~~ an effective therapy for some people.
> In 313 BCE Christianity was declared ~~to be~~ the official religion of Rome.

If you can easily omit a form of *to be*, do so.

As people put on the spot by journalists and the public, politicians some-times choose vague language to avoid committing themselves to statements they may regret later. A more cynical view suggests that abstract, indefinite language enables them to say little while appearing informed and in control. Notice the lack of specificity in the following comment by former American politician Colin Powell, reported on *Fox News Sunday* in an interview with Chris Wallace on May 16, 2004:

> "We knew that the ICRC had concerns, and in accordance with the matter in which the ICRC does its work, it presented those concerns directly to the command in Baghdad. And I know that some corrective action was taken with respect to those concerns."

When checking whether a subject fits with its predicate, ensure that the subject can perform the action that the verb describes.

Verbs and nouns are the two most important parts of speech. The verbs you choose can weaken or strengthen your prose. Choose verbs carefully, pre-ferring active to static ones and deleting verb forms like *being* and *to be* when they are unneeded.

Exercise 17.9

Read the following paragraph and underline places where you would revise verbs to make them more expressive and descriptive.

> By the 1800s, inventions were beginning to put people out of work. One of the first inventions that resulted in rebellion was in the craft guild. In 1801, Joseph Jacquard became known as the inventor of the Jacquard loom. This loom was capable of being programmed by pre-punched cards, which made it possible to create clothing design patterns. This invention led to the creation of the Luddites, who were a group made up from the craft guild. These people were

(continued)

against any type of manufacturing technology and went about burning down several factories that were using this new technology. The Luddites were around only for a couple of years, but the name Luddite is still used to describe people who are resistant to new technologies. The Jacquard loom was, in effect, an invention that replaced people. It could do great designs quickly and without making any errors. The replacement of people by machines was beginning.

Exercise 17.10

Suggest how the following passage could be improved by using more specific language and by omitting unnecessary words and phrases.

> The time period between 1985 and 1989 was a difficult one for graffiti artists in New York City. This was a time when graffiti barely stayed alive because of the harsh laws and efforts of the Metropolitan Transit Authority, which is known as the MTA. This period was called the period of the "Die Hards" because of the small number of die-hard artists who were able to keep graffiti from dying out completely. As a result of the measures of the MTA against graffiti art and artists, there was a lack of paint available for use and the level of enforcement was extremely high. The only important thing that was happening during these years was the use of markers for tagging. These tags were usually small, of poor artistic quality, and were finished quickly by the artists. These tags can be seen today at some bus stops and in some washrooms throughout the city.

Prepackaged Goods: Clichés

Expressions considered clichés today were in their prime a veritable breath of fresh air. (Did you spot the clichés in the previous sentence?) If commentary on the cliché were to be made in clichés, you would find the prose wordy and confusing:

> However, with the passage of time (more years than you can shake a stick at), they became the stuff of idle minds until after time immemorial they assumed the mantle of respectability and were accepted verbatim as par for the course. Writers worth their salt should avoid clichés like the plague or they will stop all readers with a good head on their shoulders dead in their tracks (to call a spade a spade and to give the devil his due).

Exercise **17.11**

In this short passage adapted from a travel feature, find evidence of tired and predictable writing, citing particular words and phrases that could be made more effective or accurate. Although newspaper features use informal writing, it should be descriptive and concrete. How could you make this passage more interesting?

> We're up and about at the crack of dawn, and from outside our cabin we can see the peak of a small mountain looming in the distance. Our ship glides effortlessly over the fathomless blue sea, and soon the mountain's craggy features come into view.
>
> "It's breakfast, honey," my wife, Jen, sings from inside the cabin, and soon our impeccably dressed waiter knocks softly on our door. As we sit down to partake of the delectable repast, I feel as though I could pinch myself. Yes, here we are, aboard a luxurious liner, about to drop anchor off the coast of one of the world's most fabled isles.

Clichés are overworked and unoriginal phrases. Inexperienced writers may reach for them in a vain attempt to "spice up" their writing. Clichés may be *dead metaphors*: expressions drained of their novelty through overuse. Although they may appear in some informal writing, they are poor substitutes for informative, imaginative words.

A cliché is a word or phrase that, though often true, has become overused, such as *green with envy*.

❯ Common Words That Confuse

English has many word pairs that are confusing either because the two words look similar (for example, *affect* and *effect*) or because they have similar, but not identical, uses (for example, *amount* and *number*)—or both. In most cases, the dictionary is best for problems related to meaning, but **usage** can be more complicated. The words below are the "Top Twenty-Five" that continue to give student writers the most trouble. Hints and examples are provided to help you distinguish them.

Usage is the customary and accepted way that a word is used.

For a guide to spelling, there is no better resource than the dictionary; if you have the slightest doubt about the spelling of a word, consult a dictionary—don't rely on a spell-checker.

1. accept, except. Accept is a verb meaning "to receive, to take what is offered." **Except** is a preposition meaning "other than" or "leaving out."

Hint: Think of the "crossing out" connotation of "x" in "except" to remind you that "except" means "leaving out."
Example: The bargaining committee accepted all the terms except the last one.

2. affect, effect. Affect is a verb meaning "to influence or have an effect on." **Effect**, a noun, means "a result." As a verb, effect is less often used; it means "to bring about" or "to cause"—not "to have an effect on."

> Hint: Try substituting "influence" in the sentence; if it fits your intended meaning, "affect" is the word you want.
> Example: The news of Michael Jordan's return to basketball greatly affected his fans. The effect was also felt at the box office; an immediate hike in ticket prices was effected.

3. allot, a lot. Allot, a verb, means "to portion out"; **a lot** can be an adverb (I sleep a lot) or a noun (I need a lot of sleep) meaning "a great deal." *A lot* is too informal for most academic writing; you should use the more formal *a great deal, much, many*, or similar substitutes. The one-word spelling, *alot*, is incorrect.

> Example: My parents allotted me $500 spending money for the term, which was not a lot considering my shopping habit. [informal]

4. all right, alright. All right is all right, just as "a lot" is a lot better than "alot"; **alright** and "alot" are not words.

5. allude, elude. Both are verbs, but they mean different things. **Allude** (to) means "to refer to something briefly or indirectly"; **elude** means "to avoid or escape, usually through a clever manoeuvre or strategy." *Allude* should be followed by *to*: e.g., *In the poem, Hardy alluded to the end of the century.*

> Hint: *Allude* is the verb from which the noun *allusion* (a kind of reference, see **allusion**) is formed; you can associate the *e* in *elude* with the *e* in *escape*.
> Example: In his prison memoirs, the bank robber alluded to the time in the desert when he eluded capture by disguising himself as a cactus.

6. allusion, illusion. You may have come across the literary use of **allusion**, meaning a historical, religious, mythic, literary, or other kind of outside reference used to reveal character or theme in a work. An **illusion** is something apparently seen that is not real or is something that gives a false impression.

> Hint: Since the most common mistake is misspelling *allusion* as *illusion* in literary essays, you could remember that *allusion*, meaning an outside reference, always begins with *al*.
> Examples: The title of Nathanael West's novel *The Day of the Locust* is an allusion to the book of Exodus in the Bible.
> Optical illusions often use graphics to fool our senses.

7. among, between. The simple distinction is that **between** refers to two persons or things and **among** to more than two.

Examples: The senator found himself between a rock and a hard place. Ms. O'Grady stood among her adoring students for the school picture.

Between may be the obvious choice even if more than two things are involved. For example, *Interlibrary loans are permitted between campuses.* Even though a number of campuses may be part of the interlibrary loan system, any one exchange takes place between two campuses.

8. amount, number. Use **amount** to refer to things that can't be counted; **number** refers to countable objects.

Hint: Think of using numbers when you count.
Example: The number of errors in this essay reveals the amount of care you took in writing it.

9. beside, besides. Beside is a preposition meaning "next to," "adjoining"; **besides** has several meanings as a preposition; as an adverb, **besides** means "in addition (to)."

Hint: Think of the extra *s* in besides as an additional letter to remind you of "in addition to."
Example: Beside the telephone was the telephone book, besides which she had an address book.

10. bias, biased. Bias is a noun that refers to a "tendency to judge unfairly"; **biased** is an adjective that means "having or showing a preferential attitude." A person can have a bias (a thing); be a biased person (adjective modifying "person"); or can be biased (predicate adjective after a linking verb). A person cannot be bias. Also, a person is biased or has a bias *against* (not *to* or *for*) something or someone.

Example: His bias against the Rastafarian lifestyle caused him to overlook some of its ideals.

11. cite, sight, site. To cite, a verb, is "to refer to an outside source." (The complete naming of the source itself is a citation.) **Sight** (noun or verb) refers to seeing, one of the five senses. **Site**, when used as a noun, is a location or place (usually of some importance). The most common error in essays is the use of *site* when *cite* is meant.

Hint: Remember that *cite* is a verb referring to "the act of giving a citation"; *site* is "where something is situated or sits."
Example: She said the ruins were excavated in 1926, citing as proof the historical plaque that commemorated the site.

12. e.g., i.e. E.g. is an abbreviation for the Latin *exempli gratia*, meaning "for the sake of example"; **i.e.** is an abbreviation for the Latin *id est* meaning "that is." Use "e.g." before one or more examples; use "i.e." if you want to elaborate on or clarify a preceding statement. In both cases, use a period after each letter and a comma after the abbreviation. Because they are abbreviations, they should be avoided in formal writing.

> Hint: The first letter in *example* tells you that examples should follow "e.g.".
> Example: J.K. Rowling defied the common formula for success in the children's book market by writing long novels, e.g., *Harry Potter and the Goblet of Fire* and *Harry Potter and the Order of the Phoenix*. Some of Rowling's novels have episodic plots that contain many well-developed characters, i.e., they tend to be long.

13. fewer, less. Fewer is the quantitative adjective of comparison and refers to things that can be counted; **less** is the qualitative adjective of comparison, referring to amount and things that can be measured.

> Examples: Don't believe the notice on the mayonnaise jar: "Contains 40% less calories." Calories can be counted.
> There were fewer than a dozen people at the nomination meeting.
> The less said about his defection, the better.

14. good, well. Good may be an adjective, noun, or adverb. When used as an adjective, it should clearly modify a noun (e.g., a good story) or be used as a subject complement (predicate adjective, e.g., the child was good until bedtime). It cannot be used as a predicate adjective after verbs that express an action, although it is frequently heard in speech, especially in sports (*I was hitting the ball good*).

> Incorrect: She beat the batter good.
> Correct: She is a good cook and beat the batter well.

As an adjective, **well** means "in good health" or "satisfactory." As an adverb, it has several meanings, including "thoroughly" and "satisfactorily."

> Hint: Do not use *good* as a predicate adjective after an action verb; you may use it before a noun or right after an intransitive (linking) verb.
> Examples: Making a good donation to the Children's Hospital made the corporation look good. [i.e., "appear altruistic" not "appear good-looking"]
> Although just having come out of the hospital, she looked well and continued to feel well during her recovery. [*Well* is used as an adjective after linking verbs and means "healthy."]

15. its, it's. Its is a possessive adjective meaning "belonging to it" and is formed from the personal pronoun *it*. Remember that personal pronouns are never spelled with an apostrophe. **It's** is the contraction for *it is*, the apostrophe indicating that the letter *i* is left out.

> Hint: Try substituting *it is* if you're having problems identifying the correct form; if it fits, then use *it's*; if it doesn't, use *its*. [*Its* is usually followed by a noun.]
> Example: It's foolish to judge a book by its cover.

16. lay, lie. Both are verbs. **Lay** is a transitive verb, which must always be followed by a direct object (either a noun or a pronoun). It is *incorrect* to say, "I'm going to lay down to rest." **Lie** is an intransitive verb; it is not followed by an object.

> Hint: You always lay something down, as a hen does an egg. Then it lies there.
> Examples: He lay the baby in the crib before going to lie down.
> Contrast: He had lain on the ground for 20 minutes before someone noticed him. [Lain is the past participle of lie.]
> Kim Campbell laid to rest the notion that a woman couldn't be prime minister. [Laid is the past participle of lay.]

17. led, lead. **Led** and **lead** are forms of the irregular verb **to lead** (long); the present tense is also **lead**. However, the past tense and the past participle are **lĕd** (short). Writers may become confused by the noun *lead*, the metal, which looks like *to lead*, but is pronounced like *led*. Therefore, when they come to write the past tense *led*, they may wrongly substitute the noun *lead*, rather than the verb.

> Hint: Don't be led astray by thinking there is an *a* in *led*.
> Example: Although she led in the polls by a 2:1 margin three months ago, today she leads by only a slight margin.

18. loose, lose. **Loose** is the adjective meaning "not tight"; **lose** is a verb meaning "not to be able to find," or "to be defeated."

> Hint: When you lose something, it is lost. *Lost* is spelled with one *o*.
> Example: If you don't tighten that loose button, you're going to lose it.

19. onset, outset. Both are nouns that mean a "beginning." **Outset** means "setting out," for example, on a journey or to do something; you can also use the phrase "at the outset" to refer to the early events of a narrative or play. **Onset** refers to a force or condition that comes upon one.

> Example: At the outset of my fourth decade, I experienced the onset of mild osteoarthritis.

20. than, then. **Than** is a conjunction used in comparisons (He's happier than he knows). **Then** is an adverb with temporal connotations meaning "consequently," "at that time," "after that," etc.

Hint: If you're comparing one thing to another, use *than*. *Then* "tells when."

Example: Warren said he was better at darts than Mark, and then he challenged him to a game to prove it.

21. their, there, they're. Their is a possessive adjective meaning "belonging to them"; **there** is an adverb meaning "in that place"; **they're** is the contraction of *they are*, the apostrophe indicating that the letter *a* is left out.

Hint: If you're uncertain about *they're*, substitute *they are*; *there* (meaning "in that place") is spelled the same as *here* ("in this place") with the letter *t* added.

Example: There is no excuse for the rowdy behaviour in there; they're supposed to be in their rooms.

22. to, too. To is a preposition indicating "direction towards"; **too** is an adverb meaning "also."

Hint: *To* will usually be followed by a noun or pronoun as part of a prepositional phrase; substitute *also* for *too*.

Example: The next time you go to the store, may I come along, too?

23. usage, use. Many writers overuse **usage**, which refers to "a customary or habitual pattern or practice." It applies to conventions of groups of people, such as "language usage of the English." Usage shouldn't be used simply to mean a repeated action.

Incorrect: The usage of fax machines and email has allowed businesses to increase their efficiency.

Example: I have no use for people who are always correcting my usage of *whom*.

24. who's, whose. Who's is the contraction of *who is*, the apostrophe indicating the omission of the letter *i*. **Whose** is the possessive adjective meaning "belonging to whom."

Hint: Try substituting *who is*. If it fits, then *who's* is the correct form.

Examples: Whose turn is it to do the dishes?
Who's going to do the dishes tonight?

25. you're, your. You're is the contraction of *you are*; **your** is a possessive adjective that means "belonging to you."

Hint: Try substituting *you are*. If it fits, then *you're* is the correct form.

Example: You're going to be sorry if you don't take your turn and do the dishes tonight.

Here is a list of 50 additional words that often give students trouble:

Don't Say . . .	When You Mean . . .
adolescents	adolescence (the time one is an adolescent)
aforementioned	this/previously stated
around	about (in reference to numbers)
associated to	associated with
attribute to	contribute to
avoid	prevent
base off/around	base on
conscience	conscious
continuous	continual
council	counsel
could of/would of	could have/would have
different than	different from
downfall	disadvantage
downside	disadvantage
entirety of	all
farther	further (*farther* applies to physical distance)
half to	have to
imply	infer
insure	ensure
irregardless	regardless
lifestyle	life
like	as
locality/location	place
majority of	most
man	human/humanity
manpower	resources
mindset	belief
misfortunate	unfortunate
multiple	many
none the less	nonetheless
obsess about	to be obsessed about
obtain	attain
overexaggerate	exaggerate
passed	past
popular	common
principal	principle
prior/prior to	before
references	refers to (*references* is a plural noun)
reoccur	recur
seize	cease

so	very
thanks to	due to
that	who/whom/where, etc.
thru	through
till	until
to transition	to change
upon	on
weather	whether
were	where
which	who/whom

As you progress through your course, you may find other groupings of words that you have problems with. Add them, along with definitions and correct usage, to the list above.

Exercise **17.12**

Choose 10 of the words from the lists above that you know give you trouble. Find the definitions of these words and then write sentences using the words correctly.

Example:

Amount: the quantity of something; used for non-count nouns

The amount of rain that fell in June this year is equal to all the rain that fell last year.

Number: the quantity of something; used for count nouns

It is hard to count the number of raindrops that fall into a cup.

❭ Providing Depth: Variety and Emphasis

When you revise an early draft to improve clarity, you will likely find opportunities to make your prose more interesting. Variety and emphasis in your writing will make what is competent also *compelling*. Variety and emphasis are worthwhile goals in all forms of essays: personal, literary, argumentative, and expository.

Sentence Variety

Length

You can vary the lengths of sentences for rhetorical effect. Just as short paragraphs suggest underdeveloped points, short, choppy sentences could suggest

You should avoid writing too many overly short or overly long sentences. If you see you've done this, you can use the grammatical rules to combine short sentences or break longer sentences into shorter ones.

a lack of content. On the other hand, several long sentences in a row could confuse a reader.

That doesn't mean you should write only sentences that are between 15 and 20 words long. Although sentence length alone is no measure of readability, consider revision if you find you have written more than two very short or very long sentences in a row.

To connect short sentences you can use appropriate conjunctions. Simple sentences can be joined by one of the seven coordinating conjunctions. If the idea in one sentence is less important than the idea in the sentence before or after it, use the subordinating conjunction that best expresses the relationship between the sentences. You can join independent clauses by using a semicolon or a colon.

Coordinating conjunctions are introduced on page 338; subordinating conjunctions are introduced on page 338.

Using semicolons to separate independent clauses is discussed on pages 372–3. Using colons to separate independent clauses is discussed on page 377.

To review rules for joining sentences and clauses, see page 351.

Exercise **17.13**

The following paragraph consists of too many short sentences. Using the strategies mentioned above, revise the paragraph to make it more effective.

During the earth's long history, there have been various periods of glaciation. [2] This fact is well known. [3] There is also evidence of one great glacial event. [4] It is possible that the earth was once completely covered by ice and snow. [5] Skeptics argue this is impossible. [6] They say that the earth could never have become this cold. [7] The idea of the tropics being frozen over is unlikely, they believe.

You can also join independent clauses by using a conjunctive adverb or transitional phrase, ensuring that a semicolon precedes the connecting word or phrase. You may be able to grammatically connect phrases or clauses through a parallel relationship, such as apposition. The second phrase or clause could also modify the preceding word, phrase, or clause—for example, a relative (adjectival) clause could give information about a preceding noun clause.

The rule for punctuating appositives is on pages 366–7.

Exercise **17.14**

The following paragraph consists of sentences that are too long. Using the strategies mentioned above, revise the paragraph to make it more effective.

Finding a definition for "the homeless" is difficult, but the most common definition, which is used both in the media and in current research, defines the homeless as those who lack visible shelter or use public shelters. [2] Literature about homelessness is sparse, and it was not until the 1980s that the incidence of homelessness began to be reported in the media, but homelessness has existed for centuries, and literature on the subject dates back to the feudal period in Europe.

Generally speaking, you waste space when you begin a new sentence by repeating part of the previous sentence, or by beginning a new paragraph by recapitulating part of the previous one. Although repetition can be used to build coherence, it should not create redundancy.

> In 1970, Gordon O. Gallup created the mirror test. This test was designed to determine whether or not animals are self-aware.

> Revised:

> In 1970, Gordon O. Gallup created the mirror test, designed to determine whether animals are self-aware.

When checking your work for overly long sentences, consider breaking up sentences with more than two independent clauses or one independent clause and more than two dependent clauses. See if the relationships between the clauses are clear. If they are not, divide the sentences where clauses are joined by conjunctions, by transitional words and phrases, or by relative pronouns.

Structural Variety

You can experiment with phrasal openings to sentences. Consider beginning the occasional sentence with a prepositional phrase, a verbal phrase, or an absolute phrase instead of the subject of the sentence.

A *prepositional phrase* begins with a preposition followed by a noun or pronoun; it is adjectival or adverbial and modifies the closest noun (adjectival) or verb (adverbial). A *participial phrase*, which ends in *–ing*, *–ed*, or *–en*, is a verbal phrase acting as an adjective. An *infinitive phrase*, which is preceded by *to*, can act adjectivally or adverbially. An *absolute phrase*, consisting of a noun/pronoun and a partial verb form, modifies the entire sentence.

In this short excerpt from an essay about the death of a moth, Virginia Woolf uses a prepositional phrase opening, an absolute phrase that introduces an independent clause, and two verbal phrase openings:

> *After a time*, <u>tired by his dancing</u> apparently, he settled on the window ledge in the sun, and **the queer spectacle being at an end**, I forgot about him. Then, <u>looking up</u>, my eye was caught by him. He was trying to resume his dancing, but seemed either so stiff or so awkward that he could only flutter to the bottom of the window-pane; and when he tried to fly across it, he failed.

Note the types of modifiers: *After a time*: prepositional phrase; <u>tired by his dancing</u>; <u>looking up</u>: verbal phrases; **the queer spectacle being at an end**: absolute phrase.

Creating Emphasis

Writers may create **emphasis** by presenting main points or details in a particular order. Two kinds of sentences vary in the order in which they present the main idea: periodic and cumulative sentences.

Relative clauses are discussed on pages 406–7.

Prepositional phrases are discussed on page 350.

Make sure that when you use a participial phrase at the beginning of a sentence that you include the word it is intended to modify so that it does not dangle. (See Dangling Modifiers, page 413.)

Emphasis is the importance or stress that you place on an idea. A word or phrase will have greater or less emphasis depending on where it appears in the sentence. You can begin a sentence with detail and follow with the main idea or begin with the main idea and follow with detail. These two different orders will produce contrastive effects.

Periodic sentences begin with modifiers—words, phrases, or clauses—before the independent clause. *Cumulative sentences* work the other way: they begin with an independent clause and are followed by modifying or parallel words, phrases, or clauses. While periodic sentences delay the main idea, creating anticipation, cumulative sentences develop the main idea by drawing it out. Many sentences are slightly or moderately periodic or cumulative, depending on whether the writer has begun with modifiers or ended with them. However, a writer can employ either periodic or cumulative sentences to create a specific effect. Independent clauses are shown by italics below.

Periodic:

Unlike novelists and playwrights, who lurk behind the scenes while distracting our attention with the puppet show of imaginary characters—and unlike the scholars and journalists, who quote the opinions of others and take cover behind the hedges of neutrality—*the essayist has nowhere to hide* (Scott Russell Sanders, "The Singular First Person").

Cumulative:

The root of all evil is that we all want this spiritual gratification, this flow, this apparent heightening of life, this knowledge, this valley of many-colored grass, even grass and light prismatically decomposed, giving ecstasy (D.H. Lawrence, *Studies in Classic American Literature*).

A writer can delay the main idea generating tension also by beginning with a prepositional phrase:

Behind the deconstructionists' dazzling cloud of language lie certain more or less indisputable facts (John Gardner, *The Art of Fiction*).

Other ways to achieve emphasis include parallel structures and repetition—techniques that also help in paragraph coherence—and rhythms that call the reader's attention to important ideas. The end of a sentence in itself provides emphasis, since a reader naturally slows down when approaching the last part of a sentence and pauses slightly between sentences.

The two paragraphs below employ parallel structures, repetition, and rhythm for emphasis.

When the subject is delayed in this kind of construction, ensure that the verb agrees with the subject, which will follow the verb rather than precede it. (See Finding the Subject, page 388.)

A. My professors, many of whom were to become very famous, did not tend to be philosophic and did not dig back into the sources of the new language and categories they were using. They thought that these were scientific discoveries like any others, which were to be used in order to make further discoveries. They were very much addicted to abstractions and generalizations, as Tocqueville predicted they would be. They believed in scientific progress and appeared (there may have been an element of boasting and self-irony in this) to be convinced that they were on the verge of a historic breakthrough in the social sciences, equivalent to that scored in the sixteenth and seventeenth centuries in the natural sciences . . . . These teachers were literally inebriated by the unconscious and values. And they were also sure that scientific progress would be related to social and political progress (Allan Bloom, *The Closing of the American Mind*).

Bloom employs the most common structural pattern of subject–verb–object in all his sentences, establishing a predictable rhetorical pattern that complements the predictability and uniformity of his professors that he wants to stress. Thus, *my professors*, the subject in the first sentence, is replaced by the pronoun *they* in the following three sentences; in the fourth sentence, *they* is the subject of two clauses. To avoid too many identical openings, Bloom continues with the same rhythm but varies the subject slightly: the last two sentences begin with *these teachers* and *and they*, respectively.

> **B.** Tales about Pythagoras flew to him and stuck like iron filings to a magnet. He was said, for example, to have appeared in several places at once and to have been reincarnated many times. Taken literally, this idea can be consigned to the same overflowing bin which contains the story that he had a golden thigh; but taken figuratively, it is an understatement. Pythagoras—or at least Pythagoreanism—was everywhere and still is (Anthony Gottlieb, *The Dream of Reason* 21).

The most obvious technique in paragraph B is the use of figurative language: Gottlieb uses a simile in the first sentence (*like iron filings to a magnet*) and a metaphor in the third sentence (*overflowing bin*). However, he effectively uses sentence length and rhythm to make the paragraph more appealing still. The paragraph is framed by short simple sentences that stress Pythagoras's importance. The middle sentences develop the main idea through examples. Gottlieb's final sentence, though the shortest, contains strong stresses: the use of dashes allows the writer to repeat the name Pythagoras without seeming redundant, while heavy accents fall on the final two words.

〉 Proofreading: Perfection *Is* Possible

In publishing, *editing* refers to the revising of a work before it is formatted, whether for a book, a newspaper, a magazine or journal, or other medium. **Proofreading** refers to the final check of the formatted material—done either on screen or in the form of paper "proofs" printed from the formatter's electronic files.

While someone who edits and suggests revisions to a document is mainly concerned with improving it, the proofreader is looking for errors. The proofreader is the document's last line of defence before it falls under the public eye. Ironically, poor proofreading may be the *first* thing noticed in the published document.

In spite of its importance, the last proofreading to ensure that there are no errors is usually one of the neglected stages for student writers working under deadline to submit an essay. Exhausted from the final efforts of putting the

When you *edit* or revise, you try to improve your work's structure and readability, or solidify your ideas; when you *proofread*, you try to catch all mistakes to provide a clean copy for your reader. Doing so will make a favourable first impression.

essay together, students may think that tiny errors are unimportant compared to other parts of the process stressed throughout the term. However, distracting errors may strike your instructor in a completely different light. They could be seen as careless, a sign of a lack of effort. Your instructor could become annoyed by many small mistakes and even become more critical of other parts of the essay.

Whether or not proofreading is seen as tedious, it is best performed as a mechanical process. By taking a thorough and systematic approach to the essay at this stage, you can be more confident that the work of many hours, days, or even weeks will be more readable to the person marking it.

You may think that tiny errors are unimportant compared to other parts of the process stressed throughout the term. However, your instructor could see them as careless, a sign of a lack of effort.

Proofreading Methods

Documents may be read *in teams* with one person reading aloud while the other follows the printed copy silently. When it is your work being proofread, it is best if you read aloud since you may more easily catch errors you've missed as a writer. This method works on the principle that two readers are twice as likely as one person to spot errors. It may also be more enjoyable than working alone. Clearly, it works only if a second reader is available and both readers are knowledgeable about writing and committed to the task.

Reading forward is the method of reading the paper aloud or to yourself but more slowly and carefully than you would usually do, paying attention both to the words and to the punctuation. Because it can be hard to concentrate solely on the words apart from the meaning, it's best to read through the essay at least once for meaning and then at least once again for spelling and other errors.

Reading backward is the method by which you start at the end and read to the beginning word by word or sentence by sentence. This technique forces your attention on the writing; it works well for catching spelling errors. However, it is time-consuming, and you may miss some punctuation and other "between the words" errors, as well as words that are dependent on their context.

Reading syllabically, you read from the beginning, breaking every word into syllables. This is faster than reading backward, works well for catching internal misspellings, and is quite effective for catching missing and extra words and for correcting word endings (which may be overlooked when you read forward). However, it is a slower method than reading forward word by word, requires some discipline to master, and can be hard on the eyes if done for a long time.

Guidelines for Proofreading

- Probably the main reason for essays with careless errors is that not enough time was allotted for proofing. The half hour *not* set aside for proofreading can undo the work of several hours.
- Plan to let at least a few hours pass before you look at the essay for the final time (overnight is recommended).

- Having someone else go over the essay can be helpful but is no substitute for your own systematic proofing. Instructors are not likely to be sympathetic to the cry of baffled frustration, "But I had my roommate read it over!"
- Use a spell-checker but don't rely on it. A spell-checker will not catch the difference between *there house is over their two* and *their house is over there too*.
- Do not rely on auto-correct. Look carefully at the suggested words and chose the correct one. Many students have included the word *defiantly* in their essays rather than the intended *definitely*.
- Experiment with the different proofreading methods discussed above and use the one(s) you feel most comfortable with and that works best for you. When you start proofreading using one particular method, though, you should use that same method until you finish reading.

Common Errors

Here are categories of typical errors to watch for and correct in your writing.

- all areas where consistency is required—spelling, capitalization, abbreviations, hyphenation, numbers, internal punctuation, and other places where choices pertaining to the mechanics of writing may be involved
- proper nouns (especially unfamiliar names), acronyms, etc. Are all references to authors and titles spelled correctly?
- middles and endings of words, for spelling and for agreement
- small words, such as articles and prepositions (*a, an, the, of, to, in, at, and, or, as, if, it*, etc.)
- words that have different spellings but the same pronunciation (homophones) (*to/too, their/there/they're, role/roll, cite/site, led/lead, manor/manner*, etc.)
- font style (italic, bold, Roman: applied correctly and consistently? applied to *all* necessary words?). Have you used italics for the titles of complete works, such as books and films, and put quotation marks around the titles of works contained in larger works, such as essays, articles, short stories, and poems?
- end punctuation (periods and question marks)
- quotation marks. Are they applied appropriately? Are both opening and closing quotation marks present? Have double and single quotation marks been alternated correctly? Are periods and commas inside and colons and semicolons outside? Similar checks can be made for parentheses.
- all citations, both in-text and on the final page of the essay. Check both for accuracy (author, title, journal name, date, and page numbers) and for consistency. Are all citations documented according to the style of your discipline—including capitalization, punctuation, and other conventions?

❯ Essay Presentation

Your audience and purpose are relevant to how you present your essay; for example, a scientific or engineering report probably would look quite different from an essay for English class—for one thing, it might have headings, whereas the English essay would probably not. A research essay, too, must conform to the documentation style of your discipline; on the other hand, if you are writing a personal essay and not using references, presenting your essay may mostly be a matter of following directions for title, typeface, margins, spacing, indentation, page numbering, and identifying information.

Although document design can vary, you can be sure of one thing: if your instructor asks you to format your essay a certain way, he or she will look to see that you followed these instructions. Therefore, if you are unsure about essay presentation, ask for help.

Unless you are told otherwise, you can refer to the following; it is based on MLA guidelines:

- Most instructors require essays to be typed. Use good-quality white paper, printing on one side. If you wish to conserve paper by printing on both sides, check with your instructor first.

- Leave 1-inch margins (2.5 cm) on all sides. The first page should include identification information positioned flush left (i.e., starting at the left margin). List information in the following order: your name and student ID if applicable; instructor's name (use the title that your instructor prefers—e.g., Professor Robert Mills, Dr. M. Sonik, Ms. J. Winestock, etc.); course number and section, if applicable; submission date. Double-space, then insert the essay's title, centred.

- Double-space the text of your essay; this makes it much easier for the instructor to correct errors and add comments. Also double-space any Notes, the Works Cited page, and block quotations.

- Indent each paragraph one half inch (1.25 cm)—do *not* use additional spaces to separate paragraphs, and leave a single space (not two spaces) after each period before beginning the next sentence.

- Number pages using Arabic numerals in the upper right-hand corner preceded by your last name; place this line about one half-inch (1.25 cm) from the top and flush right; you can probably create this kind of header automatically using the Insert or a similar function on your computer. If you need to include prefatory pages (such as a Contents page or a formal outline), use lower-case Roman numerals (i, ii, iii) for those pages.

- A title page is usually optional, though some instructors require it. Position the essay's title down one-third of the page with your name about half-way down; near the bottom of the page include the course number, instructor's name, and submission date. All items should be centred. Begin your essay on the second page (numbered 1) under the centred title.

- No illustrations or colours, other than black and white, should be on any pages unless you use graphics directly relevant to your essay—for example, charts or diagrams for a scientific study. Use a paper clip to attach the pages (some instructors ask for stapled pages)—especially, don't fold over a corner to keep them together. Don't use folders, clear or coloured, unless asked for. (If you do use a folder, the left-hand page margin should be slightly wider than the other margins to allow for the binding.)

- Prefer common fonts, such as Times New Roman, Arial, or Garamond (not Courier New or cursive ones). Use 10- to 12-point type size. *Do not* justify lines to the margins in academic papers or reports (i.e., set the paragraphing for flush left and an uneven line at the right margin). Finally, ensure that the text of your essay is easy to read. An essay printed in draft mode or from a cartridge that is almost out of ink will not be easy to read.

Ensure that the text of your essay is easy to read. An essay printed in draft mode or from a cartridge that is almost out of ink will not be easy to read.

■ Chapter Review Questions

1. Why is clarity important in writing?

2. Why is formal writing clearer than informal writing?

3. How is conciseness different from precision?

4. Find examples from business writing (such as advertising) that illustrate concepts discussed in this chapter, such as doubling up. Can you rewrite the samples so they are more formal and could be used in academic writing?

5. What are clichés? List some examples. Why should you avoid clichés in formal writing?

6. What is euphemistic language? Why are euphemisms confusing?

7. How are editing and proofreading different? Why are both important?

8. What are some things to look for when you proofread?

9. What message do you send to the reader if your paper has spelling mistakes or typos?

10. Why should you not rely solely on your spell-checker?

Appendix A
Tense Encounters with Verbs: A Summary

Tense refers to time when the action or condition expressed by the verb took place (or is taking place, or will take place). Each tense can take one of four *forms*:

- simple
- progressive
- perfect
- perfect progressive

These forms further describe the aspect of the verb, as to when its action began, and its duration or completion.

The auxiliary (helping) verb for most forms determines the complete form of the verb. The auxiliary verb for the progressive tenses is *to be* (*is, was, will be*); for the perfect tenses, it is *to have* (*has, had, will have*).

〉 1. Present Tenses

Simple Present (action or situation exists now or exists on a regular basis):

I call	we call
you call	you call
he/she/it calls	they call

I usually *call* for the pizza; you *call* for it this time.

Present Progressive (action is in progress):

I am sending	we are sending
you are sending	you are sending
he/she/it is sending	they are sending

Mr. Kahn *is sending* the package to you by courier.

Present Perfect (action began in the past and is completed in the present):

I have eaten	we have eaten
you have eaten	you have eaten
he/she/it has eaten	they have eaten

I *have eaten* the apple you gave me.

Present Perfect Progressive (action began in the past, continues in the present, and may continue into the future):

I have been hoping	we have been hoping
you have been hoping	you have been hoping
he/she/it has been hoping	they have been hoping

We *have been hoping* to receive news from the Philippines.

2. Past Tenses

Simple Past (action or situation was completed in the past):

I saw	we saw
you saw	you saw
he/she/it saw	they saw

Garfield *saw* the moon rise last night over his burrow.

Past Progressive (action was in progress in the past):

I was talking	we were talking
you were talking	you were talking
he/she/it was talking	they were talking

James and Beth *were talking* about storms when the hurricane warning flashed onto their computer screen.

Past Perfect (action was completed in the past prior to another action in the past):

I had finished	we had finished
your had finished	you had finished
he/she/it had finished	they had finished

Alex *had finished* the second assignment when the storm knocked out power to his computer.

Past Perfect Progressive (action in progress in the past):

I had been practising	we had been practising
you had been practising	you had been practising
he/she/it had been practising	they had been practising

The golf team sophomores *had been practising* for the tournament all summer, but when school, started their coach announced his resignation.

3. Future Tenses

Simple Future (action will occur in the future):

I will see	we will see
you will see	you will see
he/she/it will see	they will see

I *will see* the Rocky Mountains on my way to Vancouver.

Future Progressive (action will be continuous in the future):

I will be walking	we will be walking
you will be walking	you will be walking
he/she/it will be walking	they will be walking

Norm and Martee *will be walking* in the Marathon of Hope next Saturday morning.

Future Perfect (action in the future will be completed):

I will have gone	we will have gone
you will have gone	you will have gone
he/she/it will have gone	they will have gone

Sally *will have gone* around the moon several times before the ship leaves its lunar orbit.

Future Perfect Progressive (actions are ongoing up to a specific future time):

I will have been studying	we will have been studying
you will have been studying	you will have been studying
he/she/it will have been studying	they will have been studying

With the completion of this assignment, they *will have been studying* verbs for 13 years.

Remember that verbs can reflect mood (conditional, subjunctive) and voice (active, passive), and auxiliary verbs can be used to indicate conditions, such as necessity (I should go), obligation (you must go), and possibility (he may go).

Exercise

In the following passages, some of the verb forms are correct, but others need to be changed. All verbs are underlined; correct those that are incorrect.

A.

Nature <u>was</u> a precious gift. It <u>provide</u> energies that <u>affect</u> society today. Although it <u>is</u> a gift, nature <u>needs</u> our attention and care because it <u>is</u> fragile and easily destroyed. I never <u>paid</u> much attention to nature because I <u>thought</u> humanity's impact on the natural world <u>was</u> not important. A few years ago, an encounter with a squirrel <u>has changed</u> my view. I <u>walk</u> home one day, and I <u>saw</u> a gray squirrel picking up loose pine cones in the garden. I <u>am watching</u> the squirrel hopping joyfully around the yard. Suddenly, it <u>starts</u> to run across the street. But before it <u>reached</u> the other side of the street, a car <u>hit</u> it and <u>killed</u> it. I <u>am devastated</u> that the driver <u>didn't even slow down</u>, as if the life of a squirrel <u>is</u> worthless.

We <u>should always respect</u> what nature <u>has offered</u> us. The natural world <u>is</u> an important factor in maintaining a healthy life cycle. If this life cycle <u>is</u> not protected, the balance in the life cycle <u>is</u> destroyed, which <u>will bring</u> serious consequences to the lives of all human beings.

B.

I <u>remember</u> a camping trip that I <u>was going on</u> with a few of my friends. We <u>were</u> very unprepared and <u>run</u> into a few mishaps along the way. The trip <u>occurred</u> during the rainy season, and we <u>have not brought</u> any firewood. We <u>have</u> a hard time getting the fire to start, even after we <u>borrowed</u> wood and an axe from the campers next door. Of course, we <u>forgot</u> to bring a can opener, so we <u>had</u> to try stabbing at the tins with a Swiss army knife to get them open. We <u>spend</u> the night around our Coleman stove, trying to keep warm.

That night <u>made</u> us realize how much we <u>took</u> nature for granted. In our homes everyday we <u>had</u> many household appliances that <u>made</u> our lives easier for us. It <u>is</u> easy to forget that some people <u>live</u> in the world without these conveniences and <u>relied</u> on nature from dawn to dusk. This camping trip <u>occurred</u> a long time ago when I <u>am</u> much younger. But the memory of that long night in the nature <u>stays</u> with me ever since.

Appendix B
A Checklist for EAL Writers

The following are some English idiomatic expressions and rules for usage organized alphabetically by the major parts of speech. Although articles are not a major part of speech, their usage can be confusing for EAL writers, so they have been allotted a separate section, beginning on page 478.

Adjectives

One-word adjectives usually precede the word(s) they modify, except predicate adjectives that follow linking verbs (see page 335). However, **relative (adjectival) clauses** follow the noun they modify and present special challenges for writers.

Adjectives as participles

When a participle ending in –*ed* or –*en* precedes a noun and acts as an adjective, don't drop the ending it requires as a past participle:

> Although Patrick lived a *fast-paced* [not fast-pace] life, he had the *old-fashioned* [not old-fashion] habit of stopping and reading a newspaper every day work.

Adjectives and present versus past participles

In verbs related to feeling or emotion, the present particle (ends in –*ing*) is used when the subject *causes* the feeling; the past participle (ends in –*ed* or –*en)* is used when the subject *experiences* the feeling.

> The surprise ending of the football game was *exciting*; the few fans left in the stadium were *excited*.

Ago: When you want to refer to a time in the past and relate this time to today, you can use the adjective *ago*; it follows the noun. To refer to a *specific* point in the past, you can give the date (month, day, year) preceded by *on*. See **Times and dates,** under **Prepositions**, below.

The first truly successful cloning of an animal occurred almost *twenty years ago*.
The first truly successful cloning of an animal occurred *on July 5, 1996*.

Comparatives and superlatives

Use the comparative of adjectives and adverbs when you want to compare one person or thing to another person or thing. Usually, the suffix *–er* is added if the quality being compared is one syllable, while the word *more* precedes a word of two or more syllables:

In BC, summers are usually *drier* than they are in Ontario.
According to *the most recent* statistics, it is *more dangerous* to drive a car than to take an airplane.

Use the superlative of adjectives and adverbs when you want to compare more than two of something. The definite article is usually not used with comparisons, but it is used with superlatives (see **Articles—*A, An,* and *The*,** below).

In my opinion, BC is a *better* province than Alberta [there are two provinces]; in my friend's opinion, Alberta is *the best* of the western provinces [there are four].

Few vs. a few

Both can precede nouns that can be counted, but few means "not many," and a few means "some."

Few Canadians know how to play cricket. However, *a few* people on my listserv said they would be interested in learning how to play it.

Much vs. many

Use *much* before nouns that cannot be counted and *many* before countable nouns.

The Canadian television channel *MuchMusic* features *many* different kinds of music.

Plurals as adjectival phrases concerning distance, money, and time

When these kinds of plural nouns appear in hyphenated phrases before other nouns, they drop the final "s," as in the following examples:

a *10-kilometre* run (*not* a 10-kilometres run), a *30-day* refund policy, a *70-year-old* man.

Relative (adjectival) clauses

A relative clause modifies the noun it follows (known as the *antecedent*). These clauses begin with a relative pronoun (usually *who, whom, that,* or *which*). Make sure you include the relative pronoun at the beginning of the clause. Below, the complete relative clause is underlined, the relative pronoun is bolded, and the antecedent is italicized:

> In China, there is a *high school* **that was** painted green because green is considered a relaxing colour.

When you use a phrase like "in which" to introduce a clause, do not repeat the preposition at the end of the clause:

> Happiness for some people is measured by their success in the society in which they live in.

Relative clauses, agreement

The antecedent of the relative pronoun determines whether the verb in the relative clause is singular or plural. The relative pronoun is bolded in the sentence below, the verb is underlined, and the antecedent is italicized:

> The Hyundai hybrid car has a small *engine* **that** consumes less fuel than ordinary cars.

Adverbs

Adverbs with adjectives

Adverbs can modify adjectives and other adverbs, along with verbs. Ensure you always use the correct adverbial form. In the sentence below, "environmental" is the adjectival form; "environmentally" is the adverbial one:

> The average Canadian household has become more environmental*ly* conscious than in the past.

The few adjectives that end in –*ly* (e.g., *friendly, fatherly, cowardly)* cannot be made into adverbs.

Comparative and superlative of adverbs

See **Comparatives and superlatives**, under **Adjectives**, above.

Articles—*A, An,* and *The*

Indefinite articles precede some singular nouns, and definite articles precede some singular and plural nouns. Context often determines whether an article precedes a noun or whether it is omitted; idiom also can determine usage. Here are some guidelines for article use.

The indefinite article

General rule: Use the indefinite article *a* or *an* if you want to identify a general or nonspecific noun. Use *an* rather than *a* if the noun begins with a vowel that is not pronounced or with a silent "h."

> When I was bird watching, I looked for *a* Rufus hummingbird. (no specific bird is referred to)
>
> When *the* hummingbird saw me, it darted into the trees. (a specific bird is referred to)

The indefinite article is *not* used before most uncountable concrete nouns, nor do these nouns form plurals. It is easier to remember these nouns if you divide them into categories:

- *Kinds of liquids*: beer, blood, coffee, milk, oil, soup, water, wine, etc.
- *Kinds of food*: bread, cheese, corn, flour, food, fruit, lettuce, meat, pasta, popcorn, rice, sugar, etc.
- *Names of languages*: Arabic, Mandarin, Dutch, French, Japanese, Vietnamese, etc.
- *Names of areas of study*: biology, economics, geography, mathematics, etc.
- *Names of gases*: hydrogen, methane, ozone, oxygen, etc.; air, fire, smoke, and steam also belong here
- *Sports and games*: baseball, bowling, football, hockey, jogging, surfing, tennis, etc. But, baseballs and footballs (the objects, not the sports) are countable.
- *Others*: chalk, clothing, equipment, feedback, furniture, health, help, homework, housework, laughter, luggage, mail, money, research, scenery, soap, software, weather, wood, work, etc.

However, if preceded by a word like "piece" or "item," such nouns may be countable: *a piece* (or *pieces*) *of chalk, an item* (or *items*) *of furniture, a glass of water.* As well, many nouns can be used adjectivally before countable nouns: *a cheese stick, a hockey game, etc.*

Some of the nouns above can be used in a countable sense if they can be divided into different types:

> Red *wine* in moderation can be beneficial to one's health.
> Different *wines* are classified by their place of origin.

Note: Although *mail* is an uncountable noun, *email* can be used as a countable noun; thus, you can talk about receiving *an* email. As a noun, email can also be pluralized:

> Flora was shocked to see that she had received more than 100 *emails* over the weekend; as a result, she vowed to get rid of her *email* by the end of the week.

See also **Uncountable and countable nouns,** under **Nouns,** below.

The definite article

General rule: Nouns that refer to a specific person, place, or object are usually preceded by the definite article, *the*:

> Please give me *the* pen on *the* table.

A specific pen (distinct from other pens) on a specific table is requested.

> Please give me *a* pen on *the* table.

This request implies that there is more than one pen on the specific table.

> Please give me *a* pen.

Any pen from anywhere will do.

> Young children, especially in *the* 3–5 age group, are always asking questions.

Other age groups exist, making the reference specific.

Including definite articles before nouns:

a) *First versus second reference:* Use *a* when something is first mentioned, *the* when the same noun is mentioned again (it can now be identified). For example:

> Mike found *a brown bottle* that had washed ashore. When he cleaned it up, he saw that *the bottle* had *a note* inside.

b) *Nouns that refer to a species or class of objects*: Use the definite article before this group; an example is "the definite article" in this sentence. Here is another example:

> In her English class, Izumi studied *the argumentative essay* before *the research essay*.

c) *Unique nouns*: If the noun has a unique identity, precede it by the definite article.

Examples:

- *Specific eras or time periods*: *the* Industrial Revolution, *the* Age of Reason, in *the* twentieth century, etc.
- *the* Sun, *the* Moon, *the* North Star (unique celestial objects)
- *Newspapers, museums, theatres, and hotels*: *The* Vancouver Sun (newspaper), *the* Royal Ontario Museum, *the* Imax theatre, *the* Banff Springs Hotel

d) *Superlatives:* (see also **Comparatives and superlatives**, under **Adjectives**, above).

> I have found that *the best courses* at college are usually *the most challenging ones*, and they are taught by *the best teachers*.

e) *Ordinals: the first, the second, etc.* (vs. cardinal numbers: one, two, etc.)

> Maria was *the first* to cross the finishing line; Linden was *the second*. They finished one and two, respectively.

Omitting definite articles before nouns.

When using nouns that fall into the following groups, omit the definite article. However, there are exceptions to the guidelines.

a) Omit before most *plural nouns*:

> If animals have no consciousness, it is meaningless to discuss whether eating meat is immoral.

> "Animals" is a plural noun; "meat" is an uncountable noun.

b) Omit before *proper nouns*, though there are many exceptions to this general rule. For example, the article is used before some geographical names: Examples:

- *the* Pacific Ocean, *the* United States, *the* Philippines, *the* Arctic
- *National, social, and cultural groups:* Canadians, Americans; but *the* English, *the* Japanese, *the* middle class, *the* Inuit peoples

> Lonnie is a member of *the* Chipewyan First Nations and lives near Prince Albert in northern Saskatchewan.

c) Omit before *abstract nouns* unless a prepositional phrase follows the noun; abstract nouns are usually uncountable and also cannot be pluralized. Abstract nouns include *advice, anger, curiosity, employment, enjoyment, evidence, freedom, fun, health, information, intelligence, justice, knowledge, love, music, peace, pollution, reality, research, respect, truth, wealth, weather,* etc.

> *The reality of the situation*, unfortunately, is that *justice* does not always prevail.

> A prepositional phrase follows "reality" but not the abstract noun "justice."

d) Common nouns that often result in errors in article use include *government*, *nature*, *society*, *Internet*, and *media*:

- *Government*: if you are referring to a *specific* government, use the definite article; otherwise, do not use "the":

The government [meaning, for example, the government of Ontario] has no right to raise student tuition fees.

- *Nature*: If you are referring to the natural world, the noun *nature* is *not* preceded by "the." If the sense is of a quality, essence, or habit, "the" may be required.

It has been *the nature* of previous generations [their habit] to take *nature* [the natural world] for granted.

- *Society*: It is *not* preceded by "the" if the reference is a general one. Note that *society* is usually singular and requires the singular verb form. If the reference is specific, "the" may be required (for example, if it is followed by a phrase that particularizes society):

Society does not look kindly on those who fail to respect *its* rules.
I find *the society of like-minded individuals* boring and unrewarding.

- *Internet/media*: When used as a noun, *Internet* is preceded by "the" as is *media* when it refers to *the news media* as a form of mass communication, such as television, radio, newspapers, and magazines; it usually takes a singular verb form when used this way.

With the rise of *the Internet, the media has* become even a more powerful influence on *society*.

For article use with gerunds, see **Gerunds**, under **Nouns**, below.

Nouns

The following nouns often give students trouble:

Human: This noun can be used in the singular or the plural, but possessive forms should be avoided.

It is a *human* [*not* a human's] need to aim for perfection.

Humanity: *Humanity* is not preceded by the definite article (or possessive adjective) unless it refers to an inner quality (see *Nature*, under **Omitting definite articles before nouns,** above).

One quality that *humanity* shares with other organisms is the need to solve problems.
She demonstrated *her humanity* [an inner quality] by forgiving her enemies.

Opinion, express an opinion: Don't say, "In my point of view," "As for myself," or "As far as I am concerned . . . ." The most direct way of stating your opinion is simply to say, "*In my opinion . . .*" or, "*I believe that . . .*", and follow with a clause that states your opinion.

Every + noun

"Every one of," like "each one of," "either one of," etc., will be followed by a plural noun but a *singular* verb form. But when one of these words is followed directly by a noun, that noun will be *singular*, not plural (and the verb will be singular, too):

Almost *every* drafting *course* in schools *involves* computers.

Using "every one of" would result in a plural noun in the "of" phrase: *Every one of the* drafting *courses.*

Gerunds

Gerunds are incomplete verb forms that act as nouns in a sentence (they end in *–ing*). They are *always singular* and *are usually not preceded by articles.*

Learning many new skills *is* enjoyable if you have the time for *it.*

Kind(s) of/type(s) of + noun

What follows *kind of* and *type of* will be a singular noun; what follows *kinds of* and *types of* will be a plural countable noun (uncountable nouns could be used with either) since more than one kind/type will be referred to. Often, a demonstrative adjective will precede *kind/type*: "this" or "that" (both are singular) can precede kind/type; "these" or "those" (plural) can precede kinds/types.

What *type of car was* Natalie driving?
Many *kinds of cars are* on the market today.

Uncountable and countable nouns

For a list of common uncountable nouns, see **The indefinite article**, under **Articles—*A, An,* and *The*,** above. The following uncountable nouns are responsible for many writing errors:

- *Clothing:* As an uncountable noun, it will never be preceded by the indefinite article and will never form a plural. "Clothes," however, is a countable noun.

People have used *clothing* to cover their body for thousands of years; however, we often choose our *clothes* today for their fashion rather than their practicality.

- *Information* and similar nouns, such as *knowledge, evidence,* and *advice,* are uncountable abstract nouns: they are not preceded by "a" or "an" and are never plural.
- *Importance:* You can never say "an importance" or "importances." You can say "*the* importance" if a prepositional phrase beginning with "of" follows.
- *Research:* A non-count noun, it is never plural. However, *researcher,* a person who *does* or *conducts* research, is a countable noun. As a verb, "research" is usually followed by a direct object (not by "about").

As an adjective, "research" can be followed by a plural noun: *research projects, research studies.*

Some nouns can be either countable or uncountable depending on context.

In their youth, most people have at least 100,000 *hairs* on their head.

If you're determined, you could count the number of hairs!

Shaving your *hair* today is more often a matter of personal choice than of hygiene.

The sense here is of hair as a mass, therefore uncountable.

For examples of countable and uncountable nouns with articles, see **Articles—*A, An,* and *The*,** above.

Prepositions

Despite; in spite *of*: Both act as prepositions, so a *noun*—not a clause—needs to follow each.

In spite of / Despite her best efforts to create interest in the performance, only a few people attended it.

Times and dates, referring to: The preposition used for time expressions will vary according to context: e.g., I will be there *for* Christmas. (I will arrive sometime *on* or *before* Christmas); I will be there *during* Christmas (I will be there for the entire time).

For specific times:
He will arrive *at* 9 a.m. *on* Tuesday; *on* December 24

For less specific times:
He will arrive *in* the morning (*in* the evening, but *at* night); *in* December; *in* 2010.

Also see **Verbs and prepositions**, under **Verbs**, below.

Verbs

The following verbs sometimes give students trouble:

Conclude: There are a few ways to express a conclusion. In most cases, a clause should follow the verb:

> One can *conclude that* commercialism destroys culture; *one can come to the conclusion [or draw the conclusion] that commercialism destroys culture.*

> To announce the conclusion of your essay, don't say, "As a conclusion." Instead, say, "*In conclusion.*"

Remember: When you are remembering something now (for example, when you're writing about an incident in the past), *remember* is put in the present tense, though the action described will be in the past tense.

> I *remember* when I was little how I *thought* my parents *knew* everything.

Verbs as modal auxiliaries

Modals are a special category of helping verb that make the meaning of a main verb more precise. They are usually followed by the bare infinitive, without "to." Some common uses of modals are given below.

- *Can* expresses capability: Clothing *can* really say a lot about a person.

- *Could* expresses capability in the past tense: When she lived near a lake, Nina *could* swim every day.

- *Should* expresses necessity or obligation: There *should be* (or *must be*) gun laws in all states in the US.

- *May* and *might* express possibility. *May* often conveys a stronger possibility than *might*: Since she has the prerequisites, Bianca *may* enroll in the second-year course.

> Although she worked late, she *might* decide to go to the party.

- *May* also expresses *permission:* Students *may* bring beverages into the study area but not food items.

- *Will* expresses probability: Since she has the prerequisites, Bianca *will* enroll in the second-year anthropology course.

- *Would* expresses a repeated action in the past: When she lived near a lake, Nina *would* swim every day.

Verbs and nouns

Because nouns are sometimes formed from verbs and often look like them, they can be confused. Use a dictionary to ensure you have used a verb where one is required and a noun where one is required. Here are two sets of commonly confused words:

Belief, believe: *belief* is a noun; *believe* is a verb. *Believe* is often followed by *in* or *that*, depending on whether a word/phrase (*in*) or a clause (*that*) follows:

> She firmly *believed in* his innocence.
> She firmly *believed that* he was innocent; this was her true *belief*.

Breath, breathe: *breath* is a noun; *breathe* (pronounced with a long ē) is a verb. You can *take* or *draw a breath*, meaning "breathe in." Somewhat idiomatically, to *take a deep breath* can mean to prepare yourself for a difficult task (whether or not a deep breath is actually taken).

> The guest speaker, Madeleine, *took a deep breath* before she entered the crowded room. After she began speaking, she *breathed* normally again.

Verbs and prepositions

The following alphabetical list includes verbs that may be confusing, usually due to idiomatic prepositional use.

Agree/Disagree with: You agree or disagree *with* someone or with a person's views or opinions on something. There are other prepositions that can follow both these verbs, but in most essays where you argue a thesis, you will use *with* following *agree* and *disagree*.

> I agree *with* space exploration in general, but I disagree *with* those who want us to spend billions of dollars per year on something with no practical benefit for humanity.

> *Agreed* followed by *to* means "to consent" (to).

> I agreed *to* give a speech on the merits of space exploration to my philosophy class.

Apply for a loan, a scholarship, a position, a job; **to apply to** (a place or situation) a school, etc.:

> Joshua *applied to* several Ontario colleges before he *applied for* a student loan.

Attend (a university, class, concert, wedding, *etc.*; this means "to be present at"); **to study at** (a university).

> Before he decided *to study at* Red Deer College he *attended* some classes at the University of Alberta.

> See **Graduate *from***, below.

Avoid vs. to prevent: When you *avoid* something, you stay away from it; the verb is usually followed by a direct object (the thing that is avoided). When you *prevent* something, you take an action so that it does not occur; *prevent* can be followed by a direct object or by a direct object + *from* and a gerund phrase (a gerund is a noun ending in *–ing*):

> You should *avoid people* when you are sick as this will *prevent others from catching* your virus.

Call/draw attention to: To *call/draw attention to* is followed by a noun and means to point something out. A noun or possessive adjective often precedes *attention*, as in the following sentence:

> The *Intergovernmental Panel on Climate Change* (*IPCC*) was founded in 1988 in order to *draw* world *attention to* the link between climate change and human activity.

> To *pay attention to* means to take note of or to look at closely.

> All Canadians should *pay attention to* the next *IPCC* report in 2014.

> To *get attention*, meaning to attract notice, is not usually followed by a preposition:

> After failing to *get* the teacher's *attention* any other way, Harmon shouted "fire!"

> See **Pay (for)** and **Point out**, below.

Care: To care *about* means to be concerned about (see **Concern,** below):

> She cares *about* good grades.

> To *care for* or *take care of* means to look after:

> Thomas *took care of* his sister when his mother was working.

Commit: A person can *commit a* crime, *a* murder, *an* error, but a person *commits suicide* (no article). Another meaning of the verb *commit* is "to dedicate to" or "resolve to do something"; it is *often* followed by the reflexive pronoun and the preposition *to*.

> After *committing a* serious crime, he thought briefly about *committing suicide*, but decided instead to *commit himself to* a life of helping others.

Compare and contrast: When you compare, you focus on similarities; when you contrast, you focus on differences. *Compare* is usually followed by *to* or *with*:

> In our class assignment, we were asked to *compare* the Canadian system of government *with* the system in another country.

Note that what follows *compare* (or *contrast*) is the direct object; *with* or *to* then follows, and the indirect object follows *with* or *to*.

If you use the verb phrase *make a comparison*, the preposition you use is *between*:

> He made a comparison *between* one political system *and* another.

Compared to/with: In this construction, the grammatical subject is what is being compared:

> *Compared to* the small town that I grew up in, Saskatoon seems like a big city.

"Saskatoon" is the subject as it is being compared to the small town.

Compete for (something); Compete *against* (someone):

> They *competed for* the honour of being named captain of the team. Mohammed *competed against* his friend to see who could get the higher mark.

Concern: The meaning you want determines the preposition to use:

To be concerned about means to be troubled or worried about *something*.
To be concerned for means to be worried about *someone* (or, occasionally, *something*).

> She *was concerned about* the implications of the new driving regulations; specifically, she *was concerned for* her daughter, who would soon be getting her licence.

When it is not followed by a preposition, *concern* means "applies to" or "is relevant to":

> The matter I have to discuss, Yuto, *concerns* your future with this organization.

Consider, Discuss, Mention: When you consider something, you think carefully about it, usually in order to take some kind of action. *Consider*, like *discuss* and *mention*, is followed by a direct object—not by *about*. Unlike *discuss*, however, *consider* and *mention* may be followed by a clause beginning with *that*.

> Before Yoshi decided to get married, he *considered the matter* by talking it over with his married friend Eizad. Then he *discussed it with* Sanjeet. Before Yoshi *discussed* his marriage plans with his fiancée, he *mentioned* to Eizad and Sanjeet *that* he was considering marriage.

See **Think, below**.

Depend, Rely, Count: These verbs can mean "*have confidence in someone or something*" and are followed by *on* + a noun that states who or what is depended/relied on. They may then be followed by *for* + another noun that expands on the first noun:

> Shaun *depends on* email *for* most of his business.
> Maheen *relies on* her friend Amy *for* fashion advice.

Discuss: See **Consider, Discuss, Mention**, above.

Encourage/discourage: You encourage someone *to* do something, but you discourage someone *from* doing something.

> Raising tuition may *discourage* students *from* enrolling in other courses. The president of the students' union is *encouraging* all students *to* protest the tuition increase.

Note that an infinitive follows *to*, but a gerund follows *from*.

Graduate *from* university, etc.; **to be a graduate *of*** (this is the noun; the second ă is a short vowel); to have/get/obtain/pursue *an* education:

> After Kasey *graduated from* college, she went to graduate school and became a *graduate of* ubc.

Hire (someone; *employers* hire); **to be hired by** (someone, a company, etc.; *employees* are hired):

> After applying for several positions during the summer, Teh *was hired by* another company.

See **Apply for**, above.

Know *something*: This means to have information or expertise *about* something; **to know *someone*:** the person's name should follow the verb as the direct object.

> When I got *to know Tey*, I learned about computers, and I now *know* everything *about* them.
> Shelley *knows* that she has a test tomorrow.

Lack: As a verb, it is followed by a direct object; as a noun, it is usually preceded by an article or other determiner (e.g., *its*, *that*, *this*, *your*) and followed by *of*:

> The first thing she noticed about the bedroom was *its lack of* privacy.
> The kitchen also *lacked* dishes and other utensils.

Lead to: This means the same as *result in* (see below). In both cases, a result or consequence follows the preposition.

> The cloning of animals, according to many people, is certain *to lead to* (or, result in) the eventual cloning of humans.

Look at/around/for/into/over:

> *look at* (examine): In my essay, I will *look at* solutions to the problem of homeless people.
> *around*: Dazed by the accident, he slowly sat up and *looked around*.
> *for* (search): Simon *looked for* his lost notes on his messy desk.
> *into* (investigate): After being laid off for the second time this year, Natalie began to *look into* self-employment.
> *over* (scan): She *looked over* her notes from the previous class.

Mention: See **Consider, Discuss, Mention**, *above*.

Participate in: You participate *in* something—activities, sports, etc.:

> Dong Hun often *participates in* classroom discussions.

Pay (for): *Pay* means to give (usually money) what is due for goods, services, or work, etc. *For* + a noun may follow if you want to indicate what was purchased:

> She *paid* less than $80 *for* all her textbooks since she bought them used.

Point out: This verb means to call attention to (something). It is generally followed by a noun/pronoun or a clause beginning with *that*. One of the meanings of *to point* is to indicate, to single out, using a finger; it is followed by *to*.

> Ruji *pointed out* her sister among the bystanders.
> Ruji *pointed out that* her sister was always late for a meeting.
> Ruji *pointed to* her sister, who was standing in a crowd.

Refer: *Refer* is followed by *to* when the meaning is "to make a reference or to make mention of something." If a clause beginning with *that* follows, a noun such as *fact*, *idea*, etc. should intervene between the verb *refer* and the clause.

> In his letter of recommendation, he *referred to* the many occasions in which Duy had demonstrated his sense of humanity and compassion. Specifically, he *referred to the fact that* Duy had often volunteered for work in local hospices.

Result in/result from: When you use the verb *result*, you must be careful about the preposition you use after it. To result *in* means that what follows the verb will be a *result* or consequence; to result *from* means that what follows the verb will be a *cause*.

> Being convicted of the crime of murder *usually results in* long prison terms.
>
> Prison terms are the consequence.
>
> Most murders in the US *result from* the use of guns.
>
> Guns are a cause.

Stress and **emphasize:** They mean the same thing and are usually followed by direct objects (not prepositions). But if you want to use the verb phrase "put stress/emphasis *on*," note the preposition that is required. A *that* clause may also follow these verbs.

> The writer *emphasized* the main point of her argument by providing examples.
> The writer *put emphasis on* the main point of her argument by providing examples.
> The instructor *stressed that* all students should arrive on time for class.

Think is a verb with many uses. To think *about* means to "reflect on," and to think *over* means to "consider"; note the word order of *it* in the sentence below. Use *think* + a clause beginning with *that* if you want to refer to a belief or opinion.

> William originally *thought that he would take a commerce class* in the second term, but when he thought *about it* [or *thought it over*], he decided to enroll right away.

Verbs and their subjects (subject–verb agreement)

Always ensure that you use the singular form of any verb that has a singular subject. But if the subject is plural (indicating more than one of something or someone), the verb should be plural. Remember that the third-person *singular* form of a *verb* usually ends in "s."

Appendix C
Peer Edit Forms

❯ Peer Edit Form: Formal Outline

The essay outline provides the structure on which the essay itself will be built. Therefore, as an editor, you should pay special attention to the relation among the parts (Introduction, body paragraphs, Conclusion), to the order of arguments (weakest to strongest? strongest to weakest? some other logical order?), as well as to the strength and effectiveness of each main point. Is each adequately developed? Is the claim supported?

Instructions

Use the check boxes below to record the fact that you have considered and evaluated the criteria. Use the space following to add suggestions, comments, questions, and advice.

Introduction

- ❑ What kind of formal outline has been used? Topic or sentence? Other (such as graphic)?
- ❑ Does the introduction attract your interest?
- ❑ Does it announce the topic?
- ❑ Does it contain a two-part direct thesis statement announcing the topic and commenting on the topic?
- ❑ Is the claim one of fact, value, or policy?
- ❑ Is the thesis statement interesting, specific, manageable, and clearly expressed?
  - ❑ interesting?
  - ❑ specific?
  - ❑ manageable?
  - ❑ clearly expressed?

❑ Does each paragraph contain at least one main idea that can be easily identified as such? If not, which paragraph(s) don't do this?

❑ Does each paragraph contain at least two sub-points that help develop the main point? If not, which paragraph(s) don't?

❑ Has the writer been able to provide support for his/her argument? If not, suggest ways that he/she could use kinds of evidence to do this (e.g., examples, facts/statistics, personal experience, outside sources, etc.).

❑ Do the paragraphs appear to be organized using any of the rhetorical patterns discussed in Chapter 6 (e.g., definition, cause/effect, problem solution, compare and contrast)?

❑ Are the main points ordered in a logical and persuasive way? If not, what could you suggest as an alternative arrangement?

❑ Are there at least two levels represented in the outline (main points and sub-points)? Is parallel structure applied to main points and the levels of sub-points?

Conclusion

❑ Does it successfully summarize or restate the argument without sounding repetitious?

❑ Does it go beyond the introduction by enlarging on the implications of the thesis, by urging a change in thought or call to action, or by making an ethical or emotional appeal?

Final Comments or Suggestions?

Writer's Name: _____
Editor's Name: _____

› Peer Edit Form: Argumentative Essay First Draft

Your first draft is the stage at which you make the transition from large-scale structural concerns to those focusing on your developing argument—in your final draft, you will work further on these areas, along with clear expression, grammatically sound prose, etc., responding to editorial suggestions as well as your clearer idea of your argument as a result of having written the draft.

Instructions

Use the check boxes below to record the fact that you have considered and evaluated the criteria. Use the space following to add suggestions, comments, questions, and advice. In addition, *underline places in the essay where you would like to draw the writer's attention to possible grammatical problems* (such as fragments, comma splices, apostrophe problems, lack of parallelism, misplaced or dangling modifiers, pronoun agreement, case, and/or consistency) *or stylistic problems* (such as passive constructions or other instances where the writing could be made more concise, direct, or forceful—you should also note possible spelling errors along with errors in mechanics and presentation).

Introduction

- ❏ Does the introduction function successfully?
  - ❏ Is it interesting?
  - ❏ Does it announce the subject and contain a thesis statement? **Is the claim arguable?**
  - ❏ Does it suggest the main way the argument will be organized (e.g., definition, cause/effect, time order, division, compare and contrast, question/answer, etc.)?
- ❏ Does the writer establish himself/herself as credible and trustworthy? How?

Body Paragraphs

- ❏ Does the argument seem complete, and does the order of the paragraphs appear logical?
- ❏ Look at paragraphs individually. Are any too short? Too long?
- ❏ Is each paragraph unified (relates to one main idea)? If not, which ones aren't?
- ❏ Is each paragraph coherent? If not, which ones aren't?
- ❏ Do paragraphs contain topic sentences?
- ❏ Is the order of the sentences natural?
- ❏ Are there appropriate transitions between sentences, enabling you to see the relationship between consecutive sentences?
- ❏ Does the writer successfully use repetition, rephrasing, synonyms, or other devices to achieve coherence?
- ❏ Does each paragraph seem developed adequately?
- ❏ Are there different organizational methods used to develop the argument? Which ones? Are they effective?

(continued)

❑ What kinds of evidence are produced? Are they used effectively? You don't have to refer to specific paragraphs—only note if they appear to be present to help support the thesis:
  ❑ examples, illustrations
  ❑ personal experience
  ❑ analogies
  ❑ precedents
  ❑ outside authorities/secondary sources
  ❑ other
❑ Are there points where the argument seems strained, weak, incomplete, and/or illogical? Are there any fallacies (e.g., cause/effect fallacies, fallacies of irrelevance, emotional/ethical fallacies)?

Conclusion

❑ Is the conclusion satisfying? Does it summarize and/or generalize?

Other Criteria

❑ Has the arguer presented himself/herself credibly?
  ❑ Conveys knowledge?
  ❑ Seems trustworthy and reliable?
  ❑ Appears to be fair?
❑ Is the opposing view acknowledged?
❑ Is the writer's voice objective?
❑ Are there any examples of slanted language?
❑ Is the opposing view successfully refuted (as in the point-by-point method)?
❑ Are specific argumentative strategies used? Common ground? Appeal to reader interest? Concessions? Emotional appeals? If not, could any of these be helpful?
❑ Are there any places in the draft where the language seemed unclear or where a point was unclear due to the way it was expressed?
❑ If the writer used sources, are they integrated smoothly and grammatically? Are all direct quotations, summaries, paraphrases, and ideas acknowledged?

Final Comments or Suggestions?

Writer's Name: _____
Editor's Name: _____

❯ Peer Edit Form: Research Essay First Draft

Your first draft is the stage at which you make the transition from large-scale structural concerns to those focusing on integrating your research with your own ideas—in your final draft, you will work further on these areas, along with the attempt to achieve conciseness, clear expression, grammatically sound prose, etc.

Instructions

Use the check boxes below to record the fact that you have considered and evaluated the criteria. Use the space following to add suggestions, comments, questions, and advice. In addition, *underline places in the essay where you would like to draw the writer's attention to possible grammatical problems* (such as fragments, comma splices, apostrophes, lack of parallelism, misplaced or dangling modifiers, pronoun agreement and/or consistency) *or stylistic problems* (such as passive constructions or other instances where the writing could be made more concise, direct, or forceful—you should also note possible spelling errors along with errors in mechanics and presentation).

Introduction

- ❏ Is the introduction successful?
  - ❏ Is it interesting?
  - ❏ Does it announce the subject and contain a thesis statement with a claim of fact, a hypothesis to be tested, or a question to be answered?
  - ❏ Does it suggest the main way the argument will be organized?
- ❏ Does the writer establish himself/herself as credible and trustworthy? How?

Body Paragraphs

- ❏ Does the essay seem complete, and does the order of the paragraphs appear logical?
- ❏ Look at paragraphs individually. Are any too short? Too long?
- ❏ Is each paragraph unified (relates to one main idea)? If not, which ones aren't?
- ❏ Is each paragraph coherent? If not, which ones aren't?
- ❏ Do paragraphs contain topic sentences?
- ❏ Is the order of the sentences natural?
- ❏ Are there appropriate transitions between sentences, enabling you to see the relationship between consecutive sentences?

(continued)

❑ Does the writer successfully use repetition, rephrasing, synonyms, or other devices to achieve coherence?

❑ Does each paragraph seem well developed?

❑ Has the writer used secondary sources effectively? Note any exceptions.

❑ Do all the sources seem reliable?

❑ Does the writer use a sufficient number of sources? Is there an over-reliance on one source? Which one?

❑ Does the writer show familiarity with the sources used?

❑ Do the secondary sources appear to be relevant to the points discussed?

❑ Is each reference integrated smoothly into the essay?
  ❑ stylistically?
  ❑ grammatically?

❑ Has the context been made sufficiently clear in each instance?

❑ Do brackets and ellipses appear to have been used correctly?

❑ Have all sources been cited? (Identify any that may not be.)

❑ Do the citations appear correct and consistent?

❑ Are any other kinds of evidence present in addition to secondary sources (for example, analogies, personal experience, illustrations, or examples)?

❑ Does the essay appear to be fundamentally focused on exposition (explaining) rather than argumentation (persuasion)?

Conclusion

❑ Is the conclusion satisfying? Does it summarize and/or generalize?

Other Criteria

❑ Has the writer presented himself/herself credibly?
  ❑ Conveys knowledge?
  ❑ Seems trustworthy and reliable?

❑ Is the writer's voice objective?

❑ Are there any places in the draft where the language seemed unclear or where a point was unclear due to the way it was expressed?

Final Comments or Suggestions?

Writer's Name: _____
Editor's Name: _____

Appendix D
Partial Exercise Answer Key: Chapters 14, 15, 16

Exercise 14.4. Read the following paragraph and identify the following:

- 5 nouns: road, street, slum, car, stop, house, bungalow, garden, fountain, middle, arrangement, flamingoes, penguins, windows, bars, door, grandmother, driver, horn, woman
- 2 pronouns: we, that, any, it, them, she
- 6 verbs: left, turned, were, came, was, had, did, toot, stepped, saw, nodded, smiled, went
- 3 adjectives: main, narrow, extended, better, well-kept, cemented, garish, marble, plastic, heavy, iron, front
- 2 adverbs: far, out, imperiously, immediately, back, inside
- 4 prepositions: in, in front of, from, around, across, with, of
- 2 conjunctions: and, once, when

Once we left the main road and turned down a narrow side street, we were in nothing more than an extended slum. The car came to a stop in front of a house that was far better than any of the others around it. Set back a little from the street, it was a well-kept bungalow. The cemented front garden had a garish marble fountain in the middle, with an arrangement of plastic flamingoes and penguins around it. The windows had heavy bars across them, and even the front door had an extra door of iron bars in front of it. My grandmother did not get out; instead she had the driver toot his horn imperiously. A woman stepped out of the front door, and when she saw the car, she immediately nodded and smiled and went back inside.

Exercise 14.5. Which of the following are complete sentences? Draw a line between the subject and the predicate. Mark with an "S" those that contain only a subject and with a "P" those that contain only a predicate. Indicate an "N" if there is neither subject nor predicate.

1. The empty cup on the bench. S
2. Signed his name to the bottom of the petition. P

3. A spider in the web. S
4. Dropped the egg while running the egg and spoon race. P
5. A ripe-smelling orange. S
6. Faith | heals. Complete sentence
7. Is unable to drive to school today. P
8. The high levels of the lake. S
9. Can grammar rules be bent? Complete sentence [question structure]
    Grammar rules | can be bent. [rearranged as statement]
10. Thousands of tourists around the world. S
11. (You) | close the window! Complete sentence [imperative sentence]
12. A parasite. S
13. (You) | don't eat pizza every day Complete sentence [imperative sentence]
14. All dressed up with no place to go. N
15. This grammar | should be easy to master! Complete sentence [exclamation]

Exercise 14.7. To the remaining fragments in Exercise 14.5 add a subject and/or predicate to create grammatically complete sentences. Other options exist than the ones below.

Questions 1–5:

1. The empty cup on the bench belongs to Todd; I was surprised to see the empty cup on the bench.
2. The irate parent signed his name to the bottom of the petition.
3. A spider in the web is a wonderful sight; If you look carefully, you can see a spider in a web while walking in the woods.
4. My partner dropped the egg while running the egg and spoon race.
5. A ripe-smelling orange makes my mouth water; Nothing is as good as a ripe-smelling orange.

Exercise 14.8. The following may or may not be sentences. If they are not, identify what kind of fragment they illustrate (lacks subject or predicate, add-on fragment, *–ing* fragment, dependent clause fragment). If they are fragments, make them into complete sentences with a subject and a predicate and needing nothing else to complete them.

Italics show material added to make complete sentences. Other options exist for turning the fragments into complete sentences.

1. Completing the test on time *is very important*. [*–ing*]
2. Huge tears rolled down his cheeks.
3. Being that she worked late, *she had to make sure the office was securely locked*. [*–ing*] [A better sentence: Because she worked late, she had to make sure the office was securely locked.]

4. Whenever they called her into work, *she was about to leave town for a holiday.* [dependent clause]

5. He promised to call on her tomorrow *to* see if she was still all right. [add-on]

6. He must be guilty *since* he's already confessed. [dependent clause]

7. I won't watch TV tonight unless I find something interesting. [dependent clause]

8. *The party president is* introducing our next prime minister. [–*ing*]

9. A murder of crows, along with a flock of sheep, *blocked the road.* [no predicate]

10. Swimming on her back, *she eventually reached the shore.* [–*ing*]

Exercise 14.9. The following passage contains four sentence fragments. Underline them. Then, correct them by joining them to complete sentences or by adding information.

[1.]When considering college or university [dependent]. Many students must decide where to live. If they are going to school close to home, they may decide to continue living with their families. [2.]Listening to their parent's advice.[-ing] However, if the school is far away and commuting is not possible, students must decide whether to live in the school residence or in an apartment. Residences are convenient. [3.]Especially if there is a meal plan available. [add on][4.] Meal plans that are nutritious. [add on] Apartments might be a better idea though, especially if students need to work. Not all residences are close to where jobs are. Privacy might be an issue in residence. Not all students can get their own rooms. Apartments may provide privacy, but only if there is no need for roommates. Many factors need to be considered when choosing where to live.

Corrections to above errors:

1. When considering college or university, many students must decide where to live.

2. If they are going to school close to home, they may decide to continue living with their families, often listening to their parent's advice.

3 & 4. Residences are convenient, especially if there is a meal plan that is nutritious.

Exercise 14.10. First, identify the word groups in parentheses as adverbial, adjectival, noun, or verb phrases. Then, identify the subject of the sentence.

1. Tomorrow, (the class time) will be changed (for the rest) (of the semester).
                    noun phrase   adjectival   adjectival
       S = the class time

2. (Some of the food) (in the fridge) (has spoiled).
            noun   adjectival   verb
     S = Some of the
     food in the fridge

3. The store (in the mall) (with the latest fashions) (has closed).
                adjectival   adjectival   verb
   S = The store in the mall with the latest fashions

4. A search (of the abandoned house) (turned up) several cartons
                       adjectival   verb
   (of stolen goods).
      adjectival
   S = A search of the abandoned house

5. (The 2018 hockey season) (will belong) (to the Leafs).
             noun   verb   adjectival
   S = The 2018 hockey season

Exercise 14.11. Identify all independent and dependent clauses in the following sentences by underlining independent clauses and placing parentheses around any dependent clauses. For help, you can refer to the list of subordinating conjunctions, page 346; these kinds of conjunctions introduce dependent clauses. Remember that pronouns, such as *I* or *it*, can serve as subjects.

1. (Despite the professors giving harder tests,) students are still passing.
2. (Even though I was born in Canada,) I don't like winter.
3. I ran through the rain (after I realized I'd left my umbrella at home.)
4. In most parts of North America, Daylight Saving Time begins in March. [*In most parts of North America* is a phrase modifying the verb in the independent clause.]
5. The struggle for democracy will continue (until all the rebels are captured.)

Exercise 14.12. Examples of the simple, compound, and complex sentence types appear below. For compound and complex sentences, underline independent clauses, circle conjunctions, and put parentheses around dependent clauses. Identify each sentence type.

1. The class average was low in the first semester, (but) it has gone up this semester. [compound]
2. Until a few months ago, she had never eaten Thai food. [simple—*until* is a preposition in this sentence]
3. Summer is the time for outdoor sports, (and) winter is the time to hibernate. [compound]
4. Tom wanted to give Jane a gift (but) had no money. [simple—*but* is joining *wanted* and *had*, two verbs. You can see that it is not joining two independent clauses as *had* has no separate subject from *wanted*.]
5. Salmon oil is a supplement (that lowers cholesterol). [complex]
6. An essay should convince someone about a point of view (or) teach him or her a new idea. [simple—see 4]

7. <u>Mandarin is spoken in mainland China</u>, (and) <u>it has become popular in North American schools</u>. [compound]

8. <u>His library privileges have been suspended</u> (until he pays his fines). [complex]

9. <u>She looked her subject up on Wikipedia</u> (and) <u>has not gone further</u>. [simple—see 4 and 6]

10. <u>She is convinced</u> (that she will get an "A" in the course). [complex]

Exercise 14.13. To demonstrate your familiarity with the different kinds of clauses and joiners, construct compound, complex, and compound-complex sentences from the independent clauses (simple sentences) below. After you have joined the clauses in the most logical way, identify the sentence type: compound, complex, or compound-complex. Ensure that you have at least one example of each type of sentence. Small changes can be made so that it is easier to make up complex sentences, and sentence order may be changed.

1. They intended to eat at Benny's Bistro.

   They saw a long line-up outside Benny's.

   They went to Kenny's Kitchen instead.

   They intended to eat at Benny's Bistro, but they saw a long line-up outside Benny's, so they went to Kenny's Kitchen instead. [compound]

   Alternative with minor changes: As soon as they saw a long line-up outside Benny's Bistro, they went to Kenny's Kitchen instead, even though they had intended to eat at Benny's. [complex]

2. There may be nearly two million kinds of plants in the world.

   There are likely at least as many different kinds of animals.

   No one can know how many species have evolved, flourished, and become extinct.

   Although there may be nearly two million kinds of plants in the world, and there are likely at least as many different kinds of animals, no one can know how many species have evolved, flourished, and become extinct. [compound-complex]

Exercise 14.14. Fix the sentences by using a period to make two separate sentences (if you already know the rules for using other forms of punctuation to join independent clauses, you can use them). Also, identify whether the sentence is a run-on or a comma splice.

1. I read two books in two days. I did nothing else but read. [run-on]
2. I couldn't use my laptop today. I forgot to plug it in before the battery was dead. [comma splice]

3. I was frightened during my first driving lesson: the instructor yelled at me. [run-on]

4. It's easy to punctuate sentences: just put a comma whenever you pause. [comma splice]

5. She finished watching the movie then took the bus home. [correct]

6. Magazine are available for digital download. This is better for the environment. [comma splice]

7. Technology continues to evolve but we can't always predict whether this is good or bad. [correct]

8. Humans are imitators. Conforming is something they are good at. [comma splice]

9. Many immigrants want to learn about Canadian culture. They take courses about it. [run-on]

10. Binge drinking is a serious problem. Many students engage in this behaviour. [comma splice]

Exercise 14.15. Determine what is wrong in the following sentences. It could be a fragment or a run-on sentence, or it could contain a comma splice; then, make the correction.

1. comma splice—corrected: He managed to pass the year though he seldom did his homework. What will happen to him next year is anyone's guess.

2. fragment—corrected: The opening ceremonies were delayed on account of rain.

3. fragment——corrected: She has decided to work at a fast-food restaurant: not a great place for tips.

4. comma splice—corrected: Movies provide entertainment for people; different people prefer different genres such as horror.

5. fragment—corrected: She's been very happy since she bought the new tablet.

6. fragment—corrected: The only way a person can learn is to pay attention to what is going on in class.

7. fragment—corrected: He was too tall and thin to excel at sports— except basketball, of course.

8. comma splice—corrected: The concept that "bigger is better" is part of our culture. It is promoted by both advertisers and the media these days.

9. fragment—corrected: I have trouble understanding the theory of relativity and its impact on our daily lives.

10. comma splice—corrected: Justin Trudeau may eventually be as well known as his father. Pierre had charisma and charm.

Exercise 14.16. Identify the sentence errors in the following paragraph; they may include fragments, run-on sentences, and comma splices. Then, correct them.

The "Freshmen 15" is not a recent phenomenon this refers to the weight students typically gain during their first year at college or university. [run-on] What concerns doctors now is the amount of weight gained during this time. In the 70s and 80s, students typically gained 5 pounds, now it is up to 15. [comma splice] This is a very unhealthy weight gain. Once the weight is gained. [fragment] It is very hard to lose. Because of this. [fragment] Cafeterias are starting to offer more nutritional meals with fewer calories. Student councils are beginning to be proactive, and inform students of the dangers of excess weight gain. School gyms are offering more classes to help students battle this weight gain. In the future, many hope that the "Freshman 15" becomes non-existent.

   Corrections:

The "Freshmen 15" is not a recent phenomenon. This refers to the weight students typically gain during their first year at college or university. What concerns doctors now is the amount of weight gained during this time. In the 70s and 80s, students typically gained 5 pounds, but now it is up to 15. This is a very unhealthy weight gain. Once the weight is gained, it is very hard to lose. Because of this, cafeterias are starting to offer more nutritional meals with fewer calories. Student councils are beginning to be proactive, and inform students of the dangers of excess weight gain. School gyms are offering more classes to help students battle this weight gain. In the future, many hope that the "Freshman 15" becomes non-existent.

Exercise 15.1. Add commas to the following sentences, if and where required. Also, name the rule category discussed above. There is one comma rule to apply in each sentence.

1. After her inaugural speech, several members of the House rose to congratulate her. [independent clause: introductory phrase]
2. The optional package includes bucket seats, dual speakers, and air-conditioning. [items in a series]
3. We have collected more than $20,000, and there is a week remaining in our campaign. [independent clauses]
4. Metaphors, similes, and personification all are examples of figurative language. [series]
5. As one can see, the tower is leaning some four-and-one-half metres to the south. [independent clause: introductory dependent clause]
6. Hardly daring to breathe, Nelson took a quick look at the valley far below him. [independent clause: introductory phrase]
7. Although many are called, few are chosen. [independent clause; introductory dependent clause]

8. The magnificent country estate is hidden behind a long, elegant row of silver birches. [miscellaneous: coordinate adjectives]
9. "We can't achieve peace in our time if we assume war is inevitable," he said. [miscellaneous: quotations]
10. Her house was a newer one with dark wood trim and large, open rooms. [miscellaneous: coordinate adjectives]

Exercise 15.2. Add commas to the following sentences, if and where required. There is more than one comma rule to apply in most sentences.

1. I had planned to go to Calgary, but my bus was delayed for more than four hours, so I decided to go back home.
2. Juliet studied medicine at the University of Western Ontario in London, Ontario, before becoming a doctor near Prince Albert, Saskatchewan.
3. Like Jane Austen's character, Emma, the heroine of *Clueless*, Cher, is less superficial than she first appears. [If the context suggested that the reader would know what Austen character is being referred to, *Emma* would be considered non-essential information (an appositive); if not, only the comma after *Emma* would be correct.]
4. Nick and Nicole were married on April 20, 1995, but they separated two years later.
5. Jessica Julep, the mayor of Nowhere, Nova Scotia, provided inspirational leadership.
6. The simple sentence, as we've seen, is easily mastered by students, but compound sentences necessitate an understanding of various forms of punctuation.
7. The waste of our resources, including the most precious resource, water, is the major environmental problem that Canada is facing today.
8. British general Sir Frederick Morgan established an American-British headquarters, which was known as COSSAC.
9. The book with the fine red binding on the highest shelf is the particular one I want.
10. Agnes Campbell Macphail, the first woman elected to Canadian Parliament, served for 19 years, beginning her career in 1921.

Exercise 15.3. Add commas in the paragraphs below, following the rule categories as discussed above and avoiding comma splices. A few commas have been included to help with comprehension, but they may be incorrect.

1. If you asked people to name the most gruelling and challenging race in the world, most of them would probably say that it was an auto race, such as the Indianapolis 500. Few people would name the Tour de France, which is a bicycle race. Thousands of cyclists, however, vie for an elite position in this annual event. Even with the modern advances in bicycle technology, cyclists still find the course very challenging.

It offers a variety of climbs, including slight inclines, hills, and steep grades. The Tour de France has a history that dates back about one hundred years. In the years to come, the race will continue to challenge, inspire, and glorify new riders.

Exercise 15.4. The following sentences are punctuated correctly. The italicized word or phrase is either an ordinary adverb acting as an interrupter or a conjunctive adverb (joiner). Rewrite the sentence by moving this word/phrase to another place in the second clause in which its function will be different. Punctuate accordingly.

1. One of my roommates rode her bicycle to school most of the time; *as a result,* she was more physically fit than my other roommate, who didn't even own a bicycle.
2. SPCA officers work for but are not paid by the government; *in fact,* it is donations that provide their salary.

Exercise 15.5. Using the rule categories discussed above, replace commas in the sentences below with the most appropriate form of punctuation (semicolon, colon, dash, parentheses). In some cases, the commas are correct and should not be replaced.

1. April showers bring May flowers; May flowers bring on my asthma.
2. A developing salmon goes through four stages: the alevin, the fry, the smolt, and the adult.
3. Every essay needs three parts: an introduction, a body, and a conclusion.
4. He paused to admire the splendid sight before his eyes: the ruins of Montgomery Castle.
5. Mayumi tended to look on the good side of things; Glenn usually saw the bad side.
6. The following is not a rule for comma use: put a comma wherever you pause.
7. It is probable (though not certain) that she will be promoted to the rank of corporal next year.
8. It was the best of times; it was the worst of times.
9. Marselina has a fine ear for music; unfortunately, she can't sing a note.
10. In my health sciences class, we studied the four main food groups: dairy products, meats, carbohydrates, and fruits and vegetables.
11. Whenever I order designer clothing for my boutique, I shop in Toronto, Canada; Buffalo, New York; and London, England.
12. The Online Dictionary defines animal cruelty this way: "treatment or standards of care that cause unwarranted or unnecessary suffering or harm to animals."
13. The tuition increase has affected many lower income families; therefore, there is an even greater demand for student loans.

14. Brian never tired of misquoting Shakespeare: "the quality of mercy is not stained."

15. Virginia Woolf had this to say about the essay: "Of all forms of literature it is the one which least calls for the use of long words."

Exercise 15.6. Correct or add commas in the following passages. Among your changes and additions, include *at least* one semicolon and one colon (two semicolons and two colons are shown below). Some commas have been included to help with reading; however, they may not be correct.

1. Cocaine, an alkaloid obtained from coco leaves, is a stimulant to the nervous system; unfortunately, it is one of the most addictive drugs, and it is possible to overdose and die on first use. Among the 3 million users today, 500,000 are highly addicted. Cocaine users describe the high as a euphoric feeling: they feel energetic and mentally alert; however, this feeling wears off in as little as 20 minutes. User responses to the drug vary but may include the following: hyperactivity, elevated blood pressure and heart rate, and increased sexual interest. Large amounts of cocaine, such as more than 100 milligrams, can cause bizarre, erratic, and violent behaviours.

Exercise 15.7. Decide which nouns in the following sentences require the possessive; then add apostrophes and make any other necessary changes.

1. In South Africa, the current crime rate is using up much of the country's GDP.
2. Parents and teachers often complain about television's influence in today's society.
3. The Crosses' house is up for sale, and its list price is $179,000. (The last name is Cross.)
4. One's education should not depend on the financial resources of one's parents.
5. The school's biggest draw for new students was the brand new recreation complex.
6. The course I took required two hours' homework a day.
7. The mayor's biggest asset is her commitment to the city's future growth.
8. In anorexia nervosa, a patient's fingernails and teeth may be damaged due to a lack of calcium.
9. Ryan's and Jessica's birthday is on the same day.
10. Apples, oranges, mangoes, and tomatoes are the store's specials today.

Exercise 15.8. Punctuate for correctness and effectiveness, using commas and other forms of punctuation as appropriate. Minimal punctuation has been provided in places to aid in understanding; however, some punctuation

may be incorrect. Correct all errors in apostrophe use. The first two paragraphs, corrected for punctuation and apostrophe use, appear below.

Reader reaction was swift and impassioned. The site's traffic, which averages 65 to 70 million views each month, experienced an additional 50,000 page views within the first 10 days of the posting. The investigation drew more than 400 letters to the editor, hundreds of emails to the message boards, and more than 16,000 responses to an online poll.

The intensity of the response surprised veteran investigative journalist Wayne MacPhail, the article's author. Although the sheer volume of letters was unexpected, it proved to him that there was an audience for online journalism in Canada. MacPhail has experimented with hypertext reporting since the late 1980s, but, outside of "Spin Doctors," he believes that, by and large, newspapers have done a "woeful job" of building an audience for Web-based investigative reporting . . . .

Exercise 16.1. In the short paragraph below, fix pronoun–antecedent agreement errors, using at least one of each of the three options discussed above.

If a child begins to perform poorly at school nowadays, he or she [option 1] will likely be sent to a school counsellor to deal with the situation. Everyone assumes that attention deficit disorder is the culprit, and ~~they~~ [option 3] just as automatically assume that drugs are the answer. On the other hand, perhaps the child is just not interested in a particular subject, or he or she does [option 1] not understand the material. Parents, in turn, treat their children as if they are [option 2] the problem instead of listening to them [option 2] to find out how they [option 2] can be helped.

Exercise 16.2. Chose the correct form of the verb and/or pronoun in the sentences and make any other necessary changes in agreement. Rewrite the sentence if that will produce a better result. (In some sentences, there may be other options than the one given.)

1. Those who supported the motion raised their hands.
2. Neither the film's director nor its producers were on hand to receive their prestigious award.
3. The instructor as well as the students thinks the room is too small.
4. It is unfortunate when a person no longer cares what others think about him or her.
5. One should never expect to succeed unless one is willing to persist—even against the odds.
6. It is the tried and true that provides the ultimate refuge in mediocrity.
7. Everyone who works during the year is obliged to file an income tax return.

8. Her set of baby teeth was complete when she was only eighteen months old.
9. He was one of those few candidates who was able to win re-election.
10. None of the company's products require testing on animals.

Exercise 16.3. Most of the following sentences contain one or more subject–verb agreement and/or pronoun–antecedent agreement errors. Correct the sentences. Alternatives are given in some cases, but other alternatives may be possible.

1. Every person in the community should have the right to attend a university and create new opportunities for himself or herself.
   Alternative: All people in the community should have the right to attend a university and create new opportunities for themselves.
2. Especially unique to adolescent depression are physical symptoms, such as headaches. [correct]
3. The tonal quality of Amati's violins is excellent, but not perfect.
4. During the past week, there have been some unexplained occurrences on the girls' floor of the residence.
5. Small class sizes and a low student population mean few opportunities to meet new people.
6. A typical poem by Emily Dickinson leaves the reader searching for another line or even another stanza to satisfy his or her craving for closure.
   Alternative: A typical poem by Emily Dickinson leaves readers searching for another line or even another stanza to satisfy their craving for closure.
7. Use of the leaves of the coca plant for its stimulant effects dates back thousands of years. [correct]
8. A coalition of neighbourhood organizations, students, and unions is currently forming to oppose the university's proposed plan.
9. Everyone who has purchased tickets is eligible for the grand prize, but he or she must be a resident of Canada to claim his or her prize.
   Alternatives: Everyone who has purchased tickets is eligible for the grand prize but must be a resident of Canada to claim the prize.
   Those who have purchased tickets are eligible for the grand prize, but they must be residents of Canada to claim their prize.
10. If a child is denied the opportunity to play, how can he or she develop emotionally and physically?
   Alternative: If children are denied the opportunity to play, how can they develop emotionally and physically?

Exercise 16.4. Rewrite the paragraph, replacing as many nouns as possible with pronouns, ensuring that it is clear what noun (antecedent) the pronoun is referring to.

Alex and his lawyer, Alan, left in Alex's limousine for Loonies Unlimited to buy Alex's landlady, Alice, a litre of light lemonade. She told them to also buy a litre of light lemonade for her long-time lodger, Alison. When they alighted at Loonies Unlimited, they were alarmed that Alex had left his loonie in his loft. So Alphonse, of Loonies Unlimited, allowed them only one litre of lemonade, along with a length of limp licorice, and he loudly lamented their laxness.

Exercise 16.7. Identify the kind of pronoun reference errors in the following sentences; then, correct the errors by making necessary revisions. In the first five sentences, the pronoun that needs to be changed is italicized.

1. According to my textbook, pronouns should always have a clear referent. [no reference]
2. Whenever a staff meeting is called, employees are required to attend. [no reference]
3. Racism is a disease that will continue to plague society until the disease is cured. [ambiguous reference]
4. Sixty per cent of our pesticides, our major ground water pollutant, are used on cotton. [ambiguous reference]
5. During Roosevelt's Pearl Harbor speech, the president identified the US as a peaceful and tolerant nation. [no reference]; During his Pearl Harbor speech, Roosevelt identified the US as a peaceful and tolerant nation.
6. I know the sign indicated *No Parking*, but I went ahead and parked there anyway. An officer gave me a $20 fine. [no reference in both sentences]
7. Her second novel, set in the remote Hebrides, was far different from her first one. [ambiguous reference]
8. Previous Afghan successes were significant victories; for example, the country last waged war against the powerful Soviet Union. [no reference]
9. Some psychologists and researchers believe in the "innate" theory of prejudice. According to this theory, ingrained prejudice is cross-cultural and awareness of race is one of the earliest social characteristics to develop in children. These findings may help account for the theory's popularity. [remote reference]
10. During the dinosaur age, dinosaurs lived in a rapidly changing environment. [no reference]

Exercise 16.8. Choose the correct form of the pronoun.

1. Management often forgets about the needs of us wage-earners.
2. Who should run for office this election?
3. I have no intention of speaking to them.
4. The person who finishes first will be rewarded.
5. You recommend whom for the position?
6. As she entered the room, a mysterious feeling came over her.

7. Margaret Laurence was a novelist who entertained her readers with well-developed plots and realistic characters.
8. People who use memory aids tend to be better spellers.
9. The instructor explained the different cases of pronouns to Gail and me.
10. "Hey, buddy, whom did you mean to refer to when you used that insulting term?"

Exercise 16.9. The following paragraph contains errors in pronoun consistency, along with some awkward use of third-person pronouns. When you rewrite the paragraph, strive for correctness and effectiveness. First decide which person you want to refer to consistently. This decision might be based on the level of formality you want to use (first- and second-person pronouns, such as *I/me* and *you*, are considered more informal than third-person pronouns, such as *he/she* and *him/her*).

Informal: You can definitely learn a lot from educational TV; you can learn things that cannot be learned from written texts. If you are a major in Commerce, for example, and if you watch the business news, you can understand the commerce textbook better by applying what you learn from the news. Similarly, watching sports programs can be exciting and can also give you a better understanding of the game. On the other hand, if you choose to watch comedy all the time, you are not going to gain any real benefits. In general, I think that comedies are meaningless.

Formal: Educational TV has many benefits and can teach people things they cannot learn from written texts. If a person is a major in Commerce, for example, and watches the business news, he or she can understand the commerce textbook better by applying what is learned from the news. Similarly, watching sports programs can provide people with excitement and also give them a better understanding of the game. On the other hand, if people choose to watch comedy all the time, they will not gain any real benefits as comedies, generally, are meaningless.

Exercise 16.10. The intended meanings of the following sentences are obscured or distorted due to modifier problems. Working in groups, identify the particular problem (misplaced or dangling modifier) and determine the grammatical (incorrect or ambiguous) meaning(s) of the sentences. Then, fix the sentences using one of the methods above.

1. misplaced—corrected: A striped, pointed hat was on his head.
2. misplaced—corrected: As we were leaving, he tearfully promised to visit us.
3. dangling—corrected: Although Sam is unambitious and downright lazy, I have never known him to break his word.
4. dangling—corrected: His ego was further inflated when he was awarded first prize in the Ben Affleck look-alike contest.
5. misplaced—corrected: Every character has a purpose, big or small, in Shakespeare's play.

6. misplaced—corrected: When asked what my favourite sport is, without any hesitation I usually say that it is running.
7. dangling—corrected: Stepping out of the airplane, she thought the fresh air was most invigorating.
8. misplaced—corrected: In his book, Gabriel Kolko describes peace in Vietnam after the war.
9. dangling—corrected: As he opened the door unexpectedly, his eyes fell upon two of his employees sleeping in front of their computers.
10. misplaced—corrected: Teacher Laurie McNamara posed for the photographer in the Cloverdale Elementary School hallway with Principal Dan Saunders, who gave her a kidney last month.

Exercise 16.11. Correct the following sentences, each of which contains a modifier error; in some instances, it will be necessary to reword the sentence for clarity and correctness. Note: Only one of the options for correcting dangling modifiers is shown below.

1. In our city, shady characters who offer a variety of drugs lurk on quiet corners.
2. Over the years, several world-class cyclists, such as Eddie Merckx and Greg LeMond, have had spectacular careers.
3. As he ran down the street without a care in the world, two pedestrians had to quickly move out of his way.
4. As I am a member of the Sikh community, my paper will be given a strong personal focus.
5. You will have a fully interactive website, built in mere minutes, for your business or for your personal use.
6. Benefits will result only from a smoke-free environment.
7. Germany has built an extensive network of highways, known as the Autobahn, through its countryside.
8. When they look for employees today, employers are stressing verbal and written communication skills more than ever before.
9. If people are caught in criminal behaviour, their rights to privacy should be forfeited.
10. In captivity, this species of snake will eat frogs, mice, and small pieces of meat.

Exercise 16.12. In the word groups that follow, there are three or four main points related to a topic. Build parallel structures in thesis statements for each topic. Make whatever changes are necessary to achieve parallelism and use whatever order of points seems natural. Other options exist for the five sentences below.

Topic 1: I like toe socks because they are warm and comfortable, come in many colours and designs, and are the latest in sock fashions.

Topic 2: Yoga offers many benefits: it enables you to relax and reduce stress, to exercise regularly, and, through yoga classes, to meet people with similar interests.

Topic 3: Computers are important to students as they provide entertainment, cut down on homework time, and enable them to obtain a wealth of information quickly.

Topic 4: Disadvantages of having roommates are that they can create a lot of mess and invade your personal space, but having a roommate gives you someone to talk to about your problems.

Topic 5: The benefits of coffee include helping you wake up, improving your mood, and improving your concentration.

Exercise 16.13. The sentences below contain parallelism errors. Identify the kind of error (series, compounds, correlative conjunctions, or comparisons) and fix the errors.

1. A good journalist is inquisitive, persistent, and attentive. [series]
2. Music can directly affect your thoughts, emotions, and feelings. [series]
3. In this essay, I will be looking at and writing about the role of women in the military. [compounds]
4. Tiddlywinks is a game not only of considerable skill but also of strategy. [correlative conjunctions]
5. Television can affect children in a variety of negative ways since children often lack judgment, are naturally curious, and are easily influenced. [series]
6. There are three main qualities that a leader must possess: a leader must be enthusiastic, organized, and creative. [series]
7. Aman never has been and never will be good at golf. [compounds]
8. She not only was the best teacher I have ever had but also was very modest. [correlative conjunctions]
9. Tremors may occur on either side or both sides of the body. [compounds]
10. There are many reasons why people choose to watch or enjoy watching television. [compounds]

Exercise 16.16. The following five paragraphs contain various errors that have been discussed in Chapters 14 to 16. Identify the errors indicated and then make corrections. Two paragraphs with errors identified and then corrected appear below.

1. Identify and correct the following:
    a. comma splice
    b. one comma use error
    c. error in pronoun case
    d. broad pronoun reference
    e. missing pronoun antecedent
    f. two pronoun–antecedent agreement errors
    g. apostrophe omitted
    h. ambiguous pronoun reference
    i. failure to use gender-neutral language

Identify the problems: In my family, my father and sister play video games as much as me [c]. They [h] have become very complex, [b] and can even improve problem-solving in children. By progressing through increasing difficulty levels, it [e] can help childrens [g] thought processes. On the one hand, if the child goes straight to the hardest setting, they [f] may feel discouraged, [a] on the other, if the child tries to systematically progress through increasing levels, they [f] can learn the mechanics of the game step by step. This [d] can help in the study of math, as the child may be more likely to persevere with a problem until he [i] finds the solution.

Rewritten with corrections: In my family, my father and sister play video games as much as I (do). Video games have become very complex and can even improve problem-solving in children. Progressing through increasing difficulty levels can help children's thought processes. On the one hand, if the child goes straight to the hardest setting, he or she may feel discouraged; on the other, if the child tries to systematically progress through increasing levels, he or she can learn the mechanics of the game step by step. This method can help in the study of math, as the child may be more likely to persevere with a problem until a solution is found.

2. *Identify and correct the following:*
    a. comma error
    b. subject–verb agreement error
    c. fragment
    d. two parallelism errors
    e. misplaced modifier
    f. dangling modifier
    g. pronoun inconsistency
    h. comma splice

Identify the problems: Having a job and earning one's livelihood is [b] a necessary goal in life, [h] it is one of the reasons you [g] acquire an education. At the place where I work [a] however, many people come in expecting to find a job lacking presentation skills [e]. Many are poorly dressed, do not know how to behave, and they may not speak grammatically [d]. Untidy, disorganized, and unprepared, [f] I still have to match them with a prospective employer. They lack the skills to present themselves to others and knowing [d] what to do in public. Although they may be highly intelligent people. [c]

Rewritten with corrections: Having a job and earning one's livelihood are necessary goals in life. They are one of the reasons one acquires an education. At the place where I work, however, many people lacking presentation skills come in, expecting to find a job. Many are poorly dressed, do not know how to behave, and may not speak grammatically. They are untidy, disorganized, and unprepared, yet I still have to match them with a prospective employer. They lack the skills to present themselves to others and to know what to do in public, though they may be highly intelligent people.

Exercise 16.17. Identify then correct the error(s) in each sentence. If there is more than one error, choose the "more than one error" option.

1. Written through the eyes of a young boy, one can see the perspective of the indigenous peoples.
   a. dangling modifier—sentence corrected: Written through the eyes of a young boy, the narrative shows us the perspective of the indigenous peoples.
2. The daily stresses of students, such as project or assignment due dates, teaches you to manage your time wisely.
   c. more than one error (subject-verb agreement: the subject, *stresses*, should agree with the verb, *teach*; pronoun inconsistency: *you* is not the same person as the noun antecedent, *students*.)
   Sentence corrected: The daily stresses of students, such as project or assignment due dates, teach them to manage their time wisely.
3. Parents sometimes push their children so hard to excel that they lose interest altogether.
   b. pronoun reference error—sentence corrected: Parents sometimes push their children so hard to excel that these children lose interest altogether.
4. My roommate thinks it would be better for society, if all drugs were decriminalized.
   c. comma error—sentence corrected: My roommate thinks it would be better for society if all drugs were decriminalized.
5. Contributors to homelessness include the lack of good-paying jobs, increasingly large families and, probably the most important factor, which is the cost of living in a large city.
   d. parallelism error—sentence corrected: Contributors to homelessness include the lack of good-paying jobs, increasingly large families and, probably the most important factor, the cost of living in a large city.

Exercise 16.18. Identify the error (a, b, c, or d) and correct it in the sentence (there is one error in each sentence).

1. c. [their] Anorexia starts when a person decides to take control of his or her body weight.
2. b. [the semicolon] There are three types of turbine engines used in aircraft: the turbojet, the turbofan, and the turboprop.
3. b. [vendors] Work songs and street vendors' cries are examples of traditional African-American music styles.
4. c. [to extend] Reforms of the UN Security Council include abolishing the veto or extending the Council beyond the current five members.
5. c. [who listened. . .] Results from a recent study showed that patients suffering from osteoarthritis reported a 66 per cent reduction in their perception of pain by listening to music for twenty minutes each day.

Appendix E
Glossary

The terms in this glossary are used in the main text. The numbers and/or letters following each term indicate the chapter(s) and/or appendix in which it appears; for page references, consult the index. Bolded and italicized terms indicate a separate entry for the term.

3-D (three-dimensional) reading 1   A three-step approach to the reading–thinking–writing process where you (1) focus on understanding; (2) use critical thinking to test the validity of the statements; and (3) analyze and evaluate the work

abstract 10   A condensed summary giving an overview of the purpose, methods, and results of an essay or article.

adjectival modifier 14   A word or phrase that functions as an *adjective*.

adjective 14   A word that describes a noun and usually precedes the noun it modifies; it can also follow a linking verb, where it modifies the subject.

adverb 14   A word that modifies a verb, an adjective, an adverb, or even an entire sentence.

adverbial modifier 14   A word or phrase that functions as an *adverb*.

agreement 16   The principle that a verb must agree with (i.e., match) its subject in number—that is, a singular subject requires a singular verb, and a plural subject requires a plural verb. A pronoun must agree in number, person, and gender with its antecedent.

analogy 7   A comparison that helps the reader to better understand the original object or ideas. It compares two things that are unlike except in the aspect being compared.

analysis 1, 7   The process of breaking something down in order to look closely at its elements or to see how the elements connect to make a whole.

anecdote 6   An informal telling of an incident or event to introduce or illustrate a point; it is used because it is interesting or striking.

annotated bibliography 10   Summarizes similar works in a field of study. It includes a concise summary of the content, focusing on the thesis statement and major points or findings. It can also include an appraisal of the study's usefulness.

antecedent 14   The noun that appears earlier in the sentence that a pronoun replaces.

antecedent–consequent 4   A method of paragraph or essay organization. An antecedent is a preceding event, condition, or cause; a consequence is a result.

APA (American Psychological Association) style 13   A citation style used for essays in the social sciences and some sciences. It uses parenthetical in-text citations and an alphabetical list of sources under the heading References.

apostrophe 15   A mark of spelling that indicates the possessive and shows where letters have been omitted in a contraction.

appeal 9   Calling on reason, ethics, or emotion to persuade a reader that an argument is valid.

appositive 14   A noun that names or expands on the previous noun. It is usually enclosed by two commas.

argument 5, 9   Persuading your audience to change its mind or to see your point of view through claims of value or policy.

article 14, B   A word such as *a, an,* or *the* that precedes and modifies a noun.

audience 2, 9   The group of people to whom you are writing, as well as their expectations and knowledge of, interest in, or opinions on the subject. Other considerations include the diction, tone, sentence structure, page format, and so on used in the essay.

authority 7, 11   An expert's findings or opinion that can be used for support.

auxiliary verb 14   See *helping verb*.

block quotation 12   A method of setting off a large quotation (four or more lines, or 40 or more words) in your essay. The quotation is set in a paragraph by itself indented one half-inch from the left margin.

body paragraphs 1   The middle paragraphs of an essay that help prove the thesis by presenting facts, arguments, or other support. Many college or university essays have at least three body paragraphs, each having one main point expanding on the thesis.

Boolean operators 11   Terms such as AND, OR, and NOT that are used to customize a database search.

brackets (or square brackets) 12   Punctuation marks in a quotation that tell the reader that a change has been made to the original passage or that something has been inserted.

brainstorming 2   A pre-writing strategy in which you write down words, phrases, or sentences that you associate with a subject in order to come up with ideas for a thesis and perhaps its main points.

case study 7, 9   A carefully selected example that is closely analyzed in order to provide a testing ground for the writer's claim.

cause–effect 4   A method of paragraph or essay organization in which a writer looks at why or how something happened (causes) and the outcomes or consequences (effects) of those causes.

chronological organization 4   A method of paragraph or essay organization in which a writer traces a topic's development over time.

circular conclusion 6   See *conclusion*.

citation 13   An acknowledgement of the source of a quotation, a paraphrase, or a summary. It includes the author name, publication date, title, and where the information came from. A parenthetical in-text citation usually gives the author name, the year of publication, and perhaps the page number, and points to a complete citation in a References or Works Cited list.

claim 7, 9   An assertion about your topic that appears in your introduction. It usually takes the form of a thesis statement. A claim of fact is supported by facts, figures, or the findings of relevant studies; a claim of value appeals to one's ethics or moral system; a claim of policy calls for action to fix a problem or improve a situation. A claim may be tentative or conclusive.

clarity 17   Writing that is clear is grammatical, concise, direct, precise, and specific.

classification 4   A method of paragraph or essay organization in which a large number of items are organized into manageable groups and analyzed. See also *division*.

clause 14–16   A group of words containing both a subject and a predicate. A clause may be *independent* or *dependent*.

cliché 17   A word or phrase that, though often true, has become overused, such as *green with envy*.

clustering 2   A pre-writing technique in which you graphically link your ideas or thoughts by circling words and phrases and connecting them to other words. It enables you to visualize the interrelations among your thoughts. Also called *mapping*.

coherence 3   In a coherent paragraph, ideas are expressed clearly and are connected to one another. The writer uses strategies to connect one sentence to the next.

colloquialism 17   A word or an expression acceptable in conversation but not in *formal writing*.

comma splice 14   A major grammatical error in which a comma alone is used to join two independent clauses.

common ground 9   A strategy in argument used to show an opponent that you share common concerns or basic values.

comparison and contrast 4, 8   A method of paragraph or essay organization in which a writer analyzes similarities and differences between things according to selected bases of comparison. The two major patterns for organizing a comparison and contrast essay are *point-by-point* and *block*.

complete subject 14   The subject together with its modifiers.

complex sentence 14   An independent clause joined to a dependent clause by a subordinating conjunction.

composing 2   Writing out your ideas in paragraph form.

compound 14   Two of the same parts of speech acting as one grammatical unit, usually joined by a coordinating conjunction.

compound sentence 14   Two or more independent clauses joined by a coordinating conjunction (one of the FANBOYS: *For, And, Nor, But, Or, Yet, So*).

compound-complex sentence 14   A compound sentence joined with a complex sentence.

compound predicate 14   Two verbs governed by one subject.

compound subject 14   Two nouns, two pronouns, or a noun and a pronoun together acting as one subject.

concession 9   A strategy in an argument in which you give up or concede a point. This enables you to come across as fair and reasonable.

conclusion 6   The final paragraph of the essay that sums up what was said in the body paragraphs. A circular conclusion reminds the reader of the thesis, while a spiral conclusion restates the thesis but also leads beyond it. See also *wrap*.

conjunction 14–16   A word that joins words, phrases, or clauses. A coordinating conjunction joins equal units, such as two independent clauses. A subordinating conjunction joins a dependent clause, which contains less important information, to an independent clause, which contains more important information. A correlative conjunction is a two-part grammatical unit that joins two parts of sentence. Both must be used in order to complete the sentence. Common examples include *either/or, neither/nor, not only/but also, both/and*.

conjunctive adverb 14   An adverb such as *however, therefore*, or *thus* that joins two independent clauses. It is preceded by a semicolon and usually followed by a comma.

connotation 1, 9, 17   The feeling or idea that a word creates for a person.

coordinate adjectives 15   Adjectives in a series that can be moved around in the list without changing the meaning of the sentence.

coordinating conjunction 14   See *conjunction*.

correlative conjunction 14   See *conjunction*.

cost–benefit 4   A method of paragraph or essay organization in which a writer analyzes the pros and cons of the topic.

credibility 7 A readers' sense that a writer can be believed, shown through a combination of knowledge of the topic, reliability/trustworthiness, and fairness.

critical response 2 A form of essay in which a writer analyzes another piece of writing and shares his or her views on it.

critical thinking 1 A series of logical mental processes that lead to a conclusion, involving weighing the evidence, analyzing, comparing, evaluating, questioning, rethinking, and other activities.

dangling modifier 16 A grammatical error in which a word or phrase is meant to modify a noun or pronoun that doesn't appear in the sentence. It thus modifies the closest noun, often giving the sentence an unintended meaning.

dangling participle 16 A *dangling modifier* that is a verb ending in *–ing* or *–ed*.

database 11 A collection of related data organized for quick access. College and university databases include *journals* in searchable interfaces, enabling you to retrieve articles linked to various kinds of search criteria, such as title, author, or *keyword*.

deductive reasoning 9 A form of reasoning in which you use a general statement and a specific statement to arrive at a conclusion. Compare *inductive reasoning*.

definition 1, 8 A method of paragraph or essay organization in which a writer explains the characteristics of a subject or term, such as an abstract concept. It can help you understand your topic better and, perhaps, help you organize your main points.

delayed subject 16, 17 A sentence construction in which the subject appears after a prepositional phrase and the verb.

demonstrative pronoun 14 A pronoun that points to a noun and makes the reference clearer: for example, *this book* versus *that book*.

denotation 1 The literal meaning of a word and the way it is defined in a dictionary. Compare *connotation*.

dependent clause 14 A clause that contains a subject and a predicate, but that expresses an incomplete thought; it needs information that is found in the independent clause. By itself, it cannot form a complete sentence. See also *independent clause*.

description 1, 7 A method of paragraph or essay organization in which a writer uses concrete, physical detail to enable the reader to understand an object.

development pattern 4 The principle or method that determines how an essay or a paragraph will be organized. Also called organizational pattern.

diction 17 The style and tone of a piece of writing. Diction is related to word choices and level of language; formal and informal writing are examples of different kinds of diction. See also *usage*.

digital object identifier (DOI) 11, 13 A number–letter sequence that begins with the number "10" and is often found on documents obtained electronically through databases. It is the last element in a citation, just like a *uniform resource locator* (URL).

direct object 14 See *object of the verb*.

direct quotation 12 Reproducing exactly the language of a source. A direct quotation requires a citation. See also *block quotation*, *brackets*, *citation*, *ellipsis (points of)*.

division 4 A method of paragraph or essay organization in which a subject is broken down into parts in order to better understand the whole. See also *classification*.

dramatic approach 6 Writing the opening of the essay so as to catch the reader's attention in an interesting or thought-provoking way.

emphasis 17 The importance or stress that you place on an idea. A word or phrase will have greater or less emphasis depending on where it appears in the sentence. A *periodic sentence* begins with a modifier, delaying the independent clause. A *cumulative sentence* begins with the **independent clause** that is followed by modifying or parallel words, phrases, or clauses that add further detail.

empirical 7, 12   Related to observing and measuring data under controlled conditions in order to reach a conclusion about a phenomenon.

euphemism 17   A word or phrase substituted for the actual name of something, usually in order to make it more acceptable or to give it dignity. It is an example of indirect writing.

evidence 7   Information used to support a claim. Hard evidence provides direct support and includes facts, statistics, and results of studies. Soft evidence provides indirect support and includes **examples**, **anecdotes**, **case studies**, and **precedents**.

example 4, 7, 9   A method of paragraph or essay organization in which a writer uses concrete details to translate an abstract claim into something the reader can more easily understand. An example is considered soft **evidence**.

expanded thesis statement 6   See **thesis statement**.

expert 7, 11   A specialist in a subject, who has published or produced significant work about that subject. See **authority**.

exposition 5, 8   Informing, explaining, describing, or defining a topic for the audience. An expository essay uses **claims** of fact.

factual claim 7   See **claim**.

fallacy 9   A misleading or unsound argument or a misuse of an appeal to emotion.

faulty predication 17   The problem that occurs where a verb cannot be logically linked to its subject.

faulty reasoning 9   An error in thinking that can result from an argument that is not valid, a lack of proof for a claim, or an opinion not clearly separated from fact.

focused reading 1   A close and detailed (i.e., word-by-word) reading of a specific, relevant passage for comprehension or analysis. See also **selective reading**.

formal writing 4, 17   Writing in which the rules of formal usage and correct grammar need to be applied. Colloquialisms and contractions should not appear in formal writing.

freewriting 2   A pre-writing strategy in which you write without stopping and without editing or censoring your ideas.

gender-inclusive language 16   Writing that includes the careful use of terms and grammatical forms that include both genders.

generalization 6, 9   A statement that is applicable to all people or things in a large category. If there are many exceptions to the statement, the generalization is considered invalid.

hard evidence 7   See **evidence**.

helping verb 14   A verb form that combines with a main verb to form a different tense.

hypothesis 7   A prediction or expected result of an experiment or other research investigation.

idiom 17   A saying whose meaning is understood only within the context of the phrase itself. For example, *his bark is worse than his bite* can be understood only by looking at the overall meaning and not by the meanings of the individual words.

illustration 7   A detailed example that usually takes the form of an **anecdote** or a brief **narrative**.

imperative clause 8, 14   A clause or sentence that issues a command. Its subject, *you*, is always understood even though it is not expressed.

incomplete verb form 14   A verb form ending in –*ing* or –*ed/en*. It cannot be joined to a subject without a **helping verb**.

indefinite pronoun 14, 16   A pronoun that can be used in place of a noun for an unspecified individual or group, such as *each*, *either*, *one*, *everyone*, and so on. It is usually considered singular and takes a singular form in *agreement*. See also *pronoun*.

independent clause 14 A clause that is equivalent to a simple sentence: it has a subject and a predicate and needs nothing else to complete it. It can stand alone as a complete sentence. See also *dependent clause*.

indirect object 14 See *object of the preposition*.

indirect source 13 A source that is cited in another source. This is second-hand information, and requires specific methods of citation in *APA* and *MLA styles*.

inductive reasoning 9 A method of reasoning that produces a general conclusion from several specific facts or examples. Inductive reasoning is sometimes called *scientific reasoning* because scientists and other researchers use it to answer questions about the natural world and make predictions about natural phenomena. See also *deductive reasoning*.

inference 1 A conclusion based on the evidence presented; the corresponding verb is *infer*.

interrogative pronoun 14, 16 A pronoun, such as *who*, *which*, or *what*, that introduces a question.

introduction 6 The opening of an essay that presents the main idea (the thesis statement) and the main organizational pattern. It is meant to create reader interest and can be developed through a *logical approach*, *dramatic approach*, or *mixed format*.

inverted pyramid 6 See *logical approach*.

jargon 1, 11, 17 The terms and expressions that are specific to a field; those involved in that field understand these terms, but others may not.

journal 11, 13 A periodical that publishes the results of experts' research.

keyword 11 A word identified by an author or a cataloguer as important in an article and used in online and *database* searches.

linear model 1 A method of writing that breaks down the task into successive stages, each of which involves characteristic activities. These stages are *pre-writing*, *research*, *outlining*, *composing*, and *revising*.

linking verb 14 A verb that joins (links) a subject to a noun or an adjective that follows the verb.

logical approach 6 A method of writing the *introduction* to an essay, beginning with the general aspect of the topic and moving to the more specific as you progress through the introduction. Also called the inverted pyramid approach, as you move from a broad to a narrow focus.

looping 2 A *pre-writing* exercise used after you have done some *freewriting*. You underline potentially useful words, phrases, or sentences; then, you choose the best one to focus on as the beginning point for more freewriting.

main verb 14 The part of a sentence that expresses an action, a condition, or a state of being.

mapping 2 See *clustering*.

mechanics 1, 17 Matters of page format, including margin size, spacing between sentences, font size and type, and page numbers; applied to writing, it includes abbreviations, capital letters, hyphenation, and numbers.

misplaced modifier 16 An *adjective*, an adjectival phrase, an *adverb*, or an adverbial phrase that is too far away in the sentence from the word it should modify, possibly giving the sentence an unintended meaning. See also *dangling modifier*.

mixed quotation format 10, 12 Combining significant words of a source (direct quotation) with your own paraphrasing.

MLA (Modern Language Association) style 13 A citation style used in the humanities. MLA in-text formats include author's last name(s) and page or paragraph number(s). Complete retrieval information is given in a Works Cited list.

modal 14, B   A verb form appearing before the main verb to express necessity, obligation, possibility, or probability.

modifier 14, 16, 17   A word or phrase that describes or limits another word. An *adjective* modifies a *noun* or *pronoun*; an *adverb* modifies a *verb*, an adjective, or another adverb. See also *misplaced modifier*.

narration 4   A method of paragraph or essay organization in which the writer relates a scene, an incident, or an *anecdote*. It may include dialogue.

non-coordinate adjectives 15   Adjectives in a series that cannot be moved around without changing the meaning of the sentence.

non-restrictive clause 15   A clause that contains information that can be left out of the sentence without affecting the meaning of the sentence.

noun 14   The name of a person, a place, a thing, or an idea. See also *subject*.

noun phrase 14   A group of words that acts as a noun in a sentence. It can be either the subject or an object in the sentence.

object of the verb 14   The receiver of the action of the verb.

object of the preposition 14   The noun that is found in a prepositional phrase and that most frequently tells for whom an action is done. Also called *indirect object*.

organization 2   Determining the order of points; outlining a piece of writing.

outline 2, 6, 9, 12   A vertical representation of your essay's points and their support. Three types are scratch, graphic, and formal. A formal outline can be a topic or a sentence outline.

parallelism 16   The principle that elements that have the *same grammatical function* are expressed in parallel structures to achieve coherence and balance. It applies to lists of three or more items, *compounds*, items joined by *correlative conjunctions*, and comparisons.

paraphrase 10, 12   Restates a source's meaning using only your own words. When you paraphrase, you include *all* of the original thought but rephrase it. A paraphrase is about the same length as the original text.

parentheses 13, 14   A form of punctuation used in pairs that enclose less important text that explains or expands on something. In APA and MLA styles, citations are enclosed in parentheses.

parts of speech 14   The names given to each word and its function in a sentence. These are *nouns*, *pronouns*, *adjectives*, *verbs*, *adverbs*, *prepositions*, and *conjunctions*.

passive construction 16   A construction in which the subject of the sentence is not doing the action. Instead, the noun that receives the action is placed at the beginning of the sentence.

peer-reviewed 11   A journal in which all articles are assessed by experts in the field before they are published.

periodical 11   A publication that is issued regularly, including newspapers, magazines, academic journals, and yearbooks; a yearbook is a book of facts or statistics published every year.

personal essay 4   An essay that focuses on an aspect of the writer's life or a relevant experience.

personal experience 4   A description of an event in your life. Personal experience can often be effective in supporting a value claim.

personal pronoun 14, 16   Refers to a person and replaces a noun in a sentence.

phrase 14   A group of grammatically linked words that lacks a subject or a predicate or both. It functions as a single part of speech. See also *prepositional phrase*.

plagiarism 12   The intentional or unintentional use of someone else's work as if it were your own. This includes borrowing someone else's words or ideas without acknowledging the source; not placing quotation marks around a *direct quotation*; or following the wording or structure of the source too closely when *paraphrasing*.

points of ellipsis 12   Three or four spaced dots (periods) used to show where text was omitted from a *direct quotation*.

policy claim 7   See *claim*.

possessive 14–16   Indicates relationships such as ownership between two nouns. The second noun belongs to the first noun. If the first noun is singular, it takes an apostrophe + *s*. If it is a plural noun ending in *s*, it takes an apostrophe alone. Some pronouns have a separate possessive case (e.g., *my* book, *their* dinner).

precedent 7   An example that refers to the way that a particular situation was dealt with in the past. Precedents are often used in *argument* to suggest similar treatment for the matter under discussion.

predicate 14   The part of the sentence that contains the verb and object (and indirect object), or subject complement. It tells what the subject is doing or what is being observed about it.

premise 7   A statement assumed to be true. In deductive reasoning, the major premise is a *generalization* that must be true in order for the conclusion to be valid.

preposition 14   A short word or phrase that often refers to place or time that joins a noun or pronoun to the rest of the sentence, adding information to the subject or predicate.

prepositional phrase 14   A group of words that consists of a *preposition* and a *noun* or *pronoun* (the object of the preposition). The phrase can act as an *adverb* to modify a *verb* or as an *adjective* to modify a noun or pronoun.

pre-writing 2   Thinking about and coming up with a topic; also called *inventing*. Pre-writing strategies include *questioning* and *brainstorming*, *clustering* or mapping, *freewriting*, and *looping*.

primary sources 7, 11   See *sources*.

problem–solution 4   A method of paragraph or essay organization in which you focus on a problem, a solution to a problem, or both a problem and solutions.

process 4, 9   The steps in a sequence.

process analysis 4, 9   A method of paragraph or essay organization in which you describe the stages of a process.

pronoun 14   A word that takes the place of a *noun* in a sentence. This noun is called the *antecedent*. See also *agreement*, *pronoun reference*, *pronoun case*, *pronoun consistency*, and *relative clause*.

pronoun–antecedent   agreement 16   See *agreement*.

pronoun case 16   The principle that a pronoun changes its form depending on its function (subject or object) in the sentence (e.g., *I/me, we/us, she/her, they/them*).

pronoun consistency 16   The principle that a pronoun must *agree* in number, gender, and person with its *antecedent*.

pronoun reference 16   The principle that a pronoun must refer clearly to its *antecedent*.

proofreading 17   The final stage of revising an essay, in which you try to catch all mistakes to provide a clean copy for your reader.

proposal 11   A description of a planned essay that announces a topic, a purpose, and research sources.

prose 2   Ordinary written language. It does not have rhythms or patterns like poetry does.

purpose 2   Your reason for writing, as well as how you will approach the task. It can encompass the skills that the assignment is intended to develop or the effect that you hope to have on your audience.

questioning 2   A *pre-writing strategy* in which a possible thesis is framed as a specific question or series of questions you will try to answer. See also ***brainstorming***.

question–answer 4   A method of paragraph or essay organization in which you pose questions—including the journalistic questions *who?*, *what?*, *when?*, *where?*, *why?*, and *how?*—and explain their answers.

reader-based prose 1   Writing that is focused on the audience, not the writer.

rebuttal 9   The part of your argument in which you raise the points on the other side, usually in order to strengthen your argument and to appear fair.

reciprocal pronoun 14   A pronoun that refers to the separate parts of a plural antecedent (e.g., one *another*).

reference 13   A citation that gives complete retrieval information for a source used in an essay.

reflexive pronoun 14   A pronoun that uses *–self* at the end, such as *himself*. It can be used only if the person has already been referred to earlier in the sentence.

relative clause 14–16, B   A *dependent clause* that functions adjectivally, modifying the preceding *noun*. It usually begins with one of the *relative pronouns*.

relative pronoun 14   A *pronoun* that introduces a *dependent clause* and connects the clause to the rest of the sentence: *who*, *which*, or *that*.

research 1, 11–13   A stage of essay-writing in which you explore a topic to find out what others, especially experts, have written or said about it; finding background information and supporting evidence. At a college or university level, it usually requires use of library resources and/or reliable online sources.

restrictive clause 14   A *dependent clause* that contains information that is necessary for the reader to understand the sentence.

revising 1, 17   Editing to achieve a polished finished version of your essay. See also ***proofreading***.

run-on sentence 14   An incorrect sentence form that has no punctuation between ***independent clauses***. See also ***comma splice***.

scanning 1   a reading strategy in which you look for key words or sections of a text.

secondary sources 11   See ***sources***.

selective reading 1   a reading strategy with a goal, such as scanning for main points or reading for details.

sentence 14   A group of words containing a ***subject*** and a ***predicate*** that expresses a complete thought.

sentence adverb 14   An adverb that modifies the complete ***independent clause*** that follows it.

sentence fragment 14   A grammatical error that consists of an incomplete clause or a ***dependent clause*** on its own.

signal phrase 10, 12   A phrase that indicates that what follows is taken from another source. It names the author and a signal verb. The reference that follows usually gives the page number.

simple sentence 14   A sentence containing one ***subject*** and one ***predicate***.

simple subject 14   The main ***noun*** or ***pronoun*** alone.

simple thesis statement 6   See ***thesis statement***.

slanted language 9   Language that reveals the writer's bias, affecting his or her credibility. It should be avoided in most writing, such as ***argument***. Use objective, neutral language instead.

soft evidence 7   See ***evidence***.

sources 11   The texts that provide information for an essay, discovered through research. Primary sources are original sources and include literary texts, historical documents, surveys, questionnaires, and interviews. Secondary sources comment on primary sources and include authoritative written sources, such as books and journal articles, but can also include oral presentations and conference papers.

spiral conclusion 6   See *conclusion*.

style 13, 17   Specific aspects of a text, such as document formats or citation methods. Also, the way that one writes, including *tone* and *diction*.

subject 2, 14, 16   In grammar, the part of the sentence containing a *noun* that performs the action of the *verb*. Also, the field of study that an essay is about.

subject complement (completion) 14   A noun or adjective following the verb that gives more information about the subject.

subject–verb agreement 16   See *agreement*.

subordinating conjunction 14   See *conjunction*.

summary 10, 12   A shorter rephrasing in your own words of an original work. It restates only the main ideas of the source.

support 7   Facts and other evidence that help prove a claim and make it believable.

synonym 1   A word that means the same thing as, and can therefore replace, another word. See also *connotation* and *denotation*.

syntax 16   The way words are put together into sentences in a language.

synthesis 11   Putting together ideas from different sources and combining them with your own ideas.

thesis statement 1, 6   The main point of your essay, or what you are trying to prove in it, usually stated in the *introduction*. A simple thesis statement announces the *topic* and makes a comment on it. An expanded thesis statement gives more detail, such as the main points that will be covered in the essay.

tone 17   The choice of words and expressions that show the writer's attitude toward the subject. Tone may be familiar, objective, detached, casual, humorous, ironic, formal, informal, etc.

topic 2   The general idea that an essay is about. A topic is narrower and more focused than a *subject*, but less focused than a *thesis statement*.

topic sentence 3   The first sentence in a paragraph, which introduces the main idea of the paragraph.

transition 3   A word or phrase that connects ideas from one sentence or paragraph to the next. Transitions contribute to an essay's *coherence*.

uniform resource locator (URL) 11, 13   The address of specific Internet content.

unity 3   The principle that a paragraph should focus on one central idea announced in the topic sentence and that all sentences in the paragraph should relate to that one idea.

usage 17   The customary and accepted way that a word is used. See also *diction*.

value claim 7   See *claim*.

verb 14   A word that conveys an action, a state, or a condition. A verb combines with a *helping verb* to indicate tense, mood, and voice. A transitive verb takes a direct *object*; an intransitive verb takes an indirect object. A linking verb connects the *subject* to a *subject complement*.

verb phrase 14   A group of words that acts as the *verb* in a sentence.

working bibliography 11   A list of the *sources* that you consult as you work on an essay. It helps you keep track of the sources you have already looked at.

wrap 3   The last sentence of a paragraph that sums up the main point, recalling the *topic sentence*.

writer-based prose 1   Writing that is focused on the writer, not the audience.

Index

Some **Irregular Verb** Forms

Basic form	3rd-person singular	Past tense	Past participle	Present participle
be	is	was, were	been	being
bear	bears	bore	borne, born	bearing
beat	beats	beat	beaten	beating
begin	begins	began	begun	beginning
bite	bites	bit	bitten	biting
bleed	bleeds	bled	bled	bleeding
blow	blows	blew	blown	blowing
break	breaks	broke	broken	breaking
bring	brings	brought	brought	bringing
broadcast	broadcasts	broadcast	broadcast	broadcasting
build	builds	built	built	building
buy	buys	bought	bought	buying
catch	catches	caught	caught	catching
choose	chooses	chose	chosen	choosing
come	comes	came	come	coming
cost (have as a price)	costs	cost	cost	costing
cut	cuts	cut	cut	cutting
deal	deals	dealt	dealt	dealing
dig	digs	dug	dug	digging
dive	dives	dived, dove	dived	diving
do	does	did	done	doing
draw	draws	drew	drawn	drawing
drink	drinks	drank	drunk	drinking
drive	drives	drove	driven	driving
eat	eats	ate	eaten	eating
fall	falls	fell	fallen	falling
feel	feels	felt	felt	feeling
fight	fights	fought	fought	fighting
find	finds	found	found	finding
fly	flies	flew	flown	flying
forbid	forbids	forbade	forbidden	forbidding
forget	forgets	forgot	forgotten	forgetting
get	gets	got	got, gotten	getting
give	gives	gave	given	giving
go	goes	went	gone	going
grow	grows	grew	grown	growing
have	has	had	had	having
hear	hears	heard	heard	hearing
hide (conceal)	hides	hid	hidden	hiding
hit	hits	hit	hit	hitting
hold	holds	held	held	holding
hurt	hurts	hurt	hurt	hurting
input	inputs	input, inputted	input, inputted	inputting
keep	keeps	kept	kept	keeping
know	knows	knew	known	knowing
lay	lays	laid	laid	laying
lead	leads	led	led	leading
learn	learns	learned, learnt	learned, learnt	learning
leave	leaves	left	left	leaving
lend	lends	lent	lent	lending
let	lets	let	let	letting